VOICES AT WORK

Voices at Work

Continuity and Change in the Common Law World

Edited By
ALAN BOGG
and
TONIA NOVITZ

OXFORD
UNIVERSITY PRESS

OXFORD
UNIVERSITY PRESS

Great Clarendon Street, Oxford, OX2 6DP,
United Kingdom

Oxford University Press is a department of the University of Oxford.
It furthers the University's objective of excellence in research, scholarship,
and education by publishing worldwide. Oxford is a registered trade mark of
Oxford University Press in the UK and in certain other countries

First Edition published in 2014
Impression: 1

Published in the United States of America by Oxford University Press
198 Madison Avenue, New York, NY 10016, United States of America

British Library Cataloguing in Publication Data
Data available

Library of Congress Control Number: 2013955753

ISBN 978–0–19–968313–0

Printed and bound by
CPI Group (UK) Ltd, Croydon, CR0 4YY

Acknowledgements

We would together like to thank the Leverhulme Trust, without whose generosity the 'Voices at Work' project could not have happened. The project's inception was supported by Bob Hepple and Silvana Sciarra to whom we also owe our thanks. Many academics and activists have participated along the way and we are grateful to all of them for sharing their voices with us and with each other. It has been humbling to behold the intellectual brilliance and passionate commitment of our colleagues across the common law world. We would especially like to thank Gordon Anderson, Breen Creighton, Cindy Estlund, Anthony Forsyth, Sarah Slinn and Eric Tucker as friends of the project who assisted in supporting and organizing Voices events in Australia and Canada.

Acknowledgements from Alan Bogg

I should like to thank Tonia Novitz who has been an inspiring, good-humoured and good-natured traveller on the journey to this volume. Many miles have been travelled, both literally and metaphorically. I have learned a great deal along the way. My Oxford colleagues have been a source of support, friendship, and spirited dialogue, and I should like to thank Nick Barber, Cathryn Costello, Anne Davies, Sandy Fredman, Mark Freedland, Will Hutton, Jeremias Prassl, Jake Rowbottom and Alison Young. Many in the labour law community beyond Oxford have been most generous with their time, but I would like to thank particularly Ruth Dukes, Cindy Estlund, and Keith Ewing. I owe much to my dear friends Tan Shen Elderton and Rob Farrington. They know nothing about labour law, but Rob F knows how to skim a beautifully level ceiling using only plaster and a metal implement and Shen is wondrously wise about the things that matter. The voices that matter most of all are those of my wife, Sarah Green, and our two wonderful boys Alfie Asa and Benjamin Atticus. This book is dedicated to them all with much love.

Acknowledgements from Tonia Novitz

My first thanks must go to Alan Bogg, for his initial contact five years ago and the lively discussions that have led to the birth and growth of the Voices at Work project. I owe him a great debt for all that has followed. Other thanks go to the project administrators, Kristen Grayewski, Leanne Jeremy and Sarah Tew, as well as to my inspirational colleagues at Bristol who have offered help and encouragement throughout, especially Charlotte Villiers. A University of Bristol University Research Fellowship enabled my study leave in the second year of this project, which was of immense assistance. For both Alan and I, this project has led to the blossoming of contacts with various labour lawyers and social scientists beyond our home institutions and jurisdictions. Without listing all your names, I hope it is enough to say that your voices have shaped our endeavours and that I very much look forward to future conversations. This edited volume has been compiled alongside the protests of my sons, Alex and Kris, whose pragmatic perspectives on work now inform my thinking. Further thanks go to their father, my husband and colleague, Phil Syrpis, who has overcome considerable adversity during the life of this project with ongoing courage and humour. In this we have also had the support of our parents, my brother and our cousins. As this has been a time of recognizing the many voices in our family, this book is dedicated to all of them.

Contents

Table of Cases

INTERNATIONAL JURISDICTIONS

Inter-American Court of Human Rights

European Court of Human Rights

NATIONAL JURISDICTIONS

Australia

Canada

Decisions

European Union—Commission Decisions

European Union—Court of First Instance

European Union—Court of Justice

Israel

New Zealand

United Kingdom

United States of America

Table of Legislation

Canada

United Kingdom

Statutory Instruments

Other Measures

List of Abbreviations

ACAS	Advisory, Conciliation and Arbitration Service (UK)
ACCC	Australian Competition and Consumer Commission
ACTU	Australian Council of Trade Unions
AFL	American Federation of Labour
AFL-CIO	American Federation of Labor and Congress of Industrial Organizations
ALEC	American Legislative Exchange Council
ALP	Australian Labor Party
ARAW	American Rights at Work
AVR	assisted voluntary resolution
AWAs	Australian Workplace Agreements
BCLRB	British Columbia Labour Relations Board
BNP	British National Party
BOOT	Better Off Overall Test (Australia)
BWI	Building and Wood Workers International
CAC	Central Arbitration Committee (UK)
CALD	culturally and linguistically diverse
CAW-Canada	Canadian Auto Workers
CBA	collective bargaining agreement
CBI	Confederation of British Industry
CDM	Centro de los Derechos del Migrante
CIO	Congress of Industrial Organizations
CIW	Coalition of Immokalee Workers
CLC	Canada Labour Code
CTA	California Teachers Association
CTU	New Zealand Council of Trade Unions
CUPE	Canadian Union of Public Employees
DOL	Department of Labor
DPA	Data Protection Act 1998 (UK)
DPs	displaced persons
DWU	Domestic Workers United
EAT	Employment Appeal Tribunal (UK)
ECHR	European Convention on Human Rights
ECJ	European Court of Justice
ECtHR	European Court of Human Rights
EFF	Evergreen Freedom Foundation
EPA	Equal Pay Act 1970 (UK)
EPC	Employment Practices Code (UK)
ER Act	Employment Relations Act 2000 (NZ)
ESV	enlightened shareholder value
ETI	Ethical Trading Initiative
EU	European Union
FCAA	Federal Council for Aboriginal Advancement
FCAATSI	Federal Council for the Advancement of Aborigines and Torres Strait Islanders

FLA	Fair Labour Association
FOA	freedom of association
FOL	New Zealand Federation of Labour
FSHC	firm-specific human capital
FSIN	Federation of Saskatchewan Indian Nations
FW	Act Fair Work Act 2009 (Cth) (Australia)
FWC	Fair Work Commission (Australia)
FWO	Fair Work Ombudsman (Australia)
GFB	Good faith bargaining
GLA	Gangmasters Licensing Act (UK)
GPF	general political fund
GSP	Generalized System of Preferences
GUFs	global union federations
HRA	Human Rights Act 1998 (UK)
ICER	Information and Consultation of Employees Regulations 2004 (UK)
ICT	information and communication technology
IFAs	Individual Flexibility Arrangements
ILGWU	International Ladies Garment Workers Union
ILO	International Labour Organization
IOC	Information Commissioner's Office (UK)
IRA	Industrial Relations Act
IWJ	Interfaith Worker Justice
JCC	Joint Consultative Committee
JwJ	Jobs with Justice
KPIs	key performance indicators
LCLAA	Labour Council for Latin American Advancement
LFS	Labour Force Survey (UK)
LIUNA	Labourers International Union of North America
LPR	legal permanent resident
MMP	proportional representation electoral system
NADRAC	National Alternative Dispute Resolution Advisory Council
NAFTA	North American Free Trade Agreement
NALGO	National and Local Government Officers Association
NCC	National Competition Council
NCW	New Commonwealth
NDLON	National Day Laborers' Organizing Network
NDP	New Democratic Party (Canada)
NDWA	National Domestic Workers Alliance
NES	National Employment Standards
NGA	National Guestworkers Alliance
NGO	non-governmental organization
NILC	National Immigration Law Center
NLRA	US National Labor Relations Act
NLRB	US National Labor Relations Board
NOPEF	Norwegian oil workers union
NOWCRJ	New Orleans Workers' Center for Racial Justice
NPM	New Public Management
NRTWC	National Right to Work Committee

OHS	occupational health and safety
OLMS	Office of Labor Management Standards
PAC	political action committee
PC	Procurement Coordinator
PCC	Procurement Consultation Committee
PCP	provision, criterion or practice
RTW	right to work
SAI	Social Accountability International
SEIU	Service Employees International Union
SIGA	Saskatchewan Indian Gaming Authority
TCNs	Third Country Nationals
TEU	Treaty on European Union
TGWU	Transport and General Workers Union
TICER	Transnational Information and Consultation of Employees Regulations 1999
TUC	Trades Union Congress (UK)
TULRCA	Trade Union and Labour Relations (Consolidation) Act 1992 (UK)
TUPE	Transfer of Undertakings (Protection of Employees) Regulations (UK)
UEAPME	European Association of Craft, Small and Medium-sized Enterprises
USCIB	US Council for International Business
USSC	United States Supreme Court
UV	United Voice (Australia)
WEA	Washington Education Association
WERS	Workplace Employee Relations Survey (UK)

INTRODUCTION: THEORIZING VOICE

1

The Purposes and Techniques of Voice

Prospects for Continuity and Change

Alan Bogg and Tonia Novitz

Introduction

> Trust me, this will take time but there is order here, very faint, very human.[1]

This is a line which Michael Ondaatje advocates should be the first sentence of any novel, but perhaps is more apt as the starting point of an edited collection such as this one which tackles an enormous volume of material. In his 'poem to workers', *In the Skin of a Lion*, Ondaatje drew a picture of workers' lives in Canada at the beginning of the twentieth century. The central character, Patrick, is a silent man who experiences work as a logger, as a dyer in a tannery, and in construction (or rather destruction, as an expert in laying dynamite). He spends time self-employed as a 'searcher', looking for a missing businessman so as to seek the advertised reward, and he spends time in prison. He lives a precarious life, on the margins of the workforce. The novel begins with the tale he is finally prepared to tell to his adopted child, the daughter of a murdered trade unionist, as they travel towards her mother's friend. His is a story surrounded by immigrant workers, Finns, Italians, Greeks, Lithuanians, Macedonians, and Poles, finding commonality in poverty. Ondaatje evokes for us the conditions which necessitated the drive towards legal recognition of voice through legislative provision for trade unions and collective bargaining which offered a way to counter the indignity and dehumanization inherent in the process of industrialization. Of course, the models of state support for independent trade unions varied across our target jurisdictions, from the compulsory arbitration model of Australia and New Zealand, to the statutory certification model of the US and Canada, and finally, where the legal imprint was at its lightest, the 'voluntarist' alignment of British 'collective-laissez-faire'. Yet there was a golden thread that was woven through these very different models, namely that workers' *collective* agency through independent trade unions should be regarded as the fundamental unit of industrial relations policy.

In the twenty-first century, we face different circumstances, which render workers vulnerable but in other ways. Immigration remains a feature of Canadian and other labour markets, but its effects are compounded by globalization of production, such that we now witness interesting forms of outsourcing of supply chains between states, including deployment of 'agency' and sham 'self-employment' in a myriad of forms.[2]

[1] Michael Ondaatje, *In the Skin of a Lion* (Picador, 1987) 146.

[2] See Anne C. L. Davies, this volume. On sham self-employment, see her comment, 'Sensible Thinking about Sham Transactions' (2009) 38 Industrial Law Journal (ILJ) 318; also Alan Bogg, 'Sham

The feminization of the workforce (Ondaatje's key female characters are actresses and wives) poses challenges for the commercialization of care work and its accommodation within working life. The social realities of women's continuing care responsibilities while engaged in paid work leads to disparities of income and status, further facilitated by the contractual arrangements under which they are hired.[3] Technological innovation has not necessarily led to greater leisure or safety in the workplace, but rather dangers for workers caught inadvertently by surveillance systems or even criticizing their employer online.[4] Trade union membership is in decline, and yet labour markets are typified by a 'representation gap', such that many workers say they would prefer collective support and representation but are (for a variety of reasons) unable to access their apparent legal entitlements.[5] The ability of the vast majority of workers to articulate opposition seems progressively less effectual, judging by growing divides in income between the wealthy and the poorer workers;[6] in this sense, the legal props for traditional forms of collective bargaining and industrial action offer inadequate support. This is being reinforced by the muting of workers' political voice, especially as expressed through organized labour in the sphere of democratic politics. This muting leads to a significant loss of democratic control over the legal norms that go to constitute the regulatory framework for paid employment, and indeed the capabilities for effective voice within labour market institutions. We are moving towards a culture of silence.

It is in this setting that we conceived of the 'Voices at Work' network, funded by the Leverhulme Trust. This edited collection of essays is the culmination of our three-year project, which has sought to go beyond the scope of pre-existing excellent European comparative scholarship,[7] so as to investigate contemporary common law legal systems and labour markets in Australia, Canada, New Zealand, the United Kingdom of Great Britain and Northern Ireland (UK), and the United States of America (US)—our target countries. We began by seeking to examine the role of law in securing voice in terms of 'organization', 'representation', and 'negotiation' drawing on terms familiar to us as labour lawyers. Moreover, these analytical categories were crystallized against

Self-Employment in the Supreme Court' (2012) 41 ILJ 328. On supply chain regulation, see for example Stephanie Ware Barrientos, '"Labour Chains": Analysing the Role of Labour Contractors in Global Production Networks' (2013) 49(8) The Journal of Development Studies 1058. On palpable effects on UK immigrant workers, see Alan Bogg and Tonia Novitz, 'Links between Individual Employment Law and Collective Labour Law: Their Implications for Migrant Workers' in Cathryn Costello and Mark Freedland (eds), *Migrants at Work* (CUP, 2014).

[3] See Judy Fudge, 'Women Workers: Is Equality Enough?' (2013) 2(2) feminists@law—available at <http://journals.kent.ac.uk/index.php/feministsatlaw/article/view/63> accessed 27 September 2013; see also Nicole Busby, *A Right to Care? Unpaid Work in European Employment Law* (OUP, 2011).

[4] See Novitz, this volume.

[5] Richard Freeman and Joel Rogers, *What Workers Want* (ILR Press, 1999); Edmund Heery, 'The Representation Gap and the Future of Worker Representation' (2009) 40(4) Industrial Relations Journal (IRJ) 324.

[6] John Hills, Jack Cunliffe, Ludovica Gambaro, and Polina Obolenskaya (2013) *Winners and Losers in the Crisis: The changing anatomy of economic inequality in the UK 2007–2010*. CASE report, Reports 2. Centre for Analysis of Social Exclusion, London School of Economics and Political Science, London, UK; Elizabeth McNichol, Douglas Hall, David Cooper, and Vincent Palacios, *Pulling Apart: A State-by-State Analysis of Income Trends* 15 November 2012, Center on Budget and Policy Priorities available at <http://www.cbpp.org/cms/?fa=view&id=3860> accessed 27 September 2013.

[7] Perhaps most notably, Bob Hepple and Bruno Veneziano, *The Transformation of Labour Law in Europe: A Comparative Study of Fifteen Countries* (Hart, 2009).

a backdrop of values and assumptions that aligned worker voice with the collective activities of independent trade unions. Yet we found, as our interdisciplinary and cross-comparative discussions progressed, that we needed to consider how 'voice' was being translated beyond these traditional typographies so as to capture the dynamism of developments in this field. We also wanted to find the human element obscured by these legal terms of art.

In this project, we rapidly realized that this common law family did not possess the similarities we might imagine. We could not simply compare like with like; when even in the standard terrain of legislation regulating collective bargaining, the term 'good faith bargaining' had a meaning different in Australia to that in the UK.[8] While all states experienced the exigencies of global markets, with external market pressures to engage in chains of subcontracting, enhance agency work, and draw in access to cheaper migrant labour, again stark differences arose in terms of the political value systems and industrial histories that moulded their responses. The egalitarian frame we identified in an Australian context[9] had little relevance to the ostensibly politically neutral, liberal choice-oriented systems in the UK,[10] and attempts to superimpose this liberal value orientation had led to tensions and 'irritations' in the more egalitarian Australian system.[11] Further, the different countries in our study faced different issues associated with voice; for example, the UK alone did not have to address voices of indigenous workers; while oil and mineral rich Australia did not have to contend with a financial crisis on the same scale as the UK or the US, resulting in different policy prescriptions around public spending and a different profile and trajectory for the conduct of public sector collective labour relations.[12]

Accordingly, it became clear to us that very detailed systematic comparative study of 'representation', 'organization', and 'negotiation' (or indeed any particular feature of the industrial relation systems) in our target countries was not going to provide us with the kinds of data which would be usable, or even recognizable to participants in the project. This has led us down a different path in the study of comparative law; one which is more normatively oriented, seeking first to reflect on the legitimate purposes of worker voice and then offering an evaluation of the variety of legal mechanisms that assist and constrain voice in the light of these purposes. Such an approach has also led us to offer greater latitude to the contributors to this volume than might be found in other more methodical and structured comparative accounts; we wanted to instigate a festival of ideas, which could provoke debate and potentially set agendas, even if our

[8] Compare Forsyth and Slinn with Anderson and Nuttall, this volume. Compare again with Alan Bogg, 'Good Faith in the Contract of Employment: A Case of the English Reserve?' (2011) 32 CLLPJ 729 and Alan Bogg, 'The Mouse that Never Roared: Unfair Practices and Union Recognition' (2009) 38(4) ILJ 390.

[9] Alan Bogg, Anthony Forsyth and Tonia Novitz, 'Worker Voice in Australia and New Zealand: The Role of the State Reconfigured?' (2013) 34 Adelaide Law Review (Adelaide LR) 1.

[10] Alan Bogg and Tonia Novitz, 'Recognition in Respect of Bargaining in the United Kingdom: Collective Autonomy and Political Neutrality in Context' in Breen Creighton and Anthony Forsyth (eds), *Rediscovering Collective Bargaining: Australia's Fair Work Act in International Perspective* (Routledge, 2012).

[11] Gunther Teubner, 'Legal Irritants: Good faith in British law, or how unifying law ends up in new differences' in Francis Snyder, (ed.), *The Europeanisation of Law: The legal effects of European integration* (Hart, 2000) 243.

[12] Cameron Roles, and Michael O'Donnell, 'The *Fair Work* Act and Worker Voice in the Public Sector' (2013) Adelaide LR 93.

findings were not reducible to neatly tried and tested verifiable comparisons calibrated scientifically against 'functional equivalents' across systems.[13] Our ambition has been to challenge assumptions of straightforward continuity and face directly various possibilities of change, considering meanwhile the directions in which we might like to see change proceed. We also see this festival of ideas approach as being a fecund source of new research questions for comparative scholars interested in furthering and deepening the work that has been started here. For all its ambition, the *Voices* project has only really begun to scratch the surface of comparative enquiry in this particular domain of scholarship focused upon common law jurisdictions.

Reframing the ambitions of the project in this spirit of liberation has led us to engage with a wider variety of themes than those we had originally envisaged; with a range of approaches and methodologies that are eclectic; and we hope with beneficial results. The essays offered here have been developed from papers presented at different events throughout the life of 'Voices at Work' (2011–2013), whether in Oxford, Toronto, Melbourne, Barcelona, or London. They are by no means the only outputs of these events, which have given rise to a separate special issue on theories of voice (edited by Bogg and Novitz) in the Comparative Labor Law and Policy Journal (CLLPJ), another focusing on North-American issues (edited by Slinn and Tucker) in the Osgoode Hall Law Journal, and a collection of essays considering Australian and New Zealand concerns (edited by Bogg, Forsyth, and Novitz) in the Adelaide Law Journal. In this book we seek to offer a fuller and more holistic sample of the scholarship that has emerged through our dialogue, legal but also interdisciplinary.

In this book, some contributors have focused on a single national study (such as Davies on atypical work in the UK, Hardy on labour inspection in Australia, and Logan on US legislative attempts to prevent trade union engagement with political funding); they offer the reader the opportunity to extrapolate from their preliminary thematic findings and investigate other jurisdictions with an eye to broadly comparable issues. Others offer more detailed comparative pictures, such as Forsyth and Slinn on treatment of good faith bargaining in Australia and Canada or Fine's treatment of union engagement with migrant workers in the UK and the US. There are also essays which rehearse treatment of particular legal questions in a range of jurisdictions (such as Roth's exploration of indigenous work and Tucker on strikes). This variation of approach has, however, its own order, as we seek to probe and destabilize old assumptions and consider them afresh.

The volume is organized into four parts. The first considers 'Identities of Voice' in the workplace. Who is it who might wish to speak and how are they able to do so, if at all? The second part considers the 'institutions of voice' created for this purpose, which leads us to probe the role of trade unions, statutory entitlements, corporate governance mechanisms, courts, and even labour inspectorates. The observations here connect

[13] See Ralf Michaels, 'The Functional Method of Comparative Law' in *The Oxford Handbook of Comparative Law* (OUP, 2006); Günter Frankenberg, 'Critical Comparisons: Re-thinking Comparative Law' (1985) 26 Harvard International Law Journal 411 and the critique offered by Manfred Weiss, 'The Future of Comparative Labor Law as an Academic Discipline and as a Practical Tool' (2003) 25 CLLPJ 169.

to the third part on 'locations of voice', offering fresh perspectives on the ostensible divides between the private and the public, the individual and the collective, as well as the national and international. The fourth part addresses the specific role that law (and institutions beyond law) can play in obstructing or facilitating voice. Following an exploration of regulatory techniques by Howe, this section then considers the scope for various legal regimes to promote and obstruct various forms of voice in the contemporary labour markets that have been the subject of our study.

Workplace Voice and its Putative Objectives

In an earlier essay in the CLLPJ,[14] we identified what we understood as the key contours of 'voice', drawing on the work of Albert O. Hirschman who distinguished voice from 'exit' of an organization.[15] His writing offered a definition of voice of considerable breadth, which as we have noted, 'can be graduated, all the way from faint grumbling to violent process'[16] and can even encompass silence.[17] This variation is likewise a feature of this edited collection; for we have observed that voice does not just fit onto a scale from silence (assumed non-objection but also potentially passive resistance) to outright protest;[18] it may have a myriad of forms. Voice may take place within a workplace, such as a direct comment to a manager or an email sent to a colleague. Voice may operate through the organizational constraints and facilitation of a trade union structure; or it may take the form of open spontaneous resistance to certain managerial practices. Voice may not occur within the enterprise at all, but may be exercised externally in terms of complaints to an inspectorate, a tribunal, or a court;[19] and it may also be exercised in the broader political sphere, in an attempt to influence not merely one workplace but many.[20]

Hirschman's work remains foundational in terms of the normative base he offers to understanding the role of 'voice' in organizations. Hirschman's central idea is that voice can promote improvement of and loyalty to an organization, thereby circumventing exit. He gives the example of the ever-present threat of potential exit of a member or customer of a firm, which he suggests can be deterred by voice.[21] Arguably, if we see the employer as an investor in a firm, we can identify this as a rationale for the common law assumption that capital must be pacified through 'voice'. The employer, having invested in a commercial enterprise, must have the ability to control the terms of the investment, and hence the workforce hired, or they will exit the enterprise. More familiar, however, is the usage that Richard Freeman is renowned for; namely that unionization is negatively correlated to workers' quit rates, such that voice enhances workers' loyalty to the

[14] Alan Bogg and Tonia Novitz, 'Investigating "Voice" at Work' (2012) 33 CLLPJ 324.

[15] Albert O. Hirschman, *Exit, Voice and Loyalty: Responses to Decline in Firms, Organizations and States* (Harvard University Press, 1970).

[16] Hirschman 16 (n 15).

[17] Linn van Dyne et al., 'Conceptualizing Employee Silence and Employee Voice as Multidimensional Constructs' (2003) 40 Journal of Management Studies 1359 at 1362.

[18] For comment on the silence of care workers, see Cooper, this volume. For more direct forms of action, see Tucker, also this volume.

[19] See Creighton, Hardy, and Mantouvalou, this volume.

[20] See Ewing and Logan, this volume.

[21] Hirschman (n 15) for e.g. ch. 3.

organization in which they work and, thereby, profitability.[22] In the CLLPJ, we recognized that alongside this economic narrative lay another, in which the material welfare of workers (rather than their employers) and their income relative to that of those who hired them (egalitarian in nature) also constituted key objectives of their voice through collective bargaining and industrial action. Herein lies the older labour law tradition. The legislative measures that workers secured during the twentieth century (in order to utilize these industrial tools) have been thought to be grounded in universal suffrage and access to political representation; but subsequent capture of government by key financial interests seems to be undermining that political accommodation.[23] This highlights the pressing need for labour lawyers to be as attuned to the values and doctrines of constitutional law as they are familiar with classical 'labour law' concepts such as bargaining units, trade union membership, and the contract of employment.

For today, this story is further complicated by broader objectives of democracy and the protection of human rights—claimed both by workers and their employers—which might be seen to shape the scope of individual and collective claims to voice (and assertions by governments and employers as to their appropriate limits). While we might, as Eric Tucker did so eloquently in this first collection of essays on 'Voices at Work' identify conflicts between constitutions respectively of capital and of labour,[24] we find that tensions arise in broader terms between economic and between the various social justifications which could serve the interests of either or both workers and their employers. What emerges from our study of this selection of common law countries is that the objectives of workplace 'voice' are the subject of considerable normative contestation, with the entry of democratic and human rights arguments into the justificatory framing of 'voice' posing challenges for traditional economic and social understandings of collective bargaining and industrial action (egalitarian, materialist, and efficiency based). As we shall see, this shift in normative grounding has the potential to close down certain arguments (for workers and their employers) while opening other vistas of opportunity.

We explored the role of a range of democratic justifications for voice in our essay in the CLLPJ[25] and they are considered again here by other contributors to this volume.[26] In particular, for workers (and their organizations) a deliberative democratic approach offers a justificatory basis for on-going engagement by workers' organizations (as 'civil society actors') in workplace level, national, and even international decision-making.[27]

[22] Richard B. Freeman, 'Individual Mobility and Union Voice in the Labor Market' (1976) 66 American Economic Association 361; Richard B. Freeman, 'The Exit Voice Trade-off in the Labor Market: Unionism, Job Tenure, Quits and Separations' (1980) 94 Quarterly Journal of Economics 643; although this claim has been viewed more sceptically in the UK. See Stephen Procter and Michael Rowlinson, 'From the British Worker Question to the Impact of HRM: Understanding the relationship between employment relations and economic performance' (2011) 43(1) IRJ 5. For a more recent analysis of the productivity benefits brought by worker voice in the corporate field, see Johnston and Njoya, this volume.

[23] Chris Howell, 'The Changing Relationship between Labor and the State in Contemporary Capitalism' (2012) *Law, Culture and the Humanities* published online 12 June 2012 available at <http://lch.sagepub.com/content/early/2012/05/10/1743872112448362> accessed 27 September 2013; see also Eric Tucker, 'Labor's Many Constitutions (and Capital's Too)' (2012) 33(3) CLLPJ 355.

[24] Tucker (n 23). [25] Bogg and Novitz 332–6 (n 14).

[26] See, in particular, Mantouvalou, this volume.

[27] Here we draw on the writing of Jürgen Habermas, *Between Facts and Norms: Contributions to a discourse theory of law and democracy*, W. Rehg (trans.) (Boston: MIT, 1997); but also the development of the

It might also be regarded as a technique of empowerment for marginalized or weakened voices by precipitating a shift *away* from the legitimacy of coercive pressure in the political process and *towards* the exchange of reasons in a civil dialogue. The sovereignty of public reason also holds out the promise of transcending the skewed power dynamics of interest-group pluralism, especially in situations of deep inequality.[28] More ambitiously, some theorists have argued that the realization of a deliberative politics raises a radical challenge to entrenched inequalities constituted by the rules of contract and property: there can be no deliberation worthy of its name without manifest political equality in the public sphere which leads to a bold political project of redistribution and the guarantee of social rights.[29]

Yet, a deliberative approach could also restrict the content and manner of speech. It is thus both empowering *and* constraining as a democratic ideology. As participants in deliberation, unions are to give due weight to the perspectives of others, including the interests of capital, and to respond constructively within that debate. For employers (and their organizations), a deliberative frame leads to accountability as key social actors, demanding 'public reasons' for their actions and avoidance of discriminatory treatment impinging on the rights of others.[30] In both instances, this democratic perspective offers opportunities but more constraint than perhaps was contemplated previously under an economic-oriented model. Often, deliberative theorists emphasize the importance of citizens deliberating in politics for the sake of the common good of a political community by exchanging reasons that differently situated citizens could reasonably accept in a process of dialogue. In republican thought, the contours and constituents of the common good are to be determined through democratic decision.[31] Obviously, claims based on the 'common good' as a source of democratic constraint should attract careful scrutiny in the realm of real (rather than ideal) political institutions. Where constitutional structures effectively privilege the access of capital to governmental processes, there is a danger that the 'common good' can provide a cover for repressive political projects that are deeply antithetical to workers' interests. The current landscape of workers' political voice in the UK and the US indicates that such concerns are not fanciful.[32]

The influence of deliberative democratic theory on our understanding of the respective role of labour market actors, although profound, is also not the only justificatory game in town. In this volume, Bogg and Estlund draw on Philip Pettit's elaboration of a

fundamental precepts that he espouses so as to ensure equal access to deliberative fora and their utilization, despite systematic power imbalances, such as that explored by Amy Gutmann and Dennis Thompson, *Democracy and Disagreement* (Harvard University Press, 1996) and Iris Marion Young, *Inclusion and Democracy* (OUP, 2000).

[28] Gutmann and Thompson 50 (n 27).

[29] Joshua Cohen, 'Procedure and Substance in Deliberative Democracy' in James Bohman and William Rehg (eds), *Deliberative Democracy* (MIT, 1997) 407.

[30] See Hayes, this volume, for the ways in which employers but also trade unions are held accountable for the content of collective agreements—and the latter even for the methods by which they engage with their membership before the agreement is reached; also see Mantouvalou, this volume, on how the views taken by the European Court of Human Rights relating to democracy can constrain trade union conduct.

[31] For the classic work in this vein, see Michael Sandel, *Democracy's Discontent* (Harvard, 1996).

[32] See the chapters by Ewing and Logan in this volume.

'republican' theory of justice, which offers up a vision of 'freedom of non-domination',[33] which has tremendous resonance in the sphere of the labour market, where the essence of the relationship between employer and employee has been recognized as one of subordination and thus the demeaning vulnerability of the employee to arbitrary treatment by the employer.[34] This vision of freedom is not at odds, but rather complements a deliberative approach, insofar as it explicates the preconditions for life within a civic community of free citizens.[35] The 'ideal speech situation', posited by Habermas, entails, as a minimum, the establishment of a framework of basic rights and liberties upon the basis of which persons are enabled to exchange their views freely. These private rights rely on public government for their existence, but also give legitimacy to that government. The two are described as co-original.[36]

Personal freedom, not only from external constraint, but to take action (such as contestation against powerful agents) is also a feature of Amartya Sen's theoretical framework based on recognition of human capabilities. The notion of 'development as freedom'[37] may be thought, at first glance, to have little relevance to Western industrialized countries, such as those which were the target of the 'Voices at Work' study, but others have realized that his work has the potential to offer significant insight to the normative grounding of law (and indeed labour laws) in all states.[38]

So, deliberative, republican, and capabilities theory seems to steer the normative foundations of voice at work more closely to a bank of human rights protections, though the content and form of particular rights is likely to be sensitive to these differences in normative basis. Of these, freedom of speech, freedom of association, a right to privacy, and even the right to property have particular pertinence to voice. Freedom of speech (or expression) is perhaps the most obvious basis of any claim by workers to speak out, not only in their workplace to their employer (who determines the terms and conditions of their employment), but in a wider political sphere to their government (which regulates the employment relationship, other facets of their social and civic life, and the proprietary, contractual, and corporate rules that determine the scope of capital freedom).[39] Freedom of association has offered workers the freedom to combine in protest (thereby complementing individual freedom of speech by creating spaces for collective contestation) but also to join organizations in their collective interest, such as trade unions, and to engage in collective activity (such as industrial action) whether

[33] Philip Pettit, *On the People's Terms: A Republican Theory and Model of Democracy* (CUP, 2012); see also by the same author, *Republicanism: A Theory of Freedom and Government* (OUP, 1997). See discussion by Bogg and Estlund, this volume.

[34] Otto Kahn Freund, *Labour and the Law*, 2nd edn (Stevens and Sons, 1977) 7.

[35] For further elaboration, see Alan Bogg, *The Democratic Aspects of Trade Union Recognition* (Hart, 2009) ch. 4.

[36] Habermas 104 (n 27). For further analysis of this relationship, see Joshua Cohen, 'Reflections on Habermas on Democracy' 12 Ratio Juris (1999) 385 at 391 ff.

[37] Amartya Sen, *Development as Freedom* (OUP, 1999).

[38] See already under the auspices of the 'Voices at Work' project, Simon Deakin and Aristea Koukiadaki, 'Capability Theory, Employee Voice and Corporate Restructuring: Evidence from UK Case Studies' (2012) 33(3) CLLPJ 427. See also Novitz, this volume.

[39] E.g. regarding public employee entitlements in the US, Toni M. Massaro, 'Significant Silences: Freedom of Speech in the Public Sector Workplace' (1978–88) 61 Southern California Law Review 1; Helen Norton, 'Constraining Public Employee Speech (2009) 59 Duke Law Journal 1.

within or outside those structures.[40] Appreciation of the significance of social context for effective exercise of freedom of association has led to recognition of those groups as independent bearers of collective rights with their own distinct interests requiring rights-based protection. A right to privacy allows scope to restrict employer access to workers' communications with each other, giving space for speech and association.[41] The right to property has the capacity to shut down voice where claimed by employers, seeking exclusive control over the spaces that they own or protection of their economic freedoms; but these claims can be juxtaposed with arguments that workers also possess 'property' in their wage and benefit entitlements, perhaps even in the very jobs themselves (or at least what they have invested in them through their labour), the dimensions of which can then be deliberated in the courts.[42]

These rights have different permutations—scope, limitations, and significance—in the different jurisdictions under review in our project. In the Australian system, where legislation and statutory procedures offer more wide-ranging protection of workers' interests than that in Canada, the UK, and the US, rights discourse seems something of an irrelevance.[43] Others have more forcibly argued that there are dangers for workers and their organizations in pursuit of rights-based claims. Kevin Kolben offers a picture of reversion to individualistic agendas and capture by elite NGOs, in which decisions are put to courts where judges presiding have little or no sympathy for the workers' experience rather than legislatures with a democratic mandate.[44] Guy Mundlak, in a sensitive discussion of a dispute over usage of information technology, highlights that collective bargaining offered both employers and workers a more nuanced outcome to a dispute, which could be beneficial to both sides, whereas the litigation allowed those external to the workplace (NGOs, judges, politicians) problematic forms of control.[45] Bogg and Ewing have defended a normative preference for ordinary democratic channels for vindicating workers' rights where those channels are not blocked to political influence by organized labour, but they have also pointed to the vital residual role for constitutional litigation where democratic politics has failed workers.[46] The desirability of these trends may be fiercely disputed, but what we do observe is that the extension of a human rights discourse as a normative reference point has, in many countries, substantially shifted the terms of debates over worker voice, particularly those relating to identity, institutions, and locations of voice.

[40] For a recent exploration of the dimensions of 'freedom of association' as a universal entitlement, see Alan Bogg and Keith Ewing, 'A (Muted) Voice at Work? Collective Bargaining in the Supreme Court of Canada' (2012) 33 CLLPJ 379; also John Hendy and Keith Ewing, 'The Dramatic Implications of Demir and Baykara' (2010) 39 ILJ 2.

[41] See Novitz, this volume.

[42] Wanjiru Njoya, *Property in Work: The Employment Relationship in the Anglo-American Firm* (Ashgate Publishing, 2007); and Tonia Novitz, 'Labour Rights and Property Rights: Implications for (and beyond) redundancy payments and pensions?' (2012) 41(2) ILJ 136.

[43] See Colin Fenwick, 'Workers' Human Rights in Australia' in Colin Fenwick and Tonia Novitz, *Human Rights at Work: Perspectives on Law and Regulation* (Hart, 2010).

[44] Kevin Kolben, 'Labour Rights as Human Rights?' (2009–10) 50 Virginia Journal of International Law 449; a perspective akin to that of Conor Gearty, 'Against Judicial Enforcement' in Conor Gearty and Virginia Mantouvalou, *Debating Social Rights* (Hart, 2010).

[45] Guy Mundlak, 'Human Rights and Labour Rights: Why the Two Tracks Don't Meet' (2012–13) 34 CLLPJ 217.

[46] Bogg and Ewing (n 40).

Identities of Voice

Trade union membership oriented towards collective bargaining has been traditionally identified with the white working class male breadwinner.[47] In her contribution to our volume, Lydia Hayes points to the ways in which UK courts can be seen, in the implementation of equal pay law, to bolster this assumption, which may in various respects be flawed;[48] while Rae Cooper investigates an Australian attempt to institute a 'low pay bargaining mechanism' which could facilitate more effective representation of predominantly female care workers through trade union engagement in multi-level bargaining, but that has not yet been achieved. Janice Fine (in the context of migrant workers) and Paul Roth (in relation to indigenous work) also point to historic failings of trade unions in our target countries in embracing a broader membership and representing them effectively. They further identify significant instances of outreach, which are motivated by a variety of factors from economic self-interest to more altruistic engagement reflected in a broader concern for social justice objectives.[49] Anne C.L. Davies highlights the significant legal obstacles to achievement of representation of a wide variety of marginalized 'non-standard' workers. She also demonstrates very effectively how workers' identities can be legally constructed in important ways, and how legal norms can even be constituted of fractured solidarities within worker constituencies. In turn, this creates the hope that appropriately designed legal norms might be used to support worker solidarity across difference. However, the foundational question remains why we should we care about the identities of voice. The answer would seem to lie in the views taken of various alternative normative justifications for enabling voice at work.

If we approach voice at work in terms of an employer's economic rationale, drawing on the conversion of Hirschman's theory into Human Resource Management (HRM) as a discipline,[50] then voice is merely a device to ensure profitability. We have argued that this has two dimensions, namely, what we have described as 'HRM1': voice as a means to keep workers from quitting and 'HRM2': voice as a means to perfect the employer's organization by means of incorporation of useful feedback.[51]

The HRM1 rationale offers a very limited basis for inclusivity of voice in the workplace, since only the most valued workers need be given voice; if their departure will not affect the employer, then they do not need a voice. There will be times of low unemployment or where there is a skills shortage in a particular industry, which, logically may lead to a voice strategy aimed at retention, but in low-skilled work, in times of recession, we might expect voice to be minimal. In one recent study, it emerged

[47] For comment, see Peter Ackers and Adrian Wilkinson, 'British Industrial Relations Paradigm: A Critical Outline, History and Prognosis' (2005) 47 Journal of Industrial Relations (JIR) 443 at 447.

[48] In *Coventry City Council v Nicholls* [2009] EWCA Civ 1449 at [45] the Court of Appeal observed 'a tendency for men to be more likely to resort to industrial action than women', without empirical support for this gendered stereotype.

[49] See Fine and Roth, both in this volume.

[50] See, for example, Rosemary Blatt et al., 'Employee Voice, Human Resource Practices and Quit Rates: Evidence from the Telecommunications Industry' (2002) 55 Industrial and Labour Relations Review 573; and Adrian Wilkinson and Charles Fay, 'New Times for Employee Voice?' (2011) 50(1) Human Resource Management (HRM) 65.

[51] Bogg and Novitz 346 (n 14).

unsurprisingly that those workers who viewed themselves as more employable tended to engage more with organizational voice mechanisms when their organization was going through 'turbulent times', but the authors do not seem to consider the possibility that they (rather than other workers) were encouraged to do so.[52]

Even the HRM2 strategy does not offer much in terms of widening the identity of worker voice, for it depends on the extent to which the identity of particular workers indicates to management that they can provide valuable input. The current emphasis on 'high performance management' and alternative voice mechanisms such as 'quality circles' seems driven by allowing individual highly skilled employees forms of discretion over how they perform tasks, leading to greater personal motivation and responsibility; but not to broader based worker involvement through collective bargaining (which would encompass a broader base of activism and engagement).[53] HRM studies currently propose that investment in training, appraisal, reward, and team-building could be a viable strategy for preventing exit, seeking to reject the desirability of trade union membership or activity.[54]

From the simple point of view of material gain and economic instrumentalism, the constitution of its membership should not matter to the trade union or its members. Simply, the aim is to get the greatest gain for its membership as a whole and the broader that membership the more collective might it can exert; hence the attraction of a closed shop and single channel representation which means that wages (and other terms and conditions) cannot be undercut. Ideally, everyone in an occupation (whether in a given enterprise or indeed industry) should be a trade union member. Societal prejudices will be carried into trade unions as they are into any other manifestation of civil society,[55] but so too the contemporary constitution of the labour market will force changes in governance. The rapid feminization of the labour market (including the fact that the majority of women are employed in the public sector and that the public sector is where trade unionism is concentrated) does now lead us to a situation where increasingly the majority of trade union members are women, although trade union governance may be struggling to catch up with this new reality.[56] Economic imperatives in a time of trade union decline may also be significant as Roth observes, noting that:

> As union density declines, it is in the interest of unions to make themselves more relevant to more workers, particularly those belonging to minority groups who may have

[52] Erik Berntson, Katharina Naswall, and Magnus Sverke, 'The Moderating Role of Employability in the Association between Job Insecurity and Exit, Voice, Loyalty and Neglect' (2010) 31(2) Economic and Industrial Democracy 215.

[53] Stephen J. Wood and Toby D. Wall, 'Work Enrichment and Employee Voice in Human Resource Management-Performance Studies' (2007) 18 International Journal of Human Resource Management (IJHRM) 1335 at 1340.

[54] Steven Si and Yi Li, 'Human Resource Management Practices on Exit, Voice, Loyalty, and Neglect: Organizational commitment as a mediator' (2012) 23(8) IJHRM 1705; also Kamel Mellahi, Pawan S. Budhwar and Baibing Li, 'A Study of the Relationship between Exit, Voice, Loyalty and Neglect and Commitment in India' (2010) Human Relations 349.

[55] Gordon W. Allport, *The Nature of Prejudice* (Addison-Wesley Publishing Company, 1979); Rupert Brown, *Prejudice: its Social Psychology*, 2nd edn (Blackwell, 2010).

[56] Catherine Le Capitaine, Gregor Murray, and Christian Lévesque, 'Empowerment and Union Workplace Delegates: A gendered analysis' (2013) 44(4) IRJ 389 at 391; Sue Ledwith, 'Gender Politics in Trade Unions' (2012) 18(2) Transfer: European Review of Labour and Research 185.

> been ignored in the past. In North America, the recent interest of unions in organising workers on tribal lands has followed hot on the trail of the lucrative Indian gaming industry.[57]

Yet, he also recognizes that there is something more afoot here, namely that union engagement with its minority members is consistent with their role as 'social progressive organisations'.[58] There is the issue not only of efficacy of action, but of social legitimacy which comes into play here.

Trade union representation of the widest possible constituency is an objective which fits fairly neatly with notions of universal democratic citizenship, and this political ideal permeates the deliberative, republican, and capabilities approaches that we distinguished earlier. Yet it remains clear that it is an objective still to be fully realized.

If our aim is to widen the base of trade union membership, then we need to address species of exclusion in the workplace which go beyond those addressed here, for example in respect of lesbian, gay, bisexual, and transgender workers.[59] Further, we may need to revisit modes of regulation which hinder access to, and incentive to join, trade unions. Davies has described the barriers which operate at a legislative level in terms of allowing 'non-standard' workers protection from trade union discrimination (as neither 'employee' nor 'worker') and also legislative provisions which regard the part-time worker as only 'half a person' when meeting thresholds for statutory information and consultation or recognition thresholds.[60] It is difficult to join a trade union if you will receive no protection from employer retaliation when you do so and you are not given full status as a legal person requiring voice.

Further, Harcourt and Lam have found data which suggest that majority union representation, institutionalized in the US (which has spill over influence in Canada, Australia, and UK systems of statutory recognition), reduces capacity for trade union membership.[61] Non-exclusive representation by minority unions might achieve an increase in worker representation by trade unions, but there might also be a trade-off with effective bargaining. How this trade-off is to be made is a question to which we will return in respect of institutions of voice. Perhaps it is also true that in 'regulatory' systems of collective bargaining operating at sectoral and national levels, where collective bargaining is conceptualized as a form of governance generating public binding norms, the dilemmas posed by majoritarianism can be transcended somewhat, just as they are in a parliamentary democracy which adopts legislation led by the will of the majority.[62]

The other imperative is non-discrimination in terms of access to freedom of speech and freedom of association. This is familiar to UK lawyers, by virtue of the entitlement to non-discrimination under Article 14 of the European Convention on Human Rights

[57] Roth, this volume at 96. [58] Roth, this volume at 97.

[59] Myrtle P. Bell, Mustafa F. Özbilgin, T. Alexandra Beauregard, and Olca Sürgevil, 'Voice, Silence, and Diversity in 21st Century Organizations: Strategies for inclusion of gay, lesbian, bisexual, and transgender employees' (2011) 50(1) HRM 131.

[60] Davies, this volume.

[61] Mark Harcourt and Helen Lam, 'How Much would US Union Membership Increase under a Policy of Non-exclusive Representation?' (2010) 32(1) Employee Relations 89.

[62] See Keith Ewing, 'The Function of Trade Unions' (2005) 34 ILJ 1.

1950 (ECHR), which is linked to the exercise of other human rights, such as those set out in Article 10 (freedom of expression) and Article 11 (freedom of association, including the right to form and join trade unions). This may be regarded as an added push to ensure that trade unions operate in as inclusive a fashion as possible for ethical as well as pragmatic reasons. Yet, the application of human rights law also has a restrictive element, having the capacity to impede the free choice of trade unions and their members as to whom they may wish to associate with; as well as augmenting the associational rights of employers and in particular their claim to *negative* freedom of association. On this basis, despite their desire for inclusiveness, trade unions cannot coerce workers to join; this is to be a voluntary freedom exercised by the worker.[63]

Further, it has been established before the European Court of Human Rights that exclusion from a trade union or dismissal from a job on grounds of political beliefs constitutes, prima facie, a breach of Article 11 ECHR, but is capable of justification where there is no abuse of a dominant position.[64] Such a finding is inherently controversial, bearing in mind the potential impact of such responsibilities on trade union autonomy and associative freedoms. Indeed, it could be argued that placing this additional burden on already fragile and vulnerable trade union structures undermines their capability to voice concerns about certain intolerant beliefs.[65] Hayes' chapter also exemplifies how equality norms, enforced bluntly by judicial institutions insensitive to the delicate ecology of workplace communities, might have the effect of stifling or even extinguishing collective voice. These regulatory effects then entrench the historic silencing of disempowered groups in the labour market.

An alternative argument is that the Court's position merely recognized the significance of the civic role played by unions, such that as social actors they have additional responsibilities to act in ways that are seen to be fair and appropriate according to general standards of 'public reason'.[66] This argument is likely to be especially powerful where trade unions operate as public regulatory actors, for example where the formulation of collectively agreed norms is akin to a public legislative act.[67] While there are relatively few examples of this 'regulatory' conception of collective bargaining in the 'Voices' jurisdictions, the Australian experiment with the low paid bargaining stream as evaluated in Rae Cooper's chapter might be regarded as an exemplar in this regard.

[63] This entitlement of the individual employee stated by the European Court of Human Rights in App Nos 7601/76, 7806/77 *Young, James and Webster v UK*, Judgment of 13 August 1981 has been recognized in other human rights systems. See, for example, *Baena Ricardo (270 Workers v Panama)*, Judgment of the Inter-American Court of Human Rights, Judgment of 2 February 2001, paras 162–165.

[64] See App No 110002/05 *ASLEF v UK*, Judgment of 27 February 2007, discussed in this volume by Mantouvalou. See re dismissal App No 47335/06 *Redfearn v UK*, Judgment of 6 November 2012, considered in Hugh Collins and Virginia Mantouvalou, '*Redfearn v UK*: Political Association and Dismissal' (2013) 76(5) Modern Law Review 909.

[65] Note re UK implementation of the same which placed considerable restrictions on trade union autonomy, Keith D. Ewing, 'Employment Act 2008: Implementing the *ASLEF* decision—A victory for the BNP?' (2009) 38 ILJ 50.

[66] See Mantouvalou this volume.

[67] For discussion, see Alan Bogg, 'The Death of Statutory Union Recognition in the United Kingdom' (2012) 54 JIR 409.

Institutions of Voice

A reconsideration of 'voice' from a normative perspective also challenges entrenched assumptions regarding appropriate institutional bases for workplace voice. The convention is to recognize, for very good reasons, that trade unions are the most useful channel for voice, as they offer through collective bargaining an effective means by which to realize workers' aspirations (in relation to terms and conditions of employment)[68] and employers' maximization of profitability (through enhancement of loyalty and minimizing exit).[69] Hence we find that International Labour Organisation (ILO) Convention No 87 does not only address freedom of association but the ability to organize and Article 11 of the European Convention on Human Rights mentions explicitly 'the right to form and join trade unions', as indeed does Article 22 of the International Covenant on Civil and Political Rights 1966. Trade union organization is the 'gold standard' of freedom of association in terms of its capacity to redress imbalances of power which lead to poor economic outputs for workers and, from an employer's perspective, low morale leading to low productivity.

As trade union membership declines and employers become more resistant to collective bargaining, an emergent institution for voice (in Australasia) has been the legislative requirement of 'good faith bargaining'. This could be seen as a mechanism merely to enhance effective collective bargaining on economic grounds, but also can be justified in broader democratic terms, insofar as it indicates that some of the precepts of deliberative engagement be followed, namely that the parties deal with each other with an open and fair mind in the mutual search for reconciliation of opposing perspectives.[70] This potential is explored by Forsyth and Slinn comparing Australia's new experimentation with such a requirement under the Fair Work Act 2009 with a longer-standing Canadian experience; followed by a more devastating critique (from Anderson and Nuttall) of what an obligation cannot repair in a New Zealand setting. This can be compared again to the negligible use made of 'unfair practices' in a UK statutory recognition context.[71]

Thus far, whether by accident or design, the measures taken in our target countries do not appear wholly successful, but the potential to return to industrial relations legislation without such provision is far from enticing. This touches the nerve of a long-standing debate in the UK context of collective laissez-faire, whether the law (however well-intentioned or well-designed) is necessarily a secondary force in labour relations.[72] Some elements of this viewpoint recur in a modern idiom in discourse on reflexive law and governance.[73] In a retreat from this strongly sceptical thesis, all four authors look towards

[68] For which see Sidney Webb and Beatrice Webb, *A History of Trade Unionism* (Longmans, 1897), as discussed in Richard Hyman, *The Political Economy of Industrial Relations* (1989) at 63; see also Bogg and Novitz 327–30 (n 14).

[69] See n 22. [70] See Bogg 257–8 (n 35).

[71] Alan Bogg, 'The Mouse that Never Roared: Unfair Practices and Union Recognition' (2009) 38(4) ILJ 390.

[72] Otto Kahn-Freund, 'Legal Framework' in Allan Flanders and Hugh Clegg, *The System of Industrial Relations in Great Britain* (Basil Blackwell, 1954) 44; see also Otto Kahn-Freund, 'Labour Law' in Otto Kahn-Freund, *Selected Writings* (Stevens, 1978) 8.

[73] For discussion, see Bogg and Novitz 337 (n 14).

the improvement, rather than the abandonment, of such provisions. And indeed there are examples in this collection of certain legal developments having tangible voice-enhancing effects, such as Brodie's analysis and evaluation of recent common law developments in some of our target jurisdictions. Nevertheless, the utility of, say, highly developed legal good faith norms, can only be evaluated in the total regulatory context. Where capital freedoms are accorded wide latitude in the web of contract, property, tort, and corporate legal rules, piecemeal statutory interventions, however well-designed and enforced, are unlikely to advance worker voice in any significant way. It is therefore important to contextualize the trials and tribulations of core labour law techniques such as 'good faith' bargaining.

Mantouvalou considers how interventions by the European Court of Human Rights (ECtHR), which she contends betray an appreciation of trade unions' democratic role, have the potential to shape justifications for voice at work. What emerges is an acute sensitivity of the Court to the significance of pluralism, namely the expression of different political views within a healthy democratic society, entailing recognition of the key role played by trade unions in this regard. Arguably, this appreciation of the context in which Article 11 is to be applied has thereby led the Court to state explicitly that the guarantee of freedom of association under Article 11 encompasses both a right to collective bargaining (including the right to enforce a public sector collective agreement)[74] and a right to strike.[75] However, the ECtHR's jurisprudence, again following a pluralist doctrine, seeks to ensure that neither employers nor trade unions abuse a dominant position, in their role as key civic actors.[76] In this way, its jurisprudence also limits trade union autonomy in ways not previously contemplated. Her study illustrates the ways in which institutional protection of human rights (and their democratic framing) can mould afresh the entitlements and obligations of trade unions. While these insights are especially pertinent for UK labour lawyers, the wider relevance of Mantouvalou's analysis should not be underplayed. The ECtHR's approach gains normative traction from its engagement with a wide range of international sources, not least the instruments and constitution of the International Labour Organisation. In this respect, the dynamics of adjudication in relation to freedom of association provides interesting parallels in other jurisdictions where labour rights are highly constitutionalized, such as Canada.[77]

Yet, what do we do where trade union activity is not an option for workers under current statutory frameworks? One example is the UK system, where there may be insufficient numbers of workers (or trade union support amongst those workers) to achieve a very high statutory threshold.[78] Given the experiential deficit amongst many workers and employers who may have had no experience of the representational activities of trade unions, the mustering of positive support as a prelude to trade union

[74] App No 34503/97, *Demir and Baykara v Turkey*, Grand Chamber Judgment of 12 November 2008.

[75] App No 68959/01, *Enerji Yapi-Yol Sen v Turkey*, Judgment of 21 April 2009.

[76] See Virginia Mantouvalou, 'Is There a Human Right Not to Be a Trade Union Member' in Fenwick and Novitz (n 43) and Mantouvalou in this volume in discussion of App No 11002/05 *ASLEF v UK*, Judgment of 27 February 2007.

[77] See Bogg and Ewing (n 40).

[78] See the UK Trade Union and Labour Relations (Consolidation) Act 1992, Sch. A1, as discussed in Bogg (n 35) and the critique of the legislation offered in Tonia Novitz and Paul Skidmore, *Fairness at Work: A Critical Analysis of the Employment Relations Act 1999 and its Treatment of Collective Rights* (Hart, 2001).

representation is likely to be very difficult.[79] These majoritarian methods have long been regarded as being in breach of ILO principles, which clearly advocate that where a 50 per cent threshold is not met, then more than one union should be recognized for bargaining purposes in respect of their members, rather than denying representation rights to all.[80] Another is the now notorious exclusion of agricultural workers from Canada's 'Wagner' model.[81] David Doorey has, in this respect, offered an appeal for 'graduated freedom of association', which envisages legislative structures allowing scope for workers to combine in employee associations (of probably less influence than a trade union might have), where the option to form a union remains (for the time being) unavailable. Perhaps a more attractive option for those who retain a vision of trade union engagement as the preferred route to voice is the 'bargaining agent' system utilized under New Zealand legislation, which would offer at least trade union representation, although arguably in a weak and attenuated form requiring coalitions between unions to be at all effective.[82]

On an entirely pragmatic level, in whatever shape, the edifice of trade unionism cannot stand alone. As Matt Finkin has observed, without basic general protections for an individual from unjustified dismissal (or we might add discrimination) the ability to join a trade union, let alone participate in collective bargaining mechanisms or take industrial action, becomes difficult to realize in practice.[83] Indeed, this is implicit in Davies' analysis of non-standard employment identified earlier.[84] For trade union action and even consultative engagement within workers' associations rest on a fundamental premise, which Bogg and Estlund in this volume identify as a 'right to contest'. This is a richer and more meaningful concept than the bare right to do collectively what one can do as an individual, as some commentators have so narrowly defined freedom of association (as a bare liberty).[85] It begs the critical normative question of which things, precisely, one ought to be protected in doing as an individual. This formal conception of freedom of association, then, is necessarily parasitic upon a deeper normative account of fundamental labour rights.

[79] Bogg ch. 6 (n 35).

[80] ILO, *Digest of Decisions of the Governing Body Committee on Freedom of Association*, 5th edn (ILO, 2006) para. 977; see Tonia Novitz, 'Freedom of Association and "Fairness at Work"—An Assessment of the Impact and Relevance of ILO Convention No. 87 on its Fiftieth Anniversary' (1998) 27 ILJ 169 at 181; and Ruth Dukes, 'The Statutory Recognition Procedure: No Bias in Favour of Recognition?' (2008) 37 ILJ 236 at 142. For criticism of the Wagner model on this basis, see Mark Harcourt and Helen Lam, 'Non-Majority Union Representation Conforms to ILO Freedom of Association Principles and (Potentially) Promotes Inter-Union Collaboration: New Zealand Lessons from Canada' (2011) 34 Dalhousie Law Journal 115; also Roy J. Adams, 'Fraser v Ontario and International Human Rights: A Comment' (2009) 14 Canadian Labour and Employment Law Journal 377.

[81] See the Agricultural Employees Protection Act 2002 and *Ontario (AG) v Fraser* [2011] 2 SCR 3 as discussed by Bogg and Ewing (n 40).

[82] See Harcourt and Lam (n 80); but for a more critical approach, see Anderson and Nuttall, this volume.

[83] Matthew Finkin, 'Employee Self-Representation and the Law in the United States' (2013) Osgoode Hall Law Journal (forthcoming).

[84] See Davies, this volume.

[85] Sheldon Leader, *Freedom of Association: A Study in Labour Law and Political Theory* (Yale University Press, 1992) 23 and 200; an approach applied by Brian Langille, 'The Freedom of Association Mess: How we got into it and how we can get out of it' (2009) 54 McGill Law Journal 177. For a critique, see Tonia Novitz, 'Workers' Freedom of Association' in James A. Gross and Lance Compa, *Human Rights in Labor and Employment Relations: International and Domestic Perspectives* (LERA, 2009) 126–8.

That formalistic treatment of freedom of association simply cannot work when analysed from a 'democratic' perspective, which focuses our attention on the role of trade unions as responsible civic actors in their own right. Coordinated collective action, by virtue of its scale, has much greater effect than that undertaken on a solo basis; so we have to appeal to a broader justificatory basis for such action. Similarly, we have to interrogate *why* it is vital to allow workers to act collectively, or, from a freedom of speech perspective, to allow even a single worker (as an individual) to voice concerns within the workplace. If we separate out too far our human rights tradition from the societal values and norms that they are intended to encapsulate, we stray into an abstract formalism that lacks any kind of sense for the actual people involved. It is for this reason that we are unpersuaded by Hugh Collins' attempt to derive a limited 'right to form and join trade unions' from a Rawlsian position;[86] but more by the notion offered by Sen that it is for societies to seek to deliberate on the values to which they aspire and thereby the content of the freedoms whose exercise becomes the foundation for communal understandings of human capabilities.[87] In so doing, we expect that attention will be paid to the 'actual living that people manage to achieve (or going beyond that, on the *freedom* to achieve actual livings that one can have reason to value)'.[88] Hence, Bogg and Estlund applaud the contextual virtue of Pettit's 'eyeball test' approach to the derivation of fundamental rights which attends to the corrosive realities of power and subordination on weaker parties in civil society. An abstracted, formalistic approach to freedom of association cannot assist us in this respect, but more topical examples can, so it is not so hard to place the value of a 'right to contestation' in the frame of the non-unionized low paid workers, whom Anna Pollert describes as acting spontaneously to address their terms and conditions of employment; whether one speaks or a number join voices, they would seek that entitlement.[89]

It then becomes important, in terms of voice, to think about the entitlements to voice of the individual worker. In this respect, Breen Creighton offers an explanation of 'workplace rights', which go beyond the scope of trade union protections. While questions have been raised as to the extent to which such statutory entitlements (arguably prioritizing the individual over the collective) detract from the primary role of trade unions within the Australian labour relations system,[90] he indicates their tremendous potential for the enablement of worker voice. While this part of the Fair Work Act 2009 is very much concerned with the rights of the individual rather than those of the collectivity it does provide a measure of indirect protection for collectivities by protecting the rights of individuals who join or participate in their activities.[91] As such, it offers a new and promising institution of voice.

[86] Hugh Collins, 'Theories of Rights as Justifications for Labour Law' in Guy Davidov and Brian Langille (eds), *The Idea of Labour Law* (OUP, 2011).

[87] Sen 158 (n 37).

[88] Sen 73 (n 37). For this is Sen's critique of Rawls' work.

[89] Anna Pollert, 'Spheres of Collectivism: Group Action and Perspectives on Trade Unions among the Low-Paid Unorganized with Problems at Work' (2010) 34(1) Capital and Class 115.

[90] See Victoria Lambropoulos, 'The Evolution of Freedom of Association in Australia's Federal Industrial Relations Law: From trade union security to workplace rights' (2013) *Labour History* available at <http://dx.doi.org/10.1080/0023656X.2013.804277> accessed 27 September 2013.

[91] Creighton this volume.

Tess Hardy's analysis of what can be offered by a labour inspectorate which goes beyond reliance on trade union enforcement is of crucial importance given the significant groups of vulnerable workers who are non-unionized.[92] The difficulty, however, is that the onus placed on the individual worker by the Fair Work Ombudsman to raise the issue with an employer, then lodge the complaint and participate actively in proceedings remains a barrier to access, as does the institutional emphasis on timely disposal of disputes. What she exposes is a necessary supplement to trade union intervention, but not one which offers a straightforward alternative, let alone replacement.

Locations of Voice

Drawing on the analysis we have presented here, there are obviously a variety of potential locations for worker voice, which can be challenged when we start to think about voice less in economic and more in normative terms. The essays in this book, for example, challenge the containment of voice within the workplace and consider its more political aspects. In many of the *Voices* countries, political voice through democratic citizenship was traditionally regarded as both the precondition of workplace voice and the source of its normative justification. As Keith Ewing once observed:

> The social democratic agenda for labour law is partly to untangle the contradiction identified by Hugh Collins, namely that while the principles of self-determination and democracy govern the relations between the individual and the State, 'these cherished values…appear to be eclipsed as soon as we enter the workplace', where 'we find a system of autocratic power exercised by the management over the work-force.'[93]

Hence models of political democracy often provided a normative inspiration for models of democracy translated into the particular context of economic governance.[94] That said, it was nevertheless one of the dogmas of British labour law that British trade unions achieved industrial empowerment through autonomous action before they achieved political enfranchisement, which accounts for the distinctive voluntarist orientation amongst organized labour in the UK.[95] This is a dangerous dogma insofar as it leads us to take the matter of workers' political voice too lightly.

Keith Ewing's chapter challenges this dogma head on, arguing powerfully that political voice is an essential precondition of industrial voice, even in the UK's voluntarist landscape, for two main reasons. First, political voice gives worker-citizens an opportunity to participate in shaping the intricate web of legal rules that structure and constitute the contexts within which workers undertake paid labour. This is especially important where those rules appear (superficially at least) to be at some distance from the narrow issue of terms and conditions of employment governed by collective agreements, such as the rules governing property, competition law, corporate governance, contract, restitution, and torts. Yet it is precisely those legal rules that are often most critical in determining the scope of entrepreneurial freedoms and the organizational

[92] Such as the care workers identified by Cooper in this volume.
[93] Keith Ewing, 'Democratic Socialism and Labour Law' (1995) 24 ILJ 103, 112.
[94] Mantouvalou, this volume. [95] Bogg, 4 (n 35).

capacities of workers and trade unions. If collective bargaining takes place within a legal framework that is already dramatically skewed in favour of capital, just outcomes are unlikely to be embodied in autonomous collective agreements. Secondly, political voice enables worker-citizens to secure the enactment and influence the shape of labour legislation designed to neutralize the common law and provide effective auxiliary support to trade unions' collective bargaining activities. It also enables worker-citizens to secure legislation guaranteeing a 'floor of rights' and a social wage as a foundation of decent and civilizing work regardless of trade union membership and collective bargaining coverage.

One of the most striking developments in recent years has been the growth of governmental strategies, led by right-wing neo-liberal political parties, to mute the political voice of worker-citizens as expressed through trade unions. These political attacks have been most vehement in the UK and US, though Ewing's chapter also points to parallel developments in New South Wales which may also indicate a nascent political attack in the Australian context too, that seems only likely to be strengthened by the recent change of government at federal level. These strategies have sought to limit the abilities of trade unions (and, thus, worker-citizens) to participate in the democratic process. The precise form that such strategies take depends upon the particular regulatory and constitutional context. In the UK, for example, recent political attention has been directed at limiting the scope for union expenditure on campaigning activities during the electoral process. In the US, by contrast, unions (like corporations) enjoy a constitutional right to make unlimited expenditures on political campaigning. For this reason, and as set out in John Logan's chapter, the battleground in the US has therefore focused upon attenuating the democratic nexus between individual trade union members and the trade union, by seeking legislation to prevent individual political contributions being raised through payroll deduction. While the union movement was able to repel the enactment of such legislation in California, Logan speculates that this is unlikely to be the end of the story for neoliberal proponents of 'pay check' legislation in the US.

Another facet of this muting of political voice has been the assault on the collective bargaining activities of public sector trade unions, an assault that has intensified in the wake of the economic crisis and the public discourse of austerity in respect of public expenditure. Though the character and pace of this assault has varied across the *Voices* countries, Bach and Gall identify some important general trends in public sector labour relations: 'a return to unilateralism and the erosion of employee voice; the repeal of collective bargaining arrangements; reduced scope of collective bargaining; and direct or indirect attacks on public services unionism'.[96] In this way, the neoliberal state appropriates the historic role of 'model employer' to the private sector by signalling the legitimacy of an anti-union ethos of employment relations.

Bach and Gall move beyond mere diagnosis to a series of constructive prescriptions, which focuses upon the need for mass civic mobilization around an alternative political vision of a more humane political economy. And therein lies the umbilical connection to Ewing's and Logan's chapters. For if the political voice of organized labour

[96] Bach and Gall, this volume at 331.

is successfully choked off through campaign finance regulation and paycheck legislation, will this lead to an effective entrenchment of the neoliberal paradigm? The significance of this point cannot be over-estimated. It should be recalled that the doyen of neoliberalism, Hayek, was concerned with determining a 'constitution of liberty'.[97] Hayek understood that the entrenchment of a neoliberal order could not occur in an enduring way through industrial relations legislation alone. It could only be entrenched through constitutional and political reform, and it was this that was the main focus of theoretical and practical concern in his later work.[98] In our view, the *Voices* study, which emphasizes the normative preconditions for deliberative and other forms of democratic engagement, demonstrates that there has never been a more pressing need for labour lawyers to attend to the wider constitutional context of trade union activity, especially as expressed through political voice. It is our view that the silencing of trade unions' political voice may prove to be one of the most pressing industrial relations problems of our age.

As the opportunities for worker voice through collective bargaining or the political process come under increasing pressure, litigating the common law in the ordinary courts has emerged as a new sphere of worker voice. This has been an especially challenging development for labour lawyers given the traditional reputation of the common law (and its judges) as antithetical to workers' voice, being oriented instead wholly towards employers' economic objectives, without even any inkling of the ways in which voice could potentially serve those objectives. On that traditional view, the common law consecrates the subordination of the individual employee to the managerial prerogative; it also configures forms of collective action as civil wrongs in the law of tort. This was reflected in a normative commitment to the virtue of judicial abstention where the common law intersected with the employment context; managing the common law was, for labour lawyers, an exercise in damage limitation. It must be doubted whether this traditional view is sustainable, as workers (and trade unions) have increasingly turned to the common law as a way of augmenting worker voice.

Douglas Brodie's careful analysis of what the individual contract of employment offers to an employee in this regard is telling; for across all of our target jurisdictions, the protections which may be claimed remain weak. For Brodie, the strength of the common law, as manifested in good faith and fair dealing legal techniques, is in its promotion of 'due process', such as ensuring rationality in the exercise of contractual powers. Whatever the flaws of contemporary collective bargaining, the indications are that the common law is no more likely to assist the vulnerable (assuming of course, that the worker is covered by a contract of employment). In particular, Brodie is alive to the reluctance of the common law to scrutinize the substantive fairness of the contractual bargain. Even if judges were so inclined, we might also ask whether there are political and institutional concerns with common law judges adopting such an activist role in the regulation of employment contracts, a modern day version of the 'damage limitation' theory of common law adjudication. It is likewise important to scrutinize the ways in which contractual good faith cannot operate a straightforward functional equivalent

[97] Friedrich Hayek, *The Constitution of Liberty* (Routledge, 1960).
[98] Andrew Gamble, *Hayek: The Iron Cage of Liberty* (Polity, 1996) chs 4 and 6.

to collective bargaining. Bogg and Estlund's paper identifies a right to contest employer decision-making as a fundamental labour right. Contestation is, by its very nature, a form of agonistic expression that may be conflictual in nature. Given the reach of contractual values of good faith, trust and confidence, and fidelity, the contractual paradigm is ill suited to realizing this contestatory vision. Brodie's heavy reliance on Allan Flanders' conceptualization of collective bargaining might lead to a loss of focus on this vital contestatory dimension, since Flanders' work places much less emphasis on collective conflict than other accounts of collective bargaining developed during that historical period.[99]

Mark Freedland and Nicola Kountouris offer for contemplation the possibilities offered by English public common law, namely scope for judicial review of administrative action, but while it seems that trade unions may not be denied standing as litigants,[100] there is some way to go before the judiciary can rid itself (in this context) of prejudices drawn from English private law. Ultimately, theirs is a sobering reflection on the dominance of a private law paradigm in the common law as it relates to the personal employment contract, a paradigm that is 'a firmly individualistic, libertarian, and underlyingly non-democratic judicial approach to employment relations',[101] captured in the illusionary fiction of formal symmetry between two equal contracting parties. It is this illusionary fiction that entrenches 'freedom of contract' as the guiding ideology of English private common law, which fortifies the traditional labour law view that the common law (and its prophets, the common law judges) should continue to be an object of suspicion for workers and organized labour.

If the appropriate attitude towards the common law, especially in its English guise, is one of suspicious scepticism or even hostility, there are nevertheless other ways in which courts might operate as a valuable forum for voice. We have already noted the importance of human rights, whether underpinned by a deliberative or a capabilities normative base, as a framework for developing arguments about worker voice. One element in the growing significance of human rights discourse is that the boundaries between national and international spheres are breaking down. Lance Compa's chapter outlines the pressure faced by US courts to admit the relevance of international jurisprudence, particularly but not exclusively that of the International Labour Organisation which has been enhanced in recent years. With this also comes the weight of human rights jurisprudence from the UN Covenants of 1966 and regional human rights institutions, such as the European Convention on Human Rights and the Protocol of San Salvador to the American Convention. Given the prominence of the 'integrated' approach to international human rights adjudication in international judicial forums such as the ECtHR,[102] these various instruments often interact synergistically to offer the potential for a coherent body of human rights norms at the international level. While national industrial relations systems remain embedded in their respective histories, with the

[99] Bogg 39–42 (n 35).

[100] *R (Unison) v NHS Shared Business Services* [2012] EWHC 624 per Eady J at [11].

[101] Freedland and Kountouris, this volume.

[102] See Virginia Mantouvalou, 'Labour Rights in the European Convention on Human Rights: An Intellectual Justification for an Integrated Approach to Interpretation' (2013) 13 Human Rights Law Review 529.

degree of penetration modulated by constitutional differences and national legal traditions, these external normative influences have common and compelling themes.

Nevertheless, and as the continuing controversies in Canada in regarding the relevance of ILO norms to domestic constitutional adjudication on the meaning of freedom of association in the Charter attest,[103] the social impact of constitutionalized labour rights remains a delicate matter of controversy. In Tucker's brilliant analysis of constitutionalization projects in our inaugural CLLPJ symposium, he pointed to the ways in which international labour rights, for all their substantive 'thickness' in terms of content, are simultaneously diluted through 'softness' in respect of weak enforcement mechanisms. By contrast, 'capital's constitution' at every geographic level is both thicker and harder than that of labour. Like Bach and Gall, Tucker points to the important role of popular civic mobilization as a counterweight to the neoliberal political project. As Mantouvalou's chapter implies, human rights can play a valuable part in that process of civic mobilization.[104] This shatters any illusion we might have of pristine and timeless legal autonomy, even in relation to the English common law. For lying behind all legal forms are dynamics of economic power and social struggle played out daily in the workshops, call centres, and trading floors of real societies populated by real people.

Being Heard

Voice presupposes an audience, whether that is employers, politicians, courts and judges, government agencies, other workers, or wider civil society. It is therefore important that the intended audience hears workers' voices, and this might be captured in a metric of effective democratic agency. This effectiveness might be manifested in improved terms and conditions in the workplace, more appropriate mechanisms for workplace governance, influence over the legislative or judicial process, or the shaping of public opinion in civic spaces. The fourth and final section of the book explores the various ways in which legal norms might enable (or impede) the effective democratic agency of workers.

In this vein, and drawing upon sophisticated work in regulatory and 'new governance' theories, John Howe introduces a further rationale for voice, which is neither economic nor social in its orientation, but rather that voice itself enhances the regulatory efficacy of substantive norms. This leads him to emphasize the significance not only of regulatory activity that is norm-creating,[105] but also that which is norm-enforcing. This theoretical focus is strategically important given the shifting balance between different sources of labour standards in an era marked by the declining significance of collective bargaining as a norm-creating activity. Even where social-democratic governments have achieved political power in our *Voices* countries, protective interventions in the labour market are now more likely to consist of statutory rights for individual employees rather than auxiliary legislation for trade unions. Howe's chapter is valuable

[103] See Brian Langille and Benjamin Oliphant, 'From the Frying Pan to the Fire: Fraser and the Shift from International Law to International "Thought" in Charter Cases', available at <http://www.labourlawresearch.net/Portals/0/Langille.pdf> accessed 23 October 2013.

[104] Mantouvalou, this volume.

[105] Such as that highlighted by Ewing, this volume.

in exploring the ways in which enforcement regimes can open up (and indeed close down) new opportunities for worker voice in the realm of individual statutory rights, thereby placing further disintegrative pressure on the well-worn distinction between the 'individual' and 'collective' dimensions of worker voice. It also raises afresh some of the difficult questions generated by trade unions' encounters with courts and the judicial process, especially as explored in the chapter by Freedland and Kountouris.

Our argument, in this introductory chapter, is that democratic and human rights-based justifications for worker voice are permeating the sphere of debate over workplace voice; but we have sought to identify the various ways in which the content of democratic and human rights norms have been contested amongst those theorists who are broadly supportive of the general alignment. It may be important, not only to argue for certain modes of regulation if voice is to be heard, but also for attention to be paid to the enabling and constraining effects of particular norms. So, for example, Novitz identifies in the sphere of information technology that much attention is paid to employers' capacity to engage in surveillance of an employee's communications, such that attempts are made to restrict such practices with reference to a rather individualistic notion of privacy.

Drawing upon a rich reading of Sen's and Nussbaum's 'capabilities' approach, Novitz points to the important distinction between, on the one hand, freedom as a constraint on external interference and, on the other hand, freedom as an opportunity to participate in valuable practices and activities. Once again, the tendency to adopt dichotomous thinking should be resisted. Privacy norms in human rights law, even where these inhere in individuals, can be an important technique for shielding 'affiliative' interactions with other citizens. In so doing, these 'individualistic' norms can create protected spaces for social and civic relations to be forged and nurtured. Yet this must also be complemented by the development of human rights protections based on freedom of expression and freedom of association. This might potentially encompass a more communitarian understanding of worker voice through ICT, while simultaneously emphasizing the potential of human rights norms to be engines of social change through positive and programmatic state action. This looks to the importance of positive duties of realization alongside negative duties of restraint placed upon states,[106] which seems to occupy the same conceptual orbit as the 'freedom to' and 'freedom from' distinction in human rights theory.

Novitz's chapter indicates how labour lawyers need to look outside the traditional domain of labour law (in her case, human rights law, but also data protection law) to identify the ways in which legal norms and institutions can enable workers' voices to be audible and to be heard. This is a theme that also emerges strongly in Johnston and Njoya's chapter on the role of worker voice in situations of 'hostile takeover' in corporate governance law. They identify the ways in which corporate law creates a legal structure that reduces the frictions that otherwise impede hostile takeovers. In turn, hostile takeovers shrink the time horizons for strategic decision-making within restructured companies leading to the negation of 'implicit contracts' with employees based upon

[106] For analysis, see Sandra Fredman, *Human Rights Transformed: Positive Rights and Positive Duties* (OUP, 2008).

trust, the acquisition of specialized skills, and long-term commitment to the good of the firm. The emphasis on short-term economic gains induces the restructured company to maximize its share price through 'quick wins', by implementing redundancies, increasing the reliance on a growing army of casualized labour, and hacking away at employment conditions. This results in a dismal political economy where wealthy hedge funds make rapid profits while the social costs of their activities are externalized onto employees and the wider economy, thus generating a longer-term drag on national economic performance.

The authors emphasize the importance of worker voice through mixed channels—collective bargaining, information and consultation, board level representation—as a way of introducing necessary friction into this process of restructuring. They also identify the significant economic benefits to be achieved in so doing. This friction is not stultifying. Rather, it creates the conditions for *sustainable* economic growth that looks to the long term, and a humane political economy. Their chapter also highlights the different ways in which the autonomy of labour law as a discipline needs to be carefully considered. Their sophisticated engagement with economic theory indicates the importance of interdisciplinary dialogue. The profound risk of labour lawyers reaching out to only certain disciplines identified as benign, such as fundamental human rights discourse, is the ceding of the economic case for voice rights to a dominant neoliberal ideology. Johnston and Njoya's chapter demonstrates the importance of maintaining that conversation as a way of challenging the dismal economics of neoliberalism and making the economic case for strong worker voice. The chapter also demonstrates in a most striking way that without significant reform of corporate law, voice rights for workers developed *within* the domain of labour law are unlikely to be effective. Never before, in this era of globalized hyper-capitalism, has it been so vital to acknowledge this legal porosity.

McCrystal and Syrpis' chapter explores another disciplinary frontier of importance, focusing specifically upon the UK and Australia: the borderlands between labour law and competition law. Changes in the labour market, and particularly the growth in 'self-employed' actors, mean that the norms of competition law are likely to become relevant where those actors engage in 'collusive' collective activities to augment their market power. It is an especially neuralgic point simply because the domains of labour law and competition law seem so antithetical at the level of normative objectives. While the authors identify a dominant exemption-based approach to collective bargaining in both countries, excluding the operation of competition law from the sphere of collective labour relations, they also suggest that the growth in 'self-employed' actors and other forms of atypical work is placing a disintegrative pressure on the exemption-based approach. The extending reach of discretionary tests to evaluate the 'public benefit' of collective activities, measured against the metric of competition law norms, poses a threat to collective bargaining for the dependent worker designated as 'self-employed'. The institutional dimension to this competition law creep is also important, given the pessimistic assessment in some of the chapters of the adjudicative track record of common law judges. This is additionally a context where fundamental human rights arguments become important. For if freedom of association and collective bargaining are properly characterized as fundamental human rights, such rights arise in virtue of our common humanity and should be blind to the differences between different contractual forms for the provision of personal work.

Finally, Eric Tucker's sobering chapter relocates the discussion back within the central terrain of traditional labour law, the regulation of strikes as a form of voice.[107] Once a primary mechanism for workers' voice to 'be heard', Tucker traces the sharp decline in strike frequency across the English-speaking common law world, against a backdrop of restrictive (and ever straitening) strike laws. While Tucker is cautious in ascribing excessive causal significance to the role of restrictive legal regulation to this pattern of declining frequency, it likewise seems implausible that the relentless legal project of decollectivization lacks any causal salience as an explanatory factor. Tucker is rightly dismissive of the unitarist thesis that the atrophy of collective action is a signal of utopian order in our studied countries. Any claim of that nature in the wake of the global financial crisis is difficult to sustain with a straight face. Rather, the disappearance of the strike seems indicative of radical disempowerment of workers, atomism, the erosion of civic values, and growing precarity and insecurity in labour markets in common law countries.

Obviously, it is difficult to imagine that a public policy explicitly promoting growth in strike action is politically credible. Yet the frequency and pattern of strike action does seem like a credible civic barometer for the health and vigour of a country's democratic culture. Legal reform of strike law seems an important element in a strategy of democratization, though it may more effectively be pursued through constitutional litigation rather than legislative change at the current time (with the obvious disadvantages for countries such as Australia where labour rights are not constitutionalized as compared with, for example, the fertile constitutional litigation in Canada). This must be coupled with the creative deployment of new forms of social action and the forging of new solidarities with other social movements and political groupings. Tucker observes with some justification that 'the inhospitable socio-economic climate severely limits what can be achieved'.[108] A first step in that process of civic mobilization must be for the trade union movement to renew its mission as a political movement with universal demands articulated through political voice in the public sphere.

Conclusions Relating to the Techniques of Voice: Continuity and Change

If we meet again we can say hello, we can say goodbye.[109]

The measurement of continuity and change in comparative labour law is both temporal and geographic.[110] We are interested of course in identifying important shifts in the evolution of labour law systems over time. We are also interested in identifying patterns of convergence and divergence between different legal systems. We cannot claim to have done so systematically here. Our mosaic of perspectives is but a foray into the foothills of that process of comparative enquiry and, we hope, a stimulus to other brave souls who will

[107] Note that Freeman has regarded the strike (involving temporary collective exit) as a form of voice. See Freeman 362 (n 22).

[108] Tucker, this volume at 473.

[109] Ondaatje 153 (n 1).

[110] For discussion, see Bob Hepple, 'Factors Influencing the Making and Transformation of Labour Law in Europe' in Davidov and Langille (n 86).

now go forward with the journey we have started. We hope, however, that the foray has been sufficiently productive in identifying some dominant tendencies in the countries we have studied.

For much of the twentieth century, and in all of the *Voices* countries, it could fairly be said that workers' collective agency through independent trade unions was widely regarded as the fundamental unit of industrial relations policy. Further, this was firmly entrenched in the public policy that shaped industrial relations systems. This public policy was expressed through a varied range of legal and administrative vehicles, ranging from the compulsory arbitration system of Australia through to the voluntarism of British labour law. In 2014 that historical position has altered in a myriad of ways.

As many of our chapters demonstrate, progressive political forces continue to seek legal changes to perfect and enhance existing legislative provisions relating to trade union membership, collective bargaining, and industrial action, concerned to facilitate access to trade union representation for workers. As the chapters in 'identities of voice' attest to, even this rather modest objective of a fair opportunity to access trade union representation is itself a Herculean regulatory task given the diverse and sometimes fragmented worker constituencies we see within the legal categories of personal employment. Furthermore, there is no longer a political consensus that the fundamental unit of industrial relations is collective agency. Over the last four decades, political projects influenced by forms of neoliberal ideology have achieved a significant measure of political success. For this reason, the normative underpinnings of worker voice remain intensely contested in the public sphere. This has no doubt been reflected in declining union membership, collective bargaining coverage, and strike frequency across the entire common law world, though the precipitousness of that decline has undoubtedly displayed some variation too.

In respect of collective bargaining machinery, there seems to have been a deep convergence in all of the countries studied on a particular conception of representational legitimacy, namely that the allocation of decentralized bargaining rights acquires its normative justification through tracking worker consent. Often this is implemented through a system of secret workplace ballots predicated upon a majoritarian model of democracy, variants of which can be seen in Canada, the UK, and the US. The bargaining agent system of New Zealand and the hybrid Australian system may be seen as particular manifestations of this consent-based model. This has intensified the level of comparative dialogue across these countries, though at times it is a discourse on legal reform that has been conducted in ever-decreasing circles. Much intellectual energy has been expended on technical issues about the ballot, its timing, whether and how to substitute card-check mechanisms, and the role of legal good faith once bargaining is underway.[111] It remains an open question whether progressive political movements should simply turn away from this consent-based model and explore other conceptions of representational legitimacy more supportive of 'regulatory' forms of collective bargaining.[112] As Tucker's chapter demonstrates, the other dominant legal convergence has been the alignment of strike laws with restrictive purposes and effects on autonomous collective action. These two convergent tendencies have led to

[111] See for a volume dedicated to this study, Creighton and Forsyth (n 10). [112] Bogg (n 67).

a dual compression on mechanisms of collective voice as expressed through collective bargaining.

It is understandable, therefore, that in an era of declining trade union influence attitudes have been profoundly affected by thinking afresh about the sources of legitimacy for developing forms of collective worker voice in ways that can both enhance but also restrict the scope of collective activities across the jurisdictions that have been the subject of our study. We mention just three of these attitudinal shifts.

First, the growing significance of the common law as a doctrinal method for enabling and expanding worker voice, especially through the technique of contractual good faith, has been a ubiquitous tendency. It seems to us too soon to reach any conclusions on the normative appropriateness of this development. Further empirical research is needed on the role of common law courts and judges in developing the common law as it relates to the sphere of employment. While the doctrines and concepts of the common law are surely evolving, the demographic and professional background of common law judges in appellate courts probably differs little from a generation ago.

Secondly, human rights law and theory has continued to colonize many of the areas of 'traditional' labour law, and this development has been particularly prominent in Canada and the UK where labour rights are constitutionalized in particular ways. Disagreement over the desirability of that set of developments remains intense, though on balance we agree with Mantouvalou that rights discourse has latent potential to augment worker voice. Certainly, its dynamic legal potential relative to the common law seems assured. Nevertheless, this alignment generates its own difficult questions. At the level of theory, which is the most defensible methodology for deriving fundamental labour rights? At the level of practice, what are the pragmatic and democratic concerns with the judicialization of economic conflict in the sphere of work, and how might these be mitigated? Different legal orders will undoubtedly resolve these dilemmas in different ways.

Third, the ascendancy of deliberative theories of democracy, the concerns of which are often appropriated by centrist political parties espousing ideals of 'social partnership', has undoubtedly created new sources of legitimacy for trade union voice. It is also true that the demands of public responsibility and public reason constrain the abilities of trade unions to pursue the sectional interests of their members with unrestrained vigour.

We should also note that significant change is manifest in the ways in which academics and policy makers in each jurisdiction are seeking to adjust legal mechanisms to respond to the diverse challenges of contemporary labour market situations. At the theoretical level we would identify two important tendencies that are emblematic of this response to new challenges.

Illustrating this first tendency, many of the chapters in this volume disclose a deepening appreciation of the progressive blurring of the boundaries between individual and collective labour rights. The distinction between individualism and collectivism has been a prominent feature of academic discourse in all of the *Voices* countries. It is moreover a distinction that is as evaluative as much as it is descriptive of legal structures, with 'collectivism' attracting the support of those who envisage a continuing role for collective bargaining and 'individualism' attracting their opprobrium. It is an analytical and normative distinction that is as fuzzy and contested as it is widespread. As Creighton's analysis shows, the individualism–collectivism distinction operates at multiple levels. His work is critical of the protection accorded to the worker's negative right to disassociate from the collective, which we might describe as a kind of normative individualism. It is a value orientation that can have damaging consequences for the achievement of collective solidarity amongst groups of workers. Yet the chapter also indicates the important ways in which individual rights, such as the right not to be victimized for asserting statutory rights, can create the conditions for collectivization. In this way, 'individualism' at the level of legal form can have collectivist consequences in its effective support for collective activities. Howe's chapter also explores the ways in which enforcement regimes attached to *individual* labour standards and statutory rights can augment (as well as impede) *collective* forms of voice. This further suggests that the divide between the individual and the collective is highly permeable and, often, a legal construct rather than of a natural kind. And, finally, Bogg and Estlund's defence of an individual right to contestation as a fundamental labour right demonstrates how the basic fundamental building blocks of worker voice, including collective forms of voice, may ultimately rest upon 'individualistic' foundations. To the extent that these different perspectives move us beyond formalism in the task of reimagining labour laws, this should be welcomed.

Finally, the chapters also highlight continuing challenges to the autonomy of 'labour law' as a discrete discipline. In terms of 'techniques' to achieve voice at work, 'labour law' has always been regarded as the primary source of reference. It is, after all, a compound discipline amalgamating other aspects of private and public law, so its hybrid nature could assist in its adaptation to such circumstances. It is also a compound discipline in its integration of perspectives from fields such as economics, sociology, political theory, and ethics. Nevertheless, what is perhaps striking about the essays in this collection is their reach into constitutional or public law, human rights law, immigration law, competition law, company law, and data protection law (to name but a few), all of which profoundly affect worker voice while not being species of labour law. Rather, at best, legislation governing the traditional forms of collective bargaining, agreements, and action operate as narrow and discrete exceptions to the application of these other legal disciplines—and then only partially. So, while labour law still has a role to play, much regulation of workplace voice is now clearly taking place outside the usual territory.

This encourages a panoramic perspective on discrete doctrines and institutions within the traditional apparatus of labour law. For example, there is a danger in an exclusive microanalysis of, say, good faith bargaining or recognition ballots, while losing sight of the exclusion of 'illegal' migrants from the collective labour law regime (migration law), the exclusion of the dependent self-employed (competition law), and the boundless latitude conferred on rapacious corporate entities to restructure enterprises aggressively in hostile takeover situations (company and corporate governance law). Appreciation of the legal relevance of all these disciplines to workplace voice reinforces the vital importance of workers' political voice beyond the workplace. Without the promise of equal democratic citizenship, and the corresponding ability of workers and their trade unions to exert effective political influence over these multiple domains of regulation through legal reform, worker voice 'within' the narrow confines of labour law is an endangered category. This gives renewed urgency to an approach to comparative labour law that takes the primacy of politics and the constitution as its necessary point of departure.

So, we can only offer conclusions to this chapter and not a single conclusion. It is not as simple as saying farewell to one set of techniques for legal regulation of worker voice, while welcoming another. Even identification of emergent normative perspectives on the function of voice does not permit such straightforward conclusions; for, as we have sought to explain, these remain highly contested. Rather, we contend that what is unassailable is the need for workers to find access to speak in the current debates taking place around continuity and change within industrial relations, alongside those pertaining to the multifarious legal mechanisms that seek to govern the same. We appreciate that the contours of these debates vary in some significant ways from jurisdiction to jurisdiction. Yet it does seem that the over-arching challenge, in any country, will be for workers to find a way to be heard.

IDENTITIES OF VOICE

2

'Women's Voice' and Equal Pay

Judicial Regard for the Gendering of Collective Bargaining

L. J. B. Hayes

Introduction

This chapter is concerned with 'women's voice': the potential for voices at work to be free from sex-based domination, clearly heard and able to exert influence.[1] The idea is predicated on an assumption that both law and collective bargaining are intimately connected to the exercise of worker voice by women and men. To posit 'women's voice' suggests that collective voice at work is shaped by the social relations of gender which differentiate men from women in waged and unwaged labour. Gender is the expression of sex as social status. It intertwines with other aspects of identity such as race and class to situate men and women in complex social hierarchies at work.[2] Equal pay legislation is a basis for intervention in matters of sex and pay-setting, including collective agreements and individual contracts of employment. Equal pay claims provide an opportunity to explore how law conceptualizes, articulates, and legitimates norms pertaining to 'women's voice'.

A number of 'manner and form' norms appear to have emerged from judicial regard for the gendering of collective bargaining. It would seem this regard extends legal appreciation of what constitutes a discriminatory pay outcome and is motivated by a desire to free 'women's voice' from assumed sex-based dominations associated with collective bargaining. However, it is argued here that the norms link the *process* of collective bargaining too tightly with the *outcomes* of collective bargaining than is desirable for the effective communication of 'women's voice'. Firstly, the imposition of the norms weakens the legitimacy of free collective bargaining in pursuit of bilateral pay-setting between workers and employers. Secondly, their content strengthens support for pay hierarchies based on market forces and the unilateral exercise of employer power over pay.

Sex-based pay inequality testifies to women's weak bargaining position hence 'women's voice' is allied to organizational tools which can support an agenda of economic fairness and equality. One such tool is collective bargaining; another is equal pay law. Since the

[1] Marion Crain, 'Feminizing Unions: Challenging the Gendered Structure of Wage Labor' [1991] 89 Michigan Law Review 1155.

[2] bell hooks, *Feminism is for Everybody: Passionate Politics* (Pluto Press, 2000); Patricia Hill Collins, *Black Feminist Thought: Knowledge, Consciousness, and the Politics of Empowerment* (Routledge, 1991); Judith Lorber, *Paradoxes of Gender* (Yale University Press, 1994).

Equal Pay Act 1970, UK employers must 'give equal treatment as regards terms and conditions of employment to men and women'.[3] The scope of this legislative notion of 'equal treatment' is determined in both UK and EU Courts.[4] An employer may defeat a claim on the basis of a material factor difference, which is not the difference of sex, between the claimant and her comparator. However, without a material factor defence, paying a woman less than a comparable man constitutes direct discrimination and is always unlawful. Cases of indirect discrimination concern pay provisions, criteria or practices which 'put persons of one sex at a particular disadvantage compared with persons of the other sex'.[5] Indirect discrimination is lawful if the less favourable treatment (for instance, the payment of productivity bonuses or lower hourly rates for part-timers) is not for the reason of sex and an employer can justify it as 'a proportionate means of achieving a legitimate aim'.[6]

Equal pay law attends to a trichotomy of pay regulation. The first is legislative, the second lies in unilateral management control and the third is bilateral regulation via trade unions and employers as parties to collective agreements.[7] What is overlooked is the exercise of bilateral pay-setting power via 'management as commissioner' negotiations with contractors and the organized fragmentation of labour through contracting chains. In the absence of direct employment, corporations or end-user organizations do not currently bear equal pay responsibility in law.[8] This chapter examines legal attention to the bilateral control of pay shared (however unevenly) between employers and trade unions. Relative power inequalities depend in large part on the strength of worker voice.[9] A long history of labour economics literature, particularly focused on the private sector, indicates that collective bargaining tends to raise wages above the non-union rate.[10] Less attention has been paid to wage premiums in the public sector precisely because unionization is more widespread and economists assume that members and non-members benefit from collectively bargained rates as a matter of public policy.[11] However, union influence over pay relativities in the public sector is an overwhelming concern of equal pay law.[12] Here, interest in union wage premiums lies with the potential for collective bargaining to raise men's wages above those of women.

[3] Equal Pay Act 1970, s. 1(1).

[4] Art. 157, Treaty on the Functioning of the European Union [2008] C115/01; Equality Act 2010.

[5] Directive 2006/54/EC of the European Parliament and of the Council of 5 July 2006 on the implementation of the principle of equal opportunities and equal treatment of men and women in matters of employment and occupation (recast) [2006] OJ L204/23 article 2(1)(b).

[6] Equality Act 2010, s. 69(1).

[7] C-320/00 *Lawrence v Regent Office Care* [2002] ECR I-7325, [2002] IRLR 822 (AG Geelhoed [51]).

[8] C-256/01 *Allonby v Accrington and Rossendale College* [2004] ECR I-873; [2004] IRLR 224. According to research conducted by Counsel in *North v Dumfries and Galloway Council* [2013] UKSC 45, [2013] IRLR 737 [40] there is 'no case in the Court of Justice in which the principle of equal pay has not been applied between men and women who work for the same employer'.

[9] John Forth and Neil Millward, 'Union effects on pay levels in Britain' (2002) 9 Labour Economics 547.

[10] H. Gregg Lewis, *Unionism and Relative Wages in the United States: an Empirical Inquiry* (University of Chicago Press, 1963); Richard B. Freeman and James L. Medoff, 'The Impact of the Percentage Organized on Union and Non-union Wages' (1981) 63 Review of Economics and Statistics 561; Richard B. Freeman and James L. Medoff, *What do Unions Do?* (Basic Books, 1984); David G. Blanchflower, Andrew J. Oswald, and Mario D. Garrett, 'Insider power in wage determination' (1990) 57 Economica 143.

[11] David G. Blanchflower and Alex Bryson, 'The Wage Impact of Trade Unions in the UK Public and Private Sectors' (2010) 77 Economica 92.

[12] See *Armstrong v Newcastle upon Tyne NHS Trust* [2005] EWCA Civ 1608; *Coventry City Council v Nicholls* [2009] IRLR 345, EAT.

It is established in statute that potential *outcomes* of collective bargaining are unlawful where they include unfavourable terms of collective agreements or pay differences, linked to sex, which cannot be justified.[13] However, more recently, and endorsed by the Court of Appeal, employment tribunals have regarded the *process* of collective bargaining as gendered. Men are suspected to benefit from wage advantage because of a perception that worker voice exercised in unionized male-dominated occupations is more 'voluble' than women's voice.[14] One outcome has been to extend the scope for courts to recognize discriminatory pay; another is that judicial treatment of the *outcomes* and the *process* of collective bargaining is becoming indistinguishable.

The chapter opens with a historical assessment of the relationship between equal pay law and collective bargaining. The second section considers tensions over 'women's voice', particularly in relation to achieving equal pay in the public sector. The third section is an analysis of equal pay deliberations in cases which review the exercise of workplace collective bargaining over the implementation of equal pay in local government. Accordingly, a number of 'manner and form' norms appear to flow from judicial regard for the gendering of collective bargaining. In conclusion it is apparent that these norms, whilst appealing to 'women's voice', are less emancipatory than judicial concern for the gendering of collective bargaining might otherwise suggest.

Equal Pay Law and Organized Labour

In 1970 the Equal Pay Act was heralded as a social justice measure which would address a longstanding problem of women's lower wages.[15] It targeted individual workplaces and relied on comparison between similarly situated men and women. Barbara Castle MP, Minister for Labour, emphasized to Parliament that its advent did not remove the necessity for women to join trade unions.[16] The ability of both men and women to influence their terms of work was assumed to lie with collective organization. However, prior to the Act, women in mixed sex workplaces were typically paid at 50–85 per cent of the relevant rate for men.[17]

The statute spurred trade union action where men and women worked for different rates of pay in the 'same work' or in work which had been 'rated as equivalent' in a job evaluation scheme.[18] Trade unions used provisions in section 3 EPA to refer collective agreements containing discriminatory terms to a Central Arbitration Committee (CAC) for amendment.[19] By 1976, this had delivered the largest ever narrowing of

[13] Council Directive 75/117/EEC of 10 February 1975 on the approximation of the laws of the Member States relating to the application of the principle of equal pay for men and women [1975] OJ L45/19, Art. 4. C-127/92 *Enderby v Frenchay Health Authority and Secretary of State for Health* [1993] ECR I-5535, [1993] IRLR 591.

[14] *Armstrong v Newcastle upon Tyne NHS Trust* [31] and [62] (n 12).

[15] See Hansard HC vol 795 cols 913–1038 (9 February 1970) Lena Jeggar MP 968–971.

[16] Hansard HC vol 795 col 929 (n 15).

[17] Sara Connolly and Mary Gregory, 'Women and Work since 1970' in Nicholas Crafts, Ian Gazeley, and Andrew Newell (eds), *Work and Pay in Twentieth Century Britain* (OUP, 2007) 149.

[18] Equal Pay Act 1970, s. 1(2).

[19] Erica Szyszczak, 'Pay Inequality and Equal Value Claims' (1985) 48 Modern Law Review 139.

men and women's wages as measured across the whole economy.[20] The vast majority of women entitled to equal pay as defined by the Act received it, although many women did not receive the pay that their skills and jobs merited.[21]

The EPA was politically ground-breaking but legally modest. Drawing political impetus from the 1968 strike of sewing machinists at the Ford factory in Dagenham, the statutory framework appeared to regard 'women's voice' from a perspective more suited to the conditions of motorcar manufacturing than less organized, sex-segregated, industries like shop work.[22] While the communication of 'women's voice' was tied to the exercise of collective bargaining, section 3 (4)EPA specifically prevented the extension of collective agreements to include workers 'not previously falling within' them.

Section 1(1) EPA set up the individual contract of employment as the legal crucible for the elimination of discrimination. While measures in the Sex Discrimination Act 1975 and Race Relations Act 1976 introduced statutory torts, the EPA uniquely established an equality clause as a statutory contractual provision deemed to be included in all contracts of employment 'directly or by reference to a collective agreement or otherwise'.[23] Collective agreements were key to enabling law's equality clause to modify an individual employment contract. A woman needed access to a valid male comparator as a benchmark for her contract. The opportunity to expose 'his and hers' contracting was an opportunity to reveal discrimination.[24] Because component terms relating to pay could be addressed separately, the EPA did not necessarily tackle pay as a total sum of earnings from an employment.[25] Arguably, the law appeared more concerned with contractual difference as detriment than with economic deprivation on grounds of sex.

It was not pay relations *between* men and women as a whole that the law sought to equalize, but employer treatment of men and women *within* workplace groupings legally identified as suitable for pay comparison. While section 1(2) of the Race Relations Act 1976 made it automatically unlawful for employers to segregate work groups on the basis of race, sex discrimination law did not prevent the segregation of men from women at work. The shape of equal pay law allowed employers to use sex-segregation as a reason for sex-based pay difference. To establish entitlement to equal pay, both a claimant and her comparator had to be 'in the same employment'.[26] Working for the same employer was not sufficient to meet this statutory test. Men and women also had to work 'at the same establishment' or under 'common terms' of work.[27] Judicial interpretation of 'same establishment' placed weight on the importance

[20] Antonio Zabalza and Zafiris Tzannatos, *Women and Equal Pay: The Effects of Legislation on Female Employment and Wages in Britain* (CUP, 1985); Susan Harkness, 'The Gender Earnings Gap: Evidence from the UK' (1996) 17 Fiscal Studies 1.

[21] Mandy Snell, 'The Equal Pay and Sex Discrimination Acts: Their Impact in the Workplace' (1979) 1 Feminist Review 37.

[22] Sheila Cohen, 'Equal pay—or what? Economics, politics and the 1968 Ford sewing machinists' strike' (2012) 53 Labor History 51; Bob A. Hepple, Sandra McKay, and Gillian S. Morris, *Equal Pay and the Industrial Tribunals* (Sweet & Maxwell, 1984); Zabalza and Tzannatos (n 20).

[23] Equal Pay Act 1970, s. 1(2)(3).

[24] Suzanne Goldberg, 'Discrimination by Comparison' (2011) 120 Yale Law Journal 728.

[25] *Hayward v Cammell Laird Shipbuilders Ltd* [1988] ICR 464, HL; *Brownbill v St Helens and Knowsley Hospital NHS Trust* [2011] EWCA Civ 903, [2011] IRLR 815.

[26] Equal Pay Act 1970, s. 1(2).

[27] Equal Pay Act 1970, s. 1(6); See also *Lawson v Britfish* [1988] IRLR 53 EAT.

of the same geographic 'locality'.[28] Women could be denied permission to claim pay parity with higher paid men in equal work if their employer required their work to take place in separate locations.[29] This supported the operation of 'essentially different employment regimes at different establishments'.[30] Management prerogative enabled employers to carve out groupings of employees within their workplaces, and equal pay law interpreted that prerogative as a power to set pay accordingly.

An exception however, lay with the potential for union organization to intervene through the 'common terms' element of the same employer test.[31] Collective bargaining, even if conducted separately in male and female-typed occupational groups, could produce collective agreements which constituted 'common terms'. This enabled pay comparisons across the totality of workers covered by union recognition in the same employment. With 'common terms', women were not prevented from benchmarking their contracts with higher paid men simply because they worked at a separate establishment, and employers could not rely on physical separation to limit comparison.[32] The statute respected 'women's voice' by supporting separate occupational bargaining and enabling women to evidence pay discrimination through comparison across bargaining groups.

Trade unions were fundamental to women's ability to practically engage with equal pay law. The judiciary required pay parallels to be established on the basis of 'concrete appraisals of work actually performed' by men and women.[33] There was longstanding legal and political resistance to the idea of allowing hypothetical comparators in equal pay proceedings and a stricter requirement for actual comparison in UK than in European law.[34] Collective bargaining supported connections between real workers to reveal injustice and also to negotiate with employers over equal pay. Fredman has noted that the rapid decline in collective bargaining coverage since the 1970s stripped many women of their legal rights to equal pay.[35] In the following section, I argue that women did not bring claims in law until their unions were effectively forced to support litigation. Legal developments which began in the 1980s culminated in the framing of unions as discriminatory actors and have undermined union influence in resolving equal pay issues.

Tensions Over 'Women's Voice'

A struggle for legitimacy between law and collective bargaining was perhaps inevitable in the context of the historically adversarial relationship between the British trade

[28] See *Secretary of State for Employment and Productivity v Vic Hallam Ltd* (1969) 5 ITR 108, HL, (Lord Parker, 108–10); *Lord Advocate v Babcock & Wilcox (Operations) Ltd* [1972] 1 WLR 488, HL (Lord Simon, 214).

[29] *City of Edinburgh Council v Christina Wilkinson* [2011] CSIH 70 [20].

[30] *Leverton v Clwyd County Council* [1989] AC 706, HL (Lord Bridge 746C).

[31] Equal Pay Act 1970, s. 1(6).

[32] See *British Coal Corporation v Smith* [1996] ICR 515, HL (Lord Slynn, 525H).

[33] C-129/79 *Macarthy's Ltd v Smith* [1980] IRLR 210; *Walton Centre for Neurology and Neurosurgery NHS Trust v Bewley* [2008] IRLR 588, EAT.

[34] In C32/93 *Webb v EMO Air Cargo (UK)* [1994] ECR I-3567 the ECJ established sex discrimination without a comparator.

[35] Sandra Fredman, 'Reforming Equal Pay Laws' (2008) 37 Industrial Law Journal (ILJ) 193, 197.

unions and the Bench.[36] Judicial hostility to the referral of collective agreements for arbitration by trade unions was manifested in restrictions on the CAC's power to amend wages.[37] As originally enacted, the statute did not explicitly extend to 'equal pay for work of equal value'; its architects apparently envisaged work of equal value comparison to develop as trade unions bargained over job evaluation.[38] However, the European Commission brought a successful case against the UK for failing to satisfy provisions regarding work of equal value in accordance with the Equal Pay Directive.[39] The ruling of the European Court of Justice (ECJ) took issue with the UK's voluntarist approach to job evaluation and supported the Commission's assertion that 'individuals should have the possibility of succeeding in the argument that two jobs are of equal value'.[40] One mechanism for expanding access to equal value would have been to require trade unions and employers to negotiate the contextualized meaning of equal value in each workplace. However, the ECJ simply endorsed the view that it was unacceptable for equal value to be unavailable where an employer refused to voluntarily implement job evaluation.

In response, the Conservative government of the day introduced amending legislation to include statutory attention to equal pay 'where a women is employed on work...of equal value to that of a man in the same employment'.[41] The effect was to 'write in' a new role for the courts and make prior implementation of workplace job evaluation unnecessary. Under the new section 2(1)(c) of the EPA, women could prompt adjudication directly with a request that an employment tribunal appoint its own expert and evaluate comparable worth.[42]

The amendment challenged the legitimacy of collective bargaining as a medium of 'women's voice' and expanded job evaluation as an apparently objective mechanism to resolve equal pay injustice.[43] Historically, job evaluation had proven effective as a strategy to depoliticize equal pay campaigns.[44] Strength lay in its purportedly scientific, independent, and functionalist view of wage relativity, but its impact most frequently legitimized industrial hierarchies which were already well established.[45] As a consequence, job evaluation was not a mechanism which, on its own, would radically

[36] See Michael J. Klarman, 'The Judges versus the Unions: The Development of British Labor Law 1867–1913' (1989) 75 Virginia Law Review 1487.

[37] *R v CAC ex p. Hymac* [1979] IRLR 461, QB.

[38] Kay Gilbert, 'Promises and practices: job evaluation and equal pay forty years on!' (2012) 43 Industrial Relations Journal (IRJ) 137, 147; Deborah Figart, 'Wage Setting Under Fordism: The Rise of Job Evaluation and the Ideology of Equal Pay' (2001) 13 Review of Political Economy 405.

[39] Equal Pay Directive 75/117 (n 13).

[40] C-61/81 *Commission of the European Communities v United Kingdom* [1982] ECR 2601 [288].

[41] Equal Pay Act (Amendment) Regulations 1983 SI 1983/1794 introduced by s. 1(2)(c) Equal Pay Act 1970.

[42] *Hovell v Ashford and St Peter's Hospital NHS Trust* [2009] EWCA Civ 670, [2009] IRLR 734.

[43] For details see Sue Hastings, 'Grading Systems and Estimating Value' in G. White and J. Druker (eds), *Reward Management: A Critical Text* (Routledge, 2000).

[44] See discussion of the 1943 Hillingdon dispute in Harold Smith, 'The Problem of "Equal Pay for Equal Work" in Great Britain during World War II' (1981) 53 The Journal of Modern History 652; Penny Summerfield, *Reconstructing Women's Wartime Lives: Discourse and Subjectivity in Oral Histories of the Second World War* (Manchester University Press, 1998), 129.

[45] Deborah Figart, 'Equal Pay for Equal Work: The Role of Job Evaluation in an Evolving Social Norm' (2000) 34 Journal of Economic Issues 1; Paula England and Dana Dunn, 'Evaluating Work and Comparable Worth' (1988) 14 Annual Review of Sociology 227, 245.

redefine the value of women's work.[46] Sewing machinists at Ford's Dagenham factory, who had taken strike action over equal pay in 1968, continued to be graded as unskilled workers despite the settlement of the dispute and the passing of the Equal Pay Act 1970. The new equal value provisions provided an opportunity to try and use the law to overturn the ongoing legacy of their discriminatory grading under Ford's job evaluation scheme. However, the Industrial Tribunal hearing the case in 1984 upheld the integrity of the company's job evaluation decisions and denied the women an assessment of equal value with 'skilled' men.[47] The case illustrates how 'women's voice' could be diluted by the legal regulation of women's pay which relied upon the opinions and assessment of legal and managerial experts. Frustrated at the limitations of the law, the sewing machinists engaged in extended strike action. It was this action which delivered results and they gained equal recognition as skilled workers and the equal pay that followed.

In 1986, the Conservative government repealed EPA, s. 3 provisions for the voluntary referral of collective agreements.[48] The effect was to 'write out' unions as partners in the legal establishment of equal pay. This ushered in a period of intransigence towards equal pay law which combined employer resistance to the *aims* of the law with union disenchantment at the amended *approach* of the law.[49] Reduced union influence over the substance of employment contracts was one piece of the strategic 'individualization' of industrial relations advanced by successive Conservative governments from 1979.[50] Prospects for the exercise of 'women's voice', either via law or collective bargaining, were progressively weakened by the ensuing fragmentation of work, extensive contracting out of women's public-sector jobs, and intense competitive tendering pressures on male wages.[51]

In the handful of equal value cases that came to law, it was the existence of workplace collective bargaining that connected women to potential comparators with whom equal pay might be established.[52] For example, in 1988 women who worked alongside men doing the same job, for the same pay, gained the ability to apply for an equal value assessment in respect of other higher paid men working for the same private-sector employer.[53] The following year, women were entitled to turn to public sector collective agreements as 'common terms' for the purposes of equal value comparison with men working in different jobs at different establishments.[54] By 1996, the House of Lords allowed comparison to be made on a basis of 'common terms' when terms 'broadly similar' to existing terms would apply if comparators, working for the same employer, were

[46] Patricia Findlay, Jeanette Findlay, and Robert Stewart, 'The Consequences of Caring: Skills, Regulation and Reward among Early Years Workers' (2009) 23 Work, Employment and Society (Work Employ Soc) 422, 424.

[47] *Neil v Ford Motor Company* [1984] IRLR 339, EAT.

[48] Sex Discrimination Act 1986, s. 6.

[49] Simon Deakin and Colm Mclaughlin, 'The Regulation of Women's Pay: From Individual Employment Rights to Reflexive Law?' (Centre for Business Research, Working Paper 350) 14.

[50] William Brown et al., 'The Employment Contract: From Collective Procedures to Individual Rights' (2000) 38 British Journal of Industrial Relations 611.

[51] See Margie Jaffe, Bronwyn McKenna, and Liane Venner, *Equal Pay, Privatisation and Procurement* (Institute of Employment Rights, 2008); Bronwyn McKenna, 'The Union Perspective on Equal Pay' [2008] 174 Equal Opportunities Review (EOR), 1 March.

[52] *Hayward* (n 25).

[53] *Pickstone v Freemans* [1988] 2 All ER 803, [1988] IRLR 357, HL.

[54] *Leverton v Clwyd County Council* (n 30).

to work at the same establishment as the claimants.[55] However, it was the success of equal value arguments pursued in the 1993 case of *Enderby v Frenchay Health Authority* that made union negotiation in the public sector look particularly out of place.[56]

Pam Enderby claimed that the work she and other women undertook as speech therapists was of equal value to that of higher paid men working as pharmacists and clinical psychologists in the same hospital. However, their pay-setting processes were completely unconnected, there were no discriminatory terms in either of the relevant collective agreements, and both groups were independently represented in collective bargaining. The employer argued that there was no evidence of discrimination. Yet, without calling into question a specific underpinning pay practice, the ECJ viewed the extent of the pay difference, together with the sex-typing of the two bargaining groups, as sufficient to raise a presumption of indirect discrimination which required justification. *Enderby* turned the judicial approach to collective bargaining on its head since:

> the fact that the respective rates of pay of two jobs of equal value, one carried out almost exclusively by women and the other predominantly by men, were arrived at by collective bargaining processes which, although carried out by the same parties, are distinct and, taken separately, have in themselves no discriminatory effect, is not sufficient objective justification for a difference in pay between those two jobs.[57]

Preceding cases had focused on the outcomes of collective bargaining by addressing discriminatory terms in collective agreements. Now, in the absence of a provision, criterion, or practice that could be identified as producing pay difference, separate collective bargaining was not enough to justify the existence of a pay difference (since discrimination might be hidden).[58]

It was a radical leap forward for equal pay law which prompted unions and public-sector employers to streamline their bargaining arrangements and harmonize terms and conditions.[59] In local government, there were known pay disparities between manual grade men and women; and between clerical/technical grade women and manual workers. There was also an issue of productivity bonuses in male-dominated manual work to be resolved.[60] In 1997, local government employers committed to a landmark national agreement to introduce non-discriminatory pay within a decade. Known as 'Single Status', this agreement would harmonize hours and place all workers on the same single pay spine based on local job evaluation assessments. However, implementation proved painfully slow in some parts of the country and non-existent in others.[61]

In 2003, a ruling of the ECJ prompted the UK government to increase the existing statutory limit on compensatory awards from two to six years' worth of back-pay.[62]

[55] *British Coal Corporation v Smith* (n 32). [56] *Enderby* (n 13). [57] *Enderby* [23] (n 13).

[58] TUC, *CEDAW Shadow Report* (Section 11. Supplementary information on Equal Pay, 2013).

[59] Sue Hastings, *Pay Inequalities in Local Government* (Submission to Local Government Pay Commission on behalf of the Trade Union side, 2003).

[60] *Report of the Bonus Technical Working Group* (National Joint Council for Local Government, 1998); UNISON, *Single Status, Job Evaluation and Pay and Grading Reviews. Guidance on Negotiating and Settlements* (2005); Hastings (n 59).

[61] *Unblocking the Route to Equal Pay* (Local Government Employers Association, 2006).

[62] Equal Pay (Amendment) Regulations 2003 followed C-326/96 *Levez v TH Jennings* [1998] ECR I-7835, [1999] IRLR 36 [49] to bring equal pay remedies into line with those generally available for breach of contract.

This made formal legal claims a more worthwhile financial prospect for women in low-waged, part-time employment.[63] In the face of inertia at the bargaining table, employment solicitors operating a no-win no-fee business model spotted an opportunity to represent public-sector women on a private and individual basis. Their intervention sparked 'trench warfare' with the unions.[64] The no-win no-fee strategy of seeking compensation for historic losses was in direct conflict with the embedded workplace negotiations of trade unions. Collective bargaining sought pay justice for women who had been discriminated against, without consequential job losses or contracting out, as well as the protection of comparator men and women who would be down-graded or lose pay premiums as a result of the introduction of equal pay for all.[65]

Trade unions had litigated strategically to clarify the scope of equal value and employer obligations.[66] However, the landmark no-win no-fee case of *Redcar and Cleveland Borough Council v Degnan* paved the way for tens of thousands of women to claim equal pay in relation to bonus payments to which they had not been entitled.[67] The Court of Appeal accepted that the payment of bonuses to men was to the detriment of women and, unless justified by the employer, bonuses could be regarded as ordinary pay for the purposes of comparison.[68] Bonuses had been the backbone of locally negotiated productivity settlements since the 1960s and levered between 30–100 per cent higher take home pay for men than women in equal work.[69] The task of justifying bonuses as a genuine reward for increased productivity was complicated by a legacy of privatization, tendering, and re-tendering which had encouraged local authorities to streamline calculation of labour costs into hourly 'units' to facilitate competition with private-sector contractors.[70] Bespoke work-study departments and managers employed for record-keeping had proven too costly to retain.[71] Without the paperwork and managerial evidence to justify productivity bonuses, local authorities were repeatedly found to have operated widespread de facto men's and women's rates of pay.[72]

Three quarters of local authorities failed to implement Single Status by the 2007 deadline.[73] Employer priority appeared to have shifted towards outsourcing jobs— particularly the jobs of local authority employed care workers, to whom potential equal

[63] Allison Parken, *Gaining Control of Equal Pay* (Close the Pay Gap Campaign, Equality and Human Rights Commission, 2009).

[64] David Reade, 'Current issues in equal pay in the public sector' [2009] 186 EOR 1 March. See facts on the suspension of a trade union representative for acting against the union's equal pay strategy *Hamilton v GMB (Northern Region)* [2007] IRLR 391, EAT; 'The way to achieve equal pay is through unions, not these lawyers' *Guardian Newspaper* (8 January 2008); Simon Hattenstone, 'The Most Hated Lawyer in Britain?' *The Guardian* (1 May 2010).

[65] See *Redcar and Cleveland Borough Council v Bainbridge (No. 2)* [2008] EWCA Civ 885, [2008] IRLR 776.

[66] Margaret Hallock, 'Pay Equity: What is the best union strategy?' (2000) 25 Labor Studies Journal 27.

[67] *Redcar and Cleveland Borough Council v Degnan* [2005] EWCA Civ 726.

[68] For background, Sue Hastings, 'Negative (Pay) Equity' in Jeanne Gregory, Rosemary Sales, and Ariane Hegewisch (eds), *Women Work and Inequality* (MacMillan Press, 1999).

[69] See *Report of the Bonus Technical Working Group* (n 60).

[70] See *Sunderland v Brennan* [2012] EWCA Civ 413; Hastings (n 59).

[71] See facts in *Barker v Birmingham City Council* Unreported 3921 23/04/2010 ET.

[72] *South Tyneside Metropolitan Borough Council v Anderson* [2007] EWCA 654, [2007] IRLR 715 [21].

[73] *Unblocking the Route to Equal Pay* (n 61).

pay liabilities were greatest.[74] Negotiating the implementation of equal pay going forwards, securing compensatory back-pay for underpaid women and protecting others from pay losses was an immensely complex task. For unions, maximizing compensatory awards through recourse to law ran the risk of pricing women's jobs out of the public sector. However, trading low back-pay settlements in exchange for future orientated protections ran the risk of appearing to minimize the legal entitlements of women who had suffered decades of pay discrimination. Entering into collective agreements, which might be later considered as in some way discriminatory, exposed the unions to legal challenge as parties to the bargain.[75]

The union position further deteriorated as unions themselves were found liable in sex discrimination claims brought on a no-win no-fee basis.[76] A climate of union 'anxiety' over negotiating led to the freezing of progress on equal pay at a workplace level and prompted increased litigation.[77] Lord Justice Mummery remarked that workplace negotiation 'in good faith can produce fairer, more realistic and more enduring benefits ... [than] interminable litigation between waged workers and their employers about their rights'.[78] Indeed, unions were well aware that resolving a case in law often took many years; the system of comparison set out in the Equal Pay Act did not reflect women's experience of work; and a background of public service reorganization, privatization, and contracting meant legal success was uncertain.[79] These expressed reservations, together with the lapse of more than 30 years between the Equal Pay Act 1970 and mass litigation, suggests that unions did not chose to direct their members to the courts until the unions faced little alternative. The consequences were observed to be 'prolific',[80] with litigation at 'almost epidemic proportions'.[81] More than 200,000 claims have been lodged since 2005, and liability for back-pay is estimated to exceed £5 billion.[82]

The unwillingness of central and local government to increase their overall wage bill in order to correct historic pay discrimination left unions struggling over how best to represent members' diverse interests.[83] Equal pay had to be delivered by cutting the pay of some men and women rather than by simply levelling up the wages of underpaid women.[84] On a national scale, half of the 'losers' were women (mainly in clerical and technical grades) who lost premium payments, allowances, and in some instances were down-graded in new job evaluation schemes.[85] Irrespective of their veracity, 'scare stories' about pay cuts, job losses, and privatization constituted unlawful victimization

[74] See Jaffe, McKenna, and Venner (n 51); Carole Thornley, 'Unequal and Low pay in the Public Sector' (2006) 37 IRJ 344; Jill Rubery, 'Towards a gendering of the labour market regulation debate' (2011) 35 Cambridge Journal of Economics 1103.

[75] *Unison and another v Brennan* [2008] ICR 955, EAT; *Allen v GMB* [2008] EWCA Civ 810, [2008] IRLR 690; *Brennan v Sunderland City Council* [2009] ICR 479.

[76] *Unison and another v Brennan* (n 75); *Allen v GMB* (n 75); *Brennan v Sunderland* (n 75); J. Cavanagh, 'Equal Pay: Why we should feel sorry for public sector employers and unions' [2008] 178 EOR 1 June.

[77] Reade (n 64).

[78] *Haq & Others v The Audit Commission* [2012] EWCA Civ 1621 [7]–[8].

[79] McKenna (n 51).

[80] *Sunderland v Brennan* (Lord Justice Maurice Kay [5]) (n 70).

[81] *Haq & Others v The Audit Commission* (Lord Justice Mummery [5]) (n 78).

[82] See TUC, *CEDAW Shadow Report* (n 58).

[83] See Thornley (n 74).

[84] TUC, *CEDAW Shadow Report* 1 (n 58).

[85] See Gilbert (n 38); David Thompson, 'Council Workers Facing Massive Wage Cuts' *Bury Times* (7 August 2008).

when used in an attempt to dissuade underpaid women from pursuing full compensation via legal claims.[86]

The Equal Pay Act 1970 was repealed and replaced by provisions in the Equality Act 2010.[87] This single text amalgamated existing anti-discrimination law and little priority was attached to re-examining the legal approach towards equal pay.[88] As the new legislation passed through the House of Lords, peers with a lifetime of knowledge about the weaknesses of the EPA were critical of continuing its 'minimalist approach', its lack of fit with 'the way in which labour is organised these days', and its focus on individual claims-making in the face of 'systematic' pay discrimination.[89] However, the structure of equal pay law remained largely unchanged.[90] The issue of discrimination emanating from collective agreements, which had been efficiently dealt with by collective referral in the 1970s, had returned in contemporary form. Despite the strong case for a collective framework of resolution,[91] the voluntary referral of collective agreements was never seriously considered for reintroduction.[92]

It has been observed that the 'extremely litigious' environment of recent years, in which collective bargaining has struggled for legitimacy, has been underestimated in many academic accounts.[93] It would certainly seem that to assume trade unions can implement equal pay strategies in isolation of the law fails to appreciate the significance of regulation to wider issues of inequality. As gently expressed by Lord Justice Pill, equal pay 'is best dealt with by negotiation ... but progress in this field has been sufficiently slow to make attempts to seek redress through the tribunal system on occasions legitimate'.[94] Lack of progress in the bargaining field is a direct corollary of the increasingly dominant legal framework which appears to target collective bargaining as a vehicle of male privilege warranting full judicial oversight.[95] It is a suggestion the unions vociferously reject. By 2002 women were more likely to be union members than men; in 2010 a majority of the public sector's 4.1 million trade union members were women and the largest union comprised over 70 per cent female membership.[96]

[86] *Derbyshire v St Helens Metropolitan Borough Council* [2007] UKHL 16, [2007] IRLR 540.

[87] Equality Act 2010, Pt 5 Ch 3. See Bob A. Hepple, 'The New Single Equality Act in Britain' (2010) 5 The Equal Rights Review 11.

[88] Tess Gill, 'The Equality Act and equal pay—a missed opportunity' [2010] 200 EOR 1 May.

[89] Hansard HL vol 706 col 1885–1887 (23 January, 2009) (Baroness Prosser); Hansard HL vol 706 col 1890–1894 (23 January 2009) (Lord Lester).

[90] See Maleiha Malik, '"Modernising Discrimination Law": Proposals for a Single Equality Act for Great Britain' (2007) 9 International Journal of Discrimination and the Law 73; Hepple (n 87).

[91] Trevor Phillips, Chair of the EHRC recommended the Equal Pay Act be set aside to enable class actions to replace the 'legal forest fire' see Helen Mulholland, 'Equal Pay Act "should be scrapped"' *Guardian Newspaper* (01/14/2008); also Gillian Whitehouse, 'Legislation and Labour Market Gender Inequality: An Analysis of OECD Countries' (1992) 6 Work Employ Soc 65.

[92] Aileen McColgan, *Consultation Response. Women and Work Commission, the gender pay gap* (Institute of Employment Rights, 2006); *Discrimination Law Review: A Framework for Fairness: Proposals for a Single Equality Bill for Great Britain—A consultation paper* (Dept for Communities and Local Government, 2007) 53–9; David Rowbottom, 'Rediscovering the Collective Application of the Equal Pay Act' (2007) 26 Equal Opportunities International 541.

[93] Thornley, 353 (n 74).

[94] *Suffolk Mental Health Partnership NHS Trust v Hurst and Sandwell Metropolitan Borough Council v Arnold* [2009] EWCA Civ 309 [57(b)].

[95] See *Redcar v Bainbridge (No. 2)* (n 65).

[96] James Archur, *Trade Union Membership* (Department for Business Innovation and Skills, National Statistics Publication, 2010).

'Women's Voice' and Norms of Collective Bargaining

The discussion now turns to examine three cases addressing trade union strategies to implement the Single Status agreement in local government. Each case reached the Court of Appeal; each offered a judicial review of collective bargaining and claimants were supported by no-win no-fee lawyers. The cases are analysed in consecutive order and collective bargaining norms of 'manner and form' are drawn from them. The first is *Allen v GMB*, in which a union has an obligation to promote the Equal Pay Act.[97] This suggests normative procedural conduct in bargaining. The second is *Redcar and Cleveland Borough Council v Bainbridge No. 2*, in which the sex-based composition of collective bargaining groups was explored and normative standards regarding the inclusion of both men and women in collective bargaining matters, evident.[98] Third, is the case of *Coventry City Council v Nicholls*, which introduced normative propositions about the content of union negotiations from its review of a productivity-based pay settlement.[99] The three norms, of conduct, composition and content, each address a 'manner and form' aspect of collective bargaining. They arise from judicial regard for the gendering of collective bargaining and appear to be motivated by concern for the audibility of 'women's voice'.

In *Allen v GMB* the Court of Appeal held a union directly liable for sex discrimination over a local negotiation to introduce the national Single Status agreement at a local authority. Its legal significance is to link a pay settlement outcome, which was not considered discriminatory, to a process of gaining collective agreement, which was. This blurring of *outcome* and *process* put more weight on individual rights to equal pay compensation than on collective bargaining attempts to embed a system of equal pay across a workforce. The union's overarching aim was to implement Single Status and protect those members who would lose pay from the immediate impact of a fall in income. It negotiated a deal with the employer which could only be realized if women with viable equal pay claims gave up their potential entitlement to compensation in law. The Court of Appeal characterized this as a condition of the bargain which fell within the legal definition of a provision, criterion, or practice producing pay difference (PCP). As a PCP it was subject to justification.[100] While the union's aim was accepted to be legitimate, the means it adopted were considered disproportionate. It was not the *outcome* of the bargain itself, but the *process* of delivering it which was therefore found to be discriminatory. The union had assumed the acquiescence of claimants when it made the bargain. It subsequently 'persuaded' them with 'mis-information', to forego much of their (potential) compensatory entitlement for the sake of protecting others.[101] This conduct exposed women, already the subjects of pay discrimination, to further discrimination in order to facilitate a bargain which the union believed to represent a greater good.

In what the Court of Appeal acknowledged was a difficult division of 'aims and means', its legal advance coupled the *outcome* of a negotiation with the *process* of delivering it

[97] *Allen v GMB* (n 75). [98] *Redcar v Bainbridge (No. 2)* (n 65).

[99] *Coventry City Council v Nicholls* [2009] EWCA Civ 1449.

[100] C-33/89 *Kowalska v Freie und Hansestadt Hamburg* [1990] ECR I-2591, [1990] IRLR 447, ECJ.

[101] *Allen v GMB* [16] (n 75).

through collective bargaining.[102] Previously, courts applied a justificatory principle that would 'involve the tribunal focusing on substance, rather than the form, and on the result, rather than the route taken to get to it'.[103] However, in *Allen*, the trade union was caught as a discriminatory agent in a three-way entitlement contest involving claimants with equal pay rights (who were also union members); union members in need of pay protection; and an employer seeking to control its wage bill.

Lord Justice Mummery has recently observed that equal pay law 'requires the clashing of rights, not just between employer and employee, but also as between groups of employees'.[104] The *Allen* case illuminates the potential for discordance between individual equal pay rights and collective rights to free bargaining.[105] The judgment's coincidence of outcome and process gives priority to equal pay rights and obliges trade unions to positively promote them in collective bargaining. It was expressed at the first instance tribunal, and later endorsed by the Court of Appeal that:

> A Union is not 'free' to disregard the rights of a sector of its members because it has different priorities, and to be relieved of its obligations towards those members to use its best endeavours to compel their employer to comply with its obligations under the Equal Pay Act.[106]

The statement combines judicial disapproval with an assumption that unions bear a normative duty to positively promote equal pay as defined in the Act. Indeed, a close reading might suggest there is little distance between union 'obligation' and an inference of union responsibility for equal pay compliance. Judicial regard for the gendering of collective bargaining is apparently motivated by a concern that 'women's voice', as expressed through equal pay entitlements in law, should not be silenced by collective priorities.

The principle of non-discrimination is a foundation of the European Community and applies to collective agreements.[107] There is clear scope for courts to regard collective bargaining as a conditional process which normatively links those agreements to equal pay obligations.[108] While collective bargaining rights are set out in Article 28 of the European Charter of Fundamental Rights there must be doubt about the justiciability of Article 28 in the UK due to the Protocol on the Application of the Charter of Fundamental Rights of the European Union to Poland and to the United Kingdom.[109] Nevertheless, part of ensuring adequate protection for collective bargaining is respect for equality principles.[110] It would seem reasonable to seek to balance individual equal

[102] *Allen v GMB* [29]–[30] (n 75). [103] *Ministry of Defence v Armstrong* [2004] IRLR 672, EAT [46].

[104] *Haq & Others v The Audit Commission* (n 78) [8]. For discussion, see Anne C. L. Davies, 'Identifying "Exploitative Compromises": The Role of Labour Law in Resolving Disputes Between Workers' (2012) Current Legal Problems 269.

[105] Cf *Hartley v Northumbria Healthcare NHS Foundation Trust, UNISON, Secretary of State for Health, NHS Confederation (Employers) Company* Reserve Judgment on Pre-Hearing Review, 6 October 2008 ET.

[106] *Allen v GMB* [24] (n 75).

[107] C-17/05 *Cadman v Health and Safety Executive* [2006] ECR I-9583; Art.157 TFEU [2008].

[108] C-143/83 *Commission v Denmark* [1986] 1 CMLR 44, ECJ [8].

[109] Protocol on the Application of the Charter of Fundamental Rights of the European Union to Poland and to the United Kingdom, Protocol 30 Charter of Fundamental Rights of the European Union OJ 2010/C83/02.

[110] C-427/11 *Kenny and others v Minister for Justice, Equality and Law Reform* [2013] 2 CMLR 50 (Advocate General Cruz Villalon [64]).

pay rights with the exercise of collective bargaining as a legally supported freedom. The right to free collective bargaining has been recently considered in the context of age discrimination.[111] Advocate General Cruz Villalon suggested that the protection of collective bargaining is a legitimate social policy objective and 'autonomy in collective bargaining deserves proper protection at the EU level'.[112]

Finding a correct balance between equal pay rights and a right to free collective bargaining may be more complex than the *Allen* norm of procedural conduct identified here suggests. Statute already balances autonomy in collective bargaining with equal treatment rights by ensuring that collective agreement outcomes are non-discriminatory. An alternative balance is struck in *Enderby* since collective bargaining outcomes in the form of significant sex-based pay differences are subject to the same standards of justification as apply to PCPs.[113] It is precisely those standards which are applied in *Allen* but its judicial regard for the gendering of collective bargaining imposes a norm of procedural conduct in support of the objectives of the Equal Pay Act. The formulation of this norm does not appear to account for rights of self-determination in collective bargaining even though this is particularly salient where unions attempt to draw a line in the sand and secure sustainable equal pay commitments for the future. A further problem is that the norm imposes a positive obligation towards equal pay compliance that is higher than required elsewhere. There are no procedural standards associated with equal pay for employers who do not recognize trade unions, their obligations extend only so far as non-discriminatory outcomes and there is no suggestion of a duty to promote equal treatment.[114]

The second 'manner and form' norm concerns the composition of bargaining groups and emanates from the seminal case of *Redcar and Cleveland Borough Council v Bainbridge (No. 2)*. Although the case was highly complex, the focus here is on two aspects only: justification of bonus payments in male-dominated jobs and, for a separate group of claimants, the establishment of a pay protection scheme.

Claimants were clerical workers and comparators were mechanics. Both were subject to separate collective bargaining arrangements and terms of work. Terms of work, in part, reflected worker priorities and the trade-offs, demands, and compromises they had made over many years. The mechanics received bonuses to which the clerical workers were not entitled. When challenged in equal pay proceeding, the employer could not establish a link between bonus and productivity and therefore the premiums had to be justified if they were not to be found discriminatory. In the case of *Enderby*, the existence of separate collective bargaining groups had not been enough on its own to justify pay differences. A considerable distinction in *Bainbridge* was the existence of the bonus scheme as a clear PCP causing pay difference. However, throughout the

[111] C-447/09 *Prigge v Deutsche Lufthansa AG* Opinion of Mr Advocate General Cruz Villalon delivered 19 May 2011.

[112] As per Art. 6(1) Council Directive 2000/78/EC of 27 November 2000 establishing a general framework for equal treatment in employment and occupation [2000] OJ L303/22. *Prigge v Deutsche Lufthansa AG* (n 111).

[113] *Enderby* (n 13).

[114] See *Lawrence* (n 7); *Allonby* (n 8); C-170/84 *Bilka-Kaufhaus GmbH v Weber Von Hartz* [1986] ECR 1607, [1986] 2 CMLR 701.

proceedings it was the sex-based composition of bargaining groups, rather than their impact, which captured attention.

With apparent concern that collective bargaining based on occupational demarcations could silence 'women's voice', the first instance tribunal noted that 'the existence of separate workgroups facilitates discrimination and could perpetuate it'.[115] The EAT acknowledged separate collective bargaining as an available defence 'in an appropriate case' and established such a case as one where collective bargaining groups were comprised of 'similar proportions by gender'.[116] The potential for justification apparently, 'would be otherwise where there is a marked difference in the sex balance'.[117] The Court of Appeal backed away from a suggestion that gender disparity in collective bargaining groups would lead 'inevitably' to the inference of discrimination. However, it endorsed the inference of sex-based pay discrimination from facts of gender disparity in collective bargaining groups.[118] On the bonus point then, the defence of justification could hang on the sex-based composition of bargaining groups, separately from the merits or otherwise of the PCP outcome produced through the bargain. This suggests that judicial regard for the gendering of collective bargaining would find mixed-sex bargaining more legitimate than sex-segregated bargaining.

The facts of the pay protection issue covered similar ground to the *Allen* case. Collective bargaining aimed to increase the wages of women previously discriminated against and introduce a pay protection scheme to cushion the impact of a loss of income to others. It was a necessary step for implementing the Single Status agreement. The objective of the union in the *Bainbridge* action was accepted as legitimate, it was not 'tainted by sex discrimination' and, at least at face value, the operation of the scheme had no adverse impact on claimants who were not going to lose wages as a result, but to gain.[119] The group entitled to pay protection was comprised of more women than men.[120] The claimant group however was entirely comprised of women, not aggrieved about the existence of the scheme, but their exclusion from pay protection.[121]

In its deliberations, the court took a step back from assessing outcomes to consider whether the women's exclusion from the process of collective bargaining had shaped the bargain. It reasoned that if the inclusion of the women in pay protection could have been shown to put the overall scheme in jeopardy, their exclusion could have been justified. However, there was a failure to broadly include the claimants in devising the scheme; no evidence that the views of the women had been sought or considered, the negotiation took no account of the potential for discriminatory impact and evidence about the affordability or viability of including the women had not been advanced.[122] Judicial regard for the gendering of collective bargaining on the pay protection point indicates a normative preference for unions to include women as a 'manner and form' matter in collective bargaining, whether or not the specific terms or impacts of the bargain itself are discriminatory. Once again, judicial regard for gendered process appears prior to concern about discriminatory outcomes. In this instance, excluding claimants

[115] *Redcar v Bainbridge (No. 2)* [194] (n 65).
[116] *Redcar v Bainbridge (No. 2)* [198] (n 65).
[117] *Redcar v Bainbridge (No. 2)* [198] (n 65).
[118] *Redcar v Bainbridge (No. 2)* [209]–[210] (n 65).
[119] *Redcar v Bainbridge (No. 2)* [80], [189], [207] (n 65).
[120] *Redcar v Bainbridge (No. 2)* [70] (n 65).
[121] *Redcar v Bainbridge (No. 2)* [24], [69] (n 65).
[122] *Redcar v Bainbridge (No. 2)* [71], [122], [175] (n 65).

from a pay protection scheme could not be justified, in part, because of a failure to include women in negotiations.[123]

The UK Supreme Court has recently asserted that the primary question in an equal pay claim is a question of belonging; can men and women be regarded as part of the same broad community for the purposes of comparison?[124] Equal pay comparisons cannot be based on arbitrary pairing of male and female workers to bring 'the pay of the group consisting predominantly of women to the level of that of another group also formed in an arbitrary manner so that it consists predominantly of men'.[125] Hence there is some logic in viewing the composition of collective bargaining groups as a rational basis for workplace groupings which do not give succour to 'purely fortuitous or short-term phenomena'.[126] The normative formulations in *Bainbridge (No. 2)*, regarding mixed-sex bargaining and the inclusion of women in bargaining processes, are problematic in the context of equal pay law. Part of a justification of sex-based pay differences may be the existence of separate collective bargaining groups which are not based on the reason of sex.[127] If the sex-based composition of the groups is to be determinative it does not sit easily with the principle that workplace sex-segregation is not unlawful, and sex-based inclusion/exclusion from an occupational group is not directly discriminatory without subsequent detrimental treatment.[128] Pay differences between men and women might be 'unfair' but they are lawful so long as they are not discriminatory.[129]

While equal pay law focuses on equal treatment between comparators, there are many legal avenues through which women are lawfully subjected to pay disadvantage by employer power over workplace groupings and structures. For example, it is acceptable in equal pay law for an employer to pay higher rates to attract new staff (who may be men),[130] or to fill skill shortages (including all male recruitment);[131] or to reduce women's pay by outsourcing their jobs but retaining men in direct employment.[132] In these instances, even where pay detriment is established as sex-based, the law does not require a levelling of wages in order to create a climate of pay equality.

The ability to discriminate between groups is subject to an employer's power to create those groups. Hugh Collins noted the promise of equal pay law to expose employer pay-setting power to standards of rationality and principles of justification.[133] However, the potential for law to bring this power under full review, and create a forum in

[123] *Redcar v Bainbridge (No. 2)* [140] (n 65).

[124] *North v Dumfries and Galloway Council* [22] (n 8).

[125] C-400/93 *Specialarbejderforbundet i Danmark v Dansk Industri (Royal Copenhagen)* [1995] ECR I-1275, [1996] 1 CMLR 515 ECJ [36].

[126] *Kenny and others v Minister for Justice, Equality and Law Reform* [45] (n 110).

[127] *Specialarbejderforbundet i Danmark v Dansk Industri (Royal Copenhagen)* [46] (n 125); *Reed Packaging v Boozer* [1988] ICR 391, [1988] IRLR 333, EAT.

[128] C-196/02 *Nikoloudi v Organismos Tilepikinonion Ellados AE* [2005] ECR I-1789, [2005] CMLR 54.

[129] *Redcar v Bainbridge (No. 2)* [181] (n 65).

[130] *Rainey v Greater Glasgow Health Board* [1987] IRLR 26, HL; *Enderby* (n 13).

[131] *Enderby* [29] (n 13).

[132] The dual logic of supporting pay advantage to men whilst expecting pay detriment to women to be justified is traceable in the *Armstrong* litigation, see n 12 and *Newcastle Upon Tyne NHS Hospital Trust v Armstrong (No. 2)* [2010] EWCA Civ 1203.

[133] Hugh Collins, 'Market Power, Bureaucratic Power and the Contract of Employment' (1986) 15 ILJ 1, 12–13.

which 'women's voice' may be heard, is curtailed by judicial and legislative deference to employer decision-making.[134] Take for example, the deference evident in judicial acceptance that workers may be fractured into separate groups and effective equal pay comparisons frustrated by an employer decision to devolve pay-setting to individual departments.[135] Further examples include judicial deference to employer pay-setting power in workforces partly comprised of workers transferred in from another employer. The fact of the transfer is accepted as a legitimate explanation to justify the indefinite maintenance of higher pay for men, including on-going pay rises.[136] Higher levels of experience at the point of recruitment may also be used as a between-group rule to the same effect.[137] In the case of *Allonby v Accrington and Rossendale College* the ECJ faced the question posed by Advocate General Geelhoed as to whether 'the courts must turn a blind eye to the fact that...a legal device has been used precisely, it should be noted, in order to evade the consequences of the principle of equal treatment'.[138] Whilst mildly critical, the judgment of the ECJ did not prevent employers from structuring their workers on the basis of sex to avoid liability for paying women equally to men.[139] Employers exercising unilateral power over pay-setting are not required to include women, are not required to accommodate women as a historically disadvantaged community, and they may set pay on the basis of sex-segregation. Judicial deference to unilateral pay-setting power suggests judicial regard for the gendering of collective bargaining might be similarly inclined towards support for management prerogative in pay-setting.

The final example draws on the case of *Coventry City Council v Nicholls*.[140] It questions the propriety of productivity-based wage rewards in sex-typed occupations and conceptualizes a norm of bargaining content. The claimants, supported by their union, argued it was unlawful for male refuse collectors to be paid a productivity bonus to which female workers in social services were not entitled. Accepting that the jobs of claimants and comparators were of equal value, the employer argued justification on the basis that the bonus was 'self-financing' through negotiated staff reductions and efficiencies. However, the Court of Appeal acknowledged judicial suspicion that pay-setting could be influenced by 'a tendency for men to be more likely to resort to industrial action than women'.[141] The large bonuses available to refuse collectors were thought to reflect the employers' fear of the 'political consequences of [...] industrial action, which other staff did not enjoy'.[142] Accordingly, 'collective industrial muscle' had influenced the budget for the refuse service, ensuring it was historically generous enough to accommodate periodic pay demands.[143] In social services however, the budget was pared down to a minimum. There was no slack in a wage bill which 'under-rewarded jobs occupied almost exclusively by women' and strictly adhered to managing labour efficiencies by

[134] Anne C. L. Davies, 'Judicial Self-Restraint in Labour Law' (2009) 38 ILJ 278.

[135] *Robertson v Department for Environment, Food and Rural Affairs* [2005] EWCA Civ 138.

[136] *Skills Development Scotland Co Ltd v Buchanan* [2011] Eq LR 955, EAT; *Nelson v Carillion Services Ltd* [2003] EWCA 544, [2003] ICT 1256.

[137] *Bowling v Secretary of State for Justice* [2012] IRLR 382, EAT. However the mere anticipation of higher productivity will not suffice, see C-381/99 *Brunnhofer v Bank der Osterreichischen Postsparkasse AG* [2001] ECR I-4961, [2001] IRLR 571.

[138] *Allonby* [AG43] (n 8).

[139] *Allonby* [AG43] (n 8).

[140] *Coventry City Council v Nicholls* (n 99).

[141] *Coventry City Council v Nicholls* [45] (n 99).

[142] *Coventry City Council v Nicholls* [48] (n 99).

[143] *Coventry City Council v Nicholls* [48] (n 99).

policy rather than by cash reward.[144] In a markedly robust interrogation of the departmental dynamics of local government, the 'self-financing' aspect of the bonus was held to be gendered and the difference in pay unjustified.

From a perspective of social equality, the judgment is markedly progressive since it interrogates the underlying, gendered, resource context in which pay-setting is formulated. However, from a legal perspective the extent to which the judgment accommodates context should not pass without question. Significantly, no evidence was presented to support the suspicion that a male propensity for collective action or management fears of disruption lay at the heart of the bonus scheme.[145] Similar suspicions had surfaced at the EAT in *Bainbridge (No. 2)*, inferring discrimination from an assumption that a negotiating panel were all male (recognized on Appeal as having no basis in fact), and also at the Court of Appeal in *Armstrong v Newcastle NHS Trust* where strong union organization was discussed as a factor making men's voice more 'voluble' than that of women.[146]

Where presented with such evidence, a court would presumably have the tricky task of distinguishing pay-setting decisions influenced by the lawful exercise of collective action, from pay-setting decisions influenced by the reason of sex in the lawful exercise of collective action. The difficulty inherent in such an onerous task makes established conventions of assessment on the basis of *outcomes* rather than *processes* appear attractive.

The decision in *Coventry City Council v Nicholls* did not reject justification on the content of the bargain, or its exercise, but on its context. It is possible that consideration of context strays into that which, 'can sometimes hover on the verge of non-justiciability'.[147] The bonus system was found discriminatory on the basis that slack in the system made productivity reward feasible. Since the existence of a departmental budget with slack was sex-tainted, the 'self-financing' nature of the bonus could not provide justification. However, it is difficult to envisage any productivity-based pay scheme which is not, at least in part, underpinned by arguments appealing to its self-financing nature. The inference therefore, as later taken up in *Gibson v Sheffield City Council*, is that, within mixed sex workplaces, it is unlikely that productivity bargaining for sex-typed occupational groups will produce pay settlements which can be justified unless bonuses take a form which is applicable to both male and female dominated bargaining groups.[148]

While there may be other negotiating options available to trade unions, these alternatives may be less in tune with members' interests or less likely to succeed. Moreover, since productivity bargaining appears likely to be legally contentious where men and women work for the same employer in sex-typed work, restricting productivity bargaining in such circumstances may lead to fragmentation. The result would then be less amenable to embedding equal pay as a sustainable workplace value. The formulation of *Nicholls*-type judicial norms of bargaining content, in response to judicial regard for the gendering of collective bargaining, suggests that unions may be more likely to

[144] *Coventry City Council v Nicholls* [8] (n 99). [145] *Coventry City Council v Nicholls* [54] (n 99).

[146] *Armstrong v Newcastle upon Tyne NHS Trust* [31] and [62] (n 12).

[147] *Haq & Others v The Audit Commission* (Lord Justice Mummery [13]) (n 78).

[148] *Gibson v Sheffield City Council* [2010] EWCA Civ 63, [2010] IRLR 311 (Lady Justice Smith [71]).

turn to market-based arguments for pay enhancement. It would seem that too detailed attention to context may harness concern for *process*, as a tool with which to interpret *outcomes*, and entertain the risk that 'unfortunate, unintended consequences [are] ever-present'.[149]

Conclusion

This chapter has explored how the dynamic relationship between collective bargaining and law conceptualizes, articulates, and legitimates norms pertaining to 'women's voice'. Analysis of Court of Appeal judgments which reviewed trade union attempts to resolve equal pay issues at a workplace level has suggested that three 'manner and form' norms of collective bargaining are apparent. They go further than the statutory focus on the content of collective agreements, to embrace procedural elements of conduct, composition, and bargaining content. The norms relate to 'women's voice' and represent a potentially laudable equality advance which expands the capacity of law to recognize discriminatory pay outcomes.

Taken as a whole, the cases indicate that equal pay law responds in specific ways when, nominally or substantially, employers 'share' pay-setting power with workers through collective bargaining. A suggestion that responsibility for equal pay compliance lies with unions would have little basis in law, but accords with the history of the equal pay principle presented here. The law and collective bargaining have coexisted in a relation of dynamic tension over expressions of 'women's voice' in matters of equal pay.

However, judicially imposed 'manner and form' norms may have exacerbated a turn towards mass litigation in place of previous commitments to negotiation over equal pay. These norms link concern for the *process* of collective bargaining too tightly with the statutory interest in the *outcomes* of collective bargaining than is desirable for the effective communication of 'women's voice'. One consequence is a weakening of collective bargaining in the name of equality without any countervailing support for 'women's voice' at work. Another is to strengthen employer power to set pay in reference to market forces, outside of statutory regard for the worsening of women's wages or the silencing of 'women's voice' at work. Existing judicial tendencies of deference to management prerogative suggest judicial regard for the gendering of collective bargaining might find synergy with strategies of unilateral pay-setting power on purported equalities grounds.

The purpose of equal pay legislation has never been to dismantle predominantly male and female workplace groups but to enable comparison between them. Collective bargaining remains a process which is critical to enabling such comparison to become possible. To restrict collective bargaining processes is to restrict the potential for comparison. A result is to strengthen the legitimacy of employers' unilateral exercise of pay-setting power or the establishment of market-orientated bilateral relations between commissioners and contracting organizations which stand outside the reach of equal pay law.

[149] *Haq & Others v The Audit Commission* (Lord Justice Mummery [12]) (n 78).

The fate of many local authority care workers offers a strong illustration of the need for better contemporary support in law for the collective resolution of equal pay matters. While awaiting the implementation of non-discriminatory pay over the period 1997–2007, almost half of the eligible local authority social care workforce were transferred out of direct employment into private-sector work with contractors and therefore lost the ability to compare their pay with that of male local authority manual workers.[150] Judicial regard for the gendering of collective bargaining appears to be motivated by concern for the audibility of 'women's voice'. However, if its price is to undermine collective bargaining structures, privilege market-based pay-setting, and prevent meaningful pay comparisons, the prospects that 'women's voice' will be heard in matters of pay equality are inevitably damaged.

[150] Jill Rubery and Peter Unwin, 'Bringing the employer back in: why social care needs a standard employment relationship' (2011) 21 Human Resource Management Journal 122, 123–4. Private-sector contracting in homecare services increased by 300 per cent. Figures drawn from *Community Care Statistics 2007, Homecare services for adults, England* (National Health Service, 2008) iii–iv and *Community Care Statistics 2004 Homecare services for adults, England* (National Health Service, 2005) 6.

3

Low-paid Care Work, Bargaining, and Employee Voice in Australia

Rae Cooper[1]

Introduction

This chapter examines the ways in which Australia's national industrial relations law, the 'Fair Work Act 2009' (Cth) (AUS) ('FW Act'), reregulated the 'voice' of low-paid workers in the highly-feminized aged care sector. The chapter pays special attention to a key case heard by the Full Bench of the national industrial relations tribunal, Fair Work Australia, between 2009 and 2013. This was an application for a Low-paid Bargaining Authorisation by the union representing personal care workers in the aged care sector, United Voice.[2] Women care workers are typically treated as 'vulnerable workers' in the literature. They suffer low pay, work in jobs which are dirty, dangerous, and precarious, and they are susceptible, because of their low levels of bargaining power, to ill treatment from employers. In terms of voice, vulnerable workers, including low-paid care workers, are typically viewed as 'silent' workers. They have poor access to mechanisms for voice at work, either indirectly through trade unions or directly through employer initiated channels. This silence extends beyond the workplace and into broader social and economic life and interaction. The case outlined in this chapter demonstrates that decent conditions of work for women in this sector, including their capacity to exercise voice, will not be achieved simply. In fact, the complicated mixture of factors which construct labour market vulnerability for care workers may need to be reshaped through equally complex and multi-channelled mechanisms. The chapter is structured in the following way. First, a brief review of literature on women's care work, and the capacity of these workers to exercise voice, is provided. Second, the chapter shows how the innovative Low-paid Bargaining stream fits within the broader FW Act framework. The third section of the chapter analyses the first application by the United Voice union for a Low-paid Bargaining Authorisation and details the context and outcomes of the case. Before concluding, this section also sets out the key lessons of the application for the regulation of low-paid care work and details development in the regulation of aged care workplaces

[1] I wish to thank officials of United Voice, the Australian Nursing Federation and the Australian Council of Trade Unions for agreeing to be interviewed as a part of the research for this chapter. Thanks to colleagues at Leeds University Business School and Griffith University who commented on earlier papers from the project. Thanks to my research collaborator Professor Bradon Ellem and to editors of this collection for advice on the framing of this chapter. Laura Good and Nicole Cini provided research assistance at various points on this chapter and I acknowledge their contribution. All errors are, of course, my own.

[2] The Liquor Hospitality and Miscellaneous Workers Union was renamed 'United Voice' in late 2010. United Voice (UV) was joined by the Australian Workers Union in their application, but remained the lead union. Other unions and peak councils supported UV's case, for example the Australian Nurses Federation and the Australian Council of Trade Unions. The case study of the application presented here primarily examines the UV's argument and strategy.

since the case was concluded. The chapter closes with suggestions as to other, non-legal mechanisms, such as rethinking supply chains and funding regimes, for lifting wages and improving working conditions and to strengthen the voice for care workers.

Low-paid Care Work in the Literature

A key theme in the framing of care work in the academic literature is that of labour market 'vulnerability'. This concept emphasizes the inferior labour market position of employees which is constructed by low levels of market power which, in part, results from the demand for, and the perceived value of, employee skills. Vulnerable employees rely upon minimum standards, such as the minimum wage or, in Australia, industry-based awards, as well as protective legislation, for the determination of their pay and their conditions of employment,[3] and without such intervention they would be, in Allan Flanders' words, 'at the mercy of the market'.[4] Needless to say, vulnerable employees are greatly affected at times when minimum standards regimes are reregulated, as was demonstrated in Australia, during the Work Choices period, in the mid-2000s.[5]

Regardless of the intervention of the state, vulnerable workers remain in a disadvantaged position relative to both their employers and to fellow employees who are able to exercise more labour market clout. For the purposes of this chapter, a key feature of vulnerable employment identified in the literature is that it is 'silent' work. Workplace silence, where 'workers do not have avenues to pursue issues of concern to them, either because of a failure of pre-existing voice mechanisms or because of the absence of them altogether',[6] is a feature of the jobs of most vulnerable employees. Low-paid care workers are rarely touched by independent collective mechanisms of voice, for example through trade union activity and collective bargaining,[7] and the precipitous decline in trade union membership in many contexts, including Australia, during the past 20 years has exacerbated this problem.[8] When low-paid care workers *are* organized into unions, they often number among the less vocal and most powerless of the constituencies within these organizations.[9] In Australia, like much of the Anglophone world, there is no generalized employer duty to provide mechanisms for employee voice.[10] In the absence of such an obligation, employers have chosen by-and-large to not fill the vacuum,

[3] Anna Pollert and Andy Charlwood, 'The Vulnerable Worker in Britain and Problems at Work' (2009) 23(2) Work, Employment and Society (Work Employ Soc) 343; Therese Jefferson and Alison Preston, 'Negotiating Fair Pay and Conditions: Low Paid Women's Experience and Perceptions of Labour Market Deregulation and Individual Wage Bargaining' (2010) 41(4) Industrial Relations Journal (IRJ) 351.

[4] Allan Flanders, *Management and Unions: The Theory of Reform of Industrial Relations* (Faber and Faber, 1970) 215.

[5] Barbara Pocock et al., 'The Impact of "*Work Choices*" on Women in Low-Paid Employment in Australia: A Qualitative Analysis' (2008) 50(3) Journal of Industrial Relations (JIR) 477.

[6] Jimmy Donaghey et al., 'Reconceptualising Employee Silence: Problems and Prognosis' (2011) 25(1) Work Employ Soc 51.

[7] B. van Wanrooy, 'Women at Work in Australia: Bargaining a Better Position?' (2009) 35(4) Australian Bulletin of Labour 611.

[8] Cathy Bridgen, 'Unions and Collective Bargaining' (2012) 54 (3) JIR 361.

[9] Geraldine Healy and Gill Kirton, 'Women, Power and Trade Union Government in the UK' (2000) 38(3) British Journal of Industrial Relations (BJIR) 343.

[10] Ray Markey, 'Non-Union Employee Representation in Australia: A Case Study of the Suncorp Metway Employee Council Inc. (SMEC)' (2007) 49(2) JIR 187.

or 'representation gap'[11] left by unions, by providing direct channels for employees to exercise voice. As a result, the capacity of low-paid care workers to have a 'say' over important issues for them in the workplace remains largely unfulfilled.[12]

The precarity of low-paid care work amplifies the silence of the individuals who perform it. This work is often performed under precarious (casual, contract, seasonal) employment arrangements. In fact, as Charlesworth[13] and Kaine[14] point out, relatively few care workers—less than 10 per cent in direct care roles in the aged care sector—are employed on standard full-time permanent contracts. Along with poor access to pathways such as training and development for career progression, this means that vulnerable employees are often trapped in poor quality jobs across their working lives. These factors combined accentuate the extent to which vulnerable workers are susceptible to capricious treatment from employers, in turn further undermining job quality and voice.

The non-transitory nature of low-paid employment means that vulnerable low-paid work appears to have a social exclusionary effect upon workers, compounding poor economic and social power resources, and in turn diminishing workers' broader quality of life. Put simply, low levels of workplace voice and power are echoed and compounded outside of the labour market. This generates a vicious circle of silence and exclusion in and beyond the workplace.[15]

The extant literature has constructed a solid profile of the demographics of the vulnerable care workforce. A striking feature of the workforce is its overwhelming feminization. For example, it is estimated that of the 175,000 employees working in residential aged care in Australia in 2012, over 90 per cent were women.[16] This feminization is not merely 'contextual' and, as a number of feminist scholars have pointed out, there are deep and specific interconnections between paid care and the unpaid, undervalued, labour performed by female partners, sisters, and daughters in the service of family members in the home.[17] Meagher nicely sums up the association between gender, care, skills, and pay, arguing that:

> Because their skills are 'naturalized' as feminine attributes typically exercised in the private domain, care workers, the vast majority of whom are female, receive lower pay then their skills and task warrant.[18]

[11] Mark Bray et al., 'The "Representation Gap" in Australia' (2001) 12(2) Labour and Industry 1.

[12] Marian Baird et al., 'Low-Paid Women: The Impact of Regulatory Change in Australia' (2009) 40(5) JIR 393.

[13] Sara Charlesworth, 'Decent Working Conditions for Care Workers? The Intersections of Employment Regulation, the Funding Market and Gender Norms' (2012) 25(1) Australian Journal of Labour Law (AJLL) 108, 112.

[14] Sarah Kaine, 'Collective Regulation of Wages and Conditions in Aged Care: Beyond Labour Law' (2012) 54(2) JIR 204, 206.

[15] Baird (n 12); Heather Boushey and Shawn Fremstad, 'The Wages of Exclusion, Low-wage Work and Inequality' (2008) 17(2) New Labor Forum 9; Vicky Lovell et al., 'More than Raising the Floor: The Persistence of Gender Inequalities in the Low-wage Labor Market' in Dorothy S. Cobble (ed.), *The Sex of Class: Women Transforming American Labor* (ILR Press, 2007) at 35; Stephanie Luce and Eve Weinbaum, 'Low Wage Women Workers: A Profile' (2008) 17(2) New Labor Forum 3; Pocock (n 5).

[16] Kaine 207 (n 14).

[17] Sarah Kaine, 'The Regulation of Work and Wages in Aged Care: An analysis' Submission in *United Voice and the Australian Workers Union of Employees Queensland Application for Low-Paid Bargaining Authorization* (Attachment E, 3 September 2010b 1); Paula England et al., 'Wages of Virtue: The Relative Pay of Care Workers' (2002) 49(4) Social Problems 455; Julie Connelly et al., 'Tracking Pay Equity: The Impact of Regulatory Change on the Dissemination and Sustainability of Equal Remuneration Decisions' (2012) 54(2) JIR 114.

[18] Gabrielle Meagher, 'What Can We Expect From Paid Carers?' (2006) 37(1) Politics and Society 33.

Organizations and governments are not merely passive recipients of broader social and economic events and processes, like the undervaluation of care skills, in fact as Palmer and Eveline point out, each plays their own part in making and reconstituting practices which frame skills and work.[19] In Australia, a key theme in scholarship on care work has been attempting to understand the ways in which the peculiar Australian wage-fixing system has interacted with the 'valuation' of paid care skills. The historical model of compulsory conciliation and arbitration came to embody the gendered assumptions that existed at the time the system crystallized. 'Harvester Man' is viewed as having been alive and well in the operation of the arbitration system for more than a century after Justice Higgins gave him a central place in his 1907 judgment about the national 'living wage'.[20] In this case, a male 'breadwinner' was assumed to be supporting a non-working wife and three children and should expect a wage which would allow him to live in a condition of 'frugal comfort'.[21] Feminist scholars have pointed to the ways in which assumptions about, among other things, labour market engagement, models of working time, the value of jobs, and payment systems more broadly, permeated the institutional architecture of Australian industrial relations, even after conciliation and arbitration fell away.[22]

Low-paid Care Work in the Context of the Fair Work Act 2009

The FW Act became fully operational in January 2010, having been introduced in two waves from mid-2009. This headline industrial relations legislation was a key policy promise of the incoming Australian Labor government, after a landslide victory in the November 2007 general election. This followed an election campaign which focused squarely on industrial relations issues. By way of background, following the 2004 Federal election, where the conservative Howard government won a working majority of both houses of the Australian Parliament, a rare occurrence in recent history, a series of radical changes in industrial relations were enacted. The effect of these changes was to lower minimum standards, to reduce employee protections in the context of making individual contracts and collectively bargained agreements, to significantly reduce the circumstances in which unfair termination action could be taken by employees, and to wind back the capacity of unions to take other action on behalf of members.[23]

[19] Elyane Palmer and Joan Eveline, 'Sustaining Low Pay in Aged Care Work' (2012) 19(3) Gender Work and Organization 254.

[20] Marian Sawer, 'Waltzing Matilda: Gender and Australian Political Institutions' in Geoffrey Brenna and Francis Castles, *Australia Reshaped: 200 years of institutional transformation* (CUP, 2002) 148; Tim Harcourt, 'The Economics of the Living Wage' (1997) 30(1) Australian Economic Review 194; Laura Bennett, 'Job Classification and Women Workers: Institutional Practices, Technological Change and the Conciliation and Arbitration System 1907–72' (1986) 51(1) Labour History 11.

[21] Mark Hearn, 'Securing the Man: Narratives of Gender and Nation in the Verdicts of Henry Bournes Higgins' (2006) 37(127) Australian Historical Studies 1.

[22] Sara Charlesworth and Alexandra Heron, 'New Australian Working Time Standards: Reproducing the Same Old Gendered Architecture?' (2012) 54(1) JIR 164; Belinda Smith, 'What Kind of Equality Can We Expect from the Fair Work Act' (2011) 35 Melbourne University Law Review (Melb UL Rev) 545.

[23] Bradon Ellem et al., '"Work Choices": Myth-making at work' (2005) 56(1) Journal of Australian Political Economy 13.

The changes built upon the industrial relations policy agenda of the government from 1996 which had focused on the 'de-collectivising' of the industrial relations system.[24] As the effects of 'Work Choices',[25] as the Howard government's 2005 legislative and policy framework was known, became evident, community sentiment turned decisively against the government and its policy in industrial relations. Much of the disquiet came from community displeasure with details of cases where Work Choices had been used to detrimental effect on some of the most vulnerable workers in the labour market; prominent among these were low-paid women.[26] Australian unions orchestrated an impressive media and online campaign, the 'Your Rights at Work' campaign, which exploited community concern for the plight of vulnerable workers and emphasized the need to secure individual employment rights. The campaign, coordinated by the national peak council, the Australian Council of Trade Unions (ACTU), is credited as having been the decisive factor in the victory of the Australian Labor Party (ALP) over the Coalition parties in the November 2007 election.[27]

Labor leader, Kevin Rudd, and his then deputy leader and industrial relations spokesperson, Julia Gillard, campaigned on a platform of restoring 'fairness', balanced with 'flexibility', to industrial relations policy.[28] After considerable negotiation both internal to the ALP, within the broader labour movement and, later, more with business groups and state governments, the FW Act emerged.[29] The changes ushered in by the new Act included the introduction of a 'good faith' bargaining framework,[30] the re-regulation of the national minimum standards in the form of ten National Employment Standards, and the introduction of the 'Better Off Overall Test' (BOOT), designed to ensure that employees were not disadvantaged in the negotiation of workplace arrangements.[31] While the Act did allow for the negotiation of individual arrangements, in the form of Individual Flexibility Arrangements (IFAs), Australian Workplace Agreements (AWAs), statutory individual contracts, one of the more controversial aspects of the Work Choices and preceding Howard legislative agendas, were removed.[32] IFAs differed from AWAs in

[24] Rae Cooper and Bradon Ellem, 'The Neoliberal State, Trade Unions and Collective Bargaining in Australia' (2008) 46(3) BJIR 532.

[25] Workplace Relations Amendment (Work Choices) Act 2005 (Cth) (AUS).

[26] Marian Baird et al., 'Low-paid women: the impact of regulatory change in Australia' (2009) 40(5) IRJ 393.

[27] Bradon Ellem, 'Peak Union Campaigning: Fighting for Rights at Work in Australia' (2011) 51(1) BJIR DOI: 10.1111/j.1467-8543.2011.00878.x.

[28] Australian Labor Party, Forward with Fairness, (Australian Labor Party Industrial Relations Policy Platform, Canberra, 2007).

[29] Rae Cooper, 'The "Bargaining Power" of Women Employees in the Low-Paid Personal Care Sector: A Brief Review of the Concepts and the Evidence in Australia', Submission in *United Voice and the Australian Workers Union of Employees Queensland Application for Low-Paid Bargaining Authorization* (Attachment D, 3 September 2010a) 1.

[30] Breen Creighton and Anthony Forsyth, 'Rediscovering Collective Bargaining' in Breen Creighton and Anthony Forsyth (eds), *Rediscovering Collective Bargaining: Australia's Fair Work Act in International Perspective* (Routledge, 2012).

[31] Jill Murray and Rosemary Owens, 'The Safety Net: Labour Standards in the New Era' in Andrew Stewart and Anthony Forsyth (eds), *Fair Work: The New Workplace Laws and the Work Choices Legacy* (Federation Press 2009) 40; Carolyn Sutherland, 'Making the BOOT fit: Reforms to Agreement-Making from Work Choices to Fair Work' in Andrew Stewart and Anthony Forsyth (eds), *Fair Work: The New Workplace Laws and the Work Choices Legacy* (Federation Press, 2009) 99.

[32] Stewart and Forsyth (n 31); Rae Cooper et al., 'The Fair Work Act and Individual Flexibility Arrangements' (Community Work and Family Conference, Sydney, July 2013).

that they were not registered statutory contracts and, unlike AWAs, they sat on top of the substantially expanded safety net.[33]

In the parliamentary debate on the Act in March 2008, ALP Ministers and Members constructed a narrative around the need for industrial relations change and addressed the plight of low-paid employees, especially women in care-focused occupations. For example, Greg Combet, by now having moved from his role as ACTU Secretary, and into the national Parliament, recalled the impact of Work Choices and pointed to the potential remedies of the new Act:

> the harshest impact—as usual with these things—was on the lowest paid, who are always the most vulnerable to such pressure in the workplace ... This bill is important in addressing the patent unfairness of the industrial relations system of the former Howard government.... [it] will simply begin the process of ensuring that there is a fairer set of rights and responsibilities for employees and employers in the workplace.[34] (Greg Combet, Parliamentary Secretary for Defence Procurement)

Did the provisions designed to support voice mechanisms for vulnerable workers, in particular, the trade union-initiated multi-employer collective bargaining provisions, deliver real access for workers to better jobs and 'voice' as was envisaged by Combet? The following section examines the intentions and actions of the government, employers, and unions around the 'Low-paid Bargaining stream'.

Low-paid Care Work and the Low-paid Bargaining Stream

The Low-paid Bargaining stream is one of the key policy innovations of the FW Act. The key provisions of the stream are set out in Division 9[35] of the FW Act. Whilst its name suggests a singular link to low pay, this stream allows for collective bargaining across a broad spectrum of workplace and employment issues, not only pay, as would also be possible in 'mainstream' enterprise bargaining. However, it differs from other types of bargaining provided in the FW Act in some significant ways. Firstly, in order to access this stream, employees, or their representatives, must demonstrate those who would potentially be covered by an agreement meet the criteria of being 'low-paid'. The FW Act does not define what is meant by 'low-paid' and leaves this to the discretion of the institution tasked with administering the stream, Fair Work Australia.[36] Rather more detail as to the intention of the framers of the stream can be gleaned from the FW Act's Explanatory Memorandum. This document cites numerous examples of the types of employees, who, it was intended, might have access to and potentially use the scheme in bargaining. It states that the provisions are designed to assist employees, and employers, in occupations and industries such

[33] Stewart and Forsyth (n 31).

[34] House of Representatives Debates, Workplace Relations Amendment (Transition to Forward With Fairness) Bill 2008, 13 March 2008, 1689.

[35] Fair Work Act 2009 (Cth) (AUS), ss. 241 to 246.

[36] The Act established Fair Work Australia. Amendments to the Fair Work Act in early 2012, at the time this chapter was written, renamed the institution the Fair Work Commission. For ease of discussion the FWC is referred to as Fair Work Australia throughout this chapter, as this was its name throughout the hearing of the first test case of the Act.

as: 'child care, aged care, community services, security and cleaning, who are often paid the relevant minimum wage rate entering into the bargaining stream'.[37]

These employees were thought to need assistance in accessing collective bargaining due to lack of bargaining power, low skill levels, and because of the absence of other incentives to bargain in their sectors. The Explanatory Memorandum made it clear that evidence of the experience of workers during Work Choices was a motivating force in the development of the stream. It argued that low-paid employees, during this period, were subject to impulses of unrestrained managerial prerogative and, because of their low levels of workplace power and voice, had been subjected to a 'take it or leave it'[38] approach to employment matters.

The capacity for multi-employer bargaining under the Low-paid Bargaining stream stood in stark contrast to the principal forms of collective bargaining within the FW Act which were squarely focused on workplace-by-workplace bargaining, rather than sectoral or industry arrangements. As numerous scholars have charted, from the late 1980s onward, Australia's system of industrial relations policy followed a decentralizing—and many would argue, a more complicated—trajectory. We witnessed movement from a reliance primarily on industry-based awards and arbitration, to a mixture of award regulation and enterprise-based bargaining and, later, to a mixture of regulation via awards, enterprise-based bargaining, *and* individual contracting.[39] From the late 1980s to the mid-1990s it was policy orthodoxy that enterprise-based bargaining, underpinned by awards, was the most desirable mechanism for the regulation of the terms and conditions of employment. From 1996, with the introduction of Australian Workplace Agreements (AWAs) via the Howard government's Workplace Relations Act, the focus of 'ideal' regulation was shifted to the individual scale, with less and less underpinning regulation and standard-setting at the national and industry scale.[40]

The FW Act provided that after an application to make an agreement was made by an employee bargaining representative, Fair Work Australia would determine whether to make a Low-paid Authorisation.[41] Fair Work Australia needed to be satisfied in relation to a number of issues, perhaps most pertinently for our purposes, they must consider the extent of the exposure of the employees concerned to bargaining, including the history of bargaining and the bargaining strength of those involved.[42] In the process of deciding whether to issue an Authorisation, Fair Work Australia needed to specify the

[37] Fair Work Bill 2008 (Cth) Explanatory Memorandum (AUS) s. 194.

[38] Explanatory Memorandum, s. 112 (n 37).

[39] Mark Bray et al., *Employment Relations: Theory and Practice* (McGraw Hill, 2011), 327–74; Mark Bray and Peter Waring, 'The Rhetoric and Reality of Bargaining Structures under the Howard Government' (1998) 9(2) Labour and Industry 61; Harry C Katz, 'The Decentralisation of Collective Bargaining: A Literature Review and Comparative Analysis' (1993) 47(1) Industrial and Labor Relations Review 3.

[40] Peter Gahan and Andreas Pekarek, 'Collective Bargaining and Agreement Making in Australia: Evolution of the Legislative Framework and Practice' in Creighton and Forsyth (n 30); Mark Bray and Johanna MacNeil, 'Individualism, Collectivism and the Case of Awards' (2011) 53(2) JIR 149.

[41] It is perhaps worth noting that 'agreement making' does not require union involvement in the Fair Work system, nor does the Act require particular mechanisms for consultation or negotiation with employees. It is not, thus, collective bargaining as is known in other contexts.

[42] FWA must also take into account matters relating to the likely success of collective bargaining, including factors such as the productivity improvements which may result from an agreement, the number of bargaining representatives, the views of those who would be covered by a proposed agreement, and the extent to which the terms and conditions of the relevant employees are controlled by external parties or forces (s. 243).

particular employees and employers who would be covered by any potential agreement. The FW Act provided for Fair Work Australia to hold a compulsory conference with the aim of assisting the bargaining process.[43] Importantly, this was not limited to a conference between the parties directly concerned with agreement making but might include parties who could exert considerable influence on the outcome of bargaining, for example head contractors or funding bodies.[44]

After these processes had been entered into and if parties reached a stalemate, Fair Work Australia was empowered to arbitrate an outcome through a 'low-paid workplace determination'. This could take the form of either a 'consent' or 'special' determination made upon application of one or all of the parties.[45] It was to be more difficult to make a 'special' low-paid workplace determination.[46] The inclusion of potential arbitration, without the consent of both parties in the stream, appears to have been the result of intense argument within the federal parliamentary Labor caucus in late 2008. Their policy position swung away from no access to arbitration in September, to Minister Gillard announcing in November that having 'listened carefully to the views of the representatives of low-paid workers on how to ensure the success of the scheme' arbitrated outcomes on the application of one party would be made available.[47] Interviews with key parliamentary representatives involved in these discussions within the Labor caucus, suggest that arguments hinged on advocates for potential to access arbitration demonstrating that an absence of recourse to arbitration would lead to intractable bargaining disputes, effectively neutering the stream. This was a departure from the decades-long rejection of centralized arbitral industrial regulation.

Low-paid Care Work and the United Voice Aged Care Case

At the time of writing, August 2013, only two applications for Low-paid Bargaining Authorisations had been lodged with Fair Work Australia; one by the union representing aged care attendants, which will be discussed in detail later, and one by the Australian Nursing Federation to cover nurses working in the offices of general practitioners and medical centres. This second case was lodged in November 2011, and was dismissed on 17 June 2013.[48] The first case was an application made by the United Voice union on 10 May 2010. The union sought a Low-paid Authorisation to cover over 300 aged care employers in United Voice's area of constitutional coverage in three of the six Australian states: South Australia; Western Australia; and South East Queensland. The application was to

[43] Fair Work Act 2009 (Cth) (AUS), ss. 240 and 246.

[44] For an overview of the mechanics of the stream see Richard Naughton, 'The Low-paid Bargaining Scheme—An interesting Idea, but can it work?' (2011) 24(1) AJLL 214.

[45] See n 38, ss. 260–262.

[46] A Full Bench of FWA must be satisfied that the parties have genuinely been unable to reach agreement; that there is no reasonable prospect of agreement being reached; the employment conditions of the employees who would be covered by the agreement are substantially equivalent to award minima; and any employer who would be covered by a determination is not, or has not previously, been covered by a collective agreement or equivalent instrument (s. 263).

[47] Julia Gillard, 'Forward with Fairness' (Speech to the National Press Club, 17 September 2008); Julia Gillard, 'Address to the Australian Labour Law Association' (Speech to the Australian Labour Law Association, 14 November 2008).

[48] *Australian Nursing Federation v IPN Medical Centres Pty Ltd & Ors* [2013] FWC 511.

potentially 'cover' workers engaged in personal care and ancillary roles in aged care facilities. Upon lodgement of the application, the union claimed that it would pursue wage increases of between '$8 and $10 per hour' in addition to a range of other issues including 'fair workloads, minimum staff to resident ratios, government funding dedicated to wages'.[49]

As set out earlier in the chapter, the stream was intended for use by employees who 'are low-paid and those who have not historically had access to the benefits of collective bargaining'.[50] The intention was both to recognize the low levels of bargaining power and voice in sectors such as aged care and to provide a stimulant to bargaining, which, it was reasoned, would lift wages, improve conditions and, in turn, build productivity. The union pursued a strategy of attempting to 'capture' as many employers as possible in their application. Their application included a considerable number—around half of the 300 employers named in the application—who had previously, or who were currently, covered by operational enterprise agreements. On the face of it this seemed a brave move, but the union reasoned that even those employees who were covered, or had been covered, by enterprise agreements remained low-paid, because the rates of pay in extant enterprise agreements were so close to award rates that they were barely distinguishable from the minimum and, as such, despite agreement coverage the employees remained low-paid and continued to need assistance because of their difficulty in bargaining. The union's case relied on evidence not only as to the conditions set out in these agreements but also in relation to the conditions under which they were negotiated. Many agreements were made during the period of Work Choices, and the union argued that this meant that they had been subject to less scrutiny from the tribunal than they would have been under the new Fair Work system. In addition, as numerous relevant agreements were non-union agreements,[51] the union reasoned that they were not, in effect, bargained on a collective basis. The union presented numerous other arguments in relation to the dimensions of the low pay of the workers concerned. For example, aged care workers concerned were argued to be low-paid in terms of spending power, relative to the skills and competencies they held and exercised, in the light of the important tasks they performed for society and the economy, in relation to community expectations as to the wages such jobs should attract, and relative to average weekly earnings. A range of demand and supply-side explanations were advanced for why employees were low-paid, including low levels of bargaining power, historical undervaluation of care work, the feminization of this work, precarity of employment, and the nature of supply chains in the sector.[52]

[49] Liquor, Hospitality and Miscellaneous Workers Union (LHMU) 'Low-paid Bargaining fact sheet' (LHMU National Office, Sydney, 10 May 2010).

[50] See n 33, s. 169.

[51] Non-union collective bargaining was an oddity of the Australian enterprise bargaining system. These agreements were available from 1993 through to 2009, and were made in the absence of trade union representation and bargaining. See Rae Cooper and Chris Briggs, '"Trojan Horse" or "Vehicle for Organising"? Non-Union Collective Agreement Making and Trade Unions in Australia' (2009) 30(1) Economic and Industrial Democracy 93. The Fair Work Act 2009 removed the distinction between union and non-union agreements, but it remains possible for employers to make agreements with their employees without bargaining at all with unions.

[52] Ian Watson, 'Low-paid workers in the Aged Care Industry', Submission in *United Voice and the Australian Workers Union of Employees Queensland Application for Low-Paid Bargaining Authorization* (Attachment C,

A year later, on 5 May 2011, the Full Bench of Fair Work Australia signalled in its Decision that it would grant a Low-paid Bargaining Authorisation, but called for further submissions as to who should potentially be covered by that Authorisation.[53] The decision noted that the Bench agreed with United Voice to a point, having been convinced that aged care employees were indeed low-paid and that they lacked substantially in bargaining power. It also noted that this view of low pay and bargaining power extended to aged care employees covered by 'live' enterprise agreements, as their terms and conditions remained very close to those of the relevant Modern Award. However, the Full Bench made clear that because of the 'particular circumstances of the applications we are considering'[54] that employers with operational enterprise agreements should be excluded from the planned Authorisation. As such, the Bench called for submissions in relation to agreement coverage in relevant workplaces. Later, on 29 July 2011, the Full Bench handed down its Authorisation[55] where it granted an Authorisation for multi-employer enterprise bargaining to proceed within the stream between the union and 175 aged care providers.

Officials of United Voice reacted angrily to the decision and argued that this exposed a fundamental flaw in the Fair Work legislation. The union's National Secretary, Louise Tarrant, contended that the decision showed the Low-paid Bargaining stream to be an ineffective mechanism to lift workers out of low pay and she called on the government to amend the legislation or come up with other solutions to 'ensure there is fairness for low-paid Australian workers'.[56] Subsequent to the Decision, the United Voice union embarked upon a round of, ultimately unsuccessful, negotiation conferences with employers named in the Authorisation. Fair Work Australia assisted with these conferences, providing facilitation assistance and Federal government departments became involved (having been viewed by the Full Bench to play 'a pervasive role in funding') as observers assisting the negotiations. At the time of writing this chapter, despite over 18 months of meetings, there had been no resolution and no multi-employer agreement made. It seems, absent an application for a Determination by one of the parties, that the parties had reached a legal impasse.

The seeming failure of this case highlights the difficulties of relying upon a bargaining-based approach to improve the lot and to strengthen the voice of vulnerable care workers. The limits of the legislation—its failure to incorporate access for employees with little real experience of real collective bargaining and its uncertain arbitral framework—are laid bare.

There is an interesting postscript to this case which seemed for a time to have opened a more fruitful avenue for improving the circumstances of aged care workers. The Minister for Ageing and Disability, Mark Butler announced on 5 March 2013 that a 'Compact' in aged care would be developed with the aim of building quality in the standard of aged care services across Australia. This was a recommendation of the

3 September 2010), 1; Sarah Kaine, 'Industrial Instruments and the Regulation of Employment Relations in the Residential Aged Care Sector in NSW' (2010) 16(2) International Employment Relations Review 1.

[53] *United Voice & Anor* [2011] FWAFB 2633.

[54] *United Voice & Anor* at 2638 (n 53).

[55] *United Voice & Anor* (2011) (AUS) PR512659.

[56] United Voice, 'Press release: Low-paid Bargaining Stream' (United Voice National Office, 29 July 2011).

Minister's 'Strategic Workforce Advisory Group', chaired by a Commissioner of Fair Work Australia, Anne Gooley, and including membership from across the large service providers and trade unions (including, among others, United Voice), who had reported to the Minister on 19 October 2012. The group had been convened in June 2012 as a part of a broader analysis of service provision and quality standards in the aged care sector by the government.

The Compact was ostensibly framed as a mechanism to help aged care employers to recruit and retain staff by reaching agreements with employees to make improvements in wages and conditions in the sector. Should employers meet certain standards in relation to workforce issues, interestingly for our purposes, via registered enterprise agreements which would include specified minimum standards (including wage rates above award rates, specified pathways for progression of staff, access for staff to training and development, and targets in terms of health and safety injury reduction), the employing body would achieve access to higher levels of funding from government to compensate for increased workforce expenditure. The unions welcomed these announcements[57] while many employers criticized the Compact decision as 'a cost shifting exercise', representing a 'short-sighted approach' to aged care with too much focus on workforce issues and a system 'designed to favour unions'.[58] These views were echoed by the conservative shadow minister Senator Concetta Ferravanti-Wells.[59]

At the time of writing, the federal government had not fully announced the nature of funding arrangements or the specific link between this and the mechanisms of enterprise bargaining. Nevertheless, United Voice union officials reported, in interviews, that they were hopeful that linking the funding available to aged care providers to lifting standards in the workplace would prove more of an incentive for employers in the sector to collectively bargain, and thus construct higher levels of employee voice, than had proved possible using FW Act mechanisms.[60]

[57] Australian Nurses Federation 'Big win for aged care nurses in NSW' (*Media Releases*, 3 April 2013) <http://anf.org.au/news/entry/big-win-for-aged-care-nurses-in-nsws-south> accessed 12 April 2013; Health Services Union 'Aged Care Workforce Compact announcement welcomed' (*Industrial Relations News*, 5 March 2013) <http://www.hsu.net.au/news/1362720382_20871.html> accessed 12 April 2013; United Voice, '$1.2 billion commitment to aged care workforce' (*Press Release*, 5 March 2013) <http://www.unitedvoice.org.au/press-releases/12b-commitment-build-workforce-essential-quality-aged-care> accessed 12 April 2013.

[58] Catholic Health Australia, 'Aged care pay increase needs more than Workforce Compact' (*Media Releases*, 5 March 2013) <http://www.cha.org.au/news/media-releases/367-aged-care-pay-increase-needs-more-than-workforce-compact.html> accessed 12 April 2013; Leading Age Services Australia, 'Age Services: Government Continues to Fail Older Australians' (*News Release*, 5 March 2013) <http://www.lasa.asn.au/wp-content/uploads/050313-Workforce-Compact.pdf> accessed 12 April 2013.

[59] Liberal Party of Australia, 'Workforce compact... another bad joke' (Media Releases, 5 March 2013) <http://www.liberal.org.au/latest-news/2013/03/05/workforce-compact%E2%80%A6another-bad-joke> accessed 12 April 2013.

[60] To complicate matters further, in the context of writing this chapter a federal election returned the conservative Coalition parties to power. It seems certain that government funding for the Compact has become even more uncertain.

Conclusions: Low-paid Care Work, Bargaining and Voice in Australia

The FW Act was heralded by its authors as having the potential to simultaneously make Australian workplaces more 'fair' and, at the same time, more 'flexible'. Some parts of the legislation, such as the Low-paid Collective Bargaining stream established by the FW Act, were included, in part, out of a concern for the impact Work Choices had had on the work and lives of low-paid women. Low-paid women working in direct personal care, such as aged care employees, are typically posed in the literature as 'vulnerable employees'. This is because of, among other things, their low levels of voice and bargaining power. Despite undertaking immensely socially important work, women working in paid care roles have suffered undervaluation of their work and skills, in part because of issues of feminization and institutionalized sex-based discrimination. Has the FW Act undone these circumstances? The answer is, in short, no. While politicians bemoaned the ways in which employees like the women working in aged care were 'locked out' of collective bargaining, they established a stream which effectively ensured that they remained so. Whether a system premised on enterprise-by-enterprise bargaining could ever be a catalyst for increased voice (and wages) for large groups of the workforce, such as are the numbers in the aged care sector, is another question altogether. More recent initiatives, outside of the reach of mainstream industrial relations policy and employment law, which will potentially tie increased government funding for service provision to enterprise-based collective bargaining, may offer more potential. In the meantime, low-paid employees in the aged care sector remain low-paid and they remain, to a large extent, 'silent'; both in the workplace and beyond it.

4

Migrant Workers and Labour Movements in the US and UK[1]

Janice Fine

Introduction

Migrants crossing borders in search of better economic opportunities are often able to utilize their social networks to gain employment but they face the adversities of the labour market alone unless unions and other non-governmental organizations become involved in supporting voice, not only in the workplace but in the polity as well. An institutionalized labour movement can provide protection, support, and the possibility of on-going representation for migrant workers. Indeed, migrant workers are taking advantage of increased opportunities to partner with unions, but this is happening at a time of great peril for the labour movement. While the peak labour associations in the US and UK have arguably never been more supportive overall of migrant worker organizing and inclusive immigration policies than they are at present, the terrain has seldom been more inhospitable to the protection of labour standards or to unionization as it is now. If voice is essential to assertion and enforcement of migrant worker rights, the role of unions deserves closer exploration. Historically, unions have engaged in vigorous debates regarding labour migration; even when they have adopted 'pro-migration' policy positions, approaches to organizing and representation have varied depending upon the individual culture, structure, and ideology of specific national and local unions. Of course unions do not act to influence policy or organize migrant workers in a vacuum, rather they do so within specific state contexts.

This chapter will focus on some of the key debates concerning migrant issues that unions in the US and the UK have engaged, as well as the types of organizing efforts that have been launched in recent times and the underlying impetus for these efforts. Because of its membership of the EU, Britain will be viewed within the broader institutional backdrop of European policies and issues.

In the UK and US, immigrants are often disproportionately represented in the so-called '3-D' jobs: dirty, dangerous, and demeaning, which has made them prime targets for unions interested in organizing low wage workers. Migrant workers are often subject to unsafe workplace conditions, excessive hours, low compensation, and other forms of employer victimization, firing, and deportation, and are often concentrated in sectors such as garment or light manufacturing, meatpacking,

[1] Much of the material in this chapter is drawn from articles I have co-authored with Daniel J. Tichenor; I have also drawn upon joint work written with Jane Holgate as well as a series of research papers I wrote for the Solidarity Center.

hospitality, warehousing, residential construction, domestic and agricultural work that are often *de jure* or de facto exempt from labour and employment laws and difficult to monitor for violations even when there are statutes in place. But immigration and labour and employment are often divided into two separate and often contradictory spheres of law and public policy. In the US, for example, while immigration statutes prohibit employers from hiring undocumented workers, once hired undocumented immigrants are protected by all of the basic labour standards regulations and covered by most of the remedies. Undocumented immigrants can join unions, but employers cannot be compelled to reinstate them to their jobs if they are fired for organizing activity.

Immigration has always posed difficult choices for unions that fight to defend the rights and labour market positions of workers who, globalization notwithstanding, still live and work in individual nation-states. Do they shun migrant workers who enter their industries or attempt to organize them? Historically, unions have vacillated between, on the one hand, supporting restrictive state immigration policies intended to limit labour market access and preserve existing labour standards and, on the other hand, championing more open policies in order to organize immigrant workers and preserve labour standards for all. Likewise they have vacillated between blocking migrants from becoming members of their unions and actively organizing them.

As Fine and Tichenor have argued, the choices unions make about immigration policy and immigrant worker organizing are conditioned by their own institutional legacies, ideologies, and leaderships and by their relationships to the state and to employers, but these choices are neither absolute nor permanent. National labour federations and unions often adopt policies that are a mixture of restrictive and expansive and they also shift back and forth across this continuum over time. As Hyman describes it: 'Above all else, unions are *contested* organizations: within any union can be found conflicting views of its underlying purpose, its priority objectives, the appropriate forms of action, and the desirable patterns of internal relations.'[2]

This chapter will explore the evolution toward more solidaristic positions regarding government immigration policies as well as organizational and representational strategies on the part of union federations and national unions. It is divided into two parts. The first part will review the main contemporary debates in the US and UK and summarize the major *policy shifts* made by two national federations, the AFL-CIO and the TUC in the post-World War II era. The second part will shift to a consideration of the types of efforts that have been made by individual unions in support of migrant workers and a discussion of the factors that contribute to a national union's willingness to include, organize, and represent migrant workers.

[2] Richard Hyman, 'Trade Union Research and Cross National Comparison' (2001) 7(2) European Journal of International Relations (EJIR) 207.

Restriction versus Solidarity and the Post-war National Policy Debates

Debates and policy shifts in the United States

Over the course of American political development, the US union movement has ranged between a deeply restrictive and solidaristic or expansionist position on immigration. Two issues have loomed large in the US post-war era. The first has centred on the labour movement's position on the national origins quota system, which since its introduction in 1924 had imposed a low ceiling on annual admissions, strongly favouring northern and western Europeans over southern and eastern Europeans, and all but banning Asians. For decades the American Federation of Labour (AFL) was a vigorous supporter of this policy, but this position triggered fresh debate within the labour movement after World War II. The second issue that confronted the post-war US labour movement was how to respond to unprecedented Mexican labour inflows. Union leaders were agitated by dramatic increases in labour migration from Mexico and condemned what they considered to be a failed temporary 'guest worker' program, which held workers in exploitative relationships with employers or led many to leave and become part of the undocumented labour force.[3]

Fine and Tichenor have argued that one of the early game changers in how American labour positioned itself on immigration policy was the rise of the largely pro-immigration Congress of Industrial Organizations (CIO) in the 1930s, which assailed the AFL's restrictionist positions as driven by ethnic and racial exclusion. It is not surprising that the AFL and CIO have had a long history of division over the question of immigration, with the latter looking more favourably on immigration in general and on overriding refugee quotas. Founded in 1935 as a means of organizing largely unskilled industrial workers from eastern and southern Europe as well as black migrants from the South, the CIO set itself apart from the AFL, which represented primarily established craft union workers of northern and western European origin.

In the years after World War II, rivalry between the two organizations over the immigration question intensified. Although the AFL was supportive of liberal efforts to assist European Jews and displaced persons (DPs), it also staunchly backed the McCarran-Walter bill, which sought to maintain stringent limits on Asian, African, and southern and eastern European immigration. The CIO denounced the bill, labelling it 'one of the most severe blows to civil liberties, as well as to American relations with citizens of foreign nations'[4] and called for its repeal.

In the 1950s and 1960s, much of the debate centred on the status of undocumented workers from Mexico. The AFL continued to stand by a national origins quota premised on racial and ethnic bias, and it joined other labour organizations in expressing alarm that Mexican Braceros and other unauthorized migrants had depressed wages

[3] Janice Fine and Daniel J. Tichenor, 'An Enduring Dilemma: Immigration and Organised Labour in Western Europe and the United States' in Rosenblum and Tichenor, *The Politics of International Migration*, Oxford Handbook Series (OUP, 2012) 804.

[4] *Proceedings of the Congress of Industrial Organizations*, Cornell University Archives, Ithaca, NY, 1952, 131.

and destroyed working conditions. Their warnings fell on deaf ears, with Congress passing legislation in 1951 to reauthorize the Bracero program, claiming that to do otherwise would be 'unfair to the farmer and the Mexican involved'.[5]

After failing to terminate legal guest worker programs, organized labour and the Truman administration urged Congress to impose sanctions on those who illegally smuggled aliens into the country and on employers who intentionally hired illegal aliens. In 1954, a frustrated AFL Executive Council resolved to give 'unceasing publicity'[6] to the 'wetback problem'.[7] The CIO, in contrast, opposed the racist quota system *and* temporary Mexican labour, condemning the suffering of migrant labourers. Sympathy for the plight of these workers did not blunt the CIO's frustration, however, that US farm workers 'have found themselves steadily replaced by Mexicans in those areas where cheaper "wetback" labour is abundant. In turn their enforced unemployment has been used by employers to lower the standards of employment for other US farm workers in jobs where they are still employed.'[8]

The 1955 merger of the AFL and CIO brought about an enduring shift in organized labour's role in national immigration politics. In addition to state-level challenges by Massachusetts, Minnesota, and other northern states to the AFL's restrictionist position, the ascendancy of George Meany heralded a time of liberal immigration reform. No sooner had Meany assumed the helm of the newly merged labour organization in 1955 than he promptly fired the AFL's director of legislative affairs, a longtime defender of immigration restriction. Soon after the merger, the AFL-CIO Central Committee made immigration reform a top priority, calling for 'abolishment of the national origins quota system entirely'.[9]

The AFL-CIO proved crucial in the passage of the Hart-Celler Act in 1965, which dismantled national origins quotas in favour of a new preference system emphasizing family-based immigration and for the first time placed an annual ceiling on visas for migrants in the Western Hemisphere. The admissions system that has evolved since Hart-Celler has been largely premised on family reunification, and to a lesser extent on skill.[10]

[5] David Reimers, *Still the Golden Door* (Columbia University Press, 1992) 54.

[6] *Proceedings of the American Federation of Labour National* Convention, NLC's Meany Memorial Archives, Silver Springs, MD, 1950.

[7] 'Report of the Executive Council of the American Federation of Labour for 1954', *AFL-CIO Legislative Department Papers*, Meany Memorial Archives, Silver Springs, MD, 1954.

[8] 'Resolution No. 14 Migrant Farm Labour', *Proceedings of the Sixteenth Constitutional Convention of the Congress of Industrial Organizations*, Rutgers School of Management and Labour Relations Library Archive, New Brunswick, NJ, 1954, 525–6.

[9] Andrew Biemiller interviewed by Alice M. Hoffman, 22 May 1979, George Meany Center for Labour Studies Oral History Project, AFL-CIO Merger (Collection 15), Box 1, Folder 4, Meany Memorial Archives, Silver Springs, MD.

[10] Employment-based visas are a much smaller component of overall admissions and are very strongly weighted in favour of the highly skilled, with essentially no annual quota for the unskilled. As a result, unskilled immigrants are primarily restricted to family reunification, refugee and asylum policies, and 'non-immigrant' or temporary worker programs. To the extent that family reunification allows immigrants to bring over family members, the labour movement has strong reason to support it. However, to the extent that the overwhelming bias toward family reunification makes those without eligible family members unable to come (and even those with eligible family members can face extremely long waiting periods) and leaves little room for many unskilled workers to come via legal means, the labour movement has reason to consider policy alternatives. These include raising the overall annual quotas, shifting the employment visas

In the 1960s the AFL-CIO joined a variety of ethnic, economic, and human rights groups to aid pro-immigration lawmakers to both end the Bracero program and dismantle the national origins quota system, claiming that 'the true image of America is the kaleidoscope. It is a mosaic of human beings that is always changing but encased in a basic framework of freedom, of brotherhood, of tolerance, of creativity.'[11] However, reformers did not anticipate that the new ceiling on immigration from the Western Hemisphere, combined with the end of the Bracero program in 1963, would swell unauthorized Mexican inflows. The dramatic rise in apprehensions and deportations of unauthorized migrants was unmistakable and troubling to decision makers. While organized labour had defected from the restrictionist camp on national origins quotas, Mexican immigration posed an increasing challenge.

As represented by the struggles of Cesar Chavez and the Farm Workers Association (FWA) in the early 1970s, fighting illegal immigration initially had a progressive character, with a focus on winning decent wages and working conditions for Mexican Americans through unionization of the agricultural sector. However, in 1975 the United Farm Workers (UFW) and Chavez were persuaded by Latino groups to oppose only undocumented aliens who engaged in strike-breaking activities. The UFW also announced new support for a generous amnesty program,[12] and in the same year, the International Ladies Garment Workers Union (ILGWU) began campaigning to unionize undocumented aliens. Among prominent Latino labour groups, only the AFL-CIO's Labour Council for Latin American Advancement (LCLAA) remained stridently opposed to illegal immigration. For its part, Congress was deadlocked for the rest of the decade.

The AFL-CIO looked for relief with the 1986 passage of the Immigration Reform and Control Act (IRCA), which called for sanctions against employers hiring undocumented workers. Growing evidence suggested that some employers were following a strategy of selective verification as a tool for foiling union organizing drives.[13] Several of those most involved in organizing low-wage immigrant workers, including the ILGWU, the Amalgamated Clothing and Textile Workers Union (ACTWU), the Hotel Employees and Restaurant Employees (HERE), and the Service Employees International Union (SEIU), although initially supportive of employer sanctions, began passing resolutions calling for repeal as early as 1992.[14]

Meanwhile, the Immigration Act of 1990 increased the numbers of green cards to be allotted per year, largely through family preference but also employment and 'diversity visas' for under-represented countries, as well as nonimmigrant (temporary) visas, unified ethnic groups, humanitarian organizations, labour unions and the AFL-CIO, business groups in favour of bringing in more workers to their sectors, and free market

to a greater percentage of the whole, recalibrating the distribution of visas for high- and low-skilled workers, and reform of existing temporary worker programs.

[11] Hyman Bookbinder, 'The World's Refugees—A Challenge to America', *Papers of the AFL-CIO Legislative Dept. Papers*, Box 27, Folder 26, Meany Memorial Archives, Silver Springs, MD, 1960.

[12] 'Chavez Shifts Views of Illegals', reprinted in 'Illegal Aliens', *Hearings Before the Subcommittee on Immigration, Citizenship, and International Law*, 1975, 82–3.

[13] Muzzaffar Chishti, 'Employer Sanctions Against Immigrant Workers' [2000] Working USA 71–6.

[14] Leah A. Haus, 'Openings in the Wall: Transnational Migrants, Labour Unions and US Immigration Policy' [1995] International Organization (IO) 299–304.

conservatives generally opposed to restricting admission.[15] All favoured increasing legal migration, albeit for different reasons. The same year, the AFL-CIO, having long been the most strident advocate of employer sanctions, made little effort to press for stronger enforcement amidst new illegal immigration. Instead, AFL-CIO President Lane Kirkland joined fellow members of the Leadership Conference on Civil Rights in lobbying for more vigorous enforcement of job antidiscrimination protections for Latinos, Asians, and legal aliens.[16]

Surprisingly, despite a massive wave of immigration and unprecedented numbers of undocumented workers during the 1990s, the AFL-CIO sharply reversed course at the end of that decade. Declaring the sanctions it had formerly supported ineffective, the federation called for a repeal of the sanctions in 1999. At the same time, it supported expanding the organizing rights of immigrant workers, a broad amnesty for the undocumented, and immigrant admissions based upon family reunification. The comprehensive stance can be seen as the culmination of a more gradual but decisive shift beginning in the 1970s from viewing unskilled foreign-born Latinos as unorganizable to considering them instrumental in building membership in the labour movement.[17]

This reversal spurred activism but also created tremendous division within the 'House of Labour',[18] with many still opposed to guest worker programs within a larger package of immigration reform. In 2005–2006, five AFL-CIO member unions, amounting to more than a third of American union membership, nearly 4.5 million members, formally left the federation and formed a new labour coalition, Change to Win.[19] In the months following their institutional rift, the AFL-CIO and many of the Change to Win national unions intensified their immigration work through a variety of strategies, including lobbying, strengthening the numbers of immigrant union members, as well as building partnerships with grassroots, community-based immigrant organizations.

Labour leaders within the Change to Win Coalition, which had large numbers of foreign-born workers in their ranks and sought to organize millions more,[20] concluded that the federation's hard-line opposition to a guest worker program prevented a workable policy compromise with business. In exchange for a means of legalizing roughly twelve million undocumented immigrants in the United States, they acquiesced in an expansive temporary worker program of some form. In contrast, the AFL-CIO adopted the position that once a labour market shortage and legitimate employer need for new immigrant workers was established, it should be met by increasing the number of

[15] The bill increased the total number of immigrant and non-immigrant admissions by close to 200,000 per year.

[16] Lane Kirkland letter to Lawrence Siskind, 16 February 1989, *Papers of the Coalition on Civil Rights*, Container 46, Manuscript Division, Library of Congress, Washington, DC.

[17] Leah A. Haus, *Unions, Immigration, and Internationalization: New Challenges and Changing Coalitions in the United States and France* (Palgrave Macmillan, 2002).

[18] Using occupation-level data, the authors estimate the foreign-born proportions of the core occupations of the different Change to Win unions as 24 per cent in cleaning and building services (SEIU, HERE), 16 per cent in health-care services (SEIU), and 23 per cent in construction labour (LIUNA), see Brian Burgoon and Wade Jacoby, 'Is Immigration Dividing US Labour?' Unpublished manuscript.

[19] Burgoon and Jacoby (n 18).

[20] Burgoon and Jacoby (n 18).

green cards, or legal permanent resident (LPR) visas, rather than expanding temporary programs.

The debates surrounding the Border Security and Immigration Act, which was ultimately defeated in 2007, marked a unique moment in the American labour movement's struggles over immigration. While the AFL-CIO supported the demise of the Act, which was defeated despite a last-ditch effort among some Change to Win unions to strike a deal with business and government in resurrecting the measure, the outcome proved but a pyrrhic victory for the federation. If anything, the split within the federation and the loss of so many of its strongest immigrant-friendly unions galvanized the AFL-CIO to demonstrate support for low-wage immigrant workers and engage in immigration reform in other ways.

Rather than demonstrating a clear-cut division between 'restriction' and 'solidarity' within organized labour, the 2007 debate galvanized both sides to pursue solidarity and champion immigrant rights.[21] The unions that remained with the AFL-CIO after the Change to Win split were united in their support of a legalization program for the 10–12 million undocumented workers in the US. They also sought to establish a system for 'future flow',[22] which would address how levels of employment-based temporary and permanent immigrant admissions would be set going forward. To that end, the AFL-CIO asked former Democratic Labour Secretary Ray Marshall to chair a special committee on immigration that had as its mission bringing unions together around development and adoption of a common position on immigration reform.[23] Marshall met with many national unions including construction unions like the bricklayers and ironworkers, as well as agricultural unions including the Farm Labour Organizing Committee that had long been working to unionize migrant workers in the fields. The common thread running through Marshall's conversations with national unions was the perception that immigration was undermining labour standards.

Marshall then developed the framework that would comprise the basis for labour's new immigration policy consensus. The basic tenets of the policy, which was formally adopted by the AFL-CIO in 2008, were:

1. An independent commission to assess and manage future flows, based on labour market shortages that are determined on the basis of actual need;
2. A secure and effective worker authorization mechanism;
3. Rational operational control of the border;
4. Adjustment of status for the current undocumented population; and
5. Improvement, not expansion, of temporary worker programs, limited to temporary or seasonal, not permanent, jobs.

The defeat of a comprehensive immigration reform as well as the election of Obama provided the AFL-CIO and Change to Win with added incentive to come together over

[21] Janice Fine and Daniel J. Tichenor, 'Solidarities and Restrictions: Labour and Immigration Policy in the United States' [2012] The Forum 10.

[22] Ana Avendano interviewed by Janice Fine, 31 January 2012.

[23] 'The Labour Movement's Framework for Comprehensive Immigration Reform: AFL-CIO and Change to Win' (AFL-CIO 2009) <http://www.aflcio.org/content/download/7389/79487/version/1/file/immigrationreform053111.pdf> accessed 25 June 2013.

the question of immigration and the Marshall plan provided them with a vehicle for discussion. After revising some of the wording, the AFL-CIO and Change to Win jointly put forward in the Labour Movement's Framework for Comprehensive Immigration Reform pledged in April of 2009 to 'fully protect US workers, reduce the exploitation of immigrant workers and reduce employers' incentive to hire undocumented workers rather than US workers'.[24]

For the AFL-CIO, the so-called 'future flow' component is the linchpin of the entire framework because it addresses how immigration will be managed going forward (once undocumented workers and their families have a pathway to legalization and visa backlogs are cleared) and would replace the current employer or market-driven system with a government run commission of experts for determining the numbers of permanent and temporary workers admitted into the US. The commission would assess labour market needs on an on-going basis, examine the impact of immigration on the economy, wages, the workforce, and business and, utilizing a methodology approved by the Congress, set the numbers of foreign workers to be admitted on employment visas. There would be no country caps or what is referred to as 'arbitrary'[25] caps on occupational classifications; admission numbers would be set based upon a determination of a long-term labour shortage in an industry.

In contrast to other proposals that attempted to turn the current flow from illegal to legal by providing enough visas to clear demand, the AFL-CIO proposal was not aimed at trying to equalize the number of visas with the current flow. Employers would be required to prove that they had made a strong effort to hire US workers and to 'fill those jobs at the prevailing wage and other conditions that will not cause a depression in wages or working conditions in that industry'.[26] Prevailing wages would be set by state labour departments with geographically specific data and workers would be covered by all US labour and employment laws. Once an employer's petition to hire a foreign worker was approved, the job would be listed on a computerized job bank list posted through US consulates across the globe; workers would send in applications while living in their home countries and employers would hire based upon these applications.

Hired workers would come into the US with a conditional green card that would turn into a standard green card once the government processed a worker's petition to remain in the US. As unscrupulous practices on the part of recruiters have been a source of worker exploitation, no employer or labour contractor would be allowed to recruit abroad. To function properly, the system requires congress to appropriate adequate funds to ensure against backlogs, which have been a major problem under the current system, and that 'all visas that can be distributed each year are actually distributed, under both employment and family classifications'.[27] Finally, the proposal calls for

[24] 'Guest Worker Programs and the Science, Technology, Engineering, and Mathematics (STEM) Workforce' (Department for Professional Employees, AFL-CIO 2011) <http://dpeaflcio.org/wp-content/uploads/Guest-Worker-Programs-and-STEM-20111.pdf> accessed 25 June 2013.

[25] Fine and Tichenor (n 21).

[26] 'AFL-CIO's Model for Future Flow: Foreign Workers Must Have Full Rights' (*Friends Committee on National Legislation* 2008) <http://fcnl.org/assets/model_for_future_flow.pdf> accessed 25 June 2013.

[27] 'AFL-CIO's Model for Future Flow' (n 26).

reforms to existing temporary worker programs beginning from the principle that they apply only to seasonal labour shortages, are limited in size and scope, require employers to pay the adverse wage level set by state workforce agencies and to bear the costs of recruitment fees, hiring, subsistence, and travel 'so that workers are not exposed to large debts that hinder their ability to enforce their rights'.[28] To aid workers in recovering pay they are owed, the proposal requires employers to post a bond that is 'at least sufficient in value to cover the worker's legal wages...' and mandates creation of a system that facilitates workers making claims against the bonds.[29]

Despite an enduring recession and high unemployment, organized labour at the national level in 2013 is a linchpin of the immigration reform movement, seeking, with the help of President Obama and his allies in congress, to legalize the 10–12 million undocumented immigrants in the United States today and to develop a means for continued labour migration that is simultaneously respectful of US workers and supportive of those workers seeking to migrate for better economic opportunities. Whatever differences may exist among national unions regarding issues such as mandatory employer verification, employer sanctions, and temporary worker programs, and among rank and file union members more generally regarding immigration, the AFL-CIO, in broad outlines, now has an enduringly 'pro-immigration' set-point and a strong interest in seeing that its national affiliates organize migrant workers into unions.

The United Kingdom within the context of the EU

The post-World War II period witnessed unprecedented economic growth on both sides of the Atlantic. In less than a decade, the economies of Western Europe expanded so rapidly that many countries were experiencing labour shortages in some industries. How to respond to these shortages was the first 'restriction' versus 'solidarity' policy dilemma that European labour movements faced.[30] On the one hand, they feared that migrant labour posed a threat to native and naturalized workers. On the other, as major partners in the construction of democratic welfare states, they understood migrant labour to be indispensable to economic growth.

As a consequence, from roughly 1960 to 1973 a system of temporary migrant labour evolved among most of the countries of northwest Europe and some of those bordering the Mediterranean Sea, which were the suppliers. According to Penninx and Roosblad, the temporary nature of the program made labour recruitment more acceptable for the unions, because it did not undermine their bargaining power and also seemed consistent with the preferences of the migrants themselves, who in the first phase mostly did migrate only to work temporarily and then returned home. Within a few years, however, it became clear that the majority of temporary workers had begun to settle permanently in the receiving countries and were 'becoming a structural component of western European labour markets'.[31] Between 1968 and 1973 national governments,

[28] 'AFL-CIO's Model for Future Flow' (n 26).

[29] 'AFL-CIO's Model for Future Flow' (n 26).

[30] Fine and Tichenor 806 (n 3).

[31] Rinus Penninx and Judith Roosblad (eds), *Trade Unions, Immigration and Immigrants in Europe 1960–1993: A Comparative Study of the Actions of Trade Unions in Seven West European Countries* (Berghahn Books, 2000).

largely with the support of the trade unions, responded by tightening their systems through entry policies that required workers to apply for temporary residence permits prior to their arrival, as well as employers to obtain a limited number of employment permits.

After the cessation of labour migration systems, many Italian, Spanish, Greek, and Yugoslavian migrants did return to their countries of origin, but others, particularly North African and Turkish workers, overwhelmingly remained and settled in the receiving countries. During the late 1970s and early 1980s these workers mobilized to bring family members to join them through various family reunification policies. Unions were faced with another policy dilemma: whether to embrace solidarity by supporting lenient family reunification policies; or to choose restriction by opposing these policies, on the grounds that they would increase the number of new immigrants entering the labour market. Asylum policies also challenged unions by opening admission to newcomers on human rights grounds rather than to people who were already part of settled communities and had some acquaintance with trade unions. A final struggle for unions was, and remains, what to do about undocumented labour migrants who entered countries illegally after the recruitment ban and are no longer able (as they were prior to the shift in policy in the early 1970s) to regularize their status after gaining employment.

The Treaty of Rome in 1957 altered the immigration terrain by guaranteeing the right of free movement of capital, goods, services, and persons among Member States. European Union law gives any European citizen the right to work in any Member State, but when new states become members, existing Member States have the right to adopt 'transitional arrangements',[32] which restrict the free movement of new members' workers for several years. The 1997 Amsterdam Treaty formalized an EU commitment to create a common Asylum and Migration Policy (AMP), but in practice, the EU has had great difficulty getting its members to commit to a common set of policies. An integrated European migration policy has been limited by the ability of countries to opt out of various programs (or to phase them in over an extended period), and mostly does not address national policies toward non-EU labour migrants (often referred to as Third Country Nationals, or TCNs).

A new form of labour migration has grown since the 1990s: 'posted workers',[33] whose wages are determined by the lower-wage states of origin rather than the host country. In certain sectors such as construction, posted workers from new Member States have been targets of bitter resentment. In 1996 the EU adopted the Posted Workers Directive (PWD) as part of the provision of services framework of the EC Treaty, which was intended to ensure that EU workers are covered by basic labour standard protections in any EU member country in which they are performing work. The PWD requires that minimum pay and working conditions in effect for a Member State be applicable both to native labourers and those from other EU states who are posted to work

[32] Andrew Geddes, *Immigration and European Integration: Beyond Fortress Europe?* (Manchester University Press, 2008).

[33] Torben Krings, 'A Race to the Bottom? Trade Unions, EU Enlargement and the Free Movement of Labour' [2009] EJIR 49–69.

there. Tensions still arise, because companies based in countries with lower pay rates still bring their workforces with them into other member countries to perform jobs at wages cheaper than would be the case for workers in the host state; moreover, enforcement and cooperation among Member States has been weak.

In many ways, the ambivalence that characterized European organized labour's stance in general was mirrored in the specific labour history of the UK. The immediate postwar stance of the Trades Union Congress (TUC) was at best contradictory. A 1955 resolution condemned discrimination against migrants from former colonies but argued that immigrants would form a cheap labour pool and undermine union bargaining power for white workers. There was a strong current of racism in some UK unions, and 'colour bars'[34] operated in certain industries in the 1940s and 1950s. Although the TUC opposed discrimination, it did not support legislation to that end, claiming that 'conciliation was better than the law and that industrial relations might suffer'.[35] Gradually, however, the unions' position began to shift: by the 1970s the TUC had adopted a strong stance in favour of individual statutory protections and assumed an important role in shaping these policies. Nevertheless, the TUC did not resist laws passed in 1968 and 1971, which were broadly perceived as racially biased and had the effect of keeping out nonwhite citizens of the New Commonwealth (NCW) countries while allowing white colonial citizens to enter the United Kingdom (in 1973, the TUC did pass a resolution condemning the 1971 Act).

In subsequent decades a significant policy shift occurred in the TUC. In 1981 it established a charter for member unions that encouraged them 'to defend the interests of foreign workers in their negotiations and to welcome them into their organizations on a broader basis'.[36] The TUC urged unions to adopt systems for greater internal representation through the organization of black workers' sections and conferences. By 1990, it was endorsing 'the principle of dismantling barriers between nations and allowing the free movement of all persons to the greatest extent possible'.[37] Later conventions passed strident resolutions denouncing immigration laws that had been passed in the 1970s and 1980s and opposition to new laws being proposed in the 1990s. Unions such as the National and Local Government Officers Association (NALGO), the National Association of Teachers, and UNISON sponsored resolutions that condemned immigration controls at the UK and EU levels, arguing that they would yield a large pool of unauthorized workers without rights and undermine the ability of unions to defend their members and organize the newcomers. The TUC came to strongly embrace more open immigration policies within the United Kingdom and the EU as necessary to providing support for unauthorized workers within the European Community to organize.

From 1995 through 2000, the TUC unequivocally opposed both national and EU attempts to strengthen immigration controls. In the year leading up to passage of the 1996 Asylum and Immigration Act, the TUC argued that it would have the perverse effect of strengthening employers' hands and weakening migrant workers' ability to take

[34] Gamze Avci and Christopher McDonald, 'Chipping Away at the Fortress: Unions, Immigration and the Transnational Labour Market' [2000] International Migration (IOM) 199.

[35] John Wrench, 'British Unions and Racism: Organisational Dilemmas in an Unsympathetic Climate' in Penninx and Roosblad 135 (n 31).

[36] Avci and McDonald (n 34).

[37] Avci and McDonald 201 (n 34).

collective action to better their situations. After it was passed, the TUC campaigned for its repeal as well as against administrative measures taken by the Conservative government to crack down on what it claimed were widespread abuses of the social welfare system by the unauthorized. In the late 1990s the TUC continued to lobby for repeal, launched a training initiative for member unions on how to mitigate the Act's harmful effects, provided support to workers charged under it, and took part in broader efforts to oppose the increased use of enforced detention of asylum seekers. It opposed the 1999 Asylum and Immigration Act and also pursued solidaristic policies at the European level through the European Trade Union Confederation.

At the EU level the TUC increasingly promoted liberal immigration policy. Although the right of workers to 'look for and take up employment in another member state'[38] is set out in Article 39 of the EC Treaty, accession agreements allow existing Member States to impose transitional restrictions on freedom of movement for up to seven years to guard against job displacement and downward pressure on wages. The TUC came out in opposition to Britain adopting transitional measures for A8 workers who were part of the EU enlargement in 2004. 'On general principle we felt that we were part of a broader European movement and that the EU shouldn't be a club for capitalism', explained Sean Baumford, a TUC policy officer.[39] 'But we had pragmatic reasons too, because restricting access to certain labour markets, we argued, was a recipe for creating lots of undocumented workers in the EU especially because transitional measures could not be applied to self-employed people. We didn't want undocumented workers because they are vulnerable to exploitation and can have the effect of undercutting existing members.'[40]

After May 2004, workers of the eight accession states were given full access to the UK labour market but were required to register prior to beginning work. The TUC negotiated an arrangement with the Home Office to mail out a pamphlet prepared by the union federation on the workers' rights along with every registration certificate. In September 2005 the TUC reached another agreement, with the Home Office and the Confederation of British Industry (CBI), to work together on supporting a program of managed migration in which the government pledged to 'consult employers and trade unions about migration policies that are in the interests of Britain'.[41] The CBI pledged to 'promote the case for legal and managed migration, support measures to eradicate illegal working and help companies and employees move from the illegal economy to the legal economy'.[42] In turn, the TUC pledged to 'provide migrant workers with information about their legal rights, assist its affiliates to organise migrants and represent their interests in the workplace, promote equality of pay and conditions for migrant workers and harmonious relations between workers from different countries of origin'.[43]

[38] Madeleine Sumption and Will Somerville, 'The UK's new Europeans Progress and challenges five years after accession' (Equality and Human Rights Commission, 2010) <http://www.equalityhumanrights.com/uploaded_files/new_europeans.pdf> accessed 25 June 2013.

[39] TUC Policy Officer Sean Baumford interviewed by Janice Fine, 16 July 2009.

[40] Sean Baumford interviewed by Janice Fine (n 39).

[41] 'Managed Migration: Working for Britain—A Joint Statement from the Home Office, CBI and TUC', TUC press release, 2005.

[42] 'Managed Migration: Working for Britain' (n 41).

[43] 'Managed Migration: Working for Britain' (n 41).

During debates in 2006 on how to control non-EU migration, the TUC supported a policy of managed economic migration, arguing for the importance of basic International Labour Organization (ILO) rights and the right of workers to bring their families into the United Kingdom. At the same time, the TUC supported residential labour market tests and the exclusion of tier 3 nonskilled workers to avoid substitution and undercutting of wages. 'The idea is we don't want any more in from outside of the EU because there are all these people coming in from Eastern Europe who will do the work so at the moment tier 3 is closed down', said Baumford.[44] Nevertheless, the TUC strongly objected to the Immigration, Asylum and Nationality Act of 2006 and its requirement that employers police immigration status.

In the same period, the TUC defended immigration opportunities despite rising anti-immigrant sentiment during a period of unemployment and slow economic growth. It issued a spirited statement in defence of open migration within the EU, including support for the accession of Bulgaria and Romania, with no transitional restrictions. TUC General Secretary Brendan Barber objected to government plans to limit the rights of Bulgarians and Romanians to work in the United Kingdom once their countries joined the EU, arguing that 'the UK Government cannot stop the free movement of new EU citizens, nor can it prevent them from working as self-employed once they are here.... The right response to EU enlargement is properly enforced rights that prevent the exploitation of anyone working in the UK, not measures that are more likely to increase the bad treatment of workers.'[45]

In 2007, as the civil penalty regime and criminalization provisions of the Immigration, Asylum and Nationality Act of 2006 were being implemented, the TUC asserted, 'Don't penalise, regularise!'[46] Pointing to the harmful impact on migrant workers' rights of the Immigration Reform and Control Act (IRCA), a similar law passed in the United States in 1986, the union federation argued that a rights-based approach, focused on helping migrants to remain within the labour market legally or to regularize their status, would be much more effective than a penalty-based one. Noting that the AFL-CIO ultimately pushed for the repeal of IRCA, the TUC cited the American objections to the measures, namely that 'even though the object of employer sanctions was to punish employers who knowingly hire undocumented workers and not the workers themselves, in reality employers have manipulated the program to violate federal and state labour laws and to discriminate against workers'.[47] Consequently, the TUC advocated a policy of legalization of the current undocumented workforce and urged the Home Office to reject the proposal for employers to have to repeatedly check employees' papers and to abandon employer penalties. It argued that requirements to carry out checks would spur discrimination, with British ethnic minorities targeted for special scrutiny. Other employers, concerned about possible fines and criminal proceedings, would abandon the idea of employing migrants altogether. 'The proposed penalties will not deter many employers who employ undocumented workers because of their vulnerability. This market for

[44] 'Managed Migration: Working for Britain' (n 41).

[45] 'TUC on EU Work Restrictions', TUC press release, 2006.

[46] 'Don't Penalise, Regularise!' (TUC, 2007) <http://www.tuc.org.uk/international/tuc-13568-f0.cfm> accessed 26 June 2013.

[47] 'Don't Penalise, Regularise!' (n 46).

undocumented workers can only be dealt with by taking steps to minimize the vulnerability of these workers.'[48]

The enduring recession, along with the election in 2010 of a coalition government dominated by the Conservative Party has led to a pronounced shift toward a more restrictionist policy regime focused on lowering levels of immigration viewed as having become excessive. The TUC, perhaps due to internal political pressure, is viewed by knowledgeable observers as having shifted away from a strongly expansive position and is seen to be focusing more on helping to lower unemployment and upskill the existing workforce.[49] Nevertheless, the organization has continued to advocate for the rights of migrant workers.

Beyond the policy work of the national federations, as traditional sectors of union strength have declined and the service sector has expanded, some national unions in both the US and the UK have come to view immigrant workers as attractive new recruits with the potential to restore labour to its former glory. Just as unions have become more supportive of legalization programs and advocated for other policy measures that protect the rights of immigrants, they have also ratcheted up efforts to organize. The following section is drawn from comparative research of union organizing of migrant workers in the US, UK, France, Germany, Jordan, and the Dominican Republic.

Unions Organizing with Migrant Workers

Varieties of union engagement with migrant workers and migrant worker organizations

Although Federations play a central role in policy, when it comes to organizing and representation, national unions and their local affiliates are where migrant workers most directly 'encounter' the labour movement. Engaging with migrant worker issues almost always involves a combination of the following: (1) *research*—shining a spotlight on exploitative practices in different sectors; (2) *education*—working with migrant workers to problematize their experiences and learn their rights and with unions to better represent them; (3) *policy intervention*—developing specific proposals to improve migrant workers' rights; (4) *organizing*—supporting workers who take action on their own behalves; (5) *global alliance-building*—organizing on an international scale through bi-national networks and the support of global institutions. Collective bargaining agreements are crucial, but given the complex challenges surrounding migrant worker employment, a variety of strategies and actions are necessary.

Research

Poor working conditions and abuses often go unreported by virtue of language barriers, the nature of the jobs and sectors in which they are concentrated, limited governmental capacity, and sometimes migration status itself. Unions increasingly have

[48] 'Don't Penalise, Regularise!' (n 46).
[49] Camilla Devitt, 'Labour Migration Governance in Contemporary Europe: The UK Case' [2012] Fieri.

worked with experts to conduct research reports that document migrants' working conditions, using the data to mobilize members in their own ranks as well as to raise awareness among the broader public. The Commission on Vulnerable Employment, established by the TUC in 2007, highlighted the difficult conditions faced by migrant workers in the UK and, as Tapia reports 'opened space for trade union debate and action concerning the integration of migrant workers'.[50] The TUC followed the report by funding affiliates to launch projects aimed at precarious workers, many of whom were immigrants. During this same period, UNISON developed a discussion paper on international labour migration and the role of migrant workers in the UK economy, in part intended to lay the groundwork for campaigns to ratify international conventions and strengthen domestic legislation. The union has followed up with several case studies of vulnerable workers who are performing jobs that have been outsourced as well as an evaluation of the effectiveness of the union's efforts to organize and represent migrant workers.

Research has played a similar role in the US. In 2009, three academics closely allied with the labour and immigrant rights movements released a groundbreaking study that documented the high incidence of labour standards violations in low-wage sectors that has been widely cited as the justification for a range of actions on the part of the labour movement.[51] That same year, the AFL-CIO, National Immigration Law Center (NILC), and American Rights At Work released 'Iced Out'[52] a report documenting examples of where immigration enforcement by the federal government has had a chilling effect on labour organizing. In a different vein, over the past decade, in connection with its organizing campaign at the Hyatt Hotels, HERE, the hotel workers union, has released several studies that document the physical toll of certain hotel company labour practices on their largely immigrant and female housekeeping workforces.

Education

Union members often feel threatened when first confronted with migrant workers in their sectors. While many national union leaders have concluded that supporting migrant workers and organizing together is the most sensible response to globalization and lean production, to become active allies, they know that they need to convince their members. In the US, EU, Latin America, the Middle East, and South Africa, unions and federations are developing training materials and presenting workshops and plenaries to their members about why workers migrate, the problems they face and basics on migrant worker rights. They are also developing programs for migrant workers.

[50] Maite Tapia, 'The United Kingdom: Dialectic Approaches to Organising Migrant Workers; Post-war to 2010' in Lee Adler et al. (eds), *Mobilizing for Inequality: Immigrant Workers, Unions and the Crisis of Capitalism* (ILR Press, forthcoming).

[51] Annette Bernhardt et al., *Broken Laws, Unprotected Workers: Violations of Employment and Labour Laws in America's Cities* (Center for Urban Economic Development, National Employment Law Project and UCLA Institute for Research on Labour and Employment, New York, 2009).

[52] Rebecca Smith, Ana Avendaño, and Julie Martínez-Ortega, *Iced Out: How Immigration Enforcement Has Interfered with Workers' Rights* (AFL-CIO, National Employment Law Project, and American Rights at Work, Washington, DC, 2009).

Migrant workers often arrive in destination countries without information about employment and labour laws or how to access help if they need it. In the US and Europe, NGOs have been the most common and reliable sources for education and support. In addition, some unions are establishing programs to educate migrant workers about their rights and some are working with migrants prior to their departure. In Mexico, the Solidarity Center (the international labour rights arm of the US labour movement) has partnered with the Centro de los Derechos del Migrante (CDM) to set up a program for pre-departure education. The Farm Labor Organizing Committee (FLOC), one of the farm worker unions in the US that organizes guest workers coming from Mexico, has established its own recruitment and orientation program in Mexico and the US for agricultural guest workers. FLOC has opened an office in Monterrey, near the US Embassy where workers go for visas, visits workers in their home communities prior to migration to explain their rights, and give them copies of the union contract. They also visit workers upon their return to Mexico to identify violations to the collective bargaining agreement.

Other unions are working to help develop educational programs and materials to support migrant workers in targeted sectors, in part through educating their own local staff and leaders about immigration law so that they are better able to represent their migrant members, negotiate contracts that are sensitive to their issues, and defend the rights of migrant workers during organizing drives. UNISON, the largest public sector union in the UK, found that the number of migrant workers in its ranks had nearly doubled between the 1990s and 2000s. Foreign-born workers in health, education, and other public services increased from 7.6 per cent of the workforce in 1997 to 11.3 per cent in 2007 and 12.8 per cent in 2008. UNISON also found that many of its local branches were not familiar with immigration laws. In cooperation with the TUC, Migrant Rights Network, GMB and UNITE, it published a guide for union negotiators on immigration document checks and workplace raids. Dave Prentis, UNISON general secretary, hailed the guide as 'important for all of our members, not just migrant workers. If the regulations regarding immigration controls in the workplace are not applied properly, there is a danger that workers will be discriminated against, regardless of whether or not they are migrants.'[53] Similarly in the US, the AFL-CIO General Counsel's office published a manual for union lawyers and negotiators explaining the representational rights of migrant workers, including what the union can do when they receive 'no match' letters from their employers requesting that they provide proof of their legal status.[54]

Beyond education on migrant rights, unions in the UK have tapped into the Union Learning Fund, established by the Labour government in 1998, to create a new corps of union shop stewards called 'union learning representatives' a significant proportion of which are black and migrant workers, as well as to provide funding for English language classes at unionized employers which are intended to both strengthen the social cohesion of the workforce and enhance the skills and employment prospects of migrant workers.[55]

[53] 'A Guide to Equality in UNISON' (UNISON 2012) <https://www.unison.org.uk/upload/sharepoint/Policies/Guide%20to%20equality%20in%20UNISON%20-%202012.pdf> accessed 24 June 2013.

[54] Haus (n 14).

[55] Helen Cole interviewed by Janice Fine, 23 May 2011, TUC Southwest Office.

Policy intervention

As documented in the first part of the chapter, unions are increasingly advocating with elected officials and government agencies for reforms regarding immigrant admission and regularization of status. Some have also become actively engaged in lobbying government to strengthen and expand existing labour and employment laws to better protect migrant workers.

As the number of female labour migrants has increased dramatically, some unions and union federations are recognizing the gender dynamics of labour markets and occupations and focusing greater attention on improving conditions in sectors with large numbers of migrant women workers. They are also increasingly coming to include informal sector workers and the self-employed, many of which are women, as core constituents of the labour movement. Some have taken a lead role in supporting domestic workers; the adoption by the ILO of Convention 189 in June of 2011, which recognized domestic workers' right to organize, was a watershed moment.

In addition, in 2010 after many years of publicizing abuses of nannies and domestic workers, Domestic Workers United (DWU) won passage of the New York Domestic Workers Bill of Rights, the first bill of its kind in the nation which requires a minimum of one day of rest per week, overtime pay, a minimum of three paid days off per year, anti-discrimination and harassment protections, and a study commission to explore collective bargaining for domestic workers. Domestic worker organizations led the effort by documenting the problem, drafting the legislation, meeting with elected officials, telling their stories publically across the state, and taking to the streets repeatedly, but they also were assisted by the strong backing of the state AFL-CIO, which brought its considerable political power to bear in support of the effort.

Moreover, unions are working to defend the labour and employment rights of migrant workers by helping them file suit against exploitative employers, bringing wage, occupational safety, and health cases through state and federal departments of labour, and working with these agencies to strengthen their monitoring and enforcement practices.

In the US, a janitorial watchdog organization, the Maintenance Cooperation Trust Fund (MCTF) was established in 1999 by Local #1877 of the Service Employees International Union and its signatory contractors to police the industry and assist immigrant workers who are routinely taken advantage of by some unscrupulous contractors. According to MCTF, there are more than 12,000 janitorial companies in California, but only half are registered with the state as legitimate businesses. In the supermarket sector, for example, large chains routinely contract janitorial work to cleaning contractors, who subcontract the actual work at a significant reduction, to labour recruiters. Under CL 2810, an innovative California law adopted in 2003 through union advocacy efforts, it is illegal to subcontract services without adequate funding. For the California labour department to bring cases under this provision, however, workers needed to come forward with qualifying claims. MCTF and its staff of twelve more than quadruple the state's investigative capacity in the janitorial sector. Since its inception in 1999, MCTF has assisted in the collection of more than $26 million in unpaid wages for more than 5,000 janitors.[56]

[56] Janice Fine, 'Solving the Problem from Hell: Tripartism as a Strategy for Addressing Labour Standards Non-Compliance in the United States' OHLJ (forthcoming).

In Britain, in addition to taking stands on immigrant admissions and legalization issues, the TUC has also worked for stronger regulation of labour subcontractors. In 2004, following the tragic drowning deaths of 21 Chinese workers who were part of an exploitative cockle-picking gang,[57] the TUC advocated passage of the Gangmasters Licensing Act (GLA), which created a licensing authority and inspectorate for labour subcontractors in agriculture, forestry, horticulture, and food processing. The law states that workers are entitled to safe working conditions and fair treatment; requires that they receive the national minimum wage; and requires that they be given a written contract, decent housing, and safe transportation. Operating without a licence or violating these rules can lead to a ten-year prison term. While the GLA was hailed as a major step forward in regulating labour subcontractors, steps have been taken recently to weaken its reach. Up until October of 2013, the GLA required that all those applying for a licence were automatically subject to labour inspection to ensure that agency workers were working under safe conditions and receiving their proper pay, but the Coalition government took steps to end the automatic inspection process and dramatically limit its purview.[58]

Organizing

Unions have worked at a variety of levels to organize migrant workers. As essential as it is to have pro-immigration leadership at the top, for most American unions the action in terms of organizing is really at the local and regional levels. While there have been important campaigns, there are still many challenges, particularly with respect to building successful alliances between unions and migrant organizations and advocacy groups.

Asbestos removal was a fairly new industry essentially created as a result of 1980s state regulations passed first in New Jersey and later in New York, which required abatement and removal. When the Mason Tenders lost control of the industry, it became largely non-union with wages declining from 30 dollars an hour to as low as 10 by 1991, which is the condition the Labourers International Union of North America (LIUNA) found it in when they began their whole market organizing effort in 1995. LIUNA organizers honed a strategy based on an in-depth understanding of the local industry and labour market actors—especially the role of labour brokers who were acting as asbestos removal subcontractors—but believed they could not win unless they drew non-union immigrant workers into active participation in the campaign and worked with union members to overcome their biases against immigrants. The union scanned its membership for any bilingual members (who spoke Spanish or Polish) who could work as organizers, hired leaders who emerged among the non-union workers, and then moved the organizing through one-on-one recruitment, tapping into existing immigrant workers' social networks and contacts, holding spirited mass meetings simultaneously translated into Spanish and Polish and direct action on the job.

[57] The gangmaster was found criminally negligent, convicted on twenty-one counts of manslaughter, and sentenced to 14 years in prison.

[58] 'New Gangmasters Licensing Authority Inspection Rules will see More Rogue Agencies, says TUC' (TUC, 2013) <http://www.tuc.org.uk/industrial/tuc-22401-f0.cfm> accessed 24 July 2013.

In this way, LIUNA established a network of activists for the union who were embedded within the industry at important contractors. The earliest job action was undertaken by Peruvian workers from Jackson Heights who had previously conducted a sit-in strike inside a Boston high-rise. Polish workers, who were the most recent entrants into the industry at a time when wages hit rock bottom, overwhelmingly supported the union as well.

Within six months, LIUNA had successfully organized 2,500 semi-skilled, low-wage immigrant workers in the entirely non-union NYC asbestos industry and won employer recognition and collective bargaining agreements with many of the major contractors. The lessons of this campaign regarding immigrant workers' interest in unionization, willingness to take action, and the solidity of their social networks for organizing reverberated throughout the union.

Since 2011, Change to Win, the labour federation formed in 2005 by a coalition of national unions, with an eye toward either eventually organizing Walmart workers or substantially raising their wage standards, has embarked upon a campaign to organize warehouse workers in California, Illinois, New York, and New Jersey who are part of large retailers' logistics supply chains. Warehouse workers labour in close proximity to large seaports where imported goods bound for retail behemoths, including Walmart, Target, Barnes & Noble, and K-Mart, are received, unloaded, and then re-loaded onto trucks destined for warehouses and distribution centres. Upon arrival at these warehouses and distribution centres, the goods are once again unloaded, sorted, packaged, and then reloaded onto truck and rail containers for shipment to stores across the United States.

These facilities are operated and managed by Third-Party Logistics Firms (3PLs) whose main function is to manage the movement of imported goods from the ports to regional retail markets. Although nominally independent entities, most 3PLs, according to Jason Rowe, 'owe [...] their existence and market size to the big-box retailers that drive the sector'.[59] Many 3PLs contract or work exclusively with one or more of the giant retailers and require hundreds of workers, some hired directly but many more provided through networks of temporary employment agencies operating out of modest storefront offices, concentrated in cities and neighbourhoods with high proportions of immigrant Latino residents. The unspoken value of these employment arrangements is that large companies don't have to be involved in hiring and operating their warehouses. They can insulate themselves from liability for hiring undocumented workers while keeping their costs low on the assumption that workers will come cheaply and keep their mouths shut about substandard employment conditions.

In New Jersey, home to the second largest port in the US, Rowe has worked with New Labour, a ten-year-old worker centre based in New Brunswick, to document extraordinary rates of non-payment of wages and overtime, injury, and employment discrimination. Through New Labour, workers have been coming together to learn their rights, map the industry, and develop strategies for improving wages and working conditions. The partnership with New Labour, and specifically the knowledge of its membership

[59] Jason Rowe, 'New Jersey's Supply Chain Pain: Warehouse and Logistics Work Under Walmart and Other Big Box Retailers' [2012] New Labour.

base, enabled Change to Win to deconstruct the complex composition of the logistics supply chain and identify the processing locations and players responsible for movement of the big box retailers' products to market. In turn, through its relationship to Change to Win, New Labour was able to access modest funding for its efforts and join forces with others to mount a national campaign it hoped would eventually build enough leverage to raise standards for its membership. In the Fall of 2013 however, Change to Win reduced the scope of the campaign and stopped funding New Labour and a sister organization in Chicago. They are now seeking a new union with an interest in organizing the workforce.

Unions in the UK have also become involved in organizing migrants. Building upon the East London Citizens Organization's powerful living wage campaign that was launched in 2001, the TGWU (which has since become UNITE) launched a drive to unionize the cleaners at Canary Wharf's financial centre. With the help of the Service Employees International Union (SEIU), creators of the Justice for Janitors campaign in the US, UNITE succeeded in organizing close to 2,000 cleaners. As Maite Tapia has documented, UNITE also partnered with London Citizens in an effort to unionize low-wage migrant hotel workers in the Hyatt and Hilton chains but this campaign met with less success. Tapia argues it failed not only because of strong employer opposition but also because 'there was inadequate involvement of the migrant workers themselves, and... the union treated migrant workers as workers, without acknowledging their specific situation'.[60] Additionally, UNITE's Migrant Workers Support Unit, which was where the union's expertise and experience with migrant workers was concentrated, had only a tenuous relationship with the hospitality branch of the union.[61]

Global alliance-building, bi-national networks, and leveraging the support of global institutions

Some US unions in recent years have sought the support of European unions in their efforts to organize migrant workers. The Property Services Division of SEIU sought the support of service unions for its effort to organize Securitas, a Swedish company and Wackenhut/Securicor. The support of the Swedish transport workers union was instrumental to winning neutrality and a card-check agreement covering US operations.[62] SEIU also worked closely with the TGWU and UNITE on the campaign to organize migrant cleaners in London, referenced earlier. Additionally, it coordinated worldwide campaigns in the property services sector for global agreements akin to card-check neutrality pacts. One such effort targeted Group 4, the second-largest private sector employer in the world after Walmart. It became a multi-country campaign with thirty partner unions across the globe and resulted in Group 4 agreeing to recognition

[60] Tapia 45 (n 50).

[61] For more on the challenges of building alliances between migrant workers, migrant worker organizations, and trade unions in the UK, see Miguel Martinez Lucio and Robert Perrett, 'The Diversity and Politics of Trade Unions' Responses to Minority Ethnic and Migrant Workers: The Context of the UK' [2009] Economic and Industrial Democracy 324–47.

[62] Adrienne Eaton, Janice Fine, Allison Porter, and Saul Rubinstein, 'Organizational Change at SEIU, 1996–2009', Report for the SEIU, 2010, 62–3.

agreements in the United Kingdom, Malawi, Nepal, Uganda, and elsewhere in Europe and Africa.[63]

Some national unions and global union federations (GUFs) have been working to establish cross-border networks for the purpose of teaching workers their rights and connecting them to unions before they migrate, defending migrant workers rights and helping them to organize. In the US, the Farm Labor Organizing Committee (FLOC) and the United Farm Workers (UFW) have negotiated collective bargaining agreements for agricultural guest workers and the United Food and Commercial Workers (UFCW) in Canada has also organized agricultural guest workers. FLOC's efforts are unique in that it is the only union that has opened an office in the workers' country of origin, Mexico, to enforce the seniority and other contract rights of workers in Mexico, confront the exploitative practices of labour recruiters, educate workers about their rights under US labour and employment law, and also to organize Mexican farmworkers in Mexico.[64] In recent years, UNITE has set a goal of becoming known as *the* migrant workers' union and is in the process of developing an internationally transferable membership card.[65]

The Building and Wood Workers International (BWI), the GUF for construction, forestry and wood-working unions, launched an Asia-Pacific migration project in 2004 to encourage migrant worker organizing partnerships between origin and destination country member unions. An agreement was signed in 2007 between BWI affiliates in Nepal, an origin country, and Malaysia, a receiving country, to develop a joint organizing campaign, which resulted in 1,500 migrant workers becoming members of the Malaysian union. Jennifer Gordon has researched these efforts as well as other projects to establish migrant worker local unions in destination countries such as Hong Kong.[66]

In a nutshell, so far, national and local unions have been better *advocates* for migrant workers—documenting the issues they face, providing educational resources to help them understand their rights, and providing political muscle in policy campaigns—than *organizers* providing a trade union home with a collective bargaining contract and union benefits for them. As discussed later, this is due to a combination of structural, cultural, and ideological factors within the labour movement but most importantly this is a consequence of labour's inability overall to adequately respond to sweeping changes in industrial organization and employment arrangements. Organizing within supply chains is a very tough business, whether the workforce is foreign or native born. Nevertheless, despite the many difficulties faced in bringing campaigns to fruition, a growing number of unions are showing an interest in organizing and representing immigrant workers.

[63] Eaton et al. 62–3 (n 62).

[64] Jennifer Gordon, 'Towards Transnational Labour Citizenship: Restructuring Labour Migration to Reinforce Workers' Rights: A Preliminary Report on Emerging Experiments' [2009] Social Science Research Network (SSRN) 39–40.

[65] Gordon 14, 45 (n 64). [66] Gordon 36–8, 56 (n 64).

Factors Contributing to Unions' Willingness to Include Migrant Workers

Certainly, structural forces that have led to a precipitous decline in sectors of traditional union strength such as manufacturing and construction combined with the dramatic rise of the service sector have led to increased interest among unions in organizing low-wage immigrant workers. With private sector unionization rates at their historically lowest points in many parts of the world, the old argument that unions must oppose migration in order to defend their labour standards is becoming less and less defensible.

Changes in the structure and composition of the labour market and labour unions

In the US, the rise of mass production led to a spirited debate within the US labour movement about the need to adopt an industrial union model. Between 1936 and 1942, the Congress of Industrial Organizations (CIO) grew to 2.5 million members,[67] many of whom were first generation immigrants. 'Within the brief span of six years, American workers in the basic industrial sector of the nation witnessed the transformation of their bargaining structures from relatively impotent bodies into equal partners in the industrial relations system', writes Walter Galenson in his definitive account of the CIO's rise.[68] 'It is no exaggeration to say that there was a fundamental, almost revolutionary change in the power relationships of American society.'[69] AFL unions, led by the Machinists and the Teamsters, were also transformed by the rise of mass production, evolving from strict craft unions of skilled workers. As Tomlins has shown, the AFL strongly responded to the challenge posed by the CIO, growing from 2,317,500 members in 1933, to 3,516,400 in 1936, to over 4 million members in 1940.[70]

Transformation took place during the Thatcher era in the UK when economic sectors of traditional union strength underwent dramatic contraction and five major pieces of legislation restricting the role of trade unions were passed between 1979 and 1990.[71] Over time, the Conservative government dismantled corporatist consultative arrangements, made it unlawful to enforce the closed shop, made it possible for employers to seek significant damages awards against unions engaged in unlawful industrial action, and banned secondary picketing.[72] David Marsh argues that the cumulative effect of the Thatcher years on both private and public-sector unions at the local and national

[67] Christopher L. Tomlins, 'AFL Unions in the 1930's: Their Performance in Historical Perspective' [1979] Journal of American History 1023.

[68] Walter Galenson, *The CIO Challenge to the AFL: A History of the American Labour Movement 1935–1941* (Harvard University Press, 1960) 73.

[69] Galenson 73 (n 68). [70] Galenson 62 (n 68).

[71] David Marsh, 'British Industrial Relations Policy Transformed: The Thatcher Legacy' [1991] Journal of Public Policy 291–313.

[72] Marsh argues that the most damaging features of the legislation were the removal of blanket immunity which made unions liable for civil actions in tort which meant that companies could pursue claims for damages for losses incurred in an illegal strike directly against the funds of unions and the fact that employers began taking out injunctions directly on trade unions rather than individual unionists, see Marsh 294 (n 71).

levels was that they were forced into a much more defensive role than they had been in prior to 1979 when the Labour government had encouraged union recognition and membership. Total union density fell from 59 per cent in 1978 to 47 per cent in 1988, while density of TUC affiliated unions fell from 55 per cent to 39 per cent during this same period.[73] The decline of traditional industries of strength including mining and manufacturing and more recently, the public sector, combined with the rise of the traditionally less unionized service sector has given rise to an imperative on the part of some unions to organize migrant workers.

Shifts in immigration flows

From 1901 to 1920, the flow of legal immigrants into the United States was approximately 600,000 per year. Between 1921 and 1950, however, the flow of legal immigrants into the United States was only 100,000 per year (excluding Mexicans coming through Bracero). During the time when the nation's gates were all but closed to newcomers from southern and eastern Europe, unskilled workers who had arrived earlier in the century were organized and incorporated into unions as never before. Ironically, it was the low levels of immigration mandated by the national origins quota acts—the major policy legacies of labour's virulently restrictionist period during the early 1900s—that helped facilitate labour's enduring reorientation toward expansionism. In the UK, in contrast to longstanding restrictions on non-Commonwealth 'alien' admissions (opened only slightly in 1953 during labour shortages), post-war immigration policy welcomed citizens of Commonwealth countries through the 1950s before a graduated set of restrictions were imposed largely on the basis of race.[74] Up until 1990, net emigration almost always exceeded net immigration, but post World War II, Britain also experienced significant immigration. The largest proportion of immigrants to the UK has been from former colonies; however the balance of people coming from the 'Old Commonwealth' countries of Canada, Australia, and New Zealand as well as from Ireland shifted after the 1960s to the 'New Commonwealth' countries of the Indian Subcontinent and the Caribbean. Although publicly opposed to any immigration control that was racially biased, the UK labour movement did not oppose 1968 and 1971 laws that were broadly perceived as racially biased and had the effect of keeping out nonwhite citizens of the New Commonwealth countries while allowing white colonial citizens to enter the UK. With the post-war settlement of significant New Commonwealth migrant communities in Britain, trade unions recognized the importance of recruiting these workers into unions (who also had a strong propensity for joining them)—even if most stood by while they were assigned the worst shifts and lowest paid positions.[75] As described next however, these workers engaged in industrial action and launched powerful campaigns for equal treatment within their workplaces and unions. By 1990, a significant policy shift had occurred in the TUC and it became a strong supporter of open immigration

[73] Marsh 307 (n 71).

[74] Martin A. Schain, *The Politics of Immigration in France, Britain and the United States: A Comparative Study* (Palgrave Macmillan, 2008) 127–9.

[75] John Wrench, 'British Unions and Racism: Organisational Dilemmas in an Unsympathetic Climate' in Penninx and Roosblad 136 (n 31).

policies. This position has not reversed despite the recession, the broad European economic crisis, or the accession to power of the Conservative Party.

Dynamics of state capacity and state/labour union relationships

In his comparative study of trade union involvement in economic restructuring in Europe, Turner has argued that institutions, in this case the rules and structures of industrial relations, condition the impact of intensified economic competition.[76] Likewise, Fine and Tichenor argue that institutional rules and structures strongly influence how unions in different countries view and respond to migration.[77]

The labour movement's relationship to the state, positive or negative, and its sense of the state's capacity to protect it[78] has a significant impact on its electoral and policy actions. In the case of the United States, as previously discussed, it was the strongly *pro-union disposition of the state* during the 1930s and 1940s that influenced labour's policy stance in favour of abolishing the restrictive national quota acts, and this position had staying power even during the federal government's most anti-union period under Ronald Reagan.

In the UK, however it was the *anti-union disposition of the state* as part of a broader rejection of social democracy during the 1980s under Margaret Thatcher that eviscerated British unions. Under Thatcher, a series of laws directly weakening the power of trade unions was enacted, along with the regime's general embrace of neoliberal economic policy including sweeping privatization of state-run enterprises in iron and steel, coal, gas, electricity, water, airlines, telecommunications, railways, and trucking along with a strict monetarist economic approach, which paved the way for steep union decline. Membership went from 13 million in 1979 to 8 million in 1995 and the number of strike days went from 29.5 million in 1979 to 415,000 in 1995.[79] This process continued under the 'New Labour' platform of the Labour Party, which worked to reduce the influence of unions on the party and whose continued embrace of neoliberalism further weakened unions. The deteriorating relationship with the state was marked by the collapse of traditional bargaining institutions and the loss of influence under Conservative and Labour governments combined with radical labour market shifts. These changes contributed to the TUC's embrace of a solidaristic position in favour of defending the interests of foreign workers in their negotiations with employers in 1981, supporting the free movement of labour across the European Union in 1990 and rejecting employer sanctions in 1996. Thus in both the US and UK, while the disposition of the state toward unions was important in influencing their stance on migration, it was not decisive in the same way.

[76] Lowell Turner, *Democracy at Work: Changing World Markets and the Future of Labour Unions* (Cornell University Press, 1991).

[77] Janice Fine and Daniel J. Tichenor, 'A Movement Wrestling: American Labour's Enduring Struggle with Immigration, 1866–2007' [2009] Studies in American Political Development 218–48; Fine and Tichenor (n 3).

[78] Haus argues that unions alter their immigration policy positions to become less restrictionist in part because they concluded that the state lacked the capacity to enforce restrictionist policies, see Haus (n 17).

[79] Peter Dorey, 'Thatcherism's Impact on Trade Unions' [1991] CBH.

Changing racial and ethnic attitudes toward immigrants

Shifting racial attitudes toward migrants have had a major influence on the labour movements' policy stances in the US and the UK, with both starting out with xenophobic views but becoming more tolerant over time. In the UK after World War II, labour migrants came from former British colonies without restriction and went to work in the transport industries in major cities, in healthcare, the textile mills in the North, and the foundries in the Midlands. According to Wrench, although they had equal rights in theory, migrant workers suffered discrimination that led to their being confined to a 'relatively restricted spectrum of occupational areas, over-represented in low paid and insecure jobs, working unsocial hours in unhealthy or dangerous environments'.[80] While the TUC professed sympathy with the colonial exploitation of workers from the New Commonwealth countries (who, as Pakistanis, Indians, and West Indians were all people of colour), it opposed immigration and called for immigration control.[81] The TUC expressed concern about these workers' failure to integrate and did not campaign against racially biased national immigration policies passed in 1968 and 1971, which made it harder for nonwhite citizens of the New Commonwealth countries to emigrate. During the 1960s and 1970s however, NCW workers joined unions in large numbers and waged major battles for civil rights including equal treatment inside the labour movement. The first challenge to immigration controls within the TUC came from rank and file union members at the 1969 TUC Congress but it was not until 1973 that a motion was passed calling upon the next Labour government to repeal the 1971 Immigration Act.[82] By the 1980s, the TUC adopted more aggressive anti-racist positions and pushed its affiliates to drop discriminatory policies, and it came to oppose restrictive immigration measures as well. This stance was further reinforced with the onset of European integration as the TUC came to view open labour migration as inevitable. As a result, the TUC opposed employer sanctions legislation and called for its affiliates to adopt aggressive organizing strategies.[83]

In the US, as mentioned in the previous section, the newly united AFL-CIO in 1955 championed the abolition of racist national origins quotas and the Bracero program and strongly supported the civil rights movement's policy agenda but what this meant for immigrant workers was rather complicated. The AFL-CIO's strong embrace of employer sanctions during the 1970s and 1980s, although eventually used by employers to keep immigrant workers from organizing, was not originally racist or anti-Mexican. In fact, support for an aggressive enforcement regime and for employer sanctions was viewed as a means of ensuring that low-wage foreign-born and African-American

[80] John Wrench, 'British Unions and Racism: Organisational Dilemmas in an Unsympathetic Climate' in Penninx and Roosblad 133–56 (n 31).

[81] Jane Holgate, 'Listening to Marginalised Voices in Trade Unions: Research Methodology and Practice' in *Organising Black and Minority Ethnic Workers: Trade Union Strategies for Recruitment and Inclusion* (TUC, 2004).

[82] Holgate (n 81).

[83] Fine and Tichenor (n 3); Jane Holgate, 'Black and Minority Ethnic Workers and their Experience of Trade Unions in Britain: an Historical Perspective and the Relevance to Organising Today' in *Organising Black and Minority Ethnic Workers: Trade Union Strategies for Recruitment and Inclusion* (TUC, 2004).

workers would be able to find work, form unions, and be compensated fairly for their labour. With the emergence of a sophisticated union-busting industry that utilized employer sanctions to strategically rid companies of pro-union workers and make organizing the growing numbers of Latino workers extremely difficult, as well as the passage of NAFTA, labour changed its position to one of support for legalization and abolition of employer sanctions.

Union identity

Union strategies are strongly conditioned by *union identity*, defined by Hyman as '...inherited traditions that shape current choices, which in normal circumstances in turn reinforce and confirm identities'.[84] Inherited traditions can shape a union's organizational model, ideology, and leadership orientation. In the US, industrial unionism was, for the CIO, both an ideology and a model, and it conditioned the organization's outlook on immigrant workers and immigration policy. In the US, the establishment of the CIO was motivated by the desire of key national unions to organize the largely unskilled immigrant workforces of the new mass production industries and those unions' impatience with the AFL's craft-union approach. The CIO provided a vehicle for organization and security to the millions of immigrants from southern and eastern Europe who had arrived prior to World War I and to the black migrants from the South who came north after the flow of migration abated as part of the Great Migration. These workers occupied the bottom ranks of mass production labour in the unorganized industries, while AFL trade unions largely were composed of older Germans, Danes, Scots, and the English. It is perhaps not surprising then, that the CIO from the start looked more favourably than the AFL on immigration. Identity played a strong role in shaping national union approaches to immigration as well.

From the time of its founding in 1900, the International Ladies Garment Workers Union (ILG) adopted a progressive outlook which included advocacy of independent political action, support for the Socialist Party, and industrial militancy.[85] Two famous strikes: the 1909 shirtwaist makers' strike in 1909, known as the 'uprising of the 20,000' and the 1910 cloakmakers' strike which catalysed the 'Protocol of Peace' which established a six-day work week and abolished home work and inside subcontracting, helped the union to establish itself.[86] Fink argues that the union's political and industrial stance could be attributed in part 'to the high percentage of Jewish and East European immigrants comprising the union's membership'.[87] During the 1930s, the union played a central role in supporting industrial unionism. In the late 1970s according to Haus, the ILG was among the first national unions in the AFL-CIO to take a position in support of amnesty for undocumented workers.[88]

In the UK, for decades, 'colour-blindness' was the official doctrine of UK unions. They insisted that their organizations treated all workers the same way, and refused to

[84] Hyman (n 2).

[85] 'Garment Workers' Union: International Ladies (ILGWU)' in Gary M. Fink (ed.), *Labour Unions* (Greenwood Press, 1977) 120–3.

[86] 'Garment Workers' Union' in Fink 120–3 (n 85).

[87] 'Garment Workers' Union' in Fink 120–3 (n 85).

[88] Haus 78 (n 17).

examine the actual treatment of NCW workers within the workplace as well as their own institutions. The disparities were especially pronounced with respect to trade union support for industrial actions taken by NCW workers. In 1972, when 500 South Asian workers employed at Mansfield Hosiery in the Midlands went on strike, complaining of being excluded from promotions and confined to the lowest paid jobs on the basis of race, their union refused to support them. The workers relied on the support of local community organizations, political groups, and Asian workers from other factories. Even when the union shifted its position to official support for the strike, it did not call upon its white members in the factory to support their striking co-workers. Similarly, in 1974, the TGWU refused to support striking Asian workers at the Imperial Typewriter factory in Leicester, who were objecting to disparities in treatment of Asian versus white workers.

Holgate argues that the trade union movement was not moved to engage in deep self-analysis until the MacPherson Report of 1999, which was undertaken by the government in response to the murder of a black teenager, Stephen Lawrence, by racists in south London. The TUC responded to the Report's call for institutions to examine their own policies and practices in order to guard against disadvantage by establishing the Stephen Lawrence Task Group which was charged with developing a set of initiatives that would challenge 'the pernicious effects of institutional racism in the workplace as well as the trade union movement'.[89] In 2001, the TUC Congress adopted a rule change that required all TUC affiliates to demonstrate their commitment to equality as a condition of their affiliation to the TUC. In particular, unions are required to audit their membership to establish breakdowns by ethnic origin and to monitor services to members, structures, and collective bargaining by ethnicity as well and to report their progress every two years to the TUC Congress.[90]

Global links

As we have already highlighted, in recent years, decisions on the part of US and UK union federations and individual unions to focus on migrant workers have been supported through contact with ILO programs, the European Trade Union Federation, and GUFs. They are able to play a legitimizing role because as labour insiders, they know how to make the case for organizing migrant workers within the paradigm of labour organizations. They also embrace a universalizing framework that places migrant worker issues in a labour rights and better work for all contexts. Supranational labour organizations play a central role in exposing unions to broader practices beyond their borders and also in helping those unions that are innovating to join with others to have more global policy impact.

As we have seen, union positions regarding migrant workers are strongly influenced by what is happening in the labour market and the polity as well as within the

[89] Jane Holgate, '"Race", Class and the Politics of Identification: Unifying Struggles for Economic and Social Justice' in *Organising Black and Minority Ethnic Workers: Trade Union Strategies for Recruitment and Inclusion* (TUC, 2004) 29.

[90] Holgate 29 (n 89).

organizations themselves. Beyond the individual factors discussed in this section, it is really the *interrelationship* between external variables, such as shifting labour and product market dynamics, immigration flows, and the disposition of the state toward unions, and internal variables—union history, ideology, leadership, and global ties—that have shaped union responses to migrant workers over time.

Conclusion

The US and UK labour movements have now solidly embraced a solidaristic position on immigration policy but the particulars of policy as well as policy implementation will continue to fluctuate based upon the party in power, economic conditions, and the perceived size of immigration inflows. Strikingly in both countries, the issue of actually organizing migrant workers and integrating them into the ranks of the unions remains a significant challenge. In other work, I have documented the emergence in the US of worker centres—low-wage, immigrant worker organizations, which have arisen almost entirely separately from labour unions. As of 2013 there were 215 such organizations and an emergent set of national sectorally-specific federations. Some of the most promising migrant worker organizing seems to be taking place through partnerships between the AFL-CIO, national unions, and these national worker centre federations.[91]

Beyond the nascent projects emerging between worker centre federations, the AFL-CIO, and specific national unions in the US, comparative research shows that unions still most often begin their engagement with migrant worker organizing *reactively*. In many cases unions are aware of migrant workers and some of their issues but not in direct relationship with them. Engagement usually begins as *a series of 'one-off' encounters and expands to a more prolonged relationship*: a union leader is approached to help a group of workers, provides support during a crisis, shows up at a picket line, speaks at a rally, signs an appeal, and then begins to share the union's resources such as providing a meeting space, donating food, dispatching a union attorney, tapping union allies to help out as well, leveraging union power resources like access to elected officials, on the migrant workers' behalf. In some cases, migrant workers are being employed on a union jobsite or in a unionized or previously unionized sector, in other situations they are in a more isolated setting like a person's home or a small workplace.

It takes a long while for the activities of a few at the margins of the organization to migrate to the centre of the union. In truth, in the early stages neither side seems to know what to do with the other: the migrant worker or workers are embroiled in a particular struggle and appreciative of the support but not usually thinking about long-term strategy; likewise the support from the union is improvisational. In almost all cases where unions begin organizing the migrant workforce it is not because the roadmap to permanent organization is crystal clear—rather they decide to take a leap

[91] Janice Fine, 'New Forms to Settle Old Scores: Updating the Worker Centre Story in the United States' [2011] RI/IR.

of faith and do it despite the lack of clarity, in Myles Horton and Paolo Freire's memorable phrase, 'to make the road by walking'.[92]

It is in the process of engagement that episodic support has the possibility of evolving into a longer-term program and the union begins to create pathways to organization and affiliation. But the passage is far from direct. With the rise of economic liberalization, privatization, and deregulation and the decline of centralized collective bargaining regimes, labour finds itself in a weaker position across the globe. In this period of crisis, unions are faced with twin and sometimes opposing pressures, on the one hand being driven to redefine their interests and broaden their agendas and their alliances, on the other, being circumscribed by extremely challenging economic conditions. As we have seen, even when labour is open to organizing migrant workers, all sorts of structural and cultural impediments must be overcome. This is the context within which the movement's relationship to migrant workers is evolving.

[92] Paolo Freire and Myles Horton, *We Make the Road by Walking: Conversations on Education and Social Change* (Temple University Press, 1990).

5

Indigenous Voices at Work

Paul Roth

Introduction

Four countries in the 'Voices at Work' project contain populations of Indigenous peoples: New Zealand, Australia, the United States, and Canada. In the colonization process, many Indigenous people lost possession of their lands, with the result that they were deprived of resources and the basis of their traditional economies. Government policies, such as moving Indigenous people to reserves far from urban centres of employment, as well as widespread racism and lack of access to capital, affected the ability of Indigenous people to engage in mainstream economic activities.[1] The historical marginalization of Indigenous people is reflected today in generally higher levels of unemployment and lower wages for Indigenous workers in comparison to other workers, together with other poor outcomes in such social measures as education, healthcare, and incarceration rates.

The literature on the working lives and voices of Indigenous peoples is not a large one. They have tended to fall outside the purview of trade unions in most places until relatively recently because of their working predominantly in the primary sector and their location away from manufacturing centres.[2] They have also been viewed at various times and places with suspicion as potential competitors to settler workers who could potentially undercut wages and other conditions.[3]

Unions have only recently developed any interest in Indigenous people. Although recognition and advocacy of Indigenous peoples' rights, both within and outside the workplace, have become important elements in the social justice agenda in New Zealand, Australia, and Canada, there is also an element of self-interest. As union density declines, it is in the interest of unions to make themselves more relevant to more workers, particularly those belonging to minority groups who may have been ignored in the past. In North America, the recent interest of unions in organizing workers on tribal lands has followed hot on the trail of the lucrative Indian gaming industry.

[1] Bryan D. Palmer, 'Nineteenth-Century Canada and Australia: The Paradoxes of Class Formation' (1996) 38 Labour History 16, 21 comments: 'any sustained attempt to argue for the integration of aboriginal peoples into the broad national labour market is destined to falter on both sides of an equation bounded by native people's resistance and white antagonism: class formation was embedded in racial exclusion'.

[2] Tom Murray, Kerry Taylor, Joe Tepania, and Nora Rameka, 'Towards a History of Māori and Trade Unions' in John E. Martin and Kerry Taylor (eds), *Culture and the Labour Movement: Essays in New Zealand Labour History* (Dunmore Press, 1991) 50.

[3] For example, in the late nineteenth century the New Zealand branch of the Amalgamated Shearers' Union of Australia 'quickly recognized that Māori were potential members, although perhaps for rather negative reasons. The Union feared that Māori might undermine union rates for the job through not being aware of the Union's agreement and rules': Murray et al. 51 (n 2).

Union support of Indigenous people, however, is consistent with their character as socially progressive organizations. This is even where there are relatively few Indigenous workers to organize or 'live' industrial issues involving them, as in Australia, where major current concerns include the return of land and reparations for past injustices. Although there is a distinctive Indigenous voice in relation to workplace matters, there can be tension, if not outright conflict, between worker and Indigenous voice, particularly where the Indigenous voice belongs to employers or only a section of the workforce, as illustrated in New Zealand and North America. Moreover, there can be more than one Indigenous voice, as, for example, where an independent approach is taken to that of a tribal hierarchy, or an assimilationist position is adopted.

In the four countries considered, Indigenous people comprise only a small minority, with the exception of New Zealand, where Māori constitute a significant minority and have an important cultural and political presence. They therefore have a correspondingly stronger voice than Indigenous people elsewhere. Māori make up 15.4 per cent (682,200) of the total New Zealand population.[4] Australian Aborigines and Torres Strait Islanders number 2.5 per cent (548,370) of the total population.[5] Canada has an Indigenous population of 3.75 per cent (1,172,790) of the total population.[6] The United States has an Indigenous population of 2.1 per cent (about 6.4 million) of the total population.[7] These totals can be broken down to those of mixed and pure Indigenous ancestry, but generally the figures refer to those who self-identify as Indigenous.[8]

Two international instruments relate specifically to Indigenous peoples. Each contains provisions that relate to Indigenous workers, The International Labour Organisation's Indigenous and Tribal Peoples Convention 1989 (No. 169) addresses the social and economic position of Indigenous peoples generally.[9] It promotes the right of Indigenous peoples to preserve their identity and pursue traditional occupations and

[4] This is according to the most recent census in 2006: Statistics New Zealand, 'Statistics NZ releases updated Māori population estimates' <http://www.stats.govt.nz/tools_and_services/services/media-centre/additional-releases/maori-population-estimates-15-nov-2012.aspx> accessed 10 September 2013.

[5] This is according to the most recent census in 2008: 'Aboriginal and Torres Strait Islander Australia revealed as 2011 Census data is released', Australian Bureau of Statistics (21 June 2012) <http://www.abs.gov.au/websitedbs/censushome.nsf/home/CO63?opendocument&navpos=620> accessed 10 September 2013.

[6] This is according to the 2006 census. These consist of nearly 700,000 First Nations people, 50,000 Inuit, and 390,000 Métis peoples: Statistics Canada, Table 2, 'Number and percentage of population reporting Aboriginal identity, Canada, provinces and territories, 2006' <http://www12.statcan.ca/english/census06/analysis/aboriginal/tables/table2.htm>; and Figure 1, 'Percentage of Aboriginal people in the population, Canada, provinces and territories, 2006' <http://www12.statcan.ca/english/census06/analysis/aboriginal/charts/chart1.htm> both accessed 10 September 2013.

[7] This is according to the 2010 census. These comprise American Indian and Alaska natives (5.2 million) and Native Hawaiian and other Pacific peoples (1.2 million): United States Census Bureau, *Overview of Race and Hispanic Origin 2010* (Census Briefs, March 2011) 7, <http://www.census.gov/prod/cen2010/briefs/c2010br-02.pdf> accessed 10 September 2013.

[8] Compare Article 1(2) of ILO Convention 169 concerning Indigenous and Tribal Peoples in Independent Countries (1989), which provides that '[s]elf-identification as indigenous or tribal shall be regarded as a fundamental criterion for determining the groups to which the provisions of this Convention apply', and Article 32(1) of the United Nations Declaration on the Rights of Indigenous Peoples (2007), which provides that 'Indigenous peoples have the right to determine their own identity or membership in accordance with their customs and traditions'.

[9] This Convention replaces ILO Convention 107 on the Protection and Integration of Indigenous and Other Tribal and Semi-Tribal Populations in Independent Countries 1957, which took an outmoded paternalistic and assimilationist approach.

strategies for utilizing native resources. It is also aimed at combating discrimination, child labour, and forced labour. Only twenty-two countries, however, have ratified this convention. New Zealand, Australia, the United States, and Canada have not ratified it, nor are they likely to. Indeed, Indigenous groups themselves have not supported the Convention, which does not recognize aspirations to self-determination and expressly (in Art 1(3)) does not acknowledge Indigenous populations as 'peoples' entitled to self-determination at international law in terms of Articles 1(2) and 55 of the United Nations Charter.[10]

The United Nations Declaration on the Rights of Indigenous Peoples 2007 addresses various rights relating to Indigenous peoples, including individual and collective rights, cultural rights, and rights to identity.[11] In particular, the Declaration upholds the right of Indigenous peoples to remain distinct and to pursue their own priorities in economic, social, and cultural development. Article 17 focuses on labour rights. It provides that Indigenous individuals and peoples are entitled to enjoy fully all labour law rights under applicable international and domestic law; children must be protected from exploitation and any harmful work; and individuals have the right to be free from discrimination. Although 144 states voted in favour of the Declaration, four voted against it:[12] Australia, New Zealand, Canada, and the United States, all of whom have since changed their position and endorsed the Declaration.

New Zealand

The New Zealand Council of Trade Unions (CTU), the country's umbrella union organization, has about 400,000 members, 60,000 of whom identify as Māori.[13] Unemployment is somewhat higher for Māori than other groups. For the year ended March 2012, the labour force participation rate for Māori was 66.3 per cent (291,400), compared with a participation rate of 68.44 per cent for all people out of a working age population of 439,000 (15 years and over).[14] Of those Māori in the labour force, 86 per cent (252,700) were employed, and 13.3 per cent (38,700) were unemployed.

[10] See Russel L. Barsh, 'Making the Most of ILO Convention 169' (1994) 18(1) Cultural Survival Quarterly <http://www.culturalsurvival.org/publications/cultural-survival-quarterly/bolivia/making-most-ilo-convention-169> accessed 10 September 2013. For example, when questioned by the Committee on Economic, Social and Cultural Rights as to why New Zealand had not ratified ILO Convention 169, the New Zealand delegation responded that 'following consultation with Māori representatives, it had been found not to conform to a model of the State and relations with indigenous peoples that complied with the provisions of the Treaty of Waitangi, which had constitutional status': Economic and Social Council, Summary Record of 9th meeting, Consideration of New Zealand's third periodic report under the Covenant on Economic, Social and Cultural Rights, E/C.12/2012/SR.9, 1 November 2012, para. 28. The implication was that the ILO Convention could cut across recognition of Māori sovereignty.

[11] Adopted by a General Assembly resolution on 13 September 2007: General Assembly A/RES/61/295, 2 October 2007.

[12] There were eleven abstentions.

[13] Sharon Clair, Vice President Māori, New Zealand Council of Trade Unions, 'Key Note Address' (ACTU Indigenous Conference 2008, Adelaide, 19 May 2008).

[14] New Zealand Department of Labour, 'Māori Labour Market Factsheet—March 2012' <http://www.dol.govt.nz/publications/lmr/quick-facts/lmr-fs-maori-mar12.pdf> accessed 10 September 2013.

The integration of Māori into the political and legal system

Over the past generation, some Indigenous elements have become integrated within the general law. This reflects the importance of Indigenous people and culture in New Zealand, which stems from a number of historical and political factors. Māori play a much greater part in mainstream political and economic activities than their counterparts in the other countries, and they enjoy a voice in the workplace through the support and promotion of Māori values by the state,[15] the union movement, as well as conventional employment law.

Provision is made for promoting political participation by Māori through both Māori and general electoral rolls, and there are a number of measures that are intended to promote Māori economic and cultural interests. As an ILO report has noted, 'the political system satisfies the multicultural model by recognising indigenous identity, working towards the elimination of direct and indirect discrimination and at the same time, promoting integration of Māori in the New Zealand society.'[16]

Māori is an official language of New Zealand alongside English.[17] One consequence is that the legal system, including the specialist employment law institutions,[18] gives people the right to speak Māori in court, and Māori translation must be provided if requested.[19]

Māori values have a particularly important place in public sector employment. The legislation governing such employment sets out a number of 'good employer' obligations, which include

> Recognition of—
> (i) The aims and aspirations of the Māori people; and
> (ii) The employment requirements of the Māori people; and
> (iii) The need for greater involvement of the Māori people in the Public Service.[20]

Māori and trade unions

Māori did not enjoy much of a voice in union affairs until the last quarter of the twentieth century. For much of modern New Zealand history, Māori lived rural lives and agricultural workers mainly fell outside of the union movement, though Māori did

[15] The basis of British sovereignty in New Zealand was the Treaty of Waitangi, signed by representatives of the Crown and Māori in 1840. Although not incorporated into New Zealand law, the treaty is of constitutional significance and imposes obligations on the state entailing partnership with Māori and support of Māori culture.

[16] Alexandra Xanthaki and Dominic O'Sullivan, *Good Practices of Indigenous Political Participation: Māori Participation in New Zealand Elective Bodies*, Case Study 5, Research on Best Practices for the Implementation of the Principles of ILO Convention No. 169, Programme to Promote ILO Convention No. 169 (International Labour Office, Geneva, 2007) 66.

[17] *Māori* Language Act 1987, s. 3.

[18] *Māori* Language Act 1987, s. 3. The first instance Employment Relations Authority and the Employment Court were added by legislative amendment to Sch. 1 in 2000.

[19] This right may be exercised even if the person concerned understands and knows how to communicate in English: *Māori* Language Act 1987, s. 4.

[20] State Sector Act 1988, s. 56(2)(d).

become members of shearers' unions,[21] with some becoming delegates and executive members.[22] The short-lived late nineteenth-century Knights of Labour movement in New Zealand attempted to organize Māori, along with other workers, and routinely supported Māori land rights as well.[23] From the early twentieth century, Māori were active in unions in the shearing, waterfront, and meat freezing industries.[24] It has been noted that it was significant that these industries tended to be seasonal, as they 'served as a transitional point for Māori in the process of integration into the Pakeha [white] capitalist economy, straddling the boundary between the Māori and Pakeha economy, until well into the twentieth century'.[25]

In the post-war period, many Māori young men migrated to urban manufacturing areas. They mainly performed unskilled or semi-skilled labour, and though they might have been union members, they were not generally involved in union affairs.[26] One suggestion is that they were alienated by the culture of Pakeha-dominated unions.[27]

In the late 1960s and 1970s, there was a rise in Māori rights activism. There were marches and occupations in support of Māori land rights, often supported by unions. For example, during the occupation of Auckland's Bastion Point in 1977–1978 in connection with a local tribal land claim, the Auckland Trades Council imposed a 'green ban' in the face of a government proposal to build high-income housing on the site. In 1978, workers at the Petone Gear Meat works hired a bus to carry them to Parliament in Wellington in order to support the Tainui Awhiro people in a campaign to demand the return of land from a local authority.[28]

Although Māori by this time had significant union involvement at lower levels, participation at the higher levels was patchy. In 1983, the New Zealand Federation of Labour (FOL), a national labour umbrella organization established in 1937, set up a Māori and Pacific Island Advisory Committee to provide leadership on the national level. In 1985, the Committee focused entirely on Māori issues. Change, however, came too slow for some, and a few Māori proposed establishing a separate Māori union movement. The proposal was discussed in a 1986 meeting of over 400 Māori delegates at the Hui a Nga Kaimahi ('the meeting of New Zealand workers'). The meeting rejected a separate Māori union, but it demanded that the FOL and Combined State Unions (CSU) lend their support to Māori self-determination, increase Māori representation

[21] There was a high percentage of Māori in the shearers unions. About one quarter of members in 1914 were Māori, not only because there were many Māori working in the industry, but also because it was feared that if left unorganized, employers might offer them inferior terms and conditions, undermining the position of all workers.

[22] Murray et al. 52 (n 2). See also Richard Beresford Nightingale, *Māori at Work: the Shaping of a Māori Workforce within the New Zealand State 1935–1975* (PhD thesis, Massey University, 2007) 161; John E. Martin, *Tatau Tatau: One Big Union Altogether: the Shearers and the Early Years of the New Zealand Workers' Union* (New Zealand Workers' Union, 1987); 'Ngā uniana—Māori and the union movement', *Te Ara, The Encyclopedia of New Zealand* <http://www.teara.govt.nz/en/nga-uniana-maori-and-the-union-movement> accessed 10 September 2013.

[23] Robert E. Weir, *Knights Down Under: The Knights of Labour in New Zealand* (Cambridge Scholars Publishing, 2009) 43–5.

[24] Murray et al. 59 (n 2). [25] Murray et al. 59–60 (n 2). [26] Murray et al. 162 (n 2).

[27] Murray et al. 162 (n 2).

[28] The land, used as a golf course, had been taken temporarily from the tribe during the Second World War. See Cybele Locke, *Workers in the Margins: Union Radicals in Post-war New Zealand* (Bridget Williams Books, 2012) 48.

in union power structures, engage in regular consultation with Māori, and take action on Māori issues. When the FOL and the CSU combined in 1987 to form the current CTU, the national Māori committee remained in place and had two representatives on the national executive.[29]

The CTU organizational structure currently includes the CTU Runanga,[30] the representative body for Māori workers whose unions are affiliated with the CTU. Unions are represented within the Runanga by at least one person, who is responsible for ensuring that the views of Māori workers in their union are included in the discussions and decision-making of the group. Each union that is affiliated with the CTU in turn has its own Runanga whose task is to ensure that Māori have a voice in the union's operations.[31] The CTU Runanga meets about four times a year. One priority of the Runanga is to implement change within the CTU based on Treaty of Waitangi principles,[32] which includes consultation and partnership with Māori.

Workplace issues relating to Māori

There are a number of workplace issues that affect Māori in particular, including the following:[33]

- Most workplaces operate in accordance with non-Māori cultural values and assumptions, with the result that Māori can feel excluded or marginalized. For example, Māori have a wider concept of the family (*whanau*) than non-Māori, and a wider set of obligations that are owed to one's *whanau*. This has implications for domestic purposes and bereavement leave.[34]
- Where workplaces recognize the importance of Māori values and issues, there is an expectation that Māori workers should provide guidance and leadership.[35] There is

[29] 'Ngā uniana—Māori and the union movement', *Te Ara, The Encyclopedia of New Zealand* <http://www.teara.govt.nz/en/nga-uniana-maori-and-the-union-movement> accessed 10 September 2013.

[30] See the CTU website at <http://www.union.org.nz/runanga> accessed 10 September 2013. 'Runanga' is defined as a 'council, tribal council, assembly, board' in the online *Māori Dictionary* <http://www.maoridictionary.co.nz> accessed 10 September 2013.

[31] See, for example, New Zealand Public Service Association, *Māori Enterprise Delegate Guide* (November 2009), which deals with the role and functions of Māori delegates within the Te Runanga o Nga Toa Awhina structure, the congress of PSA members who identify as Māori <http://www.psa.org.nz/Libraries/Delegate_Zone/Māori_Enterprise_Delegate_Guide.sflb.ashx> accessed 10 September 2013.

[32] See n 15. For a copy of the Treaty, and discussion, see the Waitangi Tribunal website at <http://www.waitangi-tribunal.govt.nz/treaty> accessed 10 September 2013.

[33] See New Zealand Public Service Association 11 (n 31).

[34] Other examples of Māori values that may be ignored in mainstream workplaces are: the importance of maintaining people's dignity and dealing with them on the basis of openness, consultation, and give-and-take (*mana*); the observance of spiritual protocols, such as in relation to the construction or opening of premises (*wairuatanga*); and respecting demarcation zones in relation to people, places, and objects in particular contexts (*tapu* and *noa*).

[35] See *Waters v Aupouri Māori Trust Board*, Employment Tribunal, AT279/95, 22 December 1995, where a Māori social worker was unjustifiably dismissed, inter alia, for an inadequate understanding of *tikanga Māori* when the employment was on the basis that training and guidance would be provided; and *Scott v Chief Executive, Department of Corrections*, Employment Relations Authority, WA29A/06, 13 March 2006, where a Māori employee complained of unjustified disadvantage in her employment because she was required to deliver Māori cultural training even though she had told her employer that she lacked the relevant knowledge.

also the related issue as to the terms upon which such extra contributions should be made, and whether there is to be any recognition or compensation for it.

The role played by Indigenous values within a mainstream common law legal system raises some challenging issues. When the promotion and implementation of Indigenous culture in the workplace relates to the treatment of employees, situations can arise where Indigenous values do not always sit comfortably alongside the law of general application. Where employers seek to uphold Indigenous values or processes, the law may intervene to protect the rights of workers. This approach is consistent with Article 17 of the United Nations Declaration on the Rights of Indigenous Peoples, which implicitly renders Indigenous values subject to domestic and international labour law, as well as Article 46, which subjects Indigenous rights to domestic and international human rights standards. These aspects of the international standards have not always found favour with Indigenous people.[36]

There can be instances when there is a tension between Indigenous and non-Indigenous values. One flashpoint is the right to be free from sex discrimination. For example, female conservation workers are prohibited from working in areas that are *tapu*.[37] In one case,[38] a female employee of the Department of Corrections was forbidden to sit in the front row or speak at a workplace celebration for Māori graduates of a prison programme. She disrupted the ceremony because of her treatment, and her conduct attracted a complaint from the workplace Māori Staff Network. Although a tribunal made a finding of sex discrimination, no remedy was awarded.[39] The decision in this case skirted around the difficult issue of how an employer should accommodate more than one voice where there is an incompatibility between their expression.

Employers are expected to accommodate Māori values where workplaces recognize a commitment to them. Such workplaces tend to be Māori in nature (such as language schools and Māori media), or public sector agencies, particularly those with a particular Māori connection or relevance (Ministry of Māori Development, Department of Corrections, Ministry of Education). For example, some employment agreements provide for cultural leave,[40] or contain problem resolution processes that, while compatible

[36] The prioritization of conventional international human rights standards over Indigenous values has been criticized as stemming from a Eurocentric perspective: Sharon Venne, 'The New Language of Assimilation: A Brief Analysis of ILO Convention 169' (1990) 2(2) Without Prejudice 53, 60, and Catherine Iorns, 'Australia Ratification of International Labour Organisation Convention No. 169' (1993) 1(1) E Law, Murdoch University Electronic Journal of Law <http://www.austlii.edu.au/au/journals/MurUEJL/1993/1.html> accessed 10 September 2013.

[37] Defined as 'sacred, prohibited, restricted, set apart, forbidden' in the online *Māori Dictionary* <http://www.maoridictionary.co.nz> accessed 10 September 2013.

[38] *Bullock v Department of Corrections*, Human Rights Review Tribunal, Decision No 4/08, 19 March 2008. The tribunal has an overlapping jurisdiction with the specialist employment law institutions in relation to workplace discrimination and harassment.

[39] The Tribunal recognized that the employer was in a difficult position and was taking steps to try to reconcile Indigenous rights with other rights. The employer's concern for respecting Māori culture and following proper Māori protocol in this instance should be viewed in light of the fact that relative to their numbers in the general population, Māori are over-represented in the criminal justice system. About half of the male prison population, and about 60 per cent of female prisoners, are Māori: see *Over-representation of Māori in the criminal justice system: An exploratory report*, Policy, Strategy and Research Group, Department of Corrections (Wellington, September 2007) 6.

[40] This is sometimes offered as paid leave. The Secondary Teachers' Collective Agreement 2013 provides for paid leave (for up to six weeks) for 'recognized cultural activities within New Zealand or outside

with ordinary employment law principles, provide for the resolution of employment problems in a 'Māori context and manner'.[41] In the Māori Studies Department of a Polytechnic, there was a clause in the contract that provided for *hui*[42] to resolve interpersonal problems involving probationary staff.[43]

In the leading case in this area,[44] the Employment Court held that an employer's obligations to accommodate Māori values are heightened where there is an express policy to that effect, and a matter concerns a Māori employee working in a Māori setting. The employee in that case was a Māori mental health worker for a hospital's Māori mental health unit who sought three days' leave to attend a Māori festival where she was responsible for the provision of health services. The employer had granted her leave to attend this event for the previous 17 years. After some delay, she was denied leave at the last minute, having already made arrangements to have her work covered and attend the festival. She attended the festival, and was summarily dismissed on her return. The dismissal was found to be unjustified on the basis that it was unreasonable and unfair that the employee had been refused leave to attend the festival since the refusal was notified too late and without considered justification. Moreover, the employer failed to accept that attendance at the festival, and the importance of keeping her word to the festival organizers, was culturally important to the employee. The dismissal process was also defective, as it was conducted with undue haste and in a culturally insensitive manner.[45] Overall, the court's approach fell within mainstream employment law principles, in that individual circumstances, including cultural factors, are relevant considerations when an employer is making a decision to dismiss an employee.

Despite the recognition of Māori values in the workplace, conventional employment law rights still apply to disciplinary processes, so that any Māori-based values or policies must be consistent with basic requirements of reasonableness and fairness. Where the customary Māori way of dealing with employment issues has been adopted, discussions (variously called *hui* or *wānanga*[46]) are held to discuss the matter and reach a

New Zealand' (cl. 6.6.5) <http://www.ppta.org.nz/index.php/collective-agreements/stca/92-part-six> accessed 10 September 2013.

[41] See the Secondary Teachers' Collective Agreement 2013–2015, cl. 3.5.1(b), where 'Māori context and manner' is defined as relating to the following features: 'meetings can be held on a marae; there is face-to-face engagement; there can be *whanau* (extended family) support for everyone involved; guidance and advice may be provided to everyone concerned by *kaumatua* (elders) and *kuia* (female elders)' <http://www.minedu.govt.nz/NZEducation/EducationPolicies/SchoolEmployment/TeachersPrincipals/SecondaryTeachers/CollectiveAgreement/PartThree.aspx#3.5> accessed 10 September 2013.

[42] Defined by the online *Māori Dictionary* as 'gathering, meeting, assembly, seminar, conference' <http://www.maoridictionary.co.nz> accessed 10 September 2013.

[43] *Fraser v Manukau Polytechnic*, Employment Court, AEC 71/96, 31 October 1996. Such *hui* were not intended to be disciplinary in nature.

[44] *Good Health Wanganui v Burberry* [2002] 1 ERNZ 668. *Tikanga* is defined in the online *Māori Dictionary* as 'correct procedure, custom, habit, lore, method, manner, rule, way, code, meaning, plan, practice, convention' <http://www.maoridictionary.co.nz> accessed 10 September 2013.

[45] The court found that the onus was on the employer to be culturally sensitive, not on the employee to assert her *mana* Māori. 'The fact that an employee is Māori and is working in a Māori setting should have been sufficient to alert them to a need for an appropriate procedure': *Good Health Wanganui v Burberry* [58] (n 44). This was in response to the employer's objection that the employee had not asked for cultural support or procedures in relation to her dismissal interview.

[46] Defined by the online *Māori Dictionary* as 'seminar, conference, forum' <http://www.maoridictionary.co.nz> accessed 10 September 2013.

binding resolution by consensus. In a dismissal case,[47] the *wānanga* process involved discussion conducted by a *whanau* group of the two employees concerned, with everyone enjoying unlimited speaking rights, until a binding resolution was framed and unanimously agreed to by all concerned. The Employment Court commented that this was 'no more than a process, like any other process that an employer may choose when considering termination of employment'. The court, however, went on to caution:

> The fact however that certain actions which are the subject of a grievance claim and challenged for fairness, were performed validly in a customary context cannot throw up a shield preventing the eyes of the Court from probing the customary actions to see if they complied with the law's requirement that they be fair... [What] the Court must decide...is not whether the employer has justified the terminations of employment by showing they occurred in a valid customary way, but whether the terminations complied with the law.[48]

Traditional processes may be followed, but they must still be consistent with conventional employment law standards of fairness.[49]

Australia

The economic and social fabric of Aboriginal society was irreparably harmed by the colonizing power's dispossession of Aborigines from their land. This made them dependent on settler landowners for their sustenance and vulnerable to economic exploitation for their labour. Until only recently, Indigenous people fell outside the scope of labour laws that protected non-Aboriginal workers. What pittances they were entitled to are currently being sought through the current struggle for reparations for 'stolen wages'.

It has been only since the 1960s that Australia's Indigenous people began to realize rights generally, including workplace rights. The initial struggle was for equal pay and terms and conditions of work. According to the Australian Council of Trade Unions (ACTU),[50] the workforce participation rate among Aborigines and Torres Strait Islanders is currently 53.8 per cent, compared to 75 per cent for the entire population, and the unemployment rate is 16.6 per cent, which is four times the national rate. Many Indigenous workers are employed only casually or part-time in precarious employment.

[47] *Te Whanau a Takiwira Te Kohango Reo v Tito* [1996] 2 ERNZ 565.

[48] The issue in the case centred on whether the employees concerned had freely consented to termination of their employment. The court accepted that in some circumstances even reluctant acceptance of the will of the majority of the *whanau* could be considered to amount to free consent to termination by mutual agreement, but this did not occur in the present case.

[49] In *Skipwith-Halatau v Ngati Kapo (Aotearoa) Inc*, Employment Court, AEC 72/97, 18 July 1997, the employee successfully contended that the *hui* that led to her dismissal did not require an agenda to be notified in advance, and thus she had no notice that her continued employment would be considered by the *hui*. The court recognized that procedural flaws in the use of *hui* in dealing with employment disciplinary matters can lead to an unfair result. In *Rerekura v Presland*, AC 68/03, 17 December 2003, the Employment Court dealt with a suspension and disciplinary investigation based on a procedurally flawed *hui*.

[50] ACTU website, 'Indigenous Workers' <http://www.actu.org.au/Issues/Indigenous/default.aspx> accessed 10 September 2013.

The modalities of Indigenous voice

Indigenous people have lacked much of a voice in the workplace because of their low numbers in the workforce, their precarious position in it, as well as their historical concentration in the more remote parts of Australia. They have had a voice through organizations that focus specifically on Indigenous concerns, civil society, and unions.

The Victorian Aboriginal Advancement League, founded in 1957, claims to be the oldest Australian Aboriginal organization, on the basis that a decade after its foundation, it was fully run by Aboriginal people.[51] In 1958, the Federal Council for Aboriginal Advancement (FCAA) was established in Adelaide by delegates from around Australia, including peace activists, feminists, communists, and Christians, as well as representatives from organizations concerned with Aboriginal rights and welfare, such as the Aboriginal Advancement League.[52] Among its campaigns was the fight for equal wages, which it pursued through its Equal Wages for Aborigines committee, established in 1963.[53] The FCAA did not become an Indigenous-controlled organization until 1973, but it was wound up in 1978 after the federal government withdrew its funding.[54]

Union support for Aborigines began with a conventional focus on wages and working conditions from the late 1940s onwards. It was not always so, with unions earlier supporting a 'White Australia' policy.[55] The first significant union support for Aborigines was in the 1946 Pilbara strike, which at three years was Australia's longest strike.[56] It

[51] See 'Victorian Aborigines Advancement League' <http://www.indigenousrights.net.au/organisation.asp?oID=14> accessed 10 September 2013. The League grew out of two existing organizations, the Australian Aborigines League (established in Melbourne in 1934), and the Save the Aborigines Committee, which was established to address the Warburton Ranges Crisis in 1957, when nomadic Aborigines were found wandering ill and malnourished in the Central Desert where the Commonwealth was testing rockets and nuclear weapons: see 'The Warburton Ranges Controversy, 1957' <http://www.indigenousrights.net.au/section.asp?sID=1> accessed 10 September 2013.

[52] Among the organizations represented were the Council for Aboriginal Rights, the Western Australian Native Welfare Council, and the Queensland United Council for Aboriginal Welfare; see 'Federal Council for the Advancement of Aborigines and Torres Strait Islanders (FCAATSI)' <http://www.indigenousrights.net.au/organization.asp?oID=*> accessed 10 September 2013.

[53] Shirley Andrews, a tireless campaigner for Aboriginal rights, was instrumental in setting up this committee and pushing for equal wages for Aborigines: see Shirley Andrews, *Wages and Employment of Aborigines*, Federal Council for Aboriginal Advancement, Equal Wages for Aborigines Committee (April 1964). She was a member of the Communist Party of Australia, which was the only political party in the 1950s that had a policy on Aboriginal matters. In 1963, she and others successfully lobbied the ACTU to adopt a policy to end wage discrimination.

[54] This was due to the proliferation of other Aboriginal and Torres Islander organizations, and the establishment of the Department of Aboriginal Affairs and the National Aboriginal Consultative Committee.

[55] As noted by former ACTU President Jennie George, 'Unions have been products of their times and have sometimes reflected the ignorance and, in some cases, racist views of society at large': 'Reconciliation in the Community—How do we make it a reality?' (National Reconciliation Convention, Melbourne, 26–28 May 1997) <http://www.austlii.edu.au/au/other/IndigLRes/car/1997/3/speeches/seminar1/george.htm> accessed 10 September 2013.

[56] The strike lasted from 1 May 1946 to August 1949. It was planned and led by Don McLeod, an Australian Workers' Union delegate and member of the Australian Communist Party, together with two Aboriginal workers, Dooley Bin Bin and Clancy McKenna. The Australian Workers' Union was formed in 1894 after the merging of earlier unions. It originally covered workers in the pastoral and mining industries. In general, see Don McLeod, *How the West Was Lost: The Native Question in the Development of Western Australia* (Port Hedland, 1984).

was over fair wages and working conditions.[57] The strike was supported by nineteen Western Australian unions, seven federal unions, and four Trades and Labour Councils. The Western Australian branch of the Seamen's Union of Australia put a black ban on the shipment of wool from the Pilbara region. In the result, wages and conditions were improved at two stations, and these were declared as setting the standard.

In 1965, the North Australian Workers' Union applied to the Commonwealth Conciliation and Arbitration Commission to remove a clause that discriminated against Aboriginal people in the Northern Territory's pastoral award.[58] This resulted in the inclusion of Aboriginal stock workers under the award so that they would be paid the same as non-Aboriginal workers. However, this was made subject to some important qualifications,[59] including the inclusion of a 'slow worker clause', which empowered employers to pay Aboriginal employees less than the standard wage when they were deemed to work less efficiently. The implementation of equal pay also was delayed for three years to give Aboriginal people time to 'adjust' to the change. Following the Commission's ruling, about 200 stockmen and domestic workers walked off the Wave Hill cattle station.[60] This was known as the Gurindji strike of August 1966, and it lasted for seven years.[61] The action turned into a campaign for the return of Aboriginal land, as among the effects of the cattle industry were the fencing off and fouling of local water holes and the decimation of local wildlife.[62] Eventually, there was wide public support for the action, as well as other moves towards Aboriginal rights. In 1975, the Whitlam Labour government gave the Gurindji back some of their land.

In 1971, there was a strike over pay and working conditions at the Noonkanbah cattle and sheep station in Western Australia. The Aboriginal inhabitants of the area, the Yungngora, worked on the station. The walk off became a struggle for the land when the government allowed an oil exploration company to drill on sacred sites. Although the strike was respected by unions, in 1980 the Premier of Western Australia,

[57] This action involved about 800 Aborigine cattlemen working in the Pilbara region of West Australia. Such Aboriginal pastoral workers had traditionally not received wages, but were paid 'in truck' with tobacco, flour, and other commodities. Moreover, their freedom of movement was restricted. If they left the station, they were pursued and brought back by the Police.

[58] *Re Cattle Station Industry (Northern Territory) Award* (1966) 113 Commonwealth Arbitration Reports 651.

[59] See Gillian Whitehouse, 'Justice and Equity: Women and Indigenous Workers' in Joe Isaac and Stuart Macintyre (eds), *The New Province for Law and Order: 100 Years of Australian Industrial Conciliation and Arbitration* (CUP, 2004) 207.

[60] The organizers of the strike were Dexter Daniels, president of the Northern Territory Council for Aboriginal Rights, formed in 1962, and an organizer in the North Australian Workers' Union; and Lupna Giari, whose tour of east coast cities to seek support for the strikers from unionists and public meetings was subsidised by the Building Workers Industrial Union and Actors Equity: National Museum Australia, 'Dexter Daniels <http://www.indigenousrights.net.au/person.asp?pID=963>, and 'Lupna Giari' <http://www.indigenousrights.net.au/person.asp?pID=1034> both accessed 10 September 2013.

[61] Aborigines had been forced off the land and moved onto the cattle stations in order to receive rations once they were cut off from their sources of sustenance. As workers, they received rations, but living conditions were extremely poor. Unlike non-Aboriginal workers, they did not enjoy a minimum wage. They were subject to a maximum wage, but their actual wages were less than that and a mere pittance when compared to the wages of non-Aboriginal workers. See generally, Frank Hardy, *The Unlucky Australians* (Pan Books, 1978).

[62] See Lyn Riddett, 'The Strike that Became a Land Rights Movement: A Southern "Do-Gooder" Reflects on Wattie Creek 1966–74' (1997) 72 Labour History 50.

Charles Court,[63] insisted that the drilling should continue, and forty-five non-union rigs were sent into the area protected by police. In the end, no oil was found, the station was bought by the Aboriginal Land Fund, and in 2007 native title over the land was recognized.

The ACTU adopted an anti-discrimination policy in 1963, and 40 years later it formally committed itself to developing a partnership with Aboriginal and Torres Strait Islander peoples. In the 2000s, ACTU sought to increase its Indigenous membership and incorporate them in union structures. In 2001, ACTU established the Aboriginal and Torres Strait Islander Committee, made up of one representative from each affiliated union, and one representative from each State and Territory Labour Council.[64] The Committee's main aim is to: '[p]rovide culturally appropriate and accountable leadership, support and advice to the ACTU executive and affiliates in relation to Indigenous employment and Social Justice issues and strategies affecting the lives of Aboriginal and Torres Strait Islander peoples'.[65] It seeks to ensure that 'issues of Aboriginal and Torres Strait Islander rights and social justice permeate the ACTU's policy frameworks and its operations'.[66] As the ACTU Secretary stated in 2011, 'Australian unions will do what we can—with an emphasis on encouraging engagement with communities, strengthening the voice of Indigenous Australians—and standing up for their rights at work.'[67]

In 2008, the ACTU Indigenous Committee launched a Charter of Indigenous Employment Rights at the ACTU Indigenous Conference in Adelaide.[68] The Charter was based on international human rights standards,[69] and contains provisions on the right to decent work; the right to cultural recognition and respect at work; the right to freedom from discrimination at work; the right to development; and the right to appropriate education and training.

The most obvious example of workplace recognition of Indigenous culture is that some employment agreements and collective awards provide for cultural or ceremonial leave for those of Aboriginal and Torres Islander descent. Typically, provision is made for 10 days' unpaid leave per year.[70] There may also be paid leave for attendance

[63] Andrea Mayes, 'Sir Charles Court dead at 96' Perth Now (23 December 2007) <http://www.news.com.au/perthnow/story/0,21598,22966125-2761,00.html> accessed 10 September 2013.

[64] 'Role and Function of the Aboriginal and Torres Strait Islander Committee', para. 3 <http://www.actu.org.au/Images/Dynamic/attachments/2360/RoleandFunctionofCommittee.pdf> accessed 10 September 2013.

[65] 'Role and Function of the Aboriginal and Torres Strait Islander Committee', para. 1.

[66] 'Role and Function of the Aboriginal and Torres Strait Islander Committee', para. 4. The Committee's functions are advisory; providing assistance to ACTU officers; leadership development; and networking and communications.

[67] Jeff Lawrence, ACTU Secretary, 'Opening Address' (ACTU Indigenous Conference, Darwin, 16 February 2011) 3.

[68] ACTU Indigenous Committee, *Charter of Indigenous Employment Rights* (19 May 2009) <http://www.actu.org.au/Publications/Other/CharterofIndigenousEmploymentRights.aspx> accessed 10 September 2013.

[69] Including the Universal Declaration on Human Rights 1948, the ILO Indigenous and Tribal Peoples Convention 1989 (No 169) (not ratified by Australia), and the United Nations Declaration on the Rights of Indigenous Peoples 2007 (endorsed by Australia in 2009).

[70] See, for example, Australian Public Service Award 1998, cl. 33 <http://www.fwc.gov.au/consolidated_awards/ap/ap766579/asframe.html>; Nurses Award 2010, cl. 33 <http://www.fwc.gov.au/documents/modern_awards/award/ma000034/default.htm>; and Clerks' (South Australia) Award 2010, cl. 7.9 <http://www.industrialcourt.sa.gov.au/index.cfm?objectid=7B790E51-E7F2-2F96-33619241928110ED> all accessed 10 September 2013. Compare 'cultural leave' in New Zealand.

at official activities during National Aboriginal and Islanders Week in July.[71] The Queensland Industrial Relations Act 1999 makes provision for up to five days' unpaid cultural leave.[72]

In 2012, the ACTU Congress endorsed an Aboriginal and Torres Strait Islander Policy that was aimed at developing and implementing 'effective recruitment, retention and activism strategies specifically targeted at Aboriginal and Torres Strait Islander peoples within the union movement'.[73] The policy goes beyond traditional workplace issues and encompasses wider social, economic, and cultural matters affecting Indigenous people.

Reparations for 'stolen wages'

The 'stolen wages' issue emerged in recent years through increased pressure by Aboriginal people and their supporters.[74] 'Stolen wages' refers to wages and other benefits that were not given directly to Aboriginal people, but to others—government, police, and church authorities—to administer for them, with only some 'pocket money' given to the individuals concerned. It could involve the non-payment or underpayment of wages, savings and pension payments put into trust accounts, or the redirection of welfare payments and other entitlements.[75] Paternalistic motives underlay many of the practices, but money was sometimes withheld as a punishment.[76]

Stolen Wages Working Groups are active in major Australian cities.[77] Members include Aboriginal elders and community representatives, claimants and family members, as well as union representatives and members of Australians for Native Title and Reconciliation (ANTaR)[78] and other community groups.

Three Australian States have established reparation schemes to address the issue. Although they differ in detail, all have been criticized for:

- putting the burden on claimants to come forward, and to do so within a limited period despite cultural, educational, and physical obstacles;
- placing the burden of proving claims on Indigenous people when they had not been at fault for the situation;

[71] See, for example, cl. 7.8, Clerks' (South Australia) Award 2010, cl. 7.8 <http://www.industrialcourt.sa.gov.au/index.cfm?objectid=7B790E51-E7F2-2F96-33619241928110ED> accessed 10 September 2013.

[72] Section 40A(1).

[73] *ACTU Indigenous and Torres Strait Islander Policy* (ACTU Congress 2012) <http://www.actu.org.au/Images/Dynamic/attachments/7659/Aboriginal%20and%20Torres%20Strait%20Islander%20Policy%20-FINAL.pdf> accessed 10 September 2013.

[74] On the stolen wages issue generally, with a state-by-state analysis, see Rosalind Kidd, *Hard Labour, Stolen Wages: National Report on Stolen Wages*, (Australians for Native Title and Reconciliation, January 2007). In the United States, an analogous pursuit of missing income from Indian trust assets was successfully pursued in *Cobell v Norton*, filed in 1996 and settled for $1.4 billion in 2009. It was reportedly the largest class-action suit against the United States in history.

[75] See Margaret Thornton and Trish Luker, 'The Wages of Sin: Compensation for Indigenous Workers' (2009) 32(3) University of New South Wales Law Journal 647, 647, and Senate Standing Committee on Legal and Constitutional Affairs, *Unfinished Business: Indigenous Stolen Wages* (Commonwealth of Australia, 2006).

[76] As was done by the Aboriginal Protection Board in Victoria.

[77] See <http://www.creativespirits.info/aboriginalculture/economy/stolen-wages> accessed 10 September 2013.

[78] See, for example, the work of the Queensland ANTaR at <http://www.antarqld.org.au/node/19> accessed 10 September 2013.

- relying on documentary evidence when the state or other institutions were at fault for either not keeping proper records, or losing or destroying them;
- not consulting, or consulting sufficiently, Indigenous people; and
- not reflecting the actual amounts that were lost to Indigenous people.

The reparations scheme in Queensland was precipitated by lawsuits brought under anti-discrimination legislation. These actions related to the period between 1975, when the Racial Discrimination Act came into force, and 1986, when Queensland begin to pay equal wages. The first case, decided in 1996, involved Palm Island settlement workers.[79] Six plaintiffs won $7,000 compensation each before the Human Rights and Equal Opportunity Commission (HREOC).[80] Following the awards of compensation, some claims were settled out of court,[81] and 350 further claims were lodged with the HREOC.[82] Another employment discrimination case involved Aborigines living at Lutheran Church missions.[83] Damages and costs amounting to between $17,000 and $85,000 were awarded to each of the eight applicants.

Facing an increasing number of complaints, the Queensland government established the Underpayment of Award Wages Process in 1999. This involved setting aside $25 million to pay $7,000 each to thousands of Indigenous people who had been employed by the government on Aboriginal reserves at under-award rates between 1975 and 1986. In 2002, Queensland established the Indigenous Wages and Savings Reparations Offer, which involved setting up a fund of $55.4 million that was to be distributed to former workers covered under the Aboriginal Protection Acts,[84] but the offer did not extend to the families of deceased workers. The scheme closed in 2006, after less than half of the number of expected claims was received. The low uptake was partly due to the inability of some claimants to provide documentary proof of their entitlements. The amount of compensation offered was only $2,000 to $4,000, and recipients were required to waive any legal claims for further compensation.

New South Wales established the Aboriginal Trust Fund Repayment Scheme in 2004 to reimburse monies owed to claimants and their descendants from trust funds operated by the NSW Aborigines Protection Board[85] between 1900 and 1968.[86] Claims could

[79] *Bligh v State of Queensland* (1996) EOC ¶ 92-848.

[80] Aboriginal people and their union supporters had complained to the government about exploitation since the late 1950s: *Bligh v State of Queensland* 79,288. They undertook a political campaign and went on strike demanding equal wages in 1957. This was described in the media as a 'native disturbance' and attracted an increased police presence on the island.

[81] See, for example, *Douglas v State of Queensland (No 2)* [2006] FCA 1288, which involved seventeen people who lived at a mission run by the Christian Brethren.

[82] Rosalind Kidd, *Trustees on Trial: Recovering the Stolen Wages* (Aboriginal Studies Press, September 2006) 3.

[83] *Baird v Queensland* (2006) 156 FCR 451 (on appeal to the Full Court, Federal Court of Australia).

[84] Aboriginal Protection and Restriction of the Sale of Opium Act 1897 and 1901, and Aboriginals Preservation and Protection Act 1939.

[85] Later called the Aborigines Welfare Board.

[86] This money (wages, pensions, benefits, and compensation) had been collected by the Boards and placed in 'Trust Accounts'. For general information about the scheme, see the ATFRS website at <http://www.atfrs.nsw.gov.au/home> accessed 10 September 2013. The scheme was set up after consultation with Indigenous people and has a panel of three Indigenous advisors appointed by the state government to make recommendations to the Minister for Aboriginal Affairs about repayments. The panel plays a key role in determining repayments by reviewing claims. It can meet with claimants to hear additional oral or written evidence.

be made until 31 March 2009, but very few claims were successful because they lacked documentary support.[87] In response to criticism, the scheme was altered in 2009 so that lump sum payments of up to $11,000 could be made. This was to take into account non-documentary evidence for claims and streamline the process. Unlike the Queensland scheme, the scheme was set up after consultation with Indigenous people; the amount of compensation, paid in current values, was not capped; and claimants were allowed to pursue other remedies.

In 2006, the Commonwealth Parliament Senate Standing Committee on Legal and Constitutional Affairs recommended that all states should act on the issue of 'stolen wages'.[88] This impelled Western Australia and Victoria to take steps, which resulted in a reparations scheme in the former, but not the latter.

In Western Australia between 1905 and 1972, employers, including the state government, held money and property belonging to Aboriginal people in trust accounts administered by the then Department of Native Welfare.[89] Up to 75 per cent of an individual's earnings were held, but there was little or no evidence that wages were ever returned. In 2007, the Western Australian government approved a Taskforce to examine the matter.[90] It found that because of limited and unreliable documentation, the number of affected individuals and the amount owing were unknown. The Western Australia Stolen Wages Reparation Scheme, established in 2012, involved the ex gratia payment to living Aboriginal people of up to $2,000,[91] acceptance of which would not affect any reimbursement sought by individuals through other legal avenues. Applications for the payment closed on 30 November 2012, only nine months after the scheme was publicly announced.

The Victorian government took a staged approach to its investigation into 'stolen wages'. The first stage determined whether it was legally possible for the government to have withheld wages or entitlements, and it found that there were several ways in which wages and entitlements could be controlled by State government authorities under legislation between 1869 and 1974.[92] The second stage assessed whether wages were systematically withheld, but the conclusion was that this did not happen.[93] It was

[87] Records of the Boards were often incomplete or missing, which hampered the progress or success of claims through no fault of the claimants or their descendants.

[88] See Senate Standing Committee on Legal and Constitutional Affairs (n 75), recommendations 4 and 5, paras 8.26–8.27.

[89] The Aborigines Act 1905 and the Native Welfare Act 1963 governed the arrangement.

[90] The Taskforce undertook an extensive public consultation through meetings in many towns and it received submissions: Western Australia Stolen Wages Taskforce, 'Reconciling the Past: Government Control of Aboriginal Monies in Western Australia 1905–1972' (2008) <http://www.dia.wa.gov.au/en/Stolen-Wages/> accessed 10 September 2013.

[91] The requirements were that they had to have been born before 1958; lived at a government Native Welfare Settlement in Western Australia; and while residing there experienced direct Western Australian government control over their income and all or part of their income was withheld from them.

[92] *Indigenous Stolen Wages Preliminary Investigation, Stage One: Establishing the Legal Framework, Final report to Aboriginal Affairs Victoria & Public Record Office Victoria* (September 2009) <http://www.trove.nla.gov.au/work/157215987?q&versionId=171371309> accessed 10 September 2013.

[93] This part of the investigation involved researching records held at the National Archives of Australia and Public Record Office Victoria. It focused on the period after 1918, since this would take potential living claimants into account who could provide evidence of their experiences; see *Indigenous Stolen Wages Preliminary Investigation, Stage Two: Determining Implementation, Final report to Aboriginal Affairs Victoria & Public Record Office Victoria* (September 2009) <http://www.trove.nla.gov.au/work/157215987?q&versionId=171371309> accessed 10 September 2013.

recommended that a third stage of research, dealing with individual case studies, was not necessary, 'on the basis of the nature of the available records in custody and in light of the findings of stages one and two'.[94] This result has been criticized for relying on the dearth of documentary evidence and failing to consult or engage with the Aboriginal community.[95] Several groups are currently involved in attempting to progress the stolen wages issue in Victoria.[96]

North America

The position of Indigenous people in North America can generally be distinguished from that in New Zealand and Australia. Points of similarity are that the Indigenous people have suffered because of loss of land and the basis of their traditional economies; many live in isolated areas, away from industrial centres and union activity; and they have been the object of paternalistic government policies, often operating to their disadvantage. As in Australia, some policies were directly or indirectly genocidal in nature.

The position of Indigenous peoples in the United States and Canada is broadly similar and can be distinguished from that in Australasia in two main respects. Firstly, there appears to be greater engagement by unions with Indigenous concerns in Australasia than in North America. This may be due to the size of the respective countries, and the visibility and prominence of Indigenous peoples in Australasia in comparison with other disadvantaged minority groups. While North American unions have been generally exclusionist until recently, of the two, however, Canadian unions appear to be more responsive to equity issues involving Indigenous people than American unions.[97] For example, the AFL-CIO website contains few mentions of Native Americans and no reference to a specific Indigenous policy. In contrast, the Canadian Labour Congress website contains information describing its work and policy in relation to Aboriginal people,[98] and it is

[94] *Indigenous Stolen Wages Preliminary Investigation Stage Two*, ch. 5 Recommendations, 49 (n 93).

[95] See 'Stolen Wages…where to now for Indigenous Victorians' <http://www.pilch.org.au/Indigenous/stolenwages/> accessed 10 September 2013.

[96] For example, the Wampan Wages ('Pay back wages') Victorian Stolen Wages Working Group, an informal research and lobbying group, worked with two researchers at the Centre of Australian Indigenous Studies at Monash University who undertook research into instances of stolen wages in Victoria: Andrew Gunstone and Sadie Heckenberg, *The Government Owes a Lot of Money to Our People: A History of Indigenous Stolen Wages in Victoria* (Australian Scholarly Publishing, December 2009). The research indicated the shortcomings in relying on the written record, as often haphazardly preserved in archives, as opposed to oral histories involving the people concerned. PILCH (Public Interest Clearing House) (Victoria) closely monitored government actions on the stolen wages issue, and advocates a wider investigation and greater consultation on the issue: see <http://www.pilch.org.au/Indigenous/stolenwages/> accessed 10 September 2013.

[97] Gerald Hunt and David Rayside, 'Labor Union Response to Diversity in Canada and the United States' (2000) 39(3) Industrial Relations 401.

[98] The website states that the CLC directs its work on Aboriginal rights in two main areas: promoting workplace Aboriginal Rights and anti-racism, and 'working with Aboriginal workers to strengthen their voices and presence in the Canadian labour movement' through caucuses, forums, conferences and workshops. The CLC also engages in more general policy and advocacy work on the impact of government social and economic policies on Aboriginal communities. See Canadian Labour Congress, 'Aboriginal Workers' <http://www.canadianlabour.ca/human-rights-equality/aboriginal-workers> accessed 10 September 2013.

evident that a number of Canadian unions are devoting resources to better organize and represent Aboriginal workers.[99]

Secondly, many[100] Indigenous people in North America live on tribal reserves that enjoy a degree of sovereignty and self-determination that is jealously guarded. This sovereignty, however, has in recent times come under pressure from unions, which are seeking to come onto tribal lands to organize Indigenous workplaces. These are supported by federal authorities (in the United States) or provincial law (in Canada). The main impetus for this recent attention is the lucrative Indian gaming industry, sometimes termed 'the new buffalo',[101] which has brought jobs and prosperity to Indigenous reserves, as well as many non-Indigenous workers. The attempt by Indigenous peoples to exercise sovereignty in the face of outside union and regulatory pressures forms a major distinction between North America on the one hand, and Australasia on the other.

Indians in the United States perceive it as vital to preserve their tribal sovereignty and traditional hierarchies from government and union encroachment. One American Indian labour activist comments:

> I continue to believe in and support unionism—but, in any conflict between unions and tribal sovereignty, I am fully on the side of sovereignty. If a union is able to genuinely respect the tribe and its culture and the people, willing to take plenty of time (which certainly includes much respectful listening), hire tribal members (locally and otherwise) as full union staff—and forego presumed 'quick fixes' such as trying to use NLRB against the tribe—well, unions may be able to play a positive role in Indian Country. If unions try quick, shortcut approaches in relating to the tribes, the unions, in the last analysis, will never make it.[102]

In Canada, attitudes within the Indigenous community appear to be more divided, perhaps because of the different legal situation. Canadian law provides that labour matters on reserves fall squarely under provincial jurisdiction unless it relates to 'Indianness', in which case it comes under federal jurisdiction and the Canada Labour Code 1985.[103]

[99] See, for example, the Canadian Auto Workers website, 'Aboriginal Workers & Workers of Colour' <http://www.caw.ca/en/services-departments-aboriginal-workers-workers-of-colour.htm>; and Canadian Union of Public Employees (CUPE) 'Aboriginal Issues' <http://www.cupe.ca/aboriginal> both accessed 10 September 2013. More generally, see Suzanne E. Mills and Louise Clarke, '"We will go side-by-side with you." Labour union engagement with Aboriginal peoples in Canada' (2009) 40 Geoforum 991.

[100] About 34 per cent in the United States, see Stella U. Ogunwole, *We the People: American Indians and Alaska Natives in the United States, US Census Bureau* (February 2006) 14 <http://www.bia.gov/cs/groups/public/documents/text/idc-001819.pdf>; and about 40% in Canada, see Statistics Canada, '2006 Census: First Nations people' <http://www12.statcan.ca/census-recensement/2006/as-sa/97-558/p16-eng.cfm> both accessed 10 September 2013.

[101] Ambrose Lane, *Return of the Buffalo: The Story Behind America's Gaming Explosion* (Bergin & Garvey, 1995).

[102] Hunter Gray, 'Unions, Natives, Tribal Sovereignty' (16 February 2002, updated 24 June 2005) <http://www.hunterbear.org/Unions,%20Workers,%20Tribal%20Sovereignty.htm> accessed 10 September 2013. He also comments: 'efforts to unionize under the National Labor Relations Act are attacks on Native sovereignty', and observes that 'there does seem to be a basic obtuseness by union leaders about Native sovereignty, and the successful unionizing efforts, by drawing on preemptive US law, do in fact seem to undermine sovereignty'. He states that his basic position is that 'Native sovereignty is sacrosanct, absolutely critical to Native survival and enhancement'.

[103] The federal government has jurisdiction over 'Indians, and lands reserved for the Indians' under s. 91(24) of the Constitution Act 1867.

Thus, the notion of Aboriginal sovereignty does not apply with the same legal force. The result is that there is more of an ideological clash between unionism and indigeneity, between outside settler values inherent in the class struggle, and Native hierarchies attempting to preserve their authority.

United States

Indian reservations largely operate as sovereign self-governing areas,[104] and as such they are able, within limitations that have not yet been conclusively determined, to regulate their own labour relations. As one legal commentator has remarked, 'Whether the sovereignty of Indian nations will prevail to control labor and employment relations in Indian country or be swept aside by federal authority has yet to play out.'[105] Indians have a strong voice in determining their own regulation in this area, but with the economic prosperity and increased number of non-Indian employees on reservations brought by the gaming industry,[106] tensions have emerged between Indian self-regulation and mainstream collective labour law.

The application of federal law on Indian reservations depends on whether or not Congress has expressly included or excluded tribes from the scope of the law, failing which resolution of the issue must be determined by decisions of the federal courts, which are not always consistent. With one exception,[107] these federal laws cannot be enforced by private individuals, since Congress has not expressly waived the sovereign immunity of tribes in respect of such lawsuits.[108] They may, however, be enforced by such federal agencies as the Department of Labor and the Occupational Safety and Health Administration.

There are three categories of federal laws that are relevant to employment issues on reservations, some of which may have their own laws on the particular matter.[109] It is in a tribe's interest to have their own regulations on employment matters in order to deflect the court's application of federal law where its application to Indian tribes is ambiguous, or to preempt the application of federal employment protection law.

Firstly, there are federal civil rights laws that cover employment discrimination. While Title VII of the Civil Rights Act of 1964[110] and the Americans with Disabilities

[104] See, for example, Supreme Court Chief Justice John Marshall's famous description of tribes as 'domestic dependent nations' in *Cherokee Nation v Georgia*, 30 US (5 Pet) 1 (1831). In *California v Cabazon Band of Mission Indians*, 480 US 202 (1987), an early case on Indian gaming, the Supreme Court held that Indian tribes had the power to conduct gaming activities on reservations unfettered by any state or local law. This was in accord with the overarching principle that tribes could legislate on matters so long as Congress has not limited their authority to do so.

[105] Kaighn Smith, Jr, *Labor and Employment Law in Indian Country* (Drummond Woodsum MacMahon, 2011) 1.

[106] Native Indian gaming enterprises can be found on nearly half of the 561 federally recognized tribal lands in the United States: see Harvard Project on American Indian Economic Development, *The State of the Native Nations: conditions under U.S. policies of self-determination* (Malcolm Wiener Center for Social Policy, New York, 2008) ch. 8 'Gaming'.

[107] Employment Retirement Income Security Act of 1974, as amended, 29 USC §§ 1001–1461 (2006).

[108] See Smith (n 105) ch. 4 'Defensive Tribal Sovereignty: Sovereign Immunity and Tribal Employment Disputes'.

[109] Smith (n 105) ch. 8, on tribal law on employment discrimination; ch. 10, on employment preference laws for tribal members; and ch. 9, on tribal law on unions and collective bargaining.

[110] 42 USC §§ 2000e-2000e-17 (2006); the exclusion is at § 2000e(b).

Act of 1990[111] are expressly excluded from application to Indian tribes, employment discrimination is covered under the Indian Civil Rights Act of 1968.[112] The Age Discrimination in Employment Act of 1967[113] does not expressly exclude application to Indian tribes, but three attempts at invoking it against tribal entities failed in US Courts of Appeals on the basis that the cases involved intramural matters that related to the tribe's self-governance.[114]

Secondly, there are labour laws of general application that govern working conditions.[115] While not mentioning Indian tribes,[116] their application tends to depend on whether or not the activity concerned relates to tribal self-government, tribal proprietary interests, or intramural affairs.[117] One commentator has observed:

> A consistent emerging consideration for all courts... is whether the imposition of the federal law in question may infringe upon the exercise of tribal sovereignty. If the imposition of federal law upon a reservation employment relationship would undermine tribal regulatory authority exercised in accordance with established principles of tribal sovereignty as expressed in a tribal employment law, courts may be more hesitant to allow the federal law to apply.[118]

Thirdly, there is the law governing unions and collective bargaining in the private sector,[119] the National Labor Relations Act of 1935 (NLRA).[120] Traditionally, the NLRA

[111] 42 USC §§ 1201-12213 (2006); the exclusion is at § 12111(5)(B)(i).

[112] 25 USC §§ 13-1-1303 (2006), which, with the exception of *habeas corpus* petitions, the Supreme Court held could only be enforced in tribal forums: *Santa Clara Pueblo v Martinez* 436 US 49 (1978).

[113] 29 USC §§ 621-634 (2006).

[114] *Equal Employment Opportunity Commission v Karuk Tribe Housing Authority*, 260 F 3d 1071 (9th Cir 2001); *Equal Employment Opportunity Commission v Fond du Lac Heavy Equipment and Construction Company*, 986 F 2d 246 (8th Cir 1993); *Equal Employment Opportunity Commission v Cherokee Nation*, 871 F 2d 937 (10th Cir 1989).

[115] This legislation includes the Occupational Safety and Health Act of 1970 (OSHA) and the Fair Labor Standards Act of 1938 (FLSA).

[116] There is one exception, the Employment Retirement Income Security Act of 1974, as amended, 29 USC §§ 1001-1461, at §1002(32) (2006), which applies to certain retirement plans of Indian tribes.

[117] Three federal circuit courts of appeal have applied OSHA to tribal enterprises (*Donovan v Coeur d'Alene Tribal Farm*, 751 F 2d 1113 (9th Cir 1985), *Reich v Mashantucket Sand & Gravel*, 95 F 3d 174 (2d Cir 1996), and *Menominee Tribal Enterprises v Solis*, 601 F 3d 669 (7th Cir 2010)) on the basis that the activities concerned were not intramural or related to self-government (commercial purposes and employment of non-Indians); and one excluded the application of OSHA (*Donovan v Navajo Forest Products Industries*, 692 F 2d 709 (10th Cir 1982)), on the basis that the tribe had a sovereign right to manage its own affairs. In the *Mashantucket Sand & Gravel* case, the court noted that the Mashantucket Pequot Tribal Nation could still enact its own laws governing safety and health on the reservation, as long as they were not inconsistent with OSHA. In relation to the FLSA, the court in *Reich v Great Lakes Indian Fish & Wildlife Commission*, 4 F 3d 490 (7th Cir 1993) and *Snyder v Navajo Nation*, 382 F 3d 892 (9th Cir 2004) did not apply the legislation to tribal game wardens and law enforcement officers respectively because they dealt with intramural matters and involved self-governance. In *Solis v Matheson*, 563 F 3d 425 (9th Cir 2009), however, the Ninth Circuit applied the FSLA wage and hour standards to a reservation smoke shop run by a tribal member, on the basis that the intramural principle did not apply as the tribe had not 'acted on its right of self-governance in the field of wage and hours laws and specifically with respect to overtime' (433). See generally Ann Richard, 'Application of the National Labor Relations Act and the Fair Labor Standards Act to Indian Tribes: Thwarting the Economic Self-Determination of Tribes' (2005) 30(1) American Indian Law Review 203.

[118] Smith 150–1 (n 105).

[119] Collective labour relations in the public sector is governed separately by federal and state law, the latter of which can vary, for example, in relation to the legality of strike action.

[120] 29 USC §§ 151–169 (2006), and the amending Labor Management Relations Act of 1947, 29 USC §§ 141–197 (2006).

was not considered to apply to Indian tribes or enterprises located on reservations,[121] but this changed with the growth of the Indian gaming industry.

The Indian gaming industry arose in the late 1970s as gambling generally became more acceptable, with state governments setting up their own lotteries, federal policies promoting Indian self-determination, and courts recognizing limits to the jurisdiction of states over Indian reservations.[122] While the federal government stepped in to legislate state and some federal oversight over Indian gaming,[123] the position in relation to labour law has been left to be worked out by the courts.

The Indian gaming industry became so successful in generating employment, both Indian and non-Indian, that external pressure was brought to bear upon reservation labour practices.[124] The turning point came in 2004, when the National Labor Relations Board, which had long ignored labour practices on reservations, determined that tribal enterprises were subject to the NLRA, and therefore had to abide by federal law relating to union organizing.[125] The decision in *San Manuel Indian Bingo & Casino v NLRB* was upheld by a federal court of appeals,[126] which agreed that Indian gaming, as a purely commercial business with mainly non-Indian employees, did not fall under traditional tribal sovereignty. Other federal courts, however, have held differently. In the earlier case of *NLRB v Pueblo of San Juan*,[127] the federal court upheld a Pueblo right-to-work law that gave employees within the jurisdiction the right to work without having to join a union. The court held that the NLRA did not displace the tribe's jurisdiction over economic relationships within its territory.[128] Accordingly, the state of the law is currently uncertain.

[121] See *Fort Apache Timber Co*, 226 NLRB 503 (1976), which first considered the issue and held that tribal reservation entities, like state and federal governmental entities, fell outside the jurisdiction of the NLRB.

[122] Harvard Project on American Indian Economic Development 146 (n 106). On Indian gaming law in general, see Kathryn R. L. Rand and I. Stephen Andrew Light, *Indian Gaming Law and Policy* (Carolina Academic Press, 2005); Stephen Andrew Light and Kathryn R. L. Rand, *Indian Gaming and Tribal Sovereignty: The Casino Compromise* (University Press of Kansas, 2007). The first litigation that endorsed tribal jurisdiction over gaming was *Seminole Tribe of Florida v Butterworth*, 658 F 2d 310 (5th Cir 1981), upheld in 455 US 1020 (1982).

[123] See the Indian Gaming Regulatory Act 1988, passed by Congress after the Supreme Court decision in *California v Cabazon Band of Mission Indians*, 480 US 202 (1987), which had upheld the right of tribes to determine their own gaming regulations unless these were inconsistent with state criminal law.

[124] Moreover, as D. Michael McBride, III and H. Leonard Court cynically observe, 'In recent years as unions have witnessed their ranks diminish and as the [NLR] Board has become more aggressive in perpetuating its existence tribal governments and their expanding casinos have become targets': 'Labor Regulation, Union Avoidance and Organized Labor Relations Strategies on Tribal Lands: New Indian Gaming Strategies in the Wake of *San Manuel Band of Indians v National Labor Relations Board*' (2007) 40 John Marshall Law Review 1259, 1304.

[125] *San Manuel Indian Bingo & Casino v NLRB*, 341 NLRB 1055 (2004). At 1056, the NLRB commented: 'As tribal businesses have grown and prospered, they have become significant employers of non-Indians and serious competitors with non-Indian owned businesses.' For analysis of the decision, see Kelly E. W. Grez, 'Stepping onto the Reservation: the National Labor Relations Board's New Approach to Asserting Jurisdiction over Indian Tribes' (2005) 57(4) Administrative Law Review 1153.

[126] *San Manuel Indian Bingo & Casino v NLRB*, 475 F 3d 1306 (DC Cir 2007). The decision has been much criticized; see, for example, Bryan H. Wildenthal, 'Federal Labor Law, Indian Sovereignty, and the Canons of Construction' (2007) 86(2) Oregon Law Review 413, and 'How the Ninth Circuit Overruled a Century of Supreme Court Indian Jurisprudence—And Has So Far Gotten Away With It' [2008] Michigan State Law Review 547.

[127] 276 F 3d 1186 (10th Cir 2002).

[128] On the apparent inconsistency between the *San Manuel* and *San Juan* decisions, see Vicki J. Limas, 'The Tuscar organization of the Tribal Workplace' [2008] Michigan State LR 467.

Tribes have legislated on labour matters both before and after the *San Manuel* decision.[129] In California, sixty tribes signed compacts with the state in 1999 to adopt a uniform Tribal Labor Relations Ordinance that 'provides limited organizational rights to workers at tribal gaming establishments and related facilities that employ 250 or more employees'.[130] Both the Choctaw[131] and Eastern Cherokee[132] had labour relations laws in place prior to the *San Manuel* decision, and after the decision, a number of other tribes put such laws in place, such as the Mashantucket Pequot Tribal Nation[133] and the Little River Band of Ottawa Indians.[134]

In the wake of the *San Manuel* decision, tribes are being advised of various strategies for avoiding union organizing in their workplaces,[135] which is viewed negatively as interference with sovereign rights over tribal self-government and the allocation of tribal resources.[136] Tribes are increasingly making laws governing labour law on their reservations in an attempt to preempt the application of the NLRA within their jurisdictions. Where there is no tribal law on collective bargaining, or where tribal law prohibits collective bargaining entirely, then the NLRB will assert regulatory control over the matter.[137]

Canada

Indigenous peoples were involved in the nineteenth and early twentieth centuries in unions in primary industries such as trapping, fishing, cannery work, and forestry.[138] As in Australia, but from an earlier date, the early 1930s onwards saw unions being

[129] Generally, see Smith (n 105) ch. 9 'Developing Tribal Law: Unions and Collective Bargaining'.

[130] See *In re Indian Gaming Related Cases*, 331 F 3d 1094 (9th Cir 2003) for the background to the compacts entered into by the tribes.

[131] Mississippi Band of Choctaw Indians, Labor Organizations, title XXX: <http://www.choctaw.org/government/tribal_code/TITLE%2030%20LABOR%20ORGANIZATIONS.pdf> accessed 10 September 2013.

[132] Eastern Band of Cherokee, Labor Organizations, art. III <http://www.narf.org/nill/Codes/ebcicode/95wages.pdf> accessed 10 September 2013.

[133] Mashantucket Pequot Tribal Laws, title 32, ch. 1 <http://www.mptnlaw.com/laws/2007-2008%20Supplement.pdf> accessed 10 September 2013. The tribe was the first to enter into a collective bargaining agreement (with the United Auto Workers) under tribal law.

[134] Little River Band of Ottawa Indians, Chapter 600 Employment, Title 003 Fair Employment Practices Code <http://www.lrboi-nsn.gov/index.php/government/tribal-code> accessed 10 September 2013.

[135] See, for example, McBride and Court (n 124); and Seyfarth Shaw LLP, *Maintaining Union-Free Status after* San Manuel Indian Bingo and Casino v NRLB (2007) <http://www.nafoa.org/pdf/MaintainingUnion-Free-Status.pdf> accessed 10 September 2013.

[136] For an account of union organizing amongst the Navajo while appropriately respecting tribal sovereignty and local culture, and using the union as 'a vehicle for self-determination', see David Kamper, 'Organizing in the Context of Tribal Sovereignty: The Navajo Area Indian Health Service Campaign for Union Recognition' (2006) 30(4) Labor Studies Journal 17, 35.

[137] Smith 256–7 (n 105); but see Ezekiel J. N. Fletcher, 'De Facto Judicial Preemption of Tribal Labor and Employment Law' (2008) Michigan State LR 435, who argues that whereas once federal law acted as a gap-filler in the absence of labor law, some federal courts and the NLRB are attempting to preempt positive tribal law.

[138] See Rolf Knight, *Indians at Work: An Informal History of Indian Labour in British Columbia, 1858–1930* (New Star Books, 1996). Many Indigenous people participated in union activity early in the British Columbian fishing industry: see Miriam Wright, '"Building the Great Lucrative Fishing Industry": Aboriginal Gillnet Fishers and Protests over Salmon Fishery Regulations for the Nass and Skeena Rivers, 1950's–1960's' (2008) 61 Labour/Le Travail 103, and Percy Gladstone, 'Native Indians and the Fishing Industry of British Columbia' (1953) 19(1) Canadian Journal of Economics and Political Science 20.

used for political purposes to push for land rights after amendments to the Indian Act in 1927 made it illegal to use band funds for pursuing land claims against the federal government.[139] And as in New Zealand and the United States, the post-war period saw an increase in migration to urban areas, though this was not reflected by an increase in Indigenous unionization, as low skill levels and discrimination kept Indigenous people out of jobs in industry.[140] One commentator described the cause behind the lack of labour consciousness in this period as the result of several different but intersecting factors:

> Federal Indian policies of the late twentieth century encouraging Indian urban assimilation were coupled with Native people being taught agrarian skills in an increasingly industrialized society. These skills were applicable to the very reserve environment people were, ironically, being encouraged to abandon. When Native people did obtain union membership, they often found these agents embraced class structures that reflected societal trends promoting Native's peoples' physical and societal marginalization. Eventually, those same trends led to the inculcation of attitudes equating Native people with poor workers. This barrier to gainful employment also hindered the generational transfer of a labour consciousness.... That Native people see little value in seeking skilled, permanent employment or aggressively pressing for re-inclusion in unions that until recently failed to provide them sanctuary should come as no surprise.[141]

Recent union interest in greater inclusiveness of diverse groups and a wider social justice interest in the situation of Aboriginal people in Canada, however, have brought unions such as the Teamsters, the Canadian Auto Workers, and the Canadian Union for Public Employees onto reserves seeking certification to represent workers.

Indian casino gaming is also a powerful magnet attracting unions onto reserves. The situation in Canada is broadly similar to that in the United States, except that both gaming and labour matters fall under provincial authority rather than Aboriginal jurisdiction in the first instance. Canadian First Nations do not enjoy the same degree of 'domestic sovereignty' as do Indians in the United States. In Canada, there is a presumption that labour relations fall under provincial authority unless the nature of an entity's operation can be characterized as federal on application of a 'functional test'.[142] Moreover, the majority of casino workers on reserves are usually

[139] The Native Brotherhood of British Columbia was set up as a labour union in 1931, bargaining for fishermen and cannery workers; it was a successor body to the Allied Tribes of British Columbia, which had attempted to settle land claims. See Paul Tennant, *Aboriginal Peoples and Politics: The Native Land Question in British Columbia, 1849–1989* (University of British Columbia Press, 1990).

[140] Yale D. Belanger, 'Labour Unions and First Nations Casinos: An Uneasy Relationship' in Yale D. Belanger (ed.), *First Nations Gaming in Canada* (University of Manitoba Press, 2011).

[141] Belanger 286 (n 140).

[142] *Communications, Energy and Paperworkers Union of Canada v Native Child and Family Services of Toronto* [2010] 4 CNLR 279, where the Supreme Court of Canada upheld the setting aside of an order of the Canada Industrial Relations Board certifying the union as the bargaining agent for the employees of a society providing services to Aboriginal families. The Union argued that the Aboriginal character of the employer's operation meant that it was a federal undertaking in terms of s. 91(24) of the Constitution Act 1867, which concerns the powers of the Canadian Parliament in respect of Indians and their reserves. The provision of child welfare services, however, was held to fall under provincial jurisdiction. The identity of the clients as Aboriginals did not alter the essential nature of the service.

non-Native, as the reserves tend to have smaller Indigenous populations than in the United States.[143]

After having first failed to convince the courts that casino gambling was an Aboriginal self-government and treaty right under section 35(1) of the Constitution Act 1982,[144] and therefore was not covered by provincial law, Indigenous employers failed at their second line of defence, which was to challenge, on the basis of the Aboriginal nature of their enterprises, the certification of unions seeking to organize casino workers. In *Saskatchewan Indian Gaming Authority (SIGA) v National Automobile, Aerospace, Transportation and General Workers Union of Canada (CAW-Canada)*,[145] SIGA sought to quash the CAW's certification to bargain for employees of the Northern Lights Casino in Prince Albert. In response to the CAW's certification, the Federation of Saskatchewan Indian Nations (FSIN), which represents the band council chiefs of member First Nations in Saskatchewan, exercised its purported tribal jurisdiction over reserve labour relations to draft a labour code that proposed to cover all band members. The intention was 'to immunize member bands from federal and provincial labour laws while simultaneously empowering the Chief's Assembly to certify unions'.[146] In court, SIGA argued that the Saskatchewan Labour Relations Board lacked jurisdiction under the Constitution Act 1867[147] to grant the certification as the matter fell under exclusive federal jurisdiction because it was an 'Indian' business.[148] SIGA, however, failed to establish that there was an Aboriginal right to operate casinos.[149] The CAW's certification under provincial labour law was upheld.

Having been certified in 1999, the CAW was subsequently decertified in 2003 after a ballot, despite the union getting its members a 30 per cent wage increase through the Saskatchewan Labour Relations Board. The rejection of unionism was based on economic and ideological rationales advanced by the FSIN. The economic argument rested on the potentially harmful effects to Aboriginal jurisdiction over reserve activities and collective financial stability.[150] Ideologically, union organization of workers was attacked as foreign and 'un-indigenous', as it would harm the 'conciliatory manner of dealing with issues of concern'.[151] Brock Pitawanakwat, an Aboriginal commentator,

[143] For example, only 85 out of 1,150 employees of the Great Blue Heron Casino were Mississaugas of Scugog Island (which only had a population of 173), and in the early 2000s, only 700 of 3,700 employees of Casino Rama were Mnjikaning First Nations: see Belanger 295 (n 140).

[144] *R v Pamajewon* [1996] 2 SCR 821; 138 DLR (4th) 204. The case, which proceeded up to the Supreme Court, involved members of the Shawanaga and Eagle Lake bands of northern Ontario. For comment on the case, comparing United States law, see Bradford W. Morse, 'Permafrost Rights: Aboriginal Self-Government and the Supreme Court in *R v Pamajewon*' (1997) 42 McGill Law Journal 1011. The result was that Indian gaming fell under provincial law.

[145] [2003] 3 CNLR 349.

[146] Belanger 288 (n 140).

[147] Section 91(24), the Canadian Parliament's jurisdiction over 'Indians, and lands reserved for the Indians'.

[148] And therefore it fell under the Canada Labour Code 1985, rather than under provincial labour legislation, the Trade Union Act 1978.

[149] The decision of the Saskatchewan Queen's Bench was upheld by the Saskatchewan Court of Appeal at [2000] SKCA 138.

[150] Belanger 288 (n 140).

[151] Brock Pitawanakwat, 'Indigenous Labour Organizing in Saskatchewan: Red Baiting and Red Herrings' (2006) 58 New Socialist 32 <http://www.zoominfo.com/CachedPage/?archive_id=0&page_id=1781940748&page_url=//newsocialist.org/newsite/index.php?id=1037&page_last_updated=2009-09-26T08:07:08&firstName=Brock&lastName=Pitawanakwat>.

strongly criticized this approach as self-interested, misleading, and taking advantage of an Indigenous culture of resistance:

> The FSIN chiefs used this false front of nationalism as a red herring to maintain their power over labour relations in indigenous institutions. This form of red-baiting is a classic divide-and-conquer technique to prevent marginalized people from organizing to confront their oppressors. Indian reserves in Canada are rife with oppression that replicates the colonial order, and band councils are a classic example of indirect colonial rule.

Indian band councils were really no less 'foreign' than unions. The contemporary tribal governance and economy do not have a traditional form, but a different structure that 'put in place a system of indirect rule that created colonizing agents among indigenous people', with a new, non-traditional class of elites that controls non-traditional institutions, like the casinos. The result is that:

> [t]he emerging capitalist class in indigenous communities has exploited ongoing and deep-seated fears of assimilation amongst our peoples. Indigenous organizations have used a nationalist and xenophobic propaganda campaign to oppose labour unions.

Pitawanakwat also commented that the FSIN's 'use of non-native lawyers to argue in non-native courts based on non-native law that the colonizer's constitution should reinforce the band councils' ability to deny their own workers the right to organize' was hypocritical. On the other hand, he observed that Indigenous labour relations are complicated by the ambivalent Aboriginal attitude towards unions, particularly those that benefit from the resource extraction industry, which typically brings non-Indigenous workers into conflict with Indigenous people, whose land may be appropriated for development and exploitation. Moreover, 'class-based ideologies generally view any ethnic or national identity as a threat to class unity.' Pitawanakwat concluded, however, that union empowerment of Indigenous workers is not necessarily bad, and that '[i]nforming our perspectives on these issues with a critical traditionalism, rather than a naïve cultural nationalism, would go a long way towards ensuring that our self-determination efforts do not end up replicating the structures of domination that we seek to transform.'

Similar hostility towards the unionization of casino workers occurred in Ontario, where the Mississaugas of Scugog Island rejected CAW union certification by the Ontario Labour Relations Board at its Great Blue Heron Charity Casino. The First Nation unsuccessfully contended that it had an Aboriginal or treaty right to govern labour relations on its reserve lands.[152] After the CAW was certified, the First Nation formulated its own labour code, closely based on the Canada Labour Code. The CAW challenged the validity of this code, however, as it included several dubious provisions that were claimed to constitute unfair labour practices.[153] The Divisional Court and the

[152] *National Automobile, Aerospace, Transportation and General Workers Union of Canada (CAW-Canada), Local 444 v Great Blue Heron Gaming Co* [2005] 1 CNLR 147 (Ontario Labour Relations Board), upheld by the Divisional Court in *Mississaugas of Scugog Island First Nation v National Automobile, Aerospace, Transportation and General Workers Union of Canada (CAW-Canada), Local 444* [2006] 3 CNLR 46, and upheld on appeal to the Ontario Court of Appeal at [2008] 1 CNLR 71.

[153] These included prohibiting the right to strike; requiring a $3,000 fee that unions had to pay in order to speak to workers; requiring hearings to take place in a tribunal based on a traditional model; and prohibiting negotiation with unions that were not certified under the code.

Ontario Court of Appeal found that the First Nation had no right under section 35 of the Constitution Act 1982 to regulate its own labour relations. This was on the basis that there was no corresponding distinctive ancestral custom, practice, or tradition of regulating labour relations that could be said to have existed, continuing down to the present. Accordingly, provincial labour law applied.

Having failed to prevent unions from coming onto tribal lands to organize by legal argument, First Nations leaders have had to resort to other means of preventing union certification on their reserves. One strategy, as already noted, is to persuade their people to reject unionization by appealing to purported Aboriginal interests and values. Another tack is intimidation. When union organization was attempted in 2002 at SIGA's Painted Hand Casino in Yorkton, Saskatchewan, it failed a certification ballot. A subsequent case brought by two unions alleged unfair labour practices involving the dismissal of two casino workers who were involved in organizing.[154] This reportedly had a chilling effect on other employees who wished to join the organizing drive,[155] leading one of the unions to conclude that it would be unable to get majority support for certification because of employee fear of 'negative employment consequences'.[156] Aboriginal employers have also tried to preempt unions by offering good wages and benefits. Non-unionized workers, however, look to the terms and conditions achieved through collective bargaining, and this creates a continuous pressure to unionize.[157]

Although it may be too early to tell, the recent engagement between unions and Aboriginal people has the potential to blossom.[158] It may be difficult for First Nations leaders to continue their hostility towards mainstream workers' rights, particularly in the face of wage increases that have followed certification.[159] The arguments based on Aboriginal sovereignty and self-rule do not have the same foundation in Canada as they do in the United States, but that may equally mean that the Indigenous leadership might wish to hold on to what they have for as long as they can.

Conclusion

The Indigenous peoples discussed in this chapter live and work in diverse contexts, but they generally share a distinctive Indigenous experience and voice. Colonization deprived many of their land, the basis of their traditional cultures and economies, and

[154] See *Saskatchewan Joint Board, Retail, Wholesale, and Department Store Union v Saskatchewan Indian Gaming Authority Inc carrying on business as the Painted Hand Casino; Canadian Union of Public Employees v Saskatchewan Indian Gaming Authority Inc carrying on business as the Painted Hand Casino*, Labour Relations Board, Saskatchewan, Labour Relations Board, Saskatchewan, 29 August 2003.

[155] *Saskatchewan Joint Board Case*, para. 10 (n 154).

[156] *Saskatchewan Joint Board Case*, para. 12 (n 154). The case also mentioned that in 2001, during an earlier organizing campaign at the casino, a union organizer was temporarily banned from the casino: see para. 9. The temporary ban was subsequently cancelled, but the union nevertheless decided to postpone its organizing drive in 2001.

[157] Belanger 286 (n 140).

[158] See, for example, the alliance between the Assembly of First Nations and the CAW for the joint infrastructure project 'Make Poverty History for First Nations', media release (25 October 2007) <http://www.caw.ca/assets/pdf/AFNjointProjects.pdf>.

[159] As had occurred, for example, at the Northern Lights Casino in Saskatchewan and the Great Blue Heron Charity Casino in Ontario.

set them on the road to social and economic marginalization. Indigenous people have historically lacked much of a voice in the workplace because of their location away from urban centres, their concentration in the primary sector, and their low numbers in the industrialized workforce and their precarious position in it. They were sometimes regarded as potential competitors by settler workers; excluded from employment due to a lack of education, skills, and training; and were victims of racism and discrimination. For all of these reasons, they tended not to be of much interest to trade unions nor, conversely, did they develop much of a labour consciousness.

Recent times, however, have been kinder to disadvantaged minority groups. Unions have taken a greater interest in them, whether it is to advance their social justice agendas, both within and beyond the workplace, or to address declining union densities by increasing their diversity.

Land is never far from Indigenous concerns. There have been recent struggles to regain native land, and unions have been supportive. In North America, where Indigenous people were allowed some measure of sovereignty over reserves when they were regarded as being of little economic value, that jealously guarded sovereignty is now under pressure from unions seeking to organize workers in the lucrative Indian gaming industry. Union activity on tribal reserves causes tension not only between Indigenous and non-Indigenous workers (who commonly comprise the majority of workers on reserves), but also within tribes, between those who wish to maintain sovereignty over their land against perceived interlopers from outside, and those who wish to challenge traditional Indigenous hierarchies. These conflicts, with their various cultural, economic, industrial, and political dimensions, are complex, and unlikely to be satisfactorily resolved through an assimilationist approach. Thus far, the law has not imposed a definitive solution that trumps Indigenous sovereignty, but the various parties and factions have been largely left to work out the issues themselves.

Tension between worker and Indigenous voice has arisen not only in North America, but also in New Zealand, where the Indigenous voice may belong to an employer or only a section of the workforce. This raises a complexity that must be approached in a culturally sensitive manner, as traditional Indigenous values do not always sit comfortably alongside contemporary workers' rights. Although there is a distinctive Indigenous workplace voice, that ethnic consciousness must sometimes compete with class and gender consciousness.

6

'Half a Person'

A Legal Perspective on Organizing and Representing 'Non-Standard' Workers

*A. C. L. Davies**

Introduction

It is generally accepted that individuals with 'non-standard' working arrangements, such as casual, agency, or temporary work, are less likely to join unions or take part in other forms of collective activity at work. Their often precarious experience of work on the margins of the labour market may leave them with little time, money, or energy to invest in workplace participation, and a perception that to do so would bring them few immediate benefits. Indeed, they might reasonably fear that joining a union will make it harder to get and keep work because of hostility from potential employers. Thus, people who are already vulnerable for economic and legal reasons are unlikely to have access to the protection and support that collective labour relations can bring.

In this chapter, my aim is to investigate English law's treatment of 'non-standard' workers in the collective context. This is a neglected topic in the literature which—not surprisingly, given 'non-standard' workers' generally low levels of collective participation—focuses primarily on their access to individual employment rights. I will explore three different areas of law. First, I will examine whether the freedom of association of 'non-standard' workers is adequately protected. Second, I will consider how 'non-standard' workers are counted when deciding whether a firm is big enough to be a candidate for collective consultation or the statutory trade union recognition procedure. I will argue that 'non-standard' workers are not always counted, or counted appropriately, with the consequence that some firms are treated by the law as being much smaller than they are in reality. This limits the law's scope of application. And third, I will assess the legal rights of worker representatives to obtain access to information from the employer about 'non-standard' workers. I will argue that the law should give special attention to ensuring that information is provided about these workers because they are particularly vulnerable and would benefit from collective support to tackle problems such as unequal treatment when compared with 'standard' workers.

Of course, in presenting these arguments it is important to emphasize that the law's role in this area is limited, in two central respects. First, both the statutory regime for trade

* Professor of Law and Public Policy, University of Oxford; Garrick Fellow and Tutor in Law, Brasenose College, Oxford. The quotation in the title of this chapter is the title of a song by The Smiths. The chapter considers developments up to 16 May 2013. I would like to thank the editors for their helpful comments on an earlier draft. Responsibility for errors remains my own.

union recognition and those for consultation have had a relatively low impact in general terms, for a variety of reasons. The statutory recognition procedure is cumbersome and only helps unions where they already have a very high level of support or membership in the workplace. The consultation procedures are unfamiliar and, again, cumbersome to invoke. Second, the problems with persuading 'non-standard' workers to engage with collective participation mechanisms—for example, by joining a union—are primarily practical rather than legal in nature. Thus, statutory reform in this area would not be a panacea.

However, the inquiry is still worth pursuing. 'Non-standard' workers have the same rights to participation at work as workers with 'standard' working arrangements: for example, Article 11 of the European Convention on Human Rights (ECHR) guarantees freedom of association to 'everyone'. As a minimum, the law should reflect this by ensuring that 'non-standard' workers are not excluded from the design of collective labour law regimes. And ideally, the law should acknowledge their particular vulnerability by giving special emphasis to their protection via this route.

'Non-Standard' Workers

This section sets the scene for the rest of the chapter. I begin by defining 'non-standard' work and exploring some difficulties with the terminology. Then I examine some of the empirical data (both quantitative and qualitative) concerning 'non-standard' workers and their trade union membership.

Definitions

Terms such as 'non-standard' or 'atypical' work are widely used in the literature to refer to people whose working arrangements deviate from the 'standard' or 'typical' case.[1] This 'standard' or 'typical' case is a person who has the legal status of an employee (as opposed to worker or self-employed), who works full-time, who has a contract of indefinite duration, and who is employed directly by the employer rather than via an agency. In this section, I will explain some of these elements in greater detail, before noting some difficulties with the (nevertheless ever-popular) terminology.

A key form of 'non-standard' work emerges where the individual's legal status is something other than 'employee'. English law affords the full range of employment rights to people who are classified as 'employees' employed under a contract of employment. Those who are not 'employees' may either be 'workers', entitled to a subset of the employment rights given to 'employees', or they may be 'self-employed', with virtually no entitlement to employment rights.[2]

[1] For a detailed account of the law in this area, see Simon Deakin and Gillian S. Morris, *Labour Law*, 6th edn (Hart, 2012) ch. 3. There is a large critical literature. See, for example, Hugh Collins, 'Independent Contractors and the Challenge of Vertical Disintegration to Employment Protection Laws' (1990) 10 Oxford Journal of Legal Studies (OJLS) 353; Sandra Fredman, 'Labour Law in Flux: The Changing Composition of the Workforce' (1997) 26 Industrial Law Journal (ILJ) 337; Mark Freedland and Nicola Kountouris, *The Legal Construction of Personal Work Relations* (OUP, 2011); Bob Hepple, 'Restructuring Employment Rights' (1986) 15 ILJ 69.

[2] Equality Act 2010, s. 83(2), was long thought to include some self-employed people in the scope of equality law, but the decision of the Supreme Court in *Jivraj v Hashwani* [2011] UKSC 40, [2011] 1 WLR 1872 has cast doubt on this.

An employee is defined in statute as a person working under a contract of employment.[3] The contract of employment is a common law concept, and although its precise boundaries are uncertain, the individual must normally satisfy a number of requirements in order to show that he or she is an employee. The employer must either shoulder the risk of profit and loss,[4] or control the employee's activities (depending on the exact test applied by the court),[5] the terms of the contract must be consistent with employment (including an obligation of personal service)[6] and there must be mutuality of obligation between the parties (in the sense that the employer promises future work and the employee promises to perform it).[7]

The concept of a 'worker's contract' as defined in statute includes contracts of employment, plus any contract to do work personally for another person who is not the customer of a business run by the alleged worker.[8] The worker concept was used in several key pieces of legislation from 1997 onwards as a way of affording some basic protections (for example, in areas such as the minimum wage[9] and working time[10]) to individuals who did not meet the stringent tests developed by the courts for identifying 'employees', but who could not be regarded as genuinely self-employed. Anyone who falls outside both the 'employee' and 'worker' categories is, by default, self-employed.

Special problems arise in relation to those who work on a casual basis. This group includes many people with what are popularly known as 'zero hours contracts', arrangements under which the employer does not guarantee any particular level of work to the individual in a given week.[11] It is important to distinguish two types of claim that these individuals might make: a claim that can be made whilst working (such as the right to a rest break during the working day[12]) and a claim that depends on having a longer-term relationship with the employer (such as unfair dismissal[13]). The first type of claim requires the tribunal to assess the individual's status during the wage-work bargain. The best view seems to be that the individual is an employee during this time,[14] though tribunals might also find worker status (for example, where there is insufficient control[15]) or self-employment (for example, where the highly casual nature of the arrangement suggests no employment relationship at all[16]). The second type of claim requires the tribunal to determine whether a series of wage-work bargains can be linked together into a 'global' or 'umbrella' contract. This can be done either by means of statutory continuity, which (if certain conditions are met) links a series of contracts of employment together into a period of continuous employment,[17] or by means of 'mutuality of

[3] Employment Rights Act 1996, s. 230(1) (hereafter 'ERA').

[4] *Market Investigations v Minister of Social Security* [1969] 2 QB 173.

[5] *Ready Mixed Concrete (South East) Ltd v Minister of Pensions and National Insurance* [1968] 2 QB 497.

[6] *Express and Echo Publications v Tanton* [1999] ICR 693; *MacFarlane v Glasgow CC* [2001] IRLR 7.

[7] *O'Kelly v Trusthouse Forte* [1984] QB 90; *Carmichael v National Power* [1999] 1 WLR 2042.

[8] ERA, s. 230(3).

[9] National Minimum Wage Act 1998, s. 1.

[10] Working Time Regulations 1998, SI 1998/1833, r. 2.

[11] See Matthew Pennycook, Giselle Cory, and Vidhya Alakeson, *A Matter of Time: The Rise of Zero-Hours Contracts* (Resolution Foundation, June 2013).

[12] Working Time Regulations 1998, SI 1998/1833, r. 12.

[13] ERA, s. 94.

[14] For an excellent discussion, see *Quashie v Stringfellow Restaurants Ltd* [2012] EWCA Civ 1735, [2013] IRLR 99 [10]–[14] (Elias LJ).

[15] *Quashie v Stringfellow* [10]–[14] (n 14).

[16] *O'Kelly v Trusthouse Forte plc* [1983] ICR 728.

[17] ERA, s. 212, and see *Cornwall CC v Prater* [2006] EWCA Civ 102, [2006] ICR 731.

obligation', explained previously. The latter option is difficult for people working on a casual basis to satisfy because their alleged 'employer' does not normally promise them work in the future. Mutuality has been held to be a requirement for worker as well as employee status, even though it does not feature in the statutory definition.[18] The justification for this is that mutuality is necessary for the presence of a contract (of any kind), though as I have argued elsewhere, the better view is that mutuality is necessary for the contract to be one of employment.[19] On a practical level, this may not matter very much, since most of the rights that require a longer-term employment relationship are available only to employees anyway.[20] But it is worrying on two counts: depending on how the legislature uses the worker concept, it may become significant in future, and (as we saw previously) it may 'infiltrate' tribunals' assessment of the individual's status during the wage-work bargain.

The recent case of *Hospital Medical Group v Westwood* suggests that the worker concept may also suffer from being over-inclusive.[21] Here, the court was called upon to consider the status of a doctor who provided his services to patients via a private clinic. Confusingly, the court held that the doctor was self-employed and ran his own business, but should be treated as a worker because he was 'integrated' into the clinic's activities and because the clinic could not be regarded as his 'customer'. If this line of reasoning is followed, the worker concept will include some genuinely self-employed people. It is unfortunate that the court in the *Westwood* case refused to provide general guidance on the interpretation of the worker test.[22]

Historically, the courts focused on the written contract between the parties when determining the nature of their relationship.[23] But in its highly significant ruling in the *Autoclenz* case, the Supreme Court emphasized the importance of identifying the 'true agreement' between the parties.[24] This was intended to address the concern that unscrupulous employers might draft contract documents so as to suggest that the individual was not an employee in order to deny him or her employment rights even though the documents did not reflect the reality of the parties' relationship. This ruling should help to ensure that employment relationships are classified more accurately. However, a person claiming to be an employee or a worker will still need to show that he or she meets the relevant legal tests.

This three-tier structure generates two boundary lines—between employee and worker, and between worker and self-employment—applicable in two contexts (the wage-work bargain and the longer-term relationship). Both sets of boundaries are highly contested because of the uncertainty surrounding the worker test. Mapping the concept of 'non-standard' work onto these concepts is not a straightforward exercise. Anyone who is an employee counts as being in 'standard' employment, with access to

[18] *Byrne Bros (Formwork) v Baird* [2002] ICR 667 [25].

[19] A.C.L. Davies, 'The Contract for Intermittent Employment' (2007) 36 ILJ 102.

[20] It is worth noting that the Agency Workers Regulations 2010, SI 2010/93, which use 'worker', adopt a statutory approach to continuity.

[21] *Hospital Medical Group Ltd v Westwood* [2012] EWCA Civ 1005, [2013] ICR 415.

[22] *Hospital Medical Group v Westwood* [20] (n 21).

[23] See, for example, *Consistent Group v Kalwak* [2008] EWCA Civ 430, [2008] IRLR 505.

[24] *Autoclenz Ltd v Belcher* [2011] UKSC 41, [2011] ICR 1157.

the full range of employment rights. In theory at least, the idea of 'non-standard' work is used to refer to all those who are not employees but who ought to be within the scope of labour law: in other words, those who are not genuinely self-employed (though some commentators would contest this[25]). But we cannot say for certain that, where a statute extends protection to 'workers', it accurately captures all those who are not genuinely self-employed, even though that is its objective. Thus, although later in this chapter I will argue that collective labour law should use the worker concept, so that it includes as many 'non-standard' workers as possible, I do so in full acknowledgment of the fact that the test as currently applied is far from perfect.

This set of issues about employment status does not exhaust the idea of 'non-standard' working. People may count as 'non-standard' workers for other reasons: because they work part-time rather than full-time, because they have a fixed-term rather than an indefinite contract, or because they work via an agency rather than directly for the person to whom they provide their services. These types of 'non-standard' work cut across the employment status issue, in the sense that a person might be a part-time employee or a part-time worker, and so on. Moreover, these types of 'non-standard' work give rise to a range of different concerns not necessarily related to employment status or entitlement to employment rights. For example, part-timers may experience uncertainty about their hours of work,[26] and fixed-term workers experience insecurity about the possible renewal of their contract.[27] And all the workers in these categories may encounter discrimination, such as lower hourly rates of pay, because they are 'non-standard' workers, or on other grounds (part-time working is more prevalent among women, for example), or both.[28]

The terminology of 'non-standard' (or 'atypical') work is problematic for two reasons. First, as this section has demonstrated, people's working arrangements may be 'non-standard' in many different ways. It is wrong to assume that all 'non-standard' workers experience the same difficulties in the labour market. For example, the problems encountered by an agency worker with unclear employment status may be very different to those experienced by a part-time employee. Second, terms such as 'non-standard' work may have a tendency to imply that these forms of work are unusual and that the majority of people enjoy 'standard' working arrangements. However, it is difficult to know for sure what proportion of the workforce is employed in which type of job.[29] For example, while people can be asked about agency or fixed-term work, employment status is so unclear that it is difficult to conduct reliable surveys on the matter. For the purposes of this chapter, I will continue to use 'non-standard' work for convenience, but where appropriate I will try to use more precise terminology referring

[25] See, for example, Freedland and Kountouris (n 1).

[26] See Mark Jeffery, 'Not Really Going to Work? Of the Directive on Part-Time Work, "Atypical Work" and Attempts to Regulate It' (1998) 27 ILJ 193, 199.

[27] See the Fixed-term Employees (Prevention of Less Favourable Treatment) Regulations 2002, SI 2002/2034, r. 8.

[28] Fixed-term Employees (Prevention of Less Favourable Treatment) Regulations, r. 3. See also Part-time Workers (Prevention of Less Favourable Treatment) Regulations 2000, SI 2000/1551, r. 5, and Agency Workers Regulations 2010, SI 2010/93, r. 5.

[29] Brendan Burchell, Simon Deakin, and Sheila Honey, *The Employment Status of Individuals in Non-Standard Employment* (URN 99/770, Department of Trade and Industry, 1999).

to particular types of 'non-standard' work. In doing so, I make no assumption about their prevalence in the labour market.

Trade union membership among 'non-standard' workers

Since the focus of this chapter is on 'non-standard' workers in collective labour law, it may be helpful to provide some context by examining some of the data regarding the participation of these workers in collective activities. Since there is very little data available about consultation, this section will focus on trade union membership.

The definitional problems discussed in the previous section make it difficult to draw clear empirical conclusions about the extent to which 'non-standard' workers are members of trade unions. If we cannot tell what proportion of the workforce is 'non-standard', it is no surprise that we cannot tell what proportion of the 'non-standard' workforce is unionized. However, data from the Labour Force Survey (LFS) tend to confirm the widely-held view that 'non-standard' workers are less likely to be members of a union than their 'standard' counterparts. According to the LFS, trade union density for all employees is 26 per cent.[30] As is well-known, this marks an important divergence between the public and private sectors, with trade union density at 14.1 per cent in the private sector and 56.5 per cent in the public sector.[31] But for my purposes, the statistics highlight two important points. First, where they do pick out 'non-standard' forms of work, union density is lower than the average for the labour market as a whole. For example, trade union density among temporary workers is 14.2 per cent.[32] Second, union density is low in relation to certain types of work or worker that we commonly associate with 'non-standard' working. Of course, these connections are speculative and must be used with appropriate caution. For example, it is generally thought that 'non-standard' working is common in certain sectors of the economy. Union density in the LFS category of 'accommodation and food service' is 3.6 per cent, and in 'construction' it is 14.8 per cent.[33] At least anecdotally, we would associate the former sector with a high incidence of casual work, and the latter sector with a high incidence of contracts which are (or purport to be) for self-employment. Similarly, we know that many migrant workers end up in 'non-standard' jobs, often because they seek work through agencies, and union density among those whose nationality is not British is below average at 11.8 per cent.[34]

A rich industrial relations literature on the topic of 'non-standard' workers identifies a number of (linked) explanations for the difficulties unions face in organizing them.[35]

[30] Nikki Brownlie, *Trade Union Membership 2011* (Department for Business, Innovation and Skills 2012) 24.

[31] Brownlie 26 (n 30). [32] Brownlie 32 (n 30). [33] Brownlie 31 (n 30).

[34] Brownlie 32 (n 30).

[35] See, for example, Ian Fitzgerald and Jane Hardy, '"Thinking Outside the Box"? Trade Union Organizing Strategies and Polish Migrant Workers in the United Kingdom' (2010) 48 British Journal of Industrial Relations (BJIR) 131; Rebecca Gumbrell-McCormick, 'European Trade Unions and "Atypical" Workers' (2011) 42 Industrial Relations Journal (IRJ) 293; Edmund Heery, 'The Trade Union Response to Agency Labour in Britain' (2004) 35 IRJ 434; R. MacKenzie, 'Why do Contingent Workers Join a Trade Union? Evidence from the Irish Telecommunications Sector' (2010) 16 European Journal of Industrial Relations (EJIR) 153; Susanne Pernicka, 'Organizing the Self-Employed: Theoretical Considerations and Empirical Findings' (2006) 12 EJIR 125.

One problem is tension between a union's 'traditional' constituency of 'standard' workers and the emergence of a group of 'non-standard' workers who may be perceived as a threat to their terms and conditions or even their jobs.[36] A firm's use of agency or casual workers may be seen as a way of undercutting those with 'standard' jobs. For example, in a study of the Irish telecommunications industry, MacKenzie shows that although the union was attempting to organize 'non-standard' workers, some 'standard' workers were opposed and the members with 'non-standard' jobs felt that there was a hierarchy in terms of the way different types of members were represented.[37] Another problem is the lack of connection between 'non-standard' workers and a particular workplace, which is usually the focus of union organizing.[38] Many people join unions because of encouragement from colleagues who are active members. But it is difficult to build up relationships with 'non-standard' workers where they work from home or have a casual or short-term working arrangement. Yet a further problem is the attitudes of non-standard workers themselves. They may not perceive that there are any benefits from trade union membership, for various reasons. Of course, there may be a view—as discussed previously—that unions represent the interests of those with permanent jobs. But there are other problems too: workers whose jobs are precarious may not have much investment in improving their terms and conditions, or they may feel vulnerable to employer discrimination if they try to organize. And for low-paid workers in particular, a union subscription bringing uncertain future benefits may not be a manageable expense. More profoundly, certain types of 'non-standard' worker, particularly self-employed people, may see themselves as individual entrepreneurs for whom union membership is inappropriate.[39] As Dickens puts it: 'Individualization may be seen as inherent in certain non-standard forms of work that are not embedded in the organization in terms of space and time.'[40]

MacKenzie found some evidence that certain 'non-standard' workers felt that they had 'broken free' of both the union and the employer by ceasing to be employees.[41]

Of course, it is important to qualify these remarks in two respects. First, the industrial relations literature also shows that unions are adopting innovative strategies in order to reach out to 'non-standard' workers for recruitment purposes and are giving much greater thought to how to represent them, particularly where there are conflicts with members on 'standard' contracts.[42] Second, although trade unions are membership organizations, they are generally treated as having the capacity to represent people who are not members in both collective bargaining and wider political campaigns.[43] Thus, for example, it is accepted that employers will extend the benefits of a collective agreement to everyone in the relevant bargaining unit regardless of their union membership. And the trade union movement has played an important role in negotiating the EU directives on 'non-standard' work, both at European and national levels.

[36] Heery (n 35) offers a useful typology of union responses, from exclusion to engagement.

[37] MacKenzie 160–1 (n 35).

[38] Linda Dickens, 'Problems of Fit: Changing Employment and Labour Regulation' (2004) 42 BJIR 595, 609.

[39] See Pernicka (n 35). [40] Dickens 608 (n 38). [41] MacKenzie 162 (n 35).

[42] There are many good examples in the literature cited in n 35.

[43] See, for example, *ASLEF v UK* (2007) 45 EHRR 34 [50].

Nevertheless, both the quantitative and qualitative material suggests that recruiting 'non-standard' workers continues to pose significant challenges for the trade union movement. In the remainder of this chapter, I will examine the extent to which collective labour law's treatment of 'non-standard' workers contributes to these challenges.

Freedom of Association

I will begin by considering a foundational issue in collective labour law: freedom of association. To what extent are 'non-standard' workers protected when they seek to form and join trade unions?

From the international materials, it is clear that 'non-standard' workers have the same rights to organize as workers with standard jobs. As the ILO Digest on Freedom of Association puts it: 'All workers, without distinction whatsoever, whether they are employed on a permanent basis, for a fixed term or as contract employees, should have the right to establish and join organizations of their own choosing.'[44] Freedom of association is also required to be guaranteed by the relevant ILO conventions governing home work,[45] part-time work,[46] agency work,[47] and domestic work.[48]

At the most basic level, then, this suggests that 'non-standard' workers should not be prohibited from joining unions and should be protected against discrimination by the employer on grounds of their trade union membership. Historically, the UK's provisions on discrimination against trade unionists applied to employees.[49] However, in 2004, new ss. 145A (dealing with inducements to give up trade union membership) and 145B (dealing with inducements to give up collective bargaining) were introduced using the worker definition. At the same time, s. 146 (dealing with detrimental treatment on grounds of trade union membership) was amended so that it now uses the worker definition. Section 152 (dealing with dismissal on grounds of trade union membership) still applies only to employees, but this reflects the fact that unfair dismissal is an 'employee-only' right. A worker could potentially rely on s. 146 to challenge the termination of his or her employment relationship since this is an obvious form of detriment.[50] The only significant gap in protection is s. 137, dealing with refusals to offer employment on grounds of trade union membership. This still applies only to offers of a contract of employment, under s. 143(1), and it is very difficult to imagine what the justification for this might be.

We saw earlier that, even where the worker definition is used, it may not capture all the people in need of the law's protection. This raises the interesting question of whether it is necessary to have an understanding of personal scope for the purposes of

[44] ILO, *Freedom of Association: Digest of Decisions and Principles of the Freedom of Association Committee of the Governing Body of the ILO* (5th edn, 2006) [255].

[45] C 177, Home Work Convention (1996), Art. 4 (not ratified by the UK).

[46] C 175, Part-Time Work Convention (1994), Art. 4 (not ratified by the UK).

[47] C 181, Private Employment Agencies Convention (1997), Art. 4 (not ratified by the UK).

[48] C 189, Domestic Workers Convention (2011), Art. 3 (not ratified by the UK).

[49] For a powerful critique of these provisions, see Alan L. Bogg, 'Employment Relations Act 2004: Another False Dawn for Collectivism?' (2005) 34 ILJ 72.

[50] This would appear to follow from s. 146(5A), which ensures that an employee who is dismissed must invoke s. 152.

freedom of association. Why not protect 'trade union members' against discrimination, or even 'everyone', rather than 'workers'? While individual employment law might need to be able to delineate people's entitlement to rights in a precise way, surely these technicalities are irrelevant when collective activities are at issue?

In my view, this superficially attractive proposition in fact conceals two quite deep problems. First, although the role of employers' associations is much reduced in modern industrial relations, the law assumes a clear dividing line between those who are members of trade unions and those who are members of employers' associations.[51] The inclusion of some self-employed people would blur this line, at least where they are the employers of others.[52] Second, one of the crucial achievements in the history of the trade union movement is the exemption of trade union activities from regulation by competition law.[53] This exemption is challenged by the inclusion of self-employed people in trade union activities. An agreement between businesses—even micro-businesses—to fix a price for the services they offer may fall foul of competition law in a way that a collective agreement to fix the price of labour currently does not. Thus, the dividing line between employment broadly conceived and *genuine* self-employment does have a role to play in collective labour law.[54] The focus of attention should therefore be on ensuring that the worker concept is defined in an appropriately inclusive way.

Workplace Size Thresholds

The second issue I will examine is rather different. The statutory procedure for trade union recognition for the purposes of collective bargaining and the EU rules on workplace consultation apply only to large workplaces. These are defined by reference to the size of the workforce. In this section, I will show how the law fails to count 'non-standard' workers properly when determining how many people are employed by a particular firm. This can mean that collective labour law treats some firms as smaller than they really are, with the result that the scope of application of this body of law is potentially much reduced.

Of course, the policy of confining statutory support for recognition, and for consultation, to larger firms is, in itself, controversial.[55] Successive governments have been keen to limit or reduce the 'burden' of regulation for smaller firms, as a means of encouraging enterprise. Moreover, it is often argued that formal voice mechanisms are unnecessary or even inappropriate in smaller firms, where owners or managers interact with staff in informal ways on a day-to-day basis.[56] They are only required in larger

[51] See, for example, the definition of an employers' association in TULRCA 1992, s. 122.

[52] It is possible that a factor underlying the controversy surrounding UEAPME's exclusion from the EU social dialogue was its capacity, as an organization of artisans and small businesses, to blur this divide: Case T-135/96 *Union Européenne de l'Artisanat et des Petites et Moyennes Entreprises (UEAPME) v Council* [1998] ECR II-2335.

[53] TULRCA 1992, s. 11.

[54] This is not consistent with the ILO *Digest* [254] (n 44), which includes the self-employed, though it is arguable that the intention is to include those who are technically self-employed but, in reality, workers.

[55] The ILO Committee of Experts on the Application of Conventions and Recommendations has criticized the 21-worker threshold for statutory recognition: Individual Observation Concerning Right to Organise and Collective Bargaining Convention, 1949 (No 98), United Kingdom (2007).

[56] Department of Trade and Industry, *Fairness at Work* (Cm 3968, 1998) [4.17].

firms where senior managers may not be in regular contact with all staff. Against this, it can be argued that we do not know what proportion of smaller firms are, in reality, run in a friendly way, and that in those instances where workers would prefer more formal representation mechanisms, the law should support them just as it does those who are employed by bigger firms. But this is a debate for another day.

The discussion in this section will begin by examining the law's use of the employee and worker concepts in this context, before turning to the particularly odd phenomenon of treating part-time workers as 'half people' for the purposes of the rules on workplace consultation.

Employee or worker?

I will begin by setting out the legal provisions before examining their consequences and the interesting question of whether they might be open to challenge under EU law.

The statutory trade union recognition procedure laid down in Schedule A1 of the Trade Union and Labour Relations (Consolidation) Act 1992 (TULRCA) applies to firms with more than twenty-one workers.[57] The law on consultation, by contrast, tends to use the narrower 'employee' concept. Thus, the Information and Consultation of Employees Regulations 2004 (ICER), which provide the possibility of workplace consultation, apply only to firms with fifty employees or more (averaged over the previous 12 months).[58] The Transnational Information and Consultation of Employees Regulations 1999 (TICER), which provide for the possibility of information and consultation in pan-European firms, apply only to firms with at least 1000 employees within the EU and at least 150 employees in each of at least two Member States (averaged over the previous 24 months).[59] However, the use of the term 'employee' is subject to an exception. Where the firm in question is an employment agency, the term 'worker' is used instead.[60] This reflects the requirements of the Directive on Temporary Agency Work.[61] This requires Member States to ensure that agency workers count towards firm size thresholds, with a choice of counting them as against the agency or counting them as against the end user.[62] The UK government has chosen to count them against the agency.[63] Because the Agency Workers Regulations 2010 use the worker concept throughout (and because agency workers are highly unlikely to be employees of the agency) it was necessary for the government to amend the law on consultation so that, in agency settings, the worker definition could be used.[64] This makes the use of 'employee' in ICER 2004 and TICER 1999 seem even more strange.

As we saw earlier, although the worker concept is imperfect in its application, it does at least represent an attempt to delineate the scope of labour law in a broad way so as to exclude everyone other than the genuinely self-employed. Where the term 'employee' is used, 'non-standard' workers (defined to include those who are not employees in

[57] TULRCA 1992, Sch. A1, para. 7. [58] SI 2004/3426, rr. 3–4. [59] SI 1999/3323, r. 6.

[60] ICER 2004, r. 3A; TICER 1999, r. 2(4C). [61] Directive 2008/104/EC.

[62] Directive 2008/104/EC, Art. 7.

[63] Organizing a shifting population of agency workers is likely to be difficult but not impossible, as CAC Case TUR1/503 *Public and Commercial Services Union v Adecco Ltd* (2006) illustrates.

[64] SI 2010/93, r. 3.

law but who are not genuinely self-employed either) are not counted. It is important to be precise about the effect of not counting 'non-standard' workers. At first glance, this might imply that such workers are not covered by collective representation arrangements, but this is not necessarily the case. One reason for this is that not all collective representation depends on the statutory frameworks. A smaller firm might engage in collective bargaining or set up a consultation process without being obliged to do so by statute, in which case the thresholds would not matter at all. The other reason is that the thresholds are over- as well as under-inclusive. So, for example, if a firm has more than fifty employees and a large number of 'non-standard' workers, that firm would fall within the scope of ICER 2004 and, if a consultation procedure was set up, the 'non-standard' workers would benefit from it. My concern is with the under-inclusiveness of the thresholds. For example, it is not improbable to imagine a firm with a core of ten employees and a periphery of ninety 'non-standard' workers. This firm would not be big enough for ICER 2004 to apply even though in a non-technical sense we would regard it as a large firm, where both the employer and the workforce might benefit from the introduction of formal consultation procedures. The use of the term 'worker' (despite the difficulties already noted) would be preferable here.

Since ICER 2004 and TICER 1999 implement EU directives,[65] it is worth asking whether there is any scope for arguing that the UK is in breach of its obligation to implement the directives properly in its choice of the (arguably) narrower employee terminology. In general terms, it is a matter for the Member State when implementing a directive to determine its personal scope of application, in accordance with national law. However, this discretion is not unlimited and it may be possible to make a case that the choice of definition impedes the effective implementation of the directive by excluding large groups of people who ought to be protected by the relevant EU provisions. An argument of this kind succeeded in the recent *O'Brien* case, in which part-time judges challenged their exclusion from a pension scheme as discrimination against them on grounds of working part-time.[66] The claimant had to show that he was a 'worker' in order to bring the claim. The Court of Justice held that the concept of worker was used to distinguish those in need of protection from self-employed people, and suggested that it was unlikely that judges were self-employed.[67] The Supreme Court then held that Mr O'Brien was a 'worker' for the purposes of the claim. However, it remains to be seen whether this decision—which addressed quite special facts—will facilitate broader claims about the effective implementation of directives when 'employee' rather than 'worker' is used.

[65] Directive 2002/14/EC establishing a general framework for informing and consulting employees in the European Community and Directive 2009/38/EC on the establishment of a European Works Council or a procedure in Community-scale undertakings and Community-scale groups of undertakings for the purposes of informing and consulting employees (Recast), respectively.

[66] *Department of Constitutional Affairs v O'Brien* [2013] UKSC 6, [2013] 1 WLR 522.

[67] C-393/10 *O'Brien v Ministry of Justice* [2012] 2 CMLR 25.

Part-time employees

Another concerning feature of ICER 2004 and TICER 1999 is their treatment of part-time employees, who may be counted as 'half a person' for the purposes of the firm size thresholds in both legal regimes:

> For the purposes of the calculation in paragraph (2) if, for the whole of a month within the twelve-month period, an employee works under a contract by virtue of which he would have worked for 75 hours or less in that month—
>
> (i) were the month to have contained 21 working days;
> (ii) were the employee to have had no absences from work; and
> (iii) were the employee to have worked no overtime,
>
> the employee may be counted as representing half of a full-time employee for the month in question, if the employer so decides.[68]

Importantly, this only applies to the calculation of the size of the firm. Under ICER 2004, there is a 'trigger' provision requiring 10 per cent of the employees to make a formal request to the employer to open negotiations about information and consultation.[69] Part-timers count as whole people for this purpose.

As we saw previously, the relevant directives provide that it is for the Member State to determine the method for calculating whether or not the firm size thresholds have been met.[70] Moreover, EU law adopts the 'pro rata' principle in the Directive on Part-Time Work, so it could be argued that the half a person rule reflects that well-established principle.[71] A person working 75 hours or fewer per month can be said to be working around half of normal full-time hours. Indeed, we might argue (along the lines of a school maths problem) that a firm employing 100 half-timers might produce the same output as a firm with fifty full-timers, assuming each employee is equally productive, making the two firms in some sense the same size. Thus, it can be argued that the UK government's decision to implement the two directives in this way is both legitimate and in compliance with EU law.

However, as we saw before, one of the justifications for firm size thresholds is that formal mechanisms for bargaining and consultation are only regarded as appropriate for larger firms, where casual or informal interaction with management is not practicable. But this justification casts doubt on the strategy of treating each part-timer as half a person. A firm employing 100 half-timers may be notionally the same size as one employing fifty full-timers, but in terms of interacting with the workforce it seems likely to have a much greater need of formal representation mechanisms, for the obvious reason that it is more difficult to communicate with and listen to a larger group of people. It might be argued that effective channels of communication are even more important for part-timers precisely because they spend less time in the workplace. Moreover, given that part-time work tends to be dominated by women, it might

[68] ICER 2004, r. 4(3). The equivalent provision in TICER 1999 is r. 6(3).
[69] ICER 2004, r. 7; TICER 1999, r. 9.
[70] Directive 2002/14/EC, Art. 3(1); Directive 2009/38/EC, Art. 2(2).
[71] Directive 97/81/EC concerning the Framework Agreement on part-time work, Annex, cl. 4(2).

be arguable that making it more difficult for part-timers to access collective representation is a form of indirect discrimination on grounds of sex.

Information about 'Non-standard' Work

In this section, I will focus on a third aspect of collective labour law: the provision of information to workers' representatives. Effective collective activity—whether in the form of collective bargaining or consultation—depends on the employer giving workers' representatives access to information about relevant issues, such as the state of the business or terms and conditions of employment. To that end, English law on collective bargaining and consultation provides workers' representatives with legal rights of access to appropriate information. Of course, as is generally true in this area, workers' representatives are often reluctant to enforce these rights by legal means, for fear of disrupting their relationship with the employer, but their existence may have an important 'shadow' effect in some cases.

In relation to 'non-standard' work, the key question is whether the relevant provisions are sufficient to ensure that workers' representatives are aware of the situation of these workers and are able to represent them appropriately. Of course, it might be asked why 'non-standard' workers warrant particular attention in this regard, but I would suggest that there are at least three reasons for this. First, it is generally acknowledged that these workers are particularly vulnerable and may require additional help and support. Second, particularly for part-time, fixed-term, and agency workers, the law provides rights not to be discriminated against on grounds of having that status.[72] Information provided at the collective level could be used to help discover and eliminate such discrimination. Third, and perhaps more controversially, the provision of information on 'non-standard' working may encourage unions in particular to reach out to workers in this group. In turn, this may help unions to recruit more 'non-standard' workers to membership, given that people are much more likely to join if they can see that the union brings them specific benefits.[73]

The initiative for making special provision for 'non-standard' workers in the law on information has come from the EU. The Directives on Part-Time and Fixed-Term Work both mention the issue, but in very vague terms. For example, clause 5(3) of the social partners' agreement on part-time work states: 'As far as possible, employers should give consideration to... the provision of appropriate information to existing bodies representing workers about part-time working in the enterprise.'[74] The UK government took the view that this phrasing was merely exhortatory and thus did not require specific implementation in domestic law.[75] The Directive on Temporary Agency Work took a tougher line: under Article 8, obligations to provide information to workers' representatives

[72] See n 28. Of course the same point might be made about gender and other grounds of discrimination, a point recognized to some extent (albeit not in the collective context) in the ill-fated s. 78, Equality Act 2010.

[73] A point powerfully made by Alan Bogg, *The Democratic Aspects of Trade Union Recognition* (Hart, 2009), ch. 6.

[74] See n 71. See also Directive 1999/70/EC concerning the framework agreement on fixed-term work, Annex, cl. 7(3).

[75] For discussion, see Jeffery 197 (n 26).

must be amended to include 'information on the use of temporary agency workers'. In response, the UK government has amended the provisions relating to collective bargaining and to consultation so that agency work is expressly included. Thus, s. 181(2) TULRCA, on information for the purposes of collective bargaining, now provides:

> The information to be disclosed is all information relating to the employer's undertaking *including information relating to use of agency workers in that undertaking* which is in his possession, or that of an associated employer, and is information—
>
> (a) without which the trade union representatives would be to a material extent impeded in carrying on collective bargaining with him, and
> (b) which it would be in accordance with good industrial relations practice that he should disclose to them for the purposes of collective bargaining.[76]

In ICER 2004, the default information and consultation provisions have been amended so that the employer is required to disclose 'suitable information relating to the use of agency workers' in the undertaking.[77] The concept of 'suitable information' is defined as:

> (a) the number of agency workers working temporarily for and under the supervision and direction of the employer,
> (b) the parts of the employer's undertaking in which those agency workers are working, and
> (c) the type of work those agency workers are carrying out.[78]

It is arguable that the employer's duty to disclose information, whether for consultation or collective bargaining purposes, is already broadly framed, so that it would not preclude workers' representatives from using it to seek information on 'non-standard' workers. However, the express inclusion of information about agency workers helps to clarify the extent of the employer's obligations and may also encourage representatives to seek information on this topic. Now that the drafting is in place, it would perhaps be helpful to add express references to fixed-term and part-time workers.

During the process of implementing the Directive on Temporary Agency Work, the TUC campaigned for the amendments to include a requirement to disclose agency workers' terms and conditions of employment.[79] It is arguable that this proposal was misguided. Under s. 181 TULRCA, information about terms and conditions of employment is central to collective bargaining and it should be possible to obtain this information for agency workers without express provision to that effect. Under ICER 2004, it could be argued that information about terms and conditions of employment is too specific for the consultation process, which is envisaged as a forum for discussion about the future of the business. However, there was an important message underlying the TUC's campaign. One of the core features of the Directive on Temporary

[76] Emphasis added. Similar changes have been made in s. 188, TULRCA, dealing with consultation on collective redundancies. This was the subject of a successful claim in *Unison v London Borough of Barnet* (Case 3302128/2012; judgment 4 February 2013).

[77] ICER 2004, r. 20(1). [78] ICER 2004, r. 2.

[79] Department for Business, Innovation and Skills, *Implementation of the Agency Workers Directive: Response to Consultation on Draft Regulations* (2010) [7.10].

Agency Work is the right it gives agency workers to equal treatment with the end user's directly hired workers.[80] This right—like other equality rights—depends on individual workers obtaining information about unequal treatment and bringing litigation. Given the vulnerability of these workers, it seems unlikely that many will feel able to enforce their rights. Enabling worker representatives to obtain better information about agency workers' terms and conditions would offer an alternative route to enforcement. It would not be perfect: one obvious problem is that the information would be given to worker representatives at the end user enterprise, whereas the law encourages agency workers to seek collective representation at the agency, so the information would not necessarily end up in the hands of the *agency workers'* representatives. But it would help to draw attention to instances in which the end user was in breach of its legal obligations. Similar arguments might be made about part-time and fixed-term workers, who are also entitled to equal treatment with full-time or indefinitely-hired workers respectively.[81] If worker representatives had a clear right of access to information about their terms and conditions, this would offer another way of encouraging firms to rectify instances of non-compliance.

The discussion so far has concentrated on the provision of information about particular types of 'non-standard' work—agency, fixed-term, and part-time—because these are the types of work addressed by EU law. Some of the same arguments could also be made about people who have 'worker' status as opposed to 'employee' status, since they also occupy a position of disadvantage. Indeed, in some cases, a requirement to disclose information about all forms of 'non-standard' work might discourage employers from taking people on as workers rather than employees. However, the uncertain boundary between the employee and worker categories would make it difficult for employers to comply with, and worker representatives to police, this obligation.

Conclusion

I noted at the outset of this chapter that changing collective labour law in order to include and protect 'non-standard' workers would not be likely to bring about radical changes in practice. Even if we had a broader understanding of who counts when deciding how big a firm is, so that more firms would fall within their scope, the trade union recognition procedure and the collective consultation arrangements under TICER 1999 and ICER 2004 remain cumbersome and difficult to invoke. And even if rights to information expressly included information about 'non-standard' workers' terms and conditions, effective collective bargaining or consultation arrangements would need to be in place in order for worker representatives to invoke these rights. This is a field in which it is especially important to bear in mind the limits of what can be achieved through legal reform.

Nevertheless, reform in this area would have value. All workers, standard or otherwise, have the right to participate in collective activities at work. The law should require employers to provide worker representatives with information about the terms and

[80] See n 28. [81] See n 28.

conditions of 'non-standard' workers, and it should take an inclusive and non-technical approach to 'counting' them for the purposes of firm size thresholds. This would bring more firms within the compass of the legal regimes on consultation and collective bargaining and would encourage worker representatives to include them in their bargaining strategies. If 'non-standard' workers could see benefits to getting involved in collective activities at work, this might help to increase the level of union membership in this group. Moreover, at the symbolic level, these reforms would send out an important signal that our attitude towards 'non-standard' workers is to include and protect them, not to devalue and marginalize them.

INSTITUTIONS OF VOICE

7

Freedom of Association and the Right to Contest

Getting Back to Basics

Alan Bogg and Cynthia Estlund

Introduction

British and North American labour lawyers have become inured to the discourse of crisis in respect of collective worker voice. Collective bargaining through independent trade unions is in precipitous if not terminal decline, especially in the US private sector.[1] This has led to a renewed focus on 'freedom of association' (FOA), a principle with a venerable international law pedigree, as a potential source of normative support. Whatever else FOA means in the labour context, it surely protects the freedom to form and join a trade union. For some theorists, the content of FOA as a fundamental labour right begins and ends there.[2] Yet there has been a good deal of work on the possibilities of FOA both above and below this platform of a freedom to form and join trade unions.

Much recent work seeks to build up from that platform, in what we call a strategy of 'ascent': how much *more* does FOA protect above and beyond union formation? Does it, for example, entail a right to strike? A duty on employers to bargain with the employees' chosen trade union representative? Does it require at least the rudiments of a legal system (for example, along Wagner-like lines) for enforcing the duty to bargain? Constitutional litigation has been fertile in this regard in Canada and Europe, even if scepticism remains about the social impact of legal victories in the rarefied arena of constitutional courts.[3]

In parallel with this debate, however, there is also serious engagement with the question of what might lie underneath and prior to the freedom to join and form trade unions (rather than above and beyond it). This enquiry—we call it a strategy of 'descent'—implies that there is a deeper substrate beneath the protection of basic trade union freedoms—something that is logically and practically prior to the formation of a union, and that is independently deserving of protection. In short, does FOA have anything to offer to workers acting outside the ambit of unions, and to workers with

[1] For a recent summary of trade union density levels in a range of countries, see the OECD figures at <http://stats.oecd.org/Index.aspx?QueryId=20167>.

[2] Hugh Collins, 'Theories of Rights as Justifications for Labour Law' in Guy Davidov and Brian Langille (eds), *The Idea of Labour Law* (OUP, 2011) 137, 151.

[3] In the Canadian context, the most recent constitutional battle was fought in *Fraser v Ontario (Attorney General)* [2011] 2 SCR 3. In the European context, see *Demir and Baykara v Turkey* [2008] ECHR 1345, discussed in John Hendy and Keith Ewing, 'The Dramatic Implications of Demir and Baykara' (2010) 39 Industrial Law Journal (ILJ) 2. For a sceptical view of the potential of constitutional litigation to bring about social and economic change, see Harry Arthurs and Brent Arnold, 'Does the Charter Matter?' (2005) 11 Review of Constitutional Studies 37.

little prospect of, or perhaps even desire for, union representation? Our own enquiry is firmly within this latter stream of labour law theory.

If FOA entails only the rights to form and act through unions, it risks becoming vestigial in a world in which unions are receding, even fading, from the scene—and that is what most private sector workers in the US, UK, and Canada face today. To begin with, the formation of a trade union in that world is itself often very challenging. We think that is partly due to the inadequate protection of workers' rights to act as individuals and through informal groups to contest employer power. Unionization is often the culmination of a longer process of identifying and learning to promote shared aims. Rights of individual and informal contestation are very likely necessary (at least in a mostly non-union world) for workers to be capable even of forming a union. The freedom to form and join independent trade unions thus requires a practical underpinning of rights to contest employer power both individually and collectively (perhaps in informal or spontaneous groups) outside the institutional context of a trade union. One can thus reason 'down' from the traditional FOA to an entitlement to engage in less formal forms of contestation that are under-protected in all three of the labour law systems on which we focus.

But our argument here is grounded not only in positive international labour law and what is practically necessary for its realization; it is grounded as well in a more fundamental normative premise: citizenship in a free and democratic society entails the right to be free from 'domination' by others. As elaborated most fully by Phillip Pettit, 'freedom as non-domination' requires not merely non-interference in individuals' life choices (including their contractual choices); it requires the ability to contest the decisions of others, both public and private actors, who wield power over one's life and livelihood.[4] In the employment context that entails a basic right of individuals to challenge employer decisions free from the threat of reprisals; and it also entails a right to do that in association with others, through a union or otherwise.

So we seek here both to reason 'down' from the traditional FOA to its practical prerequisites, and to reason 'up' from the idea of 'freedom as non-domination' to individual and collective rights to contest employer power, including but not limited to the right to form a union for the purpose of bargaining with the employer. 'Freedom as non-domination' provides a strong normative underpinning not only for the contestatory rights of individuals and informal groups but also for the traditional FOA itself—the right to form and join a union, certainly, and perhaps also rights to bargain collectively and to strike. This theory helps give content to the traditional but rather opaque invocation of 'unequal bargaining power' as a justification for the right to act through trade unions.[5] Given the economic power that employers have over workers (at least most workers most of the

[4] There is a rich literature. The most recent statement of Pettit's views is set out in Phillip Pettit, *On the People's Terms: A Republican Theory and Model of Democracy* (CUP, 2012). There have been some innovative attempts to work through the implications of Pettit's political theory within the labour law context: see, for example, Virginia Mantouvalou, 'Human Rights and Unfair Dismissal: Private Acts in Public Spaces' (2008) 71 Modern Law Review (MLR) 912; Nien-he Hsieh, 'Workplace Democracy, Workplace Republicanism, and Economic Democracy' (2008) 9 Revue de philosophie économique 57.

[5] We will return later to this issue. But note for now one problem with the traditional justification for protecting unionization: it is not after all bargaining 'equality' that is sought or achieved through unionization; it is more like 'enough' bargaining power; but then how much is enough?

time), the right to form a union is necessary to ensure worker-citizens' freedom from domination by their employers.[6] Necessary but not sufficient. Even more basically, freedom as non-domination requires that individuals or informal groups of workers have the right to contest—question, criticize, disagree with—employer decisions about the organization, terms, and conditions of work without risking employer reprisals.

The second part of the chapter sets out a two-dimensional taxonomy of rights of contestation: on one axis, from individual to more collectivized forms of contestation, and on the other axis from the 'thinnest' version of freedom from state interference and coercion through 'thicker' protections requiring state intervention on behalf of employee rights. This part will then use this taxonomy to briefly describe the positive law of our three target countries, the US, UK, and Canada.

The third part of the chapter briefly reviews some of the extant arguments seeking to ground rights of individual and informally concerted contestation in positive labour law, especially in North America. These arguments seek to reason 'down' from FOA, and the statutory right to engage in trade union (or other concerted) activity, to a right to engage in informal or individual protest activity. While these 'top down' arguments may carry the day under positive law, and may carry weight with those who begin with a commitment to the traditional FOA, we think these arguments beg crucial questions about the normative basis for individual workers' rights to oppose or complain of employer actions.

The fourth part of the chapter sets forth our own argument for the recognition of individual and informal rights of contestation. We begin by contending, with Pettit, for a normative commitment to individual freedom, understood as 'non-domination'. From that foundation, we seek to build upward to collective rights of contestation, including the right to contest employer power through a union. We maintain that the 'bottom up' argument brings crucial normative heft both to the arguments for individual and informal rights of contestation and to the traditional FOA (that is, the right to form and act through trade unions). In the fifth part of the chapter, we offer some concluding reflections on the implications of our analysis.

A Taxonomy of Contestation Rights, and Their Status in the US, UK, and Canada

We will shortly turn to the normative case for a 'right to contest' in the workplace context. But it may be useful first to distinguish two dimensions along which rights of contestation might be arrayed. The first dimension is 'collectiveness'—from the individual dissenter (A) to small, informal groups of dissenters (B)—in both cases with no union in the picture—to groups claiming or seeking union representation. One may divide the latter into those who seek to organize a union (C) and those who claim workforce-wide (even 'exclusive') union representation based, for example, on a majority vote of workers (D). The second dimension is what we might call 'thickness'; it runs from purely negative rights against state interference (1), to state protection of negative rights

[6] Pettit himself defends such a view, in Phillip Pettit, *Republicanism: A Theory of Freedom and Government* (OUP, 1997) 95.

against employer reprisals (2), to an affirmative employer duty to bargain in good faith, enforced by the state (3), to an employer obligation to make reasonable concessions (for example, through mandatory interest arbitration) (4).

It would obviously be possible to divide up these rights differently, and to multiply categories of activity or protection. Our categories are chosen with an eye to the salient features and major variations of US, UK, and Canadian labour law, and even so are quite rudimentary. For example, those who claim union representation on a members-only, non-exclusive basis might be squeezed into row C, or might warrant a separate row. In addition, the taxonomy here leaves out one important type of contestation—the right to withdraw one's labour or to strike. That is not because it is unimportant but because it is too important to squeeze into this taxonomy. We think the 'right to strike' is best conceived as a hybrid of the right to contest and the right to exit or quit, and that it could be usefully decomposed along the same two axes. But we must leave that project for future work.

The most libertarian conception of employee rights would recognize only those in Column 1: the freedom of individual workers to speak up for themselves and contest employer decisions, and to some degree the freedom to do those things in association with others, without state interference.[7] In US law, those rights against state interference (or 'state action') are enshrined in the federal Constitution; Canada and the UK have equivalent protections of these fundamental civil liberties. But most modern market societies, and certainly our three Anglo-American regimes, go further and grant some degree of affirmative state protection of at least some forms of employee contestation. At a minimum, they protect some employee contestation rights against *employer* interference and reprisals (column 2)—and that requires affirmative state intervention on behalf of employee rights.

All three regimes recognize the traditional core of FOA—the right to form and act through a union—as against employer interference (2C and 2D) and all of them protect those rights against employer reprisals. The regimes vary in how broadly and how effectively they protect that right, but that is not our concern here. They all afford formal protection of the right to form trade unions and, subject to majority rule, the right of workers to act through the union to pursue grievances or seek improvements. (Most of the recent constitutional controversies within Canadian labour law concern the 'thickness' of that right—that is, whether and to what extent to populate Column 3 of Rows C and D.)

We are more concerned here, however, with the question whether employees are protected when they act outside the context of a union or union organizing effort—whether they do so as a precursor or as an alternative to union organizing (that is, cells 2A and 2B). Our three regimes vary in the scope of that protection, and they vary in somewhat surprising ways.

To begin with, of the three, the famously liberal US regime appears surprisingly to include the most robust rights of employee contestation. (Perhaps less surprisingly, that appearance turns out to be misleading.) The US labour law regime is the only one of

[7] For a philosophical defence of this libertarian conception, see Richard A. Epstein, 'A Common Law for Labor Relations: a Critique of the New Deal Labor Legislation' (1983) 92 Yale Law Journal 1357.

the three regimes to explicitly protect not only trade union activity, but also informal 'concerted activity' by two or more workers, without any trade union representation or involvement, against employer reprisals (cell 2B).[8] That includes both verbal contestation and strikes. The iconic case is *Washington Aluminum*: several unrepresented workers were fired for walking off the job in protest of cold temperatures; the NLRB, affirmed by the Supreme Court in 1962, held that their work stoppage was protected 'concerted activity', and ordered their reinstatement.[9] That remains the law.

The right to engage in informal concerted activity under the NLRA is not a particularly 'thick' right within our scheme; employers have no duty to bargain with a group of workers, even if they do claim union representation, unless the workers have surmounted the hurdle of majority support and exclusive representation. (Professor Charles Morris has vigorously contended that this is a misinterpretation of the NLRA, and that the duty to bargain should extend to workers who claim union representation on a members-only basis; but the mistake, if it is one, is a fairly entrenched one.[10]) The employer is free to just say no to unrepresented workers' demands; but under the NLRA, the workers cannot be punished merely for voicing them or seeking to bargain.

By contrast, the labour laws of Canada and the UK would not define this informal collective voice as protected activity, even if the employees were merely petitioning the employer for improvements, because protected labour activity is defined in terms of trade union involvement. That is reasonably plain from the face of the Canadian statute, though it is difficult to find cases to illustrate the point.[11] In the UK, the statutory formula explicitly protects an employee who 'had taken part, or proposed to take part, in the activities of an independent trade union'.[12] In *Chant v Aquaboats Ltd*, for example, an employee (who was a trade union member) organized a petition regarding health and safety concerns in the workplace.[13] The petition was vetted but not explicitly authorized by the union before it was presented to the employer. Following his dismissal, the court concluded that there was an insufficient nexus between his individual actions and the trade union; rather, his activities were the (unprotected) activities of an individual trade unionist. In other words, the statutory versions of FOA in Canada and the UK are explicitly confined to the core of trade union activity, with the UK position perhaps representing an extreme example of that tendency.

So US labour law is broader than that of many developed countries in its formal protection of informal concerted activity.[14] But the surprisingly broad protection of

[8] NLRA Sec. 7, 29 USC §157.

[9] *National Labor Relations Board v Washington Aluminum Co.*, 370 U.S. 9 (1962).

[10] See Charles J. Morris, *The Blue Eagle at Work: Reclaiming Democratic Rights in the American Workplace* (Cornell University Press, 2004).

[11] We are grateful to Professor David Doorey for a very helpful discussion of this point.

[12] See Trade Union and Labour Relations (Consolidation) Act 1992, s. 152.

[13] [1978] 3 All ER 102.

[14] Those formal protections are confined to statutory 'employees', and fail to protect many workers' basic FOA; and they are backed up with an enforcement and sanctions regime that fails to deter unlawful reprisals. See Lance Compa, *Unfair Advantage: Workers' Freedom of Association in the United States under International Human Rights Standards* (Cornell University Press, 2000). Moreover, other aspects of formal US labour law are peculiarly crimped. US law on the 'right to strike'—which allows employers to 'permanently replace' most lawful strikers although not to fire them—takes a bigger toll on employees' rights than what is added by the generous conception of 'concerted activity' and is identified by some scholars as a major culprit in union decline in the US. See Julius Getman, *The Betrayal of Local 14: Politics, Paperworkers, and Permanent Replacements* (Cornell University Press, 1999).

'concerted activity' in the US operates against the stark background of employment at will, which generally allows employers to fire employees for no reason. So while it is unlawful under the NLRA for an employer to fire an employee for walking off the job with several co-workers as in *Washington Aluminum*, it is lawful to fire a employee for politely (but singly) questioning a change in work schedules. Employment at will, together with the 'concerted' requirement of the NLRA's protections, leaves individual dissenters, however reasonable their concerns and their means, without a legal leg to stand on.

While UK and Canadian labour laws do not expressly protect either informal collective protest or individual protest outside the confines of union activity, those regimes may afford some indirect protection by way of their unjust dismissal laws (even if those laws are rather weak by international standards). Employers' obligation to justify discharge and serious discipline, or to pay a statutorily prescribed severance stipend, probably affords a measure of indirect protection to workers' non-disruptive forms of contestation, whether they speak up as individuals or in concert with co-workers. It is hard to find cases on point (in part because it is usually much cheaper for employers to pay the modest severance amounts required for unjustified dismissal than to contest the matter in court). But it is almost certainly true that some dismissals based on individual or collective presentation of grievances would be deemed arbitrary and unjustified under these laws.

It is in some ways puzzling that the right to form a union is more firmly and widely established in Western labour law systems, including those on which we focus here, than is the right of individuals to protest injustice, whether alone or in concert with others. Employee contestation rights are most likely to be protected against employer reprisals when they are most likely to disrupt employer interests and most likely to be backed by employees' own collective power. We will argue in what follows that an individual right of contestation is at least as deserving of legal protection—that it is more 'fundamental' than the right to form a union as a matter of first principles, and that it is more necessary given the power imbalance in the non-union setting. But if a puzzle is presented by our survey so far, it is one that is replicated in international labour law itself, which defines the FOA entirely in terms of the formation and freedom of action of trade unions.[15]

When we move further to the right side of the diagram toward a thicker conception of employees' right to contest employer power—the duty to bargain in good faith or even to make concessions to employees—the priority of collective contestation seems more logical, if not inevitable. It is one thing to constrain employers from retaliating against individuals or small groups who raise their voices against employer decisions; it is another thing to affirmatively oblige the employer to bargain with every such individual or group. The resulting imposition on employer discretion and resources, and the limited gains for 'industrial peace', make it unsurprising that these affirmative obligations usually arise only when workers have reached some collective consensus about their grievances and demands.

[15] See e.g. ILO Right to Organise and Collective Bargaining Convention, 1949 (No. 98).

An employer duty to bargain or consult in good faith with individual employees or small groups of employees, without union representation, is neither inconceivable nor unprecedented in Anglo-American law.[16] Professor Matthew Finkin has pointed to a smattering of US laws that obligate employers to meet and confer with employees regarding potential accommodation of employee disabilities, medical needs, or family obligations.[17] Other countries have gone further in requiring employers to deal with unrepresented employees, either as individuals (in the notable case of New Zealand[18]), or through works councils or other mandatory consultation procedures (especially in the EU, including the UK). By and large, however, in the US, UK, and Canada, it is only when a majority within the relevant employee group has chosen union representation that employers acquire affirmative obligations to bargain in good faith, and often to provide relevant information.

Grounding Rights of Individual and Informal Contestation: The arguments internal to labour law

We are obviously not the first to argue for broader protection of both informal concerted activity and individual worker voice, either as prelude to trade union activity or for its own sake. Given the intensity of the crisis in North America, it is no surprise that the leading protagonists in the debate over non-union forms of employee voice are drawn from these jurisdictions. If worker voice is to have a future as well as a glorious past, it is going to have to take forms that fall outside the realm of trade union activity. Indeed, if worker voice *through trade unions* is to have any kind of future, then protecting less institutionalized forms of contestation is equally critical. Given the obduracy of labour law regimes (especially but not only in the US), one crucial question is whether one can ground the protection of those new forms of voice within the existing legal sources.

In the US, positive labour law protects 'concerted activity... for mutual aid or protection', but not (as far as the US courts are concerned) the 'FOA' in international labour law. Canadian law, by contrast, explicitly recognizes the FOA in its Charter, informed by international law; but its labour statutes protect only 'trade union' activity. North American scholars have sought to ground rights to individual and (in Canada) informally concerted activity in those instruments.

Let us begin north of the US border with Professor David Doorey's recent work on 'graduated freedom of association'.[19] Doorey begins with an appealing case for protection: X and Y join a grassroots advocacy group in order to press their temporary employer—a fairground operator—to respect norms of decent work, and are dismissed

[16] As noted previously, Morris argues that the NLRA, properly construed, compels employers to bargain on a members-only basis with employees who choose to be represented by a union.

[17] Matt Finkin, 'Employee Self-Representation and the Law in the United States' Osgoode Hall Law Journal (2013).

[18] For discussion, see Gordon Anderson, 'Good Faith in the Individual Employment Relationship in New Zealand' (2011) 32 Comparative Labor Law and Policy Journal (CLLPJ) 685.

[19] David Doorey, 'Graduated Freedom of Association: Worker Voice beyond the Wagner Model' (2012) 38 Queen's Law Journal 515.

for their trouble. X and Y have no remedy under the Canadian labour relations statutes because they were not engaged in *trade union* activity; unlike US law (but like UK law), there is no statutory protection for informal concerted action outside the union setting. Doorey argues trenchantly that the 'FOA' under the Charter requires at least this much protection for all employees, regardless of statutory coverage. In giving content to this 'thin' version of FOA, Doorey takes as his model the 'much-maligned' Agricultural Employees Protection Act 2002 (AEPA),[20] which protects employees from reprisals for joining and acting through an employee association, and obligates the employer to consider representations and engage in a 'meaningful dialogue' with an employee association. Doorey argues that this 'thin' FOA should operate as a basic floor for all workers, not as a substitute for the traditional Wagner model (as the AEPA is for agricultural workers), but as a supplement. That is, the 'thin' FOA would protect all workers unless or until they had formed a union, at which point it would be displaced by the 'thicker' statutory version of FOA, and exclusive collective bargaining, when its requirements are met.

Given the non-protection of informal, non-union concerted activity under Canadian law, Doorey's argument makes an important contribution to the Canadian debate. Yet the argument seems to beg the question: what right is it that is being exercised in concert, or in association, with others? Is it an individual right to make collective representations to the employer, and to have those representations considered in a process of meaningful dialogue? (That seems nonsensical. How could one have an *individual* right to make *collective* representations?) Or is it an individual right to dissent or to make contestatory demands? If it is the latter, it would seem to require further normative grounding from outside FOA. So argues Professor Brian Langille in the Canadian constitutional context: the FOA, properly understood, is nothing more nor less than the freedom to do with others that which one is at liberty to do as an individual.[21] Let us put aside for now the hotly debated question whether the FOA can, *contra* Langille, serve as a platform from which to ascend to more fulsome trade union rights, such as a right to compel the employer to bargain in good faith through the imposition of correlative duties.[22] But we think Langille is onto something in arguing that, as a conceptual matter, FOA tells us nothing about which things we are entitled to do as an individual.[23] That enquiry depends upon a separate normative theory of an individual's entitlements. Once those individual entitlements are identified, FOA then extends protection when we exercise our individual rights or liberties in concert with others.

The special value of FOA, then, is that it underscores the need to protect individuals when they choose to exercise their liberties or rights with others. One might ask why this is necessary: if the individual action is protected either as liberty or right, doesn't

[20] SO 2002, c 16, as construed in *Ontario (AG) v Fraser*, 2011 SCC 20, [2011] 2 SCR 3.

[21] Brian Langille, 'The Freedom of Association Mess: How we got into it and how we can get out of it' (2009) 54 McGill Law Journal 177, which draws upon the earlier work of Sheldon Leader, *Freedom of Association* (Yale University Press, 1992).

[22] For a defence of the view that it can serve as a platform, see Alan L. Bogg and Keith Ewing, 'A (Muted) Voice at Work? Collective Bargaining in the Supreme Court of Canada' (2012) 33 CLLPJ 379.

[23] That is, which things we are at liberty to do or have a right to do. One might still contend on empirical, practical grounds that the FOA requires the protection of individual and informally concerted activity.

this individual protection protect the group in an aggregative way? But historically the collective dimension itself has often drawn reprisals. That is shown by the laws condemning conspiracy and 'combinations' in restraint of trade, and the application of both to collective labour activity; that is good reason in itself to underscore the entitlement to act collectively when it exists. Moreover, concerted action by employees is often more threatening than individual protest to managerial prerogatives, and more likely to trigger reprisals. For that reason, too, it may be necessary to expressly affirm legal protection for concerted activity through FOA. But we should be sceptical of attempts to derive those individual rights that are being exercised collectively from FOA itself.

The enquiry may seem like an esoteric quibble, but much can be lost by failing to take it on. For example, Doorey suggests that his version of 'thin' FOA does not imply an individual right to strike. That makes sense; one cannot ground such a right in FOA alone—i.e., in the liberty to do with others what one is entitled to do alone. But if there is (as we believe) a deeper basis for an individual right to withdraw labour, then FOA *can* protect individuals' right to withdraw labour in concert with others.[24] Similarly, we think Doorey's argument for (at least) the 'thin' freedom of workers to associate with others peacefully to pursue shared aims seems to assume a more basic individual right peacefully to pursue one's own aims. We do not think that the 'thin' collective freedom he advocates can be derived from 'above', that is, from FOA itself.

It may be more fruitful to start from the more concrete statutory rights to engage in trade union activity and, in US law, 'other concerted activity'. One may be able to reason 'down' from the right to form and join a union to informal concerted action (or 'down' from the right to engage in concerted activity to rights of individual dissent) based on legislative purpose.[25] One such argument, previewed earlier, is practical, and is based on the apparent psychology of collective action: it often takes someone who is willing to stand up to the employer, even alone, to plant the seeds of concerted activity and eventually union organizing. That appears to be the instinct underlying cases like *Washington Aluminum* in the US: informal concerted activity may be the early stirrings of collective impulses that may lead to union organizing. We think these psychological arguments gain persuasive power as union density falls. In the old days, workers who were dissatisfied with workplace terms and conditions might be expected to consider unionization as a matter of course; unionization was familiar and normal, and dissident impulses were quite likely to flow into union channels. That is no longer true for many non-union workers. So even if FOA means the right to form and join trade unions, that right, to be effective, might require the protection of 'pre-union' forms of employee dissent.

A different sort of argument can be found in the US labour board's erstwhile theory of 'constructive concerted activity': individual employee complaints about a breach of

[24] And if there is an individual right to withdraw labour in protest of employer action under some circumstances (a hybrid of the right to quit and the right to contest), and to be free from employer reprisals in doing so, then the FOA may protect a right to strike in association with others. As noted earlier, we think these issues require more elaboration than we can give them here.

[25] Langille is thus wrong, we think, to the extent that he argues that the FOA *cannot* mean anything more than the liberty to do in concert what one is entitled to do as an individual. A particular enactment of that language might mean more than that as a matter of positive law.

public statutory regulations were treated by the NLRB for a time as 'concerted activity' because such complaints were *presumed* to be of concern to employees as a group and to have been made on behalf of those workers.[26] The idea of 'constructive concerted activity' captures a functional truth that individual activity in fact can advance collective interests. The argument was rejected by most courts on textual grounds, and has since been abandoned by the NLRB. But much like the 'group psychology' argument, this is an attempt to derive an individual right of dissent based on its kinship with group dissent (without putting either one on a firm normative footing).

Professors Gorman and Finkin in their important 1981 article begin to fill that gap.[27] They argue that the statutory language does not require the paradox of permitting the dismissal of an individual employee who voices a grievance about her salary while protecting a group of employees who voice the same grievance. They contend that the historical proponents of workers' foundational legal rights assumed that individual worker protest was lawful and entitled to protection, but that they insisted on singling out 'concerted' activity in order to repudiate a history of heightened legal hostility to concerted worker action. Gorman and Finkin conclude that the statutory distinction between individual and concerted action 'proceeds upon a false dichotomy, for at the core of the freedom of the individual to protest in a group necessarily lies the freedom of the individual to protest at all'.[28] But why 'necessarily'? Theirs is chiefly a masterful argument about the proper interpretation of the NLRA's Section 7 given the particular history behind that language; they do not, because they do not have to, probe the normative basis for protecting individual protest against reprisals. But they argue that, for the statute's proponents, the answers lie in the contemporary meaning of 'industrial democracy' and 'industrial citizenship', which animated the framers of the NLRA and thus illuminate the purpose of the statute.[29] In that they come very close to what we consider the heart of the matter.

In more recent work, Finkin configures the 'right to complain' more broadly in terms of enabling individual contractual agency, a form of individual self-representation, not as a precursor to union representation but as a substitute (for some employees and some topics).[30] He begins by pointing to strong evidence that many employees prefer individual bargaining to group bargaining, especially on topics that implicate privacy concerns. Finkin shows that, in the epic New Deal shift from the old regime of individual liberty of contract, and the well-nigh irrebuttable presumption that individuals were capable of bargaining for themselves, to the embrace of government support for collective bargaining, US law missed the intermediate step of attempting to ensure that individuals actually could bargain or at least speak up for themselves. By leaving intact the employment at will presumption, subject to the right to bargain (mainly through a union) for protection against arbitrary dismissal, unrepresented individuals were left again without a leg to stand on in dealing with their employer.

[26] For discussion, see Robert A. Gorman and Matt W. Finkin, 'The Individual and the Requirement of "Concert" under the National Labor Relations Act' (1981) 130 University of Pennsylvania Law Review 286, 289–310.

[27] Gorman and Finkin (n 26).

[28] Gorman and Finkin 345 (n 26).

[29] Gorman and Finkin 343 (n 26).

[30] Finkin (n 17).

The focus of Finkin's recent article is not on the normative case for a right to complain but mainly on where it can and cannot be found in US law and elsewhere. He describes US law on the matter as a formless mishmash of assorted protections that add up to much less than a robust 'right to complain', or right of self-representation. And he argues in short—going back to our taxonomy—that the law should complete its very halting and partial move from Box A/1 to Box A/2, and guarantee the protection of individual complaints and suggestions against employer reprisals. The article is highly provocative, and productive, for its rehabilitation of an individual bargaining right and the attempt to identify and fortify its legal manifestation. But it does not go as far as the earlier co-authored article does in identifying the normative foundations of the individual right to complain.

What is still missing is a sustained normative defence of an individual right to complain. Without that normative defence, it might easily be caricatured as a charter for the disgruntled and disaffected. With a proper normative defence, the individual right to complain could become a sturdy basis upon which to build upward—to ground both existing and as-yet unrecognized rights to engage in informal concerted activity, and even to more firmly ground existing rights to engage in trade union activity.

Non-domination as a Basis for Fundamental Labour Rights

We think that there is a deeper conceptual foundation for these individual and informal contestation rights, one that clarifies their relation to the conventional FOA right to form and act through a trade union, and that grounds the case for the full range of employee contestation rights up to and including union activity. We find that conceptual foundation in Professor Philip Pettit's influential elaboration of a 'republican' theory of political justice, the foundation of which is his conception of 'freedom as non-domination'.[31] Using this framework, we derive an *individual right of contestation* that provides a possible method for refining and clarifying the foundations in the strategy of descent as developed by Doorey and Finkin.

On Pettit's theory of *freedom as non-domination*, a citizen's freedom is compromised where other agents (individual or collective) enjoy a capacity to interfere arbitrarily in her choices. 'Being unfree does not consist in being restrained; on the contrary, the restraint of a fair system of law—a non-arbitrary regime—does not make you unfree. Being unfree consists rather in being subject to the potentially capricious will or the potentially idiosyncratic judgement of another.'[32] Even if there is no actual interference in choices, the vulnerability to interference is a form of unfreedom, for it forces one to anticipate and accommodate oneself to the other's desires, backed as they are by the power to interfere. Moreover, and especially where there is a shared awareness of this vulnerability, it is a shaming and demeaning status to occupy. The dominated citizen might resort to strategies of deference or subterfuge in order to placate the powerful.

[31] See, particularly, Pettit (2012) (n 4). [32] Pettit (1997) 5 (n 6).

By contrast, the free citizen enjoys that status in virtue of laws, institutions, and social norms that impose effective external constraints on the capacity of other agents to interfere in her choices arbitrarily or with impunity. 'Freedom... requires the capacity to stand eye to eye with your fellow citizens, in a shared awareness that none of you has a power of arbitrary interference over another.'[33] Pettit distinguishes this view from liberalism's insistence on 'negative' freedom from interference, and on the centrality of 'consent' to justify the exercise of authority over others.[34] 'Freedom as non-domination' shifts the focus—helpfully, we think—from consent to contestability.

We do not pretend to offer a full defence of Pettit's theory here; he does that rather well himself. But one of its attractive features is that it puts the employment relationship, and the characteristic asymmetries of power inherent in that relation, near the centre of democratic theory (where we think it belongs).[35] To see why, consider Pettit's basic heuristic for judging whether freedom as non-domination is ensured:

> [P]eople should securely enjoy resources and protections to the point where they satisfy what we might call the eyeball test. They can look others in the eye without reason for the fear or deference that a power of interference might inspire; they can walk tall and assume the public status... of being equal in this regard with the best.[36]

Its application is conditioned by the local circumstances in a given political community. Where the citizen's 'basic liberties' are supported by a mix of legal protections and public resources that meet this 'eyeball test', it can be said that the citizen is 'the liber, or "free person", in the republican tradition.'[37]

Pettit goes on to elaborate a number of basic liberties that are necessary to fulfil this 'eyeball test', several of which go directly to the ability of the *employee* to look into the eye of her employer without fear or hesitation: the freedom to express what one thinks; the freedom to associate with others who are likewise willing to associate; and the freedom to change occupation and employment.[38] We want to argue that, if and only if these three basic liberties are secured, then employees are sufficiently free from domination by their employer so as to meet the requirements of republican citizenship. Moreover, we want to argue that 'freedom as non-domination' supplies a normative foundation for individual and informally concerted employee contestation of employer power, as well as for the freedom to form and act through trade unions.

The freedom to change occupation and employment

We begin, albeit just briefly, with the employee's freedom to quit the employment relationship and to choose to enter contractual relations with other employers. In our view, the importance of this labour freedom cannot be gainsaid. But we leave for another day

[33] Pettit 5 (1997) (n 6).

[34] And he sees elements of the republican view lurking in the more attractive versions of liberalism.

[35] Pettit (2012) 114–15 (n 4). In Otto Kahn-Freund's canonical reflections on law and power, and the subordinate nature of the employment relation, we detect an alignment with Pettit's core ideas of non-domination. For further discussion, see Alan L. Bogg, *The Democratic Aspects of Trade Union Recognition* (Hart, 2009) 146–7.

[36] Pettit (2012) 84 (n 4). [37] Pettit (2012) 82 (n 4). [38] Pettit (2012) 103 (n 4).

the elaboration of this freedom and in particular its relation to the 'right to strike'. For now we simply observe that the 'eyeball test' heuristic may put in doubt the legitimacy of various contractual devices for limiting the employee's freedom to quit, such as post-termination restrictive covenants or extensive notice periods.[39]

The basic liberty to quit and change jobs or occupations, suitably protected and resourced, is a necessary but by no means a sufficient safeguard in ensuring non-domination in the employment relationship.[40] Nor is it the case, as Richard Epstein contends, that respect for the employee's right to quit requires respect for the employer's right to fire at will. On the contrary, the employer's right to fire an employee arbitrarily typically enables 'domination', and thus threatens the freedom, of the latter in ways that the employee's freedom to quit does not enable the employee to dominate the employer.[41] Even good employers in an at-will world are a dominating presence in the lives of their employees because they have *the capacity to interfere for ill* in their employees' choices. Such a state of affairs would fail to meet the 'eyeball test'.

The fundamental 'freedom from domination' offers a rationale for much of what Pettit identifies as the 'standard approach' to regulating in spheres such as employment, that is, imposing 'legal duties on the presumptively stronger party . . . and thereby establishing the corresponding rights of the weaker'.[42] Conventional labour rights regulating the minimum wage and working time, for example, put a floor on the employer's power to modify elements of the employment relation unilaterally, and thus curtail the employer's capacity to interfere in the employee's choices. But the link between 'freedom as non-domination' and employment protections is especially clear with regard to measures 'restricting or regulating the right of an employer to fire at will' as a way of 'screening out various options for the stronger'.[43] As already observed, even if there are economic incentives for employers to behave well towards employees, and even if most employers do behave well towards employees, the absence of legal restriction on arbitrary dismissal comports with domination.

The freedom to express what one thinks, or to contest employer power

The point is underscored when we turn to the 'freedom to express what one thinks'. An employee who can be fired for no reason is subject to the employer's arbitrary interference in her choices; but among the choices in which the employer is free to interfere is the choice to protest or contest employer policies or decisions. We agree that general

[39] It may also cast doubt on immigration restrictions that tie the right to remain in a territory to employment with a single employer, and may require provision public resources in the form of a system of public unemployment insurance. See Pettit (2012) 113–15 (n 4).

[40] Cf Richard A. Epstein, 'In Defense of the Contract at Will' (1984) 51 University of Chicago Law Review 947.

[41] Economically-minded critics might respond that 'domination' (just like 'inequality of bargaining power') is all a matter of labour market forces, which might in any particular case favour the employee. We think that employees' ability to 'dominate' an employer is a rare exception that should not distract from the far more usual case of employer domination. Even a highly skilled employee usually experiences far more economic and social dislocation in the event of discharge than an employer experiences in the event of an important employee's departure, in part because of the virtual impossibility for the employee of diversifying her investment of her own 'human capital' or of storing it up for future use.

[42] Pettit (2012) 115 (n 4).

[43] Pettit (2012) 115 (n 4).

legal protection from arbitrary dismissal is necessary to ensure non-domination. It limits the scope for the most oppressive forms of arbitrary treatment in the workplace, and in so doing it creates a milieu where employees can begin to meet their employer's eye. In our view, however, something more is needed to ensure non-domination. This is the employee's right to *challenge* and *contest* the employer's discretionary decision-making as it relates to the situation of the employee: let us call this the individual right to contestation. It is only where there is an individual right to contestation, protected against reprisals, that the employee is free from employer domination in her working life. While 'for cause' protection creates a moral environment that does not pervasively chill expressive activity in the workplace, neither does it guarantee specific protection for a right to contestation.[44]

The employee's right to contest is a workplace-specific instantiation of the basic liberty to express one's thoughts. The right promotes the employee's freedom by checking the employer's prerogative. The employee's right to contest is more precise than the more general basic liberty of free expression from which it is derived. It singles out for special protection speech that is by its nature agonistic and that is likely at times to be very unwelcome to employers. In our view, the republican theory of freedom as non-domination provides a compelling normative justification for Gorman and Finkin's idea of a 'right to complain'. That is not surprising, for Gorman and Finkin rely on strains of early twentieth-century US labour thought to inform the historic meaning of workers' basic statutory rights; and those strains of thought were self-consciously carrying forward the 'republican' tradition from which Pettit draws his own theory of freedom as non-domination.

Of course, the right to contest is rather abstract and we know of no legal systems that recognize and protect an abstract 'right to contest' as such. Rather, the abstract right to contestation is implemented in more specific domains of regulatory activity in different legal systems. The contours of implementation will vary across the following range of parameters:

(a) Substantive scope of contestation. What sorts of employer decisions or actions should employees have the right to contest? This issue resembles scope issues arising under existing labour law, for example, in defining what counts as 'mutual aid or protection' with regard to which employees may engage in 'concerted activity' under the NLRA. We think the right to contest should encompass at least the following sorts of topics, mostly familiar within our family of legal systems: (i) employee contestation of union *and non-union* governance structures, including employees' campaigning for or against trade union representation, participating in any statutory procedures for determining whether consultative arrangements enjoy the requisite employee approval, and contesting unilateral employer decisions to establish non-union forms of employee representation; (ii) employees' assertion of statutory employment rights against employers; (iii) employees' presentation of grievances or complaints regarding terms or conditions of employment. It is an interesting and important question whether

[44] That is, without a right to contest, contestation could be considered 'cause' for discipline or discharge. Of course, the right to contest might be secured through an unjust dismissal regime by a stipulation that reasonable exercise of contestation rights would not constitute just cause for dismissal.

employees' right to contest extends beyond terms and conditions of employment to matters of concern to the public (such as violation of environmental or securities laws or threats to public, patient, or customer safety). We think it should, but we recognize such an extension might require additional pillars of support beyond what is presented here.

(b) Legal protection. What should be the form (or 'thickness' as per the horizontal dimension of Table 7.1) of legal protection?

Table 7.1 A two-dimensional taxonomy of contestation rights

A Two-Dimensional Taxonomy of Contestation Rights

Employee Contestation: Level/thickness of protection → (from least to most protection) **What type of contestation is protected?** (from least (bottom) to most collective)↓	**(1) Employee (Ee) contestation is free from state sanctions (but unprotected vs. Employer (Er) reprisals)**	**(2) Employee contestation is protected by state vs. Employer reprisals**	**(3) Employer is req'd to bargain in good faith (may include duty to provide info, e.g.)**	**(4) Employer is req'd to reach agreement or submit to state-imposed resolution of disputes/ mandatory interest arbitration**
(D) Majority of Ees in relevant bargaining unit who choose U representation	(1/D) Majority of workers w/ in workplace/ bargaining unit may lawfully choose to be rep'd by U, speak thru U	(2/D) . . . & it is unlawful for Er to coerce/ retaliate against Ees making that choice	(3/D) Er must confer/ bargain in GF w/U that rep's majority of its Ees	(4/D) Mandatory arbitration of interest disputes w/majority U representative
(C) Any Ees who seek or choose U representation (U organizing & minority U/'members-only')	(1/C) Any group of Ees may lawfully associate w/a Union & present grievances thru U	(2/C) . . . & it is unlawful for Er to coerce/ retaliate against Ees who do so	(3/C) Er must confer/ bargain in GF w/U that rep's any of its Ees	(4/C) Mandatory arbitration of interest disputes w/ any group of Ees rep'd by U
(B) 2 or more individual Ees acting in concert ('concerted activity')	(1/B) Ees may lawfully associate w/ fellow workers & act peacefully in concert	(2/B) . . . & it is unlawful for Er to coerce/ retaliate against Ees for engaging in such concerted actions	(3/B) Er must confer in GF w/any 2+ Ees who present shared grievances	(4/B) Mandatory arbitration of interest disputes w/ any 2+ Ees
(A) Individual Ee	(1/A) Ee cannot be punished by state for speaking up, presenting grievances	(2/A) . . . & it is unlawful for Er to coerce/ retaliate against Ees who do so	(3/A) Er must confer in GF w/ individual Ees	(4/A) Mandatory arbitration of interest disputes w/ any single Ee

(i) Clearly a right to contest would fail to meet the 'eyeball test' were it not accompanied by robust safeguards against employer victimization (i.e., Column 2), whether through dismissal, threatened dismissal, or other forms of coercive interference. The scattered manifestations of the right to contest in existing law (which mainly protect employees who disclose or protest violations of statutory rights or public interests) tend to be shielded by prohibitions against employer retaliation. In US law these legal protections stand as important exceptions to employment at will; in other jurisdictions such protections often augment those entailed by unfair dismissal laws,[45] or add remedies to mark the special seriousness of the violation. The republican 'eyeball test' would also be astute to the procedural and institutional context to the right's enforcement, such as provision for legal representation, attorney fees, and costs, and standing rules that enable bodies such as trade unions to participate in the legal process.

(ii) The 'eyeball test' might militate in favour of more affirmative support for the 'right to contest'. Apart from imposing on employers a duty to consider in good faith employees' proposals or criticisms (which we consider later), we can imagine a case for other forms of affirmative support, such as the public provision of sufficient resources to ensure that the right to contest is a real right rather than a mere paper right. Those resources might consist in legal rights to information, without which an employee may not know when contestation is warranted.[46] The provision of expert assistance can also enhance employees' capacities to engage in contestation in an assured and effective way, either directly as under the European Works Councils legislation,[47] or through providing access to trade union support in specific contexts.[48] The republican 'eyeball test' would also countenance public support, perhaps through favourable tax subsidies, for community-based labour initiatives such as the 'labor-community' organizations, religious groups and worker advice centres.[49] These new groups can be a valuable source of moral support and expertise for employees engaged in workplace contestation.

We concede that, in reciting this 'wish list' of affirmative entitlements, we have gone beyond what might be defended as a minimum constellation of employee rights consistent with the 'eyeball test'. The non-domination principle is robust enough to

[45] In UK law, the concept of 'automatically unfair reasons' is marked out as a special protective category in unfair dismissal legislation, protecting employees from victimization for asserting statutory rights. This ensures that such dismissals cannot ever be justified as reasonable in all the circumstances.

[46] Cynthia Estlund, 'Just the Facts? The Case for Workplace Transparency' (2011) 63 Stanford Law Review 351.

[47] See, for example, Transnational Information and Consultation of Employees Regulations 1999, SI 1999/3323, reg. 16 (5)–(6).

[48] See, for example, the right to a trade union companion in certain grievance and disciplinary contexts, set out in s. 10 of the Employment Relations Act 1999. Another resourcing technique is the legal entrenchment of paid time off rights for training purposes, especially for designated employee representatives.

[49] See Katherine Stone and Scott Cummings, 'Labor Activism in Local Politics: From CBAs to "CBAs"' in Guy Davidov and Brian Langille (eds), *The Idea of Labour Law* (OUP, 2011) 273.

generate norms and desiderata as well as minimum requirements for a decent 'republican' regime of workplace rights, but our present focus is on the latter.

(iii) One form of 'affirmative support'—that is, state enforcement of employer duties of engagement—calls for separate consideration. One can certainly argue that it is not sufficient to prevent employers from victimizing employees who exercise their right to contest, and that the mutual respect that underpins non-domination requires that the contestation is taken seriously by the employer as the beginning of a dialogue. That is consistent with New Zealand's recognition of the employer's duty to consider even individual complaints and proposals in good faith.[50] At the same time, we have already conceded that, for purely practical reasons, a duty to consider employee proposals or protests in good faith is bound to be narrower with regard to individual or informal contestation than it is with regard to contestation through a trade union with majority support among the workers.

We applaud the New Zealand law, as well as Finkin's proposal for a broader right of self-representation, both of which entail a correlative employer duty to bargain with individuals. But we view a legal duty to bargain in good faith with individuals as reaching beyond minimum standards toward a more fulsome realization of the aspirations of 'freedom as non-domination'. Such legal duties are clearly permissible, and are often good policy, but in our view they are not part of the minimum set of entitlements that is necessary to support employee freedom, understood as non-domination.

This concession in regard to the 'thickness' of the individual right to contest makes sense, we think, only in view of some further implications of 'freedom as non-domination', and especially the collective dimension of the individual right to contest. The latter will bring us back to the scope of the duty to bargain in good faith.

The freedom to associate with others who are willing to associate[51]

We agree with Langille that the freedom of association as a basic normative principle entitles individuals to do in concert with others what each has the right to do individually (though we disagree with the implication that positive international or national law on FOA does not or cannot expand upon this protection). That means that individual employees are entitled to join with their fellows to contest employer decisions and conduct, and thereby to bring social pressure to bear on an employer, free from employer reprisals. We think the freedom to engage in collective contestation—with one or two or many co-workers—is a vital element to ensuring non-domination in the workplace setting. At a minimum that entails a collective right to cease work (as a hybrid of the right to quit and the right to do so in association with others).[52] As noted previously, however, we leave for another day the question of how far these basic principles go in requiring protection of a 'right to strike'.

[50] Anderson (n 18). [51] Pettit (2012) 103 (n 4).

[52] For an exploration of the linkages between freedom of speech and the right to strike, see Tonia Novitz, *International and European Protection of the Right to Strike* (OUP, 2003) 71–3.

There are two dimensions to the basic liberty of association with others.

(a) The republican conception of freedom of association would envisage a robust set of legal protections for the basic form of concerted activity where X and Y associate with each other for a permissible purpose, and in particular for the purpose of contestation. Recall Doorey's powerful example of temporary fairground employees meeting clandestinely with community organizers in order to avoid the employer retaliation that would be perfectly lawful under Canadian labour law. This quite obviously fails to meet the threshold of sufficiency set by the 'eyeball test'. That is partly because, for ordinary employees, individual contestation is unlikely to be effective; it is unlikely to enable employees to meet their employer's eye in presenting grievances. That is the practical importance of affirming X's and Y's freedom to associate with each other as willing citizens.[53] As Pettit observes, concerted action leads to 'a form of civility which leads [citizens] to work at organizing the group and at articulating shared grievances',[54] which in turn leads to the emergence of groups in civil society that act as checks on dominating power. For these reasons, only US law (as a formal matter) meets the 'eyeball test' in its protection of basic, informal concerted activity. Canadian and UK law, in protecting only the narrower category of trade union activity, do not.

(b) We would nevertheless expect to see specific protections for trade union rights in the sphere of freedom of association. Pettit himself acknowledges that 'legalizing the unionization of employees and recourse to strike action' is a necessary element in a legal system that tackles employer domination effectively.[55] And we have already noted that basic forms of concerted contestation evolve into more familiar patterns of trade union association and activity; indeed, trade unions are the paradigmatic form of contestatory associational activity in the workplace. The basic employee liberty as non-domination, and its 'eyeball test', provide strong normative grounds for requiring robust protection of union organizing, collective bargaining demands, and collective action (that is, doing together what one has the basic right to do as individuals) against employer reprisals.

(c) By contrast, the basic liberty may not include an employer duty to bargain in good faith. In other words, it would appear that the strategy of descent—that is, of discerning rights that are less formal and less institutionalized than trade union activity—has a firmer philosophical basis in Pettit's theory than does the strategy of ascent—that is, of 'thickening' the rights of trade unions. For example, Pettit says that 'basic liberties' 'cannot extend to liberties on the part of anyone to determine how others act';[56] and he argues against laws that entrench the rights of existing groups in freedom of association 'since this would favour those who already happen to have formed such groups and would fail to treat people equally.'[57]

[53] As Pettit has argued in *On the People's Terms* (n 4, 129), law is only likely to be constitutive of non-domination when 'being disposed to approve of compliance and to disapprove of deviance, citizens can become non-intentional sources of enforcement, as they observe one another's behaviour, and form attitudes of approval and disapproval in response'.

[54] Pettit (1997) (n 6). [55] Pettit (2012) 115 (n 4). [56] Pettit (2012) 94 (n 4).

[57] Pettit (2012) 95 fn 14 (n 4).

A conception of the basic liberty that is neutral between different forms of association, and sceptical of the particular privileges of existing 'trade unions',[58] would open the field of employee representation to new forms of association that employees might choose to represent them. That would be a good thing. On the other hand, it might rule out a fundamental *right* to collective bargaining that entails duties on employers to bargain in good faith with a trade union.[59] That might discourage some labour lawyers from embracing non-domination as an animating ideal for labour law. But it is important to observe that this animating ideal might nonetheless permit positive law (*including positive international law*) that imposes on employers a duty to bargain with trade unions or other employee associations, and that imposes a higher duty to bargain with associations that meet a threshold level of support among employees (as the Wagner model does). We think that is the case even if 'liberty as non-domination' does not require such a duty as a normative matter.[60]

Fortifying or Undermining the 'Freedom of Association'? On the Supportive Role of an Individual Right to Contest

We anticipate an important objection to our claim that individual rights of contestation, exercised singly or in concert with others, should be regarded as the basic substrate of FOA.[61] The objection begins with positive international labour law, which protects a specific form of concerted activity, trade union activity, rather than concerted activity as such.[62] But the objection it is grounded in a deeper concern that excavating the foundations of the traditional FOA right to engage in trade union activity might end up undermining that right—that 'deconstruction' such as we undertake might lead toward destruction.

It is important to acknowledge that FOA as it is embodied in the ILO instruments and committee decisions should not be regarded as some kind of Platonic form. Like any legislated standard, ILO conventions (and the ILO's tripartite governance structure itself) reflect the concerns of the constituencies that participated in their

[58] Compare, however, Stuart White, 'Liberal Neutrality and Trade Unions' (2012) 33 CLLPJ 417.

[59] See Langille (n 21) and cf Bogg and Ewing 393–7 (n 22).

[60] That view may be consistent with Doorey, who argues that the FOA under international and Canadian labour law should entail an employer duty to consider in good faith proposals presented by employees through some kind of association, and to engage in 'meaningful dialogue' with such an association. (Again, that is roughly what the Canadian *Agricultural Employees Protection Act 2002* provides, albeit as a substitute for Wagner-like protections rather than, as Doorey proposes, a supplement.) This would impose a lesser duty at a lower threshold of formality than the existing statutory duty to bargain exclusively and in good faith, and with an eye to reaching an agreement, with a majority-backed trade union. We think that strikes a fair balance of interests, and may reflect positive international law on FOA, whether or not the duty to bargain is required as a matter of fundamental normative principles.

[61] We thank Professor Mark Freedland for pressing this objection in a seminar discussion in Oxford. We also note that Doorey anticipates a very similar objection, or set of objections, to his idea of 'graduated FOA'. See Doorey 538–42 (n 19).

[62] Take Art. 1 of ILO Convention 98, for example, which specifies that 'workers shall enjoy adequate protection against acts of anti-union discrimination in respect of their employment'.

negotiation and the bargaining power that trade unions have historically exercised in shaping these institutions. Those historic circumstances, and the resulting language and institutions of international law, are obviously entitled to great respect as legally binding norms, and they carry with them a bundle of (admittedly mostly 'soft' and quite weak) legal consequences. For those who already embrace the trade-union-centred version of FOA, that may be all that is needed. Those readers may or may not be persuaded by the arguments of others, which we review and support in the third part of the chapter, for deriving rights to individual and informally concerted activity from this positive law protection of FOA. But they do not need to be persuaded as to the essential need to protect trade union activity itself.

The problem is that, as trade union membership and political power wane, more and more of the crucial participants in debates that affect labour rights are asking that very question (whether expressly or not). Why protect trade unions and trade union activity as such? Invocations of 'unequal bargaining power' do not answer that question for sceptics; inequalities, just and unjust, abound in the world, and do not necessarily call for the intervention of international law. Proponents of the FOA, understood solely as the right to form and act through trade unions, portray the FOA as a 'human right', alongside the freedom from forced labour, from the worst forms of child labour, and from discrimination. But that does not quite answer the 'why' question. The right to act through a historically particularized institution—one that exercises power and enjoys various rights even as it is embattled—can easily be caricatured by opponents as a reflection of the political power of that institution rather than of basic human rights. Its foundations are perhaps less self-evident than basic prohibitions of child labour or forced labour—at least to those who are not already believers.

It is partly in hopes of fortifying those foundations that we offer our own argument about freedom from domination and what it requires in the context of work. The idea of freedom from domination by others as a basic entitlement in a decent society aims in part to show why the right to form and act through trade unions, the traditional FOA, is fundamental. But that fundamental right is itself built up from other more basic rights that are logically prior to it, and that are under-protected or even ignored in most legal regimes we know about. So as the case for the traditional FOA meets resistance, as it is increasingly likely to do if current trends continue, it is important not only to be able to explain why the traditional FOA is fundamental, but also to begin to make the case for broader protection of the rights on which the FOA builds.

But that leads to the second dimension of the anticipated misgivings about our argument. For the choice to start with trade union activity (as in the Canadian and UK systems) may reflect both a deeper normative concern and a practical political concern. The normative concern might be that the protection of basic concerted activity is the protection of a highly individualized form of FOA. As a political matter, if the substrate of FOA is individualized in this way, it arguably constitutes a precarious and unstable foundation upon which the more collective forms of FOA may totter and even collapse. Individual and informally concerted contestation might be regarded by many as an adequate substitute for trade union activity, and to undermine the case for protecting the latter. That would be very undesirable, certainly from the perspective of non-domination as a baseline principle.

Thus stated, the objection is important but not unanswerable. Leaving aside the point that even group rights are based ultimately upon individuals and their interests,[63] there are three more specific responses. First, as we and others have already argued, basic forms of concerted activity are often the prelude to the emergence of trade union activity. Workers learn to collectivize through shared endeavour and it is often a natural next step to form or join a trade union.[64] In this way, the protection of trade union activity is practically dependent upon the protection of basic concerted activity.

Secondly, if there is a concern that basic concerted action might serve to undermine the cohesiveness and solidarity of trade union organization, for example by encouraging fragmentation of workers' collectivities, this can be curtailed through smart regulatory design. One possibility would be to limit (though not eliminate) legal protection for basic concerted activity in situations where there is a certified majority union. It should also be remembered that the protection of contestatory rights can serve a useful function in allowing workers to challenge non-union structures where these are regarded as contrary to the workers' interests.[65]

Finally, we should keep in view the analytic distinction between, on the one hand, the protection of concerted activity through FOA and, on the other hand, the specific individual right or entitlement that is being exercised collectively. We have argued in defence of an individual right to contestation as a fundamental labour right. Where *this* is the individual right that is being exercised collectively, the relation between basic concerted activity and trade union activity is likely to be mutually reinforcing. By contrast, the risks of destabilization of collective interests might be more pronounced where 'individual contractual agency' is taken as the relevant base right (as in Finkin's more recent work).

Conclusion

We view this chapter as illuminating an important research agenda in comparative labour law, rather than providing any definitive answers. Understanding the ways in which a fundamental right to contestation is implemented and impeded in these various jurisdictions is a vital mapping exercise and one that is worthy of the attention of comparative labour lawyers. Also important are the ways in which FOA is configured in these different systems, and the ways in which FOA and the right to contestation interact in specific regulatory contexts.

At a deeper level, we see this work as provoking a vital methodological engagement with the issue of how to identify 'fundamental labour rights'. In an important recent contribution to the topic, Hugh Collins has deployed a Rawlsian 'original position' approach to the identification of fundamental labour rights, which leads him to specify FOA as the right to form and join trade unions simpliciter.[66] This is a controversial

[63] Bogg and Ewing 401–8 (n 22).

[64] See e.g. the facts in *Palomo Sanchez v Spain* [2011] ECHR 1319, where informal concerted contestatory activity developed quite naturally into the formation of, and acting through, a trade union.

[65] See, for example, the ballot procedures in the Information and Consultation of Employees Regulations 2004, reg. 8 and reg. 30(6).

[66] Collins (n 2).

move, not least because Rawls himself was careful to confine that methodology to ascertaining the 'basic structure' of liberal societies rather than resolving discrete normative issues in the sphere of work. By contrast, we have started to work through the very different implications of Pettit's republican 'eyeball test'. On this alternative approach, rather than sitting blindfold behind the veil of ignorance, the worker is invited to sit and look her employer squarely in the eye, and to explore what rights and resources would make that possible given the power dynamics of real workplaces.

8

Promoting Worker Voice through Good Faith Bargaining Laws

The Canadian and Australian Experience

Anthony Forsyth and Sara Slinn***

Introduction

Worker voice through collective bargaining has been a mainstay of the Canadian industrial relations system for the last 70 years. However, 'enterprise bargaining' is a more recent innovation in Australia, emerging in the 1990s to overshadow conciliation and arbitration[1] as the principal basis for determining employment conditions—and as a vehicle for employee voice.[2] Good faith bargaining (GFB) obligations have formed part of federal and provincial collective bargaining laws in Canada almost since their inception. GFB is, again, a concept adopted much more recently in Australia—finding its fullest expression in the statutory collective bargaining framework introduced as part of the former Labor government's 'Fair Work' reforms in 2009.[3]

GFB obligations are a feature not only of Canadian and Australian labour law. They also form part of the United States and New Zealand collective bargaining systems, although each has taken different statutory approaches to implementing GFB. In the US and Canada the GFB is coupled with an explicit statutory obligation on parties to bargain.[4] Under the US NLRA the GFB is expressed as obligation 'to confer in good faith',[5] while in Canada GFB provisions typically impose a double obligation on parties: to bargain in good faith and to 'make every reasonable effort to conclude a collective agreement'.[6] In light of this limited statutory guidance, the scope and content of

* Professor, Graduate School of Business and Law, RMIT University, Melbourne, Australia. The authors would like to thank Lara Anderson of the BCLRB for providing administrative data for this project.

** Associate Professor, Osgoode Hall Law School, York University, Toronto, Canada.

[1] Collective bargaining operated as an adjunct to the traditional conciliation and arbitration system from its establishment in 1904, mainly through the practice of 'over-award bargaining': Breen Creighton and Andrew Stewart, *Labour Law*, 5th edn (Federation Press, 2010) 292–4.

[2] See further Alan Bogg, Anthony Forsyth, and Tonia Novitz, 'Worker Voice in Australia and New Zealand: The Role of the State Reconfigured?' (2013) 34 Adelaide Law Review 1.

[3] Andrew Stewart, 'A Question of Balance: Labor's New Vision for Workplace Regulation' (2009) 22 Australian Journal of Labour Law (AJLL) 3.

[4] National Labor Relations Act 29 U.S.C. §§ 151–169 (2000) (NLRA), ss. 8(a)(5) and 8(b)(3). See e.g. s. 47, British Columbia Labour Relations Code (Code).

[5] The NLRA, s. 8(d) definition of 'collective bargaining' also indicates limits to the GFB, providing: 'For the purposes of this section, to bargain collectively is the performance of the mutual obligation of the employer and the representatives of the employees to meet at reasonable times and confer in good faith with respect to wages, hours, and other terms and conditions of employment, or the negotiation of an agreement, or any question arising thereunder, and the execution of a written contract incorporating any agreement reached if requested by either party, but such obligation does not compel either party to agree to a proposal or require the making of a concession…'

[6] See e.g. ss. 11(1) Code.

the obligations have largely been determined by labour tribunal and court decisions. In contrast, the Antipodean approach, though influenced to varying degrees by US and Canadian GFB,[7] involves detailed statutory definitions and guidance to the scope and content of the GFB.[8] The New Zealand legislation provides for one or more additional 'codes of good faith' to be established as further guidance to parties in meeting their GFB obligations.[9]

A second point of departure is with regard to the degree of compulsion to conclude an agreement that is included in the GFB. Neither the Australian nor US legislation impose any obligation on parties to settle while, as already noted, Canadian legislation tends to require parties to make 'every reasonable effort' to reach an agreement.[10] In contrast, New Zealand's GFB provisions explicitly require bargaining parties to 'conclude a collective agreement unless there is a genuine reason, based on reasonable grounds, not to' and set out statutory guidelines for what might constitute such reasonable grounds.[11]

Although GFB is commonly an element of decentralized, enterprise-based models of collective bargaining,[12] the statutory requirements differ among jurisdictions (including among Canadian jurisdictions, as discussed later) and the precise definition and scope of the duty to bargain in good faith have long been contested in all of these jurisdictions. For example, the US formulation of GFB[13] has been the subject of extensive litigation over its 65 years of existence. This has involved examination of questions such as the 'state of mind' with which negotiating parties must approach negotiations for an agreement;[14] and whether the good faith obligation is simply procedural in nature, or also connotes a requirement to make substantive proposals and ultimately to conclude an agreement.[15] These have also been key contested issues in the evolution of GFB obligations in Canada and Australia, as the discussion in this chapter will show.

[7] See n 74 and Gordon Anderson, 'Transplanting and Growing Good Faith in New Zealand Labour Law' (2006) 19 AJLL 1 at 2.

[8] Australia, Fair Work Act 2009 (Cth) (FW Act), s. 228 (addressed further later). The New Zealand Employment Relations Act 2000 (ERA) imposes a 'duty of good faith' on a variety of specified employment relationships (s. 4(2)), including the employer and union relationship when bargaining a collective agreement (s. 4(2), (4)(a)). The statute provides explicit direction on the scope and content of the GFB duty (ERA, ss. 4(1)–(4), 31–33).

[9] ERA, s. 31(b).

[10] US legislation explicitly provides that the GFB 'does not compel either party to agree to a proposal' (NLRA, s. 8(d)).

[11] ERA, ss. 31(aa), 33.

[12] See e.g. the later discussion of the shift to enterprise bargaining in Australia in the early 1990s (which was accompanied by the introduction of a limited statutory GFB duty in 1993); and see Gordon Anderson, *Reconstructing New Zealand's Labour Law: Consensus or Divergence?* (Victoria University Press, 2011) 74–5, 142–4, discussing the operation of GFB in the context of the policy of 'enterprise confinement' first introduced under New Zealand's Employment Contracts Act 1991 (this concept endures as the basis for the collective bargaining framework under the Employment Relations Act 2000).

[13] Under the NLRA; see further later in the chapter.

[14] See e.g. Brian Bemmels, E.G. Fisher, and Barbara Nyland, 'Canadian-American Jurisprudence on "Good Faith" Bargaining' (1986) 41(3) Relations Industrielles 596, 597–8, referring to US case law requiring negotiations to be conducted 'with the view of reaching agreement if possible' (footnote omitted).

[15] See Bemmels, Fisher, and Nyland 604–5 (n 14), noting that although the US duty of good faith expressly specifies that negotiating parties are not required to make concessions, an employer must 'make *some* reasonable effort in *some* direction to compose [its] differences with the union' (footnote omitted).

There have been many studies of the (in)effectiveness of North American collective bargaining statutes, highlighting their failure to deliver increased coverage of collective agreements and to extend the practice of collective bargaining much beyond unionized sectors of the economy.[16] However, these studies have mostly focused on the limitations of the scope and processes of statutory union recognition operating in the USA and Canada, rather than the duty to bargain in good faith. Given its novelty, there is (as yet) no in-depth study of the effectiveness of the Australian formulation of GFB published in the academic literature.[17]

In this chapter, we seek to add to this body of evidence by providing a comparative assessment of the Canadian and Australian experience with GFB laws. In relation to Canada, we base our analysis on data drawn from administrative records of a provincial labour tribunal, the British Columbia Labour Relations Board (BCLRB), for the 1 January 2003–31 December 2012 period, and from the published decisions of the BCLRB. For Australia, we utilize data obtained from a recent research project conducted through a research partnership with the Fair Work Commission (FWC; formerly Fair Work Australia), which examined the statutory collective bargaining scheme over its first three years of operation (1 July 2009–30 June 2012).[18]

Canada

History of good faith bargaining in Canada

Before 1900 little labour legislation had been passed in Canada and what did exist was heavily influenced by the British voluntarist approach to labour relations.[19] The first elements of compulsion introduced into Canadian labour law were drawn from Australian labour relations and focused on compulsion in dispute resolution. This produced an early Canadian system centred on conciliation and arbitration, including limited use of compulsory conciliation and arbitration.[20] There existed no requirement to bargain.

[16] The literature is voluminous. See e.g. Roy J. Adams, 'The North American Model of Employee Representational Participation: "A Hollow Mockery"' (1993) 15 Comparative Labor Law Journal 201; Karen Bentham 'Employer Resistance to Union Certification: A Study of Eight Canadian Jurisdictions' (2002) 57(1) Relations Industrielles/Industrial Relations 159; Michele Campolieti, Chris Riddell, and Sara Slinn 'Labor Law Reform and the Role of Delay in Union Organizing: Empirical Evidence from Canada' (2007) 61 Industrial and Labour Relations Review 32; Judy Fudge and Harry Glasbeek, 'The Legacy of PC 1003' (1994–1995) 3 Canadian Labour and Employment Law Journal (CLELJ) 357; Chris Riddell 'Union suppression and union certification success' (2001) 43 Canadian Journal of Economics 396; Sara Slinn, 'An Analysis of the Effects on Parties' Unionization Decisions of the Choice of Union Representation Procedure: The Strategic Dynamic Certification Model' (2005) 43 Osgoode Hall Law Journal 407.

[17] Although see the preliminary assessments in Anthony Forsyth, 'The Impact of "Good Faith" Obligations on Collective Bargaining Practices and Outcomes in Australia, Canada and the United States' (2011) 16(1) CLELJ 1; Breen Creighton and Pam Nuttall, 'Good Faith Bargaining Down Under' (2012) 33(2) Comparative Labor Law and Policy Journal (CLLPJ) 257; Alex Bukarica and Andrew Dallas, *Good Faith Bargaining under the Fair Work Act 2009: Lessons from the Collective Bargaining Experience in Canada and New Zealand* (Federation Press, 2012); Rosalind Read, 'Direct Dealing, Union Recognition and Good Faith Bargaining under the Fair Work Act 2009' (2012) 25(2) AJLL 130.

[18] Anthony Forsyth, Peter Gahan, John Howe, and Ingrid Landau, *Fair Work Australia's Influence in the Enterprise Bargaining Process*, Fair Work Australia Research Partnership Project, Final Report, 30 September 2012. The present authors are grateful to the co-authors of the FWC-commissioned study, and to the FWC, for permission to utilize parts of the Final Report in this chapter.

[19] Harry D. Woods, *Labour Policy in Canada* (MacMillan of Canada, 1973) 43.

[20] Woods 46 (n 19).

Unlike Britain, Australia, or Canada, labour law as it developed in the early twentieth century in the United States centred on establishing the framework for bargaining relationships: recognition of defined bargaining units and compulsory bargaining.[21] Nonetheless, a duty to bargain was only an implicit element of US labour legislation until the 1947 Taft-Hartley amendments to the 1935 National Labor Relations Act (commonly referred to as the 'Wagner Act' after its sponsoring senator) introduced an express obligation to bargain, and a definition of 'collective bargaining' which included an obligation on employers 'to meet at reasonable times and confer in good faith with respect to wages, hours, and other terms and conditions of employment'.[22]

It was not until the mid and late 1930s that the American notion of compulsory bargaining was tentatively introduced into Canadian labour law in some short-lived provincial labour legislation, and it did not gain widespread application until the Second World War. Temporary wartime federal labour legislation passed in 1944, referred to as 'PC 1003' and widely adopted across the country, incorporated Wagner Act principles, including compulsory bargaining. PC 1003 provided an express right to collective bargaining reinforced by an explicit obligation on parties to 'negotiate in good faith with one another and make every reasonable effort to conclude a collective agreement'.[23] Violations of these provisions were offences and subject to monetary penalties, although labour board consent was required to prosecute.[24]

Post-war, the federal government replaced PC 1003 with the 1948 Industrial Relations and Disputes Investigations Act which incorporated the main components of the predecessor legislation.[25] Shortly thereafter the provinces reclaimed jurisdiction of labour relations with provincial statutes which also substantially emulated the key parts of PC 1003—including some version of a duty to bargain in good faith or make reasonable efforts to agree—leading to similar labour legislation across the country. Different jurisdictions adopted a variety of formulations for bargaining obligations. British Columbia (BC), for instance, included an obligation to bargain in its legislation, but only required parties to make every reasonable effort to conclude an agreement, with no reference to good faith in negotiations.[26] BC's legislation retained this formulation, with minor amendments, until 1973 (addressed later).[27]

The duty to bargain in good faith in North American labour law is regarded as a mechanism implementing the principle of compulsory collective bargaining, a necessary foundation for union recognition as exclusive bargaining agent for a group of employees,[28]

[21] Woods 49 (n 19).

[22] Taft-Hartley Act as ss. 8(a)(5), 61 Stat. 141 (1947), 29 USC ss. 158(b)(3) (1952). The Taft-Hartley Act also added 61 Stat. 142 (1947), 29 USC ss. 158(d), a definition of 'collective bargaining'. For a comprehensive history of GFB in the United States, see Russell A. Smith, 'The Evolution of the Duty to Bargain' [1941] 39 Michigan Law Review 1065.

[23] Wartime Labour Relations Regulations [1944] UKPC 1003, ss. 4(3), 10(2).

[24] Wartime Labour Relations Regulations, s. 42.

[25] Industrial and Disputes Investigation Act S.C. 1948, c. 54.

[26] Industrial Conciliation and Arbitration Act 1947, S.B.C. 1947, c. 44, ss. 2(1), 13–16.

[27] Labour Code of British Columbia Act, S.B.C. 1973, c. 122.

[28] The Labour Law Casebook Group, *Labour Law: Cases, Materials, and Commentary*, 4th edn (Industrial Relations Centre, Queen's University, 1986) 233, citing Archibald Cox, 'The Duty to Bargain in Good Faith' [1958] 71 Harvard Law Review (Harv L Rev) 1401, 1407–9.

and the 'logical extension of the idea of compulsory recognition'.[29] The 1969 Woods Task Force Report (regarded as the intellectual basis for modern Canadian labour legislation) concluded that collective bargaining 'works more effectively and yields more satisfactory results when both sides to the negotiation act in good faith' and that where one party fails to bargain in good faith 'the disease is usually contagious'.[30] The Report explicitly rejected adopting the American approach of developing 'elaborate jurisprudence' on the good faith standard, regarding the good faith obligation as a minimal, procedural obligation and expressing concern that following the American approach would simply lead to developing unenforceable law or law that encouraged token compliance or litigation.[31]

In 1973 British Columbia was the first Canadian jurisdiction to introduce labour legislation effectuating the Report's recommendations and marked a new approach to labour relations regulation in Canada (1973 Code).[32] One aspect of this new regime was the consolidation of jurisdiction for labour relations in a specialized administrative tribunal, the Labour Relations Board, instead of the courts. Consequently, the 1973 Code not only conceptually relocated GFB violations from being a civil offence to regulation as an unfair labour practice, but removed GFB enforcement from the courts and brought it within the Labour Relations Board's exclusive authority to apply the standard and award remedies, subject to judicial review. This approach to labour relations regulation was soon mirrored, to varying degrees, in labour legislation across the country.

BC's 1973 Code required employers and unions to act in good faith and to make 'every reasonable effort to conclude a collective agreement' in bargaining.[33] This two-part GFB obligation has persisted, without substantial changes, through numerous amendments and replacements of the legislation. Today, section 11(1) of the Labour Relations Code (Code) requires that '[a] trade union or employer must not fail or refuse to bargain collectively in good faith in British Columbia and to make every reasonable effort to conclude a collective agreement'.[34] Although it is a two-pronged duty, it is generally simply referred to as the 'duty to bargain in good faith' (GFB).

The BCLRB, like other Canadian labour relations boards, has broad authority to make remedial orders for a breach of the Code, including GFB violations.[35] The key limits on this authority are that remedies are to be compensatory and restorative, not punitive in nature, and that there must be a clear connection between the violation, its consequences, and the remedy awarded.[36] Remedies are also shaped by the BCLRB's

[29] Harry D. Woods, 'Canadian Collective Bargaining and Dispute Settlement Policy: an Appraisal' [1955] 21 Canadian Journal of Economics & Political Science 447 at 450.

[30] Canada Taskforce on Labour Relations and Harry D. Woods, *Canadian Industrial Relations: The Report* (Privy Council Office, 1968) para. 544.

[31] *Canadian Industrial Relations: The Report*, para. 547 (n 30).

[32] Labour Code of British Columbia Act, SBC 1973, c. 122.

[33] Labour Code of British Columbia Act, SBC 1973, c. 122, s. 6.

[34] Labour Relations Code, RSBC 1996, c. 244, s. 11(1). Also relevant to the GFB duty was a new feature introduced by the BC Code: first contract arbitration. This permitted a party to apply to the labour board for arbitration of a first collective agreement. Among the matters the board was explicitly permitted to take into account when deciding whether to require arbitration was whether, and to what degree, parties had bargained in good faith (BC Code 1973: s. 71).

[35] Code, ss. 14(4), 133(1); *National Bank of Canada v Retail Clerks' International Union* [1984] 1 SCR 269; *Royal Oak Mines v Canada (Labour Relations Board)* [1996] 1 SCR 369.

[36] *Roberta Scott* et al. *(Target Resources)*, (1993), 16 CLRBR (2d) 65; *National Bank of Canada v Retail Clerks' International Union*, [1984] 1 SCR 269.

explicit statutory duties, which include encouraging the 'practice and procedure of collective bargaining between employers and trade unions', 'cooperative participation between employers and trade unions in resolving workplace disputes', and 'the use of mediation as a dispute resolution mechanism'.[37]

By the 1980s, commentators widely criticized GFB as having had little practical effect in regulating collective bargaining.[38] Some commentators attributed this to the emphasis on conciliation rather than compulsory bargaining that characterized Canadian labour law until the 1970s. They contended that this caused the GFB concept to be 'obscured' and fail to develop.[39] Others were sceptical of this explanation, particularly because labour relations actors had virtually abandoned the conciliation process by the 1970s.[40]

A second explanation pointed to the difficult enforcement procedures and inadequate remedies available for bad faith bargaining as the reason for lack of development of GFB law. Until the 1970s, most jurisdictions provided for GFB enforcement through quasi-criminal procedures in provincial criminal courts, subject to the criminal standard of proof and requiring labour tribunal consent to prosecute. The only available penalty was a small fine.[41] Beginning in the 1970s, GFB enforcement was brought exclusively within labour board jurisdiction and became subject to broader labour board remedies.

Finally, others suggested that GFB is a fundamentally unworkable concept. Earl Palmer condemned the GFB duty as a 'harmful fiction' distracting parties from constructive negotiations, and asserted that 'good faith is not a part of the bargaining process and, indeed, seems impossible of attainment under the conditions of the existing economic system' involving self-interested negotiating parties.[42] Brian Langille and Patrick Macklem focused their critique on GFB's fundamental reliance on distinguishing between self-interested employer behaviour (regarded as an essential part of the bargaining process) and bad faith employer behaviour in bargaining. They rejected this distinction as largely non-existent, and concluded that this approach allowed rational and powerful employers to avoid GFB obligations by claiming to act in self-interest, thereby allowing such employers to 'effectively... step outside the collective bargaining regime'.[43]

In a similar vein, Michael Bendel pointed to a survey study undertaken for the Woods Task Force Report in which the authors found 'a widespread feeling among

[37] Code, ss. 2(c), (d), (h). In this regard BC differs from some labour legislation in some other Canadian jurisdictions lacking a purpose or 'duties' clause (see Sara Slinn, 'Untamed Tribunal? Of Dynamic Interpretation and Purpose Clauses' (2009) 42 University of British Columbia Law Review (UBC L Rev) 125).

[38] See e.g. Brian A. Langille and Patrick Macklem, 'Beyond Belief: Labour Law's Duty to Bargain' [1988] 13 Queens Law Journal 62; Bernard Adell, *The Duty to Bargain in Good Faith: Its Recent Development in Canada*, Research and Current Issues Series No. 48 (Industrial Relations Centre, Queen's University, 1980); Michael Bendel, 'A Rational Process of Persuasion: Good Faith Bargaining in Ontario' [1980] 30 University of Toronto Law Journal 1; Earl E. Palmer, 'The Myth of "Good Faith" in Collective Bargaining' [1965–1966] Alberta Law Review 409.

[39] Palmer 409 (n 38). [40] Adell 2 (n 38).

[41] Palmer 416–17 (n 38); Adell 2 (n 38). Bendel (n 38) at 2 notes that, in contrast, the American National Labor Relations Board had always heard and been able to make cease and desist orders or 'take affirmative action to repair the prior failure to bargain'.

[42] Palmer 418 (n 38). [43] Langille and Macklem 80–1, 93 (n 38).

labour relations practitioners that "good faith" cannot be generated by legislation'.[44] As Bernard Adell describes it '...the uncomfortable feeling has persisted from the start that the duty [to bargain in good faith] is at worst a contradiction in terms and at best unenforceable'.[45]

Operation of British Columbia's duty to bargain in good faith: 2003–2012

In Canada, responsibility for labour law is divided among the federal and ten provincial governments. The Constitution allocates primary responsibility for labour relations to the provinces, and labour relations matters fall within federal jurisdiction only for specified industries and employees of the federal government or federal Crown corporations.[46] Consequently, in Canada there are eleven separate labour relations jurisdictions with provinces, rather than the federal government, responsible for labour relations in most industries.

In order to offer the most meaningful comparison between Australian and Canadian data, it would be preferable to use cross-Canada data covering comparable numbers of employees, industries, and workplaces as the Australian FWC data. However, practical limits exist in terms of Canadian data availability. Cross-national data is not available because few Canadian labour tribunals have the capacity to collect and provide substantial individual case-level data. The BCLRB is one of these tribunals, as is the federal Canada Industrial Relations Board. Given the limited range of industries within federal jurisdiction, we judged that data from one of the largest provincial labour tribunals capable of providing this information is a better source for this comparative exercise. Therefore, this section of the chapter employs administrative data from the provincial BCLRB.

A further consideration in selecting the Canadian data was the time period for the study, and our decision in this regard was governed largely by the relative numbers of cases available from the two jurisdictions (Australia and BC) to allow for a meaningful comparison. The Australian data was available for the first three years of operation of the new legislation (July 2009–June 2012). As BC is a much smaller jurisdiction than Australia it was to be expected that, in order to obtain sufficient number of BCLRB GFB cases for analysis, it would be necessary to use a longer time period for the BC data. The GFB duty is a long-standing element of the Canadian and BC labour relations systems, therefore substantial historical data is available. Consequently we selected the 2003 to 2012 period for the BC data.

[44] Bendel 2 (n 38), citing Canada Task force on Labour Relations, Innis Christie and Morley Gorskey, *Unfair Labour Practices: An Exploratory Study of the Efficacy of the Law of Unfair Labour Practices in Canada* (Queen's Printer, 1968) 54.

[45] Adell 1 (n 38).

[46] These industries include: aeronautics, air transport and airports, atomic energy, banking, customs, grain elevators, inter-provincial transportation, most railways, postal services, shipping and navigation, telecommunications, television and radio broadcasting, and account for approximately 10 per cent of the workforce. Canada's three territories (Yukon, Northwest Territories, and Nunavut) have elected to adopt the labour legislation of other Canadian jurisdictions, instead of establishing their own labour relations legislative systems.

The BCLRB provided individual case-level data on the 315 GFB complaints that were filed and disposed of under section 11(1) of the Code between 1 January 2003 and 31 December 2012.[47] The full data set was used for most of the analysis that follows, and subsets of the data (specified in what follows) were used for specific analyses.

Using this data we present a series of descriptive statistics offering an overview of the operation of the section 11(1) Code GFB provisions over the 2003–2012 period. This includes descriptive analysis of the identity of applicants, outcomes of GFB complaints, and stage of the bargaining relationship at which GFB complaints arose. This is followed by a brief discussion of GFB case law.

Good faith bargaining: analysis of Canadian data

Applicants and outcomes

Over the 2003–2012 period a total of 315 GFB complaints were filed and disposed of by the BCLRB, an average of 31.5 such cases per year (see Figure 8.1). Over 80 per cent of these complaints were filed by unions (253 or 80.8 per cent), whilst fewer than 20 per cent were filed by employers (57 or 18.1 per cent). Less than 2 per cent of cases were filed by another party or multiple parties (see Figure 8.2).[48]

The great preponderance of complaints were settled, regardless of the identity of the applicant. Overall, 69.2 per cent of GFB complaints were settled, 16.5 per cent were granted and 13.3 per cent dismissed, with the remaining few cases accounting for less than one per cent of the total were either withdrawn or not proceeded with (see Figure 8.3).

When the frequency of each category of outcome is examined based on the identity of the applicant, the results reflect the fact that unions file nearly four times the number of GFB complaints compared to employers, and complaints filed by other parties or multiple parties are negligible. Union-filed GFB complaints accounted for more than quadruple the number of GFB complaints granted by the BCLRB, compared to those filed by employers (80.8 per cent compared to 19.2 per cent of the total). Similarly, far more settled (78.9 per cent compared to 18.8 per cent of the total) or dismissed (85.7 per cent compared with 14.3 per cent of the total) cases arise from union complaints

[47] A GFB obligation appears in a variety of roles in the BC Code in addition to its primary statement in s. 11(1), reflecting the central role of compulsory bargaining in the Wagner-modelled BC Code. These associated provisions include the s. (1) definition of 'collective bargaining'; s. 2(c) imposition of a duty on the board and other persons exercising powers and performing duties under the Code to encourage 'the practice and procedure of collective bargaining'; the s. 47(b) requirement to 'commence to bargain collectively in good faith, and make every reasonable effort to conclude a collective agreement' once a party has given notice to commence bargaining; and, the s. 54(1)(b) obligation on employers and unions to 'meet, in good faith, and endeavor to develop an adjustment plan' where the employer 'introduces or intends to introduce a measure, policy, practice or change that affects the terms, conditions or security of employment of a significant number of employees to whom a collective agreement applies'. This study examines only cases arising from the s. 11(1) GFB duty.

[48] In one case both a trade union and one or more individuals filed the GFB complaint. In four other cases the applicant was other than a single employer or union (e.g. multiple employers, unions or individuals, or another configuration). Note that these anomalous applicant situations are not included in many subsequent calculations involving cases with single employer or trade union applicants, and which are the overwhelming majority of cases.

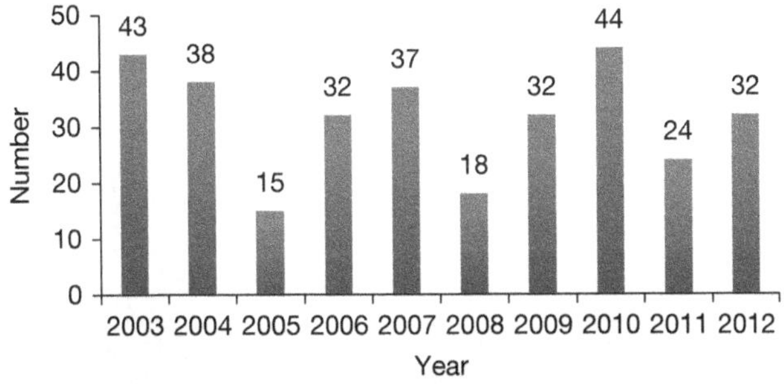

Figure 8.1 GFB cases filed and decided, 2003–2012

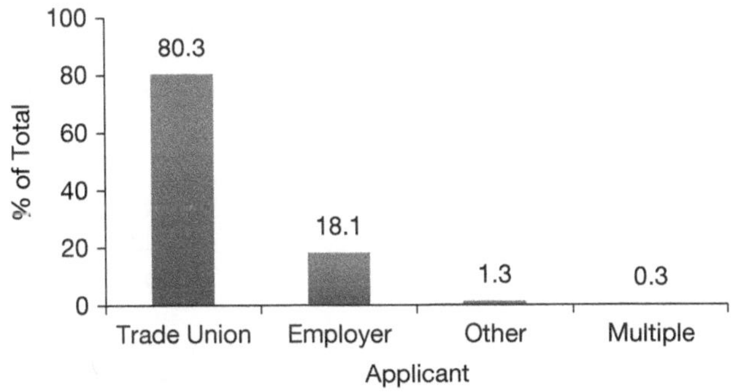

Figure 8.2 GFB complaint applicant, 2003–2012

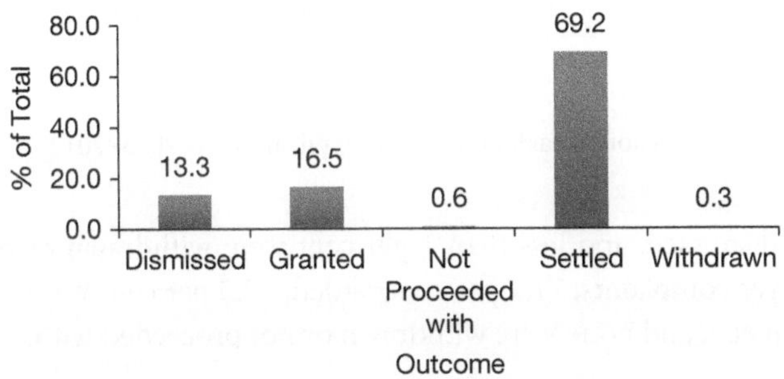

Figure 8.3 GFB Complaint outcomes, 2003–2012

compared to employer GFB complaints. All cases that were withdrawn or not proceeded with in the study period were associated with union-filed complaints.

Perhaps more illuminating is to consider the frequencies of each outcome category within the set of cases filed by unions and by employers (see Figures 8.4 and 8.5). When outcomes are examined with respect to the identity of the applicant, for complaints filed by a union or employer, the breakdown of outcomes for each of the two types of applicants is similar to each other and to the overall distribution of outcomes described earlier. Among complaints filed by unions, 68 per cent settled, 16.6 per cent were granted, 14.2

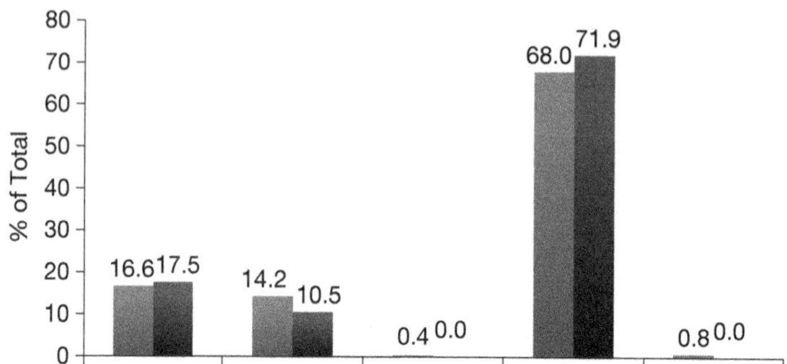

	Granted	Dismissed	Withdrawn	Settled	Not proceed
Union	16.6	14.2	0.4	68.0	0.8
Employer	17.5	10.5	0.0	71.9	0.0

Figure 8.4 Complaint outcome by applicant type, 2003–2012

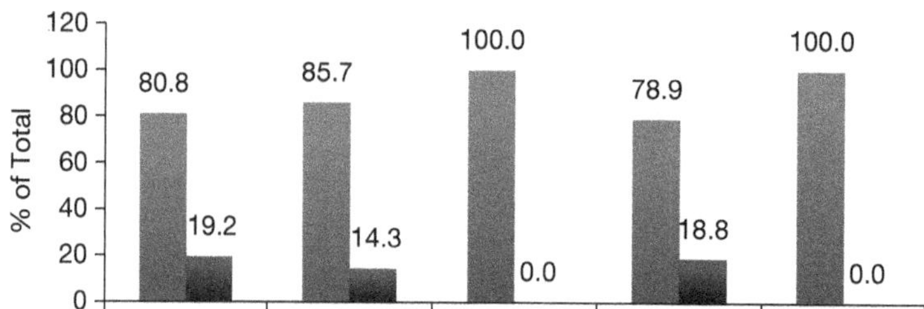

	Granted	Dismissed	Withdrawn	Settled	Not proceed
Union	80.8	85.7	100.0	78.9	100.0
Employer	19.2	14.3	0.0	18.8	0.0

Figure 8.5 Proportion of each outcome by applicant type, 2003–2012

per cent were dismissed, and less than 1 per cent were withdrawn or did not proceed. Among employer complaints, 71.9 per cent settled, 17.5 per cent were granted, 10.5 per cent were dismissed, and none were withdrawn or not proceeded with.

Stage of bargaining relationship

Bad faith bargaining occurring in the period after a bargaining relationship is newly established may have very different consequences and a very different complexion, than bad faith bargaining occurring during negotiations for a renewal collective agreement by parties with a more established relationship. In particular, the former situation may be a continuation of pre-certification employer resistance to union representation or a reflection of one or both parties' lack of negotiating experience. Either may jeopardize the long-term success of the bargaining relationship. In order to get a sense of the stage of collective bargaining relationships at which GFB complaints arose, we examined the data in two ways.

First, we sought to examine the relative proportions of GFB complaints filed early in the bargaining relationship compared to those filed at a later stage. Ideally this would involve distinguishing complaints that arose while the first collective agreement was being negotiated from those filed during subsequent bargaining rounds. Given that the average length of a collective agreement is approximately three to four years, within the ten-year span of the BC data it could be expected that many of the bargaining relationships would bargain one or more renewal agreements during the study period.[49] However, lacking individual case data about the time to reaching a first contract or evidence of the average time to first contract, we designated a two-year period from the date of certification as an approximation of the first contract negotiation period. We then examined a subset of the data using this two year period to categorize complaints as those likely filed during the first agreement negotiating period ('FA') and those likely filed after the first agreement was settled ('post-FA').[50] This assumes that most first collective agreements would be reached within two years of the date of certification.

Among the 258 GFB complaints filed by either an employer or union and decided during the 2003–2012 period for which the certification date is available, slightly less than one third (82 per cent or 31.8 per cent) were FA complaints, filed within two years of certification.[51] While the proportion of FA complaints filed each year over the study period ranged from 11.5 per cent to 53.9 per cent of all GFB complaints, on average, FA complaints made up 32.3 per cent of the total number of GFB complaints filed in each year of the study period (see Figure 8.6).

When GFB complaints are broken down by whether they are FA or post-FA complaints and by applicant, notable differences are evident (see Figure 8.7). First, as noted earlier, unions were substantially more active GFB applicants than employers, and this difference exists for both FA and post-FA complaints. With few exceptional years, both unions and employers filed fewer FA than post-FA complaints. This latter result might be expected since the data set includes bargaining relationships established many years (and in some cases many decades) prior to 2003.

Among union-filed FA complaints, 15.6 per cent were granted, 8.2 per cent dismissed, and 75.6 per cent settled. Meanwhile, no employer FA complaint was granted, 11.1 per cent were dismissed, and 88.9 per cent settled. No FA complaints were filed by other or multiple parties. Among post-FA complaints filed by unions, 16.6 per cent were granted, 17.9 per cent were dismissed, and 63.6 per cent were settled, with the remainder withdrawn or not proceeded with. Among such cases filed by employers, 16.7 per cent were granted, 8.3 per cent were dismissed, and 75 per cent settled; the

[49] The mean duration of collective agreements entered into for bargaining units of 500 or more employees and under federal jurisdiction was 36.8 months (with 40 per cent of the agreements having terms between 36 and 47 months). Between 2004 and 2012 average duration ranged from 35 to 50 months. See Canada, Human Resources and Skills Development Canada, Workplace Information Division, *Collective Bargaining in Canada 2012*. <http://www12.hrsdc.gc.ca/p.5bd.2t.1.3ls@-eng.jsp?pid=6722> 6. Collective agreement duration data is not available for BC.

[50] Note that only two more cases would be captured by a three-, instead of two-, year FA period.

[51] Not all GFB complaints are associated with a certification; therefore, not all have a certification date. Certification date is missing in one case where certification occurred; three cases where there appears to be no bargaining relationship established; and 19 where the type of collective bargaining relationship is not recorded. Additionally, cases filed by multiple or 'other' applicants are excluded from this portion of the analysis which includes only GFB complaints filed by an employer or union.

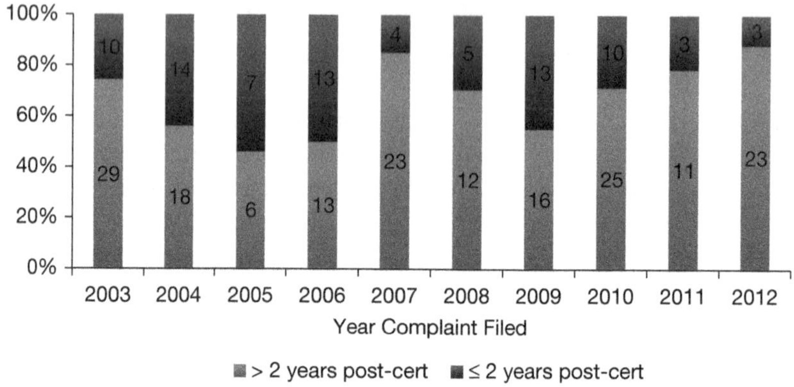

Figure 8.6 GFB complaints filed by stage of bargaining relationship, 2003–2012

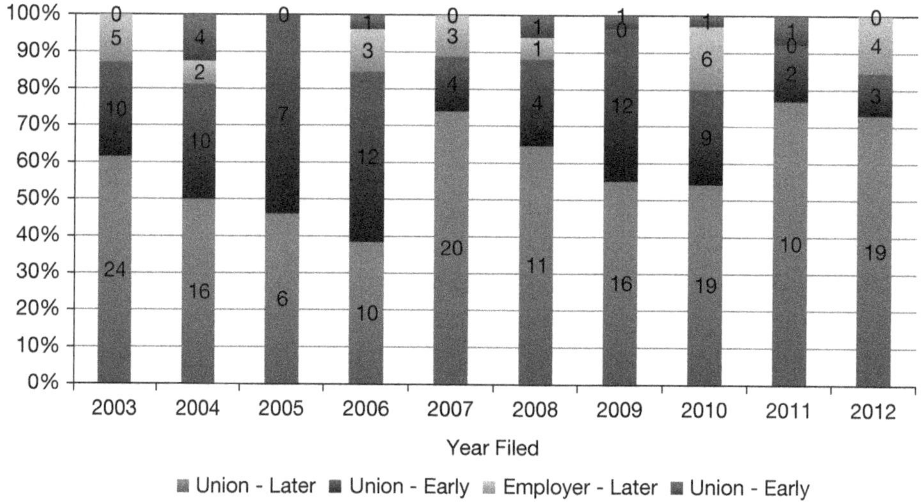

Figure 8.7 GFB Complaints filed by applicant and stage, 2003–2012

remaining cases were withdrawn or did not proceed. No such complaints were made by other parties.

Time to complaint

A different perspective on the GFB complaint phenomenon can be gained by examining the length of time after certification that GFB cases are filed, using a subset of the data.[52] This subset includes those GFB complaints filed within the study period relating to bargaining relationships certified within the study period, 2003–2012, for which the

[52] Certification is a statutory collective bargaining agent recognition process, and is a key feature of Canadian labour legislation. It is generally analogous to the 'majority support determination' process in Australian labour law (see further later in the chapter).

date of certification is available and where the GFB complaint was filed on or after the certification date. This subset includes a total of 86 cases, with a mean elapsed time of 416 days, and a range of 4 to 2,996 days between certification and GFB complaint filing. The median time elapsed is 190.5 days, with one quarter of cases filed within 84 days of certification and one quarter filed 385 or more days post-certification.

Subsequent GFB complaints

Using a subset of the data containing the 86 GFB complaint cases, where the bargaining relationship was established by certification between 2003 and 2012 allows us to examine the extent to which multiple or subsequent GFB complaints arise in a single bargaining relationship (see Table 8.1).

Twelve of these bargaining relationships saw between two and four GFB complaints filed and decided during the study period for a total of 31 GFB complaints. Unions filed

Table 8.1 Bargaining relationships and multiple GFB complaints, 2003–12

Bargaining Relationship	Stage of GFB Complaint	Applicant	Outcome
1	FA	Union	Settled
	FA	Union	Dismissed
	FA	Union	Dismissed
2	FA	Union	Settled
	FA	Union	Settled
3	FA	Union	Settled
	FA	Union	Settled
4	FA	Union	Settled
	Post-FA	Union	Dismissed
5	FA	Union	Settled
	FA	Union	Dismissed
	FA	Union	Granted
6	FA	Union	Settled
	FA	Union	Settled
	Post-FA	Union	Dismissed
7	FA	Union	Granted
	FA	Employer	Dismissed
	FA	Union	Dismissed
8	FA	Employer	Settled
	FA	Union	Settled
9	FA	Union	Granted
	FA	Union	Granted
10	FA	Union	Settled
	FA	Union	Settled
	FA	Union	Settled
11	FA	Union	Settled
	FA	Union	Settled
	FA	Union	Settled
	FA	Union	Settled
12	FA	Union	Settled
	FA	Employer	Settled

28 of the 31 complaints (90.3 per cent). All but two of these complaints were filed in the FA period (93.5 per cent), and three employer complaints were filed in this period. Most complaints were settled (20 or 64.5 per cent), with seven dismissed (22.6 per cent) and four granted (12.9 per cent).

Good faith bargaining case law

What is commonly referred to as the 'duty to bargain in good faith' consists, in BC as in most Canadian jurisdictions, of a two-part obligation: the duty to bargain in good faith and the duty to make every reasonable effort to conclude an agreement.[53] Specifically, as already noted, section 11(1) of the Code provides: 'A trade union or employer must not fail or refuse to bargain collectively in good faith in British Columbia and to make every reasonable effort to conclude a collective agreement.'

Labour boards apply a subjective standard to assessing whether the 'good faith' requirement is satisfied, while the obligation to make 'reasonable efforts' is tested against an objective standard determined by common standards and practices in the relevant industry.[54] Generally GFB applies to the bargaining process and labour boards avoid assessing the merits or reasonableness of proposals. The rationale for this approach was established and well summarized by BCLRB Chair Paul Weiler in one of the board's first GFB cases and continues to underpin application of the duty in Canadian law today:[55]

> ...It would be inconsistent with the fundamental policy of the Code—the fostering of *free* collective bargaining—for the Board to evaluate the substantive provisions of each party, to decide which is the more reasonable, and then to find the other party to be committing an unfair labour practice for not moving in that direction. That interpretation of [the GFB provision] would amount to compulsory arbitration in disguise, and without the restrictions carefully placed around [first contract interest arbitration provisions]. The theory of the Code is that each side in collective bargaining is entitled to adopt the contract proposals which are in its own interest, to stick firmly to its bargaining positions, and then to rely on its economic strength in a strike to force the other side to make the concessions.

Interpretation of GFB requirements has not undergone much development since being established soon after introduction of modern labour legislation in the 1970s, and BCLRB case decisions issued during the study period reflect these basic principles. These principles have been summarized as requiring the following:[56]

1. That the parties meet and commence bargaining.
2. That both fully discuss the issues at hand and the rationale for their positions on these issues.

[53] A minority of provinces employ different statutory GFB formulations, including requiring good faith alone, reasonable effort, or diligence and good faith, or simply requiring parties to meet and bargain and prohibiting employers from failing or refusing to negotiate with the union. George W. Adams, *Canadian Labour Law* (Canada Law Book, 1993) para. 10.1640.

[54] *Royal Oak Mines v Canada (Labour Relations Board)* [1996] 1 SCR 369.

[55] *Noranda Metal Industries Ltd* [1974] BCLRBD No 149, [1975] 1 Can LRBR 145 at 159.

[56] John Godard, *Industrial Relations, the Economy, and Society*, 7th edn (Captus Press, 2011) 286–7.

3. That neither party suppress or distort information required by the other party or intentionally mislead the other party.
4. That neither party frustrate the bargaining process by contradicting itself or simply going through the motions with no intention of making meaningful concessions—a strategy commonly referred to as 'surface bargaining'.
5. That management not attempt to circumvent the union by making an offer directly to union workers....

Remedial awards in GFB violation cases are another important aspect of the case law which, in contrast with GFB principles, themselves, have not been subject to much examination. BCLRB case management data does not record remedial awards. This information is available only in the individual case files (which were not available to us) or in published BCLRB case decisions. The BCLRB published very few GFB case decisions during the study period. Therefore, a review of the remedies granted in these two dozen published decisions offers only a limited snapshot of the BCLRB's remedial approach to GFB violations during the study period.

Declaration of violation of the Code, a cease and desist order, and a direction to parties to engage in collective bargaining in compliance with Section 11(1) are the least intrusive remedial awards available for GFB violations. A simple cease and desist order was issued in one case, and another was coupled with an order for a new employee vote to ratify a proposed agreement in another case.[57] Remedies directing parties to bargain in compliance with the GFB duty often specified that such bargaining commence within a specified number of days following the BCLRB decision.[58] Where the violation consisted of a party failing to provide relevant information during bargaining, the remedy commonly consisted of a disclosure order where the information remained relevant to negotiations.[59] Monetary damage remedies are not commonly awarded, although in one case where the employer's GFB violation included closing the workplace to avoid its bargaining obligations or an illegal lockout, the BCLRB concluded that declaratory relief and cease and desist orders would be insufficient and ordered the employer to pay lost earnings to employees.[60]

Many of the published decisions included remedies that intervened in the process and sometimes the substance of bargaining. Some decisions voided statutory votes or

[57] *Insurance Corporation of British Columbia*, BCLRB Decision No. B84/2004; *MTM Enterprise Ltd*, BCLRB Decision No. B168/2007.

[58] *Nil/Tu,O Child and Family Services Society*, BCLRB Decision No. B33/2007; *Seli Canada Inc.* BCLRB Decision No. B177/2006; *CDL Disposal Ltd.*, BCLRB Decision No. B298/2003. The following decisions contained no deadline: *B.C. Hardwood Floor Co. Ltd.*, BCLRB No. B127/2010; *Timberwest Forest Company*, BCLRB No. B124/2007 (a declaration accompanied the bargaining order). In *Westfair Foods Ltd.*, BCLRB Decision No. B175/2010 the award specified that parties were required to engage in 'rational discussion' which would include 'consideration of reasonable counterproposals'.

[59] *Pacific Pallet Ltd.*, BCLRB Decision No. B95/2008; *Hudson's Bay Co.*, BCLRB Decision No. B226/2004; *Lender Services Ltd.*, BCLRB Decision No. B289/2006; *Modern Auto Plating Limited*, BCLRB Decision No. B48/2003 (information was no longer relevant at the time of the decision; the BCLRB concluded a declaration was sufficient remedy); *Westfair Foods Ltd.*, BCLRB Decision No. B20/2010 (disclosure order accompanied by a direction to meet with a BCLRB mediator at his earliest availability).

[60] *CJS Victoria Inc. (Copperjohns)*, BCLRB Decision No. B46/2004; *G & H Noble Custom Cut Ltd.*, BCLRB Decision No. B85/2008.

agreements,[61] declared a lockout invalid and ordered compensation to an employee, or ordered a party to drop or cease and desist making specified bargaining proposals.[62] In one case where the employer violated the GFB duty by reviewing the union proposal before preparing its own, the award specified that negotiations would recommence based on the union's proposal only, and specified a collective agreement term. If the parties agreed to a longer term then bargaining could also consider the employer's proposal.[63]

In several cases the remedial award specified the format or structure of bargaining, often with BCLRB assistance, and often with explicit reference to the section 2 Code duties to foster collective bargaining and mediation as a dispute resolution tool.[64] Instances of more substantial BCLRB intervention into bargaining arose in a series of decisions stemming from a case in which both the employer and union committed GFB violations.[65] The BCLRB's remedial response was to order the parties to participate in a mediation/adjudication process, with BCLRB assistance, to establish a bargaining format. The decision set out specific steps for the parties to follow (outlining the series of counter proposals) to conclude collective bargaining and fulfil their GFB obligations. The BCLRB became actively involved in that round of negotiations, providing mediation and direction to the parties. When the parties were unable to agree, the BCLRB ultimately imposed a bargaining structure and format applicable to that round of negotiations, and a further clarification of its directions and ruling.[66]

Australia

Overview of good faith bargaining in Australia

From the early 1990s, Australia moved towards a system of enterprise-based bargaining, which has gradually overtaken the traditional framework of regulation of employment conditions through industrial awards.[67] While 'modern awards' continue to set minimum wages and conditions for many Australian employees, many more workers are now covered by enterprise agreements.[68]

[61] *MTM Enterprise Ltd.*, BCLRB Decision No. B168/2007 (voided ratification vote, ordered new vote, and made cease and desist order); *Timberwest Forest Corporation*, BCRLRB Decision No. B189/2007 (refused employer request for employee vote on its final offer); *Forest Industrial Relations Ltd.*, BCLRB Decision No. B433/2003 (declared memo of agreement of no force and effect).

[62] *VSA Highway Maintenance Ltd.*, BCLRB Decision No. B69/2007; *Coast Hotels Ltd*, BCLRB Decision No. B209/2009.

[63] *Thunderbird Winter Sports Centre*, BCLRB Decision No. B164/2004.

[64] *Forest Industrial Relations*, BCLRB Decision No. B256/2003; *Westfair Foods Ltd.*, Decision No. BCLRB No. B61/2011.

[65] *Construction Labour Relations Association of British Columbia* [2004] BCLRB Decision No. B322/2004.

[66] *Construction Labour Relations Association of British Columbia* [2005] BCLRB Decision Nos. B50/2005; B86/2005.

[67] See the special issue of the journal 'Labour and Industry' (2012, 22(3)) devoted to consideration of the evolution of the enterprise bargaining system in Australia on the occasion of its twentieth anniversary. See also Keith Townsend, Adrian Wilkinson, and John Burgess, 'Is Enterprise Bargaining Still a Better Way of Working?' (2013) 55(1) Journal of Industrial Relations (JIR) 100.

[68] Australian Bureau of Statistics, *Employee Earnings and Hours, Australia, May 2012*, Cat. 6306.0.

The provisions for GFB are a central feature of the collective bargaining framework in the Fair Work Act 2009 (Cth) (FW Act).[69] This legislation marked a return to a collectivist approach to agreement-making, replacing a system which prioritized individual negotiation between employers and employees.[70] Under the Workplace Relations Act 1996 (Cth), collective bargaining could occur—but apart from the capacity of employees and unions to take protected industrial action in support of their claims for an agreement, an employer was under no obligation to bargain. When bargaining did occur, there were no requirements on any of the parties to negotiate in good faith.[71]

Collective bargaining under the FW Act is conducted through the bargaining representatives of employers and employees.[72] Employer bargaining representatives may include the employer itself, and anyone it appoints in writing (e.g. a consultant or employer association representative). Employee bargaining representatives may include an employee's union, or an employee representing him/herself or a group of employees. This provision for individual employee representation in collective agreement negotiations sets the Australian system apart from the Canadian (and United States) approach, whereby a majority union obtains exclusive representation rights over the employees in a bargaining unit.[73]

Under section 228(1)(a)–(f) of the FW Act, the following explicit GFB obligations are imposed on the bargaining representatives for a proposed enterprise agreement:

- attending and participating in meetings at reasonable times;
- disclosing relevant information in a timely manner, although not confidential or commercially sensitive information;
- responding to proposals made by other bargaining representatives in a timely manner;
- giving genuine consideration to the proposals of other bargaining representatives, and giving reasons for any responses to those proposals;
- refraining from capricious or unfair conduct that undermines freedom of association or collective bargaining;
- recognizing and bargaining with all other bargaining representatives.

[69] Another principal feature of that framework is the capacity of unions, employees, and employers to take lawful industrial action (known as 'protected action') in support of their bargaining claims: see Shae McCrystal, *The Right to Strike in Australia* (Federation Press, 2010).

[70] Although the extent to which the FW Act truly restored a *collectivist* approach is the subject of some debate: see e.g. Breen Creighton, 'A Retreat from Individualism? The Fair Work Act 2009 and the Re-collectivisation of Australian Labour Law' (2011) 40(2) Industrial Law Journal (ILJ) 116, arguing (at 143) that the model of collective bargaining under the legislation is notably 'individualistic' in character (in part because enterprise agreements are made between employers and employees, rather than employers and unions).

[71] Ron McCallum, 'Trade Union Recognition and Australia's Neo-Liberal Voluntary Bargaining Laws' (2002) 57 Relations Industrielles 225.

[72] Anthony Forsyth, 'The Evolving Pluralistic Approach to Employee Representation at the Enterprise in Australia' in Roger Blanpain (ed.), *Systems of Employee Representation at the Enterprise: A Comparative Study* (Kluwer Law International, 2012) 1; Elyane Palmer, 'The Representative Role of Unions in the Fair Work System' (2013) 55(3) JIR 421.

[73] Clyde Summers, 'Exclusive Representation: A Comparative Inquiry into a "Unique" American Principle' (1998) 20 CLLPJ 47.

Importantly, section 228(2) qualifies these obligations, by providing that GFB does *not* require a bargaining representative to make any concessions during bargaining or to reach agreement on the terms to be included in an agreement.

There are some similarities between the content of the GFB obligations under Australian and Canadian law, although a significant difference is the absence in Australia of any equivalent to the Canadian obligation to make all reasonable efforts to conclude an agreement. The Labor government—in framing the FW Act GFB provisions—did not consciously seek to emulate North American laws on the subject.[74] This is despite the fact that, in arguing for the introduction of GFB requirements during the period of the Howard Coalition government (1996–2007), academics and the trade union movement made frequent reference to US and Canadian law.[75] In interpreting the FW Act provisions, the FWC has repeatedly indicated that overseas jurisprudence on GFB is not relevant, or at least should be treated with caution, in the Australian context.[76]

The powers of the FWC to make a bargaining order to enforce the GFB obligations[77] form part of the tribunal's supervisory role over collective bargaining.[78] Its other powers under Part 2-4 of the FW Act include:

- making a majority support determination, the effect of which is to compel a reluctant employer to engage in collective bargaining, where it is established that a majority of the relevant employees in a workplace want to bargain;[79]
- making a scope order to resolve a dispute between employee and employer bargaining representatives over the coverage of a proposed agreement;[80]
- resolving bargaining disputes on application by a bargaining representative, by conciliation or mediation or (if all bargaining representatives agree) by arbitration;[81]
- making a low-paid authorization, which provides access to multi-employer bargaining for certain low-paid employees who have not previously been able to access enterprise bargaining, and assisting the bargaining representatives in low-paid

[74] For instance, there is no explicit mention of Canadian or United States law in relevant sections of the *Explanatory Memorandum to the Fair Work Bill 2008*.

[75] See e.g. Australian Council of Trade Unions, *A Fair Go at Work: Collective Bargaining for Australian Workers* (September 2006); Anthony Forsyth, 'Worker Representation in Australia: Moving Towards Overseas Models?' (2007) 33(1) Australian Bulletin of Labour 1; Aaron Rathmell, 'Collective Bargaining after Work Choices: Will "Good Faith" Take Us Forward with Fairness?' (2008) 21(2) AJLL 164; note however the cautionary tone in George Strauss, 'Suppose Australia Copied US Employee Relations Practices' (2008) 18(2) Economic and Labour Relations Review 123.

[76] See e.g. *Finance Sector Union v Commonwealth Bank of Australia* [2010] FWA 2690 (9 April 2010) at para. 58 (National Labor Relations Board jurisprudence on GFB not taken into account, as US system of exclusive bargaining rights does not have parallels in Australia); *Endeavour Coal Pty Ltd v Association of Professional Engineers, Scientists and Managers, Australia* [2012] FWAFB 1891 (22 March 2012) at para. 21(Canadian and NZ jurisprudence, developed in different industrial and legislative contexts, should be treated with caution when considering the GFB obligations under the FW Act).

[77] FW Act, ss. 229–232. Other enforcement options include the FWC making a serious breach declaration to address serious and repeated breaches of bargaining orders, or enforcement through court orders: FW Act, ss. 233–235 and Part 4-1.

[78] Richard Naughton, 'The Role of Fair Work Australia in Facilitating Collective Bargaining' in Breen Creighton and Anthony Forsyth (eds), *Rediscovering Collective Bargaining: Australia's Fair Work Act in International Perspective* (Routledge, 2012) 68.

[79] FW Act, ss. 236–237. [80] FW Act, ss. 238–239. [81] FW Act, s. 240.

bargaining to reach an agreement (including by arbitration of a first agreement in certain limited circumstances).[82]

The operation of Australia's good faith bargaining laws: July 2009–June 2012

As indicated in the Introduction, this part of the chapter draws largely upon the data and findings of research conducted through a partnership arrangement with the FWC,[83] which examined the tribunal's role in supervising enterprise bargaining under the FW Act over the first three years of the legislation's operation (1 July 2009–30 June 2012).[84] We present here data drawn from the FWC's case management database to show the numbers of applications for bargaining orders to enforce the GFB obligations, in the context of the overall numbers of applications lodged under Part 2-4 of the FW Act over this period. We also present data on the identity of applicants for bargaining orders, the industries from which applications came, and the outcomes of the applications. This is followed by a discussion of the case law on the GFB requirements, illustrating the types of bargaining tactics and conduct which the FWC has found to be consistent with GFB—and tactics/conduct which have been found to constitute bad faith.

Good faith bargaining: analysis of Australian data

Figure 8.8 shows the number of applications made under the various provisions in Part 2-4 of the FW Act seeking assistance or a determination/order from the FWC in relation to the bargaining process. This shows that over the period 1 July 2009 to 30 June 2012, a total of 1,785 applications were lodged. The vast bulk of these applications (1,075 or 60.2 per cent) were made under section 240 (applications to the tribunal for assistance to resolve a bargaining dispute, overwhelmingly through conciliation or mediation). Applications for bargaining orders to enforce the GFB obligations were the next most-utilized mechanism, with 324 applications over the three-year period (18.2 per cent of the total number of Part 2-4 applications). In comparison, there were 274 applications for majority support determinations; 108 applications for scope orders; and only 4 applications for low-paid authorizations.

Figure 8.9 reports the number of bargaining order applications made each month over the period July 2009–June 2012. From this figure it is difficult to discern any distinctive trend in the monthly lodgement of applications for bargaining orders over the three-year period. However, annualized data show a reasonably steady flow of

[82] FW Act, ss. 241–246, 260–265.

[83] The research partnership was entered into by the authors named at n 18 and FWC (then FWA) as part of an expression of interest issued by the then General Manager in June 2011, which invited interested academics and academic institutions to submit proposals to undertake a partnership research project. The projects were to advance the understanding of issues that would inform one or more areas of the reporting requirements outlined in s. 653 of the Fair Work Act 2009. The FWC subsequently selected the authors' proposal and provided assistance to the authors by providing access to relevant (non-confidential) public case files as well as data from its case management database for purposes of the research.

[84] Forsyth et al. (n 18).

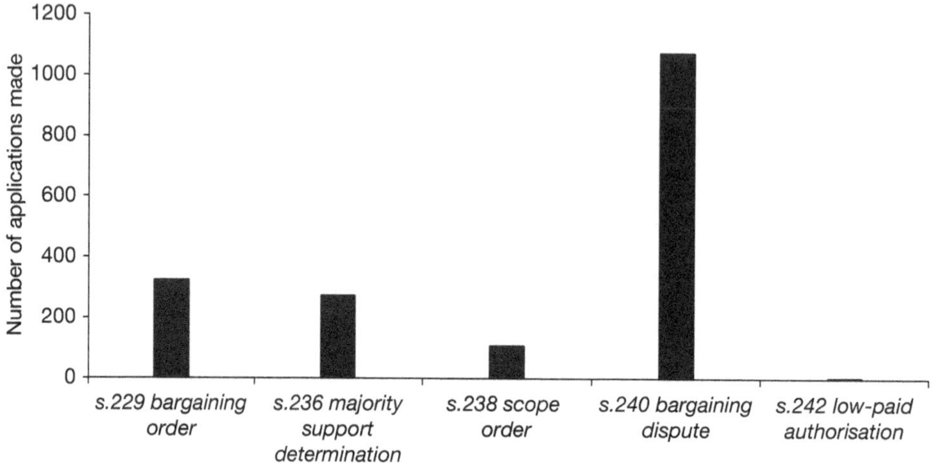

Figure 8.8 Applications lodged under Part 2-4, by type

Source: Compiled from Fair Work Commission case management database. Data are for the period 1 July 2009 to 30 June 2012.

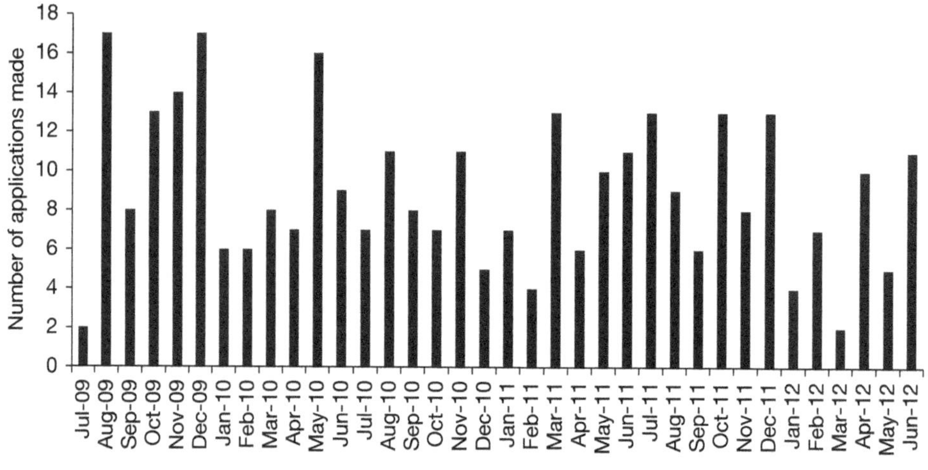

Figure 8.9 Applications for bargaining orders, monthly total

Source: Compiled from Fair Work Commission case management database. Data are for the period 1 July 2009 to 30 June 2012.

applications: in the first year of operation of the FW Act, 123 applications for bargaining orders were made; followed by 100 and 101 applications in the second and third years respectively.

Figure 8.10 indicates the identity of the applicants seeking bargaining orders.[85] The majority (252, or 77.7 per cent) of bargaining order applications over the three-year period were made by union bargaining representatives. Compared with the other types of applications to the tribunal that can be initiated under Part 2-4 of the FW Act, a

[85] A bargaining order may be sought by any bargaining representative involved in negotiations for an enterprise agreement.

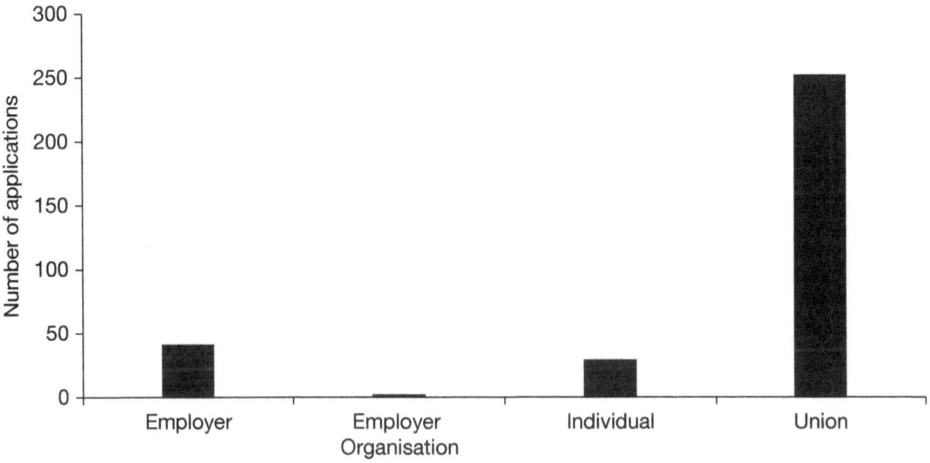

Figure 8.10 Applications for bargaining orders, by applicant type

Source: Compiled from Fair Work Commission case management database. Data are for the period 1 July 2009 to 30 June 2012.

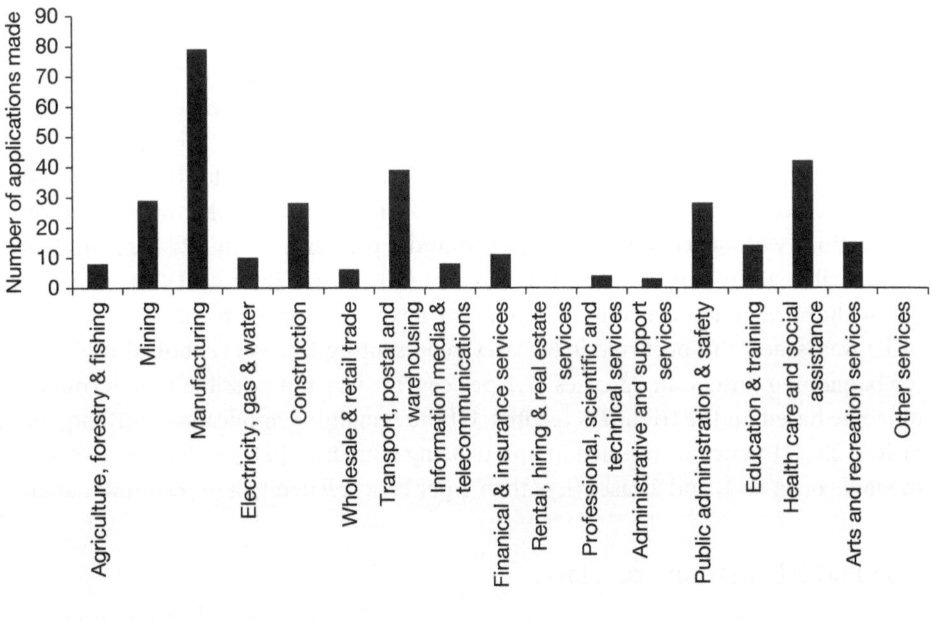

Figure 8.11 Applications for bargaining orders, by industry

Source: Compiled from Fair Work Commission case management database. Data are for the period 1 July 2009 to 30 June 2012.

larger proportion of bargaining order applications were made by employers: 43 applications (13.3 per cent of the total) were made by employers or employer associations. 29, or 9.0 per cent of all applications for bargaining orders, were brought before the tribunal by individual bargaining representatives.

Figure 8.11 shows the distribution of bargaining order applications by industry over the period July 2009–June 2012. The largest proportion of these applications were

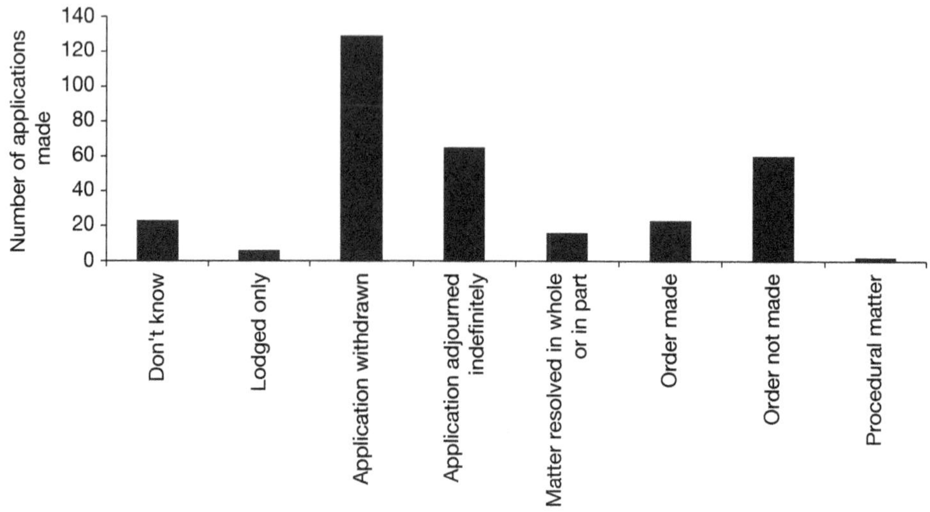

Figure 8.12 Applications for bargaining orders, by outcome

Source: Compiled from Fair Work Commission case management database. Data are for the period 1 July 2009 to 30 June 2012.

concentrated in the following industries: 79 in manufacturing (24.4 per cent); 42 in healthcare and social assistance (13 per cent); 39 in transport, postal and water services (12.0 per cent); 29 in mining (9.0 per cent); 28 in construction (8.6 per cent); and 15 in arts and recreation services (4.6 per cent).

Figure 8.12 reports outcomes associated with all applications for bargaining orders over the three-year period.[86] The key finding from this data is that bargaining order applications were successful in only 23 (around 7 per cent) of the 324 cases dealt with by the tribunal. In almost two-thirds of cases (200, or 61.7 per cent), the application was withdrawn or adjourned indefinitely. The next most common outcome was that no order was issued; this occurred in 60 cases, representing 18.8 per cent of all applications for bargaining orders. In 23 cases (7.1 per cent) it was not possible to determine the outcome based on the tribunal's records. Of the remaining applications for bargaining orders: 23 (7.1 per cent) resulted in orders being issued; 16 (4.9 per cent) were resolved in whole or in part; and 2 cases (less than 1 per cent) related to a procedural matter.

Good faith bargaining case law

With many decided cases, the first three years of operation of the good faith bargaining framework under the FW Act provide the best opportunity (to date) to examine the adaptation of good faith in the Australian context.[87] First, we consider how the FWC has interpreted the obligations in section 228(1)(a), (c), and (d) of the FW Act,

[86] In a number of these cases it was not possible to determine the outcome from the FWC's records; hence, a number of applications are recorded in Figure 8.12 as unknown ('don't know').

[87] That is, in comparison with the short-lived experiment with a duty to bargain in good faith under federal legislation between 1993–96 (see Richard Naughton, 'Bargaining in Good Faith' in Paul Ronfeldt and Ron McCallum (eds), *Enterprise Bargaining, Trade Unions and the Law* (Federation Press, 1995) 84); and the longer-standing GFB provisions under Western Australian legislation which have involved few decided

requiring bargaining representatives to attend meetings, give genuine consideration and respond to the proposals of other bargaining representatives, and give reasons for those responses. Overall, the tribunal has used these provisions in many cases to ensure an orderly bargaining process—for example, by making orders setting a timetable for negotiations and the exchange of information, proposals, and counter-offers between the bargaining representatives.[88] The FWC has also found the following types of conduct in breach of the requirements in section 228(1)(a), (c), and/or (d):

- an employer refusing to meet with union bargaining representatives at proposed times, and failing to provide reasons as to why the times proposed by the union were unreasonable;[89]
- an employer simply saying in response to a union's log of claims that they were 'unrealistic', rather than giving genuine consideration to the union's proposals;[90]
- a union refusing to meet with an employer (despite the employer having made a number of concessions), and failing to respond to the employer's proposals;[91]
- an employer purporting to withdraw from the bargaining process, by refusing to participate in further negotiations after a proposed enterprise agreement was rejected by employees in a ballot.[92]

Secondly, we look at the FWC's approach to the obligation regarding information disclosure imposed upon bargaining representatives by section 228(1)(b). This has been found to require an employer to provide a union bargaining representative with information relating to the employee classifications and pay rates under a proposed agreement. With this information, the union could properly assess the company's position and establish whether it would lead to a wage increase (so the information was both relevant to the negotiations, and not confidential because individual employees could be de-identified).[93] In contrast, it has been held that employers are not required:

- to provide a union with the consolidated financial accounts for the business and its related entities, because the employer did not assert an incapacity to pay during agreement negotiations;[94]

cases (see Michael Gillan, Donella Caspersz, and Daniel White, 'Test of Faith: Good Faith Bargaining in Western Australia' (2011) 24 AJLL 95).

[88] See e.g. *Liquor, Hospitality and Miscellaneous Union v Carinya Care Services*, PR501295 (2 September 2010); *NSW Nurses' Association v Macquarie Hospital Services Pty Ltd* [2010] FWA 6372 and PR500749 (24 August 2010); *Australian Services Union v NCR Australia Pty Ltd* PR500593 (16 August 2010). On some occasions, the FWC has ordered the parties to participate in conciliation conferences overseen by the tribunal: e.g. *Curragh Queensland Mining Pty Ltd v Communications, Electrical and Plumbing Union*, PR524980 (7 June 2012).

[89] *Australian Manufacturing Workers Union v Galintel Rolling Mills Pty Ltd T/A The Graham Group and Others* [2011] FWA 6326 (16 September 2011).

[90] *Australian Meat Industry Employees Union v T&R (Murray Bridge) Pty Ltd* [2010] FWA 1320 (26 February 2010).

[91] *Flinders Operating Services T/A Alinta Energy v Communications, Electrical and Plumbing Union* [2010] FWA 4821 (30 July 2010).

[92] *Australian Services Union v NCR Australia Pty Ltd* [2010] FWA 6257 (16 August 2010); see also *Community and Public Sector Union v Red Bee Media Pty Ltd* [2010] FWA 9253 (7 December 2010).

[93] *Community and Public Sector Union v Red Bee Media Pty Ltd* [2010] FWA 9253 (7 December 2010).

[94] *Queensland Nurses' Union of Employees v TriCare Limited* [2010] FWA 7416 (23 September 2010).

- to go to extensive efforts to provide the information requested by a union, in this instance responding to questions by the union regarding the employer's pay offer that the tribunal found were too 'broad, complex and ambiguous' (the FWC clarified that an employer's obligation under section 228(1)(b) is not to satisfy another party's request for information; rather it is to provide relevant information in a timely manner).[95]

Thirdly, we examine the tribunal's application and interpretation of the obligations in section 228(1)(e)–(f), requiring bargaining representatives to recognize and bargain with each other; and to refrain from capricious or unfair conduct that undermines freedom of association or collective bargaining. These elements of section 228(1) have given rise to by far the greatest number of decided cases.

We begin with conduct that has been found by the FWC to breach section 228(1)(e) and/or (f). In a number of decisions, the tribunal has held that an employer must not provide misleading information to employees during negotiations,[96] although this can be distinguished from information that is simply 'robust'. Employer and employee bargaining representatives have been given considerable latitude to 'forcefully put [their] account of the bargaining directly to employees for their information or to attempt to persuade them to support a proposed agreement'.[97] This permissive approach was taken to its extreme in *Liquor, Hospitality and Miscellaneous Union (WA Branch) v Hall and Prior Aged Care Organisation and Others*,[98] where the tribunal found that the use of emotive language by bargaining representatives—putting their best 'spin' on the negotiations in material distributed to employees—was all part of the 'rough and tumble' of bargaining.[99]

Various forms of 'direct dealing' by employers with employees have been ruled in breach of the GFB requirements—particularly, employers making direct offers to employees or making unilateral changes to working conditions during agreement negotiations. The rationale for this approach is that it preserves the integrity of the bargaining process, by ensuring that the employer cannot take action designed to weaken employee support for collective negotiation.[100] Such employer conduct is proscribed, even if it results in *improvements* in employees' wages or conditions, such as unilateral

[95] *Australian Services Union v Australian Taxation Office* [2011] FWA 5407 (18 August 2011).

[96] See e.g. *National Union of Workers v Ross Cosmetics Australia Pty Ltd* [2012] FWA 3252 (18 April 2012); here, the employer was found to have acted in bad faith where it provided misleading information to employees about a proposed agreement and its effect on existing entitlements, and implied in its communications to employees that certain claims by the union were unlawful. In *Transport Workers Union v Veolia Transport Queensland Pty Ltd* [2011] FWA 5691 (23 August 2011), the employer transgressed s. 228(1)(e) when it issued a series of staff bulletins including incorrect statements about the rights of union members to take protected industrial action.

[97] *National Union of Workers v Ross Cosmetics Australia Pty Ltd* [2012] FWA 3252 (18 April 2012). See also *National Union of Workers v Patties Foods Ltd* [2011] FWA 4103 (1 July 2011); *Jupiters Limited v United Voice* [2011] FWA 8317 (5 December 2011).

[98] [2010] FWA 1065 (11 February 2010).

[99] Among other things, the employer had described the union as 'just wanting to cause trouble', and being 'unfair, unreasonable and un-Australian'. For its part, the union had distributed material portraying the employer as 'the caricatured black suited, cigar smoking "fat capitalist" dragging a trolley load of money'.

[100] See e.g. the views of a Full Bench of the tribunal in *Endeavour Coal Pty Ltd v Association of Professional Engineers, Scientists and Managers, Australia* [2012] FWAFB 1891 (22 March 2012) at [55].

salary increases made in circumstances where the employer has refused to put a pay offer on the bargaining table.[101] Even more clearly constituting unfair or capricious conduct that undermines freedom of association or collective bargaining (in breach of section 228(1)(e)) is where an employer seeks to separate individual employees from the collective group—for example, by offering employees a 3 per cent pay rise if they revoked the union's status as their bargaining representative.[102] However, the implementation by employers of changes to certain employment arrangements (such as workplace policies or rosters) during bargaining has, in a number of decisions, been found not to breach the good faith requirements.[103] Further, direct dealing in the form of communications between employers and their employees about matters that are the subject of negotiation is not considered in breach of section 228(1)(e) or (f) (this is discussed further later in the chapter).

'Surface bargaining'—where a bargaining representative is simply 'going through the motions' without any real intention of reaching an agreement—has been found technically in breach of section 228(1)(e)–(f). However, difficulties have arisen concerning the FWC's powers to frame orders dealing with surface bargaining, given the limitations imposed by section 228(2).[104] The leading decision on this issue is that of Justice Flick of the Federal Court of Australia in *Endeavour Coal Pty Ltd v Association of Professional Engineers, Scientists and Managers, Australia*.[105] In this case, the union had been seeking an agreement for its members employed at the company's coal mine. From the commencement of negotiations in July 2010, the parties held twelve meetings over a 12-month period before reaching an impasse. The union then applied for a bargaining order, arguing that the company was not bargaining in good faith because it had no real intention of reaching an agreement and would not put any proposals in the negotiations. The union was successful in the tribunal at first instance and on appeal before a Full Bench, obtaining orders requiring the company (among other things) to provide it with a list of matters that it would be prepared to include in an agreement.[106]

In a further appeal by the company to the Federal Court, Justice Flick agreed with the tribunal's approach to interpreting the requirements of section 228(1)(e)–(f) and in particular their application to surface bargaining. According to Justice Flick, a bargaining representative cannot sit 'mute' during agreement negotiations or 'adopt the role of a disinterested suitor, only rejecting offers and proposals' advanced by other bargaining representatives.[107] Despite this, Justice Flick struck down the tribunal's order requiring

[101] *Finance Sector Union v Commonwealth Bank of Australia* [2010] FWA 2690 (9 April 2010).

[102] *Australian Manufacturing Workers Union v Galintel Rolling Mills Pty Ltd T/A The Graham Group and Others* [2011] FWA 6326 (16 September 2011).

[103] See e.g. *Association of Professional Engineers, Scientists and Managers, Australia v BHP Coal Pty Ltd* [2012] FWA 4435 (27 June 2012); *Australian Workers Union v Woodside Energy Limited* [2012] FWA 4332 (30 May 2012). In both cases, it was held that the employer had not acted with the intent of subverting the bargaining process.

[104] See earlier in the chapter; and note s. 255(1)(a), which precludes the FWC from making an order requiring particular content to be included or not included in an agreement (unless the parties have agreed to arbitration under s. 240(4): see s. 255(2)).

[105] (2012) 206 FCR 576.

[106] *Association of Professional Engineers, Scientists and Managers, Australia (Collieries' Staff Division) v Endeavour Coal Pty Ltd* [2012] FWA 13 (4 January 2012); *Endeavour Coal Pty Ltd v Association of Professional Engineers, Scientists and Managers, Australia* [2012] FWAFB 1891 (22 March 2012).

[107] (2012) 206 FCR 576 at [35].

the company to table the proposals it would be prepared to include in an agreement, finding that this: 'trespasses into the area of requiring Endeavour Coal to accept [the identified matters] as part of any final agreement that may be reached', contrary to the limitations imposed by section 228(2).[108] Justice Flick highlighted the tension, inherent in section 228, between the positive duty to bargain in good faith and the proviso that this does not require a party to make concessions: 'The difficulty is in the formulation of orders to give effect to [the good faith] requirements without trespassing into the prohibited territory created by s 228(2).'[109]

Turning now to conduct that has been found *not* to be in breach of section 228(1)(e) or (f), the FWC has generally permitted employers to submit a proposed agreement to a ballot of employees—even when a union or other employee bargaining representative asserts that negotiations have not yet concluded. This issue highlights a clash between the agreement-making provisions of the FW Act,[110] and the GFB requirements. After some uncertainty arising from several inconsistent decisions of the tribunal,[111] a Full Bench settled the issue in *Construction, Forestry, Mining and Energy Union v Tahmoor Coal Pty Ltd*.[112] There, it was stated that while there may be circumstances where the conduct of a ballot without the agreement of other bargaining representatives is in breach of the GFB requirements, that will not always be the case.[113] In deciding whether an agreement can be submitted to a ballot of employees, the tribunal can consider (for example): whether an impasse or stalemate has been reached in the negotiations;[114] whether the union still needs a reasonable opportunity to discuss the employer's latest proposal; or whether negotiations have reached a point where the employer is entitled to put the agreement to a ballot to see if progress can be made.[115] A number of cases illustrate that it will be particularly difficult for a union to establish a breach of section 228(1)(e)–(f), and obtain a bargaining order preventing an employer from submitting an agreement to ballot, where the union becomes involved in negotiations at a late stage.[116]

The FWC has also given employers considerable latitude in relation to direct communication with employees while bargaining is occurring. The main authority on this

[108] (2012) 206 FCR 576 at [62].

[109] (2012) 206 FCR 576 at [78]. Two other decisions illustrate the tribunal's apparent inability to deal effectively with surface bargaining: *Association of Professional Engineers, Scientists and Managers, Australia v BHP Coal Pty Ltd* [2012] FWA 4435 (20 June 2012); and *Australian Manufacturing Workers Union v Cochlear Limited* [2012] FWA 5374 (3 August 2012).

[110] FW Act, Part 2-4, Divisions 3 and 4, the provisions of which enable an employer to request employees to approve an enterprise agreement within certain prescribed time-frames relating mainly to the provision of information to employees about the proposed agreement; and then (if a majority of employees who cast a vote approve the agreement) to submit the agreement to the FWC for approval.

[111] See e.g. *Australian Services Union v Queensland Tertiary Admissions Centre Ltd* [2009] FWA 53 (29 July 2009); cf *National Union of Workers v Chep Australia Ltd* [2009] FWA 202 (11 September 2009) and *Australian Meat Industry Employees Union v T&R (Murray Bridge) Pty Ltd* [2010] FWA 1320 (26 February 2010).

[112] [2010] FWAFB 3510 (22 May 2010).

[113] [2010] FWAFB 3510 at [30].

[114] This test has been applied in a number of subsequent FWC decisions: see *Queensland Nurses' Union of Employees v TriCare Limited* [2010] FWA 7416 (23 September 2010); *Australian Manufacturing Workers Union v Coates Hire Operations Pty Ltd T/A Coates Hire Limited* [2012] FWA 3357 (19 April 2012).

[115] [2010] FWAFB 3510 at [30].

[116] *Australian Services Union v Global Tele Sales Pty Ltd* [2011] FWA 3916 (22 June 2011); *Construction, Forestry, Mining and Energy Union v Ostwald Bros Pty Ltd* [2012] FWA 2484 (23 March 2012).

issue is (again) the Full Bench decision in *Construction, Forestry, Mining and Energy Union v Tahmoor Coal Pty Ltd*.[117] In this decision, the tribunal rejected the union's claims that the employer had breached section 228(1)(e)–(f) by holding briefings with employees and sending information to their homes about agreement proposals—without informing the union. As long as the information provided to employees was not misleading,[118] the meetings were not oppressive, and the employer continued to meet with the union, the employer acted reasonably in seeking to explain its proposals to employees directly.[119] This approach has been strongly criticized from the union's perspective: drawing partly on the more restrictive Canadian position, Bukarica and Dallas argue that direct communication between an employer and its workforce undermines collective bargaining by challenging the authority of the union as the employees' bargaining representative.[120] However, this view has not found support among members of the FWC, as illustrated by the Full Bench decision in *Tahmoor Coal* and a number of single member decisions.[121]

Conclusion: Assessing the Experience of Canadian and Australian Good Faith Bargaining Laws

The British Columbia data, obtained from the BCLRB for the 2003–2012 study period, reveal a fairly stable volume of GFB complaints being filed each year, with trade unions filing the great majority of these applications. Regardless of the identity of the applicant, few complaints are granted. Most result in a voluntary settlement; few are dismissed; and a very small proportion of complaints are withdrawn or not proceeded with. It is difficult to draw implications from this pattern of outcomes. However, rather than reflecting parties' strategic use of GFB complaints, this may be an effect of the BCLRB's explicit statutory duty to promote collective bargaining, cooperative resolution of disputes, and mediation to resolve disputes, including in its remedial awards.[122]

Our findings surrounding the timing of GFB complaints suggest that, by the time a complaint is filed, sufficient time has generally elapsed since certification of the bargaining relationship to expect that some bargaining activity (or attempted bargaining) has already occurred. Meanwhile, our finding that a substantial proportion of all GFB complaints are filed within two years after certification suggests that the first round of negotiations in a newly established bargaining relationship is particularly prone to GFB disputes.[123]

[117] [2010] FWAFB 3510 (22 May 2010). [118] See earlier in the chapter.

[119] [2010] FWAFB 3510 at [28]–[29].

[120] Bukarica and Dallas 109–11 (n 17); see also Read 130, 138–40, 147–8 (n 17).

[121] *Liquor, Hospitality and Miscellaneous Union v Mingara Recreation Club Ltd* [2009] FWA 1442 (1 December 2009); *Queensland Nurses' Union of Employees v Roman Catholic Diocese of Toowoomba T/A Lourdes Home for the Aged, Lourdes Home Hostel* [2009] FWA 1553 (7 December 2009); *LHMU WA Branch v Hall and Prior Aged Care Organisation and Others* [2010] FWA 1065 (11 February 2010).

[122] Section 2, Code.

[123] Recognition of the particular difficulty of the first round of negotiations underlay BC's adoption of first contract arbitration provisions in its 1973 Code (See Harry W. Arthurs, 'The Dullest Bill: Reflections on the Labour Code of British Columbia' (1974) 9 UBC L Rev 280).

Finally, our review of remedial awards (though limited by the small number of decisions published in the study period) indicates that the BCLRB's remedial response to GFB violations is varied and carefully tailored to the particular circumstances in each case. The BCLRB employs its remedial authority to intervene directly, or through BCLRB mediators, to referee or manage bargaining to ensure GFB. In some cases this extends to the BCLRB outlining the bargaining procedure the parties are to follow in order to comply with GFB. These more interventionist responses appear to be products of the BCLRB's earlier noted statutory duties. These duties, and their resulting influence on remedial outcomes may, in turn, encourage parties to voluntarily resolve complaints.

In relation to Australia, the statistics drawn from the FWC's case management data showed that, over the first three years of operation of Part 2-4 of the FW Act, the volume of applications for orders to enforce the good faith bargaining applications was fairly consistent. However, more recent data indicates a reduction in bargaining order applications since mid-2012.[124] The tribunal's case management data also revealed that very few applications resulted in a bargaining order being made; and a high proportion of applications were withdrawn or adjourned, suggesting that the making of such applications is often a tactical manoeuvre by bargaining representatives. This last finding was confirmed by data drawn from interviews conducted with employer, union, and employee bargaining representatives as part of the FWC study.[125] The interview data also indicated that the GFB provisions—and the FWC's role in overseeing them—are having an observable 'shadow effect' on the parties' negotiating conduct and tactics.[126] For example, awareness of the good faith requirements and the availability of bargaining orders has been sufficient to keep negotiations 'on track' in a number of instances (without a formal application for an order).[127]

When we compare the BC and Australian data on GFB complaints filed with the BCLRB and the FWC respectively, we find the identity of applicants for orders to enforce the GFB obligations is strikingly similar, with unions making around 80 per cent of applications in both jurisdictions. In terms of outcomes, we can see that a substantially higher proportion of GFB complaints in BC were successful (16.5 per cent, compared with 7.1 per cent in Australia). While it is difficult to interpret this difference, it may reflect the different stages of development of this legal principle in the two jurisdictions. While the contours of the GFB obligation are well settled in BC, it was a new and developing concept in Australia during the period under study. Therefore we might expect more unsuccessful complaints in the context of less certain law. Interestingly, though, in both jurisdictions the vast majority of GFB complaints are settled, withdrawn, or adjourned definitely. This 'shadow effect' arguably points to a higher level of influence of GFB provisions than is suggested by the 'success' rates reported earlier in the chapter.

[124] See e.g. 'Dismissal claims rise, bargaining activity slows', *Workplace Express*, 13 February 2013; 'Surge in adverse action claims, bargaining quiet,' *Workplace Express*, 24 May 2013.

[125] Forsyth et al. 113–15 (n 18).

[126] The shadow effect of collective bargaining legislation is considered (in the UK context) in Gregor Gall, 'The First Ten Years of the Third Statutory Union Recognition Procedure in Britain' (2010) 39 ILJ 444.

[127] Forsyth et al. 115–16 (n 18).

Considering the decisions issued in BCLRB cases decided during the study period, it appears that the GFB principles which have been well-established for several decades continue to be applied without substantial changes. Notably, the focus of BCLRB scrutiny in GFB complaints continues to be the parties' conduct and the process of bargaining, not the substance of bargaining proposals. It also appears that the longstanding criticism of the GFB provision continues to apply: that it is unable to effectively address the sophisticated, powerful employer who thwarts constructive negotiations by cloaking bad faith, surface bargaining as self-interested and, therefore, good faith efforts.

Also interesting are the clear indications in the case law surrounding remedial awards for GFB violations that the BCLRB's primary focus in crafting a remedial order is on establishing a GFB process between the parties. Particularly notable is the BCLRB's willingness to intervene in negotiations to achieve this purpose, primarily by giving parties explicit directions for an adequate bargaining process, requiring parties to negotiate with assistance of a Board mediator, and by retaining jurisdiction to resolve any problems arising in implementing the remedial order. In light of the criticism of access to, and usefulness of, GFB remedies (as described earlier) in the earliest appearance of statutory GFB obligations in Canada, these flexible, responsive, and monitored remedies are potentially an important development.

Comparing the Australian GFB case law to established principles in BC, this developing jurisprudence also tends to focus more on the machinations of the bargaining process than on the substance of bargaining proposals. The Australian case law over the initial three-year period of the FW Act highlights several important trends. First, the process obligations (section 228(1)(a)–(d)) are operating largely as intended, ensuring an orderly bargaining process in many cases through the provision of clear ground rules for the conduct of negotiations. Secondly, the obligations which impact more directly on bargaining tactics (section 228(1)(e)–(f)) have operated to prohibit certain kinds of employer behaviour that undermine the bargaining process, such as attempts to separate employees out from the collective group through direct offers or unilateral improvements to existing conditions. Thirdly, however, a narrow interpretation of the obligations in section 228(1)(e)–(f) in some other cases has allowed employers significant latitude to (for example) communicate directly with employees during negotiations, and this is arguably not consistent with the objective of facilitating and promoting collective bargaining.[128] Fourthly, this statutory purpose is also undermined by the FWC's attitude to when an employer may submit an agreement to a ballot of employees. This approach prioritizes compliance with the *agreement-making* requirements over those applicable to good faith negotiations and *collective bargaining.*[129] Fifthly, the prevailing position on surface bargaining illustrates the inherent tension between the section 228(1) obligations and the limitation upon them contained in section 228(2). The FWC cannot enforce, through a binding order, its view that bargaining must be undertaken with the outcome of an agreement in mind.

[128] See FW Act, ss. 3(f) and 171.

[129] See also Read 142–6, 148–51 (n 17); and (outlining a broader critique of the FW Act bargaining scheme) Bukarica and Dallas ch. 4 (n 17).

This leads to a broader observation about the FW Act bargaining framework: that it can get a reluctant employer to the negotiating table (for example, through a majority support determination),[130] but it cannot compel such an employer to conclude an agreement.[131] Overall, the GFB provisions have proven largely ineffective in resolving several intractable bargaining disputes in the first three years of operation of Part 2-4 of the FW Act.[132] And in a number of more recent high-profile disputes, the good faith rules have played only a marginal role, with greater focus on utilization of the parties' rights to take protected industrial action and triggering the restricted grounds for the FWC to impose an arbitrated outcome.[133]

These conclusions as to the limited practical impact of the duty to bargain in good faith may be attributable to the 'liberal neutrality' ideology in which it is grounded in Australia, and the 'industrial pluralism' roots of the labour relations system in BC (and Canada more generally). On this view, the state does not so much *promote* collectivist forms of worker voice—rather, the state confines itself to establishing a procedural framework that enables workers to exercise *choice* about union representation and bargaining.[134] The failure to provide stronger and more unequivocal support for collective bargaining has been considered in explaining the ineffectiveness of bargaining laws in several other national settings.[135] Further, the balancing of interests inherent in the ideology of 'third way' competitiveness[136]—made explicit in the duties imposed on the BCLRB's exercise of its authority,[137] and in the collective bargaining framework under the FW Act[138]—arguably limits the efficacy of collective bargaining regulation in both jurisdictions.[139]

[130] See e.g. Bradon Ellem, 'A Battle Between Titans? Rio Tinto and union recognition in Australia's iron ore industry' (2013) 34(3) Economic and Industrial Democracy (published online).

[131] Rae Cooper and Bradon Ellem, 'Getting to the Table? Fair Work, Unions and Collective Bargaining' in Creighton and Forsyth 135 (n 78).

[132] A more positive analysis was presented by a government-initiated review of the FW Act in 2012, the independent Review Panel finding that the good faith provisions were proving to be 'flexible and responsive to the particular bargaining circumstances being considered', and that they 'encompass a balanced approach to regulating bargaining conduct'. The Panel rejected union and employer submissions arguing for amendments to the good faith rules, due to the 'relatively early stage of operation of these provisions and the unsettled nature of many of the matters at issue'; further, there were 'advantages to a less prescriptive approach' which retained discretion in the tribunal 'to address a wide and disparate range of conduct'. See John Edwards, Ron McCallum, and Michael Moore, *Towards More Productive and Equitable Workplaces: An Evaluation of the Fair Work Legislation* (Australian Government, Canberra, June 2012) 133, 138.

[133] See e.g. Anthony Forsyth and Andrew Stewart, 'Of "Kamikazes" and "Mad Men": The Fallout from the Qantas Industrial Dispute' (2013) 36 Melbourne University Law Review 785; Bukarica and Dallas (n 17), Epilogue.

[134] Bogg, Forsyth, and Novitz (n 2).

[135] See e.g. Alan Bogg and Tonia Novitz, 'Recognition in Respect of Bargaining in the United Kingdom: Collective Autonomy and Political Neutrality in Context' in Creighton and Forsyth 225 (n 78); Ruth Dukes, 'The Statutory Recognition Procedure 1999: No Bias in Favour of Recognition?' (2008) 37(3) ILJ 236; Benjamin Sachs, 'Enabling Employee Choice: A Structural Approach to the Rules of Union Organizing' (2010) 123 Harv L Rev 656; Anderson 233 (n 12) (and see 142–4, 152–5).

[136] That is, fairness for employees and productivity for employers; see further Bogg, Forsyth, and Novitz (n 2).

[137] Section 2, Code; these Code duties were informed by a 'third way' approach to the role for the labour board and labour regulation in BC (see the discussion in Slinn (n 37)).

[138] Donella Caspersz, Michael Gillan, and Daniel White, 'State, Ideology and the Emergence of "Good Faith" Collective Bargaining Regulation in Australia' (2011) 53(5) JIR 632.

[139] Perhaps best exemplified by the almost total failure of the new low-paid bargaining provisions in the FW Act: see Richard Naughton, 'The Low Paid Bargaining Scheme—An Interesting Idea, But Can It Work?'

What, then, are the future prospects for the GFB duty in Canada and Australia? GFB is an established component of statutory labour regulation in Canada. However, from its inception in labour legislation, the duty to bargain in good faith has been simultaneously acclaimed as essential to ensuring the fundamental elements of the Canadian labour relations system (collective bargaining and respect for exclusive union bargaining agency) and criticized as an unworkable concept incapable of enforcement. Nonetheless, GFB provisions have remained in Canadian labour legislation and have not been the subject of amendments, which have been primarily politically motivated over the last few decades.[140] It appears that partisan reformers view other features of the labour relations regime as more attractive targets for achieving partisan goals. In Australia, given the return to government of the conservative Coalition parties in the federal election held on 7 September 2013, we are likely to again see a swing away from state support for collectivism. While the GFB provisions of the FW Act will be retained, implementation of the Coalition's industrial relations policy[141] will provide some support for strategies of employer resistance to collective bargaining of the kind that were prevalent during the Coalition's last period in government.[142] This will inevitably lead to greater contestation over, and ultimately an attenuation of, collective bargaining as an expression of worker voice.

(2011) 22 AJLL 214; *Australian Nursing Federation v IPN Medical Centres Pty Ltd and Others* [2013] FWC 511 (17 June 2013).

[140] Regarding politicized labour legislation reform in Canada, see Kevin Burkett, 'The Politicization of the Ontario Labour Relations Framework in the 1990s' (1998) 6 CLELJ 162 and Brian Burkett, 'Reflections on Tripartism and Labour Law Reform' (2005) 12 CLELJ 261.

[141] Liberal/National Coalition, *The Coalition's Policy to Improve the Fair Work Laws*, May 2013.

[142] Rae Cooper, Bradon Ellem, Chris Briggs, and Diane van den Broek, 'Anti-unionism, Employer Strategy and the Australian State, 1996–2005' (2009) 34(3) Labor Studies Journal 339; Rae Cooper and Bradon Ellem, 'The Neoliberal State, Trade Unions and Collective Bargaining in Australia' (2008) 46 British Journal of Industrial Relations 532.

9

The Good-Faith Obligation

An Effective Model for Promoting Voice?

Gordon Anderson and Pam Nuttall***

Introduction

On 19 November 2010, twenty-nine men lost their lives in an underground coalmine explosion at Pike River on the West Coast of New Zealand's South Island. The subsequent Royal Commission Inquiry identified a number of factors contributing to the explosion but one of the more important was the lack of effective worker voice, either collectively or individually, in influencing health and safety.[1] This was a major contributor to the dangerous safety culture identified by the Commission which was so seriously weakened 'that signs of an explosion either went unnoticed or were not heeded'.[2] The Commission's concern with the lack of worker voice[3] was reflected in its recommendations which included the need for worker health and safety representatives including union appointed check inspectors with the power to halt activities when there is serious danger.[4]

In this chapter we explain the legal changes that led to the muting of worker voice in New Zealand workplaces, changes that contributed to the loss of voice in one of the world's most dangerous industries.

The muting of worker voice was a central policy objective of the neoliberal reforms of the 1990s. The next wave of reforms (in 2000) was intended to restore worker voice through an obligation to conduct employment relations in good faith. This chapter analyses the effectiveness of these reforms and questions whether effective voice is possible without collective representation.

Achieving Voice

Worker voice in New Zealand was achieved politically, as an expression of the relatively early enfranchisement of the New Zealand settler democracy[5] and as early as

* Professor, Faculty of Law, The Victoria University of Wellington, New Zealand.

** Senior Lecturer, School of Law, AUT University, New Zealand.

[1] 'Report of the Royal Commission on the Pike River Coal Mine Tragedy' (2012) ch. 7, para. 40.

[2] Royal Commission ch. 13, para. 33 (n 1).

[3] In this chapter we use the generic term 'worker' to encompass dependent contractors and the like. 'Employee' is used where the legal rights being discussed are specifically restricted to 'employees', that is those working under a contract of service.

[4] Royal Commission ch. 30 (n 1).

[5] The right to vote for all adult male citizens was achieved in 1879, plural voting based on property rights was abolished for the election of 1890 (i.e. 'one man, one vote') and full adult suffrage (i.e. including voting rights for all adult women) was achieved from 1893.

1865 political voice achieved a significant outcome when attempts to introduce an indigenous Master and Servant Act were defeated.[6] The most far-reaching political victory, however, was the Industrial Conciliation and Arbitration Act 1894 which provided the model for industrial relations for almost a century. The passage of this Act followed the defeat of organized labour in the 1890 Maritime Strike. 'Several thousand seamen, wharf labourers, coal miners and some railwaymen were involved in the strike which lasted 11 weeks and ended in total triumph for the employer.'[7] Union organization disintegrated, and involvement in union activity was often treated as grounds for instant dismissal.[8]

Industrial impotence, however, was offset by political influence in the newly-elected Liberal government which had actively courted the working class vote.[9] Several Liberal MPs were working men and others had been union-endorsed. The social upheaval which accompanied the strike also sparked widespread middle-class concern about the destructive effects of industrial conflict. These factors promoted acceptance of 'the principle that the state had a right and a duty to intervene in labour disputes and impose a settlement on the parties when they were unable to resolve their differences by peaceful negotiation.'[10] The outcome of this combination of public disquiet and support for legislative intervention on the part of the labour movement, was a statute whose purpose was to 'encourage the formation of industrial unions and associations and to facilitate the settlement of industrial disputes by conciliation and arbitration.'[11] It is interesting to note, however, that compulsory conciliation and arbitration was rejected out of hand by the labour movements in both the United States and the United Kingdom.[12] The Act was a political triumph for New Zealand unionism but also an expression of its industrial weakness.[13]

The arbitration system established in 1894 was firmly consolidated over the remaining 17 years the Liberals remained in power but under a politically conservative administration in less buoyant economic times industrial activism again began to operate outside of the arbitration system. This militant union challenge, culminating in the internecine struggle of the Waihi Strike in 1912 and the revolutionary upheaval of the defeated General Strike in 1913, made both the limits on industrial strength and the loyalty of many unionists to the arbitration system abundantly clear. While industrial unions did not abandon their preference for direct bargaining with the employer, industrial activism again turned

[6] John Henning, 'New Zealand: An Antipodean Exception to the Master and Servant Rules' (2007) 41 New Zealand Journal of History 62, 75.

[7] James Holt, *Compulsory Arbitration in New Zealand: The First Forty Years* (Auckland University Press, 1986) 21.

[8] Erling Rasmussen, *Employment Relations in New Zealand* (Pearson, 2009) 51.

[9] Holt 24 (n 7). [10] Holt 15 (n 7).

[11] Industrial Conciliation and Arbitration Act 1894, Long Title.

[12] Holt 29 (n 7). Arbitration was generally favoured by weaker unions in Britain because employers would be compelled to acknowledge and engage with the union whereas larger and more powerful unions especially in Britain were suspicious of the attitude of the courts to organized labour. In a TUC debate in 1901 the arbitration opponents were referred to as 'big dogs that can wag their own tails'. Holt cites the destruction of a compulsory arbitration system in Kansas in the 1920s by concerted strike action by opposed unions.

[13] See also Melanie Nolan and Pat Walsh, 'Labour's Leg Iron? Assessing Trade Unions and Arbitration in New Zealand' in Pat Walsh (ed.), *Work and Society: The Centenary of the Arbitration System* (Dunmore Press, 1994).

to political activity and was instrumental in the founding of the modern Labour Party in 1916.

Worker voice consequently became dependent on a sufficiently strong political voice to determine the policy of at least one major political party, traditionally the Labour Party. Although Labour did not gain power until 1935, even out of power its commitment to the arbitration system restrained radical reform,[14] and the one major threat to the system, the repeal of compulsory arbitration under a Reform-United government in 1932, was promptly reversed when Labour became the government. In two subsequent political crises, the 1951 waterfront dispute and the economic crisis of the 1970s, National governments, primarily for pragmatic reasons, were normally prepared to implement only moderate, and largely uncontentious, reforms to the arbitration system.[15]

Within the arbitration system effective industrial voice was achieved through two principal mechanisms. First, and most important, was that workers were represented by unions in conciliation and arbitration, the process which resulted in the award which determined their terms and conditions of employment.[16] Moreover, as awards covered all workers in an industry, this representation extended well beyond union members. The second form of voice, built on the award system, was voice at workplace level in the administration of the award. Most awards contained rights of entry for union officials and many allowed workplace delegates. Moreover most workplace disputes that arose were dealt with at the workplace level by union and employer (or employer association officials), familiar with the often highly complex background to the award provisions in dispute and who tended to have pragmatic and, most of the time, constructive working relationships, at that level.

Losing Voice: The Economic Revolution of 1984 to 1993

For close to a century the arbitration system provided workers with a significant degree of industrial voice, both at an occupational/industrial level and at workplace level. It might have been assumed that this history of support, or at least tolerance, would have resulted in worker voice achieving considerable resilience and that it would be incorporated into any reformed system of industrial relations. This was not the case. The neoliberal revolution of the late 1980s and early 1990s, and in particular the Employment Contracts Act 1991, had little room for any form of worker voice and was actively hostile to organized or mandated voice. This hostility was soon reflected in judicial decisions[17] and to some extent became consolidated in employer

[14] Holt 111 (n 7) commented on the 1913 dispute, that '[t]he majority [of workers] never abandoned the arbitration system…' and this remained true until at least the 1980s and helps explain the political reluctance to attack the arbitration system. In the 1951 Waterfront Dispute the peak union body, the Federation of Labour, supported the National government against the militant unions.

[15] Gordon Anderson, *Reconstructing New Zealand's Labour Law: Consensus or Divergence?* (Victoria University Press, 2011) ch. 3.

[16] In practice the great majority of awards were settled by agreement at the conciliation phase, albeit under the umbrella of the Court of Arbitration: Noel Woods, *Industrial Conciliation and Arbitration in New Zealand* (Government Printer, 1963) 103.

[17] Anderson ch. 5 (n 15).

and managerial mind-sets.[18] Within little more than two years Employment Contracts Act had swept away most of the gains of the previous century.[19]

While this victory for the neoliberal vision of employment reflected developments in other Anglo-American countries, its impact in New Zealand was exacerbated by characteristics peculiar to the political system and to weaknesses within the arbitration system. The political characteristics need not be discussed at any length but in summary a first-past-the-post electoral system, combined with a unicameral parliament, allowed a determined executive to implement a radical programme of reform at a pace that left any opposition floundering.[20] This tactic was used by both Labour and National governments in the decade beginning in 1985.[21]

The major weaknesses inherent in the arbitration system were, first, industrial voice was crucially dependent on statutory support, second, trade unions were very much creatures of the system, and finally, workplace voice, exercised through delegate structures and the like, was dependent on the relevant award. The necessity for the arbitration system had arisen originally from the industrial weakness of the union movement in the 1890s and the failure of direct industrial action. The defeat of a second wave of union militancy led by the 'Red Feds' in the early part of the twentieth century, culminating in the doomed Waihi and waterfront strikes of 1912–13, confirmed the role of the arbitration institutions (and the ballot box) as the feasible channel of worker voice in New Zealand. But because the union movement was unable to develop its own 'countervailing power' through militant action, it had to accept an effective arbitration unionism which did not engender structures for mass organization and industrial action.

Unions enjoyed industrial voice because their registration under the Industrial Conciliation and Arbitration Acts gave them monopoly representation rights in relation to the industry/occupation for which they were registered.[22] However the combination of compulsory arbitration including the prohibition on strikes, monopoly coverage and, from 1936, compulsory membership, resulted in a fragmented and weak union movement. Commentators writing in the 1960s, shortly before the arbitration system came under sustained economic and political pressure, were less than complimentary about the state of unions. Gross characterized the majority of the union movement as 'stagnant', as 'perhaps incapable of using the strike weapon', and as deprived 'of certain functions which seem essential to organisational vitality'.[23] Woods refers to

[18] Alan Geare et al., 'Workplace Values and Beliefs: An Empirical Study of Ideology, High Commitment Management and Unionisation' (2009) 20 International Journal of Human Resource Management (IJHRM) 1146.

[19] Raymond Harbridge et al., *Employment Contracts: Bargaining Trends and Employment Law Update 1995/96* (Industrial Relations Centre, Victoria University of Wellington, 1996) 51.

[20] Jane Kelsey, *The New Zealand Experiment: A World Model for Structural Adjustment?* (Auckland University Press, 1995) 33.

[21] This tactic became unfeasible when a proportional representation electoral system (MMP) came into effect in 1996.

[22] The various Industrial Conciliation and Arbitration Acts, of which the last was repealed in 1973, allowed a union to be registered on the application of seven persons and an application could be refused if potential members 'might conveniently belong' to an already existing union thus giving an existing union a virtual monopoly in the industry for which it was registered.

[23] Martin Gross, 'The Condition of New Zealand Unions—An Environmental Approach' [1961] New Zealand Journal of Public Administration 28.

some unions becoming little more than 'fee collectors',[24] and in a later and more critical assessment to 'a disintegrated, weak, poverty-stricken and untrained trade unionism...hundreds of small unions kept small and ignorant and poverty-stricken by the law'.[25]

By 1991 this picture had changed in two major ways. First, in the 1970s and 1980s unions become more organized and more militant as the arbitration system evolved into a system dominated by collective bargaining, albeit within the award structure.[26] A rejuvenating union movement did, however, come at a price. In particular the combination of high levels of industrial action and increasing political hostility to compulsory union membership resulted in a strongly negative reaction from sectors of society that might once have been neutral if not supportive of trade unions. When, in the late 1980s, the threat posed by the neoliberal agenda became clear, and unions sought to organize to counter the threats posed to the movement,[27] it proved to be too little too late. Union opposition to the Employment Contracts Bill was weak and ineffective.[28]

Moreover, at the same time workers largely lost their political voice. In the late 1980s first Labour, and then National, became captured by the new-right and its neoliberal ideology.[29] After Labour came to power in 1984, workers and their unions found themselves increasingly marginalized within the Party and unable to significantly influence a Cabinet which had been captured by an inner core of ministers determined to implement a pro-business, neoliberal deregulatory agenda. While this agenda was more muted in the case of labour market reform it was clear that Labour was also ready to abandon the core elements of the arbitration system guaranteeing worker voice. Compulsory arbitration was abolished in 1984[30] opening the way to enterprise bargaining[31] and, potentially, union-free workplaces. More damaging, however, was that Labour's economic deregulation agenda split the Party eviscerating its electoral support.[32] By 1990 a severely weakened Labour Party was defeated by a National Party implacably opposed to the existing industrial relations system.

The influence of neoliberalism had turned the National Party's grudging support of the arbitration system to open opposition to both the system and to the principal vehicle of worker voice, trade unions. National's Employment Contracts Act 1991 was based on a view of the employment relationship as purely contractual between an employer and an individual worker and, ideally, free of third party intervention.[33] The process

[24] Woods 132 (n 16).

[25] Noel Woods, 'Comments on the Industrial Conciliation and Arbitration Act 1894' (1994) 19 New Zealand Journal of Industrial Relations (NZJIR) 225, 227. This article was written after Woods, a long serving public servant, retired as Secretary of Labour.

[26] Anderson ch. 3 (n 15).

[27] Ellen J. Dannin, *Working Free: The Origins and Impact of New Zealand's Employment Contracts Act* (Auckland University Press, 1997) ch. 5; Brian Easton, *The Commercialisation of New Zealand* (Auckland University Press, 1997) 122.

[28] Dannin ch. 8 (n 27).

[29] Kelsey pt 1 (n 20).

[30] Industrial Relations Amendment Act 1984, s. 13.

[31] The Labour Relations Amendment Act 1990, s. 7 made this objective explicit.

[32] Kelsey 37 (n 20).

[33] For an account of the nature and development of the policy agenda see Pat Walsh and Rose Ryan, 'The Making of the Employment Contracts Act' in Raymond Harbridge (ed.), *Employment Contracts: New Zealand Experiences* (Victoria University Press, 1993); Dannin ch. 6 (n 27).

by which the Act was drafted also sent a clear signal of National's approach to worker voice. In marked contrast to previous post-war reforms in 1973 and 1987 which were preceded by extensive public consultation and input from both unions and employers, the Bill was drafted in secret and with only business input.[34] This lack of concern for worker voice was seen again in the final stages of the Bill's progress when, without notice or opportunity for submissions, its provisions were extended to all employees, a change that extended the Act's reach to the approximately 60 per cent of the employed workforce who were not union members.[35]

Lost Voice: The Legislative Revolution

The radical nature of the reforms in the Employment Contracts Act need not be repeated here although the mechanisms through which it collapsed worker voice should be noted. Most importantly the reforms resulted, as was intended, in the individualization of employment relationships and the de-unionization of workplaces.[36]

De-unionization and limiting collective voice

Under the Employment Contracts Act employees were entitled to choose to exercise collective voice through union membership and collective bargaining, indeed the right to exercise choice was stressed in the Act's objectives.[37] In practice real choice, and hence voice, were vulnerable both in respect of union membership and in the ability to bargain collectively.

The introduction of voluntary union membership was not only a matter of principle but a potent weapon for attacking the financial and organizational base of trade unions. Union density dropped from 41.5 per cent when the Employment Contracts Act was enacted to approximately 20 per cent by 1996, a figure which has remained roughly constant to the present time.[38] The rapid drop in membership partly reflected a genuine choice to cease membership with the repeal of compulsory unionism and also worker realization that little was to be gained from membership when bargaining became untenable. However employer hostility to membership was also an important factor as the Act provided only rudimentary protection against anti-union tactics.[39] While evidence is limited on how widespread such tactics were, it is clear that they were not negligible.[40]

[34] Walsh and Ryan (n 33).

[35] For a comment on this issue see Pat Downey, 'Work and Contract' [1991] New Zealand Law Journal 145.

[36] Gordon Anderson, 'Individualising the Employment Relationship in New Zealand: An Analysis of Legal Developments' in Stephen Deery and Richard Mitchell (eds), *Employment Relations: Individualisation and Union Exclusion An International Study* (Federation Press, 1999).

[37] Employment Contracts Act 1991, Long Title.

[38] Aaron Crawford et al., 'Unions and Union Membership in New Zealand: Annual Review for 1997' (1998) 23 NZJIR 191. The current figure is 21 per cent: 'Union Membership Return Report 2011' (Department of Labour, 2012) although private-sector density is estimated to be closer to 10 per cent.

[39] Anderson 78 (n 15).

[40] See, for example, the facts of *Adams v Alliance Textiles (NZ) Ltd* [1992] 1 ERNZ 982 (EmpC) and *United Food IUOW v Talley* [1992] 1 ERNZ 756 (EmpC).

Even when unions did retain members the sudden removal of compulsory membership severely constrained their financial and organizational resources and limited their ability to represent members irrespective of other legal barriers placed in their way. The result was that the exercise of collective voice became severely constrained and in some occupations, where union representation had been dependent on compulsory membership, largely vanished.[41] While the Act did not prohibit collective bargaining it made it considerably more difficult. Bargaining was confined to enterprise level, thus limiting the effectiveness of industrial action and increasing the difficulties of union organizing,[42] and while employees were entitled to choose a representative[43] to negotiate on their behalf there was no requirement for an employer to enter into negotiations. However, an employer was required to 'recognise the authority' of the representative, and was not free to bypass that representative and negotiate directly with the employees concerned.[44] The courts, however, allowed employers considerable latitude to discourage union membership and undermine negotiations.[45] The success of negotiations was therefore dependent on either employer willingness to negotiate or on the ability of employees to strike to reinforce their negotiating position. As will be seen in what follows, arguments that employers were legally bound to negotiate in good faith found little sympathy in the courts. As collective bargaining declined, and as remaining awards expired, rights of representation such as the right to appoint job delegates or consultation processes became ineffective. Collective voice at workplace level was increasingly muted.

The government's policy of eliminating mandatory worker voice was not confined to the Employment Contracts Act. Other avenues of voice were also restricted, most notably when a major revision of health and safety legislation made only extremely weak provision for worker involvement in health and safety matters.[46] One commentator expressed the view that the Act introduced: 'an era of voluntarism in some aspects of occupational health and safety and the removal of any statutory guarantee that employees will have effective representation regarding health and safety in the workplace'.[47]

Individualization

The most important long-term impact of the Employment Contracts Act was the individualization of the employment relationship with the result that the contract of

[41] In 1987, the last year detailed figures were available, the various hotel, hospital, and restaurant unions had a combined membership of over 49,000, clerical employees' unions over 42,000, and shop assistants' unions over 17,000: 'Annual Report of the Department of Labour for the Year Ending 31 March 1987' (1987) X AJHR. All these unions vanished within a few years of the enactment of the Employment Contracts Act.

[42] Employment Contracts Act 1991, s. 18(2).

[43] The term 'representative' is used as that was the statutory term under the Employment Contracts Act. The word 'union', and any legal recognition of unions as such, was expunged from employment legislation.

[44] *Eketone v Alliance Textiles (NZ) Ltd* [1993] 2 ERNZ 783 (CA).

[45] See generally Anderson ch. 4 (n 15).

[46] The Health and Safety in Employment Act 1992, s. 14 provided that employers shall 'ensure that all employees have the opportunity to be fully involved in the development of the procedures' related to hazard identification and the like. This requirement was not backed by effective sanctions: see Alexander Szakats, 'The Health and Safety in Employment Act' [1993] Employment Law Bulletin (ELB) 34.

[47] John Hughes, 'The Health and Safety in Employment Bill' [1992] ELB 3, 5 and generally *Mazengarb's Employment Law* (online, LexisNexis) para. 6019A.3.

employment became the centrepiece of the employment relationship. Before 1991 the contract of employment, at least for award workers, was secondary to the award. Even for non-award workers the day to day role of the contract was minimal. As in some other jurisdictions dominated by the collective determination of employment conditions, the contract of employment was undeveloped and immune to the pressures of industrial reality.[48] In New Zealand this position gradually changed from the mid-1970s[49] but the repeal of the arbitration system removed the principal barrier to the dominance of the common law and the common law courts. From the late 1980s the Court of Appeal was increasingly assertive in developing employment law at the expense of the specialist courts, a trend that gained momentum after 1991 when appeals from the Employment Court were consistently upheld.[50] The limits of individual worker voice became increasingly defined by the unsympathetic common law.

This development was important as by 1993 it had become clear that any future Labour government would not significantly alter the underlying structure of the Employment Contracts Act even if it might ameliorate its more extreme features by supporting collective bargaining and requiring employment relations to be conducted in good faith.[51] The future role for worker voice looked likely to develop at the level of the individual employment relationship even if the genesis of the legal obligation might be statutory.

Judicial retrenchment

During the 1990s a number of attempts were made to obtain a degree of worker voice through the courts. In particular it was argued that employers, as one aspect of the mutual obligation of trust and confidence, had an obligation to negotiate in good faith when entering employment contracts and, additionally, that procedural fairness required employers to consult when taking decisions to make workers redundant.[52] While some early decisions of the Court of Appeal and decisions of the Employment Court supported this argument the Court of Appeal later actively opposed such arguments on the basis that 'the 1991 Act represents a substantial departure from the collectivist principles of previous industrial relations legislation in favour of a model of free contractual bargaining'.[53] One writer commented that the court's approach provided 'ample scope for parties to engage in conduct that is dictatorial, unilateral and

[48] Margaret Wilson, 'The New Contractualism and the Employment Relationship in New Zealand' in Glyn Davis et al. (eds), *The New Contractualism?* (Macmillan Education Australia, 1997) 91 and also Alan Bogg, 'Good Faith in the Contract of Employment: A Case of the English Reserve?' (2011) 32 Comparative Labor Law and Policy Journal (CLLPJ) 729, 744.

[49] Anderson ch. 5 (n 15).

[50] The current Employment Court was established in 1991 but is the legal successor of variously named courts back to the Court of Arbitration founded in 1894. It was named the Labour Court between 1987 and 1991.

[51] See generally Alan Geare (ed.), 'Labour's New Deal: A Bargaining Framework for a New Century?' (1993) 18 NZJIR 151 and in particular Helen Clark, 'Employment Relations—the New Direction Under Labour' (1993) 18 NZJIR 153; Gordon Anderson and Pat Walsh, 'Labour's New Deal: A Bargaining Framework for a New Century?' (1993) 18 NZJIR 163.

[52] For a more extensive discussion see Gordon Anderson, 'Good Faith in the Individual Employment Relationship in New Zealand' (2011) 32 CLLPJ 685, 703.

[53] *Aoraki Corporation Ltd v McGavin* [1998] 3 NZLR 276 (CA), 286.

inconsistent with good faith bargaining'.[54] In this atmosphere there was little possibility of good faith being developed in employment law. On the contrary it became increasingly marginalized and diminished. In one case the court, referring to a statement in the Employment Court on the characteristics of good faith negotiation, stated that counsel 'properly'

> did not attempt to defend the Chief Judge's requirement . . . that each party had to regard the other as an equal contributor to the form, content and other qualities and aspects of the proposed contract. The policy and wording of the 1991 Act make it clear that either party to the negotiation may in general proceed on a take it or leave it basis . . .[55]

More immediately germane to individual voice and good faith was the Court of Appeal's re-evaluation of personal grievance law to increasingly emphasize managerial rights at the expense of worker protection. In *Brighouse Ltd v Bilderbeck* Richardson J stated that 'procedural fairness does not require that decisions on redundancy be negotiated with the employees'.[56] Later, in *Aoraki Corporation Ltd v McGavin* the majority of the court stated that although consultation might be desirable in some cases: '[t]o impose an absolute requirement of that kind would be inconsistent with the employer's prima facie right to organise and run its business operation as it sees fit'.[57]

This highly restrictive approach was to continue during the first few years of the Employment Relations Act 2000. In the first significant case on the new statutory duty of good faith reforms, *Coutts Cars Ltd v Baguley*,[58] a majority of the Court of Appeal resisted the suggestion that the new Act required a re-evaluation of its approach holding that the good faith obligation was merely a statutory formulation of the pre-existing common law term of mutual good faith and fair dealing and that it saw no reason why its decisions under the Employment Contracts Act 'should not continue to provide guidance on the applicable principles'.[59] Only one member of the court in *Baguley*, McGrath J, accepted that the new Act required some re-evaluation of the law.[60] This resistance abated after amendments strengthening the duty in 2004 and changes of personnel on the court.

Vehicle for Voice: The Legislative Duty of Good Faith

The Minister of Labour in the Labour-led government which gained power in 1999 has written that the government saw the re-establishment of cooperative relationships at the workplace and at industry and national level as critical to its overall labour market

[54] Geoff Davenport, 'The Legal Obligation to Bargain in Good Faith in the New Zealand Labour Market: Myth or Reality' (1999) 24 NZJIR 113, 149.

[55] *Tucker Wool Processors Ltd v Harrison* [1999] 1 ERNZ 894 (CA), 911. This was one of several cases where the court upheld conduct that would appear to have been the antithesis of good faith: see for example *New Zealand Fire Services Commission v Ivamy* [1996] 1 ERNZ 85 (CA).

[56] [1994] 2 ERNZ 243 (CA) Richardson J dissenting.

[57] [1998] 3 NZLR 276 (CA) at 618.

[58] *Coutts Cars Ltd v Baguley* [2002] 2 NZLR 533 (CA).

[59] *Coutts Cars v Baguley* at [42] (n 58) and see also *PSA Auckland City Council v The New Zealand Public Service Association* [2004] 2 NZLR 10 (CA). On the court's generally restrictive approach to mutual trust and confidence see Anderson 698 (n 52).

[60] *Coutts Cars v Baguley* at [42] (n 58), McGrath J at [83] dissenting on this point.

objectives of reversing low productivity and skill shortages.[61] The mechanism to achieve these changes was to be a statutory duty of good faith. Section 3(a) of the Employment Relations Act 2000 states that the object of the Act is 'to build productive employment relationships through the promotion of good faith in all aspects of the employment environment and of the employment relationship'. The need for this pervasive duty becomes clear when it is appreciated that the Act largely retained the underlying structure of the Employment Contracts Act including its emphasis on freedom of association and enterprise-based employment.[62]

The statutory duty has now been in place for well over a decade and appeared to have achieved broad political acceptance. It was significantly strengthened in 2004[63] and not subsequently amended. However, the National-led government, elected in 2008, has amended the Act to reinforce the rights of employers[64] and now proposes to reverse the specific good faith duty to conclude a collective agreement unless there is a genuine reason, based on reasonable grounds, not to.[65]

Labour also made reforms to increase voice in other areas, most importantly provisions for employee involvement in workplace health and safety including requirements for employee participation processes.[66]

The statutory duty

Although the duty of good faith is derived from well-established legal antecedents, its statutory formulation was an ambitious attempt to develop a comprehensive obligation to regulate and change behaviour in employment relationships.[67] The duty has three elements: a broad duty applying to all employment relationships requiring the parties not to mislead or deceive each other, a specific obligation requiring employers to consult with employees when making decisions that will have an adverse effect on the continuation of employment, and the duty to conduct collective bargaining in good faith. The duty is a statutory obligation which cannot be contracted out of.[68]

The general duty, set out in section 4(1)(a), requires the parties to an 'employment relationship' to 'deal with each other in good faith'. While paragraph (b) gives some

[61] Margaret Wilson, 'The Employment Relations Act: A Framework for a Fairer Way' in Erling Rasmussen (ed.), *Employment Relationships: New Zealand's Employment Relations Act* (Auckland University Press, 2004) 14.

[62] See generally Gordon Anderson, 'Just a Jump to the Left? New Zealand's Employment Relations Act 2000' (2001) 14 Australian Journal of Labour Law (AJLL) 62.

[63] Employment Relations Amendment Act (No. 2) 2004. This Act was partly a response to restrictive Court of Appeal decisions but also reflected a more supportive coalition arrangement following the 2003 general election: see Wilson 14 (n 61).

[64] Employment Relations Amendment Acts 2008, 2010, 2012 and see also the Employment Relations Amendment Bill 2013, which was given a first reading on 5 June and referred for Select Committee hearings, with a reporting date of 5 December.

[65] Gordon Anderson, '"The Sky Didn't Fall In" An Emerging Consensus on the Shape of New Zealand Labour Law?' (2010) 22 AJLL 94.

[66] Health and Safety in Employment Act 1993, Pt 2A. Such processes were mandatory if there were thirty or more employees and could be requested if there were less than thirty.

[67] See generally Gordon Anderson, 'Transplanting and Growing Good Faith in New Zealand Labour Law' (2007) 19 AJLL 1; Anderson (n 52).

[68] Employment Relations Act (NZ), s. 238.

context by providing that a party must not do anything that misleads or deceives the other, it is explicitly provided that this does not limit the general obligation. Subsection 4(1A) elaborates by providing that good faith is 'wider in scope than the implied mutual obligations of trust and confidence' and requires the parties to an employment relationship 'to be an active and constructive in establishing and maintaining a productive employment relationship in which the parties are, among other things, responsive and communicative'.[69]

Section 4(1A)(1)(c) establishes a specific obligation to consult employees when 'proposing to make a decision that will, or is likely to, have an adverse effect on the continuation of employment'. It requires employers to provide access to relevant information, and for an opportunity to comment on the information before the decision is made.

The third, element, the duty to bargain in good faith, set out in section 32, is primarily concerned with bargaining process but does contain provisions that in principle should enhance collective voice.

The duty extends to all 'employment relationships' including employer–employee and union–employer relationships,[70] and encompasses most matters likely to have a significant impact on an employee's job security or which might otherwise prejudice or affect an employee. Apart from the obvious case of collective bargaining this includes consultations about 'the effect on employees of changes to the employer's business'; 'proposals that might impact on an employer's employees including proposals to contract out work…or to sell or transfer all or part of the employer's business'; and 'making employees redundant'. Good faith is explicitly applied to bargaining for an individual employment agreement and to matters arising out of an individual employment agreement.[71]

The statutory duty of good faith is far reaching and signalled a major departure from the formalistic approach to employment law that characterized the 1990s. It might therefore have been expected that good faith would have a positive impact on employment relations, that it might significantly strengthen worker voice collectively and individually. The duty was clearly underpinned by the belief that workers had a legitimate stake in their employment and were entitled to an active voice when decisions were taken that were likely to impact on their employment. The question we now attempt to answer is whether the duty has had the impact intended and promoted collective or individual worker voice.

Good Faith Bargaining

The components of the duty to bargain in good faith are described in the Act and supported by a statutory code of good faith which elaborates and expands on these obligations. Additionally the general duty in section 4 also applies so that the obligation not to mislead or deceive, and to be active and constructive, apply to bargaining as they do to other aspects of the employment relationship.[72] The Employment Court has

[69] This wording seems specifically designed to signal a departure from the position taken by the Court of Appeal in *Auckland City Council v The New Zealand Public Service Association* [2004] 2 NZLR 10 (CA).

[70] ERA 2000, s. 4(4).

[71] ERA 2000, s. 4(5).

[72] 'Bargaining' is also defined broadly and includes all interactions relating to bargaining and communications in relation to it: ERA 2000, s. 2.

developed a strong body of authority making it clear that the parties take some risk in attempting to avoid good faith obligations.[73]

Collective bargaining is not, however, a standalone process and relies on at least two foundations: the ability of unions to initiate bargaining and their ability to conclude collective agreements. The duty to bargain in good faith is primarily a process obligation establishing how bargaining should be conducted although it does require that the parties 'conclude a collective agreement unless there is a genuine reason, based on reasonable grounds, not to'.[74] A 'genuine reason' need only be a failure to agree mutually acceptable terms. The lack of support for the two additional foundations also weakens good faith bargaining in and hence the effectiveness of collective bargaining as a conduit for worker voice. It is further handicapped by the largely ineffective provisions in the Act seeking to prevent employers undermining collective bargaining, for example by passing on agreed terms to non-members.[75]

Consultation obligations during restructuring

The most immediate impact of the statutory duty, outside collective bargaining, has been in relation to a number of matters which can be brought together under the general rubric of business restructuring. These include consultation on the effect on employees of changes to the employer's business, proposals by an employer that might impact on the employer's employees including proposals to contract out work or to sell or transfer part of the employer's business, and making employees redundant.[76] An employer proposing to make a decision that may have an adverse effect on the continuation of its employees' employment must provide those employees with access to relevant information about the decision and provide an opportunity to comment on that information before any decision is made.[77] This element of the duty overrules the approach taken by the Court of Appeal in the 1990s and makes it explicit that employees are entitled to be consulted on both the substance of a proposed decision and on its implementation.[78] A failure to properly consult is likely to lead to a finding that the dismissal was procedurally unjustified or, in some cases, a compliance order preventing dismissals until the good faith requirements have been complied with.[79] The court has stated:

> [64] ... Parliament intended to alter and prescribe the tests for justification for disadvantage in, or dismissal from, employment in general and to change the judge-made law exemplified by the judgments of the majority of the Court of Appeal in *Coutts Cars*. It addressed these latter changes by adding specific information sharing provisions in s 4. These set out a fair and reasonable employer's minimum obligations where redundancy may ensue and are thus an element of the new s103A tests of justification.

[73] See the court's judgment in *Association of University Staff v Vice Chancellor of University of Auckland* [2005] ERNZ 224 (EmpC) and generally Anderson 234 (n 15).

[74] ERA 2000, s. 33. The present government has indicated it will amend this provision to remove the expectation of concluding an agreement.

[75] ERA 2000, ss. 59A–59C. [76] ERA 2000, s. 4(4)(a)–(e). [77] ERA 2000, s. 4(1A)(c).

[78] *HP Industries (NZ) Ltd v Davision* [2008] ERNZ 514 (EmpC).

[79] Such orders have delayed restructuring plans at one major paper mill and at Air New Zealand.

> [65]... A fair and reasonable employer must, if challenged, be able to establish that he or she or it has complied with the statutory obligations of good faith dealing in s 4 including as to consultation because a fair and reasonable employer will comply with the law.[80]

The requirements for proper consultation are well established in New Zealand law[81] and were enumerated in an employment context in *Communication and Energy Workers Union Inc v Telecom New Zealand Ltd*.[82] That case makes it clear that consultation cannot be a mere formality. It requires that a proposal not be acted on until after consultation, that employees must be given sufficiently precise information to enable them to state a view, be given a reasonable opportunity to do so and that genuine efforts must be made to accommodate those views. The Employment Court has however been careful to stress that 'the consent of persons consulted is not necessary following proper consultation and that there need not be an agreement'[83] and it is now well established law that the courts will not overturn a genuine business decision that results in redundancy.[84]

The General Duty

The influence of the general duty of good faith, particularly in the context of worker voice, is less dramatic and has been most apparent in personal grievance cases where it has influenced the court's approach to procedure in disciplinary and dismissal proceedings.[85] For example the duty was held to rule out a 'blotter' approach to a disciplinary hearing where the employer was unresponsive to evidence as it was set out, the court holding that the duty emphasized a need for participatory discussion and for tentative conclusions to be outlined.[86] The full consequences of the general duty have yet to be worked through[87] but it may be that the most significant will be the incremental development of an obligation of fair management practice placing some limits on employer prerogative.[88] In practical terms employers must ensure that they have defensible and robust human resource management practices capable of surviving judicial scrutiny if a challenge arises. However, while such developments may lead to more productive employment relationships, their impact on worker voice is more marginal and largely builds on and reinforces elements of procedural fairness that are already well developed in personal grievance law.

[80] *Simpsons Farms Ltd v Aberhart* [2006] 1 ERNZ 825 (EmpC).

[81] *Wellington International Airport Ltd v Air NZ* [1993] 1 NZLR 671 (CA).

[82] [1993] 2 ERNZ 429 (EmpC). [83] [1993] 2 ERNZ 429 at [63].

[84] *GN Hale & Son Ltd v Wellington Caretakers etc IUW* [1991] 1 NZLR 151 (CA).

[85] Personal grievance procedures allow employees to challenge not only a dismissal but also a range of other disadvantageous actions: ERA 2000, s. 103.

[86] *X v Auckland District Health Board* [2007] ERNZ 66 at [153] (EmpC).

[87] For the perspective of the Chief Judge of the Employment Court see Graeme Colgan, 'Good Faith Obligations in Practice: When, What, by Whom and to Whom?' (Employment Law in the Public Sector, Wellington, 22 May 2008).

[88] Gordon Anderson and Jane Bryson, 'Developing the Statutory Obligation of Good Faith in Employment Law: What Might Human Resource Management Contribute?' (2007) 37 Victoria University of Wellington Law Review 487.

Restored Voice?

Margaret Wilson, Minister of Labour when the Employment Relations Act was passed, has written:

> [L]egislation cannot change individual values or beliefs. It can, however, influence and change behaviours. Whether legislation successfully changes behaviours depends on whether it is sufficiently practical in its application to enable those affected to conduct their affairs in an orderly and mutually productive manner.[89]

The difficulty the new approach faced was that a decade of neoliberalism and individualism in employment relations was less than conducive to the changes sought by the government. The limited research on managerial attitudes suggests however that, while changing attitudes was never going to be easy, especially among smaller employers, the task was not necessarily impossible. Human resource managers at least were open to more pluralistic approaches even if they did not necessarily apply these at the workplace.[90] A preliminary analysis of other recent research suggests that, at least among larger employers, there is a high level of commitment to employee consultation generally and to at least some level of engagement with unions.[91]

Whether a statutory duty of good faith was likely to achieve the behavioural changes sought depended, of course, on whether the incentives built into the legislation were effective. Legislation of this character is intended to achieve public policy objectives through the encouragement of private systems of self-regulation, such as internal management processes 'to infiltrate the firm's decision-making matrices and erect signposts that direct decision-makers towards the state's desired course of action'.[92] One method of achieving this result is the use of risk as a regulatory tool. If an employer perceives that non-compliance will increase reputational or brand risk, legal risk, and financial risk it might be expected to act to minimize those risks. Legal structures encourage self-regulation by rewarding its use and sanctioning non-compliance but the costs of non-compliance need to be sufficient to overcome the strong unitary forces always inherent in employment relations and which, over the decade of the 1990s, became the prevailing norm in employment practice and in the interpretation of the law.

The question then is did Labour's introduction of a statutory duty of good faith restore, at least to some degree, worker voice lost during the 1990s? This question is best addressed by considering collective and individual voice.

Collective voice

While alternative mechanisms, such as works councils or systems of internal democracy may provide some collective voice, effective voice that can influence both terms

[89] Wilson 17 (n 61).

[90] Alan Geare and others, 'Employment Relationships: Ideology and HRM Practice' (2006) 17 IJHRM 1190.

[91] Gordon Anderson et al., 'The Interface Between the Law and the Workplace: The Role of Human Resource Managers' (Labour Law Research Network, Barcelona, 15 June 2013).

[92] David Doorey, 'A Model of Responsive Workplace Law' (2012) 50 Osgoode Hall Law Journal 47, 58.

and conditions of employment and the management of the on-going employment relationship is unlikely in the absence of effective unions. To be effective unions need to be able to organize and be able to take effective industrial action if they are to bargain collectively. As the first section of this chapter makes clear these factors have historically been dependent on political voice but that since 1990 political support, most particularly from the Labour Party, has been muted. In part this reflected the need to work in coalition governments, but it is also clear, from both the Employment Relations Act and subsequent policy platforms, that Labour does not consider clear legislative support that supports strong and effective union organization to be politically viable.

(a) *Freedom of association and union organization*

The Employment Contracts Act enacted a strong form of freedom of association: any arrangement stipulating union membership or non-membership was unlawful.[93] These provisions were not amended by Labour in 2000 although Labour did allow the registration of unions as legally recognized entities[94] and provided that only unions could represent employees in collective bargaining. Notably, however, Labour did little to enhance protection for employees against employer anti-union activities. The only legal constraint on such activities was, and remains, that an employer may not 'subject an employee to duress... in relation to membership... of a union' or may not 'discriminate against an employee in the employee's employment... by reason directly or indirectly... of involvement in the activities of a union'. This remedy allows no collective legal response to anti-union activities and provides, at best, a remedy only well after the event.[95] There is for example no obligation of employer neutrality in relation to union organizing, leaving employers free to campaign actively against union membership.

(b) *Collective bargaining*

The Act requires an employer to bargain in good faith with any union representing two or more of the employer's employees.[96] Achieving employer recognition of a union is therefore not an issue. If a union can organize members in an enterprise the law will support the union through the requirement for good faith bargaining. This system is initially one of self-help but with a reasonably supportive statutory duty ensuring the parties comply with process obligations during bargaining and which constrains a range of bad faith actions relating to bargaining.[97] The remedies available to the court and Authority include financial penalties but more importantly a compliance order requiring a party

[93] See now ERA 2000, Pt 3.

[94] ERA 2000, Pt 4. In 1991 registered unions were deemed to be re-registered under the Incorporated Societies Act 1908 and the term 'union' erased from legislation.

[95] For a detailed discussion see *Mazengarb* para. ERA11.3 (n 47) and on unions generally Anderson ch. 11 (n 15).

[96] Legally this could require an employer to bargain with several different unions although it is rare for more than a few unions to be involved with any one employer. The Act also provides some mechanisms for amalgamation of bargaining.

[97] 'Bargaining' is broadly defined in the Act and includes all interactions relating to bargaining and communications in relation to it: ERA 2000, s. 2.

to comply with its good faith obligations.[98] The effectiveness of the good faith provisions has proved to be of value in a number of disputes, including drawn out industrial disputes, in placing at least some constraints on party behaviour.[99]

Such drawn out disputes, however, tend to involve unions with the industrial strength to support bargaining with industrial action. If, instead, the starting point is a weaker union, able to organize a more limited group of workers within an enterprise but not able to strike effectively, the good faith duty may still have a positive effect but it is significantly impaired by the absence of mechanisms to ensure the conclusion of a collective agreement. Where an impasse arises the Act provides access to a facilitation process[100] but this does not include third party determination of terms and conditions. Such a determination is possible, but only in the case of egregious breaches of good faith, and the statutory barriers to seeking this remedy are such that there has been no case where leave has been given to use the process.[101] What is clear is that if an employer does not wish to conclude an agreement, and a union does not have the strength to strike effectively, the employer will have little problem in meeting their good faith obligations but will eventually be able to end bargaining without an agreement.[102]

(c) Restored voice?

If increased collective voice is to be judged by bargaining density it is clear that the duty of good faith has had little impact. The available information on bargaining density suggests that density has dropped overall, particularly in the private sector, and that while union density has remained largely static since 2000 at around 20 per cent, bargaining density in the private sector continued to fall under the Act and is currently just under 10 per cent.[103] This situation may, however, be attributable to Labour's failure to enact the basic foundations necessary for the promotion of collective bargaining,[104] support for union membership, and protection from anti-union activities, rather than failings in the duty of good faith as such.

The duty to bargain in good faith is an important component of collective voice and where collective bargaining occurs it is proving valuable in ensuring that worker voice is heard during the bargaining process. However, in the absence of an employer who is willing to settle an agreement, or a union that can achieve an agreement through industrial strength, that voice is restricted. The reality in New Zealand, as elsewhere, is that

[98] A compliance order can be regarded as equivalent to an injunction: ERA 2000, s. 137.

[99] One particular example includes a drawn out, and on-going, dispute between Ports of Auckland and the Maritime Union relating attempts to de-unionize the port and to replace employees with contractors but it has also been of importance in disputes between the Meat Workers Union and the meat company, AFFCO New Zealand Ltd, as well as between the University of Auckland and the Tertiary Education Union.

[100] ERA 2000, ss. 50A–50I. [101] ERA 2000, s. 50J.

[102] For the circumstances in which facilitation may be sought, and the types of behaviours that may warrant it, see *McCain Foods (NZ) Ltd v Service & Food Workers Union Nga Ringa Tota Inc* (2009) 6 NZELR 426 (EmpC). The case illustrates the ease with which an employer may comply with good faith obligations while ensuring agreement is not reached.

[103] Percentage calculated from data in Stephen Blumenfeld and others, *Employment Contracts: Bargaining Trends and Employment Law Update 2011/2012* (Industrial Relations Centre, Victoria University of Wellington, 2012) Table 2.2. This series, which has been published annually since 1994, provides most detailed analysis of changes in bargaining patterns.

[104] Promoting collective bargaining is an express object of the Act: ERA 2000, s. 3(a)(iii).

in the absence of industrial strength, voice through collective bargaining will be ineffective without some sanction that strongly encourages agreement. It is a binding collective agreement that gives effective voice, not the bargaining process.

Individual voice

Individual voice is more difficult to define but at a minimum it involves participation in decisions that have a significant impact on an employee's working environment or job security. Most obviously it includes changes in working conditions, occupational health and safety, discipline, and dismissal as well as decisions likely to lead to restructuring and redundancy. Typically the exercise of individual voice is either through a consultative process or required as an aspect of procedural fairness. Unlike collective voice, individual voice may influence a decision but is largely powerless at the point a final decision is made. In this sense New Zealand workers have had a long experience with the exercise of individual voice, most notably in the context of personal grievances, but the scope of that voice was increasingly narrowed during the 1990s as the courts steadily restricted both the matters on which employees were required to be consulted and the range of factors employers were required to consider.[105]

While the statutory duty has not rebalanced the power relationships at the point of decision, it has influenced the strength of individual voice in the lead up to a decision. This is most apparent in section 4(1A)(c) where there are express obligations to provide information relevant to a decision. Information in turn enhances the ability to engage in consultation and the possibility of influencing a final decision. The specific obligations in the subsection, as well as the broader duty are probably the most successful example of 'infiltrating' internal management decision making. A failure to engage in proper consultation imposes considerable commercial, financial, and legal risks. Failure to consult during a significant restructuring may lead to a compliance order delaying that restructuring until consultation is properly carried out. In individual cases it will increase the possibility that a dismissal for redundancy may be held to be unjustified. In larger firms, at least, sound human resource processes tend to be taken seriously and over time change the character of decision-making. This process may be slow but eventually change can be significant as has been the case with processes around dismissal.

Has voice increased?

The statutory duty has strengthened both individual and collective worker voice, and while most of this increased strength has been retained under National-led governments, the political vulnerability of worker voice to changing political winds remains clear. National has made a number of small changes that have chipped away at elements of voice. These have included some restrictions on union access to members in their workplaces, and a narrowing of the test for justification in personal grievance cases. Further amendments, including the repeal of the expectation that the parties

[105] For a full discussion of the development of individual good faith see Anderson (n 52).

will conclude an agreement and provisions for terminating bargaining, have been signalled.[106] These amendments will be particularly significant for unions whose industrial strength is limited and are clearly intended to support employers seeking to actively resist collective bargaining. However what must be kept in mind is the very low starting point from which improved voice began. The Employment Contracts Act decimated worker voice and the process of rebuilding it, which began within unions in the second half of the 1990s, has been slow and uneasy. Labour implemented solid measures to enhance collective voice expressed through unions, but at the margins voice remains vulnerable. Individual voice has been expanded, particularly in the context of business restructuring, but again remains vulnerable and of limited influence where it is not supported by some collective expertise and strength.

Conclusion

This chapter began by referring to the Pike River tragedy. The events leading up to the explosion provide a succinct case study of why worker voice became increasingly irrelevant in New Zealand. The causes of lost voice at Pike River cannot be attributed solely to legal reforms but must be placed in the context of overall labour market deregulation. First, the composition of the labour force was one of few permanent employees and heavily reliant on contract labour. The workforce was largely non-unionized, turnover was high, and training less than adequate. Moreover employment opportunities on the Coast were limited; mining was one of the few significant employers of labour. This was an environment where voice was not encouraged and its exercise seen as unwise. An environment developed that led to known risks not being properly addressed, an ineffective health and safety committee, and a culture that tolerated high risk practices. Much of the fault for the explosion can be laid at the door of Pike River's management but the situation it allowed to develop was only possible because of the state's withdrawal from regulation of the workplace and from the lack of enforcement of what regulation did exist.[107] The Royal Commission Report is assiduous in identifying the regulatory failures from the time the mine was proposed through to the explosion, most importantly the total lack of health and safety oversight, inspection, and enforcement by the Department of Labour. The Pike River tragedy highlights the failure of the regulatory state to ensure worker voice and the most dramatic consequences of that failure, but it is the tip of an iceberg that was created in 1991 and which melted only to a limited extent in 2000.

Industrial voice in New Zealand has always been dependent on the agency of the regulatory state. Despite some successes in the period between the failure of the arbitration system and the enactment of the Employment Contracts Act, industrial action on its own has been ineffective in redressing the serious power imbalances in the

[106] Kate Wilkinson, 'Employment Relations Amendment Bill 2012—Collective Bargaining and Flexible Working Arrangements' (Office of the Minister of Labour, 3 May 2012) and now introduced as the Employment Relations Amendment Bill 2013 (n 63). At the time of writing the Bill had been reported back from a Select Committee but will not be further considered until 2014.

[107] Andrew Dallas and Rowan Anderson, 'An Injury to All: The Legal Regulation of Workplace Health and Safety in New Zealand's Coal Mines' [2012] ELB 89.

employment relationship throughout much of the history of New Zealand. While there have been some sites of concentrated industrial 'muscle', these have been insufficient to support an autonomous system of collective laissez-faire.

Effective voice for New Zealand workers was woven into the fabric of a society created by the progressive Liberal administration and the welfare state policies of the first Labour government. Its perpetuation by post-war conservative governments reflected a tripartite consensus which suited all parties in a small, heavily-protected economy, confident of secure British markets for its predominantly agricultural exports. Exposure to the world economy in the 1970s and an extremely rapid and thorough-going process of market deregulation in the 1980s and early 1990s swept almost all the structures which had created and complemented state supported worker voice. The afterglow of a mythology of the egalitarian society and the fair workplace persists, however, despite the evidence to the contrary.

This is what has made the Pike River tragedy so especially shocking to many New Zealanders. The impact of the deregulated marketplace has been starkly apparent and the virtual absence of effective government oversight of industrial safety exposed. The good faith legislative concept has provided some level of individual employment protection and created the mechanisms to support collective bargaining in the limited areas where this is still a realistic option. Industrial weakness has not quite plumbed the nadir of post-1890 industrial impotence. But as in 1890 and 1916, industrial activism must again look to political leverage to achieve the creation of effective worker voice in this jurisdiction.

The reality of employment relations is that there is a serious inequity in bargaining power between employees and employers which is only partly alleviated by collective organization. Individuals may be given rights of consultation and a voice in decisions that affect them, and this may have some impact. But that impact is almost entirely subject to the employer's discretion. Breaches of the duty to consult may attract a sanction, but that sanction will at best be limited compensation for lost employment. Attempts to increase voice without the backing of a union are likely to be doomed to failure: 'troublemakers' are not difficult to isolate and job insecurity is normally enough to restrain most employees. While Labour's reforms recognized the legitimacy of unions, it did not significantly alter the reality on the ground. Unions had continued to exist and to bargain under the Employment Contracts Act. The Employment Relations Act gave legal form to that reality: the regulation of the process of bargaining has been significantly improved but not its scope. Labour's reforms were solid but not courageous.

Overall good faith has had a positive impact but has not proved to be the game changer in employment relations. Whether a genuine game changer was politically feasible or sustainable is an open question but what is clear is that, in the absence of strong collective voice, worker voice will remain muted and of limited effectiveness. Worker voice must have strength to be effective and it must be expressed through channels that limit retaliation by employers. Historically there has only been one vehicle which can achieve this and in New Zealand at least this vehicle has required strong political support. That support became and remains highly contingent.

Loss of voice is not, however, inevitable. Australia, which until the 1990s shared New Zealand's arbitration system, has also gone through several years of major deregulatory reforms but has retained a strong underlying institutional structure and, by comparison with New Zealand, relatively strong and active unions. The reasons for the less extreme reforms in Australia are complex but include a stronger union movement, local political structures and, possibly most importantly, the legislative constraints of a bicameral federal parliament and a federal constitution. In Australia change was more measured and grew out of existing institutional structures.[108] One result was apparent in the Pike River Inquiry where the health and safety regimes in New South Wales and Queensland were regarded as exemplars and strongly influenced the Royal Commission's findings. It is the findings of the Royal Commission, and the report of the Independent Taskforce on Workplace Health and Safety,[109] that will provide the next battleground for worker voice. The Royal Commission made strong recommendations on enhanced employee participation in safety and the Taskforce recommendations reinforced these conclusions. While the majority of both the Pike River Royal Commission's and the Taskforce's recommendations have been accepted by the National government it is not yet clear that recommendations, including the right to stop work and stronger mandatory requirements for health and safety committees, will be fully accepted for larger workplaces generally, let alone for highly decentralized, but very dangerous, industries such as forestry. Resistance to worker voice on such fundamental matters as life and physical safety would suggest that further growth of worker voice will be very slow.

[108] See generally Andrew Stewart, 'Australian Labour Law in Transition: The Impact of the Fair Work Act' (2012) 37 New Zealand Journal of Employment Relations 3 and for an account of the different reform processes in the two countries Gordon Anderson and Michael Quinlan, 'The Changing Role of the State: Regulating Work Arrangements in Australia and New Zealand 1788–2007' (2008) 95 Labour History 111.

[109] 'Report of The Independent Taskforce on Workplace Health and Safety' (2013).

10

Democratic Theory and Voices at Work

*Virginia Mantouvalou**

Introduction

In Lee Hall's inspiring play 'The Pitmen Painters', set in the 1930s, a group of miners/trade unionists hire a University Professor to give them lessons in art appreciation. At some point they find themselves producing beautiful works of art. But when an art collector offers to buy Jimmy's painting, George reacts. This does not belong to the individual miner/artist, he says. It belongs to the union: '[t]he whole principle of [the union] is about collective ownership.' Intense disagreement breaks out, and when a young lad suggests putting the matter to a vote, he creates further tension:

> George: Listen, this is a democratic organisation. Nebody [sic] is voting or anything here—there are proper procedures to go through.[1]

When thinking about a voice at work, the first institutions that come to mind are workers' organizations, and first and foremost trade unions. Workers' voice was traditionally expressed through collective bargaining and industrial action.[2] In labour law theory, a common justification for a collective voice at work is democracy. On this view, workers should have a right to a voice, because this is required by democratic values. Yet both the meaning of democracy and the exact role of the institutions of voice are controversial.

Democracy is a contested concept at state level, as the first part of this chapter shows. An equal right to self-government commonly serves as a justification for the most appealing accounts of democracy. Individuals should have an equal right to participate in the making of decisions that affect their lives. Yet given that today democracy is indirect and representative, the literature places much attention on citizens' participation as a corrective to its indirect nature, which is central in accounts of democracy termed 'participatory'.[3] More recently, deliberative models of democracy dominate the literature. Participation is central here too, but a key feature of these accounts is that practical reason takes on a primary role,[4] while in order for decisions to be impartial,

* Reader in Human Rights and Labour Law, University College London (UCL), Faculty of Laws; Co-Director of the UCL Institute for Human Rights. I am very grateful to Alan Bogg, Hugh Collins, George Letsas, and Tonia Novitz for comments on a draft.

[1] Lee Hall, *The Pitmen Painters* (Faber and Faber Plays, 2008) inspired by William Feaver's *Pitmen Painters—The Ashington Group 1934–1984* (Carcanet Press, 1988) 51.

[2] Alan Bogg and Tonia Novitz, 'Investigating Voice at Work' (2011–2012) 33 Comparative Labor Law and Policy Journal (CLLPJ) 323 at 324.

[3] See, for instance, Robert Dahl, *A Preface to Economic Democracy* (University of California Press, 1985); Carole Pateman, *Participation and Democratic Theory* (CUP, 1970).

[4] See, for instance, Jurgen Habermas, *Between Facts and Norms—Contributions to a Discourse Theory of Law and Democracy*, translation by William Rehg (MIT, 1997).

an inclusive process of collective discussion is required.[5] On deliberative models, continuous deliberation, argumentation, and discussion help define, refine, and resolve moral disagreement through the exchange of reasons.

This passage from Lee Hall's play shows that the definition of democracy is not uncontroversial in the context of the workplace either, where it raises questions of workplace participation in decisions taken by the employer or the state, but also new issues involving the power of trade unions over individual members. In a way that mirrors the debate on democracy at state level, a line of scholarship talks about industrial democracy and a right to self-government at enterprise level. In classical accounts of workplace democracy that place emphasis on participation, workers have a right to a voice at work, which is grounded on the principle of equality. There is inequality of bargaining power between the employer and the workers, and there is a need to counterbalance this imbalance of power and to give workers an effective right to participate. The deliberative accounts of democracy, when applied to the workplace, place more weight on the importance of public reasoning that aims to promote impartiality, rather than interest group bargaining that is said to dominate classical pluralist accounts of democratic voice at work. On this analysis, workers' voice must above all be collective. Workers must organize to have a voice at work. The first part of this chapter presents these accounts of democracy as a justification for workers' voice.

The second part of the chapter looks at human rights law as an avenue for workers' voice, in order to assess the contribution that this makes in the theoretical debates on democracy as a justification of voice. It focuses on the European Court of Human Rights (ECtHR or Court) that has frequently said in respect of Article 11 and its protection of freedom of association that workers and their organizations should have a 'right to be heard'. Because human rights as moral principles are stringent standards, and because human rights law sets out strong legal obligations, its approach to workplace voice is important. This section discusses the European Convention on Human Rights (ECHR or Convention), given its significance for the landscape of voice in the United Kingdom. The ECtHR clearly views workers' organizations as important institutions of voice, but it does not always specify the precise avenue of workplace voice that the Convention protects. Yet the Court has in recent years supported a right to collective bargaining and a right to strike as essential avenues for workers to be heard. Workers' voice in human rights law has its limitations too, which this section explores. At the same time, the Court has had to address workers' voice not only in traditional settings of inequality of power between employers and workers, but also when it comes to conflicts *between* workers. In such instances, human rights law requires that individual workers have a right to be heard against trade unions themselves. In human rights law, state authorities may need to intervene in the internal matters of unions when liberal rights are at stake, in order to protect the individual from majoritarian preferences. The Convention then also recognizes a right to individual voice *against* the collective.

Yet workers' voice in the ECHR is secured not only through trade unions. The Court has regularly ruled that for the voice of workers to be heard, state authorities may need

[5] Carlos Nino, *The Constitution of Deliberative Democracy* (Yale University Press, 1996) 133.

to adopt legislation. There is a line of case law, which requires laws to be enacted for workers' rights to be protected and their voice to be heard. What this section finds is that the model of democracy that underlies the Convention is a liberal, anti-majoritarian model, based on the principle of equality and individual freedom. As the final part of the section shows, even though the Court does not explicitly endorse any particular model of democracy, its decisions play an important role in a deliberative account of democracy, which views courts as important fora of deliberation where the authorities are required to justify their actions. In addition, it fulfils this democratic role because its case law forms the foundation for debate at the nation-state and the European supranational level.

How does a human rights justification of workplace voice compare to the democratic justification that is prominent in labour law theory? On the one hand, there are important areas of convergence and mutual support between democratic theory and human rights law in the discussion of workers' voice. First, human rights law endorses a liberal account of democracy, where the idea of equality is central. Against this background, it embraces equal participation not only at state level against the authorities, but also in the workplace, where there is inequality of bargaining power between the employer and the worker. Conceptions of political equality range from republican models that seek to encourage or ensure active participation in the political decision-making process, to neutrality-based models that seek to make fair the background conditions of individual choice within a market economy. Likewise, conceptions of equality in the workplace range from strong participatory models that seek to ensure active worker participation in the running of the business to weaker participatory models that seek to counter the unfairness that can lead to exploitation in an unregulated employment market. It is this latter vision of equality that can be said to underlie the decisions of the Court. Second, a human rights justification that stems from the approach of the ECtHR in the cases explored here shows that there is convergence between human rights and democratic justifications both in some of the institutions of voice that are required (trade unions), and in the avenues of voice that are protected. This can be seen in areas such as the right to collective bargaining and the right to strike, both of which are essential both in human rights law and democratic theory. The areas of convergence are important to highlight, for the more the justifications of voice, the stronger its normative force.

On the other hand, there are at least two ways in which human rights principles on workers' voice can be distinguished from the dominant analyses in democratic theory. First, human rights law itself recognizes a right to a voice not only *through* trade unions, but also to individual workers *against* the power of trade unions, for example in cases of conflicts between workers. Workers' voice in human rights serves both as a sword, namely a positive right to participate, and as a shield, namely a right to be protected against the domination of employers, unions, or state authorities. Second, the ECtHR recognizes that workplace expression may legitimately be limited, if it conflicts with other workplace interests, such as good faith, trust, and cooperation. Human rights law protects workers' voice, but also recognizes that it has limitations, when it conflicts with such interests. Third, and very importantly, human rights law does not only recognize the role of unions as institutions of voice. It may also require the enactment of legislation that protects workers' rights as individual human rights, and guarantees another avenue of voice at work.

Voice and Democracy

In labour law theory, workplace voice was historically linked to associational activity. Collective action exercised through workers' organizations was traditionally viewed as the most important way in which workers' interests could be promoted. Because in general, the inequality of bargaining power between employers and workers is viewed as a key normative foundation of labour law, trade unions are seen as the key institutions to address this. The idea that '[f]ighting individually, workers lose; fighting together, workers can win' is dominant.[6] In this context, workplace voice is often said to be grounded on democracy: there is an analogy to draw between the rights of citizens to participate at state level, and the rights of workers to take part in decision-making at the level of the enterprise. What is the definition of democracy at the level of the state? What do we mean when we refer to workplace democracy and voice? I will take statist models of democracy as a starting point, as these have also been used by labour law scholars as analogies for democratic institutions in the workplace.[7]

Democracy at state level

Democracy is generally grounded on the value of self-government. At the heart of the belief in a democracy lies 'the view that in a certain kind of human association, the process of government should as far as possible meet democratic criteria, because people involved in this kind of association possess a *right*, an inalienable right to govern themselves by the democratic process'.[8] On such accounts, democracy has intrinsic importance.[9] This is based on the value of equality, on the idea that everyone's interests should be weighted equally, and that each person is the best judge of what promotes her or his interests.[10]

At state level, when reference is made to this system of governance, we do not usually have in mind direct democracy, which is aligned with participatory models of democracy where citizens are directly involved in decision-making. Democracy is today indirect and representative, where citizens elect officials that represent them in decision-making.[11] Decisions reached are rarely unanimous; they are made by majorities. To suggest that any decision reached by a majority is democratic, though, would reflect a crude and inadequate view of democracy. There are other, better, conceptions of representative democracy.

[6] Jay Youngdahl, 'Solidarity First: Labor Rights Are Not the Same as Human Rights' (2009) 18 New Labor Forum 31 at 32.

[7] See Alan Bogg, *The Democratic Aspects of Trade Union Recognition* (Hart Publishing, 2009) ch. 1.

[8] Dahl 56–7 (n 3).

[9] For a purely instrumental account of democracy, see e.g. Richard Arneson, 'Democracy Is Not Intrinsically Just' in Dowding, Goodin, and Pateman (eds), *Justice and Democracy* (CUP, 2004) 40.

[10] Robert Dahl, *Democracy and its Critics* (Yale University Press, 1989) 97–105.

[11] See David Held, *Models of Democracy*, 3rd edn (OUP, 2006) 4.

The best definitions of democracy entail not only procedural elements, which majoritarian democracy entails as it involves the expression of majorities' will through elections, but also some key substantive features: a list of basic rights that prevail over the will of majorities. This can be described as a liberal democracy. Dworkin, for instance, only sees the decision of a majority as legitimate if it is a majority in a community of equals. He draws a distinction between 'statistical' and 'communal' democracy,[12] and suggests that communal democracy is central in all charters of rights. On this understanding a democratic decision is legitimate if people have expressed their will from a position of political equality. On a liberal account, certain civil and political rights, like freedom of expression or freedom of association, are viewed as an essential prerequisite for a democracy, because they instantiate political equality. Without these rights, which may serve as constraints on majoritarian preferences, there is no democracy.

Other contemporary conceptions of representative democracy place emphasis on the value of citizens' participation in the political process.[13] These models are first, the participatory and, second, the deliberative model. According to the participatory conception, the key aim of a democracy is the participation of citizens in decision-making. Citizens' participation serves a number of functions. For Rousseau, for instance, participation promotes individual interests and good government, but it also educates individuals to be public, as well as private citizens.[14] In the participatory accounts of democracy more generally the educative function of participation is a key reason why participation is valued.[15] At the same time, though, participation plays an integrative role, and is viewed as a system of government that is more likely to lead to the acceptance of collective decisions.[16]

On the deliberative model of democracy, finally, participation is also important, but here the idea of public reasoning takes on a central role. Because there is reasonable moral disagreement, political decisions should be reached through a deliberative process, in which all those affected have a right to take part from a position of equality.[17] Citizens need to participate, and by this we mean that they must deliberate, exchange views, and provide reasons for their position on questions of public interest.[18] On this model, for decision-making to be legitimate, it ought to take account of all those who will feel the impact of the decisions reached, so as to promote impartiality. Decisions reached in this deliberative way may be better informed than in other accounts of democracy, and can also represent better the common good. Deliberative democracy places special attention on argumentation that aims to offer mutually acceptable reasons, rather than simple interest-group bargaining, which may take place in other accounts of participatory democracy. For this reason, many theorists regard it as a better account of democracy than other participatory models that do not focus on deliberation.

[12] Ronald Dworkin, *A Bill of Rights for Britain* (Chatto and Windus, 1990) 35.

[13] See Pateman (n 3).

[14] See the discussion in Pateman ch. 2 (n 3).

[15] Pateman 42 (n 3).

[16] Pateman 43 (n 3).

[17] Amy Gutmann and Dennis Thompson, *Democracy and Disagreement* (Harvard University Press, 1996) ch. 1.

[18] John Rawls, *Collected Papers* (Harvard University Press, 1999) 579–80.

Democracy at work

Theorists have applied the participatory accounts of democracy beyond the state level, in the workplace. Participatory accounts of democracy have led scholars to argue that if democracy is justified at state level, it is also justified at the level of the enterprise. Workers should have a right to self-government in the workplace, because the workplace can serve as a school for democratic citizenship at state level. Indeed, people spend most of their life at work, so participation in decision-making in the workplace can educate them and make them better citizens outside the workplace.[19]

Workplace participation does not only have instrumental value, though.[20] It also has intrinsic value.[21] The key idea here is that the workplace is a political system itself, and individuals in this political system should be able to exercise control in the way that they are governed in this context, in a manner analogous to the control that they exercise at state level.[22] In terms of institutions of voice, if self-government in the workplace is a fundamental right, then it is not sufficient to have trade unions, as Dahl argues. A voice at work requires strong institutions that are run by the workers themselves. Democratically run enterprises must be 'self-governing', as Dahl says, and workers need to have voting equality: each worker must have one vote.[23] The issues over which the workers will have voting equality involve how the revenues of the enterprise will be used: what will be invested and what will be distributed as wages. Self-governing enterprises that are run efficiently and do not violate fundamental rights of workers are, on Dahl's account, good for justice and democracy.[24]

Turning to the deliberative model of democracy, there has been some scepticism about its application in the workplace. Yet it has also been insightfully defended as a justification of voice at work. The heart of the criticism expressed in labour law scholarship is that the workplace is about conflict, and workplace voice expressed primarily through collective bargaining and strike cannot be captured by deliberative theory.[25] On this view, deliberative democracy can only serve as a justification for institutions of social partnership in the workplace. Even if deliberative processes are in place, interest-group bargaining will in reality be taking place behind the scenes, as Novitz has suggested.

We can also find a strong defence of deliberative democracy in the workplace in labour law theory, though.[26] Bogg argued that this model of democracy does not always aim to lead to consensus. Deliberation may be able to clarify the points of disagreement between different groups (workers and employers in the employment context), and disagreement thus crystallized can enrich the deliberations.[27] In addition, the interest-group bargaining analysis of industrial conflict may at times rest on a limited understanding of what is at stake. Even though it may seem that industrial conflict is about wages, for instance, what is in fact at stake is a list of deep and abstract moral values.[28] The right to strike itself, which may be viewed as primarily about negotiation against

[19] Pateman 43 (n 3). [20] Dahl 94 (n 3). [21] Dahl 111 (n 3). [22] Pateman 43 (n 3).
[23] Dahl 91 (n 3). [24] Dahl 92–3 (n 3).
[25] Tonia Novitz, *International and European Protection of the Right to Strike* (OUP, 2003) 21.
[26] Bogg 249 ff (n 7). [27] Bogg 252 (n 7). [28] Bogg 254 (n 7).

the background of interest-group bargaining, has been offered a deliberative democratic justification by Bogg.[29] It can provide a level playing field between employers and workers, whose relationship is unequal, and may also encourage deliberation. It should be explained that by saying that collective bargaining and strike can have an important function in a deliberative democracy we do not mean that in practice they always fulfil this role.[30] We mean that trade unions, through their avenues of voice, can, and also should, at a normative level, play this role in a deliberative model of democracy.

In participatory accounts of democracy discussed here, then, workplaces must be governed by workers themselves or at least trade unions must have a central role in workplace decision-making. In deliberative models of democracy, workers' associations are viewed as essential institutions of voice, and a right to collective bargaining and strike are regarded as fundamental avenues of voice. An exact analogy between the state and the industry is hard to draw, though this kind of analogical reasoning has been common amongst labour law theorists.[31] Yet that participation at state level and participation through work are closely linked comes as no surprise and has been highlighted also in the area of citizenship theory, where it has been argued that the two key rights of the status of citizenship are, first, a right to vote, and second, a right to work.[32] The idea that in a democracy, individuals should take part in decisions that affect their lives not only at state level, where there is the possibility of arbitrary exercise of power by the authorities, but also in the workplace, where they spend much of their life, and where there is also the possibility of arbitrary exercise of power by the employer because of economic dependence, is of fundamental importance.

Human Rights and Workers' Voice

What does human rights law add to the analysis of theories of democracy and workers' voice? This question is addressed here by reference to the ECHR, and the approach of the ECtHR to workplace voice and democracy, given the significance of this case law for the landscape of voice in the UK.

Democracy is a fundamental value reflected throughout the ECHR. It is also mentioned in its Preamble that reaffirms the belief of the contracting states in human rights that 'are best maintained... by an effective political democracy'. The Court has frequently addressed the links between democracy and human rights in its case law, where at times certain rights are viewed as essential for a democracy, while at other times democracy serves as a justification for restrictions to rights.[33] A good example that shows the role of democracy in the Convention comes from the context of political

[29] Bogg 255 ff (n 7).

[30] See, for instance, the critical analysis of deliberative democratic principles in strike action in the context of the UK and Australian model in Shae McCrystal and Tonia Novitz, '"Democratic" Pre-conditions for Strike Action: A Comparative Study of Australian and UK Labour Legislation' (2012) 28 International Journal of Comparative Labour Law and Industrial Relations 115.

[31] Hugh Collins, *Employment Law*, 2nd edn (OUP, 2010) 134.

[32] Judith Shklar, *American Citizenship—The Quest for Inclusion* (Harvard University Press, 1998).

[33] For an early account of democracy in the Convention, see Susan Marks, 'The European Convention on Human Rights and its "Democratic Society"' (1995) 66 British Yearbook of International Law 209.

parties. When examining state interference with political parties, the test employed by the Court tends to emphasize the importance of pluralism for democracy, which is a fundamental value of the Convention and the only political system that is compatible with it.[34] The Court has ruled that 'only convincing and compelling reasons'[35] may make a restriction of freedom of association in the case of political parties compatible with the ECHR.

The conception of democracy that the Court endorses is not majoritarian democracy, which was earlier described as a crude conception of democracy. This is unsurprising, given that a key function of human rights law is to protect individuals from majoritarian preferences. The ECtHR has frequently stated that '[a]lthough individual interests must on occasion be subordinated to those of a group, democracy does not simply mean that the views of a majority must always prevail: a balance must be achieved which ensures the fair and proper treatment of minorities and avoids any abuse of a dominant position.'[36] A strong commitment to liberal democracy underlies the case law of the Court, and has repeatedly been reiterated in its judgments.[37] The promotion of liberalism and the suppression of totalitarianism is, after all, the reason why the Convention was drafted in the first place, in the aftermath of the Second World War.

A participatory account of democracy is not unknown territory in Strasbourg jurisprudence. In the case *United Macedonian Organisation Ilinden v Bulgaria*,[38] which involved the refusal of the authorities to register an association, the ECtHR said: 'It is only natural that, where a civil society functions in a healthy manner, the participation of citizens in the democratic process is to a large extent achieved through belonging to associations in which they may integrate with each other and pursue common objectives collectively.'[39] As is evident in this passage, the reason why the Court endorses participation in civil society organizations is because it promotes participation at state level too. The justification of the importance of participation in civil society organizations is instrumental, in other words, and is based on the fundamental value of democracy as a political system at state level.

Democracy is an important value reflected in the Convention, and developed in the case law of the Court. What is the legal protection of a human right to a voice at work and what are its links to democracy?

[34] *United Communist Party v Turkey*, App No 133/1996/752/951, Judgment of 30 January 1998, para. 45.

[35] *United Communist Party v Turkey*, para. 46 (n 34).

[36] See, for instance, *Young, James and Webster v UK*, App Nos 7601/76 and 7806/77, Judgment of 13 August 1981, para. 63.

[37] For a recent example, see Hugh Collins and Virginia Mantouvalou, '*Redfearn v UK*: Political Association and Dismissal' (2013) 73 Modern Law Review 909.

[38] *United Macedonian Organisation Ilinden and Others v Bulgaria*, App No 59491/00, Judgment of 19 January 2006.

[39] *United Macedonian Organisation v Bulgaria*, para. 58 (n 38).

Associations and workplace democracy

The question of a human right to workplace voice and democracy will be addressed by first looking at Article 11 of the ECHR. The provision reads as follows:

> 1. Everyone has the right to freedom of peaceful assembly and to freedom of association with others, including the right to form and to join trade unions for the protection of his interests.
> 2. No restrictions shall be placed on the exercise of these rights other than such as are prescribed by law and are necessary in a democratic society in the interests of national security or public safety, for the prevention of disorder or crime, for the protection of health or morals or for the protection of the rights and freedoms of others. This Article shall not prevent the imposition of lawful restrictions on the exercise of these rights by members of the armed forces, of the police or of the administration of the State.

(a) Human rights as a sword: liberal democracy and workers' participation

From early on in its case law, the Court had to consider the components of the right to associate in the context of trade unionism, in order to examine the positive elements of trade union freedom. This aspect of the case law for workers' voice can be called the function of human rights law as a sword, which I contrast to its function as a shield that will be explored in the section that follows.

Given the explicit protection of trade unions in Article 11, the Court always viewed them as essential institutions in a liberal democracy.[40] What was less clear, though, was what precise avenues of voice trade unions had available to them under human rights law, in order to have an effective right to be heard. In one of the first collective labour law cases, the *National Union of Belgian Police v Belgium*,[41] the ECtHR was asked to interpret the phrase 'for the protection of his interests' in the first paragraph of Article 11 against the background of unionization. Is it redundant or does it serve a purpose in the Convention? The ECtHR said:

> These words, clearly denoting purpose, show that the Convention safeguards freedom to protect the occupational interests of trade union members by trade union action, the conduct and development of which the Contracting States must both permit and make possible. In the opinion of the Court, it follows that the members of a trade union have a right, in order to protect their interests, that *the trade union should be heard*. Article 11 para. 1 (art. 11-1) certainly leaves each State a free choice of the means to be used towards this end. While consultation is one of these means, there are others. What the Convention requires is that under national law trade unions should be enabled, in conditions not at variance with Article 11 (art. 11), to strive for the protection of their members' interests.[42]

[40] The Court has not this far examined the right to contest outside the union context, which Bogg and Estlund have developed. See Alan Bogg and Cynthia Estlund, 'Freedom of Association and the Right to Contest: Getting Back to Basics', this volume.

[41] *National Union of Belgian Police v Belgium* A19; 1 EHRR 578.

[42] Para. 39 (n 41), emphasis added.

The right to be heard, which the Court recognized in the *National Union of Belgian Police*, did not mean that the applicant trade union should be recognized for the purposes of consultation. The approach in the *National Union of Belgian Police* was typical of the way in which the Court interpreted workplace voice, and was re-iterated later on. In *Schmidt and Dahlstrom v Sweden*,[43] it ruled that the right to strike was one of the means by which unions could strive for the protection of their interests, but it was not an essential avenue of voice.[44] Finally, in *Swedish Engine Drivers' Union*,[45] the Swedish government refused to enter into a collective agreement with the applicant union, and entered into an agreement with a larger and more representative union. The Court held that Article 11 does not guarantee any particular treatment for trade unions.[46] It implies a right to be heard, but allows the contracting states a 'free choice of the means to be used towards this end'.[47] In past case law, in other words, trade unions were viewed as important institutions of voice, but no precise avenues of voice (beyond the general requirement that the trade union be heard) were recognized as essential.

The approach of the Court in the early jurisprudence reflected a limited understanding of the role of workers' associations for workplace voice, and was criticized to this effect.[48] The explicit protection of the right to form and join a trade union in the ECHR was probably founded on the understanding that there is inequality of power between the employer and the worker, and human rights law should be addressing this inequality. In that sense, the model of democracy underlying the cases was a liberal model that values the right to equal participation in decision-making. Yet because of the limited avenues of voice supported, this model was neither clearly endorsed nor developed.

In recent years the Court has recognized that the right to be heard of workers and their associations requires the protection of collective bargaining as an essential component of Article 11. In *Wilson*, for instance, it established that a trade union has a right to seek to pressurize the employer to hear its voice in one way or another.[49] The landmark decision in *Demir and Baykara* in 2008 explained that workers' voice is a developing concept in the Convention, which is in itself a living instrument.[50] Against this background, the right to collective bargaining emerged as an essential element of Article 11.[51] In *Enerji Yapi-Yol Sen*[52] and other case law that followed,[53] the Court ruled that

[43] *Schmidt and Dahlstrom v Sweden* A21; 1 EHRR 637.

[44] *Schmidt and Dahlstrom*, para. 36 (n 43).

[45] *Swedish Engine Drivers' Union v Sweden*, App No 5614/72, Judgment of 6 February 1976.

[46] *Swedish Engine Drivers' Union v Sweden*, para. 39 (n 45).

[47] *Swedish Engine Drivers' Union v Sweden*, para. 39 (n 45).

[48] See Keith Ewing, 'The Human Rights Act and Labour Law' (1998) 27 Industrial Law Journal (ILJ) 275; Novitz 238 (n 25); Lord Wedderburn, 'Freedom of Association or Right to Organise? The Common Law and International Sources' in Lord Wedderburn (ed.), *Employment Rights in Britain and Europe* (London: Lawrence and Wishart, 1991) 138 at 144.

[49] *Wilson, National Union of Journalists and Others v UK*, App Nos 30668/96, 30671/96 and 30678/96, Judgment of 2 July 2002, para. 44.

[50] *Demir and Baykara v Turkey*, App No 34503/97, Grand Chamber Judgment of 12 November 2008, paras 145–146. For analysis, see Keith Ewing and John Hendy, 'The Dramatic Implications of *Demir and Baykara*' (2010) 39 ILJ 2. On the character of the ECHR as a living instrument, see George Letsas, 'The ECHR as a Living Instrument: its Meaning and its Legitimacy' in Ulfstein, Follesdal, and Peters (eds), *Constituting Europe—The European Court of Human Rights in a National, European and Global Context* (CUP, 2013) 106.

[51] *Demir and Baykara*, para. 147 (n 50).

[52] *Enerji Yapi-Yol Sen v Turkey*, App No 68959/01, Judgment of 21 April 2009.

[53] See, for instance, *Danilenkov v Russia*, App No 7336/01, Judgment of 30 July 2009.

the right to strike is also an essential component of Article 11 of the Convention. While it said that this is not an absolute right and that it can be restricted in certain circumstances, it found that a general ban on strikes in the public sector violated the ECHR.

It can be said that the approach of the ECtHR in recent Article 11 cases is grounded on the belief that a key function of trade unions is to counterbalance the inequality of bargaining power in the workplace, a key justification of labour law.[54] The inequality of bargaining power is not stated openly in decisions of the Court as the organizing principle of associational activity under Article 11. Yet as a liberal egalitarian account of democracy underlies ECHR case law,[55] similarly such an account can be said to justify recent Article 11 cases, which recognize a richer content to the provision than in the past in order to make the associational rights of workers effective.[56]

In what sense is equality a key value here? It was said earlier that conceptions of political equality range from republican models that seek to encourage or ensure active participation in the political decision-making process, to neutrality-based models that aim to make fair the background conditions of individual choice within a market economy. Similarly, conceptions of equality in the workplace range from strong participatory models that seek to ensure active worker participation in the running of the business to weaker participatory models that seek to counter the unfairness that can lead to exploitation in an unregulated employment market. It is this latter vision of equality that can be said to underlie the decisions of the Court. In the jurisprudence, trade unions have a right to represent workers, a right to collective bargaining and strike, but workers themselves do not have a right to direct participation in running the enterprise. Even though the approach of the ECtHR falls short of Dahl's vision of self-government at work, still it can be grounded on the idea of equality that requires the protection of at least some procedural rights to participate that can protect workers from exploitation.

(b) Limitations to trade union voice

Workers' collective voice is not without its limitations in ECtHR jurisprudence. The Convention protects freedom of expression, which has been examined specifically in the workplace context, and can serve here as an example of the limitations that can be placed on the human right to a voice at work. The case in question is *Palomo Sanchez v Spain*,[57] where the Court had to assess the dismissal of trade union officers who published in a trade union newsletter a cartoon and some other publications with sexual content that involved their human resources manager. The texts and cartoon were published against the background of an industrial dispute, and the purpose of the

[54] Paul Davies and Mark Freedland, *Kahn-Freund's Labour and the Law* (Stevens, 1983) 18; Guy Mundlak, 'The Third Function of Labour Law: Distributing Labour Market Opportunities among Workers' in Guy Davidov and Brian Langille (eds), *The Idea of Labour Law* (OUP, 2011) 315.

[55] George Letsas, *A Theory of Interpretation of the European Convention on Human Rights* (OUP, 2009); Virginia Mantouvalou, 'Is there a Human Right Not to Be a Trade Union Member?' in Colin Fenwick and Tonia Novitz (eds), *Human Rights at Work—Perspectives on Law and Regulation* (Hart Publishing, 2010) 439.

[56] See *Demir and Baykara*, para. 144 (n 50).

[57] *Palomo Sanchez v Spain*, App Nos 28955/06, 28957/06, 28959/06, and 28964/06, Grand Chamber Judgment of 12 September 2011.

publications was to criticize the manager. The Court looked at the case in light of freedom of expression (Article 10 of the ECHR), which in this context had to be assessed against the background of trade union activities (Article 11 of the ECHR). Like Article 11, Article 10 permits limitations to freedom of expression, which are assessed in the case law through a test of proportionality. The majority of the Court ruled without much hesitation, and with the support of International Labour Organization materials, that the dismissal of the applicants was a legitimate restriction to their right to express themselves.

However, a powerful dissent by Judges Tulkens, Bjorgvinsson, Jociene, Popovic, and Vucinic took the opposite view to the majority. Recognizing the importance of workers' voice, and the particularities of this voice in the trade union context, the dissenting judges emphasized that views that 'shock, disturb and offend' merit the protection of the Convention, 'as an expression of pluralism, tolerance and broadmindedness, without which there is no democratic society'.[58] Workers' voice was given by the majority lower protection than other types of expression outside the employment context.[59] That the dismissal of the trade unionists was found to be compatible with the ECHR could have a 'chilling effect' on trade union activities more generally, and should therefore have been ruled to violate the Convention.[60]

The position of the majority in *Palomo Sanchez* is unfortunate, but is probably due to the particularities of the case that involved publications that could be seen as vulgar. Yet it does not cease to reflect a poorer understanding of the employment relation than the one underlying the decisions discussed earlier, and the role of workers' voice in the labour context, as the dissenting opinion insightfully argued. The dissent, on the other hand, shows a good understanding of the importance of workers' voice in a liberal account of democracy that is committed to free expression even when such expression is shocking and offensive.[61] The dissent strongly values free expression and tolerance, and holds that voice at work merits special protection because it is grounded on the inequality of power between the worker and the employer. This inequality is expressed through the ability to dismiss the worker—a power that the dissent compares to the power of the state to arrest a person,[62] drawing in this way a strong parallel between democracy and voice at state level and at workplace level.

(c) Human rights as a shield: voice in conflicts between workers

European human rights law, as developed by the Strasbourg Court, protects individuals not only against state authorities, but also against private power.[63] In the context of employment, this private power is not only exercised by the employer; it can also be exercised by the unions themselves. It is fair to say that unions, like other organizations in modern society, may exercise power over the individual, which when there

[58] Dissent, para. 10 (n 57). [59] Dissent, para. 11 (n 57). [60] Dissent, para. 17 (n 57).

[61] *Handyside v UK*, App No 5493/72 Judgment of 7 December 1976, para. 49.

[62] Dissent, para. 18 (n 57).

[63] For discussion of positive obligations under the ECHR, see Alastair Mowbray, *The Development of Positive Obligations under the European Convention on Human Rights by the European Court of Human Rights* (Hart Publishing, 2004).

are closed shop agreements in place may be as coercive as the power exercised by state authorities. In the effort to further their own and their members' interests, unions may neglect or 'sacrifice the interests of some individuals'.[64] The protection of individual workers from the power of unions can be analysed against the background of what Guy Mundlak has described as the 'third function of labour law', which is to resolve conflicts *between* workers.[65] In this context, the case law of the ECtHR has recognized a voice for individual workers against unions' power. It was said in the introduction to this piece that the human right to a voice at work can serve not only as a sword, a function that we saw in the earlier sections, but also as a shield: it is protected when the union, for instance, exercises dominating power over an individual. That we find this element in human rights law, with its focus on individual liberal rights, should come as no surprise.

The function of human rights law as a shield, in conflicts between workers, can be found in cases where decision-making by unions allows majority views to prevail at the expense of individual rights.[66] This can be seen in closed shop agreements under Article 11 of the ECHR, and emerged from early on in the jurisprudence, in *Young, James and Webster v UK*.[67] The applicants here were dismissed because they refused to join the trade unions with which their employer, British Rail, signed a closed shop agreement when they were already employed. One of the applicants disagreed with the political views of the union, while all three applicants objected to various aspects of the system as it operated at the time, because they believed that it did not promote labour interests effectively. The ECtHR said that setting no limitations to compelled association would strike at the very substance of Article 11 and stated that 'a threat of dismissal involving loss of livelihood is a most serious form of compulsion',[68] which could violate the Convention. With respect to democracy, the Court recognized explicitly that it should not be equated to majoritarianism, and that individuals and minorities must be protected from majorities' abuse.[69] A balance needs to be struck between the union's right to be heard in the negotiations with the employer, and the voice of the individual that needs to be heard when in conflict with that of the union.

From *Young, James and Webster*, but also from more recent case law,[70] it emerges that individual workers who do not want to unionize will most of the time be protected under the Convention. According to the case law, compulsory union membership will be compatible with European human rights law only if the following conditions are satisfied: first, if the union or unions are politically neutral, namely if they have no affiliation to a political party, something that is admittedly rare at least in Europe. Second, in cases where unions have political affiliations, there ought to be an effective and transparent option of non-political membership for the individuals that disagree

[64] Clyde Summers, 'Trade Unions and their Members' in Larry Gostin (ed.), *Civil Liberties in Conflict* (Routledge, 1988) 65.

[65] See Mundlak (n 54); see also Anne Davies, 'Identifying "Exploitative Compromises": The Role of Labour Law in Resolving Disputes Between Workers' (2012) 65 Current Legal Problems 269.

[66] Davies views this as a key area of conflict of interests between workers. See Davies 16 ff (n 65).

[67] *Young, James and Webster v UK*, App Nos 7601/76, 7806/77, Judgment of 13 August 1981.

[68] *Young, James and Webster*, para. 55 (n 67).

[69] See the passage accompanying n 36.

[70] *Sorensen and Rasmussen v Denmark*, App Nos 52562/99 and 52620/99, Judgment of 11 January 2006.

with the union's political aims.[71] In conflicts between workers in the closed shops context, these are essential guarantees of individual voice against union power according to the ECtHR.

Labour law scholars have been critical of the strong protection of individuals against union membership, which the Court recognized long before it protected a voice at work for trade unions themselves. Tonia Novitz said that the Court shows 'a greater interest on the defence of individual autonomy than collective solidarity',[72] and Lord Wedderburn described the case law as 'individual and formalistic'.[73] However, in terms of the discussion of a voice at work and democracy in human rights law, the closed shops line of cases should not come as a surprise. It simply confirms the liberal character of human rights and the anti-majoritarian character of the ECHR, and recognizes that the interests of labour, which are explicitly mentioned in Article 11 of the Convention, do not always coincide.[74] There may be conflicts of interest between different groups of workers, which the Court recognizes and addresses in the interpretation of the Convention, a traditional liberal document. Liberalism is committed to individual freedom,[75] which here requires that workers should always have a voice, not only against the employer, but also against workers' associations that may exercise oppressive power over them. There are limits to majoritarian decision-making by trade unions, and Convention rights show where these limits are to be found: in the protection of individual rights of workers. When unions act in ways that restrict these rights, the Court may find that there is a violation of the ECHR.

The function of human rights law in protecting individual voice in conflicts between workers is also confirmed in another case that examined exclusion from union membership of individuals, where the Court examined the compatibility of union rules with the Convention. In *ASLEF v UK*,[76] where the applicant union excluded an individual from membership because of his political affiliation and activities with an extreme right-wing party, the British National Party (BNP), the ECtHR said that abuse of the union's dominant position 'might occur, for example, where exclusion or expulsion from a trade union was not in accordance with union rules or where the rules were wholly unreasonable or arbitrary or where the consequences of exclusion or expulsion resulted in exceptional hardship'.[77] In this case, the exclusion was ruled to be justified and compatible with the Convention.[78]

For present purposes it is important that the Court examined the democratically adopted rules of the union to assess whether they resulted in the arbitrary exclusion of an individual worker. What becomes evident here is that the law should insist on internal democracy of trade unions, which should be democratic institutions, in a

[71] For further analysis, see Mantouvalou (n 55). [72] Novitz 238 (n 25).

[73] Lord Wedderburn, 'Freedom of Association or Right to Organise? The Common Law and International Sources' in Lord Wedderburn (ed.), *Employment Rights in Britain and Europe* (Lawrence and Wishart, 1991) 138 at 144.

[74] See Davies 10 (n 65).

[75] Jeremy Waldron, 'Theoretical Foundations of Liberalism' in his *Liberal Rights—Collected Papers* (CUP, 1993) 35 at 37.

[76] *ASLEF v UK*, App No 11002/05, Judgment of 27 February 2007. [77] *ASLEF*, para. 43 (n 76).

[78] For analysis, see Keith Ewing, 'The Implications of the ASLEF Case' (2007) 36 ILJ 425.

liberal sense: majorities' decisions are legitimate only when they do not violate individual rights.

What emerges at this point is that the ECHR, a traditional liberal egalitarian document, safeguards a right to a voice against the power of the employer. In this context, trade unions that are explicitly protected in the Convention are recognized in the case law as essential institutions of voice, and collective bargaining and the right to strike are viewed as fundamental avenues of voice. The protection of workers' collective voice in the Convention emphasizes the role of collective action against the background of the inequality of power between the employer and the worker. The model of democracy that prevails in this case law is a liberal egalitarian model. The anti-majoritarian character of the Convention, though, also means that individuals must be protected against the power of unions, which may sacrifice an individual's rights for the sake of the collective good. In conflicts between workers, the Court has shown in its case law that individuals have a voice at work against the power of unions, which must themselves be governed to a certain extent by liberal democratic principles.

Legislation and workers' voice

Workers' organizations are not the only institutions of voice that the ECHR recognizes and the protection of which it requires. The ECtHR has frequently heard claims of individual workers who have complained that their Convention rights have been breached, because, for instance, national law did not afford them adequate protection when their labour rights were violated. In these examples too, the Court has recognized that individual workers must have a voice at work, and that for their voice to be heard outside the union context, state authorities have an obligation to enact legislation. The ECtHR, in other words, has recognized in its case law that the enactment of legislation that complies with the Convention is another way in which workers' voice can be heard.

One example where the Court ruled that legislation is required is to be found in the case *Siliadin v France*.[79] Siliadin was a migrant domestic worker who lived and worked in appalling conditions. She took a claim to the ECtHR, arguing that her situation amounted to slavery, servitude, forced, and compulsory labour. In the landmark judgment of the Court, it was accepted that the domestic worker's situation was incompatible with the Convention. The ECtHR ruled that the fact that French law did not criminalize the employers' conduct violated Article 4 that prohibits slavery, servitude, forced, and compulsory labour. In the present case, it was criminal legislation that was required in order to make French law compatible with the ECHR. Yet it is very likely that in other cases, the Court may rule that protective labour legislation is needed in order to comply with the Convention. That legislation that is compatible with the Convention is an important avenue of voice is also evident in cases where the Court has examined claims of unfair dismissal. In this case law, the Court has found that state authorities violate the ECHR, if national law does not adequately protect workers from dismissal in breach of Convention rights.[80] Legislation that is compatible with ECHR

[79] *Siliadin v France*, App No 73316/01, Judgment of 26 July 2005.

[80] See, for instance, *Redfearn v UK*, App No 47335/06, Judgment of 6 November 2012. See analysis in Collins and Mantouvalou (n 37).

rights, in other words, is an additional avenue for workers' voice and is essential for the sufficient protection of the liberal model of human rights enshrined in the Convention. This avenue also points to the importance of workers' political voice in the wider democratic process, in shaping the legislation that governs their life at work.

Right to individual petition and workers' voice

In what has been discussed this far, it has emerged that the key model of democracy that underlies the Convention is a liberal egalitarian model. This is evident in that inequality of power between employers and workers can be described as a justification for the protection of collective labour rights in the case law. At the same time majority decisions are acceptable only if they do not infringe individual rights. While unions are protected as important institutions of voice, individual workers are also recognized as being entitled to a voice at work, both against the employer and against the power of unions themselves. In this way, unions are also required to be democratic institutions where individual rights are upheld. The model of democracy that underlies Convention case law, though, is not participatory—at least not in the way that theorists like Dahl have developed it. In addition, there is no explicit discussion of unions as fora of deliberation in the case law. Could it be said that, despite the lack of explicit recognition of these models of democracy, the jurisprudence still promotes the values that these models advance?

Labour law scholars are often sceptical of the role of courts, such as the ECtHR, in relation to workers' voice.[81] In his insightful article 'Labor's Many Constitutions (and Capital's too)', Eric Tucker discusses constitutional rights of workers (labour's constitution) and contrasts them to the constitutionalization of the neoliberal economic order (capital's constitution). He concludes by asking: 'Can labor's constitution be hardened without resort to traditional mechanisms of judicial review, but in a manner that builds democratic capacities?'[82] This contrast between judicial review and democracy is important for present purposes. Underlying Tucker's statement is the concern that there is a tension between constitutional and international human rights, on the one hand, and democracy, on the other, primarily because these rights are protected by the judiciary, and not by democratic institutions (like legislatures or workers' organizations). Yet, as the earlier sections showed, the links between workers' right to voice and democracy are complex, as indeed is the relationship between social rights and democracy,[83] and civil and political rights and democracy.[84]

[81] An excellent example of this is to be found in the work of Harry Arthurs. See, for instance, Harry Arthurs, 'The Constitutionalization of Employment Relations: Multiple Models, Pernicious Problems' (2010) Social & Legal Studies 403.

[82] Eric Tucker, 'Labor's Many Constitutions (and Capital's too)' (2011–2012) CLLPJ 355 at 377.

[83] See, for instance, Cecile Fabre, *Social Rights Under the Constitution—Government and the Decent Life* (OUP, 2000) 110; Sandra Fredman, *Human Rights Transformed—Positive Rights and Positive Duties* (OUP, 2008); Jeff King, *Judging Social Rights* (CUP, 2012) 152 ff; Virginia Mantouvalou, 'In Support of Legalisation' in Conor Gearty and Virginia Mantouvalou, *Debating Social Rights* (Hart, 2011) 123 ff.

[84] See, for instance, David Beetham, *Democracy and Human Rights* (Polity Press, 2003) 89 ff; Carole Gould, *Globalizing Democracy and Human Rights* (CUP, 2004) Part II.

In constitutional theory too Jeremy Waldron famously argues that liberal rights are valuable, but they should be left in the hands of legislatures, rather than courts, because this is what democracy requires.[85] In response to the scepticism expressed in the scholarship on the role of courts in the protection of workers' voice in a democracy, it can fairly be argued that the protection of human rights under the ECHR can play a crucial role in a deliberative model of democracy.[86] This is because the case law of courts like the ECtHR can serve as another forum of deliberation. This position has been defended, for instance, by John Rawls, who viewed constitutional courts as exemplary in this respect, for the reason that state authorities are required by them to give reasons in order to explain and justify their decisions.[87] The role of courts as deliberative fora has been analysed much in literature that views them as good institutions of deliberation exactly because they are not exposed to electoral pressures,[88] and has also been examined in social rights scholarship.[89]

On the analysis that views courts as important deliberative institutions, the ECtHR (like other courts) is not the final decision-maker, and the value of the judicial decision is not limited to the resolution of the specific conflict. Deliberation is a continuous process, and judicial decisions are only part of this process. Courts are 'an engine of public debate', a function that they are well-placed to exercise, as they may hear complaints of individuals who might otherwise be excluded from politics, and force the authorities to justify their decisions.[90] The additional value of constitutional review, then, lies in the role of the judgment and its reasoning as part of the deliberative process. In addition, the ECtHR, through its decisions that regularly attract much public attention and generate debates at national and supranational level, fulfils this deliberative function with success.

The institution of constitutional or international human rights protection through courts, on this analysis, is not undemocratic, contrary to what is sometimes suggested. It is a democratic avenue of voice, not only because it ensures that majoritarian preferences do not always prevail when workers' rights are at stake, but also because the judicial decisions themselves are an additional avenue of workers' voice in the continuous process of democratic deliberation. Without this avenue, this voice might be weak (in the case of trade unions), or non-existent (in the case of individual workers), in the context of majoritarian politics.

Conclusion

This chapter explored workers' voice through the lens of democratic theory and human rights law. It showed that workers' voice has a democratic justification, if one looks at the most appealing definitions of democracy, which are also applicable in the workplace.

[85] See, for instance, Jeremy Waldron, 'The Core of the Case Against Judicial Review' (2006) 115 Yale Law Journal 1346.

[86] Gutmann and Thompson 45 (n 17).

[87] John Rawls, *Political Liberalism* (Columbia University Press, 2005) 231.

[88] See Ronald Dworkin, *A Matter of Principle* (Harvard University Press, 1985) 70.

[89] Roberto Gargarella, 'Theories of Democracy, the Judiciary and Social Rights' in Gargarella, Domingo, and Roux (eds), *Courts and Social Transformation in New Democracies* (Ashgate, 2006) 13 at 27.

[90] As referred to earlier, 28–9.

Democratic theory justifies a right to a voice at work that can be exercised through workers' participation. Collective voice of workers also has a human rights justification, which in turn embraces democratic arguments too: above all the idea of equality, which is an essential condition of a liberal democracy. A human right to a voice at work, at least in the way that it has been developed in the case law of the ECtHR and interpreted in this chapter, empowers workers to unionize and take part in decision-making that affects their working lives. A human rights justification suggests that for workers' voice to be heard, their organizations must have certain avenues secured: a right to collective bargaining and a right to strike are two examples of the essential means by which workers' organizations can be heard. That there is an overlap in the avenues of voice supported by a human rights justification and a democratic justification of workers' voice is important to emphasize: the more the normative justifications of collective voice, the stronger the demand for powerful collective institutions of voice.

At the same time, human rights law also recognizes a right of the individual worker to be protected against unions' power if majoritarian decisions at union level violate individual rights. This can happen when, for instance, there is compulsory union membership for individuals that object to it, or arbitrary exclusion from union membership for individuals that wish to be members. Human rights law views union power as potentially threatening to limit individual freedom, and accepts the links between democracy at the level of the state and at the level of the industry. A liberal, anti-majoritarian model of democracy underlies this line of cases that recognize the importance of collective voice, but also protects individual voice against collective power through a balancing exercise. In addition, the liberal account of democracy that is reflected in the Convention sometimes requires the enactment of legislation as an essential avenue of workers' voice. Workers have a right to be heard in the ECHR both through trade unions and through the law. Finally, even though the ECtHR does not explicitly endorse a particular model of democracy, it can fairly be said that its case law serves as an important forum of deliberation, and is itself another institution of workers' voice.

Democracy is a contested concept both at the level of the state, and at the level of the industry. This chapter argued that the most appealing models of democracy are liberal egalitarian models, which value equality in decision-making but respect decisions of majorities only insofar as they do not violate individual rights. Democratic institutions—state legislatures or civic society organizations, such as trade unions—are essential institutions of workers' voice. Yet the example of European human rights law shows that the power of these institutions will be limited when individual rights of workers are infringed. The protection of both collective and individual voice is compatible with the best theories of democracy, and required under liberal principles of human rights law.

11

Individualization and the Protection of Worker Voice in Australia

Breen Creighton

Introduction

Article 1(1) of the Right to Organise and Collective Bargaining Convention 1949 (No 98) requires that 'workers shall enjoy adequate protection against acts of anti-union discrimination in respect of their employment'.[1] This points to what might be termed the traditional approach to protection of worker voice. It proceeds from the assumption that if workers are to have an effective voice in the workplace they must have the capacity to join, and participate in the activities of, trade unions without being victimized for doing so.

Australia, New Zealand, and the United Kingdom have ratified Convention No 98; Canada and the United States have not. Nonetheless, all five jurisdictions have made at least some attempt to provide statutory protection against anti-union discrimination.[2] The current iteration of the Australian protections appears as Division 4 of Part 3-1—General protections ('Part 3-1' or 'General Protections') of the Fair Work Act 2009 ('FW Act').

Division 4 provides workers with protection against 'adverse action' 'because' they have engaged in, or are proposing to engage in, 'industrial activity'—in other words, it purports to provide protection for workers who choose to express voice through joining and/or participating in the activities of an 'industrial association'. This term is defined in section 12 of the FW Act to include any association of employees, independent contractors, employees and independent contractors, or employers 'that is registered or recognised as such an association (however described) under a workplace law'. It would also encompass 'an association of employees, or independent contractors, or both (whether formed formally or informally), a purpose of which is the protection or promotion of their interests in matters concerning their employment, or their interests as independent contractors (as the case may be)'. This latter concept is sufficiently broad to encompass ad hoc groupings of employees or contractors, so long as they have the purpose of protecting or promoting the interests of their members.[3]

[1] Article 1(2) provides that such protections 'shall apply more particularly' in respect of acts calculated: (a) to make the employment of a worker subject to their not being a union member, or (b) to cause the dismissal of, or otherwise prejudice, a worker because of union membership or because of 'participation in union activities outside working hours or, with the consent of the employer, within working hours'.

[2] See Canada Labour Code, ('CLC') ss. 94–99; Employment Relations Act 2000 (NZ) ('ER Act') Part 9; National Labor Relations Act 1935 (US) ('NLRA') ss. 7 and 8(a); Trade Union and Labour Relations (Consolidation) Act 1992 (UK) ('TULRCA'), ss. 137–167.

[3] Cf the definitions of 'trade union' and 'independent trade union' in ss. 1(a) and 5 of TULRCA. See further Simon Deakin and Gillian Morris, *Labour Law*, 6th edn (Hart Publishing, 2012) 798–805.

Meanwhile, Division 3 of Part 3-1 adopts a more expansive approach to the individual expression of worker voice than Division 4 by providing protection against adverse action because the worker is possessed of, has exercised, or is proposing to exercise, a 'workplace right'.[4]

The General Protection provisions in Part 3-1 of the FW Act constitute the principal focus of this chapter.[5] They will be seen to provide a level of protection for individual voice that is clearly more comprehensive than parallel provision in the comparator jurisdictions. It is important to appreciate, however, that Part 3-1 does not expressly confer any protections (or positive rights) upon industrial associations as vehicles for the exercise of collective voice. Instead, it provides protection against adverse action for individuals who engage in industrial activity, and permits associations to initiate enforcement proceedings on behalf of their members or potential members. On the logic of Article 1(1) of Convention No 98, this in turn helps protect the organizational integrity of the collectivity. On the other hand, the fact that Division 4 of Part 3-1 provides the same protection for the right *not* to belong or participate as for the right *to* belong or participate means that in its present form this provision must inevitably compromise the integrity of the collectivity.

The Division 3 protections have even less bearing upon the exercise of collective voice than those in Division 4 in the sense that they are principally concerned with protecting the 'workplace rights' of 'persons'.[6] It is true that 'person' for these purposes can include registered industrial associations and corporations, but the main focus of Division 3 is very clearly upon protecting individuals against 'adverse action' because of their workplace rights.[7] Even though some of these rights have a collective flavour, the protections provided by Division 3 are entirely consistent with, and indeed provide further evidence of, the individualization of workplace relations, and the attendant marginalization of collective voice, which have characterized legislative developments in Australia over the last 20 years.

The Australian Context

The Conciliation and Arbitration Act 1904 ('1904 Act') was born out of a series of major defeats inflicted upon Australian (and New Zealand) unions in the early 1890s.[8] The end-result was that levels of union membership were decimated, and that employers had successfully asserted the principle of 'freedom of contract': that is, their capacity to 'negotiate' terms and conditions of employment directly with individual employees

[4] Part 3-1 provides a number of additional protections for worker voice. For an outline see text accompanying nn 58–61. For more detailed discussion, see Breen Creighton and Andrew Stewart, *Labour Law*, 5th edn (Federation Press, 2010) 557–74; also Alan Bogg and Cynthia Estlund, 'Freedom of Association and the Right to Contest', this volume.

[5] Some of the issues addressed in this chapter are also discussed in Victoria Lambropoulos and Michael Wynn, 'Unfair Labour Practices, Trade Union Victimisation and Voice: A Comparison of Australia and the United Kingdom' (2013) 34 Adelaide University Law Review 43.

[6] For further discussion of the concept of workplace rights, see text accompanying nn 55–71.

[7] For further discussion of the concept of adverse action, see text accompanying nn 28–44.

[8] See further the essays collected in Stuart Macintyre and Richard Mitchell (eds), *Foundations of Arbitration: The Origins and Effects of State Compulsory Arbitration 1890–1914* (OUP, 1989); James Holt, *Compulsory Arbitration in New Zealand: The First Forty Years* (Auckland University Press, 1986).

without the involvement of 'third parties' such as trade unions—with predictably disadvantageous consequences for the employees concerned.[9]

The 1904 Act sought to address this imbalance by providing for the registration of organizations of employers and workers; enabling such organizations (and individual employers) to make legally enforceable industrial agreements; and establishing a Court of Conciliation and Arbitration with the capacity to conciliate industrial disputes extending beyond the limits of one state and, where parties were unwilling or unable to reach agreement, to impose an outcome in the form of an arbitrated 'award'.

Section 9 of the original Act of 1904 clearly recognized the need to provide protection against victimization for workers who chose to join, or participate in the activities of, a trade union. Even before it was replaced by an expanded provision in 1914, it was remarkably advanced for its time. It provided protection both against dismissal because of union membership or office-holding, and against injury in employment or prejudicial treatment on those grounds. It also provided for the imposition of what were at the time quite significant monetary penalties, and from the outset it included a partial reversal of the onus of proof in enforcement proceedings. Both in terms of timing and content, section 9 meant that levels of legal protection for worker voice in Australia were very much in advance of the comparator jurisdictions.[10]

The 1904 Act was amended on many occasions over the years, but in expanded form, the section 9 protections remained part of the statutory structure up until the Act's repeal in 1988,[11] and with occasional exceptions they were interpreted in a way that promoted their protective purpose.[12] They were retained by the Industrial Relations Act 1988—but with a number of significant extensions. The most important of these was the addition of protection against refusal of employment to the established protections against termination of employment and prejudicial treatment within employment.[13] In a further significant development, in 1993 the 1988 Act was amended by the insertion of a protection against dismissal on grounds of *non-membership* of a trade union.[14] These changes paved the way for a much more radical restructuring of the entire system of industrial regulation in 1996 at the initiative of a newly-elected Liberal/National Coalition government.

[9] See Paul Davies and Mark Freedland (eds), *Kahn-Freund's Labour and the Law*, 3rd edn (Stevens, 1983) 18. See also Lambropoulos and Wynn (n 5).

[10] Section 6 of the Industrial Conciliation and Arbitration Amendment Act 1903 (NZ) introduced protection against dismissal 'by reason merely' of the fact that a worker was a member of an industrial union, or where it was 'conclusively proved' that the worker was dismissed 'merely because he is entitled to the benefit of an award, order, or agreement'. Protection against victimization was introduced in the United States in 1935, and in the various Canadian jurisdictions from the late 1930s onwards. However, it was not until the passage of the Industrial Relations Act in 1971 that statutory protection against anti-union discrimination was introduced in the United Kingdom for the first time.

[11] By that time the protections were set out in s. 5 of the 1904 Act, and the proscribed grounds had been extended to include: refusing or failing to join in industrial action; 'being a member of an organisation which is seeking industrial conditions, is dissatisfied with his conditions'; and being an 'officer, delegate or member of an organisation' who had done, or proposed to do 'an act or thing which is lawful for the purpose of furthering or protecting the industrial interests of the organisation or its members'.

[12] See e.g. *Eaton v McKenzie* (1916) 12 Tas LR 94; *General Motors-Holdens Pty Ltd v Bowling* (1975) 51 ALJR 235 ('*Bowling*')—cf *Pearce v WD Peacock & Co Ltd* (1917) 23 CLR 199; *Heidt v Chrysler Australia Ltd* (1976) 13 ALR 365.

[13] Industrial Relations Act 1988, s. 334(2).

[14] Industrial Relations Act 1988, s. 170DF(1)(c).

The 1988 Act was extensively amended and renamed as the Workplace Relations Act 1996 (WR Act). Whilst it retained the core organizational protections dating back to 1904, it also introduced a number of further provisions which were clearly driven by an ideological commitment to marginalizing organized labour and individualizing the labour market.[15] Prominent amongst these changes were the introduction of provision for making Australian workplace agreements (AWAs) and expanded protections for 'freedom of association', or more accurately, freedom *not* to associate.

Ostensibly, AWAs were agreements negotiated between employers and individual workers at the level of the workplace. In practice, they almost invariably consisted of pro forma documents presented to employees (or would-be employees) on a 'take-it-or-leave-it' basis.[16] Making an AWA entirely excluded the operation of any other industrial instrument such as an award or (collective) certified agreement that would otherwise have applied to the employee concerned. An AWA could derogate from the terms of any otherwise applicable award, so long as it did not leave the employee any worse off than they would have been had they not made the AWA.[17] The capacity to enter into such 'agreements', and to make doing so a pre-condition of employment, was clearly fundamentally antithetical to the effective exercise of worker voice.

In broad terms, the new freedom of association provisions required that an employer must not, for a 'prohibited reason': dismiss an employee; injure an employee in their employment; alter the position of an employee to their prejudice; refuse to employ a person; or discriminate against another person 'in the terms or conditions on which the employer offers to employ the other person'. There were originally no fewer than fourteen prohibited reasons, and this number was significantly extended over the next ten years. In many respects, the prohibited reasons replicated the protections set out in section 334 of the 1988 Act, but they also extended those protections by proscribing all conduct which was engaged in because a person 'is not, or does not propose to become, a member of an industrial association'.[18] This was markedly wider than the protection against termination on these grounds which had been introduced in 1993.

The practical application of these provisions gave rise to a number of interesting, and from the Coalition government's perspective, somewhat unexpected outcomes. These included a number of cases where the WR Act was found to afford protection to the right of individuals to have their interests represented by a trade union, and to have access to the benefits of collectively determined instruments.[19] In other cases, attempts

[15] See further Richard Naughton, 'Sailing into Uncharted Seas: the Role of Unions Under the Workplace Relations Act 1996 (Cth)' (1997) 10 Australian Journal of Labour Law (AJLL) 112; Amanda Coulthard, 'The Individualisation of Australian Labour Law' (1997) 13 International Journal of Comparative Labour Law and Industrial Relations 95.

[16] For discussion see Andrew Stewart, 'The Legal Framework for Individual Employment Agreements in Australia' in R. Mitchell and S. Deery (eds), *Employment Relations: Individualisation and Union Exclusion* (Federation Press, 1999); Ronald C. McCallum, 'Australian Workplace Agreements—An analysis' (1997) 10 AJLL 50.

[17] This was the so-called 'no disadvantage test'. It was abolished in 2005; partially resuscitated as the 'fairness test' in 2007; reinstated in modified form in 2008; and replaced by the 'better off overall test' in 2009. See further Creighton and Stewart at 327–31 (n 4).

[18] WR Act, s. 298L(1). Following further amendments in 2005, this protection was located in ss. 792–793 of the WR Act.

[19] The most significant of these was the decision of the High Court of Australia in *Patrick Stevedores Operations No 2 v Maritime Union of Australia* (1998) 195 CLR 1 ('*Patricks*'), a case which arose from a

to use the provisions in this way were unsuccessful.[20] Interestingly, however, there is little evidence of their use by non-members to challenge discriminatory treatment by reason of their non-membership.[21]

The WR Act was extensively amended by the Workplace Relations Amendment (Work Choices) Act 2005 ('Work Choices'). Amongst other things, these amendments made it much easier to erode employment protections through AWAs,[22] and further extended the reach of the freedom of association provisions to the point where there was a quite bewildering array of 'protections' scattered more or less at random throughout the WR Act. The core provisions were, however, concentrated in Part 16 of the Act.

The Work Choices amendments proved extremely divisive both socially and politically, and played a significant role in the electoral defeat of the Coalition government in 2007. The newly-elected Labor government was committed to the repeal of Work Choices, and to the re-collectivization of labour law. The FW Act purports to honour that commitment. By and large it does so—albeit in a somewhat 'attenuated' form.[23]

The General Protections

Context

The FW Act reasserts the primacy of enterprise-based collective bargaining as the means of fixing terms and conditions of employment. There is no provision for making individual statutory agreements (such as AWAs) which, according to section 3(f), 'can never be part of a fair workplace relations system'. There is legislative support for collective bargaining in the form of good faith bargaining requirements, and access to a range of tribunal orders which are intended to facilitate such bargaining. The bargaining regime is also underpinned by a 'safety net' comprising (collectively determined) 'modern awards' and legislated minimum standards in the form of the National Employment Standards (NES).[24]

The 'attenuated' character of bargaining under the FW Act is reflected in the fact that although enterprise agreements are inherently collective in character, individual

violent and bitter dispute in the waterfront industry in 1998—see further Creighton and Stewart 180–1 (n 4), and the sources cited therein. See also *Finance Sector Union of Australia v Commonwealth Bank of Australia* (2000) 106 IR 1239; *Greater Dandenong City Council v Australian Municipal, Administrative, Clerical and Services Union* (2001) 112 FCR 232 ('*Dandenong*'); *Finance Sector Union of Australia v Commonwealth Bank of Australia* (2007) 157 FCR 329.

[20] See e.g. *Maritime Union of Australia v CSL Australia Pty Ltd (No 1)* (2002) 113 IR 326; *Australian Workers' Union v BHP Iron Ore Pty Ltd* (2001) 106 FCR 482. See also David Quinn, 'To Be or Not to Be a Member—Is That the Only Question? Freedom of Association under the Workplace Relations Act' (2004) 17 AJLL 1.

[21] But see *Employment Advocate v Barclay Mowlem Construction Ltd* (2005) 139 IR 19; *Fair Work Ombudsman v Offshore Marine Services Pty Ltd* (2012) 219 IR 435 ('*Offshore Marine*'). For more general discussion of the non-membership issue in the Australian context, see Phillipa Weeks, *Trade Union Security Law* (Federation Press, 1995) 219–55.

[22] See Joel Fetter, 'Work Choices and Australian Workplace Agreements' (2006) 19 AJLL 210.

[23] See further Breen Creighton, 'A Retreat from Individualism? The Fair Work Act 2009 and the Re-collectivisation of Australian Labour Law' (2011) 40 Industrial Law Journal 116, at 142.

[24] For an outline of these provisions, see Andrew Stewart, 'A Question of Balance: Labor's New Vision for Workplace Regulation' (2009) 22 AJLL 3. For more detailed description see Creighton and Stewart at chs 10–12 and 21 (n 4).

employees can nominate any person or body they wish (including themselves) as their 'bargaining representative' in negotiations for such an agreement. If an individual does not appoint a bargaining representative, then any union of which they are a member, and that is eligible to represent their industrial interests, is treated as their 'default' bargaining representative. The individual can, however, cancel the union's authority at any time, irrespective of whether they appoint another representative. There is no formal 'recognition' mechanism for purposes of bargaining, and no union bargaining monopoly, as in North America and New Zealand.[25] Furthermore, unions cannot formally be party to an agreement—although they can (and frequently do) elect to be 'covered' by any agreement in relation to which they have acted as a bargaining representative.[26] Although there are no hard data on the point, it appears that in practice few employees appoint themselves, or anyone other than a union, as bargaining representative.[27] However, the fact that it is possible to do so is clearly indicative of the individualized character of the support for collective voice that is provided by the FW Act.

This is also reflected in the General Protections provisions. As noted earlier, Division 4 largely consists of a re-enactment of the freedom of association provisions of the WR Act—shorn of some of their more egregiously anti-union features, but still including broad-based protection of the right not to belong. Division 3, meanwhile, consolidates some of the protections that were scattered around the post-Work Choices WR Act, and introduces some significant new protections under the umbrella of 'workplace rights'. Again, these new protections are essentially individualistic in character.

Adverse action

The application of the protections provided by Divisions 3 and 4 turns on the requirement that workers not be subjected to 'adverse action' because of their 'workplace rights' or 'industrial activity'. The concept of adverse action is explained by means of a table in section 342(1) which sets out the circumstances in which a person may be found to have taken adverse action against another. As between employer and employee, they include: dismissing an employee;[28] injuring an employee in her or his employment; and

[25] For further discussion of these issues, see the essays collected in Breen Creighton and Anthony Forsyth (eds), *Rediscovering Collective Bargaining: Australia's Fair Work Act in International Perspective* (Routledge, 2012).

[26] For discussion of the distinction between 'coverage' and 'application' of industrial instruments, see Creighton and Stewart at 331–2 (n 4).

[27] However, the practice of appointing non-union bargaining representatives, including self-appointment, is certainly not unknown—see e.g. *Morcom* [2009] FWA 694; *Philmac Pty Ltd s 185 application* [2011] FWA 1639; *National Union of Workers v Pattie's Foods Ltd* [2011] FWA 4103.

[28] For example, in *Australian Licenced Aircraft Engineers Association v International Aviation Service Assistance Pty Ltd* (2011) 205 IR 396 ('*IASA*') the respondent was found to have taken adverse action against an employee by terminating his employment. Ostensibly this was because he no longer had a licence from a client airline permitting him to carry out maintenance work on their aircraft. The licence had not been renewed on the basis of an adverse report provided to the airline by IASA about the employee's work performance. This report was motivated by the employer's displeasure at the fact that the employee had raised issues about overtime entitlements under his (statutory) employment agreement; had sought assistance from the applicant union in relation to those entitlements; and, having been dismissed because of these actions, had been reinstated in consequence of a court application under the 'freedom of association' provisions of the WR Act. In *National Tertiary Education Union v Royal Melbourne Institute of Technology* [2013] FCA 451 ('*RMIT*') a university was found to have contravened Part 3-1 when it terminated the employment

altering the position of an employee to their prejudice. This last has been described as 'a broad...category which covers not only legal injury but any adverse affection of, or deterioration in, the advantages enjoyed by the employee before the conduct in question'.[29] Adverse action may also consist of discriminating between an employee and other employees of the employer,[30] refusing to engage a prospective employee,[31] or discriminating 'in the terms or conditions to which the prospective employer offers to employ the prospective employee'. According to section 242(2), adverse action also includes organizing or threatening to engage in any of these activities.

As with their immediate predecessor, the Part 3-1 protections extend to relations between principals and independent contractors, as well as between employers and employees. For example, a principal will take adverse action against an independent contractor with whom it has entered into a contract for services if it: terminates the contract; injures the contractor in relation to the terms and conditions of the contract; alters the position of the contractor to its prejudice; refuses to make use of, or to agree to make use of, services offered by the contractor;[32] or refuses to supply, or agree to supply, goods or services to the contractor.[33] Item 4 makes equivalent provision for contractors who have not yet been engaged.[34] The fact that the Part 3-1 protections uniformly apply to independent contractors is in marked contrast to the protections provided by TULRCA in the United Kingdom, which are in some instances limited to relations between employers and employees.[35]

Clearly, the concept of adverse action has the potential to capture a broad range of discriminatory conduct by employers, potential employers, principals, and potential principals. It also extends to actions taken by: employees against their employer; contractors against principals; and industrial associations (and their members or officers) against 'any person'.[36] However, simply taking adverse action is not sufficient to give

of one of its professors on what were found to be spurious redundancy grounds. The true reason for the termination was the fact that she had complained to the university and a regulator about bullying by her head of department.

[29] *Patricks* at 18 (n 19). See also *Qantas Airways Ltd v Australian Licenced Aircraft Engineers Association* (2012) FCAFC 63 ('*Qantas Case*'), which is discussed in the text accompanying n 68. Cf the approach to detrimental treatment in s. 146 of TULRCA.

[30] Section 342(1) Table, item 1.

[31] Section 342(1) Table, item 2. For example, in *Construction, Forestry, Mining and Energy Union v Pilbara Iron Company (Services) Pty Ltd (No 3)* [2012] FCA 697 ('*Pilbara Case*') the respondent was found to have taken adverse action when it refused to offer employment to a trainee after the expiry of a fixed term contract because he had engaged in industrial activity by (inter alia) raising occupational health and safety concerns with management and nominating as a health and safety representative under the relevant occupational health and safety legislation. In subsequent proceedings ([2012] FCA 894), the company was fined a total of $A35,500 and ordered to offer the employee a permanent position.

[32] See e.g. *Louka v Centrelink* (2010) 204 IR 382.

[33] Section 342(1) Table, item 3.

[34] In *Construction, Forestry, Mining and Energy Union v State of Victoria* [2013] FCA 445 the Victorian government was found to have subjected workers to adverse action when it threatened to refuse to engage their employer on a major construction project because it was party to an (entirely lawful) enterprise agreement which contained provisions that were allegedly inconsistent with a Code of Practice and associated Implementation Guidelines that applied to government procurement in the Construction industry. See also *Construction, Forestry, Mining and Energy Union v McCorkell Constructions Pty Ltd (No 2)* [2013] FCA 446 ('*McCorkell*'). Both decisions were reversed on appeal, [2013] FCAFC 160.

[35] See further Deakin and Morris at 816–55 (n 3).

[36] Section 342(1) Table, items 5, 6, and 7 respectively. For an example of an employer (successfully) seeking injunctive relief against a union which had subjected it to adverse action because of its exercise of

rise to liability under Part 3-1: it must also be taken *because* of 'industrial activity' or a 'workplace right'.[37]

The importance of this causal connection is highlighted by the decision of the High Court of Australia in *Board of Bendigo Regional Institute of Technical and Further Education v Barclay* ('*Barclay*').[38] The respondent was a workplace representative for the Australian Education Union. In that capacity he emailed union members at the Institute about concerns which had been raised with him by a number of union members in relation to employees being pressurized to provide inaccurate information in the context of an external audit of one of the Institute's programmes. Mr Barclay did not raise these issues with management before circulating the email to members. The Director of the Institute, Dr Harvey, took the view that this constituted misconduct on Mr Barclay's part, and suspended him on full pay and denied him access to IT services and the Institute's premises pending the completion of disciplinary proceedings against him. This clearly constituted adverse action. However, at first instance it was found not to constitute unlawful action because the trial judge was satisfied that Dr Harvey had not acted 'for any reason associated with… [Mr Barclay's]…union membership, office or activities'.[39]

This decision was reversed on appeal. In the course of their joint reasons Gray and Bromberg JJ stated that:

> [t]he determination of those questions [of causation] involves characterisation of the reason or reasons of the person who took the adverse action. The state of mind or subjective intention of that person will be centrally relevant, but it is not decisive. What is required is a determination of…the 'real reason' for the conduct. The real reason for a person's conduct is not necessarily the reason that the person asserts, even where the person genuinely believes he or she was motivated by that reason. The search is for what actuated the conduct of the person, not for what the person thinks he or she was actuated by (sic). In that regard, the real reason may be conscious or unconscious, and where unconscious or not appreciated or understood, adverse action will not be excused simply because its perpetrator had a benevolent intent. It is not open to the decision-maker to choose to ignore the objective connection between the decision he or she is making and the attribute or activity in question.[40]

its workplace rights, see *Laing O'Rourke Australian Pty Ltd v Construction, Forestry, Mining and Energy Union* [2013] FCA 133 ('*Laing O'Rourke*'). See also *Director of the Fair Work Building Inspectorate v Mates* [2012] FMCA 475 (safety steward on a construction site refusing to 'induct' two employees who were non-members).

[37] It should also be noted that s. 362 provides that if a person 'advises, encourages or incites, or takes any action to coerce' a second person to take adverse action for a proscribed reason, then the first person is taken to have contravened the provision in question. Section 550, meanwhile, provides that a person is taken to have contravened the FW Act where they have aided, abetted, counselled, procured, induced, conspired to effect, or 'been in any way, by act or omission, directly or indirectly, knowingly concerned in or party to' a contravention.

[38] (2012) 290 ALR 647. See also *Ramos v Good Samaritan Industries* [2013] FCA 30 (no proven connection between performance management of employee and his exercise of his workplace right to make a complaint). This is one of numerous cases where legitimate performance management processes have been found not to constitute adverse action.

[39] *Barclay v Board of Bendigo Regional Institute of Technical and Further Education* [2010] FCA 284 [54]–[55].

[40] *Barclay v Board of Bendigo Regional Institute of Technical and Further Education* [2011] FCAFC 14 at [28].

The decision of the Full Court was in turn overruled by the High Court. In the course of their joint reasons French CJ and Crennan J stated that:

> [t]here is no warrant to be derived from the text of the relevant provisions of the Fair Work Act for treating the statutory expression 'because' in s 346, or the statutory presumption in s 361, as requiring only an objective inquiry into a defendant employer's reason, including any unconscious reason, for taking adverse action. The imposition of the statutory presumption in s 361, and the correlative onus on employers, naturally and ordinarily mean that direct evidence of a decision-maker as to state of mind, intent or purpose will bear upon the question of why the adverse action was taken, although the central question remains 'why was the adverse action taken?'[41]

With respect, Gray and Bromberg JJ did not suggest that section 346 required *only* an objective inquiry. On the contrary, they clearly accepted that the 'state of mind or subjective intention' of the decision-maker 'will be centrally relevant'. In that respect their views were quite consistent with those of French CJ and Crennan J. Where the approach adopted by Gray and Bromberg JJ differed from that adopted by the High Court was their insistence that the decision-maker's subjective intention was 'not decisive', and that a decision-maker could not simply 'choose to ignore the objective connection between the decision he or she is making and the attribute or activity in question'.

The decision of the High Court means that it will often be very difficult for an applicant for relief under Part 3-1 to establish the relevant causal connection in circumstances where a respondent is able to lead credible evidence as to the subjective intentions of the decision-maker, even though an 'objective' assessment of their conduct suggests that they were motivated by a proscribed reason.

Leaving aside any difficulties emanating from the decision in *Barclay*, Part 3-1 does contain a number of provisions which can help ease some of the evidentiary difficulties which inevitably arise in the context of applying provisions such as sections 340 and 346.

First, section 360 makes clear that the proscribed ground does not have to be the 'sole' or even the 'dominant' reason for the adverse action: 'a person takes action for a particular reason if the reasons for the action include that reason'. On the other hand, it has also been determined that the proscribed ground must be a 'substantial or operative factor' in the respondent's actions.[42]

Secondly, there is a reverse onus provision in section 361 which is clearly the lineal descendent of section 9 of the 1904 Act:

> If:
> (a) in an application in relation to a contravention of this Part, it is alleged that a person took, or is taking, action for a particular reason or with a particular intent; and
> (b) taking that action for that reason or with that intent would constitute a contravention of this Part;
>
> it is presumed, in the proceedings arising from the application, that the action was, or is being, taken for the reason or with that intent, unless the person proves otherwise.

[41] [2012] HCA 32 [44]. Gummow and Hayne JJ and Heydon J delivered concurring opinions.
[42] See e.g. *Bowling* at 241–2 (n 12); *Lewis Construction Co Pty Ltd v Martin* (1986) 70 ALR 135, at 138–9.

A substantial proportion of successful general protections claims have turned upon the respondent's inability to discharge this reverse onus.[43]

Industrial activity

The core protections in relation to industrial activity are set out in sections 346 and 347 of the FW Act.

Section 346(a) stipulates that a person must not take adverse action against another because that person: 'is or is not, or was or was not, an officer or member of an industrial association'. Section 346(b) provides protection for individuals who *do* any of the things set out in section 347(a) and (b).[44] These include (inter alia): being or not being a member of an industrial association;[45] being involved in establishing an industrial association;[46] organizing or promoting 'a lawful activity for, or on behalf of, an industrial association';[47] representing or advancing the 'views, claims or interests of an industrial association';[48] and seeking to be represented by an industrial association.[49]

In contrast, section 346(c) provides protection for persons who *do not do* any of the things set out in section 347(c)–(g), including: organizing or promoting 'an unlawful activity for, or on behalf of an industrial association'; encouraging or participating in unlawful activity organized or promoted by an industrial association; complying with 'an unlawful request made by, or requirement of, an industrial association'; taking part in industrial action;[50] or making payments in respect of industrial action.[51]

Division 4 contains a number of provisions which complement sections 346 and 347. They include proscription of coercion,[52] and 'knowingly or recklessly' making a false representation about a person's obligation to engage in industrial activity, or to disclose whether they are or are not a member of an industrial association or are engaging or

[43] See e.g. *Dandenong* (n 19); *RMIT* (n 28); *Moore v Slondia Nominees Pty Ltd* [2012] FMCA 273 ('*Moore*') [86]; *Stephens v Australian Postal Corp* (2011) 207 IR 405 ('*Stephens*')—cf *Barclay* (n 38); *Construction, Forestry, Mining and Energy Union v Bengalla Mining Company Pty Ltd* [2013] FCA 267; *United Firefighters' Union of Australia v Easy* [2013] FCA 763.

[44] Cf the activities which constitute 'involvement in the activities of a union' under s. 107 of the ER Act.

[45] Section 347(a). See *Transport Workers' Union of Australia v No Fuss Liquid Waste Pty Ltd* [2011] FCA 982 ('*No-Fuss*').

[46] Section 347(b)(i).

[47] Section 347(b)(ii), (iii). See e.g. the *Pilbara Case* (n 31) (nominating as a worker health and safety representative); *Australian Municipal, Administrative, Clerical and Services Union v Shire of Mundaring* (2011) 213 IR 293 and 311 (distributing election material supporting particular candidates in a local government election).

[48] Section 347(b)(v). In *Construction, Forestry, Mining and Energy Union v BHP Coal Pty Ltd (No 4)* [2012] FCA 1454 ('*BHP Coal No 4*') the respondent was found to have contravened both s. 347(b)(iii) and (v) when it dismissed an employee who had waved an 'anti-scab' placard at non-striking workers at a coal mine. In *Construction, Forestry, Mining and Energy Union v BHP Coal Pty Ltd* [2012] FCA 1201 a differently constituted Court reached the opposite conclusion on essentially the same facts, albeit at a different mine. These decisions provide an interesting contrast with the attitude towards abusing non-strikers which was on show in *R v Druitt* (1867) 10 Cox CC 592.

[49] See e.g. *IASA* (n 28).

[50] Part 3-3 of the FW Act makes provision for taking protected industrial action. The effect of s. 347(f) is to ensure that individuals are not subjected to adverse action because they do not participate in either protected or unprotected industrial action. Section 341(2) makes clear that participating in protected action constitutes the exercise of a 'workplace right' for purposes of Division 3.

[51] See Division 9 of Part 3-3 of the FW Act.

[52] See further text accompanying n 69.

not engaging in industrial activity.[53] Section 350 meanwhile, makes it unlawful for an employer or principal to 'induce' another person to join, not join, or remain a member of an industrial association.

On its face, section 346(a) would make it unlawful to refuse employment to an employee whose name appeared on a 'blacklist' of union activists. However, it is notoriously difficult to establish the existence of such lists, let alone their content—even with the assistance of a reverse onus. In fact, formal blacklisting of union activists does not appear to be a common practice in Australia—although anecdotal evidence suggests that it is not entirely unknown, especially in the construction industry.[54]

Workplace rights

Section 340(1) makes it unlawful for a person to take adverse action against another person because that person: has a 'workplace right'; has or has not exercised such a right; or proposes to exercise or not to exercise any such right. It also makes it unlawful to take adverse action against a person 'to prevent the exercise of a workplace right by the other person'.[55] Furthermore, section 341(3) makes clear that prospective employees are taken to have the same workplace rights as they would have 'if he or she were employed in the prospective employment by the prospective employer'. This is, however, subject to an exception in section 341(5) which permits the transferee of a business to refuse to employ all or any of the employees of the transferor because they would bring with them the terms of any industrial instrument that was binding on the transferor and that would become binding upon the transferee in consequence of the transfer.[56] This appears to run directly counter to the conceptual underpinnings of the UK Transfer of Undertakings (Protection of Employment) Regulations 2006.[57]

According to section 341(1):

> A person has a workplace right if the person:
> (a) is entitled to the benefit of, or has a role or responsibility under, a workplace law, workplace instrument or order made by an industrial body;[58] or
> (b) is able to initiate, or participate in, a process or proceedings under a workplace law or workplace instrument; or
> (c) is able to make a complaint or inquiry:
> (i) to a person or body having the capacity under a workplace law to seek compliance with that law or a workplace instrument; or
> (ii) if the person is an employee—in relation to his or her employment.

[53] Respectively, ss. 348 and 349.

[54] Blacklisting has been a source of continuing difficulty in some of the comparator countries—see e.g. the discussion in Deakin and Morris at 844–9 (n 3).

[55] Section 340(2) provides that a person must not take adverse action against a second person because a third person had exercised a workplace right for the benefit of the second person. This is exactly what happened in *IASA* (n 28).

[56] See FW Act, Part 2-8. See also Creighton and Stewart at 335–7 and 613–16 (n 4).

[57] These Regulations are the latest iteration of regulations which were first (reluctantly) introduced by the Thatcher government in 1981 to give effect to the requirements of the Acquired Rights Directive 1977 (77/187/EC). See now Directive 2001/23/EU.

[58] This would include the Fair Work Commission, and its state counterparts.

The protection afforded by section 341(1)(a) would encompass employees who assert their entitlement to the benefit of enterprise agreements, awards, or the FW Act itself,[59] and also individuals who act as a bargaining representative in negotiations for an enterprise agreement,[60] or who seek to exercise their rights under occupational health and safety legislation.[61]

Section 341(1)(b), meanwhile, is clearly intended to provide protection for those who initiate or participate in a process or proceeding under the FW Act or under other 'workplace laws' such as workers' compensation or occupational health and safety legislation.[62]

Section 341(2) provides an extensive list of activities that constitute a 'process or proceedings' for these purposes.[63] As might be expected, they include participating in, or being able to participate in, court or tribunal proceedings concerning a workplace law or a workplace instrument.[64] They also include: participating in protected industrial action and in ballots to authorize such action; 'making, varying or terminating an enterprise agreement'; appointing, or terminating the appointment of, a bargaining representative; involvement in dispute settlement in accordance with a workplace law or a workplace instrument; and the exercise of a number of individual employment rights under the FW Act, or an industrial instrument.[65]

The protection provided by section 341(1)(b) is complemented by section 341(1)(c)(i). It means, for example, that making a complaint or inquiry to the Fair Work Ombudsman ('FWO'),[66] or an occupational health and safety regulator, would constitute the exercise of a workplace right. Section 341(1)(c)(ii) raises more far-reaching issues.

On its face, this subparagraph seems to protect employees who make a complaint or inquiry to literally anyone, so long as it is in relation to their employment. Clearly, this would include complaints or inquiries directed to an employer. For example, in the *Qantas Case* it extended to the airline's suspending international postings for all maintenance engineers at its Brisbane base in response to an employee's having raised queries with management about whether rostered day off entitlements accrued during a previous overseas posting.[67]

[59] See e.g. *Chileshe v E&M Business Trust T/a Yellow Brick Road Service Group* [2013] FCCA 10 (seeking to enforce wage and conditions entitlements under an award and the NES); *Moore* (n 43) (pursuing a claim for unpaid wages under the FW Act); *Fair Work Ombudsman v WKO Pty Ltd* [2012] FCA 1129 ('*WKO*') (taking unpaid parental leave in accordance with the NES); *Brown v Premier Pet t/a Bay Fish* [2012] FMCA 1089 (exercising right to refuse to work unreasonable overtime in accordance with the NES).

[60] See *Jones v Queensland Tertiary Admissions Centre (No 2)* (2010) 196 IR 241 ('*Jones No 2*').

[61] *Pilbara Case* (n 31); *Automotive, Food, Metals, Engineering, Printing and Kindred Industries Union v Visy Packaging Pty Ltd (No 2)* (2011) 213 IR 48 ('*Visy*').

[62] See e.g. *Stephens* (n 43). However, not all laws that deal with safety issues will constitute a 'workplace law'—*Australian Licenced Aircraft Engineers Association v Sunstate Airlines (Qld) Pty Ltd* [2012] FCA 1222.

[63] 'Workplace law' is defined in s. 12 to include the FW Act itself and a number of other measures. 'Workplace instrument' would include awards and enterprise agreements made under that Act and its predecessors, but not a contract of employment—*Barnett v Territory Insurance Office* (2011) 196 FCR 116.

[64] See e.g. *IASA* at 444–5 (n 28); *Fair Work Ombudsman v Wongtas Pty Ltd (No 2)* [2012] FCA 30.

[65] See e.g. *WKO* (n 59).

[66] The powers and functions of the FWO are set out in Part 2-5 of the FW Act. Relevantly, they include providing advice and assistance to employees and employers, conducting workplace inspections, and initiating court or tribunal proceedings. See further Creighton and Stewart at 140–4 and 506–7 (n 4).

[67] See also *RMIT* (n 28); *Devonshire v Magellan Powertronics Pty Ltd* [2013] FMCA 207 (complaining about underpayment of wages); *Murrihy v Betezy.com.au Pty Ltd* [2013] FCA 908 (seeking legal advice in

That said, the potential reach of section 341(1)(c)(ii) is clearly constrained by the fact that there must be a causal connection between any adverse action and the employee's 'complaint or inquiry'. It must also be constrained by the application of the subjective test endorsed by the High Court in *Barclay*. On the other hand, section 361 does mean that once an applicant has established that a respondent has subjected them to adverse action it is for the respondent to prove that they were not actuated by the applicant's workplace rights or industrial activities.

Like Division 4, Division 3 contains a number of ancillary protections. The most important of these is section 343 which makes it unlawful for *any* person to organize or take action against another with intent to coerce that person to exercise or not to exercise a workplace right, or to exercise a workplace right in a particular way. This effectively replicates section 789 of the WR Act. That provision generated a significant body of litigation, but despite that, it is still not entirely clear just what will constitute 'coercion' for this purpose. However, it does now seem relatively well settled that coercion in this context is comprised of two elements: that the impugned action was aimed at negating choice, and that it was unlawful, illegitimate, or unconscionable.[68]

The other ancillary protections include: section 344, which prohibits employers from exerting 'undue influence or pressure' upon employees in relation to decisions to exercise or not to exercise prescribed individual employment rights; and section 345 which makes it unlawful 'knowingly or recklessly' to make a 'false or misleading representation' about a person's workplace rights or 'the exercise, or the effect of the exercise, of a workplace right by another person'.[69]

Division 5 provides a further range of individual protections. They include proscription of adverse action because of a person's 'race, colour, sex, sexual preference, age, physical or mental disability, marital status, family or carer's responsibilities, pregnancy, religion, political opinion, national extraction or social origin'.[70] They also include protection against dismissal because of temporary absence from work because of illness or injury. Division 6, meanwhile, deals with 'sham contracting arrangements' in the sense of arrangements whereby an employer enters into what purports to be a contract for services, but which is in fact a contract of service.[71]

relation to unpaid contractual entitlements)—cf *Harrison v In Control Pty Ltd* [2013] FMCA 149 (complaints about the way the employer's business was run were not complaints 'in relation to' the applicant's employment).

[68] In the *Qantas Case* (n 29), the suspension of overseas postings constituted coercion in the relevant sense. In *McCorkell* (n 34), refusing to engage a subcontractor was found at first instance to constitute coercion of the subcontractor and its employees to exercise their workplace rights to vary an existing enterprise agreement. For a helpful review of the authorities under the WR Act, see *Liquor Hospitality and Miscellaneous Union v Arnotts Biscuits Ltd* (2010) 198 IR 143 [61]–[66].

[69] See e.g. *WKO* (n 59).

[70] Section 351. On the interaction between this provision and federal and state anti-discrimination legislation, see Creighton and Stewart at 543–4 (n 4).

[71] Creighton and Stewart at 569–71 and 539–41 (n 4). For an example of the practical application of these provisions, see *FWO v Metro Northern Enterprises Pty Ltd* [2013] FCCA 216.

Compliance

Sections 365 and 371 of the FW Act have the effect that where an alleged breach of any of the General Protections involves dismissal, the matter must first be referred to the Fair Work Commission (FWC), which is then required to attempt to resolve the dispute.[72] Any such application must be accompanied by the prescribed filing fee, and must be made within 21 days of the dismissal taking effect—subject to the FWC's discretion to extend this period in accordance with section 366(2).[73]

If the FWC is unable to resolve the dispute, section 369 requires that it issue a certificate to that effect. Within 14 days of such issue, the complainant may apply to the Federal Court of Australia or the Federal Circuit Court of Australia (collectively, 'Court') for the imposition of penalties and other relief. Where the alleged contravention does not involve dismissal, the matter *may* be referred to the FWC for conciliation, or the applicant may go directly to court.

Section 546 enables a person affected by a contravention, an industrial association that is entitled to represent the industrial interests of any such person, or an inspector[74] to apply to the court for the imposition of a pecuniary penalty of up to $A10,200 for individuals, and $A51,000 for corporations.[75] The court may in its discretion order that some or all of any penalty is to be paid to the individual, an applicant industrial association, or the Commonwealth.[76]

In addition to, or instead of, imposing a pecuniary penalty, section 545(1) enables the court to make 'any order the court considers appropriate if the court is satisfied that a person has contravened, or proposes to contravene, a civil remedy provision'. Such orders can include an injunction (interim or permanent) 'to prevent, stop or remedy the effects of a contravention';[77] an award of compensation (with no upper limit);[78] an order for reinstatement;[79] or any other order the court considers appropriate.[80]

[72] The FWC is the latest incarnation of the Court of Conciliation and Arbitration which was originally established in 1904. For discussion of its composition, role and procedures, see Creighton and Stewart at 122–40 (n 4).

[73] The limitation period for non-dismissal cases appears to be six years from the date of the contravention—FW Act, s. 544.

[74] See further Creighton and Stewart at 142–4 (n 4).

[75] For the factors to be taken into account in fixing a penalty, see *Kelly v Fitzpatrick* (2007) 166 IR 14 [14]; *Offshore Marine* [11]–[12] (n 21).

[76] Payment to parties other than the Commonwealth is quite common—see e.g. *IASA* (n 28) ($A10,000 to applicant union); *RMIT* (n 28) ($A37,000 to applicant union); *Burke v Serco Pty Ltd* [2013] FMCA 196 ($A16,500 to self-represented applicant).

[77] See e.g. *Jones v Queensland Tertiary Admissions Centre Ltd* (2009) 190 IR 218; *Visy* (n 61); *Laing O'Rourke* (n 36). Note, however, that the reverse onus provision in s. 361(1) does not apply to applications for interim injunctions—s. 361(2).

[78] In *IASA* (n 28), the employer was ordered to pay compensation totalling $A 94,572.02 to the employee, in addition to the penalty payable to the union (see n 76). The court did not order reinstatement of the employee because he had returned to his native Indonesia in order to try to find work.

[79] See e.g. *RMIT* (n 28); *Stephens* (n 43); *BHP Coal No 4* (n 48). On what 'reinstatement' requires, see *Blackadder v Ramsey Butchering Services Pty Ltd* (2005) 221 CLR 539.

[80] See e.g. *Pilbara Case* (n 31), where the respondent was ordered to make an offer of employment to the individual against whom it had taken adverse action. Cf *No Fuss* (n 45) at [43]–[47] where the court determined that it did not have power under s. 545 to order that a person be disqualified from being a director of a company that had been involved in a contravention of the FW Act, or that the company accept an undertaking that the director not be involved in the management of the staff of the company.

The scope of the relief that is available under the FW Act goes beyond what is available in any of the comparator jurisdictions. For example, under section 140 of the TULRCA an individual who has been denied employment because of union membership (but not activities) can obtain a declaration, compensation (subject to the same upper limit as for unfair dismissal), or a recommendation that the respondent take action to obviate or reduce the adverse effect of the unlawful conduct. Failure to comply with a recommendation may (but will not necessarily) result in an increased award of compensation. There is no provision for the imposition of a penalty, and no access to injunctions or orders that the employer must make an offer of employment. Access to relief in the other comparator jurisdictions is also much more limited than under the FW Act.[81]

Section 570(1) states that costs are not normally payable in proceedings relating to a contravention of Part 3-1, although the situation may be otherwise if the court is satisfied that:

- a party instituted proceedings 'vexatiously or without reasonable cause';[82]
- a party's unreasonable act or omission caused the other party to incur costs;[83] or
- a party unreasonably refused to participate in a matter before the FWC and the matter arose from the same facts as the proceedings.[84]

These provisions appear to be something of a 'mixed blessing' from a would-be applicant's perspective. On one hand they mean that an aggrieved party can initiate proceedings in the reasonable expectation that they will not be exposed to orders for costs so long as they have not acted vexatiously or unreasonably. On the other hand, the fact that costs are not normally available, even if an application is successful, may inhibit some would-be claimants—especially if they do not have the support of a union, and the FWO is not prepared to initiate proceedings on their behalf. The dampening effect of the non-availability of costs may, however, be partially mitigated by the capacity of the court to order that some or all of a penalty be paid to the employee or the applicant.

Using Part 3-1

After a relatively sluggish start, the number of applications to the FWC in relation to alleged contraventions of Part 3-1 has steadily increased:[85]

[81] See ER Act, Part 9. On the enforcement of unfair labour practice provisions in the United States, see Robert A. Gorman and Matthew W. Finkin, *Basic Text on Labor Law Unionization and Collective Bargaining*, 2nd edn (Thomson West, 2004) 162–5. On Canada see CLC, ss. 97–104, and Labour Law Casebook Group, *Labour and Employment Law: Cases, Materials and Commentary*, 8th edn (Irwin Law, 2011) 258–74.

[82] Section 570(2)(a). See e.g. *Khiani v Australian Bureau of Statistics* [2011] FCAFC 109 [50]–[52]; *Clothier v Ngaanyatjarra Media* [2012] FWAFB 6323.

[83] Section 570(2)(b). See *Cugura v Frankston City Council (No 2)* [2012] FMCA 530.

[84] For costs in the FWC, see s. 611, and also ss. 376, 401, and 780.

[85] These figures are drawn from the Annual Reports of the President of the FWC. They are likely slightly to understate the number of court and tribunal applications arising from Part 3-1 due to the fact that applicants in non-dismissal cases can go directly to Court. In practice most applicants do go to the FWC before initiating Court proceedings and would, therefore, be captured in these data.

Table 11.1 Applications to FWA for Part 3-1 contraventions: July 2009–June 2013

Period	Dismissal applications	Non-Dismissal applications	Total Applications	Certificates under s. 369
July 2009–June 2010	1,188	254	1,442	NA
July 2010–June 2011	1,871	504	2,375	NA
July 2011–June 2012	2,302	598	2,900	931
July 2012–June 2013	2,427	556	2,980	832

Although the figures in Table 11.1 suggest that Part 3-1 is quite extensively relied upon in practice, there are in fact many fewer such applications than under the unfair dismissal provisions in Part 3-2 of the FW Act—for example, in 2012/13 there were 14,800 unfair dismissal applications, as compared with just under 3,000 under Part 3-1. Business groups have been sharply critical of the practice (fostered by certain law firms) of making an application under Part 3-1 and using the threat of further proceedings to try to encourage the respondent (usually the employer) to settle the claim by paying 'go-away money'. Whilst the practice undoubtedly exists, it is not possible to provide any credible estimate of the number of applications that would fall into this category.

Protecting Worker Voice under Part 3-1

The protections set out in Part 3-1 are clearly more comprehensive, and more robust, than their counterparts in the comparator jurisdictions. The protections relating to 'industrial activity' in Division 4 are broader in scope than in any of the other jurisdictions, whilst those accorded to the exercise of 'workplace rights' go beyond what is formally available in any of those jurisdictions. In addition, the penalties that can be imposed under section 546, and the range of orders that may be made under section 545, go some considerable way beyond what is available elsewhere. The potential efficacy of these protections is enhanced by the fact that in addition to victims of adverse action, both the FWO and a relevant industrial association have the capacity to initiate enforcement proceedings.

Despite these positives, various aspects of the General Protections provisions give some cause for concern as to their efficacy as a means of protecting the exercise of worker voice.

First, it is not clear that Part 3-1 provides an adequate response to the problems of proof that inevitably arise in this context. The 'multiple reasons' and reverse onus provisions can certainly be of considerable assistance in some instances. As against that, the adoption of the subjective test in *Barclay* runs counter to the approach to this issue that is adopted in anti-discrimination legislation in most jurisdictions,[86] and has the potential significantly to inhibit the effectiveness of the Part 3-1 protections.[87]

[86] See e.g. *Virgin Blue Airlines Pty Ltd v Stewart* [2007] QSC 075. See also *Purvis v Department of Education and Training (NSW)* (2003) 217 CLR 92, at [142]–[166] (per McHugh and Kirby JJ) and [234]–[236] (per Gummow, Hayne, and Heydon JJ).

[87] See further Kathleen Love, Beth Gaze, and Anna Chapman, '"But Why?" "Just Because": The Causal Link between Adverse Action and Prescribed Grounds under the Fair Work Act' Paper presented at AIRAANZ Conference, Freemantle, 6–8 February 2013.

Secondly, it is important not to lose sight of the fact that the General Protections are principally concerned with protecting individual voice. It can readily be accepted that such protections are necessary—for example where there is a risk of collective voice being subverted by victimization of individuals, or where the means of collective voice are not available. This last is increasingly likely given the decline in levels of union membership and coverage in all five jurisdictions.

It is, nevertheless, important also to ensure that the protection of individual voice does not have the effect of impeding the exercise and/or legitimacy of collective voice. For example, it is possible that the FW Act has this effect by according the same level of protection to the right not to join or participate as to the right to join or participate. The fact that there have been relatively few cases where individuals have litigated in order to protect the right not to join or participate under both the WR Act and the FW Act may seem to suggest that this problem is more apparent than real. On the other hand, the relative lack of litigation may indicate that the negative protections have effectively curtailed the use of union solidarity devices such as the closed shop or union preference arrangements, thereby compromising the exercise of collective voice.[88] Furthermore, even if it were the case that the negative protections had little practical impact, there is a real possibility that the mere fact of their existence may serve to compromise the legitimacy of the exercise of collective voice.

It is not entirely clear, to this observer at least, that the protections set out in Part 3-1 strike the most appropriate balance between the need to protect the legitimate interests of individuals and the protection and promotion of collectivities as a means of giving effect to worker voice. That said, it must also be recognized that given the current climate of opinion in Australia, and in the comparator jurisdictions, it would be extremely difficult in political terms to remove protection for the right not to join, or to refuse to participate in the activities of, a collectivity. It is also important, however, to bear in mind that Article 1 of ILO Convention No 98 does not require protection of the right not to belong or participate as a corollary of the right to belong and participate: rather, this is a matter to be left to national law and practice.[89]

[88] Under the former conciliation and arbitration system, industrial awards quite frequently contained 'preference clauses'. These were award terms which accorded preferential treatment to union members in relation to issues such as hiring and retention in employment. The relevant provision was repealed at the instance of the Coalition government in 1996. See further Richard Mitchell, 'The Preference Power and the Practice of the Federal Industrial Tribunal, 1904-1970' (1987) 29 Journal of Industrial Relations 3 and 'The Rise and Fall of the Preference Power: The Practice of the Federal Commission, 1970–1987' (1988) 1 AJLL 224.

[89] See e.g. International Labour Conference, 32nd Session, 1949, *Record of Proceedings*, 468.

12

'It's Oh So Quiet?' Employee Voice and the Enforcement of Employment Standards in Australia

*Tess Hardy**

Introduction

In the past, it was often assumed that enforcement of employment standards regulation was 'unproblematic'[1] in Australia. The apparent silence on the part of employees was seen as a sign that minimum employment standards were largely respected and upheld by employers. Contrary to these common conjectures, however, there is now evidence to suggest that employer non-compliance with such standards is a significant problem.[2]

Although compliance is critical to the overall integrity of the regulatory scheme, a reduced premium has been placed on problems of enforcement which have generally been perceived as incidental to the 'key' industrial relations issues, such as recognizing and supporting trade union and collective bargaining activity.[3] However, the underlying shifts to the labour market and legislative framework across the common law world including the decline of collective bargaining and trade unionism, the growth in individual rights, the increase in atypical employment arrangements, and the pervasive spread of globalization, have led to a resurgence of interest in the regulatory role of the state and prompted a search for new forms of worker participation, representation, and agency.[4] This chapter centres on the emergence of a somewhat novel institutional vehicle for worker voice and one that has not been readily recognized in the existing literature on voice, namely the labour inspectorate.

* Law Lecturer, Graduate School of Business and Law, RMIT University; PhD Candidate, Melbourne Law School.

[1] See Laura Bennett, *Making Labour Law in Australia: Industrial Relations, Politics and Law* (The Law Book Co, 1994) 145.

[2] Historically, employer non-compliance in Australia has been found to be 'significant and sustained'. See Miles Goodwin and Glenda Maconachie, 'Unpaid entitlement recovery in the federal industrial relations system: Strategy and outcomes 1952–95' (2007) 49(4) Journal of Industrial Relations (JIR) 523, 523. This trend appears to have continued. For example, the average rate of employer non-compliance in national audits finalized by the FWO in 2011/2012 was around 25 per cent. Further, in some previous targeted campaigns—such as the audit undertaken by the FWO in the security industry in 2009—the contravention rate was as high as 47 per cent.

[3] Miles Goodwin, 'The Great Wage Robbery: Enforcement of Minimum Labour Standards in Australia' (PhD Thesis, University of New South Wales, 2003) 13.

[4] See Linda Dickens (ed.), *Making Employment Rights Effective: Issues of Compliance and Enforcement* (Hart Publishing, 2012); David Weil, 'Individual Rights and Collective Agents: The Role of Old and New Workplace Institutions in the Regulation of Labor Markets' in Richard B. Freeman, Joni Hersch, and Lawrence Mishel (eds), *Emerging Labor Market Institutions for the Twenty-First Century* (UCP, 2005); Cynthia Estlund, *Regoverning the Workplace: From Self-Regulation to Co-Regulation* (Yale University Press, 2010).

More specifically, this chapter will explore some of the ways in which the federal labour inspectorate in Australia—now known as the Office of the Fair Work Ombudsman (FWO)[5] —has sought to develop mechanisms for promoting and protecting voice outside the classical collective bargaining framework and in the context of the contemporary regulatory landscape. This chapter begins by first considering the importance of voice to employer compliance with, and enforcement of, minimum employment standards—an issue which has been largely neglected in the academic debate. It then surveys the evolution of employment standards regulation in Australia and analyses how the changing source and structure of legal norms and employment rights have influenced the compliance and enforcement position of institutional actors, such as trade unions, the federal industrial tribunal, and the federal labour inspectorate. The chapter goes on to consider the ways in which the FWO provides a possible channel for voice through their outreach activities and their new dispute resolution process. Finally, the chapter offers some reflections on how labour inspectorates, like the FWO, may seek to ensure that voice is amplified, not muted, and in doing so, provide some protection to those workers who are the least likely to speak out.

Employee Voice and Enforcement

While debates over 'voice' have an extended history, they have largely focused on a limited number of channels: traditionally, independent trade unions and industrial tribunals; and more recently, employer-sponsored schemes and statutory workplace committees.[6] However, the shift away from manufacturing to service industries, the fall in trade union membership, the increase in individualized, legislated standards, the expansion in the small business sector, and the rise in precarious working arrangements mean that, in many common law countries, the majority of workers are no longer represented by unions or covered by enterprise bargaining agreements.

These underlying shifts have led to the fracturing of worker identities and interests and strengthened the call for new locations, institutions, and mechanisms for expressing voice.[7] In particular, Harry Arthurs argues that with the decline in collective bargaining in advanced industrial economies, there is a need to 'explore new ways to provide workers with some measure of industrial justice, for promoting sensible and orderly resolution of workplace conflicts, and especially for ensuring that states, markets and employers are accurately informed about and responsive to the needs and preferences of workers'.[8]

[5] In 2006, the year Work Choices took effect, the labour inspectorate operated as an executive agency known as the Office of Workplace Services. From 2007, the labour inspectorate was transformed into a statutory agency known as the Office of the Workplace Ombudsman. This agency was later renamed the Office of the Fair Work Ombudsman from 1 July 2009 as part of the Fair Work reforms. While this chapter will touch on the work performed by these predecessor agencies, the focus is largely on the activities and approach of the FWO.

[6] For a recent overview of this literature, see John Budd, Paul Gollan, and Adrian Wilkinson, 'New Approaches to Employee Voice and Participation in Organisations' (2010) 63(3) Human Relations 303.

[7] See Ian Watson, John Buchanan, Iain Campbell, and Chris Briggs, *Fragmented Futures: New Challenges in Working Life* (Federation Press, 2003).

[8] Harry Arthurs, 'Reconciling Differences Differently: Reflections on Labor Law and Worker Voice After Collective Bargaining' (2007) 28 Comparative Labor Law and Policy Journal (CLLPJ) 155, 156.

In order to better reflect and capture the diverse needs and desires of workers, there has been a departure from traditional conceptualizations of participation which were rooted in industrial democracy.[9] In its wake, a more inclusive definition of voice has surfaced which is 'less concerned with a balance of bargaining power and material benefits for workers, but more oriented to broader social objectives in a deliberative and reflexive legal framework'.[10] Indeed, for many non-unionized or vulnerable workers, voice—in the classical sense—may not be a primary objective. For these workers, voice may be less about improving or influencing conditions at the workplace, and more about simply ensuring that the existing standards are respected and upheld. Indeed, an important, but neglected function of voice is the role it plays in compliance and enforcement. It is increasingly clear, however, that the ability of employees to raise a grievance and seek a fair resolution—either within or outside the organization—is critical. It is this particular conceptualization of voice which frames the analysis in this chapter.

When unions are weak, and collective bargaining is less dominant, it is unsurprising that minimum employment standards as prescribed by legislation grow in significance.[11] It is somewhat of a paradox then, that it is precisely when workers are not unionized that statutory rights and protections are less likely to be raised and relied upon.[12] While an absence of law can have significant implications for working standards, Otto Kahn-Freund has observed that the law cannot, on its own, guarantee satisfactory working conditions. He added:

> [a]s a power countervailing management trade unions are much more effective than the law has ever been or can ever be... Everywhere the effectiveness of the law depends on the unions far more than the unions depend on the effectiveness of law.[13]

Without access to a labour market intermediary, such as a union, employees are less likely to complain about their workplace conditions, even where they are deleterious. Factors which militate against complaining include those related to the individual, such as gender, ethnicity, education, and background, as well as the workplace environment, such as size, degree of conflict, and internal policies.[14] From an economic perspective, it has been suggested that employees are unlikely to complain where the costs outweigh the benefits of doing so. In this instance, 'costs' include those related to obtaining information about the scope and application of minimum employment standards and how such rights may be exercised and enforced. In addition, there are also the potential costs associated with employer retaliation, including possible job loss.[15]

[9] Budd et al. 304 (n 6).

[10] Alan Bogg and Tonia Novitz, 'Investigating "Voice" at Work' (2012) 33 CLLPJ 323, 324.

[11] It is worth acknowledging, however, that where unions are especially weak, particularly politically, this can lead to an erosion of legislated labour standards. The United Kingdom is a prime example of this phenomenon.

[12] Neil Gunningham, 'Occupational Health and Safety, Worker Participation and the Mining Industry in a Changing World of Work' (2008) 29 Economic and Industrial Democracy (EID) 336, 346.

[13] Otto Kahn-Freund, *Labour and the Law* (Stevens, 1977) 10.

[14] See David Weil, 'Are Mandated Health and Safety Committees Substitutes for or Supplements to Labor Unions' (1999) 52(3) Industrial and Labor Relations Review 339, 341–2.

[15] Weil 20 (n 4).

While adverse treatment of complainants by employers is prohibited under the Fair Work Act 2009 (Cth) (FW Act),[16] behavioural studies suggest that many employees abstain from speaking out because of the perceived psychological and societal costs, such as fear, guilt, and isolation by peers and community.[17] Indeed, while some of these costs may decrease after the employment ends, concerns about future employment prospects can still serve to curtail complaints about a former employer.[18]

Unions have been shown to effectively lower these costs in various ways and this can lead to higher complaint rates and improved compliance levels.[19] This trend can be linked to the fact that employees in unionized firms have an increased capacity to review and interpret legal standards, mediate and challenge their implementation by management, and attract the attention of labour inspectorates by voicing their grievances.[20] Unions assist employees in performing these functions by reducing or internalizing the costs of exercising individual rights conferred to workers—for instance, by facilitating a means for workers to make complaints anonymously.[21]

Another important feature of institutional representation is that it can help to ensure that changes at the workplace are undertaken in a way that benefits groups of employees, not just those individuals who are willing and able to explicitly raise their concerns. This overcomes one of the major weaknesses of individual voice and a heavily complaints-orientated strategy which can lead to investigations that are shaped by the specific concerns of one worker and confined to the immediate employer. In comparison, unions exercising collective voice are able to consolidate information gathered from workers to build a more intricate understanding of the network of employers or contractors which may assist in widening the enquiry beyond the scope of the initial complaint by identifying and helping others who have been similarly affected.[22] In this respect, it has been observed that 'social efficiency is enhanced where individually based rights are exercised via an agent operating in the collective interest'.[23]

Part of the reason that unions are able to perform these important compliance and enforcement functions is that they generally have the power and authority to take formal and informal action in the face of employer resistance to conform. In particular, in the Australian system, trade unions have legal standing to enforce statutory employment rights, even when those rights are individually vested.[24] While unions have access

[16] The FWO takes any allegations of victimization (known as 'adverse action' under the FW Act) seriously and has previously pursued a number of cases against employers who have taken adverse action against employees who have complained about their pay and conditions. See e.g. Fair Work Ombudsman, 'Melbourne company fined $35,000 for sacking workers who complained about pay', Media Release, 13 April 2010.

[17] Yuval Feldman and Orly Lobel, 'The Incentives Matrix: The Comparative Effectiveness of Rewards, Liabilities, Duties, and Protections for Reporting Illegality' (2010) 88 Texas Law Review 1151, 1157–8.

[18] Bennett 143 (n 1).

[19] See Weil 25–7 (n 4).

[20] See David Weil, 'Enforcing OSHA: The Role of Labor Unions' (1991) 30(1) Industrial Relations 20; Margaret Lee, 'Regulating Enforcement of Workers' Entitlements in Australia: The New Dimension of Individualisation' (2006) 17(1) Labour & Industry 41.

[21] David Weil and Amanda Pyles, 'Why Complain? Complaints, Compliance and the Problem of Enforcement in the US Workplace' (2005) 27(1) CLLPJ 59.

[22] Janice Fine and Jennifer Gordon, 'Strengthening Labour Standards Enforcement Through Partnerships with Workers' Organisations' (2010) 38(4) Politics and Society 552.

[23] Weil 23 (n 4).

[24] Section 540 of the FW Act provides that a trade union may apply for a court order in relation to a contravention or proposed contravention of a civil remedy provision in relation to an employee if: (a) the

to sanctions, such as civil penalties, through the court system, these formal powers are rarely invoked. Rather, union enforcement activity more commonly involves alternative and less formal approaches, such as direct negotiation with employers at the workplace, accessing external dispute resolution, or employing economic sanctions, including various forms of industrial action.[25]

While unions are clearly integral to the exercise of employee voice and the effective enforcement of minimum employment standards, this channel of voice is no longer available in many workplaces. The key question is whether a government agency—such as a labour inspectorate—can replicate some of the core benefits already outlined in a way that leads to enhanced employee voice and improved compliance. For example, can the labour inspectorate help employees understand, interpret, and apply their rights to be paid and employed in accordance with minimum employment standards? Is the inspectorate able to effectively shield employees from employer retribution by allowing individuals to complain anonymously or on behalf of a group of workers? Can the regulatory agency assist in delivering workplace justice by providing an informal forum for the fair resolution of disputes? The evolution of employment standards regulation in Australia, and the changing pattern of employee representation and dispute resolution, provides a useful case study in this respect.

The Evolution of Employment Standards Regulation and Enforcement in Australia

In the Australian context, 'union voice has historically been the most prominent means by which workers were organised and represented in the employment relationship'.[26] This can be linked to the conciliation and arbitration system, which was a defining feature of the Australian workplace relations regime for most of the twentieth century. This unique system of dispute settlement performed several key regulatory functions and had a number of significant effects on the power and position of regulatory actors.

First, the key driver of conciliation and compulsory arbitration was to secure industrial peace and avoid economically destructive disputes. To achieve this objective, the system entrenched a strong and distinctive tradition of resolving workplace conflict through dispute resolution mechanisms overseen and administered by an independent industrial umpire. A central outcome of this process was to impose protective standards for workers across industry sectors or occupational classes in the form of 'awards'.

employee is affected by the contravention (or will be affected by the proposed contravention); or (b) the trade union is entitled to represent the industrial interests of the employee.

[25] See Tess Hardy and John Howe, 'Partners in Enforcement? The New Balance Between Government and Trade Union Enforcement of Employment Standards in Australia' (2009) 22 Australian Journal of Labour Law (AJLL) 306.

[26] Amanda Pyman, Brian Cooper, Julian Teicher, and Peter Holland, 'A Comparison of the Effectiveness of Employee Voice Arrangements in Australia' (2006) 37(5) Industrial Relations Journal 543, 545. Throughout most of the twentieth century, union membership levels hovered around 50 per cent of the workforce in Australia, albeit with some ebbs and flows during this period. See David Peetz, *Unions in a Contrary World* (Cambridge University Press, 1997). Union density is currently around 18 per cent in Australia. See Australian Bureau of Statistics, *Employee Earnings, Benefits and Trade Union Membership* (Cat 6310.0, May 2013).

Trade unions were effectively charged with 'policing' this system, and accordingly, were afforded extensive privileges and protections, such as rights of entry and legal standing to commence court proceedings. That said, it appears that it was far more common for unions to rely on less formal avenues to resolve disputes about compliance—for example, by exercising industrial muscle and leaning on the employer or by notifying a dispute and gaining access to the arbitral powers of the federal industrial tribunal.[27]

The dominant role played by unions on the compliance and enforcement front had a profound effect on the position of the federal labour inspectorate.[28] For the first three decades of the conciliation and arbitration system, unions provided the only avenue of enforcement. The general neglect of the labour inspectorate, which persisted over the course of the twentieth century, appears to have been premised on an assumption that enforcement of employment standards regulation was more properly the role of trade unions than the government.[29]

This regulatory landscape, and the entrenched role of trade unions within it, all changed with the election of the Howard Coalition government in 1996. In its first year, the Howard government introduced the Workplace Relations Act 1996 (Cth), which encouraged individualization strategies, restricted union rights, and curtailed the powers of the federal industrial tribunal—the most significant regulatory institution within the conciliation and arbitration system. Employee voice was progressively characterized as direct and this was 'fuelled by an increasingly aggressive focus on managerial prerogative, the decline of unionism and the primacy of regulation of the employment relationship at the enterprise level'.[30] These developments were later associated with a 'significant and growing "representation gap" in Australia'.[31]

This gap soon widened with the arrival of the Coalition government's Work Choices legislation in 2006.[32] As has been well-documented,[33] the collective, award-based framework which largely defined the first century of industrial relations in Australia was displaced by an avid promotion of individual statutory agreements and the legislative entrenchment of a core set of minimum employment standards. Work Choices also sought to marginalize unions as the legitimate representatives of employees by placing limits on the capacity of unions to take industrial action, exercise rights of entry and access the dispute resolution jurisdiction of the Commission.[34]

The Work Choices legislation also had significant implications for compliance and enforcement of employment standards regulation. In particular, replacing a collectivist system with a rights-based model had the effect of elevating the role of formal

[27] Hardy and Howe (n 25); Chris Arup and Carolyn Sutherland, 'The Recovery of Wages: Legal Services and Access to Justice' (2009) 35 Monash University Law Review (Monash ULR) 96.

[28] Glenda Maconachie and Miles Goodwin, 'Recouping Wage Underpayment: Increasingly Less Likely?' (2006) 41 Australian Journal of Social Issues 328, 339.

[29] Hardy and Howe (n 25).

[30] Pyman et al. 547 (n 26).

[31] Mark Bray, Peter Waring, Duncan Macdonald, and Stephane Le Queux, 'The "Representation Gap" in Australia' (2001) 12(2) Labour & Industry 1, 25.

[32] Workplace Relations Amendment (Work Choices) Act 2005 (Cth) ('Work Choices').

[33] See generally the various articles in the special issue of the Australian Journal of Labour Law (2006) 19(2).

[34] Anthony Forsyth, 'Workplace Conflict Resolution in Australia: The Dominance of the Public Dispute Resolution Framework and the Limited Role of ADR' (2012) 23(3) International Journal of Human Resource Management 476, 478.

enforcement mechanisms utilized by the federal labour inspectorate and overseen by the courts at the expense of informal dispute resolution processes initiated by trade unions and administered by the federal tribunal. The changing dynamics between these institutional actors was further perpetuated by the fact that, during the Work Choices period, the federal labour inspectorate received an influx of resources and an unexpected flush of political enthusiasm for enforcement. Combined, these factors directly led to a boost in the inspectorate's workforce, a shift in enforcement strategy, and a spike in litigation.[35]

Soon after being elected in late 2007, the new Rudd Labor government started to unwind some of the key policy positions taken by the former Coalition government. In particular, the FW Act sought to restore the central place of enterprise bargaining and remove easy access to individual statutory agreements. Although the FW Act signalled some significant reforms, the Work Choices legacy lived on in a number of critical respects. For example, while the Fair Work reforms returned a sense of legitimacy to unions as a voice for employees, most workers remained without union membership.[36] Basic working conditions, such as leave and termination entitlements, continue to be principally secured by legislation. Minimum wages are currently set down in 'modern awards', which are no longer the product of negotiation between industrial parties, but the outcome of determination made by the Fair Work Commission (FWC)—the name now given to the federal industrial tribunal. The scope of the dispute resolution procedure administered by the FWC is also strongly influenced by the changes which took place under Work Choices insofar as the Commission only has jurisdiction to exercise private arbitration where this power is conferred upon it by the relevant dispute resolution clause.[37]

These shifts are important in a number of ways. First, one of the inherent values of the conciliation and arbitration process was the way in which it transformed informal regulation and decision-making processes into a legitimate model of corporate governance. In doing so, the award-making process, as well as the negotiation of enterprise agreements, underlined the important role of workers and their representatives in developing and implementing the normative regime of the workplace.[38] In comparison, the rise of individual employment rights prescribed by legislation positions workers and their advocates as passive beneficiaries of actions taken on their behalf by legislators, albeit trade unions and employer associations have often been active participants in the political debate and legislative processes.[39] At the same time, the promise

[35] See Tess Hardy, 'A Changing of the Guard: Enforcement of Workplace Relations Laws Since Work Choices and Beyond' in Anthony Forsyth and Andrew Stewart (eds), *Fair Work: The New Workplace Laws and the Work Choices Legacy* (Federation Press, 2009).

[36] Andrea Kirk and Eve Anderson, 'Examining the New Actor Status of Employee Assistance Programs: A Voice for Employees' in Grant Michelson, Suzanne Jamieson, and John Burgess (eds), *New Employment Actors: Developments from Australia* (Peter Lang, 2008) 267, 269.

[37] FW Act, ss. 738–739. See Joellen Riley, 'From Industrial Arbitration to Workplace Mediation: Changing Approaches to Dispute Resolution' in Stewart and Forsyth 200 (n 35).

[38] Arthurs 160 (n 8).

[39] For example, following the 2007 federal election, the Rudd Labour government established a tripartite Committee on Industrial Relations (commonly known as 'COIL') to develop and draft the Fair Work Bill 2009 (Cth) prior to its introduction into Parliament. In order to capture the various perspectives on the legislative reform package, this Committee consisted of a number of different advisory groups, including a

of individual rights often has the effect of heightening calls for their enforcement.[40] It is now the case in Australia, as it is in many common law countries, that unions frequently enforce standards set by Parliament[41] or refer matters directly to the labour inspectorate for further investigation and follow up.[42] Indeed, as legislated standards have expanded, so too has the role of the government agency responsible for upholding these standards.[43]

This touches on another critical issue—that is, the changing role of and interaction between the two key government institutions in this context—the FWC and the FWO. Traditionally, it was the industrial tribunal, rather than the labour inspectorate, which was principally responsible for the resolution of workplace grievances.[44] This traditional dispute resolution pathway is reflected in the 'model' dispute resolution clause that features in all modern awards and many enterprise agreements.[45] In particular, this 'model' clause expressly steers parties towards the Commission. However, it is arguable that this approach no longer reflects the fact that the majority of workplace disputes involve non-unionized workers. The current FWC President, Justice Iain Ross, recently acknowledged there had been a significant shift over the past 15 years away from collective disputes in favour of individual applications.[46] Furthermore, to have the Commission hear a dispute arising under the NES, a modern award, or an enterprise agreement, the applicant must ordinarily still be in employment.[47] As noted earlier, it is increasingly rare, particularly in non-union or small workplaces, for employees to bring a complaint against their existing employer because of fears of reprisal. If a worker decides to wait until after their employment ends, their options to pursue a grievance in the Commission are limited to lodging a claim under the unfair dismissal or general protection provisions of the FW Act. Such applications must not only fall within the relevant jurisdictional parameters,[48] they must also be submitted within a

business advisory group, a workers advisory group, and a small business advisory group. See 'Legal Experts Start 10 Day Review of Labor's Draft IR Laws', Workplace Express, 7 October 2008.

[40] Joellen Riley, 'Workplace Dispute Resolution under the Fair Work Act: Is There a Role for Private Alternative Dispute Resolution Providers?' (2009) 20 Alternative Dispute Resolution Journal (ADRJ) 236. This trend has been similarly observed in the UK context: see Bob Hepple and Gillian Morris, 'The Employment Act 2002 and the Crisis of Individual Employment Rights' (2002) 31(3) Industrial Law Journal (ILJ) 245.

[41] FW Act, s. 540.

[42] Trevor Colling, 'Trade Union Roles in Making Employment Rights Effective' in Linda Dickens (ed.), *Making Employment Rights Effective: Issues of Compliance and Enforcement* (Hart Publishing, 2012) 183, 185.

[43] Hepple and Morris (n 40).

[44] See Forsyth (n 34); Therese MacDermott and Joellen Riley, 'Alternative Dispute Resolution and Individual Workplace Rights: The Evolving Role of Fair Work Australia' (2011) 53 JIR 718.

[45] FW Act, ss. 146 and 186(6).

[46] According to President Ross, two-thirds of applications lodged in 1998/1999 were the result of collective disputes; this had fallen to less than 40 per cent by 2011/2012. See 'New FWC help for self-represented parties', *Workplace Express*, 6 May 2013. Similar trends have been observed in the UK. For example, in 1975, the Advisory, Conciliation and Arbitration Service (ACAS) received 2,564 requests for collective conciliation. In 2010/2011, this number had dropped to 1,054. In the same time period, the number of individual conciliation cases had substantially increased from 29,100 cases in 1975 to 74,620 cases in 2010/2011. See Nicole Busby and Morag McDermont, 'Workers, Marginalised Voices and the Employment Tribunal System: Some Preliminary Findings' (2012) 41(2) ILJ 166.

[47] See e.g. *Fairall v St George & Sutherland Community College* [2012] FWA 8847.

[48] For example, an applicant seeking a remedy under the unfair dismissal provisions must generally be able to establish that their employment was terminated at the initiative of the employer, that the termination

21-day timeframe after the triggering event. In addition, the applicant must pay a filing fee to lodge an application with the Commission, which although modest may serve to deter low-paid workers from proceeding with their claim.

In comparison to the FWC, the FWO is at much greater liberty to determine the scope and structure of the internal dispute resolution process they administer given that this process is not prescribed by legislation, but rather is at the discretion of senior management and determined by internal policy. For example, the FWO can and does receive complaints about a wide range of employment matters from disputes about minimum employment entitlements, such as minimum pay, leave, allowances, redundancy, and notice of termination, to allegations of discrimination or adverse action.[49] The majority of complaints received by the FWO are, however, concerned with underpayments of wages.[50] While the bulk of the complaints made to the FWO come from former employees,[51] the agency is also able to deal with, and encourages, complaints from existing employees. The FWO can receive complaints for up to six years following an alleged contravention, there is no applicable salary cap, and the FWO is authorized to deal with 'safety net contractual entitlements'.[52] Finally, accessing the dispute resolution services, and other assistance of the FWO, is free. In light of this, it is not surprising that employees, especially those without union support or the financial resources to engage private legal representation,[53] are increasingly turning to the FWO when seeking an institutional vehicle for voice.[54]

was harsh, unjust, or unreasonable, and that they can otherwise meet the other relevant thresholds, including that their annual salary falls below the relevant salary limit.

[49] A number of provisions in Part 3-1 of the FW Act deal with situations where one person has taken 'adverse action' against another person because: (a) they have exercised a 'workplace right' (e.g. a right, amongst others, to make a complaint or inquiry to a person or body that has the capacity to seek compliance with a workplace law, such as an inspector or trade union); (b) of their membership or non-membership of an industrial association; or (c) of their engaging or not engaging in certain industrial activities.

[50] Complaints relating to wages made up 63 per cent of the total complaints received by the FWO. See Australian National Audit Office, 'Delivery of Workplace Relations Services by the Office of the Fair Work Ombudsman' (Audit Report No 14, 2012–13), 74.

[51] A similar pattern can be observed in other common law countries. For example, Taras reports that well over 90 per cent of employment-related complaints received by the Canadian federal and provincial employment standards hotlines come from former employees. See Daphne Taras, 'Reconciling Differences Differently: Employee Voice in Public Policymaking and Workplace Policy' (2007) 28 CLLPJ 167, 175.

[52] Section 12 of the FW Act defines 'safety net contractual entitlements' to mean entitlements under an employment contract that relate to any matter also covered by the National Employment Standards or by a modern award. This may include contractual entitlements to pay or leave that are more generous than the 'safety net' prescribed by legislation or the applicable modern award.

[53] Self-help remedies are particularly difficult to access in Australia given that legal costs are not generally recoverable in this jurisdiction: FW Act, s. 570. For further discussion of the way in which costs orders may affect access to justice, see Beth Gaze and Rosemary Hunter, 'Access to Justice for Discrimination Complainants: Courts and Legal Representation' (2009) 32(3) University of New South Wales Law Journal 699.

[54] This is illustrated by the fact that the FWO received 26,366 complaints in 2011/2012. In this same year, the FWC received 18,957 applications under the provisions relating to unfair dismissal (14,027), general protections (2,901), and dispute resolution (2,029). The last figure does not include dispute resolution applications which relate to bargaining disputes or applications for informal assistance relating to agreements and industrial action. See Fair Work Ombudsman, *Annual Report 2011–2012*, 16; and Fair Work Commission, *Annual Report 2011–2012*.

The Fair Work Ombudsman and Employee Voice

The FW Act charges the FWO with responsibility to encourage and ensure compliance with national workplace laws through education initiatives, producing best practices guides and by monitoring, investigating, and enforcing workplace laws. There are very few legislative restrictions on how the agency should achieve these statutory objectives and fulfil its statutory mandate. The way in which voice is harnessed (or not) is therefore less about legal frameworks and more about internal decision-making processes and external environmental factors.

Since 2006—the year Work Choices commenced and the federal labour inspectorate rose to prominence—there has been a discernible shift in the emphasis placed on education and advice and the inclination to use litigation and other coercive sanctions. For example, in the immediate wake of Work Choices, the labour inspectorate was keen to develop a reputation as being a strong and effective regulator. They set out to achieve this objective by adopting an aggressive litigation strategy and deploying a savvy use of media—an approach potentially buttressed by broad political commitment to the regulatory agency at the time.

More recently, however, the FWO's enforcement functions and powers have been downplayed, while its role in promoting voluntary resolution through advice, education, and mediation has been accentuated. While civil remedy litigation remains 'one of the compliance tools available to the Fair Work Ombudsman', litigation activities are generally seen as 'the last resort of a broader compliance system'.[55] This recent move towards 'softer' or more persuasive approaches appears to be driven by a number of different factors.[56]

For a start, the political, economic, and social environment in which the FWO has been operating has been a challenging one. There has been a change of government following a hotly contested election which centred on workplace relations issues; there has been a major financial crisis which has had significant flow-on effects for particular industries, such as manufacturing and retail; and finally, the FWO has had to contend with the inherent complexities associated with any new regulatory regime. In particular, the renewed emphasis on cooperative mechanisms may be a response to the apparent perception in some pockets of the regulated community that the FWO was being too aggressive in its pursuit of non-complying employers, especially at a time when there had been significant legislative change and the application of instruments remained unsettled.[57]

The lobbying from business potentially gained greater traction in light of the fact that the Fair Work reforms are generally geared towards promoting conciliatory rather than adversarial approaches to the resolution of workplace relations disputes. As set out

[55] Fair Work Ombudsman, *Annual Report 2009–2010*.

[56] For further discussion of the shift in this litigation strategy, see Tess Hardy, John Howe, and Sean Cooney, 'Less Energetic, but More Enlightened? Exploring the Fair Work Ombudsman's Use of Litigation in Regulatory Enforcement' (2013) 35(3) Sydney Law Review (Sydney LR) 565.

[57] Nicholas Wilson, 'Update from the Fair Work Ombudsman' (Speech to Industrial Relations Summit, 5 March 2012).

previously, the regulatory framework in Australia was historically organized around the idea that the interests of employers and employees were fundamentally in conflict.[58] In contrast to the interest-based premise of the conciliation and arbitration system, the contemporary legislative framework expressly provides that a key function of the FWO is 'to promote harmonious, productive and cooperative workplace relations'.[59] While the concept of workplace partnerships is most commonly associated with standard-setting and bargaining, or promoted by HRM advocates interested in high performance work systems, this powerful discourse of cooperation and collaboration has important implications for compliance and enforcement practices, and partly explains the FWO's current approach to employee voice.

One of the most significant factors behind the FWO's change in approach, however, has been a drop in agency resourcing.[60] The recent decrease in agency funds has been partly justified on the basis of an assumption that the need for assistance would subside once the Fair Work system was more fully established. This assumption is somewhat misplaced, however, given that it does not properly account for the fact that in providing assistance to workers who had been largely left without recourse, the FWO has effectively generated a demand for its services which is unlikely to abate any time soon.[61]

Moreover, this substantial increase in complaints makes it more challenging for the FWO to meet managerial demands for efficiency which is manifest in the agency's key performance indicators (KPIs). While quantitative KPIs may encourage timeliness and responsiveness,[62] there is a danger that these numerical targets may cultivate a 'culture of efficiency'[63] where the success of inspectorate work is judged by meeting quotas to reduce or eliminate complaint backlogs, even where doing so may compromise investigative integrity or procedural fairness. Further, some have argued that time-sensitive KPIs generally discourage state-based enforcement in favour of a light-touch, self-regulatory approach.[64] Indeed, the adoption of informal dispute resolution processes effectively allows the FWO to better preserve resources and avoid the key disadvantages of litigation, including the formal and technical procedures for filing and presenting

[58] Stuart Macintyre and Richard Mitchell (eds), *Foundations of Arbitration: The Origins and Effects of State Compulsory Arbitration, 1890–1914* (Oxford University Press, 1989).

[59] FW Act, s. 682.

[60] 'Budget 2013: More Dollars for FWC, Less for FWBC', *Workplace Express*, 14 May 2013.

[61] In 2011/2012, the FWO recorded the receipt of 26,366 complaints, which represents an increase of 20 per cent from the 21,980 complaints received during 2010/2011. There was a slight decrease in the last financial year where the FWO recorded the receipt of 24,678 complaints. See Fair Work Ombudsman, *Annual Report 2012–2013*.

[62] Responsiveness is one of the five principles of the FWO Customer Charter. In particular, the Charter states: 'We aim to offer the best possible service and are continually looking to improve upon our performance. In addition to treating customers with dignity and respect, we are also committed to the following delivery timeframes: we will resolve 80% of complaints in 90 days; the Fair Work Infoline will resolve 80% of matters at the first contact; the Fair Work Infoline will be available 99% of the time during advertised hours; our website will be available 99% of the time.' See Fair Work Ombudsman, Customer Service Charter, 23 April 2013.

[63] Mary Gellatly, John Grundy, Kiran Mirchandani, J. Adam Perry, Mark Thomas, and Leah Vosko, '"Modernising" Employment Standards? Administrative Efficiency and the Production of the Illegitimate Claimant in Ontario, Canada' (2011) 22(2) Economic and Labour Relations Review (ELRR) 81, 96.

[64] Mary Gellatly et al. 96 (n 63).

evidence, as well as the delay and expense associated with obtaining and enforcing court orders. As Riley points out:

> The interest of governments in reducing public expenditure on court and tribunal systems, and in responding to lobbying to relieve the cost of these rights to business enterprises, goes some way towards explaining the pressure on governments to consider [alternative dispute resolution] as a means for resolving individual workplace disputes. (It is not all about concern for access to justice for ordinary workers, after all).[65]

This shift in the dominant compliance and enforcement approach of the inspectorate from a formal, litigious model to a more informal, dispute resolution approach has important implications for worker voice. The next section will explore the FWO's new compliance strategy and consider the extent to which the inspectorate is capable of providing a new channel for voice. In particular, it will assess whether the inspectorate is (or should be) performing some of the key regulatory functions performed by traditional institutional actors, including trade unions and the federal industrial tribunal.

The FWO's New Compliance Strategy

From the start of 2013, the FWO publicly moved away from the traditional compliance and enforcement model of its predecessors—which generally involved undertaking a detailed investigation of every workplace complaint that was lodged with the agency. In its place, the FWO has sought to implement a 'strategic enforcement' model—a term coined by David Weil based on his research into the US Department of Labour.[66] The key features of this model, as applied by the Australian regulator, were explained by a senior manager at the FWO as follows:

> This strategic approach seeks to resolve matters at a workplace level between the parties. In turn, the FWO is able to focus our efforts where they are most needed. Our experience under this model was that the vast majority of employers sought to do the right thing, and that matters were resolved more often than not, through assistance and education rather than through the use of statutory powers and a detailed linear investigation. This same experience tells us that each case is not the same and they do not all require the same deployment of resources, or use of statutory powers, to achieve a quality outcome.[67]

This new regulatory strategy has resulted in a number of significant changes in the way that compliance is promoted and contraventions are detected. It has also transformed the method by which employee complaints are processed and resolved by the agency.[68] Each of these regulatory functions will be considered in turn later in the chapter.

[65] Riley 238 (n 40).

[66] David Weil, *Improving Compliance Through Strategic Enforcement* (Report for US Department of Labour, 2010).

[67] Michael Campbell, 'The FWO's Approach to Compliance and Enforcement' (Speech to Ai Group National PIR Group Conference, 6 May 2013).

[68] For completeness, it is noted that the FWO also has jurisdiction to receive complaints from a range of people, including employers. Employer complaints may be received in relation to an alleged breach of provisions relating to freedom of association and/or unlawful industrial action. It is also possible that, in unusual

How does the FWO promote compliance and detect contraventions?

All new employees now receive a Fair Work Information Statement upon commencement of employment, although this document contains only the most basic information about the Australian workplace relations system.[69] As documented earlier, the pace of legislative change in Australia has meant that while the current system provides for a comprehensive set of protective standards, it is inherently complex. To address this problem, the FWO is expressly empowered to promote compliance with the FW Act. In line with this statutory objective, the inspectorate 'has invested significantly in the development of educative resources and programs that seek to resolve potential workplace issues before a complaint form is even filled out'.[70]

For example, the FWO operates a Fair Work Infoline—a telephone information service which can provide personalized assistance to the caller.[71] The website of the FWO is also comprehensive. It contains links not only to modern awards, but a plain English explanation of rights and obligations under the workplace relations laws. On the website, employees can also access an online calculator called PayCheck Plus—which is an important tool in helping employees identify whether they have been underpaid. More recently, the FWO has begun to offer a tailored email alert service to notify employees when there are any relevant changes to the modern award that covers their employment.[72]

In addition to these self-help mechanisms, the FWO has also undertaken to proactively educate employees through a number of campaigns and outreach programmes. Indeed, contrary to the dominant detection methods of past labour inspectorates, the FWO is more sensitive to the fact that some industries have higher rates of vulnerable workers which make it more prone to employer contraventions. In line with the strategic enforcement model, the FWO has increasingly placed a greater emphasis on proactive detection measures and more collaborative methods to capture less visible problems.

To this end, the FWO has frequently sought to enrol other institutions or intermediaries in order to strengthen its outreach activities and overcome some of the collective action problems identified earlier.[73] Trade unions are ideally qualified to participate in these collaborative strategies, however, their meagre presence in key sectors means that the FWO is increasingly looking beyond traditional labour market intermediaries. In particular, the FWO is progressively collaborating with a range of non-government organizations, including migrant resource networks, ethnic business

circumstances, the dispute resolution process will apply to a matter which was initially identified as part of an audit undertaken by the FW Inspectors.

[69] See FW Act, ss. 124–125. The Fair Work Ombudsman is responsible for preparing the Fair Work Information Statement, which is currently two pages long and contains the barest details about each of the prescribed rights and entitlements.

[70] See Campbell (n 67).

[71] Interpretation and other support services are also available for complainants who have difficulty understanding English or have a hearing or speech impairment.

[72] For example, when the minimum pay increases as a result of the annual wage review undertaken by the FWC.

[73] See Tess Hardy, 'Enrolling Non-State Actors to Improve Compliance with Minimum Employment Standards' (2011) 22(3) ELRR 117.

groups, community legal centres, training providers, and others as critical contact points for both awareness-raising and whistleblowing. This expansive form of collaboration is particularly important in industries where there are a high number of vulnerable employees and workplaces are less likely to be unionized or affiliated.[74] The FWO also provides both direct and indirect support and assistance to community groups through funding grants and by encouraging firms to commit to paying a specified sum to community legal centres as part of enforceable undertakings.[75] However, the level of regulatory engagement with these additional groups and networks remains in a state of development and the presence of such groups is patchy. Indeed, in comparison to the long history of community activism in the US, and the emerging regulatory role of NGOs in the UK,[76] worker advocate groups in Australia are far less developed and much less active.[77]

The absence of a non-state actor which has the necessary regulatory capacity to protect employee voice and influence compliance outcomes is a key problem in employment standards regulation and a fundamental weakness of these collaborative strategies. Without deeper and more meaningful engagement with these third party intermediaries, or greater attention and energy directed towards proactive detection, it is likely that the inherent structural barriers militating against complaints will mean that even the best informed workers may still remain quiet.

How are complaints processed and resolved by the FWO?

Notwithstanding the agency's renewed focus on proactive models of detection, the majority of the FWO's activities are still consumed with registering and resolving employee complaints. In most instances, and as a first step, the FWO encourages the complainant to directly raise the relevant issues of concern with the employer in a bid to try to resolve those issues without the need for external intervention. If this direct

[74] For instance, as part of the Cleaning Services Campaign and following a suggestion from the relevant union, the FWO sought to address the alleged exploitation of international students by translating information about workplace rights and disseminating it through twenty-two university cafes. More importantly, it sought to enrol the assistance of university student associations, private colleges and English schools through an associated email campaign. Fair Work Ombudsman, *Annual Report 2010–11*, 28. Further, in 2011, the FWO established the 'Barefoot Tutors' programme which is designed to disseminate information within the culturally and linguistically diverse (CALD) community. As part of this programme, the FWO enrols community leaders to educate members of the relevant ethnic communities in their own language about workplace rights and entitlements. See Fair Work Ombudsman, *Annual Report 2011–2012*.

[75] An enforceable undertaking is a statutory agreement which can be made between the FWO and an alleged wrongdoer which sets out a number of promises or commitments intended to rectify past contraventions and encourage future compliance. Failure to meet these commitments can lead to the enforcement of the undertaking in court. See Tess Hardy and John Howe, 'Too Soft or Too Severe? Enforceable Undertakings and the Regulatory Dilemma Facing the Fair Work Ombudsman' (2013) 41 Federal Law Review 1.

[76] For example, Oxfam in the UK is increasingly active in agitating for workplace relations reform in the domestic context. See e.g. Oxfam, 'Turning the Tide: How to Best Protect Workers Employed by Gangmasters—Five years After Morecambe Bay' (Oxfam Briefing Paper, 31 July 2009). In comparison, the Australian arm of Oxfam is generally concerned with campaigning for improved workers' rights in developing countries, but not in Australia itself.

[77] Grant Michelson, Suzanne Jamieson, and John Burgess, 'Filling the Void: Emerging Actors in Australian Industrial Relations' (2009) 13(1) Journal of Economic and Social Policy 1, 12.

method fails to achieve the desired outcome or is deemed to be inappropriate, the FWO may then make an initial assessment about the most effective and efficient way in which to respond to the complaint.

First, if the matter is outside the FWO's jurisdiction or otherwise has no merit, the complaint will be closed immediately.[78] In all other cases, a team of experienced FW Inspectors evaluates the matter using a fixed set of criteria to determine the level of resources and assistance to devote to resolving the complaint. In particular, the FW Inspector will generally consider the nature of the complaint (i.e. whether it is a 'routine' or 'complex' matter), the characteristics of the complainant (i.e. whether the employee falls within a vulnerable category),[79] and the compliance history of the relevant employer. For example, if the complainant is highly paid, is not otherwise vulnerable, and the contravention relates to a 'routine' matter, such as an alleged underpayment, the FWO may actively encourage the employee to access self-help remedies (such as initiating a small claims proceeding).[80]

Alternatively, the FWO may request the complainant to participate in the 'assisted voluntary resolution' (AVR) process administered by FW Inspectors. If these options are not suitable or are refused,[81] the matter may be referred straight to FWO's internal mediation service. In comparison, if at the initial assessment stage, the matter is deemed to be more serious and 'complex', then voluntary resolution mechanisms may be skipped in favour of a more formal investigation process. Generally, the FWO is aiming to undertake a detailed investigation in only a minority of cases.

Following this initial assessment, most complaints are referred to the AVR team. The AVR process generally involves a FW Inspector contacting both the employer and the employee separately by telephone in order to work through the issues and discuss potential solutions prior to the matter proceeding to mediation. As part of this preliminary process, the FW Inspector seeks to help both sides become better informed about the nature of the complaint and their respective rights and responsibilities under federal workplace laws.[82] While the FW Inspector may seek to verify particular claims through a review of relevant documents, the Inspector does not generally conduct field visits, undertake any detailed underpayment calculations, or dictate the terms of any resolution. Rather, the stated objective of the transformed AVR process is to provide

[78] Approximately 10 per cent of all matters are closed on this basis. See Campbell (n 67).

[79] The FWO Litigation Policy describes a 'vulnerable worker' as including: young people, trainees, apprentices, people with a physical or mental disability or literacy difficulties, recent immigrants and people from non-English speaking backgrounds, the long-term unemployed and those re-entering the workforce, outworkers, people with carer responsibilities, indigenous Australians, employees in precarious employment (e.g. casual employees) and people residing in regions with limited employment opportunities and/or with financial and social restraints on their ability to relocate to places where there might be greater job opportunities. See Fair Work Ombudsman, *Guidance Note 1—Litigation Policy*, 20 July 2011.

[80] FW Act, s. 548.

[81] AVR is deemed to be unsuitable if the allegation or complaint is: confidential; from an overseas worker employed in Australia under a visa; related to unpaid trial work or unpaid work experience; involves complex matters, such as discrimination, industrial action or right of entry; involves an employer with a history of non-compliance; is of a particularly serious nature; and/or the assessor, using their discretion, decides AVR is not appropriate or in the public interest.

[82] Fair Work Ombudsman, 'Before mediation', <http://www.fairwork.gov.au/complaints/the-complaints-process/pages/before-mediation.aspx> accessed 13 May 2013.

a quick and accessible forum for meaningful customer engagement and for parties to arrive at a mutually acceptable outcome.

While the AVR Inspector is able to escalate complaints to the Compliance branch for formal investigation, the majority of complaints that are not resolved via AVR are later referred to mediation. It seems that the agency generally believes that '[w]ith the exception of deliberate and systemic noncompliance, most matters are suitable for referral to mediation'.[83] Mediation is generally conducted over the telephone by an accredited FWO Mediator[84] on an informal, voluntary, and confidential basis. A key distinction between AVR and mediation is that the former is conducted without any extensive enquiry into whether an agreed resolution reflects the underlying legal obligations, while the latter is said to only succeed 'if both parties make an informed decision and agreement within the boundaries of what is lawfully owed to the employee'.[85] As required, the mediator may allow the parties to speak with a 'technical liaison officer' within the FWO who can provide more precise advice about the relevant legal issues.

However, the FWO Mediation Charter also makes clear that the FWO Mediator is independent and 'does not act as a judge, provide legal advice, make a determination on who is right or wrong or impose decisions on the parties'.[86] In line with this Charter, the FWO Meditator does not generally assist parties in calculating the extent of any underpayment or quantifying the loss, rather the mediation process is principally designed to help employers and employees find 'mutually acceptable' or 'flexible' solutions to workplace issues, and provide parties with a sense of ownership by allowing them to 'control the outcome'.[87]

Where a party refuses to participate in mediation, or the matter fails to settle, the complaint is then likely to be referred to the 'Resolution' team. In this team, senior FW Inspectors conduct a condensed investigation process which may (or may not) lead to rectification of any underpayment and the imposition of administrative sanctions, such as penalty infringement notices (i.e. a fine) or compliance notices (i.e. a formal direction to take certain remedial steps which is enforceable in court). Alternatively, the FWO may end its involvement at this point. In these circumstances, the complainant may then be left to take their own action, such as lodging a small claims proceeding in a relevant court.

Amplifying or Muting Employee Voice?

The internal complaints management and dispute resolution process of the labour inspectorate has largely avoided scrutiny in the past given that it is far less visible than some of the other compliance activities undertaken by the FWO, such as targeted

[83] Fair Work Ombudsman, *Annual Report 2011–2012*, 77.

[84] FWO Mediators are trained in line with National Alternative Dispute Resolution Advisory Council (NADRAC) requirements and follow the Australian National Mediator Practice Standards. Fair Work Ombudsman, 'Mediation', <http://www.fairwork.gov.au/complaints/the-complaints-process/pages/mediation.aspx> accessed 13 May 2013.

[85] Campbell (n 67).

[86] Fair Work Ombudsman, 'FWO Mediation Charter', <http://www.fairwork.gov.au/Complaints1/FWO-Mediation-Charter.doc>, 13 March 2013.

[87] Fair Work Ombudsman 'Mediation' (n 86).

campaigns and enforcement litigation. Further, the widespread use of mediation by the FWO is still relatively novel. However, given that a majority of complaints are said or predicted to 'be resolved before or during mediation',[88] it is critical to understand the benefits and drawbacks of this new process and what this may mean for employee voice in particular and employer compliance more generally.

The new complaints resolution process of the FWO is, in many respects, similar to the traditional enforcement strategy of trade unions—insofar that both are geared towards quick and informal resolution of complaints. However, in providing an alternative channel for employee voice, there is a real question about the extent to which the FWO can achieve the benefits of trade union enforcement identified earlier. For example, can it be said that the FWO has effectively empowered employees, enhanced access to justice, and improved compliance?[89] Is it possible for the FWO to maintain neutrality and independence and still deliver fair outcomes, particularly where the dispute involves potential contraventions of basic legal rights and relates to those who otherwise lack agency and representation?[90] Finally, in privatizing individual disputes, can the FWO deliver the collective benefits associated with trade union compliance practices and processes?

The first obvious difference between the approach of the FWO and that of trade unions arises in relation to its complaint registration process. As noted earlier, before an employee even lodges a complaint with the FWO, the FWO generally encourages the employee to raise the issue directly with the employer. In some respects, this preliminary step simply reflects the 'model dispute resolution process' already referred to and the approach commonly taken by unions—that is, to try to resolve the problem at the workplace level.[91]

The problem is that without access to a labour market intermediary, encouraging a complainant to first raise their concerns with their employer has the effect of pushing 'responsibility for the process back onto the parties and into workplaces but without the democratic and collective elements of socialised systems'.[92] While this step is not mandatory, encouraging self-enforcement of rights can affect the accessibility of dispute resolution procedures.[93] Part of the reason that complaints are made after the

[88] Fair Work Ombudsman 'Mediation'. Of the 26,574 complaints finalized by the FWO in 2012–13, more than 65 per cent were resolved through AVR and/or mediation. See Fair Work Ombudsman, *Annual Report 2012–2013*, 24.

[89] See Commonwealth Ombudsman, 'Better Practice to Complaint Handling' (April 2009).

[90] Hilary Astor and Christine Chinkin, *Dispute Resolution in Australia* (LexisNexis Butterworths, 2002) 42.

[91] For example, the first provision of the model dispute resolution clause for modern awards states: 'In the event of a dispute about a matter under this award, or a dispute in relation to the NES, in the first instance the parties must attempt to resolve the matter at the workplace by discussions between the employee or employees concerned and the relevant supervisor. If such discussions do not resolve the dispute, the parties will endeavour to resolve the dispute in a timely manner by discussions between the employee or employees concerned and more senior levels of management as appropriate.'

[92] This has been quite a prominent theme in the UK context, especially under the now defunct Employment Act 2002—which placed a primacy on 'dispute resolution' as a normative ideal. It was an ideal that had predictably damaging effects on worker interests. For further discussion, see Trevor Colling, 'No Claim, No Pain? The Privatisation of Dispute Resolution in Britain' (2004) 25 EID 555, 571–2; Hepple and Morris (n 40).

[93] Cf the situation in Ontario, Canada—for further discussion, see Gellatly et al. 91 (n 63).

employment ends and one of the drivers for seeking out the assistance of a government agency in the first place, is because there may be no active or powerful employee advocates available. Rather than leading to complaints being made by existing employees, it may have the opposite effect—that is, vulnerable workers, particularly those in precarious work, may be more inclined to wait until their employment ends to minimize the risk (and potential loss) associated with employer retaliation.

The accessibility of these processes is also limited by the FWO's general reluctance to accept confidential complaints.[94] Further, in many cases, each affected individual may be required to lodge a separate complaint, even where the alleged contraventions are not necessarily confined to one worker, but rather affect many other employees at the same workplace. While the FWO's policy on these matters may be driven by resourcing pressures and the practical problems of accessing the necessary employment records without revealing the complainant's identity, these difficulties must be balanced against some of the broader problems associated with complaint investigations. In particular, by confining the investigation to the resolution of an individual complaint (or by discouraging confidential complaints), the FWO's ability to identify and address more serious or systemic contraventions is likely to be constrained.[95] While it is true that complaints 'often happen because of poor communication and people not having the right information',[96] sometimes complaints signal the need for a very different compliance and enforcement approach, namely one based on detection and deterrence.

Another potential weakness—and one that is more challenging for the FWO to overcome—is that to lodge a complaint with the regulator, the employee (or their representative) must identify and articulate the relevant claims in the complaint form. This is not a straightforward task in the current regulatory environment. Additional obstacles arise for workers who may have literacy or numeracy difficulties or who are unfamiliar with the Australian workplace relations system.[97] Notwithstanding the FWO's sophisticated education tools and extensive communication activities,[98] to lodge a complaint and actively participate in its resolution, workers must not only possess information about the minimum employment standards, they must also acquire 'knowledge about

[94] While complaints are able to be lodged on a confidential basis or by a third party, such as a union representative, the FW Inspectors generally encourage and sometimes require that the identity of the complainant and the details of the complaint be disclosed to the employer. If the complainant refuses to agree to this request, the FW Inspector may suggest that the worker make the complaint after their employment ends reminding them that they have six years in which to do so. This is very different from the confidential nature of the complaints procedure which can be used in relation to the National Minimum Wage in the UK. See Department of Business Skills and Innovation, 'National Minimum Wage Compliance Strategy' (March 2010).

[95] David Weil, 'A Strategic Approach to Labour Inspection' (2008) 147 International Labour Review 349, 361.

[96] Fair Work Ombudsman, 'Before Mediation' (n 86).

[97] This problem was recently illustrated in the case of *Warrell v Walton* [2013] FCA 291 (4 April 2013), where the applicant—who was described as having 'difficulties with reading and writing and is brain damaged'—mistakenly lodged an unfair dismissal application with the FWO rather than the Commission. As a result of this error, his application was not filed with the Commission until after the relevant statutory time period had expired.

[98] For a recent discussion of the various educational initiatives undertaken by the FWO, see Australian National Audit Office, 'Delivery of Workplace Relations Services by the Office of the Fair Work Ombudsman' (Audit Report No 14, 2012/2013).

how to apply abstract legal rights to their specific conditions [and] the ability to gather evidence to prove their case'.[99]

As noted earlier, the education and empowerment of employees was one of the important regulatory functions performed by trade unions and one of the reasons for improved compliance rates in unionized firms. In comparison, when a worker is seeking to make a complaint to the regulator, a FW Inspector will not generally assist a complainant to identify relevant entitlements, except to refer them to the general Fair Work Infoline. This may be, in part, because of a reluctance to compromise the agency's position of neutrality and independence. Further, adding rather than reducing the claims set out on the complaint form may serve to hinder rather than assist the agency in achieving its objective of a speedy and mutually acceptable resolution. In practical terms, if a worker fails to comprehensively identify and set out all the relevant entitlements in dispute in the complaint form, these entitlements are more likely to be lost. This is because the AVR and mediation processes are generally conducted on the basis of resolving only those issues which are set out in this originating document, particularly now that a copy of this document is provided directly to the employer.[100] For vulnerable workers, without easy access to an employee advocate or specialist advice, the current complaints registration process may fall into the trap identified by Vosko, that is, it requires the 'precariously employed to play the protagonist [and this] works against the exercise of voice'.[101]

One of the important perceived benefits of the FWO's dispute resolution pathway is efficiency. On the one hand, the efficiency of dispute resolution and adjudication processes is an important element of ensuring access to justice. On the other hand, a focus on efficiency may reflect the 'pragmatic rationalities of managerialism'[102] and an overarching desire to reduce agency costs. The significance placed on efficiency is captured by a common mantra applied internally within the FWO, that is: 'justice delayed is justice denied'.[103] The emphasis on this phrase, and its potential to influence the processes and outcomes delivered by the agency, raises a very real question, however, about the extent to which efficiency benefits the complainant and the nature of the 'justice' being achieved when minimum employment entitlements are at risk of being negotiated away through private dispute resolution or mediation.[104] In this respect, Abel cautions that:

> [i]nformal institutions deprive grievants of substantive rights. They are anti-normative and urge parties to compromise; although this appears to be even-handed, it works to the detriment of the party advancing the claim—typically the individual grievant.[105]

[99] Gellatly et al. 91 (n 63).

[100] For example, workers may not realize that they may be entitled to redundancy pay, annual leave loading, or superannuation under the relevant industrial instrument and may not be informed of such once they have lodged a complaint form.

[101] Leah Vosko, '"Rights without Remedies": Enforcing Employment Standards in Ontario by Maximising Voice among Workers in Precarious Jobs' (2013) 50(4) Osgoode Hall Law Journal 845, 870.

[102] Busby and McDermont 181 (n 46).

[103] This statement appears to be derived from comments made by the former British Prime Minister William Gladstone. See United Kingdom House of Commons, Parliamentary Debates, 16 March 1868.

[104] Riley (n 40).

[105] Richard Abel, *The Politics of Informal Justice* (Academic Press, 1982), as cited in Mary Anne Noone, 'ADR, Public Interest Law and Access to Justice: The Need for Vigilance' (2011) 37 Monash ULR 57.

As noted earlier, informal dispute resolution is not a new mechanism for resolving workplace disputes in Australia. Rather, it was a defining characteristic of the conciliation and arbitration system. However, this traditional system of dispute resolution was premised on inherent adversarialism between established, collective interests and the methods were generally compulsory and coercive. These peculiar features served to guard against the issues identified by Abel earlier—for instance, even where unions were acting on behalf of individual members, they were often serving collective interests, and were generally better placed to resist employer pressure to make concessions.

In contrast, the dispute resolution processes adopted by the FWO largely reflects the principles of high trust HRM theory (and the ideological slant of the FW legislation) which tends to emphasize the potential for such processes to lead to cooperative, win-win solutions.[106] While it is true that informal dispute resolution processes, such as conciliation and mediation, can be quick, inexpensive, flexible, and responsive, they also carry some particular risks and 'disputes over the recognition of workplace rights manifest this risk'.[107] For example, in a bid to meet time-based KPIs, FWO staff conducting AVR and/or mediation may be inclined to seek a quick settlement rather than a fair solution which may require calculation of entitlements—a lengthy and time-consuming process. Indeed, on the basis of their research of the conciliation process conducted by ACAS, which is similar in many ways to the dispute resolution pathway adopted by the FWO, Busby and McDermont warn that quantitative performance targets may lead to a situation where:

> [d]isputes become figures; the identities of parties that should be listened to and brought together are lost. The dispute is crystallised into one issue: the negotiation of a financial compensation package which is seen as the most likely route to a positive result. The highly complex legal issues and related remedies disappear from the dispute... [with the result that] managerialism further strengthens a move away from the language of rights, this time towards the language of the possible...[108]

Indeed, this observation raises a more fundamental question about dispute resolution in this context, that is, whether 'flexible' solutions are an appropriate response to the potential contravention of minimum employment standards. The nature of these rights, and the quantification of the loss suffered as a result of these types of contravention, are often fundamentally different from the compromise necessary to resolve bargaining disputes. Riley argues that:

> [i]f rights have been considered to be so important that they require enactment in a statute, it does not make sense to allow parties effectively to contract out of those rights when put under pressure in private and confidential negotiation with the very person who refused to recognise the right.[109]

These risks are perhaps most pronounced, and concerning, where there is a power imbalance between the parties. In this context, power can not only be manifested in outward threats, acts of aggression, force, or pressure, but can also be derived from

[106] Riley 237 (n 40). [107] Riley 237 (n 40). [108] Busby and McDermont 182 (n 46).
[109] Riley (n 37).

superior education, language or literacy skills, from being of a higher social status, or from belonging to a dominant race or ethnic group. Power can also be affected by a person's ability to access critical information, financial resources, or expertise, such as legal advice.[110] More subtly, a power imbalance may arise from the fact that workers may be conditioned to internalize an employer's point of view and therefore not be able to necessarily 'articulate more fundamental challenges to the structural constraints under which they work, are paid and otherwise treated in the workplace'.[111] Indeed, an employee/employer relationship is often seen as a paradigm of inequality.[112]

Adopting a dispute resolution process which is founded on the implicit assumption that all parties are equal and should be treated the same, when this is clearly not the case, may compound underlying inequalities and perpetuate further injustice.[113] Rather than ensuring fair outcomes, mediator neutrality may mean pressures to settle fall more heavily on the party with the most to lose, namely the individual complainant.[114] Questions have been raised about 'whether impartiality/neutrality is possible or even desirable as a goal'[115] in the context of resolving disputes over workplace rights. The potential for these power differentials underlines the importance of identifying, as early and comprehensively as possible, whether the relevant complainant is 'vulnerable' and therefore whether that person should be screened out of AVR and/or mediation or provided with additional assistance in order to more fully and fairly participate in these processes.[116]

The Australian National Mediator Standards, to which the FWO publicly subscribes, recognize that some disputes may not be appropriate for mediation because of potential power issues. It is arguable that this caution applies with equal, if not greater force to AVR given that this preliminary process does not have the same level of procedural safeguards as mediation. For example, the FWO Mediation Charter expressly states that the mediation will be suspended or terminated if 'parties seek to misuse the mediation or reach an agreement that the mediator believes is unconscionable or illegal'.[117]

In addition to introducing clear and transparent criteria about when AVR and/or mediation is (and is not) appropriate, another way in which to address potential power imbalances is to ensure the relevant dispute resolution process is conducted in a procedurally fair manner. For example, it may be desirable in some circumstances for the FW

[110] Bernadine Van Gramberg, *Managing Workplace Conflict* (Federation Press, 2006) 80. Gaze and Hunter 699 (n 53), observe, in the context of discrimination complaints, that individual or small business respondents are often better resourced, often have access to legal advice via an employer organization and, in the case of incorporated companies, can claim the relevant legal fees as a tax deduction.

[111] Bogg and Novitz 335 (n 10).

[112] Anna Chapman, 'Discrimination Complaint-Handling in NSW: The Paradox of Informal Dispute Resolution' (2000) 22 Sydney LR 321, 348.

[113] Chapman 344 (n 112).

[114] Gaze and Hunter 700 (n 53). In addition, Busby and McDermont (n 46) at 179 have found, in their study of ACAS conciliations, that feelings of powerlessness are the result, in part, of the perceived impartiality of the conciliator.

[115] Busby and McDermont 180 (n 46).

[116] In practice, however, it is difficult for FW Inspectors to make a thorough assessment of whether the worker is 'vulnerable' and what assistance may be required to adequately assist the person in resolving the complaint given that the current FWO Complaint Form seeks very limited information about the complainant's background and potential needs.

[117] Fair Work Ombudsman, 'FWO Mediation Charter' (n 86).

Inspector or FWO Mediator to actively encourage participants to obtain independent professional advice or information both before and during AVR and mediation, so that they fully comprehend their legal entitlements and remedial options. For example, as part of the initial registration process, the FWO may consider providing all vulnerable workers with information about unions, generalist or specialist community legal centres, and other relevant legal services, and are referred to these services where appropriate.[118] The FWC's new pro bono representation programme provides an instructive model in this respect.[119] Providing vulnerable workers with greater access to legal representation may mean complainants have a better sense of the strengths (and flaws) of their case, which may not only enable complainants to resist undue settlement pressure,[120] but also work to deter weak cases from proceeding.[121]

A final way to ensure that alternative dispute resolution does not lead to an erosion of legislated workplace rights is to provide parties with ready access to an independent decision-maker for determination of those rights. Indeed, even if one accepts that voluntary resolution is generally preferable to litigation, and cooperation should be favoured over confrontation, it has been argued that:

> an adversarial system, grounded upon a rights based paradigm, in turn founded upon the rule of law, must remain in place, at least in some form, as a viable dispute resolution mechanism... Ultimately the collaborative paradigm falters if not grounded upon an absolute.[122]

Neither the FWC nor the FWO have the authorization or constitutional power to finally determine disputes about the application of minimum employment standards; rather this jurisdiction is exclusively reserved for the courts. Although the FWC is arguably in a stronger position to guard against some of the risks identified earlier. For a start, the dispute resolution processes undertaken in the Commission generally occurs in the 'shadow' of FWC arbitration.[123] Further, in exercising its arbitral powers, the FW Act expressly provides that the Commission must not make a decision that is inconsistent with the

[118] Law Reform Committee, *Inquiry into Alternative Dispute Resolution and Restorative Justice* (Parliament of Victoria, 2009) 87.

[119] This programme is designed to match eligible self-represented applicants appearing before the Commission with pro bono legal services provided by private employment law firms. The pro bono programme was designed to improve access to justice and ensure that self-represented applicants could adequately deal with complex legal issues. See 'New FWC help for self-represented parties', Workplace Express, 6 May 2013.

[120] There is recent case law relating to unfair dismissal applications which suggests that procedural fairness can be compromised by a stronger party having access to legal representation when the weaker party does not. See *Warrell v Walton* [2013] FCA 291 (4 April 2013); *Azzopardi v Serco Sodexo Defence Services Pty Limited* [2013] FWC 3405 (29 May 2013).

[121] Gaze and Hunter 723 (n 53).

[122] J. S. Wolfe, 'Across the Ripple of Time: The Future for Alternative (or, is it "Appropriate?") Dispute Resolution' (2001) 36 Tulsa Law Journal 785, 794, as cited in Julian Gruin, 'The Rule of Law, Adjudication and Hard Cases: The Effect of Alternative Dispute Resolution on the Doctrine of Precedent' (2008) 19 ADRJ 206, 211.

[123] For example, s. 739(4) of the FW Act provides that: '[i]f, in accordance with the [dispute resolution term set out in the enterprise agreement, contract of employment or other written agreement], the parties have agreed that FWC may arbitrate (however described) the dispute, the FWC may do so.' A note to this section adds: 'FWC may also deal with a dispute by mediation or conciliation, or by making a recommendation or expressing an opinion (see subsection 595(2)).' MacDermott and Riley (n 44).

FW Act, a modern award, or an enterprise agreement that applies to the parties.[124] As noted earlier, recourse to the Commission, and the residual threat of arbitration, was an important part of the traditional trade union compliance strategy. This is reflected by the FWO's guide on effective dispute resolution which describes a 'best practice dispute resolution process' as one that provides the Commission 'the necessary discretion and power to ensure settlement of the dispute if the dispute remains unresolved after the early stages of the dispute resolution procedure have been attempted'.[125]

Lack of easy access to an independent decision-maker empowered to determine the relevant rights is one of the challenges facing complainants who participate in assisted voluntary resolution and/or mediation undertaken by the FWO. In this context, the alternative dispute resolution processes are undertaken in the shadow of a formal investigation, the threat of administrative sanctions, and ultimately enforcement litigation through the courts. While the FWO has an option to refer all relevant complaints from existing employees to the FWC for dispute resolution (and possibly arbitration),[126] most complainants will be barred from this course as their employment has already come to an end at the time of making their complaint. For these workers, the lack of access to arbitration, combined with the fear of having to fend for themselves, may mean that complainants engaging in the FWO's dispute resolution processes are potentially under more pressure to surrender their legislated rights in order to avoid the evidentiary problems, costs, uncertainty, and stress which often plague investigations and enforcement litigation.[127]

A final criticism made regarding alternative dispute resolution in the literature is their confidential nature. On the one hand, confidentiality is seen as an essential part of informal dispute resolution processes. A primary attraction for many employers is that the confidential nature of most dispute resolution process minimizes reputational damage and the potential 'spill-over effect' (i.e. where settling one matter elicits similar claims from others.) From the perspective of employees, confidentiality may help preserve their dignity throughout the process. The inherent secrecy of such settlements, however, presents a dilemma for public regulators, such as the FWO.[128] Indeed, a critical benefit of institutional representation and enforcement through union channels is the fact that the benefits arising from successful resolution of an individual complaint are not confined to one member, but generally extend to other workers who may have been similarly affected in the relevant workplace or sector.

While the FWO dispute resolution model may be quick and cost-effective in solving individual complaints, the privatization of the deliberations and outcomes means that these processes may do little in terms of developing and legitimizing norms of

[124] FW Act, s. 739(5).

[125] Fair Work Ombudsman, 'Best Practice Guide 10—Effective Dispute Resolution', <http://www.fairwork.gov.au/BestPracticeGuides/10-Effective-dispute-resolution.pdf> accessed 10 May 2013.

[126] FW Act, s. 739. An added benefit of this approach is that a party who unreasonably refuses to participate in the dispute resolution process before the FWC may be liable for costs if enforcement proceedings are later issued in relation to the same facts: FW Act, s. 570(2)(c).

[127] Arup and Sutherland (n 27); and Therese MacDermott and Joellen Riley, 'ADR and Industrial Tribunals: Innovations and Challenges in Resolving Individual Workplace Grievances' (2012) 38(2) Monash ULR 82, 98.

[128] Riley (n 37).

workplace practice beyond the individual employer.[129] They diminish the diffusion of best practice and fail to develop jurisprudence about how the rights should be interpreted and applied.[130] Private settlements also tend to 'limit the exemplary power of the law; that is the extent to which justice is *seen to be done*'[131] and therefore fail to enhance specific or general deterrence of future contraventions. This can lead to a sense that there is a low probability of detection and sanction which can have the effect of emboldening employers and silencing workers.[132]

One way in which to ease the tension between publicity and confidentiality is for the FWO to publish—in a de-identified form—illustrative case studies and reports on issues which have arisen in the context of AVR or mediation which are in the public interest.[133] Routinely recording the outcomes of dispute resolution is also a useful way for the inspectorate to identify repeat players and map some of the more systemic drivers of non-compliance. This can work to ensure that the FWO's proactive or coercive activities, including workplace audits and litigation, are properly targeted. Tracking and integrating the FWO's various compliance activities is important to ensure that dispute resolution by the agency goes beyond mere customer service and does more than just help the immediate worker involved.[134]

Conclusion

The foundation of employment regulation in Australia has irreversibly shifted in the past century. The overarching changes to the legislative framework, combined with underlying developments in the labour market, have weakened the position and power of trade unions to make and enforce workplace norms on behalf of workers. Regulation of minimum employment standards in Australia and various advanced economies elsewhere can now be described as 'a system which institutionalises conflicts into individual, justiciable disputes'.[135] This has prompted a search for alternative actors that can assist employees to understand, exercise, and enforce their rights in the workplace. Out of this representational vacuum has emerged a somewhat unlikely candidate in Australia, namely the federal labour inspectorate.

Although statutory protections in Australia are relatively comprehensive, the increased vulnerability of workers, and the absence of trade unions in many small enterprises, has meant that many workers are 'unwilling or unable to invoke their statutory protections as individuals'.[136] To address this issue, the FWO has taken various steps to improve employee awareness, knowledge, and capability through targeted campaigns, collaboration with unions and community organizations, and innovative use of old and new media. Arguably, one measure of its success is the fact that the number of employee complaints continues to be substantial. However, the escalation of employee complaints at a time of contracting resourcing creates a separate challenge

[129] Riley (n 37). [130] Riley 240 (n 40). [131] Colling 573 (n 92). [132] Taras 185 (n 51).
[133] Law Reform Committee 84 (n 118). [134] Weil 77 (n 66).
[135] B. Simpson, 'British Labour Relations in the 1980s: Learning to Live with the Law' (1986) 59 Modern Law Review 769, 809.
[136] Gunningham 354 (n 12).

for the FWO—how to preserve precious funding and achieve agency KPIs, while still ensuring that employee voice is protected and promoted.

To meet this challenge, the FWO has recently redesigned its complaint management and dispute resolution processes on the basis of a model of strategic enforcement. The prioritization of complaints makes sense from a resources perspective. The focus on voluntary resolution is also largely consistent with idealized models of regulatory enforcement. Moreover, an emphasis on dispute resolution reflects historical trends in industrial relations and more recent developments in the legal system generally. However, implementation of these new processes is not without risk. In particular, privatizing and individualizing workplace disputes about minimum employment standards can have the effect of masking 'the vastly unequal power dynamics embedded within the relationship between employer and worker'.[137] Making vulnerable workers effectively responsible for securing their own employment rights is especially problematic. It is therefore incumbent upon the FWO to ensure that in encouraging quick and 'mutually acceptable' solutions, it does not compromise procedural or substantive fairness or undermine its broader objective of promoting and enforcing compliance with minimum employment standards.

[137] Gellatly et al. 99 (n 63).

LOCATIONS OF VOICE

13

The Importance of Trade Union Political Voice

Labour Law Meets Constitutional Law

K. D. Ewing

Introduction

Why is a political voice essential for free trade unionism?[1]

The answer seems obvious, particularly in the jurisdictions covered by this volume. These jurisdictions are characterized as being common law jurisdictions where trade unions are regarded as being in restraint of trade and their activities a conspiracy to injure. It is necessary to overcome a hostile legal framework by legislation, which in turn requires a measure of political power to which politicians feel constrained to respond. A political voice is necessary for industrial freedom.

But effective trade unionism needs more than simply freedom from restraint. Trade unions also need the support of the state to facilitate and support their activities. The unique feature of trade unionism is the principle of collective bargaining, the practice of which is unlikely without strong government support. That support may be provided by either administrative or legislative mechanisms, in the absence of which employers are free to eschew collective bargaining in favour of other means of setting terms and conditions of employment.

It continues. Political action is necessary not only to establish the structures within which trade unionism can operate, but also to deal with those questions that are unlikely to be dealt with effectively without some dedicated legislative support. Health and safety, discrimination and equality, and dismissal and redundancy are thought to fall into this category, with legislation again being necessary at least in the latter two cases to counteract strong common law rules that enhance employer power at the point of recruitment and termination (and every stage in between).

Trade unions thus must be engaged politically in order to secure legislation that will enable them to challenge the power of the employer, as well as legislation that will directly regulate the conduct of the employer in its dealings with their members. But trade unions are concerned not only with the needs of members in the workplace. They have an interest in the social wage—the health and well-being of their members, the education of their children, and the circumstances in which they are housed, as well as the conditions of their retirement.

[1] For the classic answer, see Sidney and Beatrice Webb, *Industrial Democracy* (Longmans, 1920 edn) ch. 4. Here I am referring to a political voice for instrumental reasons (on which see the ultra-instrumental account in Irving Richter, *Political Purpose in Trade Unions* (Allen & Unwin, 1973)), without prejudice to the wider question about the nature of trade unions as political organizations, an issue brought into sharp relief for lawyers by the litigation in *ASLEF v United Kingdom* [2007] ECHR 184, (2007) 45 EHRR 34.

All of this means that trade unions must have a political voice, without which they would be unable to function, and without which they would fail properly to represent the interests of (in the United Kingdom) their six million members. Indeed the need for that political voice is now greater as the forces of neoliberalism strip away at trade union industrial power, removing union bargaining activity and leaving workers vulnerable to exploitation. In the modern world that exploitation finds formal expression in low pay and irregular working hours.

It is thus unfortunate—but perhaps inevitable—that trade union political action should now be vulnerable, at a time of greatest need. The purpose of this chapter is to trace the nature of that vulnerability and to show how the erosion of trade union industrial voice and working conditions are paralleled by determined efforts to erode trade union political voice. The re-emergence of common law constitutional values explained in what follows directly reflects the re-emergence of common law contractual values. Indeed, the former appear consciously designed to cement the latter.

The Common Law Constitution

So just as embryonic trade union industrial activity encountered legal problems, so embryonic trade union political activity encountered constitutional problems in the courts and elsewhere. These problems provide a nice illustration for both public lawyers and labour lawyers of how constitutional law serves and sustains economic interests and has to adapt as the balance of economic forces evolves.[2] In the case of trade union political activity, the attack was launched soon after trade unions had secured significant results by political action by means of the Trade Disputes Act 1906, which overturned three major decisions of the House of Lords.[3] Not the least of these was the *Taff Vale* case,[4] in which the railway companies by litigation had established that trade unions were legal persons and liable for the wrongful acts of their servants and agents. This gave rise to a bitter argument subsequently about what Parliament had intended in 1871 and 1876 when it had legalized trade unions,[5] an argument won by Lord Loreburn who drafted and took charge of what was to become the Trade Disputes Act 1906.[6]

Common law constitution and trade unions

The legal and constitutional challenge to trade union political engagement was laid bare in the *Osborne* judgment, where in common with other unions the Amalgamated Society of Railway Servants (ASRS) had introduced a compulsory levy of its members

[2] This is a point made forcefully by others in the past. See Ralph Miliband, *The State in Capitalist Society* (Merlin Press, 1968 reprinted 2009).

[3] Specifically *Taff Vale Railway Co Ltd v Amalgamated Society of Railway Servants* [1901] AC 426, *Quinn v Leathem* [1901] AC 495, and *South Wales Miners' Federation v Glamorgan Coal Co* [1905] AC 239.

[4] *Taff Vale Railway Co Ltd v Amalgamated Society of Railway Servants* (n 3).

[5] On which see the text accompanying n 11.

[6] For an account of Lord Loreburn's constitutional promiscuity, see K. D. Ewing, 'The South Shields Case—Subverting the Trade Disputes Act 1906?' in K. D. Ewing (ed.), *The Right to Strike: From the Trade Disputes Act 1906 to the Trade Union Freedom Bill 2006* (IER, 2007) ch. 5.

for the purposes of parliamentary representation.[7] The money raised in this way was to be used to pay the election expenses of ASRS candidates at an election, and to pay them a salary if elected to Parliament. The rules also provided that parliamentary candidates nominated by the union 'shall sign and accept the conditions of the Labour Party and be subject to their whip', while the Labour Party constitution in turn provided that parliamentary candidates and members 'must accept this constitution; [and] agree to abide by the decisions of the parliamentary party in carrying out the aims of this constitution'.

ASRS Rules

1. For the maintenance of parliamentary representation a fund shall be established by the society. The subscription to be 1s. 1d. per year per member, to be paid quarterly, and forwarded to the head office with the quarter's dues.
2. The objects of the fund shall be
   (a) to provide for representation of railwaymen in the House of Commons as the annual general meeting may from time to time determine. All candidates shall sign and accept the conditions of the Labour Party and be subject to their whip.
   (b) To contribute to the Labour Representation Committee such sums as the executive committee or the annual general meeting may from time to time direct so long as the society remains affiliated to such committee.
3. A separate account shall be kept of this fund, and the money invested in the names of the trustees of the society.... Such funds shall be used for the objects herein stated.
4. Candidates adopted in accordance with object (a) must be and remain bona fide members of the society....
5. In the event of a candidate being selected for a constituency his election expenses shall be defrayed....
6. Should a candidate be elected he shall be paid a salary of 250l. a year and third-class return fare to his constituency so long as he remains a member of Parliament. He shall reside at such place as the executive committee or annual general meeting may consider necessary for the proper discharge of his duties. During the time Parliament is not sitting his services shall be at the disposal of the society, as the executive committee or general secretary may direct, and be subject to the conditions laid down for organizing secretaries.
7. The executive committee shall make suitable provision for the registration of a constituency represented by a member or members, who may be candidates responsible to and paid by this society.

These arrangements were held to be unlawful principally because they were *ultra vires*, in the sense that they went beyond the purposes for which the Trade Union Acts 1871–6 recognized trade unions. But in forming that decision as to legality, it is quite clear that some judges in both the Court of Appeal and the House of Lords were influenced by constitutional arguments that made such arrangements unsustainable. This is a time when constitutional arguments were being deployed more generally against

[7] *Amalgamated Society of Railway Servants v Osborne* [1910] AC 87. For a full account, see Michael J. Klarman, 'Osborne: A Judgment Gone Too Far?' (1988) 103 English Historical Review 2.

trade unions, with a key protagonist being Sir George Farwell who occupied a key role in the three major labour law cases of the decade.[8] Although never a member of the Lords himself, Sir George was nevertheless clearly influential, setting the ball rolling at first instance in *Taff Vale*, where in holding for the plaintiff he did so on the remarkable but revealing basis that trade unions were 'irresponsible bodies with such wide capacity for evil'.[9]

As Sir George was later rightly to acknowledge, it was 'common knowledge' that trade unions were 'dissatisfied' with the *Taff Vale* judgment.[10] However, Parliament's response in the form of the Trade Disputes Act 1906 left Sir George more than 'dissatisfied', expressing himself in strong terms about a measure he clearly thought to violate constitutional principle. In his view, the Act was 'in entire contradiction of those doctrines of personal freedom and equality before the law which have hitherto been its main aim and object'.[11] But although wedded to Dicey-esque notions of the rule of law,[12] as I have written previously on this case Sir George was bound by a more fundamental rule of law, namely the rule of parliamentary sovereignty.[13] This led him to lament that

> [i]t was possible for the courts in former years to defend individual liberty against the aggression of kings and barons, because the defence rested on the law which they administered; it is not possible for the Courts to do when the Legislature alters the law to destroy liberty, for they can only administer the law. The Legislature cannot make evil good, but it can make it not actionable.[14]

A few months later Sir George was present in the *Osborne* appeal, the court at first instance having held that the activity complained of was lawful.[15] Taking the view that trade unions were monsters and that their activity was protected by legislation that violated constitutional principles (in the sense that the Trade Disputes Act 1906 violated the rule of law), it is hardly surprising that he should move to liquidate the trade union political power that had made such legislation possible. Here again the common law provided an opportunity, for just as the industrial activities of trade unions were sustained by legislation that violated constitutional principle, so the means by which that legislation was secured violated constitutional principle, that is to say the principles of the common law constitution. It is true that in developing these arguments Sir George Farwell was not alone. But his arguments on this—albeit secondary—aspect of the decision were the most fully articulated.

This aspect of the case provoked a fierce response from four judges in particular: Fletcher Moulton and Farwell LJJ in the Court of Appeal, and Lords James of Hereford and Shaw of Dunfermline in the House of Lords, several of whom were influenced by the work of Blackstone and Locke, thereby giving us a real insight into the true nature of the common law constitution, the values it reflected, and the power it

[8] See Ewing (n 6). [9] *Taff Vale Railway Co Ltd v Amalgamated Society of Railway Servants* (n 3).
[10] *Conway v Wade* [1908] 2 KB 844. [11] *Conway v Wade* 854 (n 10).
[12] See A. V. Dicey, *Law and Public Opinion in England* (1905, 2nd edn, 1915). [13] Ewing 110 (n 6).
[14] [1908] 2 KB 844, at 856.
[15] *Amalgamated Society of Railway Servants v Osborne* [1909] 1 Ch 163. The first instance judge (Neville J) was bound by the earlier decision in *Steele v South Wales Miners' Federation* [1907] 1 KB 361. The SWMF was not affiliated to the Labour Party at the time (though that ought not to have been relevant in subsequent decisions).

sustained. According to Sir John Fletcher Moulton in the Court of Appeal, the arrangements were not illegal but 'wholly illegal',[16] while for Sir George Farwell they were not unconstitutional, but 'utterly unconstitutional'.[17] There were two reasons for this, one being identified by both Fletcher Moulton and Farwell. This was the concern that the arrangements violated a 'deep seated' legal principle that 'the position of a representative is that of a man who has accepted a trust towards the public, and that any contract, whether for valuable consideration or otherwise, which binds him to exercise that trust in any other way than as on each occasion he conscientiously feels to be best in the public interest is illegal and void'.[18]

This was an argument grounded in the duties of the elected representative. The other objection is the one identified specifically by Sir George Farwell, which related to the duties of the elector, and in particular the individual trade union member obliged by membership of the union to subscribe to political causes to which he or she disapproved. Drawing on Blackstone (who expressed himself against universal suffrage because of the weakness of mind of the working man) rather that 'any statutory provision',[19] Sir George said that '[such] compulsion is utterly opposed to the whole theory of representative government'.[20] According to Blackstone, 'As it is essential to the very being of Parliament that elections should be absolutely free, therefore all undue influences upon the electors are illegal, and strongly prohibited.'[21] Inspired also by Locke,[22] Farwell LJ continued in this vein as follows:

> It is not enough to say that a man's vote has not been influenced. It is also necessary for his freedom that he shall not have been coerced into supporting by money or otherwise the candidate whom he wishes to oppose. It is really ludicrous to suggest that this choice is confined to voting on the day of the poll. A man who throughout desires the return of A., and yet wittingly and willingly assists to return B., by subscription or otherwise, stultifies himself and ranks in point of intelligence with the man who votes at the poll for both of the opposing candidates. To constrain a man to such imbecility is both to injure and to insult him, and is, besides, an injury to the community in preventing freedom of election. Unless freedom of choice is to be reduced to an absurdity

[16] *Amalgamated Society of Railway Servants v Osborne* 188 (n 15).

[17] *Amalgamated Society of Railway Servants v Osborne* 196 (n 15).

[18] *Amalgamated Society of Railway Servants v Osborne* 187 (n 15). (Fletcher Moulton LJ, who had been a Liberal MP until 1906, when he was appointed to the Court of Appeal. He became a peer in 1912.)

[19] *Amalgamated Society of Railway Servants v Osborne* 194 (n 15). It would never have occurred to Blackstone that women might vote.

[20] *Amalgamated Society of Railway Servants v Osborne* (n 15).

[21] Blackstone, *Commentaries on the Laws of England*, vol. 1, 171.

[22] The following passage—which had been cited by Blackstone—was said to be 'applicable' to the *Amalgamated Society of Railway Servants v Osborne* case (n 15): 'Thus to regulate candidates and electors, and new-model the ways of election, what is it but to cut up the government by the roots, and poison the very fountain of public security? For the people, having reserved to themselves the choice of their *representatives,* as the fence to their properties, could do it for no other end, but that they might always be freely chosen, and so chosen, freely act, and advise, as the necessity of the common-wealth, and the public good should, upon examination and mature debate, be judged to require. This, those who give their-votes before they hear the debate, and have weighed the reason on all sides, are not capable of doing. To prepare such an assembly as this, and endeavour to set up the declared abettors of his own will, for the true *representatives* of the people, and the law-makers of the society, is certainly as great a *breach of trust*, and as perfect a declaration of a design to subvert the government, as is possible to be met with' (John Locke, *An Essay of Civil Government* (CUP, 1960 edn), para. 222).

it must extend to the whole conduct of the elector towards the candidate from beginning to end.[23]

Labour Party Rules

I. Affiliation.—(1.) The Labour Party is a federation consisting of trade unions, trade councils, Socialist societies, and local Labour associations....

II. Objects.—(1.) To organize and maintain a Parliamentary Labour Party with its own whips and policy; (2.) to secure the election of candidates for whose candidature an affiliated society has made itself financially responsible, and who have been selected by a regularly convened conference in the constituency.

III. Candidates and Members.—

(1.) Candidates and members must accept this constitution; agree to abide by the decisions of the parliamentary party in carrying out the aims of this constitution; appear before their constituencies under the title of Labour candidates only; abstain strictly from identifying themselves with or promoting the interests of any party not eligible for affiliation; and they must not oppose any candidate recognized by the executive committee of the party.

(2.) Candidates must undertake to join the Parliamentary Labour Party if elected.

IV. Executive.—The executive shall consist of thirteen members, nine representing the trade unions, one the trade councils and local Labour associations, and three the Socialists....

Creating constitutional space for labour

The consequence of the *Osborne* judgment was effectively to find the Labour Party unlawful. In response, the threat to the existence of labour representation was addressed in two ways. The first was the introduction in 1911 of the payment of MPs, a step taken without the need for legislation, but which was necessary to protect Labour parliamentarians from the impact of *Osborne*.[24] The other was the introduction in 1913 of legislation partially to reverse the *Osborne* judgment to permit trade unions to continue to support the Labour Party.[25] In restoring the power of trade unions to engage in such activity, the then Liberal government struck a compromise that was influenced in part by the constitutional reasoning of the courts in *Osborne*, at least so far as it related to the rights of the individual who objected to making a contribution towards his or her union's parliamentary representation.

The Trade Union Act 1913 effectively cemented in statute and made obligatory the practice of the ASRS that was challenged in the *Amalgamated Society of Railway Servants v Osborne*, provided each union could secure the authority of its members in a ballot to adopt political objects, defined in effect so as to include affiliation to the Labour Party and support for Labour MPs. Having secured this authority, trade unions would now be required to establish a separate political fund from which any such objects would

[23] *Amalgamated Society of Railway Servants v Osborne* 195 (n 15).

[24] See William B. Gwyn, *Democracy and the Cost of Politics* (Athlone Press, 1962).

[25] On the enactment of this legislation, see Michael J. Klarman, 'Parliamentary Reversal of the *Osborne* Judgment' (1989) 32 Historical Journal 893.

be supported, and to raise a separate political levy of the members by which the fund would be sustained. Crucially, any member who objected to contributing to the fund would have a right not to do so under mandatory rules of the union, and a right not to suffer disadvantage or disability on account of his or her having contracted out. In addition, union rules were to provide a right of complaint to the Chief Registrar of Friendly Societies for members aggrieved by a union's breach of its political fund rules.[26]

Although this took the unions most of the way home, it did not take them all of the way. There was still the issue addressed by a majority in the Court of Appeal and by a minority in the House of Lords relating to the obligation of the MP sponsored by a trade union to support the Labour Party. Although we might consider it bizarre today that the idea of a political mandate should be questioned in this way, this nevertheless remained an uncertain threat to trade union action. The Labour Party changed its rules to abate the threat,[27] though a number of unions continued to make acceptance of the Labour whip a condition of sponsorship of MPs.[28] While sponsorship was no longer necessary for the MP's salary (now provided by the state), it was valuable in terms of selection as a candidate, the payment of election expenses, and support in the constituency after the election.

This settlement has been remarkably enduring, yet also remarkably vulnerable. It is enduring in the sense that the structure of what was put in place in 1913 remains in legislation to this day,[29] and indeed the legislative settlement of 1913 has influenced the law of a number of other common law jurisdictions, most notably the United States.[30] It is vulnerable, however, in the sense that the form of protection for the individual trade unionist's 'constitutional' rights has been only grudgingly accepted, the compromise broken in 1927 when as part of the reparations for the General Strike in 1926 the then Conservative government changed the rules to require trade unionists to contract in to paying the political levy rather than contract out. Although explicable from a perspective of liberal democracy advanced judicially in *Osborne*, it is less explicable from a perspective of social liberalism in which it was recognized that space had to be found in the political system to accommodate the voice of organized labour.

The law on the political levy was restored in 1946, and with it the financial fortunes of the Labour Party, the income of which from affiliation fees had declined by about a third as a result of the move to 'contracting in' in 1927. This of course raises

[26] For a full account of this regime, see K. D. Ewing, 'The Trade Union Question in British Political Funding' in K. D. Ewing, Jacob Rowbottom, and Joo-Cheong Tham (eds), *The Funding of Political Parties—Where Now?* (Routledge, 2012) ch. 3.

[27] Robert T. McKenzie, *British Political Parties*, 2nd edn (Heinemann, 1964) 473–5.

[28] See K. D. Ewing, *Trade Unions, the Labour Party and the Law—A Study of the Trade Union Act 1913* (Edinburgh University Press, 1983) 32.

[29] Its essential features are to be found in the Trade Union and Labour Relations (Consolidation) Act 1992, Part I, Ch. 6. The Certification Officer has replaced the Chief Registrar of Friendly Societies as the person by whom appeals are heard; and since 1984 the authority of a trade union to operate a political fund must be renewed every 10 years.

[30] See *Brotherhood of Railway Clerks v Allen*, 373 US 113 (1963), where the Trade Union Act 1913 is appended the decision as providing the basis of a solution to the same problem in the United States. The jurisprudence in the United States has evolved greatly since then and predictably has led to a very complex outcome. See most recently in this train of decisions, *Knox v SEIU, Local 1000*, 567 US (2012). But compare the much more permissive approach in Canada: *Lavigne v OPSEU* [1991] 2 SCR 211.

questions—confronted most recently by the US Supreme Court in *Knox v SEIU, Local 1000*[31] —about whether the trade union political voice should be sustained by the contributions of members (and in the United States dues' payers) who are passive rather than active participants. But although this clearly offends some on the liberal side of the house (albeit that it was a Liberal government that produced what became the Trade Union Act 1913), it is an arrangement that is perfectly consistent with a social democratic constitutional model, with an emphasis on collectivism to enhance the power of the relatively weak (industrially and politically) individual, and democracy to legitimate the existence and exercise of that collective power.[32]

In the United Kingdom it is difficult to fault the democratic authority for trade union participation in politics. Since 1984 trade unions have been required to ballot their members every 10 years for authority to continue to operate their political funds.[33] Clearly designed by the Thatcher government to undermine this activity,[34] trade unions have weathered three rounds of political fund ballots and are now in the process of a fourth. No major union has had to wind up its political fund as a result of a political fund ballot. Having voted in the ballot, members are entitled to contract out of paying the political levy, the arrangements for doing so being contained in the rule book of every union, which will normally be uploaded on the union's website, easily available by keying the name of the union into a search engine.[35] And if that is not enough, no one is required as a condition of employment to be a trade union member.

From Liberal to Social Democracy

There are various points of entry to the political process, which follow the structure of government in liberal democracies. These points of entry are progressive, in the sense that they begin with *electoral politics*, in which trade unions seek to mobilize the electoral power of their members to secure the return of certain candidates and parties, and the extraction of pledges and commitments from these candidates and parties. Moving up a gear, trade unions may seek *direct representation in the legislature* as a platform for promoting their members' interest. This may be done either by working through established parties, or by establishing a new party that presents candidates with a trade union background and interest. Moving up another gear, trade unions may also seek to

[31] *Knox v SEIU, Local 1000* (n 30).

[32] Indeed some of those on the liberal side of the house want to go further still. Regarding trade unions as political cash cows, there is a view circulating that trade unions should be required to ask their members to which political party their political levy should be allocated. Trade unions would effectively become collecting agencies for all political parties, including those out to harm them. See Committee on Standards in Public Life, *Political Party Finance*, Cm 8208, 2011, at 110–11. Such a requirement would be difficult to reconcile with Convention rights following *ASLEF v United Kingdom* (n 1). If a trade union cannot be required to take BNP members into membership, on what ground can they be required to raise money for the BNP?

[33] See now Trade Union and Labour Relations (Consolidation) Act 1992, ss. 73–81.

[34] See Frederich A. Hayek, *1980s Unemployment and the Unions* (IEA, 1980) 57: 'A political party in which trade unions have a major constitutional role cannot strike at the source of their power.' See also *Daily Telegraph*, 1 August 2013 reflecting on Cabinet papers released by the National Archives. The headline is enough: 'Thatcher Government wanted Labour's relationship with trade unions "reduced out of all recognition" by 2000'.

[35] See for example, <http://www.unitetheunion.org/uploaded/documents/Rule%20Book%20to%20Dec%20201211-5667.pdf>.

make *contact with the government* in order to influence the government's political priorities and to secure benefits for members. The history of trade union political activity has so far followed this evolutionary and progressive trajectory.

From electoral campaigning to parliamentary representation

The first political method is electoral, whereby citizens and other groups seek to influence the outcome of elections. Trade union electoral activity will be dedicated to securing the return of candidates or parties who are sympathetic to the trade union cause and who will undertake to promote workers' interests. For this tactic to be effective, it is clearly preferable (though perhaps not necessary) that workers should be enfranchised, the votes of individual workers creating a reservoir of political power if effectively mobilized.[36] In the United Kingdom, some trade unionists were enfranchised at a relatively early stage,[37] and this power has been mobilized effectively on a number of occasions since the election in 1868, in the wake of the first franchise extension to cover skilled workers.

The mobilization of electoral power meant that both of the established political parties were constrained to respond to the trade union interest. As a result, trade unions secured important statutory concessions in the form of the Trade Union Act 1871 and the Conspiracy and Protection of Property Act 1875, the first providing protection from the common law doctrine of restraint of trade, and the second providing protection from criminal liability for industrial action.[38] Indeed in the immediate aftermath of franchise reform in 1867 (which brought in a number though by no means all trade unionists), it appears that trade unions used their new electoral power opportunistically, with Pelling recording that trade unionists presented a number of 'Test Questions' to parliamentary candidates in 1874 and in some cases encouraged their members to vote Conservative as a result.[39]

But perhaps the best known example of electoral mobilization to secure political results related to the Trade Disputes Act 1906, with the TUC Parliamentary Committee winning an agreement with the Liberals to reverse the *Taff Vale* decision (holding trade unions vicariously liable for the tortious acts of their servants and agents), and securing pledges from Liberal candidates (some of whom were miners) to support the reversal of the latter decision. Quite whether the test question and pledges would be as effective today from non-Labour candidates is open to question. Electoral mobilization is based on a capacity to deliver, and while workers in the nineteenth century may have had a sufficiently common identity to respond to the advice of their union on the matter of union freedom, it is not clear if in the modern world workers would be similarly motivated. Nor indeed in the more highly disciplined party system would candidates be able to give meaningful pledges of this kind.

[36] On electoral power without the franchise, see Henry Pelling, *A History of British Trade Unionism*, 3rd edn (Macmillan, 1976) 62–3.

[37] Beginning with the Representation of the People Act 1867, on the significance of which see George D. H. Cole, *British Working Class Politics 1832–1914* (Labour Book Service, 1941) 29.

[38] See Pelling 70–6 (n 36).

[39] Pelling 74 (n 36).

In any event, in revealing the virtues of an electoral activity as a means of expressing political voice, John Saville makes clear that the experience of enacting the 1906 Act also laid bare its limitations.[40] It is one thing to secure electoral pledges and even legislation on the back of these pledges. But without effective parliamentary representation, these pledges can be diminished in the implementation. In the aftermath of an election, the pledges enter a political process from which will emerge a synthesis reflecting the views of different interests. On trade union rights, the pledges will inevitably be mediated by the views of civil servants and employers whose interest will be well represented in government, and elsewhere in the political process. The important lesson of the parliamentary proceedings leading to the Trade Disputes Act 1906 was that trade unions were able skilfully to deploy representation in Parliament to take advantage of a divided government to secure maximum protection possible.[41]

Along with the mobilization of electoral power, parliamentary activity thus allows for the mobilization of parliamentary power where trade unions individually or collectively have some form of parliamentary representation. Again it is probably not essential to parliamentary engagement that there is direct parliamentary representation. It is the case that many interests seeking to change the law do so without formal representation in Parliament. In the nineteenth century non-enfranchised and non-represented workers developed the skill of parliamentary lobbying and worked to influence the proceedings of parliamentary committees, submitting evidence and appearing as witnesses.[42] On the other hand, however, it was felt deeply by trade unionists throughout the nineteenth century that direct parliamentary representation was essential in order to convey the 'disadvantages, difficulties, and hardships' endured by the 'working man'.[43]

The first trade unionists elected to Parliament (Thomas Burt and Alexander McDonald) were miners' leaders who were elected as Liberals in 1874.[44] The number of trade unionists has swollen since, and the trade union interest has been represented in Parliament by the Trade Union Group of Labour MPs, which historically has been a powerful group of Labour backbenchers.[45] This presence not only enabled the views of trade union members to be represented, but it also provides a residue of parliamentary power that can be deployed politically to advance the interest of trade union members. While the experience of the Trade Disputes Act 1906 shows that this parliamentary power can be mobilized in a positive manner to promote legislative proposals, more recent experience (such as the debate over *In Place of Strife* in 1969) reveals that it is just as likely to be mobilized in a defensive manner to modify—or in extreme cases block—an anti-union government initiative.[46]

[40] John Saville, 'The Trade Disputes Act of 1906', in Ewing ch. 4 (n 6).
[41] Saville (n 40).
[42] See R. Page Arnot, *The Miners—A History of the Miners' Federation of Great Britain, 1889–1910* (George Allen & Unwin Ltd, 1949).
[43] Page Arnot 292 (n 42).
[44] Page Arnot 289–90 (n 42).
[45] For a historical account, see William D. Muller, *The Kept Men? The First Century of Trade Union Representation in the British House of Commons, 1874–1975* (Hassocks, 1977).
[46] See Lewis Minkin, *The Contentious Alliance: Trade Unions and the Labour Party* (Edinburgh University Press, 1991). *In Place of Strife*, Cmnd 3888, 1969, was a White Paper issued by the Labour government in 1969 proposing a number of controls on trade union freedoms. It was successfully resisted by the trade unions, the Parliamentary Labour Party playing a key part in the process. See Peter Jenkins, *The Battle of Downing Street* (Knight, 1970). A more recent—and poignant—example is the mobilization of trade union

From parliamentary representation to a government focus

Although there are clearly opportunities to be had in undertaking parliamentary activity, as a political strategy it too is very limited. Without a sympathetic government to advance the cause, parliamentarians have little power to initiate change. It is true that they may initiate private members' legislation, as when John McDonnell MP introduced the Lawful Industrial Action (Minor Errors) Bill 2010.[47] But without government support, measures of this kind have no chance of success in a hostile parliamentary environment.[48] An effective political voice needs a government focus, that is to say a focus designed to influence the policy and behaviour of government. Plainly, both electoral and parliamentary activity respectively contribute to such a focus, and plainly both overlap with a government focus. But they are not enough.

A government focus may take two forms, the first being to secure the election of a political party that is sustained by trade unions and which will be expected to represent the interests of trade unions and their members in government. This requires workers to identify heavily with workplace questions when exercising their rights as citizens, and to do so in large enough numbers. Given the nature of electoral politics in Westminster systems with single member constituencies, it is unlikely that any political party could secure government on its own, when the party in question is composed only of trade unions and trade union members. As a result it is generally necessary for a trade union government strategy of this kind to be exercised through a political party which is a coalition (sometimes a very uneasy coalition) of trade unions and other interests, as is typically the case of Labour parties in common law jurisdictions.

But although the trade union influence is diluted in such arrangements, they nevertheless provide opportunities for trade union representation at Cabinet and other senior levels within government. During the war-time Coalition, Attlee was instrumental in bringing Ernest Bevin into government as Minister of Labour. It was only when Bevin was appointed Foreign Secretary in the post-war Labour government that he resigned as General Secretary of the TGWU. Indeed, such was the significance of the TGWU that Bevin was not the only General Secretary to be appointed to Cabinet level, with Harold Wilson inviting Frank Cousins to join his Cabinet in 1964, a move that was the political equivalent of an appointment from the Bar to the Supreme Court. The significance of this appointment was not lost on a man who was later to succeed Cousins, with Jack Jones stressing 'the importance of having an authentic trade union voice inside the Cabinet'.[49]

MPs (among others) to oppose party funding reforms proposed by Sir Hayden Phillips in 2007. See Hayden Phillips, *Strengthening Democracy: Fair and Sustainable Funding of Political Parties* (HMSO, 2007). The story of that campaign has yet to be written.

[47] HC Debs, 22 October 2010, col 1211.

[48] Thus, although topping the private members' ballot, the Bill was talked out by filibustering on the part of Tory backbenchers.

[49] Jack Jones, *Union Man: An Autobiography*, 2nd edn (Warren and Pell, 2008) 160. Jones also highlights the power senior trade unionists had to influence other appointments: for example Michael Foot as Secretary of State for Employment.

The other form that a government focus may take is one in which trade unions engage directly with the government of the day, regardless of its political composition. For trade unions to engage in political action of this kind, however, it is essential that they have power, which is usually power of an economic nature that governments need to manage. Thus it was a particular feature of western democracies in the post-war era that constitutional space was made for trade unions (and in some cases employers) communicating with government as social partners. To this end trade unions would be engaged on matters of economic management and while much of the dialogue was informal, formal structures were also put in place.[50] These include the National Economic Development Council (established by a Conservative government), a development of perhaps greater symbolic than political importance.[51]

Although by no means unprecedented (trade unions had been involved in economic management during the First World War), trade union involvement in economic management was thus institutionalized after 1945. One of the best examples of trade union engagement at this level was the Wage Restraint Bargain of 1948.[52] This is a measure celebrated by the Harvard historian Samuel Beer. According to him the bargain was reached at a time of 'intimate symbiosis between the unions and the Labour party',[53] and was 'remarkable as much for the way in which it was reached as for its contents and results'.[54] This was a *tripartite* agreement (involving government, business, and the TUC); also according to Beer:

> The bargain was not itself embodied in any legislative instrument such as a statute or statutory order. Yet it achieved a regulation of an important aspect of the British economy that no such legislative instrument by itself could have done. Indeed, one may think of it as a kind of extra-governmental regulation.[55]

The culmination of this particular government focus was the Social Contract of 1974, which was a *bilateral* agreement between the then Labour government and the TUC on economic policy.[56] In procedural terms (without any judgment as to substance), this was perhaps the apotheosis of a trade union government focus, and the apotheosis of trade union political influence. The bulk of the British trade union movement was formally affiliated to the Labour Party, in the sense that the largest trade unions were members of the party (and as such involved in the making of party policy). Their party was now in government and it was with the leadership of this party that they were now negotiating terms that would see concessions being given on pay restraint in return for legislation on trade union and workers' rights, as well as beneficial policies on other matters.[57] As the

[50] Trade unions were not alone in securing such access, which gave rise to a number of sympathetic accounts of pressure group politics in the US and the UK as being consistent with liberal democratic principles.

[51] See Jones 307 (n 49) ('a useful talking shop').

[52] For details, see Samuel H. Beer, *Modern British Politics* (Faber, 1965) 205–7. See also Victor L. Allen, *Trade Union and Government* (Longmans, 1960) 286.

[53] Kenneth O. Morgan, *Labour in Power 1945–1951* (OUP, 1984) 79.

[54] Beer 204 (n 52).

[55] Beer 205 (n 52).

[56] To the extent that it was tripartite, it was the Labour party and not the CBI that was the third party.

[57] The legislative benefits—in the Trade Union and Labour Relations Act 1974 and the Employment Protection Act 1975—were at the time considerable, and would combine greatly to enhance worker voice industrially.

experience of the Social Contract perhaps reveals, the two approaches to a government focus for political activity described here are not mutually exclusive, with the impact of the second being strengthened by the effective deployment of the first.

Levels of Political Engagement—The European Union

The main focus of this chapter is with trade union political activity at national level. As well as national Parliaments and national governments, however, trade union political activity also requires parallel forms of engagement at sub-national levels of government, whether it be state or devolved governments and legislatures, or local government. All are important for a coherent trade union political strategy.

So too are forms of engagement with supra-national levels of government, most notably the EU. The evolution of the EU has provided opportunities for effective political engagement at electoral, legislative and governmental levels, both to expand workers' rights and now—in a different economic and political climate—to defend them.

An interesting feature of the EU as it has evolved is the extent to which it has entrenched a legislative and governmental role in the TFEU for trade unions and employers by the process of social dialogue, as a means of creating labour standards on a pan-European basis, a procedure which has produced a number of important outcomes (such as parental leave) (TFEU, Arts 154, 155).

Perhaps inevitably, this procedure has been challenged, essentially on the ground of its lack of democratic legitimacy. In sharp contrast to the (extra-judicial) approach taken to such arguments in the United Kingdom, these concerns were rebuffed judicially in the context of the EU.[58] The long slow death of this EU constitutional procedure will thus be for economic rather than constitutional reasons.

The Fresh Challenge of Liberalism

Although social democratic theorists saw social democracy as the progressive evolution of liberal democracy, these developments nevertheless revealed a tension between the two. Social democracy is based on the collective representation of individuals through organizations, and on the acceptance of the legitimacy of their collective power. Liberal democracy is blind to the imbalance of economic resources and insists on the political representation of individuals in an individual capacity, emphasizing the personal autonomy of the individual and the atomization of collective power. Trade union political voice constantly has been trapped by this tension, which re-emerged during the Social Contract with an appeal to liberal constitutional values by the latter's critics, reflecting the depth of liberalism's economic roots.[59] The United Kingdom may not have a written constitution; but it does have unshakeable constitutional principles that are as effective a restraint on political evolution as the formal constitutional structures of other western democracies.

[58] See Brian Bercusson, 'Democratic Legitimacy and European Labour Law' (1999) 28 Industrial Law Journal (ILJ) 153.

[59] On varieties of liberalism, see Alan L Bogg, 'New Labour, Trade Unions, and the Liberal State' (2009) 20 King's Law Journal 403.

Corporatist structures—constitutional principle

An early casualty of the liberal revival has been trade union participation in the structures of government. The second of the forms of government focus referred to earlier has largely perished (at least in the United Kingdom), in the sense that there is now no meaningful engagement with government on economic questions. It is true that under the Blair and Brown governments a limited form of tri-partism took place. But this was very discrete (relating for example to the implementation of EU Directives), and did not appear seriously to address macro-economic questions. The principal reason for this was that government economic policy since the late 1970s has largely contained trade unions, so that in discussions with government trade unions had little collective institutional power that needed to be controlled.

The revival of economic liberalism was accompanied by—and was in part justified by—a revival of liberal constitutionalism.[60] The two are closely intertwined: liberal constitutionalism needs different structures than social democratic constitutionalism. The former simultaneously provides a demand for certain forms of economic arrangement and the containment of economic actors, while also providing the structures to sustain these arrangements and means to contain these actors. As a result, the values of collective representation and voice, which were a feature of the social democratic structures and practices developed in the post-war period, were displaced by a renewed emphasis on the principles that had inspired some of the judges who sat in the *Osborne* case.

The Social Contract was thus vulnerable on two fronts, the first relating to a variation of Sir George Farwell's anxiety about representative government. This concern was highlighted forcefully in the pages of *The Times*, at a time when *The Times* was widely respected and influential than it is today. The response to the budget of 1976 provides a good example of this concern, with *The Times* feigning alarm less by its content than by the process by which it was determined:

> For the first time the Budget has ceased to be an act of Government, dependent for its authority only upon Parliament, and has become a matter of negotiation between the Government and an outside body representative of only one section of the community, an important minority, but a minority nevertheless. This constitutional innovation must tend to increase the authority and prestige of the TUC and correspondingly to reduce the authority and prestige of the Government and of the House of Commons.[61]

It was suggested in the same column that the Budget presented by Denis Healey was conditional on negotiations with the TUC on collective bargaining outcomes. This led *The Times* to thunder that 'there is no country in which the Budget is announced in a

[60] For an early consideration of this question, see K. D. Ewing, 'Trade Unions and the Constitution: The Impact of the New Conservatives' in Cosmo Graham and Tony Prosser (eds), *Waiving the Rules—The Constitution under Thatcherism* (Open University Press, 1988) ch. 8. See also K. D. Ewing, 'The Politics of the British Constitution' [2000] PL 405, from which much of this account draws freely.

[61] *The Times*, 7 April 1976.

conditional form subject to negotiations with the trade unions'; to exclaim that 'the TUC by virtue of their power had become a second House of Parliament, a second Chamber with power and authority the House of Lords has long since lost'; and wryly to observe that while 'governments governed by armies are common', 'governments governed by trade unions are a rarity'.[62] There then followed an attack on this 'corporate constitution':

> In any event this corporate constitution would be inferior to the old free constitution of Britain, inferior because it is less free and less democratic. A Chancellor of the Exchequer ought to take into account the views and interests of all sections of society; he ought to be free to make his own decisions in the light of the whole national interest and not of any limited part of it. Mr Healey is the representative of every adult voter in the country because we all had an opportunity to vote for a member of Parliament at the last General Election.... We may or may not approve of what he does, but he is the result of our democratic choice. Mr Len Murray, Jack Jones and even that admirable figure Mr Tom Jackson are simply the representatives of their members and of nobody else. To have one's taxes fixed by Mr Healey may be an agony, but to have them fixed by Mr Len Murray is an insult.[63]

But just as an appeal to the principles of representative government was used to justify the dismantling of the structures of government into which trade unions had drawn themselves, the same appeal was made to attack the fruits of these processes. One of the outcomes of the Social Contract negotiated with the TUC was the repeal of the Industrial Relations Act 1971, and its replacement with the Trade Union and Labour Relations Act 1974 and the Employment Protection Act 1975. The effect of these latter measures was to impose new demands on employers to recognize trade unions for the purposes of collective bargaining, require individuals to join a trade union (on pain of dismissal) where a union membership agreement was concluded between the employer and the trade union, and restore the protection of trade unions from liability in tort in the event of unprotected industrial action.

These measures (which would sustain trade union strength and legitimacy as partners in the Social Contract) were a clear affront to common law principles and led to renewed conflict between the trade unions and the courts, in which the legislation was seriously diminished.[64] Recalling the judgments of Sir George Farwell in the early years of the twentieth century, Lord Denning announced in a public lecture on the eve of the general election in 1979 that 'the greatest threat to the rule of law is posed by big trade unions', adding for good measure that 'one of the biggest problems is how to restrain the abuse or misuse of their power'.[65] Here he was simply the ventriloquist's dummy, with more robustly Farwellian views having been expressed by Hayek and his disciples in the

[62] *The Times*, 7 April 1976. [63] *The Times*, 7 April 1976.

[64] For an account of this conflict, see Lord Wedderburn, 'Industrial Relations and the Courts' (1980) 9 ILJ 65.

[65] Lord Denning, *The Closing Chapter* (OUP, 1983) 321. Lord Denning had earlier expressed the view that he had wished the courts had had the power to refuse to apply to legislation while his battle raged with the trade unions. See Lord Denning, *What Next in the Law?* (OUP, 1982).

right wing think tanks.[66] Having previously lamented 'a pronounced decline in the rule of law in the field of labor',[67] Hayek was later to reflect that

> [s]o long as general opinion makes it politically impossible to deprive the trade unions of their coercive powers, an economic recovery of Great Britain is also impossible.[68]

The Trojan Horse

Apart from the strength of orthodox principle, the other way liberal constitutionalism now challenges trade union political action is to be found in party funding laws. This is an area of the law that offers a menu of regulatory options for policy makers, designed to reduce the risk of corruption on the one hand and unfair electoral competition on the other.[69] As such it is a discipline which cannot be ideologically neutral, and it is one which is moved in part by the same concerns that were displayed in the judgments of Sir John Fletcher Moulton and Sir George Farwell in *Osborne*, and in particular their concerns about representative government and the role of the representative, for which today read political party. Indeed to the extent that the concern is that by large donations corporations and others are able to buy favours from government, it is difficult to argue with those who contend that such conduct should be contained.

One way of dealing with these concerns is to impose a cap on the amount of money that any individual or corporation may receive from any donor in a defined period, usually a year. The gap in the income of the political parties that this inevitably causes is then usually filled by the taxpayer in the form of state funding. This is thought to be 'clean' money. Such arrangements have obvious dangers for trade union-based political parties, it being impossible to make a case that trade unions should be excluded from the regulatory regime completely, if at all. If, however, the cap was to apply to trade unions it would mean that the principle whereby trade unions affiliate to a political party based on the size of the union would be fatally undermined and that the social democratic structure of trade union-based political parties would be in effect 'utterly illegal'.

This in fact has been the impact of party funding reforms in a number of common law jurisdictions, with New South Wales being the most recent prominent example. It is, however, possible to legislate in a way that respects the origins and diversity of party structure and organization without eliminating trade union-based parties on the altar of the liberal constitution. This can be done by lowering the regulatory ambitions by controlling donations through the medium of transparency and spending controls (the former supposing that publicity will act as a self-restraint, the latter supposedly reducing the demand for large donations). But although this is the British model (a social

[66] See Frederich A. Hayek, *Trade Unions—The Biggest Obstacle* (IEA, 1980), and Hayek (n 34). Also Charles G. Hanson, *Taming the Trade Unions* (IEA, 1991), and Frederich A. Hayek, *Economic Freedom and Representative Government* (IEA, 1973).

[67] Frederich A. Hayek, *The Constitution of Liberty* (Routledge, 1960) ch. 18: trade unions had become 'uniquely privileged institutions to which the general rules of law do not apply'.

[68] Hayek 64 (n 34).

[69] For a full account, see K. D. Ewing, *The Cost of Democracy—Party Funding in Modern British Politics* (Hart, 2007) ch. 2.

democratic model of party funding regulation consciously designed to accommodate the Labour party's structure),[70] it is one that is increasingly under pressure and will almost certainly change in the near future.

Right of centre parties have been the main engine of change in those jurisdictions that so far have yielded to the liberal democratic model of party funding regulation. Now in the United Kingdom, it is the Labour Party itself that presents a threat to the traditional model of a trade union political response centred on a political party as the focus of its legislative and governmental engagement. Here the desire of the Labour Party leader—Ed Miliband—is not to use legislation to alter the relationship between the trade unions and the Labour Party, but to do so by a process of internal party reform in which the position of the individual trade unionist will be enhanced at the expense of the collective voice of the union.[71] This is a revealing move that draws back to one of the limbs of liberal constitutionalism emphasized by Sir George Farwell in his defence of the individual as the only legitimate agent in liberal democracy.

This initiative by the Labour leader is the latest development in what has been a long campaign on the part of one wing of Labour's historic but fragile coalition to reduce the trade union voice in Labour Party affairs. Historians will no doubt provide a full explanation in the fullness of time. For present purposes, however, it can at least be said that this conflation of economic and political liberalism in the Labour Party is a mark of the loss of trade union influence and voice industrially. The Labour Party can continue with the historic process of diminishing the role of trade unions within its ranks not only because it is electorally expedient to do so, but also because for Labour it is ideologically appropriate to do so. It is thus by no means clear why senior trade unionists (albeit a small minority) should agree that there is some 'moral justification' in the Labour Party leadership's plan to require trade unions to affiliate to the Labour Party only those individuals who have expressed a desire to be associated with Labour.[72]

Although it is protested that these proposed reforms are not designed to alter the historic nature of the collective relationship between Labour and the trade unions, it is difficult to see how that relationship could survive. To the extent that there is trade union support for these proposals, it can only be on a basis (informed or otherwise) that anticipates a different political voice for trade unions, one based on working to ensure that a number of sympathetic MPs are elected to Parliament rather than one based on securing influence in a party of government. This may be characterized as a move back to a legislative rather than a governmental political strategy, one that accepts a diminished political voice to reflect a diminished industrial voice. But as the ghost of Sir George Farwell

[70] See Political Parties, Elections and Referendums Act 2000. This was based largely on Committee on Standards in Public Life, *The Funding of Political Parties in the United Kingdom: Report*, Cm 4057–1, 1998. The report's recommendations were consistent with the proposals of the Labour Party on key questions. See App V.

[71] In a speech on 9 July 2013, the Leader of the Labour Party said: 'We do not need to change that law on the right of Trade Unions to have political funds. But I do want to change the way individual Trade Unionists are affiliated to the Labour Party through these funds. At the moment, they are often affiliated automatically. I do not want any individual to be paying money to the Labour Party in affiliation fees unless they have deliberately chosen to do so. Individual Trade Union members should choose to join Labour through the affiliation fee, not be automatically affiliated'. See <http://www.labour.org.uk/one-nation-politics-speech>.

[72] *BBC News*, 13 July 2013.

reminds us, that diminished voice is not necessarily a more legitimate one if the battle of morality is to be fought on the impoverished terrain of the liberal constitution.

Electoral Voice

There is a sense that we are moving back to where we started. Economic and political liberalism is trumps; social democracy has been trumped, and with it the social democratic institutions it sustained have been removed or are in the process of being removed. But there is one difference between now and the early efforts of trade unionism to secure a political voice, in the sense that steps have now been taken to diminish the trade union voice further by attacking the capacity of trade unions to mount an effective electoral campaign, alongside the attacks on their capacity to mount effective legislative or government focused activities.

Silencing the electoral voice

Briefly, these restraints on electoral activity are to be found in controversial legislation enacted in 2014, which introduces tight spending limits on trade union electoral activity. It is true that hitherto trade unions did not engage actively as 'third parties' in elections, with the exception of UNISON, which has two political funds—following the merger of three trade unions with two different political traditions.[73] UNISON raises substantial funds for its general political fund (GPF), which—unlike the affiliated political fund (APF)—is used for independent campaign expenditure rather than affiliation fees or donations to the Labour Party.

Since the large-scale party funding reforms in 2000, such expenditure by trade unions has been capped at just under £1 million nationally *in the year immediately before the general election* (with similar caps applying to other elections).[74] The cap represented 5 per cent of the money the largest political parties are permitted to spend and did not seriously challenge the practices of any electoral participant, striking a fair balance between the need to respect freedom of expression guarantees in the ECHR, Art 10 and the need to promote a level playing field between candidates, parties, and others in an election.

In an extremely controversial move, however, changes introduced by the Coalition government in 2014 seek to contain latent trade union electoral power.[75] Thus the amount of permitted 'controlled expenditure' is cut so that trade unions will be free to spend no more than £390,000 nationally for electoral purposes.[76] Where, however, the 'controlled expenditure' is 'targeted' in support of a particular party (or may

[73] Two of the unions (COHSE and NUPE) had political funds and were affiliated to the Labour Party; the other (NALGO) had a political fund but was not affiliated to the Labour Party, using its political fund principally for election campaign purposes only.

[74] Political Parties, Elections and Referendums Act 2000, s. 94, Sch. 10.

[75] Transparency of Lobbying, Non-party Campaigning and Trade Union Administration Act 2014, Part II. For the response of the Joint Committee on Human Rights to the Bill, see HL Paper 61/ HC 755 (2012–13).

[76] Transparency of Lobbying, Non-party Campaigning and Trade Union Administration Act 2014, Part II.

reasonably be regarded as intended to support that party), the limit is slashed to £39,000 nationally.[77]

Under these proposals, a union will be able to spend more of its 'controlled expenditure' as 'targeted expenditure', but only if it secure the agreement of the Labour Party.[78] However, 'targeted expenditure' by a union approved by the Labour Party will count towards the party's permitted election campaign expenditure, as well as towards the union's permitted 'controlled expenditure'.[79] At the same time, trade union expenditure will be 'sliced and diced', in the sense that a union will be unable to spend no more than £9,000 controlled or targeted expenditure in a single constituency.[80]

It may be of course that some aspects of this new legislation will violate human rights principles. There is reason to believe that a legal challenge on this ground may have some prospect of success, notwithstanding a recent decision of the ECtHR in which it was held that a ban on political advertising did not violate the right to freedom of expression.[81] This, however, does not affect the promising line of inquiry opened up by the earlier decision in the *Bowman* case,[82] where the ECtHR held that a tight restriction on third party election spending at constituency level violated freedom of expression, partly on the basis that there were no comparable controls on the press.[83]

It may also be that—following the enactment and implementation of this legislation—trade unions will adapt to the new regime and make fuller use of those forms of action that remain uncontrolled (such as direct communications with their 6 million members).[84] Nevertheless, at a time when efforts are being made to push them out of the Labour Party, the introduction of the Transparency of Lobbying etc Act 2014 will greatly diminish trade union capacity to engage with the electorate in the 12 months before an election. The retreat along three political fronts (government, legislative, and electoral) will be complete, in a manner that invites comparisons with the restrictions introduced by *Osborne*.[85]

[77] Transparency of Lobbying Act, Part II (n 76).
[78] Transparency of Lobbying Act, Part II (n 76).
[79] Transparency of Lobbying Act, Part II (n 76).
[80] Transparency of Lobbying Act, Part II (n 76).
[81] *Animal Defenders International v United Kingdom* [2013] ECHR 362(GC), (2013) 57 EHRR 21. See J. Rowbottom, 'A surprise ruling? Strasbourg upholds the ban on paid political ads on TV and Radio', *UK Const L Blog*, 22 April 2013 (<http://ukconstitutionallaw.org>).
[82] *Bowman v United Kingdom* [1998] ECHR 4, (1998) 26 EHRR 1. For an account of the implications of this decision, see Committee on Standards in Public Life, *The Funding of Political Parties in the United Kingdom: Report*, Cm 4057-I, 1998.
[83] *Bowman v UK* para. 47 (n 82). Expenditure by newspaper companies is expressly excluded from the definition of 'controlled expenditure'.
[84] Such communications are expressly excluded: Transparency of Lobbying, etc Act 2014, amending the Political Parties, Elections and Referendums Act 2000, by inserting a new Sch. 8A.
[85] The comparison is not implausible. Ewing 217 (n 28) refers to advice by the Lord Chancellor to the Prime Minister after *Osborne* that a trade union would not be allowed to subscribe to a free trade campaign or one for reform of the process by which electors were registered to vote, or to spend money on a Hyde Park demonstration. Despite his constitutional promiscuity, the Lord Chancellor (Loreburn) did not sit in *Osborne*, as he had earlier in *Conway v Wade* [1909] AC 606.

Does the Labour Party Link Still Matter?

It is unlikely that trade unions will ever recover the political influence they had in the 1970s. But still they need political influence. Should they be relaxed about the proposed Miliband reforms and reduce their role within the Labour Party? One option would be to accept a change in the relationship with the Labour Party and to focus on the government in power. But that can only happen when there is reason for the government to deal with trade unions. This may arise where trade unions have industrial power that needs to be managed, or where there are shared political values that give trade unions a legitimate political voice. Neither is the case in the United Kingdom.

In terms of a government strategy, a relationship with a political party with the capacity to form the government is the only alternative. Again the influence that trade unions have within that party will depend in large measure on their power and/or the existence of shared values. At a time when the social democratic consensus has fractured, it is the former rather than the latter that will underpin that relationship. Because of weak industrial power and declining memberships, however, trade unions need to rely on political leverage to underpin the relationship. That comes down to the capacity to mobilize members electorally and the capacity to pay the bills. Hence the big push from others for state funding of political parties.

In the absence of any alternative government strategy, it would be bold if not reckless for trade unions to accept a further dilution of their role and influence in the Labour Party. Although there are widespread concerns about the arrangements not working well and about trade unions 'not getting enough' from the relationship, it may be short-sighted and self-defeating to accept a change that will lead to the rewriting of a party constitution that provides a structured framework for representation at an institutional level. It will never be replaced, and once lost it will never be recovered. The diminished outcomes for trade unions within this constitutional arrangement are a reflection not only of reduced industrial power but also of determined and persistent political opponents.

New lines of defence?

As a result of these latter changes, it is unlikely that we will ever see in Britain the type of campaign for workers' rights mounted by the ACTU to oust John Howard's government in Australia in 2007.[86] It looked unlikely that we would ever see that campaign repeated in Australia, following legislation recently introduced by the Liberals in New South Wales,[87] which may well have become a model for other governments (in Australia and elsewhere) to follow. The legislation in question read not unlike the legislation introduced by the UK's Coalition government referred to earlier, and indeed may well have been an inspiration for the latter.

Under the NSW legislation, only individuals could make contributions to political parties, in what looks like a tight embrace of the kind of constitutionalism on display in *Osborne*. The Explanatory Notes made clear that affiliation or membership fees by trade unions were now unlawful.[88] Trade unions could, however, continue to be affiliated to

[86] For an account of the campaign, see Bradon Ellem, 'Peak Union Campaigning: Fighting for Rights at Work in Australia' (2013) 51 British Journal of Industrial Relations 564.

[87] Election Funding, Expenditure and Disclosures Amendment Act 2012 (NSW).

[88] Election Funding, Expenditure and Disclosures Amendment Bill 2011, *Explanatory Note*: 'As a result of the amendments, it will be unlawful for a corporation or other entity (including an industrial organisation) to pay annual or other subscriptions to a party for affiliation with the party.'

the Australian Labor Party;[89] but if they did remain affiliated to the party any union campaign expenditure would be treated as expenditure by the party, whether or not the party had approved the expenditure, and whether or not it agreed with it.[90]

As in the United Kingdom, this attempt to silence the trade union political voice was most certainly being done for reasons of naked political opportunism, rather than for any principled constitutional reason. This is not to say that the political reasons of the NSW Liberals and the Labour Party leadership in the UK are the same. As also with the Labour Party internal reforms proposed by the party leadership in the United Kingdom, the NSW legislation nevertheless also dances coincidentally to a traditional constitutional tune, which has been conspicuously revived, and which gives the legislation a measure of intellectual legitimacy.

But in seeking to diminish the political voice of trade unions in this way, the legislator faces a hurdle that did not exist in 1909 when Sir George Farwell and his colleagues were developing the application of ultra-liberal constitutionalism. This is the question of fundamental rights already alluded to, rights which present in most countries as human rights (in this case freedom of association and freedom of expression). The question now is whether these new restrictions on trade union political representation and electoral engagement are consistent with the modern fundamental freedoms by which liberal government is purportedly sustained.

Australia famously does not expressly include fundamental rights of this latter kind in its constitution (at least to the extent that they can be enforced in the courts).[91] The High Court of Australia has, however, implied such rights (such as the right to freedom of political communication) into the constitution of the Commonwealth through the medium of the principle of 'representative government' (again) by which the Commonwealth Constitution is said to be underpinned.[92] As a result, in 1992 the court held legislation relating to party political broadcasting to be unconstitutional.[93]

In a constitutional challenge to this legislation by Unions NSW in 2013, the question now for the High Court of Australia was whether the legislation violated these latter principles of representative government, a question that takes us back to where we started. Implicitly, it required the court to consider whether the constitutional principle of representative government is to take a meaning similar to that given by Sir George Farwell, or whether it is to take a meaning that—by diversity of political party structure—permits or encourages the widest representation of interests in the process of government.

[89] The organization of the ALP is similar to that of the Labour Party in the United Kingdom. This legislation applies only to its NSW branch.

[90] Election Funding, Expenditure and Disclosures Amendment Act 2012 (NSW).

[91] See now the fascinating and much neglected Human Rights (Parliamentary Scrutiny) Act 2011 (Cth), which appears to be shunned by lawyers because it does not provide for judicial scrutiny. It is nevertheless a very important and impressive document especially in relation to the human rights instruments against which legislation is to be scrutinized. For comment, see David Kinley and Christine Ernst, 'Exile on Main Street: Australia's Legislative Agenda for Human Rights' [2012] European Human Rights Law Review 58.

[92] *Australian Capital Television Pty v Commonwealth* (1992) 177 CLR 106.

[93] Though with the benefit of hindsight the legislation created a much fairer allocation of broadcasting time than the chaos by which it was replaced, giving rise to the need for the scrutiny of judicial decisions after the event, in the same way that there are calls for post-legislative scrutiny. But no one has risen to my suggestion.

Conclusion

It is particularly poignant that this matter should present in the modern era for the first time in Australia, given that the ALP not only existed before the Commonwealth Constitution was created, but in 1910 also produced the world's first majority Labour/Labor government. It is surely not the case that the ALP thought that it was signing up to the ideas advanced by Sir George Farwell and his colleagues, when subscribing to the Commonwealth Constitution in 1900, and to what since has been claimed judicially to be the latter's commitment to representative government.

It is true that *Osborne* was received in NSW with a warm embrace in 1918;[94] but the NSW Court of Appeal received it only on the narrow ground of statutory interpretation, without dancing to Sir George's tune about constitutional government.[95] It is also true that the High Court of Australia was the first highest court in the common law world to have in the past decided unequivocally in favour of the legitimacy of trade union political activity; but that was in connection with legislation relating to a unique labour law system.

The decision in question was *Williams v Hursey*,[96] where members of the Democratic Labour Party objected to their union's support for the ALP, and claimed that it violated Commonwealth rather than state law. Yet although the claim was strongly rejected by the High Court, it did not necessarily follow that trade union political action could not be expressly prohibited. In a remarkable decision that swims against the tide of modern history, however, the High Court of Australia in *Unions NSW v New South Wales* held that the NSW legislation was unconstitutional as violating implied constitutional rights.[97]

In so holding the High Court offered a different vision of democracy and the role of trade unions in modern democratic arrangements from that of the government. But although enthusiastically celebrated by trade unions, the latter is a decision that will come too late for some jurisdictions, notably in Canada where the union link with the NDP has been irretrievably sacrificed on the altar of extreme party funding laws.[98] These contain tight controls on donations and expenditures and make no allowance for diversity in party structure and organization, a template of liberal constitutionalism offered to the common law world that has strongly influenced political actors in several jurisdictions, including Australia.[99]

The crucial point about Canada—which is missed in many countries—is that the changes took place with the agreement of the NDP and within the NDP of the trade

[94] *Allen v Gorten* (1918) 18 SR (NSW) 202.

[95] Amending legislation was duly passed by the NSW Parliament, and in other states. See Ewing ch. 8 (n 28).

[96] (1959) 103 CLR 30 (R C Tadgell (1960) 2 MULR 405).

[97] [2013] HCA 58 (18 December 2013).

[98] For a full account, see Ewing ch. 9 (n 69). This is somewhat ironic given the Canadian Supreme Court's decision that the use of union dues for political purposes was not unconstitutional: see *Lavigne v OPSEU* [1991] 2 SCR 211. The legality of the action did not protect it from restriction.

[99] They also have a strong influence in the United Kingdom: Stephen Crone, *Reforming Political Party Funding in the UK: Lessons from Canada* (Democratic Audit, 2011). For the most recent official proposals on party funding reform (from which a former Labour minister on the Committee dissented), see Committee on Standards in Public Life 2011 (n 32).

unions affiliated to it. This was no doubt a rational position for the latter, given that the NDP never had been and showed no likelihood of ever becoming a party of government (at least at federal level). In these circumstances it seemed sensible that the state should support the party through quarterly allowances, releasing union money to be spent on other political priorities. But what is understandable in Canada is not necessarily rational elsewhere.

The 'Canadian solution'—at least on the question of political donations—does not form the basis of a coherent political strategy for trade unions in all Westminster style liberal democracies where labour parties are stronger. If the Farwellian vision of democracy is to prevail in the United Kingdom, the trade union political voice will be gagged, with opportunities for limited electoral and legislative engagement. At elections they will be free to engage with their members but not effectively with the wider public, and after elections free perhaps to engage with a small but largely powerless caucus of sympathetic MPs.

The silencing of trade union political voice is an inevitable consequence of neoliberalism and the decline of trade union industrial power.

14

The Movement to Eliminate Labor's Political Voice

Proposition 32 and 'Paycheck Protection' in the United States

John Logan

Introduction

In November 2012, Californians voted 56.1 per cent to 43.9 per cent to reject the nation's most sweeping effort to date to undermine organized labour's political voice. The pro- and anti-Proposition 32 camps spent a combined total of over $135 million on a campaign that was organized labour's top priority in California, and, along with the re-election of President Obama, one of its highest priorities nationwide.[1] Labour unions spent $75.1 million on the 'No on Proposition 32' campaign, while conservative organizations spent $60.5 million on the 'Yes' campaign. The 2012 election marked the third time in 15 years that California voters have rejected a so-called 'paycheck protection'—legislation restricting how unions can raise and spend money on political activities—ballot initiative. In 1998, in what the then AFL-CIO president John Sweeney called a 'modern political miracle', California voters rejected Proposition 226, the highest-profile paycheck protection ballot measure of the 1990s. And in 2005, in an early attempt to constrain the political activities of public-sector unions, Californians voted down the highest-profile paycheck measure of the 2000s, Proposition 75.

The defeat of Proposition 226 slowed paycheck's momentum in the late 1990s and early 2000s. But since 2011 paycheck protection has, once again, become a high priority for conservative politicians and anti-union organizations. After the failure of Proposition 32 at the ballot box, its principal backers—primarily conservative activists and out-of-state Super PACs (political action committees) stressed that the initiative was part of longer-term effort in California and the rest of the nation to neuter organized labour's political activities. While disappointed that they had failed to win the hard-fought battle against California's 'most powerful and well-funded special interest', its labor unions, they were nonetheless 'grateful for the incredible support' they had received from voters across the state: 'We started a grassroots effort to take California back and it doesn't end here.'[2]

[1] Proposition 32 had four main provisions: a ban on direct contributions by unions and corporations to candidates in state and local elections; a ban on union and corporate funds raised by payroll deduction for political purposes; a requirement that unions receive annual written permission from employees who wish to make voluntary contributions for political activities, providing the funds were not raised by payroll deductions; and a ban on state contractors making contributions to any political official involved in the awarding of that contract.

[2] Daily Labor Report, 'California Initiative Fails to Ban Union Payroll Deductions for Political Purposes', 7 November 2012.

As supporters of the Proposition 32 campaign indicated, paycheck protection—conservatives' favourite state-level anti-union initiative in the 1990s—has once again become a national cause for American conservatives. In the 2011 legislative session, for example, conservative lawmakers and activists in fifteen states attempted to enact paycheck legislation: Alabama, Arizona, Florida, Kansas, Minnesota, Missouri, Mississippi, New Hampshire, New Jersey, New York, Oregon, Pennsylvania, South Dakota, Tennessee and Texas. Legislation was passed in two states, Alabama and Arizona, but in 2012 both laws had injunctions against implementation. Paycheck legislation or ballot initiatives were defeated in seven states: Florida, Missouri, Mississippi, New Hampshire, Oregon, South Dakota, and Texas. And paycheck legislation was carried over to 2012 in six states: Kansas, Minnesota, New Jersey, New York, Pennsylvania, and Tennessee.

Paycheck protection bills have not been limited to state-level legislation. Since the 1990s, the national Republican Party has consistently supported paycheck legislation—the 2012 official Republican Party platform contained prominent support for paycheck legislation—and the US Congress has voted on a federal 'Paycheck Protection Act' on several occasions, but the legislation has never become law.

In a related development, thirteen states saw efforts in 2011–2012 to enact bills prohibiting the automatic deduction of union dues from the paychecks of public sector employees, a provision which is often part of paycheck bills or accompanies efforts to enact paycheck legislation: Arizona, Iowa, Idaho, Indiana, Michigan, Minnesota, Missouri, North Carolina, New Jersey, Oklahoma, Rhode Island, Tennessee, and Wisconsin. Two states, North Carolina and Wisconsin, enacted this legislation, while it was defeated in eight states—Arizona, Iowa, Idaho, Indiana, Missouri, New Jersey, Rhode Island and Tennessee—and carried over in three states—Michigan, Minnesota, and Oklahoma. Conservative legislators continue to try to enact these measures. In June 2013, Missouri's Democratic Governor vetoed legislation that would have required public-sector unions to obtain workers' written consent each year before deducting dues and before using fees for political activities. Republicans in the US House of Representatives have introduced legislation that would end the automatic deduction of union dues for federal and District of Columbia government employees.[3] These paycheck protection and dues deduction bills are part of a nationwide strategy to eliminate organized labour's political voice.

This article examines five major issues related to paycheck protection legislation. First, it analyses the political agenda of promoters of paycheck legislation. Second, it examines the transparency and amount of money that unions spend on politics. Third, it examines whether workers support their unions' political agenda and the legal rights afforded to dissenting employees. Fourth, it discusses whether unions could raise money for political activities through means other than payroll deduction. And finally, it analyses the effectiveness of paycheck legislation in the five US states that currently

[3] Daily Labor Report, 'Missouri Governor Vetoes Measure to Block Automatic Deduction of Public-Union Dues', 27 June 2013; Daily Labor Report, 'House, Senate Bills Would End Automatic Deduction of Union Dues for Federal Workers', 8 June 2011.

have it. While the focus of the article is on Proposition 32, and on previous efforts to enact paycheck legislation in California, most of these issues apply equally to every other state.

The battle over unions' political spending has intensified after the Supreme Court's 2010 *Citizens United* decision[4] —which stated that corporations and unions have a constitutional right to make unlimited independent expenditures, so long as they are not coordinated with candidates' campaigns—and will likely remain a contentious issue for several years. Although they are vastly outspent,[5] unions are the only organized group whose political expenditures—overwhelmingly in support of progressive causes and candidates—are anywhere near the level of spending by employer associations, corporations, and conservative billionaires, which is why union spending has become the principal target of several right-wing organizations. In June 2013, the Heritage Foundation and forty state-level conservative groups launched the 'National Employee Freedom Week' to publicize 'the little-known fact that unionized employees have the legal right to opt out of... their union's political activities'. According to these organizations, workers 'don't want unions playing politics with their money. Many union members want their union to focus on work, but instead, union bosses are using members' dues money for political purposes.'[6]

The battle over union political spending in the US provides an interesting comparison with recent developments in the UK, where unions are required to establish a separate political fund and ballot members every 10 years to reauthorize the political levy. Individual members can opt out of paying the political levy, but those who do not opt out cannot influence how the union uses their contribution, which is decided by union policy. In 2013, the future of union financial support for the Labour Party became a national political issue. Labour leader Ed Miliband proposed changing party policy to permit individual members, but not unions, to affiliate with the Labour Party, a position supported by the party's largest union funder, Unite. The Coalition government, in contrast, has proposed changing the funding of political parties—including union funding of the Labour Party—through legislation, which the unions oppose.[7]

Paycheck Protection's Conservative Agenda to Weaken Unions

Starting with the very first state paycheck measure in Washington State in 1992, a network of conservative and anti-union organizations has promoted paycheck legislation through ballot initiatives and state bills. By the late 1990s, paycheck protection was a key component in the campaign to constrain unions' political spending. In common with

[4] 130 S. Ct. 876 (2010).

[5] Center for Responsive Politics, '2014 Overview: Business-Labor-Ideology Split in PAC & Individual Donations to Candidates, Parties Super PACs and Outside Spending Groups' (no date). Available at <http://www.opensecrets.org/overview/blio.php> accessed 15 July 2013.

[6] Available at <http://EmployeeFreedomWeek.com> accessed 7 September 2013. Daily Labor Report, 'Heritage Foundation Joins Union "Opt-Out" Effort' 5 June 2013.

[7] Doug Pyper, 'Trade Union Political Funds and Levy' (House of Commons Library, Standard Business Note: SN/BT/593, 8 August 2013).

state-level paycheck and dues-deduction bills in 2011–2012, most paycheck bills introduced in the late 1990s and early 2000s were based on 'model ALEC legislation'.[8]

The main promoters of paycheck protection have always been conservative and anti-union organizations. According to one analysis '[t]he lineup of proponents includes an array of ideologically conservative groups and right-wing benefactors. Among them are the Christian Coalition, Family Research Council, Heritage Foundation, National Right-to-Work Committee, Americans for Tax Reform, and the American Legislative Exchange Council.'[9] A similar alliance of conservative organizations continues to promote paycheck legislation today. Paycheck bills have always been an attempt to tilt the balance of political power in favour of conservative politicians who promote them, not about protecting the rights of individual union members and non-union employees.[10]

Numerous observers have commented on the partisan goals of paycheck legislation. The *Sacramento Bee*'s editorial against Proposition 226, California's 1998 paycheck protection ballot initiative—the most important paycheck measure prior to Proposition 32—explained that the controversial ballot initiative 'hides behind the rhetoric of political reform, but at its heart is the most old-fashioned kind of political power play. It is an effort by conservatives to use the power of government to muffle the political influence of labor unions.'[11] McClatchy Newspapers called the claim that paycheck protection represented an effort to protect individual rights against union coercion 'The Big Lie'. [12]

Most academics agreed that, in common with other paycheck protection measures, the real purpose of Proposition 226 was to weaken the political voice of union members, not to protect their money against misuse. One academic expert wrote: 'The passage of Proposition 226 . . . would immediately weaken one of the core constituent groups of the Democratic Party. . . . Ultimately, this, rather than the rights of workers, appears to be the primary motivation behind the phenomenon of paycheck protection.'[13]

Then President Bill Clinton best captured the view that Proposition 226 was, at heart, a battle over political power: 'This is not a real problem. This is an attempt to create the impression that individual members are being put upon when they aren't. And it's being

[8] Formed in 1973, ALEC brings together conservative state legislators and business together on a host of economic and social policy issues. ALEC has been the principal force behind the state level anti-union legislation in the past two years. The ALEC 'Voluntary Contributions Act' states: 'The Voluntary Contributions Act requires labor organizations that engage in political activities to keep a segregated fund for political contributions. It further specifies that contributions to that fund will be on a voluntary basis and the contribution shall be made directly by the donor. In addition, the Act prohibits payroll withholding of funds to be used for political purposes.' In what is the largest concerted legal attack on union rights since the New Deal, conservative lawmakers in thirty-one states attempted to limit collective bargaining rights for public sector employees in 2011. Legislation was passed in eleven states, defeated in twenty states, and carried over to the 2012 legislative session in ten states. These bills were based on ALEC's 'Public Employee Freedom Act'.

[9] Marick F. Masters, Raymond Gibney, and Thomas J. Zagenczyk, 'Worker Pay Protection: Implications for Labor's Political Spending and Voice' (2009) 48(4) Journal of Labor Research 565.

[10] David S. Broder, *Democracy Derailed: Initiative Campaigns and the Power of Money* (Harcourt Inc., 2000) 91–161.

[11] Sacramento Bee, Editorial, 'No on Proposition 226: Phony Arguments Hide a Political Power Grab', 6 May 1998.

[12] Quoted in Broder 116 (n 10).

[13] Paul Clark, 'Using Members Dues for Political Purposes: The "Paycheck Protection" Movement' (1999) 20(3) Journal of Labor Research (J Labor Res) 340.

done to alter the balance of power in the political debate.' [14] And when paycheck protection became a national conservative movement in the 1990s, most commentators viewed it as a partisan power play. The *Washington Post* editorialized that the amount of money in politics should be reduced but not through 'disingenuous' paycheck protection measures that aim to take unions out of politics: 'In fact what it seeks to do in the name of solicitude for workers is weaken unions. This is the wrong way to have a battle about unions and the wrong way to have the battle about campaign finance as well.'[15]

Supporters of paycheck protection, in their own words

Journalists, politicians, and academics are not alone in stressing the partisan goals behind paycheck legislation. Several paycheck supporters have made the same basic point.

Paycheck protection as political payback

Support for paycheck protection has, at times, been motivated by straightforward political retribution, either against the labour movement generally or against a particular union. During the Proposition 226 campaign in 1998, for example, an internal memo from one of the initiative's major financial backers, the California Restaurant Association, explained why the group was supporting the paycheck protection initiative so vigorously: 'The association took this action because restaurant owners in California have been under attack for years by union officials, most notably when unions sponsored Proposition 210 that added $1.50 to the minimum wage.' [16] Likewise, the only national business organizations to support the measure, the National Federation of Independent Business, wrote on Proposition 226: 'Your business is under siege. The union bosses demand: Minimum-wage increase, mandated health insurance, opposition to legal reform. You can fight back. Vote yes on Proposition 226.'[17]

Conservative activists have backed paycheck legislation for similar reasons. James Righeimer, one of the conservative activists who initiated Proposition 226, sought to eliminate the political voice of the 325,000-member California Teachers Association (CTA). Righeimer had been a major sponsor of a 1993 California proposition to introduce school vouchers in public education. The CTA, he complained, 'spent $20 million to cream the measure'. Proposition 226 was direct political payback.[18] Then Governor, Pete Wilson, also supported Proposition 226 in an attempt to undermine public-sector unions.[19] And Governor Arnold Schwarzenegger promoted Proposition 75 in 2005 because public-sector unions vigorously opposed his radical reform agenda.

[14] Daily Labor Report, 'Clinton Opposes California Proposition 226; Sees "Significant Disadvantage" for Unions' 5 May 1998.

[15] Washington Post, 'Not Paycheck Protection' (editorial), 29 May 1998.

[16] Quoted in John Jacobs, 'Unmasking 226's "paycheck protection" masquerade' Sacramento Bee, 28 May 1998.

[17] Quoted in Broder 132 (n 10).

[18] Quoted in National Education Association, *The Real Story Behind Paycheck Protection* (Washington, DC, 1998) 47.

[19] Broder 98–9 (n 10). In December 2012, Adelson, who spent $100 million supporting Republicans in the 2012 election, told the Wall Street Journal that he would double his spending next time round and

Another major paycheck supporter, casino mogul Sheldon Adelson, adopted it as a cause to punish the Hotel and Restaurant Employees union (HERE), with which he had clashed in Las Vegas over his new 'Sands' casino. In addition to funding a failed effort at paycheck protection in Nevada, Adelson became a major backer of two failed paycheck initiatives in California—Proposition 226 in 1998 and Proposition 75 in 2005.[20] For these business groups, politicians, and conservative activists, paycheck legislation was 'payback time'—a vehicle for punishing against their political adversaries in the labour movement.

Not all employer organizations have embraced paycheck so enthusiastically. The largest business groups in the California, including the Chamber of Commerce and the California Manufacturers Association, have declined to support paycheck protection politically or financially. One spokesperson explained their reticence: 'We were asked to support Prop. 226 but said no. This is a war nobody needed. We have basically had labor peace in this state, and once you start a war like this, it never ends. We tried to tell the proponents...but they wouldn't listen.' The opposition of California's major business associations showed that paycheck legislation was 'a solution in search of a problem'. [21]

In most other states, however, Chambers of Commerce and other business organizations have supported paycheck protection initiatives. In a 2013 campaign in Kansas for a bill that would prevent public sector unions using money raised by payroll deduction for political activities, for example, a lobbyist for the state Chamber of Commerce explained his goal: 'I need this bill passed so we can get rid of public sector unions.'[22]

Paycheck protection as a mechanism to eliminate Labor's political voice

Other supporters of paycheck protection have sought to use it to fundamentally weaken all unions. Conservative powerbroker Grover Norquist, Founder and President of Americans for Tax Reform, has spoken openly about the agenda behind the paycheck protection movement. Norquist has said that the opportunities provided by the Supreme Court's 1988 *Beck* decision (which established private-sector employees' right to opt-out of union political contributions) 'will enable us break the unions' and that paycheck protection measures at the state level would 'crush labor unions as a political entity'. Norquist has argued that under paycheck protection, every worker who did not opt in to the union political fund 'is another worker who doesn't pay $500 a year to organized labor's political machine'.[23] Likewise, David Horowitz, president of the right-wing Center for the Study of Popular Culture, stated in an interview in the *LA*

that he would 'continue funding state-by-state efforts to curtail organized labor's power'. Quoted in Alicia Mundy, 'Adelson to Continue Betting on the GOP', Wall Street Journal, 4 December 2012.

[20] Jon Ralston, 'The short unhappy life of the Paycheck Protection Act' Las Vegas Review-Journal, 21 June 1998. In Oregon, another failed attempt to pass a paycheck protection initiative modelled on Proposition 226 was the brainchild of another longtime conservative activist, Bill Sizemore.

[21] Quoted in Broder 108, 157 (n 10).

[22] Quoted in 'Kansas Chamber: Bill will help destroy public-sector unions' in Topeka Capital-Journal, 23 January 2013 <http://cjonline.com/news/2013-01-23/kansas-chamber-bill-will-help-destroy-public-sector-unions> accessed 15 June 2013.

[23] Grover Norquist, 'The Democratic Party is Toast' Washington Monthly, September 2004, available at <http://www.washingtonmonthly.com/features/2004/0409.norquist.html>.

Times: 'We want to take [unions] out of politics, not just in California, but in every state in the union.'[24]

In 2012, California's Proposition 32 was promoted and funded by conservative activists, Republican front organizations, and out-of-state groups with a strong partisan agenda. The initiative was written by two of the leading lawyers of the California Republican Party, Michael Capaldi and Thomas Hiltachk, who specialize in ballot initiatives that are 'the opposite of what they sound like'.[25] The principal backer of the measure was the right-wing Lincoln Club of Orange County, a group that played a key role in the Supreme Court's *Citizens United* decision.[26] And the main funders of the measure were libertarian billionaire Charles Munger Jnr, and two Republican front organizations that do not disclose their donors—the Iowa-based 'America Future Fund' and the Arizona-based 'Americans for Responsible Leadership'. The America Future Fund receives its funding from the Koch brothers, right-wing billionaires who fund a variety of conservative groups, including ALEC, while the *Tucson Citizen* called Americans for Responsible Leadership 'a Koch brothers "dark money" front group.'[27] For these conservative groups and activists, Proposition 32 was an effort to diminish unions' political influence and choke off a major source of funding for progressive causes and candidates—what conservative columnist George Will calls 'transmission belts conveying money to the Democratic Party'. [28] Opposed to Proposition 32 were not only unions, but also 'good government' organizations: Common Cause, the League of Women Voters, Public Citizen, as well as the state's leading consumer and environmental organizations.

Union spending political

Conservative supporters of paycheck protection claim that the legislation is needed because unions spend too much of their members' dues money on political activities they do not support, and that members do not know how much of their money is being spent on politics. So how transparent is union political spending and how much do they spend?

Union financial transparency

As a result of revised and expanded financial disclosure LM-2 forms adopted by the Bush Department of Labor (DOL) in 2005, American unions with revenues over $250,000 per year are now among the most transparent organizations in the country when it comes to spending on politics. They are required to disclose 'direct and indirect disbursements to all entities and individuals...associated with political disbursements or contributions in money'. Large US unions are also more transparent in their political spending

[24] Quoted in National Education Association 49 (n 18).

[25] Hendrik Hertzberg, 'Votescam', New Yorker, 6 August 2007.

[26] *Citizens United v Federal Election Commission*, 558 U.S. 310 (2010).

[27] Kenneth P. Vogel and Tarini Parti, 'Inside Koch World', Politico, 6 June 2012; Tuscon Citizen, 'Americans for Responsible Leadership—a Koch brothers "dark money" front group', 27 October 2012.

[28] George Will, 'Where the Money Comes From', Washington Post, 24 August 2011.

when compared with unions in most other advanced Anglophone countries.[29] These LM-2 forms, filed each year with the Office of Labor Management Standards (OLMS) at the DOL, contain detailed information on a comprehensive range of political activities—including unions' political communications with their membership—not just information on direct donations to candidates for political office, which is contained in union filings with the federal election officials. Schedule 16 of the expanded LM-2 form ('Political Activities and Lobbying') requires unions to disclose a broad range of activities related to politics, including polling fees, money spent on internal political communications, and even the cost of bratwursts used to feed workers in Wisconsin protesting a controversial law eliminating public sector bargaining at the state capitol in early 2011.[30]

In contrast with unions, US corporations do not disclose a broad range of their political spending activities. Unreported activities include, for example, corporate donations to the political wing of the US Chamber of Commerce, currently the single largest lobby in the country. In the 2012 election cycle, the Chamber spent more than $136.3 million on electioneering, overwhelmingly on Republican candidates and causes.[31] Those spending activities that corporations are required to disclose, moreover, are not easily found in one or two government databases, in contrast with union political spending.[32]

Unlike union members, employees, customers, and shareholders have no legal right to opt out of paying for corporate political expenditures. The same groups that have promoted paycheck protection measures have opposed giving shareholders opt-out rights when it comes to corporate spending on politics. In addition, most public employees, who have no legal right to opt out, help fund corporate political speech. One recent analysis of compelled corporate political speech explains the problem:

> [A] significant portion of the money that corporations are spending on politics is financed by equity capital provided by public pension funds—capital contributions that the government requires public employees to finance with their paychecks.... Contrast this situation with how the court treats political spending by unions.... If the public employees union were to spend any of the money raised through dues on politics... the dues requirement would amount to forced political speech.... [T]he court has held that no union may use an employee's dues for political purposes if the employee objects.[33]

Thus, public sector employees are forced to subsidize corporate political speech through pension contributions—they cannot choose stock or avoid compelled speech associated with stock choices—but no employee is forced to subsidize union political speech.

[29] John Lund and John McLuckie, 'Labor Organization Financial Transparency and Accountability: A Comparative Analysis' (2007) 58(4) Labor Law Journal 251–66; John Lund, 'Financial Reporting and Disclosure Requirements for Trade Unions: A Comparison of UK and US Public Policy', (2009) 40(2) Industrial Relations Journal 122–39.

[30] Tom McGinty and Brody Mullins, 'Political Spending by Unions Far Exceeds Direct Donations', Wall Street Journal, 10 July 2012.

[31] Center for Responsible Politics, '2012 Outside Spending, By Group' (no date). Available at <http://www.opensecrets.org/outsidespending/summ.php?cycle=2012&chrt=V&disp=O&type=A> accessed 30 April 2013.

[32] McGinty and Mullins (n 30).

[33] Benjamin I. Sachs, 'How Pensions Violate Free Speech', *New York Times*, 12 July 2012.

In addition, compared with unions, corporations spend much of their political funds on external lobbying, while unions spend more on internal political communications with their members. This lack of corporate transparency is especially significant because in recent years, corporations and other business organizations have significantly outspent unions in politics. Since the 1980s, states one recent study, 'political spending by corporations has dwarfed union political donations. In such an environment, it is impossible for organized labor to "buy" legislative support from Congress.'[34]

Businesses organizations currently dominate all aspects of political spending. In California, according to the non-partisan Center for Investigative Reporting, business interests spent almost $700 million on contributions to candidates, parties, ballot initiatives, and independent expenditures from 2001 to 2011. Unions spent $284 million during the same ten-year period, with two major unions, the California Teachers Association and the State Council of the Service Employees International Union, spending well over half of organized labour's total amount. Wealthy individuals, most of whom support conservative candidates and causes, have spent $231 million. The vast majority of these expenditures, moreover, go to ballot initiatives or independent expenditures, spending that would have been completely unaffected by Proposition 32's prohibition on direct donations to candidates by corporations or unions.[35]

Thus, when it comes to financial transparency, the situation is clear: union spending on political activities is transparent and detailed information on their spending is easy to access; corporate spending is neither transparent, nor is the information easy to access.

How Much Money Do Unions Spend on Politics?

How much of their members' dues money do American unions spend on politics? Contrary to what is often assumed, the actual answer, as a percentage of total union dues, is relatively little. In 2006, for example, unions spent a total of $413 million on all political activities, including national, state, and local elections—out of a total dues income that year of almost $9.7 billion. Thus, according to the expanded LM-2 financial disclosure forms filed with the Office of Labor Management Standards at the DOL, only 4.3 per cent of unions' total income for the year 2006 was spent on political activities.[35a]

Internal union communications to members, which constitute a significant amount of labour's overall political spending, are not reported in filings with the Federal Election Commission (FEC), but must be included in the financial reporting to the OLMS. Unions' most important role in politics is arguably not to spend directly on candidates or campaigns—although they certainly do this—but to increase turnout among union members and union households and to increase the percentage of union members and

[34] Marick F. Masters and John T. Delaney, 'Organized Labor's Political Scorecard' in James T. Bennett and Bruce E. Kaufman (eds), *What Do Unions Do? A Twenty-Year Perspective* (Transaction, 2007) 503, 507.

[35] Coulter Jones and Elizabeth Titus, 'State's top 100 political donors contribute $1.25 billion', California Watch, 4 June 2012. Available at <http://californiawatch.org/money-and-politics/states-top-100-political-donors-contribute-125-billion-16436> accessed 15 June 2013.

[35a] Masters and Delaney 507 (n 34).

union households voting for labour-endorsed candidates and causes. According to several studies, unions have achieved considerable success in both of these goals.[36]

What do the DOL's revised LM-2 financial disclosure forms tell us about union political spending? Out of the top twenty largest unions by membership, eleven spent fewer than 5 per cent of total dues and other income on political activities in 2006. Only five international unions out of twenty spent over 10 per cent of their total income on political activities, all of them entirely or partly public-sector unions. One union that has repeatedly been attacked by state-level conservative organizations over its allegedly lavish spending on politics, the National Education Association, spent only 9.03 per cent of its total income on politics.[37]

Moreover, the total amount of money unions have spent on political activities over the past two decades, 'when adjusted for inflation, has not increased, even after the huge increase in so-called 'soft money' expenditures on political campaigns' in the late 1990s and early 2000s. One academic analysis concluded that, in real dollars, 'union contributions peaked in 1992 and fell to their lowest level in the past decade in 2002'.[38] Union political spending, moreover, constitutes a tiny proportion of the increase in wages that employees secure as a result of unionization. Union membership provides workers with a wage premium of approximately 17 per cent—unionized workers earn 17 per cent more than their non-union counterparts—while union dues average only 1.25 per cent of employees' total monthly wages.[39] Only about 4 per cent of those dues are spent on political activities, and much of that amount is devoted to internal communications with union members. Thus, given that political activity is increasingly central to unions' ability to deliver for their members, union spending on politics is good value for money, even though it has failed to win federal labour law reform. Union political spending has increased since 2007—especially post-*Citizens United*—but it remains a small percentage of total interest group spending on both federal and state elections and lobbying. As a percentage of total expenditures, unions spend most on state elections and ballot initiatives (about 10 per cent of the total spent), less on federal election cycles (about 5 per cent), and least of all on lobbying (less than 2 per cent).[40] Are members coerced into supporting unions' political activities?

Unions are democratic organizations

In California and the rest of the country, workers cannot be forced to join a union as a condition of employment. Under federal law neither union officials nor employers can require employees to join unions.[41] For those workers who choose to join unions,

[36] Masters and Delaney 507–8 (n 34). See also Robert Bruno, 'Voting the "New Union" Label: Illinois Labor and The Return to Class Politics' (1998) 23(2) Labor Studies Journal 55–84.

[37] Masters, Gibney, and Zagenczyk 569–70 (n 9). [38] Masters and Delaney 505 (n 34).

[39] David G. Blanchflower and Alex Bryson, 'What Effect Do Unions Have on Wages Now and Would Freeman and Medoff Be Surprised?' in *What Do Unions Do? A Twenty-Year Perspective* 79, 84 (Transaction, 2007); David Card, 'The Effect of Unions on the Structure of Wages: A Longitudinal Analysis' (1996) 64(4) Econometrica 957, 974.

[40] Marick F. Masters, 'Union Power: The Role of Labor Money in American Politics', Paper presented at the 2013 annual meetings of the Labor and Employment Relations Association on 5 January 2013 in San Diego, CA.

[41] *NLRB v General Motors Corp.*, 373 U.S. 734 (1963).

members control the organization. Unions are small 'd' democratic organizations—the Office of Labor Management Standards at the Department of Labor regulates internal union elections for private-sector unions, while public sector unions are regulated under state laws—that have elected local and national leaders.[42] If they are unhappy with the performance of union officials, members can vote out the leadership. The performance of local and national union leaders in contract negotiations and in the political realm, and continued membership support, is critical to their ability to remain in office.

These democratically elected national and local officers decide union political endorsements by a vote, and funding for political activities comes from financial assessments approved by the membership. If the membership does not approve of union officers' actions in political endorsements, it can vote them out of office, and thus local and national leadership must be responsive to their members' political views. Academic studies demonstrate that union leaders frequently adopt political positions that reflect the range of their members' beliefs on politics.[43]

Under existing law, dissenting workers enjoy strong protections

Existing US labour law in both the public and private sectors prohibits unions from forcing workers to make political contributions. Under federal campaign finance law, unions can contribute to Congressional or Presidential campaigns, but must do so through a segregated political action committee (PAC) fund, which is funded through separate, voluntary contributions by individual members. The law prohibits unions from forcing members into contributing to this separate, voluntary federal election fund.[44]

Workers also enjoy extensive protections when it comes to union political activities in state and local politics. First, workers can gain employment wherever they want without having to pay for political activities they oppose. Second, if they gain employment at a unionized workplace, workers have the option of becoming 'agency fee payers'—who pay fees that cover only the costs of representing them in the bargaining unit—thereby opting out of supporting union political activity with which they disagree.[45] Even if they opt out of the union's state political activities, dissenters will continue to benefit economically from the union's activities on behalf of all bargaining unit members. Moreover, in both the public and private sectors, employees can object to the use of their dues money for general political purposes. They do not need to object

[42] George Strauss, 'What's Happening Inside U.S. Unions: Democracy and Union Politics' (2000) 21(2) J Labor Res 211.

[43] Hebert B. Asher et al., *American Unions in the Electoral Arena* (Rowman & Littlefield Publishers, Inc., 2001) 21.

[44] *NLRB v General Motors Corp.*, 373 U.S. 734 (1963); *Communications Workers of America v Beck*, 487 U.S. 735, 745 (1988). Beck states the private-sector unions can require non-member contributions for collective-bargaining activities but not for political activities.

[45] Kenneth G. Dau-Schmidt, 'The Right to Choose: Protecting Union Workers from Forced Political Contributions' Testimony before the House Committee on Oversight and Government Reform, 8 February 2012. Available at <http://oversight.house.gov/wp-content/uploads/2012/02/2-8-12_Full_Dau-Schmidt.pdf> accessed 30 April 2013.

to specific political activities of the union. And their right to 'opt out' of union political spending extends to most forms of political lobbying, not only to direct electoral spending.[46]

Protections for dissenting employees do not end there. Under the National Labor Relations Act, private-sector unions must send 'Hudson Notices' every year to non-member agency fee payers who do not contribute to the union's political fund. These Hudson Notices provide dissenters with details of the union's spending—including union spending on political activities—and explain how their reduction in the agency fee as dissenters has been calculated. Hudson Notices provide dissenters with a minimum of 30 days to challenge the union's assessment of their reduced agency fee. If they disagree with the union over the level of the agency fee, they can file a complaint with the National Labor Relations Board (NLRB), which must investigate, if it finds merit in that complaint.[47] Moreover, a recent court decision significantly expands the rights of dissenting employees and places additional restrictions on unions' political spending. In June 2012, in a decision that has potentially sweeping implications for union political speech, the Supreme Court ruled in *Knox v SEIU Local 1000*[48] that when unions levy a special mid-year political assessment, they must issue dissenters with an additional Hudson Notice and require them to opt in, rather than opt out, of the new fee for political activities.[49]

When calculating the agency fees of non-members, unions can charge objecting employees for costs associated with the negotiation and administration of collective agreements, but they cannot charge dissenters for costs associated with the union's political activities. Thus, by claiming that it will protect employees' dues money from being used for political purposes they do not support, paycheck protection legislation pretends to confer a right that already exists.[50] In addition, the financial reports that unions file with the OLMS include information on the number of dissenting employees and the amount of dues money that the union has returned to them. Finally, unions cannot deduct union dues or other union fees from employees' paychecks without first receiving written permission.[51] Thus, existing legal protections extend to the way in which non-member employees pay their agency dues or other fees. Unions or employers cannot force employees to have money for representation or political activities automatically deducted from their paycheck without authorization. In the absence of authorization, automatic deductions are illegal.[52]

[46] *Abood*, 431 U.S. at 240–2. Abood states that public-sector unions can require non-member contributions for their collective-bargaining activities but not for their political activities.

[47] Dau-Schmidt (n 45).

[48] 132 S. Ct. 2277, 2296 (2012).

[49] Catherine L. Fisk and Erwin Chemerinsky, 'Political Speech and Association Rights After *Knox v SEIU Local 1000*' (2013) 98(6) Cornell Law Review (forthcoming). The authors argued that the Supreme Court's decisions in *Citizens United* and *Knox* have 'significantly increased the political influence of corporations and significantly decreased the political influence of unions'. They also state that the sweeping implications of *Knox* call into question 'the constitutionality of collective bargaining based on exclusive representation and majority rule'. Knox essentially argues that an opt-out system provides insufficient protection for workers' First Amendment right against forced speech.

[50] *Chicago Teachers Union, Local No. 1 v Hudson*, 475 U.S. 292, 304–6 (1986).

[51] Dau-Schmidt (n 45).

[52] Dau-Schmidt (n 45) 29 U.S.C. § 186(c)(4).

Federal law provides strong legal safeguards against union coercion of both members and non-members. Employees enjoy a federally protected right to opt out of funding union political activity. No one can be forced to join a union as a condition of employment. Non-members who pay an agency fee have a legal right not to contribute to unions' political activities. Unions cannot force employees to contribute to costs for political actions that are unrelated to the negotiation and administration of collective agreements. Paycheck protection does not change or add to these existing legal rights.[53]

Thus, existing law already protects workers when it comes to forced political contributions. They enjoy a clear right to refrain from paying for the union's political activities that are unrelated to the negotiation and administration of collective agreements. But paycheck protection legislation deprives choice from members who want a union with an effective political voice. Most paycheck protection measures replace the current 'opt-out' system, whereby workers can choose not to contribute to the union's political fund, with an 'opt-in' system, which requires that unions get written permission from every worker each year before using dues money for politics. Under an opt-in system, even members who support their unions' political platform will likely delay, procrastinate, or be tempted to become 'free riders'—i.e., enjoy the benefits derived from the union's political activism without having to pay for it.[53a] Moreover, some members who support their union's political activity would likely miss annual filing deadlines under paycheck laws. Thus, inertia and the 'problem of collective action'[54] would make it difficult for unions to participate effectively in politics, and their ability to deliver economic benefits for their members would consequently be impaired. The current opt-out rule is designed to ensure that unions are able to participate effectively in the political arena despite the opposition of the dissenting minority. But it also ensures that dissenters need not finance the union's political speech.[55] As the Supreme Court has stated, 'the majority…has an interest in stating its views without being silenced by the dissenters'.[56]

No evidence of widespread union coercion

Supporters of paycheck legislation consistently state that these laws are needed to ensure that workers are not forced to contribute to political causes they do not support. Thus, paycheck protection, they argue, is not an ideological attack on unions but a targeted effort to advance the freedom of individual employees. But they have failed to provide evidence that significant numbers of union members either disagree with the political agenda of their unions or feel coerced into contributing to their union's political activities.

[53] *Communications Workers of America v Beck*, 487 U.S. 735, 745 (1988); *Abood v Detroit Board of Education*, 431 U.S. 209, 235–6 (1977).

[53a] Dau-Schmidt (n 45).

[54] Mancur Olson, *The Logic of Collective Action: Public Goods and the Theory of Groups* (Harvard University Press, 1971).

[55] Benjamin I. Sachs, 'Unions, Corporations, and Political Opt-Out Rights After Citizens United' (2011) 112 Columbia Law Review 863.

[56] Quoted in Fisk and Chemerinsky 11 (n 48).

First, paycheck supporters have provided anecdotal stories of individual union members who disagree with the political platform of their union. No doubt these stories are real. 14.3 million workers in the US are union members. California has almost 2.5 million union members—more than any other single state in the nation—and thus it would be remarkable if one could not find individual cases of union members who complain of 'coercion' or who oppose the political agenda of their union. But these anecdotal stories do not amount to compelling evidence of a widespread problem of union coercion.

Second, supporters of paycheck protection argue that unions' political activities are separate from and unrelated to their bargaining and contract negotiation functions. The notion that a union's economic and political concerns are distinct and separate is outdated and incorrect. Political activity is increasingly important to unions' collective bargaining function, and central to their ability to deliver for their members.[57] Indeed, the ability of unions to represent their members' economic interests is arguably increasingly dependent as much on national, state, and local politics as events at the bargaining table. As government regulation of both internal union operations and external workplace relations has grown significantly over the past half century, the importance of unions' political activities has also grown in importance. As a result, there no longer exists a clear 'line of demarcation' between unions' political and collective bargaining activities.[58] The more success unions have in state and national politics, the better able they are to deliver economic benefits and workplace protections for their members.[59] To deliver for their members, it is essential that unions participate in the political process.[60]

Third, paycheck supporters state that in order to remedy coercion, public policy must make it as difficult as possible for unions to get non-members and members to finance union political activities by requiring that workers give annual written permission. Then, when union revenues fall because of the apparent effectiveness of paycheck measures, they claim this provides evidence that members do not support the political agenda of their unions. In reality, it provides evidence only of the efficacy of paycheck measures in stopping unions raising money for politics. It tells us nothing about the preferences of individual members concerning support for unions' political activities. The Supreme Court has stated that employee dissent must not be 'presumed—it must affirmatively be made known to the union by the dissenting employee'.[61] Conservative arguments concerning the lessons from paycheck protection measures assumes widespread dissent on the part of union members, but they do not demonstrate it. These arguments tell us nothing about member support for union political activities.

Fourth, right wing think tanks have produced policy briefs that repeat figures cited by other conservative organizations claiming to prove that union members object to their

[57] Reuel E. Schiller, 'Waning of Union Strength' (1999) 43 Berkeley Journal of Labor and Employment Law 63, quoted in Sachs 805 (n 55).

[58] Joseph Rauh, 'The Legality of Union Political Expenditures' (1960–61) 34 Southern California Law Review 152 at 163, quoted in Sachs 850 (n 55).

[59] Hebert B. Asher et al., *American Unions in the Electoral Arena* (Rowman & Littlefield Publishers, Inc., 2001) 47.

[60] Sachs (n 55).

[61] *International Assn. of Machinists v Street*, 367 U.S. 774.

dues being used for politics. A widely quoted 2012 brief from the Heritage Foundation, for example, states that '[f]ully 60 percent of union members object to their dues being spent on political causes'. The evidence cited to back up the claim is a poll of a 'representative sample of 760 union members' conducted by Word Doctors, the focus group firm of conservative strategist and paycheck protection advocate, Frank Luntz.[62]

Thus, supporters of paycheck legislation assert and assume widespread objection on the part of union members, but fail to provide compelling evidence of its existence. There is no evidence of coercion in relation to workers joining a union; in relation to workers contributing to union political spending; in relation to workers using automatic payroll deductions; or in relation to workers making voluntary contributions to unions.

When it comes to union coercion, the situation is clear: no worker can be forced to join a union as a condition of employment—the 1947 Taft Hartley Act outlawed the closed shop—and no worker can be forced to contribute to a union's political activities as a condition of employment. Some workers want to join the union—so they can vote on contracts that will decide pay, benefits, and conditions—but do not want to abide by the majority's decision when it comes to the union's political activities. Some workers will always disagree with some of the union's actions in the political realm, just as some will always disagree with its activities in bargaining. In politics, paycheck advocates want the interests of the dissenting minority to trump those of the non-objecting majority. But most observers agree that when membership in the union and contributing to political activities are voluntary, majority rule concerning the funding of union political activities is fair. Under existing federal law, workers currently enjoy an extensive right to opt out from union expenditures for political activities.[62a] Paycheck protection legislation does not revise, supplement, or strengthen that existing right.

Union members are happy with their unions

While we have no evidence that significant numbers of union members feel they are being coerced into supporting union political activities, we do have evidence that, by a significant margin, union members are content with the representation that their unions provide. Thus, far from representing a workplace necessity or a genuine effort to protect the interests of individual members, paycheck protection is designed to weaken unions at the ballot box. It is payback for union support for progressive candidates and causes, not an attempt to defend individual members or non-member employees against coercion.

The biggest survey of union members' attitudes in the past three decades is *What Workers Want* by Freeman and Rodgers. Based on evidence from the Worker Representation and Participation Survey, Freeman and Rodgers conclude that over 90 per cent of workers have a 'positive' or 'very positive' view of their union, and

[62] James Sherk, 'Backgrounder: Unelected Unions: Why Unions Should Be Allowed to Choose Their Representatives', The Heritage Foundation, 27 August 2012. Available at <http://www.heritage.org/research/reports/2012/08/unelected-unions-why-workers-should-be-allowed-to-choose-their-representatives> accessed 15 June 2013.

[62a] Dau-Schmidt (n 45).

90 per cent of union members would vote for a union if a workplace election were to take place tomorrow. Underlying these voting intentions are workers' experiences with unions: 'Just 5% of unionists described their experiences as bad, and just 2% describe them as very bad.'

The percentage of workers who approve of their union's positions on 'national political issues' is lower, but still relatively high, and the percentage of workers who approve of the performance of local officers in politics is higher than those who approve of national officers. According to Freeman and Rogers, 68 per cent of workers are either 'very satisfied' or 'somewhat satisfied' with their national union's involvement in politics. Only 25 per cent state that they are 'not too satisfied' or 'not satisfied' with the union's involvement in politics, which is the same percentage that say they are 'not too satisfied' or 'not satisfied' with their union's performance on bargaining for wages and benefits.[63]

Given that political activity is a charged area—more so, arguably, than bargaining over wages and benefits—it is notable that 68 per cent of union members, in a poll in which only one third of respondents self-identified as Democrats, say that they are satisfied with their unions' political activities. Freeman and Rogers' research provides a stark contrast with studies by right-wing think tanks finding that 60 per cent of union members object to union political activities. Conservative arguments that a majority of union members are dissatisfied with their union's political platforms, and feel they are being coerced into funding political activities that they do not support, do not stand up to scrutiny.

Could Unions Raise Money for Politics through Means Other than Payroll Deduction?

The short answer is only with great difficulty and expense, and likely with little success.

Proposition 32 would have outlawed the use of union money raised through payroll deduction—which is how the overwhelming majority of unions raise funds—for political activities, even if unions were to receive annual written permission from their members. While Proposition 32 would have imposed similar payroll deduction restrictions on corporations, this is not how most corporations raise money for political contributions. Instead of using money raised through payroll deductions, corporations rely overwhelmingly on funds from their general treasuries. Standard paycheck protection measures, in contrast, often allow the use of money raised through payroll deduction for political activities, providing unions receive annual written permission from employees.

Proposition 32 supporters argued that, if workers support their agenda, unions could raise money for political activities through alternative means, such as bank account or credit card deductions. The actual evidence on this point, however, suggests otherwise, for two main reasons: first, those union members who have access to bank accounts and credit cards are often reluctant to use them this way, even when it comes to paying for union membership dues. Second, many low wage and immigrant workers often lack

[63] Richard B. Freeman and Joe Rogers, *What Workers Want* (Cornell University Press, 1999) 70, 78.

adequate access to bank accounts and credit cards and thus would be unable to pay in this way.

Even among unions whose members have bank accounts and credit cards, many would likely be reluctant to contribute to their union's political funds in this way. According to interviews with local and state-level union officials in California, union officers believe that, even though the majority of their members have access to bank accounts and credit cards, it would be extremely difficult for their unions to raise money for politics through these mechanisms. Union members have the option of paying their monthly dues by using credit cards or bank accounts but almost none of them do so. Overwhelmingly, union officials report, members in California have expressed opposition to paying in this way, even though they are happy to give the union permission to deduct money automatically from their paychecks. Quite simply, they do not like giving their bank account and credit card information to the union—or to anyone else.[64]

More importantly, the argument that unions could raise money through mechanisms other than payroll deduction ignores that reality that several unions in California represent low paid, and often immigrant, workers who are unbanked, underbanked, or who lack proper access to credit cards. Unbanked households are those that lack any kind of bank account at an insured depository institution. Underbanked households are those that hold a bank account of some sort, but who also frequently rely on a range of alternative financial services providers, including payday loans and even pawnshops. The percentage of households in each category—both nationwide and in California—is relatively high.

The 2011 Federal Deposit Insurance Corporation (FDIC) national survey of unbanked and underbanked households, which has the most comprehensive statistics, reports that 8.2 per cent of American households overall are entirely unbanked, and 7.8 per cent of California households are entirely unbanked, up from 7.6 per cent in 2009. Fully 28 per cent of all US households are unbanked or underbanked, while 25.8 per cent of California households are unbanked or underbanked. Moreover, 22 per cent of 'foreign-born non-citizens' are entirely unbanked, as are 28 per cent of US households earning less than $15,000 per year. 37 per cent of US Spanish-only households, who are represented in high numbers by certain service-sector, healthcare, and construction unions in California, are entirely unbanked.[65] Also addressing the percentage of unbanked households, the Richmond Federal Reserve concluded that 46 per cent of blacks and 34 per cent of Hispanics born in the US are entirely unbanked. Among immigrant groups, 53 per cent of Mexicans and 37 per cent of other Latin American immigrants are unbanked, and 20 per cent of Asian immigrants are unbanked.[66]

These figures indicate the significant challenges faced by unions such as the Service Employees International Union, United Food and Commercial Workers, Laborers

[64] Phone interviews conducted by the author with local and state-level union officials in California between August and October 2012.

[65] *2011 FDIC National Survey of Unbanked and Underbanked Households* (Federal Deposit Insurance Corporation September 2012):<http://www.fdic.gov/householdsurvey/2012_unbankedreport.pdf> accessed 15 May 2013.

[66] Vanessa Sumo, 'Bringing in the Unbanked' (Richmond Federal Reserve, Winter 2007). Available at <http://www.richmondfed.org/publications/research/region_focus/2007/winter/pdf/feature3.pdf> accessed on 15 June 2013.

International Union of North America, and UNITE HERE when it comes to collecting funds by mechanisms other than payroll deduction. These unions represent many low wage and immigrant workers for whom contributing through banks accounts and credit cards is not a realistic option. Their members often lack credit cards and bank accounts, and cash remains their primary way of paying for most services. Moreover, because many banks fail to provide adequate services for low paid and immigrant workers, these workers often pay exorbitant sums for check cashing and remittance services, which makes it difficult for them to pay for union dues and services in this way. Most mainstream banks do not offer the financial products these workers need: their services are 'expensive, inconvenient, and difficult for immigrant workers to access'.[67]

Thus, the arguments of Proposition 32 supporters concerning readily available alternatives to payroll deduction fail to reflect the reality facing unions in California. California's unions represent almost 2.5 million workers, including tens of thousands of low-wage and immigrants in janitorial, security, hospitality, building trades, and healthcare jobs, among others. Some large locals of national unions represent members who are overwhelming from low-income and immigrant households. For workers in these unions, payroll deduction is often the only realistic way to contribute to the union's political fund; bank account or credit card deduction is simply not a realistic option. Prohibiting the use of payroll deduction for political purposes would seriously undermine the ability of these unions to raise funds and participate in politics. What Proposition 32 and similar measures do is *take away* the ability of a union member to contribute to the union's political fund by payroll deduction. Proposition 32 would have banned the practice outright, even for those union members who want to contribute that way.

The Cost to Unions of Complying with Paycheck Laws would be Substantial

Under legislation such as Proposition 32, the costs to unions of record-keeping compliance and the costs of constructing new methods of raising revenue for politics would be substantial. Both supporters and opponents of paycheck legislation have noted the onerous administrative and financial burden this legislation imposes on unions, thereby undermining their effectiveness. Indeed, for some of its supporters, paycheck legislation's primary value lies with its role as a 'paperwork expansion act' because every dollar that unions are required to spend on administration to raise funds and legally comply with paycheck measures is a dollar that they cannot spend on politics or other union activities. One advocate of Proposition 75, California's 2005 failed paycheck protection initiative, stated that, rather than protecting the dues money of dissenting employees, 'its real value is as a paperwork-creation initiative' that would impose a new layer of bureaucracy on unions and curtail their ability to participate in politics.[68]

[67] Janice Fine, 'Organized Labor, Worker Centers and the Contemporary Search for Alternative Forms of Organization for Low Wage Immigrant Workers', Paper presented at the 65th Conference of the Midwest Political Science Association, 12 April 2007.

[68] Tim Cavanaugh, 'Paycheck Protection Racket', Reason Magazine, 4 November 2005. Available at <http://reason.com/archives/2005/11/04/paycheck-protection-racket> accessed 15 June 2013.

California has almost 2.5 million union members. American's most populous state added 110,000 new union members in 2012, even while union membership fell by 368,000 in the nation as a whole. Getting annual written permission from each member would transform labour officials into bureaucrats who run around the state collecting millions of permission slips, rather than advocating for their members, and would bury them in an enormous mound of paperwork. Indeed, promoting paycheck legislation in states that already have right-to-work laws—and a majority of paycheck bills in 2011–2012 have been in right-to-work (RTW) states, where union dues are already voluntary—seems to be motivated solely by the desire to impose an administrative burden on unions. Workers in unionized workplaces in RTW states already receive the benefits of union membership without paying for politics or representation costs.

In addition to collecting 2.5 million permission slips every year, the cost of constructing alternative methods of raising money from the state's members would be prohibitively expensive. If Proposition 32 had become law, California unions would almost certainly have needed to reassign existing staff members from their representation and advocacy roles to administrative functions, hire outside consultants to help them comply with the law, and devise new methods of rising money, drastically revise their existing administrative, accounting, and fundraising procedures, and, for some unions, hire additional staff members to implement these changes. For large unions—those with revenues in excess of $250,000 dollars per year—this would likely cost hundreds of thousands and possibly millions of dollars per year; for medium-sized organizations with revenues between $10,000–250,000 per year, it would cost tens of thousands of dollars; and for small organizations with revenues of under $10,000 per year, it would cost thousands of dollars per year. Few unions could devote significant additional resources to administrative tasks and still participate in the political process in any meaningful way.[69]

Impact of Paycheck Protection Measures in Five States

Five US states currently have some limited form of paycheck protection legislation: Washington, Wyoming, Idaho, Utah, and Michigan. Ohio had a paycheck protection law in the 1990s, but the Ohio Supreme Court twice struck it down. Idaho's law has also been partially struck down by the courts, and as a result it no longer covers local government employees. Washington amended its 1992 paycheck law in 2007 to significantly narrow the definition of union political activities covered by the legislation. Arizona and Alabama passed paycheck measures in 2011, but the courts have blocked both measures. In March 2013, a federal district court ruled unconstitutional

[69] While we do not have accurate figures on how much it would have cost unions to comply with Proposition 32's 'opt-in' provision, we do have figures on how much it cost unions to comply with the more extensive financial reporting forms introduced by the George W. Bush DOL, a considerably easier financial burden than collecting permission slips from every member. According to the DOL, the cost for submitting the new LM-2 was $24,271 per respondent in the first year, $17,387 per respondent in the second year, and $17,262 per respondent in the third year. The total annual cost to respondents for the revised Form LM-2 was $116.0 million in the first year, $83.1 million in the second year, and $82.5 million in the third year.

the 'Protect Arizona Employees' Paychecks From Politics Act', which was enacted in April 2011.[70]

While we have limited empirical evidence on the actual impact of these laws, on balance, that evidence indicates that they have impaired unions' ability to engage in core political activities. These laws vary considerably but are significantly more limited in scope than was Proposition 32. Some laws cover only public sector unions; others (in common with Proposition 32) cover both public and private sector unions. Some laws contain a narrow definition of political activities, covering only electoral contributions; others (in common with Proposition 32) adopt an expansive definition of political activities. Some laws cover only non-member agency fee payers; others (in common with Proposition 32) cover both union members and non-members. 'Opt-in' provisions in some laws (in common with Proposition 32) require annual written permission from both members and non-members before dues money is used for political activities, while others contain an 'opt-out' mechanism for members and non-members. Given its sweeping scope and broad definitions, Proposition 32 would have had a major impact on unions' ability to engage in core political activities.

Some anti-union organizations, such as the National Right to Work Committee (NRTWC), argue that unions continue to find ways around paycheck legislation to raise and spend members' dues money on politics. According to one conservative critic of paycheck, '[m]any RTW supporters have regarded paycheck-protection legislation as, at best, a diversion of resources, effort, and attention' from more fundamental issues.[71] Thus, NRTWC has argued that a national right-to-work bill—which would outlaw union security agreements in the twenty-seven states that do not currently have right-to-work laws[72] —along with repeal of the National Labor Relations Act and the Railway Labor Act, is the only effective way to overcome the problem of 'union coercion'.

Even among anti-union organizations, however, opposition to paycheck protection is a minority position. Both supporters and opponents of paycheck protection, along with most academic commentators, believe that paycheck bills are (or can be) effective in stopping unions from engaging in their core political functions. One of the principal promoters of paycheck legislation, the Heritage Foundation—which has connections with many state-level organizations that have championed paycheck legislation—argues that legislation in the five states that have it 'has had a clear effect on public sector union contributions for state legislative offices. These laws reduce union campaign donations by approximately 50 percent', thus demonstrating the effectiveness of paycheck protection initiatives in undermining unions' ability to raise money for politics.[73]

[70] Daily Labor Report, 'Federal Court Strikes Down Arizona Statutes, Including Check-off and Picketing Restrictions' 5 April 2013.

[71] Charles W. Baird, 'Paycheck Protection in California: What Went Wrong?' The Freeman: Ideas on Liberty 48:11 (November 1998). Available at <http://www.thefreemanonline.org/columns/paycheck-protection-in-california-what-went-wrong/> accessed 1 June 2013.

[72] In September 2013, a state judge struck down Indiana's right-to-work law, which had been signed into law in February 2012. Thus, at the time of writing, twenty-three states have right-to-work laws, but the state's Attorney General will appeal the decision and the Indiana ruling may be overturned on appeal.

[73] James Sherk, 'What Do Union Members Want? What Paycheck Protection Laws Show About How Well Unions Reflect Their Members' Priorities', Heritage Foundation, 30 August 2006. Available at <http://www.heritage.org/research/reports/2006/08/what-do-union-members-want-what-paycheck-protection-laws-show-about-how-well-unions-reflect-their-members-priorities> accessed 15 June 2013.

Another conservative organization that advocates for paycheck legislation, the Florida-based James Madison Institute, believes that Utah's law in particular has had a profound impact on unions' political activities. Utah's 'Voluntary Contributions Act' has had 'a serious effect' on public sector worker contributions to the Utah Education Association's segregated PAC fund. Utah's language is the 'gold standard' for other states to emulate. It also states that Washington's paycheck measure (Initiative 134) has constrained the Washington Education Association's (WEA) political fundraising, and calls 'a myth' the argument that paycheck is 'ineffective and doesn't really control union spending'.[74]

One organization that played a key role in the enactment of paycheck legislation in Washington state, the Evergreen Freedom Foundation (EFF), believes that the legislation has been effective at constraining unions' ability to raise money for politics: 'The law had an immediate and dramatic effect on unions' ability to collect political dues.' The money raised by the WEA fell by almost 90 per cent after one year of the new law. Since then, the EFF argues, funds raised by the WEA have never exceeded 20 per cent of the pre-paycheck law level. In Idaho, paycheck legislation has also had a profound impact; according to the EFF, political funds raised by unions fell by over 70 per cent. In common with the Madison Institute, however, the EFF reserves most praise for Utah's paycheck protection legislation: 'The amount of money raised by Utah unions for politics fell from $155,000 to $40,000—a 75 percent drop. In 2001, the UEA had over $600,000 in its PAC. In every election year since then, UAE has been forced into deficit spending.' [75]

Given the totality of the evidence on the impact of these measures, academics have concluded that paycheck protection does seriously hinder unions' ability to participate in politics. A national paycheck protection law, one study concluded, would have 'substantially hindered' unions' ability to participate in the 2008 election cycle. Paycheck legislation 'clearly has the potential to shrink Labor's capacity to spend money on politics by large amounts', without which it is difficult to compete in politics.[76]

Considering it had a broad definition of union political activities, the fact that it applied to public and private unions and to members as well as non-members, required annual written permission, and, most importantly, prohibited the use of money raised through payroll deduction, even with annual written permission, the impact of Proposition 32 would have been greater than any of the existing five state paycheck protection laws. Given the amount of money currently being spent on California politics by business interests and wealthy individuals, Proposition 32 would almost certainly have made it impossible for California unions to compete effectively in state and local politics.[77]

[74] The James Madison Institute, 'Backgrounder: A Paycheck Protection Primer for Florida', March 2006, No. 48. Available at <http://www.jamesmadison.org/pdf/materials/467.pdf> accessed 15 June 2013. The Washington Education Association also reported that the paycheck law had a 'dramatic negative impact' on its ability to raise money for politics. Quoted in Broder 97 (n 10).

[75] Michael Reitz, 'Paychecks Unprotected: Lessons Learned in California and Other States' *Capital Research Center: Labor Watch*, January 2006. Available at <http://capitalresearch.org/pubs/pdf/LW0106.pdf> accessed 15 June 2013.

[76] Masters, Gibney, and Zagenczyk 574 (n 9).

[77] Jones and Titus (n 35). California Watch, 'The Rainmakers: California's top political donors, 2001–2011' (no date). Available at <http://rainmaker.apps.cironline.org/> accessed 15 June 2013.

Conclusion

For the past two decades, California has been at the epicentre of right-wing efforts to enact paycheck protection legislation, which would seriously impair the ability of American unions to participate in politics. In 1998, the defeat of Proposition 226 slowed the nationwide conservative push for paycheck protection legislation. Proposition 75, which was voted down in 2005, represented an early effort to constrain the influence of public sector unions, before the slew of anti-public sector union legislation since 2011. In November 2012, Californians rejected the most sweeping paycheck protection measure yet proposed, Proposition 32, in what was the most expensive and high profile campaign the country has ever seen. In the months leading up to the election, the pro and anti-Proposition 32 sides spent over $135 million on the bitterly contested electoral campaign.

But the defeat of Proposition 32 is unlikely to slow the push for paycheck legislation in the way that the defeat of Proposition 226 did in the late 1990s. In the past two years, as part of a much broader state-level assault on public sector unions, almost half of the states in the country have considered or are considering legislation that would restrict unions' ability to raise or spend money on politics. Although only a few states have thus far enacted this legislation, and unions have successfully challenged most of these laws in the courts, paycheck protection legislation remains a central goal for conservative organizations in the United States. Paycheck protection laws do not offer any significant new legal protections for dissenting employees or respond to a documented problem of employee objections to union political spending, but they restrict the ability of unions to effectively participate in politics.

15

Public Service Voice under Strain in an Era of Restructuring and Austerity

Stephen Bach and Gregor Gall

Introduction

Traditionally, the public services has been viewed as one of the most secure locations for the expression of voice by workers and this has been reflected in high levels of union density and collective bargaining coverage in the vast majority of industrialized countries.[1] In historical perspective, the public services only became a stronghold of union presence from the 1960s onwards. This was linked to the expansion of public services, the increased willingness of public services workers to join unions in periods of government wage restraint, and the uneven spread of collective bargaining rights for many public services workers in countries such as Australia, Canada, and the United States.[2] But it was also linked to government encouragement of union membership and collective bargaining for the public services in a number of other countries like Britain and Germany, indicating that the notion of the state as a model and fair employer held some sway in this former period. Public services reforms over recent decades, however, notably privatization, marketization, and managerialism, coalescing around a New Public Management (NPM)[3] have altered the climate for the expression of employee voice. The strengthening of managerial prerogatives and redrawing the line between state and market provision has created a far less conducive context for employee voice, although in some regions, notably the Nordic countries, commitment to public services voice remains intact. The onset of the economic and financial crisis from 2007–2008 reinforced and intensified many of these existing trends and marked the start of more systematic and concerted attempts to erode traditional forms of employee voice in the public services in many jurisdictions.[4]

It has been the transformation of a crisis that originated in the dysfunctional operation of financial and capital markets into a sovereign debt crisis centred on public expenditure that has encouraged governments—and been used by governments

[1] Lorenzo Bordogna and Roberto Pedersini, 'Public sector industrial relations' in *Industrial Relations in Europe 2012* (European Commission, 2013). Available at: <http://ec.europa.eu/social/main.jsp?catId=738&langId=en&pubId=7498>.

[2] Tiziano Treu, *Public Service Labour Relations: Recent Trends and Future Prospects* (International Labour Organisation, 1997).

[3] Christopher Hood, 'A Public Management for All Seasons?' (1991) 69(1) Public Administration 3.

[4] International Labour Office, *Collective Bargaining in the Public Service: A Way Forward* (ILO, 2013) 125–6.

influenced by neoliberalism—to justify the curtailment of public services employment and wages, usually implemented unilaterally by government without recourse to social dialogue and collective bargaining.[5] These measures have emboldened other governments with an ideological antipathy towards the public services and collective models of employment regulation to attempt to overturn longstanding patterns of public services voice as has occurred in many US states, Britain, and elsewhere.

This chapter examines the current state of employee voice in the public services and the challenges it faces in the aftermath of two decades of managerialism, neoliberalism and the more recent impact of the debt crisis. Voice is a term that was popularized by Hirschman in his analysis of exit, voice, and loyalty, where he defined voice as any attempt to 'change, rather than to escape from, an objectionable state of affairs, whether through individual or collective petition to the management directly in charge'.[6] Subsequently, voice has been used broadly to denote the ability to have a say or express a view but in itself this tells us little about the forms of employee voice, the level at which voice is exercised, or the scope for worker influence over decision-making (especially as having 'a say', i.e., voice, is not synonymous with being listened to and/or exercising influence in order to effect change).[7]

In this chapter, we concentrate upon the most important forms of employee voice in the public services, especially representative (indirect) forms of voice, particularly collective bargaining, but we also note the growth of forms of employer-initiated direct voice. We assume that 'voice at work' for public services workers has a dual purpose. First and foremost, to facilitate a rudimentary form of democracy in the workplace for workers by which the conditions of employment and the organization of work are co-determined. Second, and flowing from this that under such conditions levels of efficiency and effectiveness will—all other things being equal—be enhanced and so deliver for citizens, the end users or consumers, better standards of service provision.[8] As alluded to already, the existence and form of voice at work should not be conflated per se with the processes and nature of voice for the institutions of voice can become hollowed out and eroded such that they have little effect if the original political values underpinning them are discarded and replaced by contrary ones. The consequence of the hollowing out may result in increased inequality vis-à-vis gender, age, and race.

The main focus of this chapter in this regard is the core public services that remain publicly funded and regulated and to some extent (still) publicly provided and owned (although the degree of provision and ownership has declined under the contracting out to—and commissioning of—services from the private sector). These services—central government, local government and the regions, health, and education—constitute

[5] Stephen Bach and Roberto Pedersini, 'The Public Sector in the Crisis' in *Industrial Relations in Europe 2012* (European Commission, 2013). Available at:<http://ec.europa.eu/social/main.jsp?catId=738&langId=en&pubId=7498>. See also Daniel Vaughan-Whitehead, 'Public Sector Shock in Europe: Between structural reforms and quantitative adjustment' in Daniel Vaughan-Whitehead (ed.), *The Public Sector in Shock* (ILO, 2013).

[6] Albert O. Hirschman, *Exit, Voice and Loyalty* (Harvard University Press, 1970) 30.

[7] See also Alan Bogg and Tonia Novitz, 'Investigating "Voice" at Work' (2012) 33(3) Comparative Labor Law and Policy Journal 101 for extended discussion of the application of 'voice' to the workplace.

[8] Alan Bogg, Anthony Forsyth, and Tonia Novitz, 'Worker Voice in Australia and New Zealand: the role of the state reconfigured?' (2013) Adelaide Law Review (forthcoming).

an increasingly important location of voice at work as private services collective bargaining and union membership shrink in the majority of countries.[9] The public services increasingly comprise the bedrock of the union movement and this is exemplified by the increased proportion of union members that are women and employed within occupations such as teaching, nursing, and social work.

Employee Voice in the Public Services: A Distinctive Model?

It has long been recognized that the regulation of employment relations in the public services and the adoption of systems of employee voice that include the right to collective bargaining raise a number of issues that do not arise in the private services. These issues and their attendant complexities stem from the frequently conflicting roles that the state plays in its multiple roles as employer, regulator, provider of finance, and policy maker. The state within the bargaining process is, therefore, simultaneously: the employer who seeks to recruit and retain its workforce whilst also responsible for raising revenue to reward its workforce; the policy maker responsible for sound public finances and economic growth; and the regulator of industrial relations. As such, some intellectual traditions and models of public services employment are underpinned by an assumption that these competing roles are incompatible with the establishment of full collective bargaining rights for public services workers. This underscores the distance travelled since the era when national states under some political traditions (like social democracy) sought to act as a model employer, whereby they set standards of employment and employment relationships which they encouraged private services employers to emulate. (Of course, under neoliberalism, the state as employer seeks to emulate and proffer a different type of exemplar.)

In addition to bargaining and concertation in the political arena (often termed 'political exchange'), whether on local, regional, or national scales and directly with governments or indirectly through affiliation to political parties, unions in the public services have since the late 1960s developed forms of workplace unionism which have complemented their national bargaining activities (even if they never attained the advanced state of development of workplace unionism found in the private services). The development of extensive workplace unionism is of particular note given that worker voice at only—or predominantly—the national level suffers from a democratic deficit in terms of membership, union participation, and co-determination of workplace governance (for example, implementation of national agreements, work organization, local issues etcetera). As with the erosion of the efficacy of national bargaining for unions, the rise of NPM has also undermined the efficacy of local bargaining for unions as the managerial prerogative has been asserted in a unilateral manner often guided by the ideology of unitarism.

This perspective of public services peculiarity was expressed most forcibly by US commentators in the 1960s and 1970s in a context of public services union membership growth and the establishment of public services collective bargaining. Wellington and Winter and Summers argued that public services collective bargaining differed

[9] Bordogna and Pedersini (n 1).

fundamentally from the private services because it was primarily a political rather than an economic process.[10] The implication was that it potentially distorted the democratic process because it gave one interest group, public services workers and their representatives, privileged access to state officials via the bargaining table and excessive influence over budgetary decisions in the wage negotiation process. They did not conclude that collective bargaining should be prohibited but cautioned that private services labour law doctrine should not be transferred to the public services without modification.[11]

Although seldom articulated in such stark terms in a European context, a questioning of the legitimacy of public services collective bargaining has surfaced in recent years with austerity measures such as unilaterally imposed wage cuts and wage freezes often legitimized by reference to public services workforces' so-called 'privileged' terms and conditions that stem from their economic and political influence in the bargaining process. The contentious nature of public services collective bargaining has been especially pronounced in some countries, as recent developments in the United States testify (see later). By contrast it is widely acknowledged that collective bargaining balances the needs of employers for flexibility with worker concerns to minimize uncertainty and risk. By establishing clear rights of—and obligations on—both parties, it establishes understandings between the actors and prevents arbitrary intervention as well as facilitating involvement, enabling wider ownership and greater legitimacy for decisions.[12]

In general, collective bargaining has become a feature of public services employment regulation in many industrialized countries with major implications for employee voice and union practice. In some respects, public services unions retain considerable organizational advantages compared to their private services counterparts. Traditionally, they have operated in contexts in which union presence is more accepted, with less overt hostility from employers, and there are fewer organizational constraints as membership is often concentrated in large employer units. Public services unions can leverage political influence, articulating particular claims as legitimate public interests, recognizing that governments are often sensitive to the electoral consequences of public service workforce dissatisfaction.[13] Finally, although the public services have been the target of outsourcing, here unions are threatened less directly by the process of globalization. Many public services are less amenable to transfer overseas, although public service offshoring is not unknown.[14]

Union density in the public services is with a few exceptions higher than in the private services, and sometimes by a wide margin.[15] This is evident in the current cases in

[10] Harry H. Wellington and Ralph K. Winter, *The Unions and the Cities: Studies of Unionism in Government* (Brookings Institute, 1971); Robert Summers, 'Public Sector Bargaining Substantially Diminishes Democracy' (1980) 1 Government Union Review 5 but compare Allan Flanders, 'Collective Bargaining: a theoretical analysis' (1968) 6(1) British Journal of Industrial Relations (BJIR) 1.

[11] Compare Bob Hepple, 'Labour law and public employees in Britain' in W.T. Murphy and Kenneth William Wedderburn (eds), *Labour Law and the Community: Perspectives for the 1980s* (Institute for Advanced Legal Studies, 1983) 67.

[12] Susan Hayter, 'Introduction' in Susan Hayter (ed.), *The Role of Collective Bargaining in the Global Economy* (Edward Elgar, 2012) 1.

[13] Paul Johnston, *Success While Others Fail: Social Movement Unionism and the Public Workplace* (ILR Press, 1994).

[14] K.-H. Yu and Frank Levy, 'Offshoring Professional Services: Institutions and professional control' (2010) 48(4) BJIR 758.

[15] See for example David Blanchflower 'International Patterns of Union Membership' (2007) 45(1) BJIR 6.

Britain (57 per cent v 15 per cent), Greece (64 per cent v 19 per cent), and Ireland (67 per cent v 21 per cent) but also in the Nordic countries as well[16] with a similar polarity in Australia (43 per cent v 13 per cent) and Canada (69 per cent v 15 per cent). Wide gaps also exist outside of Europe such as in the United States (41 per cent v 8 per cent).[17] Moreover, the majority of union members in many of these countries are now to be found in the public services, and this primarily accounts for the greater coverage of collective bargaining in the public services sector than in the private services sector.[18] In other words, the heartland of labour unionism is now to be found in the public services and not in manufacturing as it once was. A main exception to high public services union density is amongst the former communist countries of central and eastern Europe where union density in countries such as the Czech Republic and Poland is well below ten per cent.[19]

Despite relatively high union density, public services collective bargaining is complicated by the distinctive role of the state that influences the process and outcomes of collective bargaining. In some countries the state has been unwilling to grant collective bargaining rights to public servants that are viewed as an organic and integral part of the state (e.g. Germany in relation to the *Beamte*) rather than as employees with their own distinct interests.[20] Even if collective bargaining rights are granted, the state has a dual role in the bargaining process; it is one of the parties that negotiates the substantive rules of an agreement, but it also regulates the procedural rules that define the relationship between the parties. This provides considerable latitude for the state to limit the role of collective bargaining. There is scope to use other methods such as legal regulation or executive decisions to define the employment relationship and to alter collective bargaining unilaterally as economic and political circumstances alter.

Sovereign and model employer traditions

It is conventional to distinguish between two main public services employment relations traditions labelled by Beaumont,[21] namely, the sovereign employer approach and the model employer approach. In the sovereign model tradition, public servants are regarded as distinct from other wage earners because they are servants of the state and, therefore, no differentiation exists between the interests of the state and those that work for it. Consequently, a conventional pluralist industrial relations model of differentiated interests, and the acceptance of collective negotiations, does not hold sway.

[16] See Bordogna and Pedersini (n 1).

[17] Richard C. Kearney, 'Public Sector Management Relations: Change or status quo?' (2010) 30(1) Review of Public Personnel Administration 89. And within the USA itself the variation of public sector union density by state ranges from 73 per cent in New York to 8 per cent in North Carolina (Chris Edwards, 'Public Sector Unions' (2010) 61 Tax and Budget Bulletin (Cato Institute)).

[18] See Susan Hayter, *Social Dialogue Indicators—International Statistical Inquiry 2008-09: Technical Brief* (ILO, 2011) 13–14 for overall bargaining coverage by country and European Commission, *Industrial Relations in Europe 2012* (Social Affairs and Inclusion Unit B.1 2013) 47 for comparison of overall and public service bargaining coverage in Europe.

[19] See Bordogna and Pedersini (n 1).

[20] Brendt Keller, 'After the End of Stability: Recent trends in the public sector of Germany' (2011) 22(11) International Journal of Human Resource Management (IJHRM) 2331.

[21] Phil Beaumont, *Public Sector Industrial Relations* (Routledge, 1992).

Instead, employment regulation is founded upon unilateral state control of the conduct of employment relations by laws and the adoption of specific public service statutes. Statutory regulation determines terms and conditions of employment and the right to collective bargaining and the associated right to strike has been absent or severely circumscribed. The corollary is that state employees are granted special employment status and rights in relation to pay, pensions, and employment security. This highly prescribed model of employment regulation with a strong legal basis has been associated strongly with many continental European countries, such as France[22] and Germany, and countries such as Japan.[23] In the United States, federal employees have the right to bargain over workplace issues but not wages, whilst at state and local level there is considerable variation in the extent to which collective bargaining rights are granted and the occupational groups covered by collective bargaining.[24]

By contrast, the model employer tradition is based less on isolating the public services from processes of joint regulation and more on the state seeking to establish standards that other employers can emulate. It is based upon a common law tradition that does not draw a sharp distinction between systems of employment regulation in the public and private services and is more associated with Anglo-Saxon countries. In Britain, the difference between public and private services employment regulation has always been less marked than in many countries with collective bargaining arrangements established in each main public services industry. In New Zealand, the separate employment statute of public services workers was abolished in the late 1980s and the Employment Relations Act 2000 promotes collective bargaining, but there is no obligation upon the parties to conclude an agreement. In Australia, the Public Service Act 1999 provides for the delegation of employment relations responsibilities to agencies and worked in tandem with the implementation of the neoliberal *Work Choices* programme of the conservative National-Liberal coalition governments of 1996–2007.[25] The trend was only partly reversed by the Labor governments (2007–2013) under their *Fair Work* programme.[26] Canada also has a well-established tradition of public services collective bargaining.[27]

[22] Lorenzo Bordogna and Stefano Neri, 'Convergence towards an NPM Programme or Different Models? Public Service Employment Relations in Italy and France' (2011) 22(11) IJHRM 2311; and W. Kickert, 'Public Management Reform in Countries with a Napoleonic State Model: France, Italy and Spain' in Christopher Pollitt, Sandra Van Thiel, and Vincent Homburg (eds), *New Public Management: Adaptation and Alternatives* (Palgrave, 2007).

[23] ILO 146 (n 4).

[24] Stephen Bach and Rebecca Kolins Givan, 'Varieties of New Public Management? The reform of public service employment relations in the UK and USA' (2011) 22(11) IJHRM 2349; and Richard Freeman and Eunice Han, 'The War Against Public Sector Collective Bargaining in the US' (2012) 54(3) Journal of Industrial Relations 386.

[25] David Peetz and Janis Bailey, 'Neo-liberal Evolution and Union Responses in Australia' in Gregor Gall, Adrian Wilkinson, and Richard Hurd (eds), *International Handbook of Labour Unions: responses to neo-liberalism* (Edward Elgar, 2011) 62.

[26] Rae Cooper and Bradon Ellem, 'Getting to the Table? Fair Work unions and collective bargaining' in Breen Creighton and Anthony Forsyth (eds), *Rediscovering Collective Bargaining: Australia's Fair Work Act in International Perspective* (Routledge, 2012) 135.

[27] ILO (n 4); and Mark Thompson and Daphne Taras, 'Employment Relations in Canada' in Greg Bamber, Russell Lansbury, and Nick Wailes (eds), *International and Comparative Employment Relations* (Sage, 2011).

The distinction between sovereign and model employer traditions highlights different traditions of public services employment regulation, but does not fully capture the variety of systems of employee voice because some countries blend elements of unilateralism with forms of collective bargaining. In broad terms, collective bargaining prevails in Australia, Canada, the United States, New Zealand, all the Nordic countries, Ireland, Netherlands, Italy, and Spain. In other countries, such as parts of central and eastern Europe, collective bargaining institutions exist, but in practice unions and employers associations are often weak, unrepresentative and have limited autonomy resulting in a very uncertain status for collective bargaining in countries such as Hungary.[28] In some countries hybrid systems exist that blend collective bargaining and unilateralism. Germany is a notable case because of its dualistic structure with a sizeable group of *Beamte* that are excluded from collective bargaining.[29] Britain is also a distinctive case because it combines predominantly industry-level collective bargaining practices with a system of pay review bodies, which comprise neither unilateral regulation nor collective bargaining in a strict sense. Employers and unions submit evidence and commission their own research and this encourages a form of arm's-length bargaining, but with the important caveat that the government retains authority to amend, delay, or reject review body recommendations. In recent years, governments in Britain have often rejected—or ignored—the recommendations of pay review bodies.

Even if collective bargaining rights are conceded, controlling the public services pay bill and ensuring orderly industrial relations is a preoccupation for central government. Collective bargaining institutions and practice, therefore, only imperfectly resemble the idea of 'free' collective bargaining. Restrictions may exist on the scope of bargaining, for example, the exclusion of wages from negotiations as occurs in countries as diverse as the Czech Republic, the United States (federal employees), and in Greece for civil servants. Governments also often intervene directly or indirectly in the bargaining process, limiting the autonomy of the parties. In some jurisdictions governments have to approve the outcomes of negotiations and any agreement reached may not be binding on the government that may amend or ignore any agreement. These systems therefore are more akin to unilateral regulation than collective bargaining (e.g. France, Japan). There is also considerable variation in the coverage of collective bargaining and limitations are often extended to curtail the expression of voice through strike action. Restrictions are commonly applied to the armed forces, police, and the judiciary but also it is not unusual for career civil servants to be prohibited from taking industrial action. Even if industrial action is permitted, specific regulations impose notice periods required prior to strike action, minimum service levels to be provided during strikes, and other provisions that usually apply to what are termed 'essential' public services.[30] A final and frequent component of state regulation relates to the establishment of special procedures and institutional arrangements to resolve collective disputes.

[28] S. Hámori and J. Köllő, 'Hungary: Public sector labour market from crisis to crisis' in Daniel Vaughan-Whitehead (ed.), *The Public Sector in Shock* (International Labour Office, 2013).

[29] Keller (n 20).

[30] Bordogna and Pedersini (n 1); and Carmen La Macchia, 'The Protection of the Strike in the Internal National Legal Systems' in Carmen La Macchia, *The Right to Strike in the EU* (Ediesse, 2011).

Trends

Such distinctive features of public services employment regulation under the sovereign model were partly eroded in the 1960s and 1970s with the growth of union membership accompanied by pressure to concede bargaining rights to these members' unions. Public employment in areas such as education, health, and social work grew rapidly, eclipsing employment in traditional civil service functions associated with distinctive forms of employment regulation.[31] In the subsequent decades reforms of the public services were widespread, eroding further differences with private services employment regulation but in a context in which employee voice was starting to retreat rather than advance. These trends have been associated with the adoption, in many countries albeit to varying degrees, of NPM reforms in the 1980s and 1990s that encouraged public services employers to emulate private services practice, advocated as a way to boost efficiency and effectiveness.[32] These reforms have been associated with the spread of neoliberalism that assigned primacy to the development of market relations. Opportunities increased for public–private partnerships with government and for commercial enterprises to provide core public services. This process required an interventionist state to roll back its activities and reach, challenging institutions associated with the Keynesian welfare state such as centralized collective bargaining. It also required state policies to roll out and embed a neoliberal approach to governance such as the establishment of more autonomous commercially orientated hospitals or competition rules intended to encourage provider diversity and competition.[33] Using the example of Britain, this agenda had three main components.

First, privatization and marketization were widely adopted, even if the timing and government motives varied.[34] In Britain, a far-reaching programme of privatization occurred with most nationalized industries and public enterprises transferred into the private sector. Collective bargaining remained the dominant form of pay determination in privatized companies, but it became more decentralized, and widespread enterprise restructuring was reflected in more disparate bargaining structures. The ability of unions to mobilize their members diminished, and senior- and middle-management grades were often excluded from collective bargaining.[35] The remaining public services were subject to a process of market-testing. The initial emphasis in the early 1980s on cleaning and refuse collection was extended to incorporate white-collar 'back-office' functions such as IT and payroll services. The Workplace Employee Relations Survey

[31] Treu (n 2).

[32] Stephen Bach and Giuseppe Della Rocca, 'The Management Strategies of Public Service Employers in Europe' (2000) 31(2) Industrial Relations Journal 82; Organisation of Economic Cooperation and Development, *Governance in Transition: Public Management Reforms in OECD Countries* (OECD, 1995); and Christopher Pollitt and Geert Bouckaert, *Public Management Reform: a Comparative Analysis. NPM Governance and the Neo-Weberian State* (OUP, 2011).

[33] Jamie Peck and Adam Tickell, 'Neoliberalizing Space' (2002) 34(3) Antipode 380; and Dexter Whitfield, *In Place of Austerity: Reconstructing the Economy, State and Public Services* (Spokesman, 2012).

[34] Harvey Feigenbaum, Jeffrey Henig and Chris Hamnett, *Shrinking the State: The Political Underpinnings of Privatization* (CUP, 1998).

[35] Andrew Pendleton 'What Impact has Privatisation had on Pay and Employment? A review of the UK experience' (1997) 52(3) Relations Industrielles 554.

(WERS) indicated that by 1990, 98 per cent of central government workplaces outsourced some services, a higher figure than for any other services in the economy.[36] Regardless of whether a service was retained in-house or outsourced, this policy led to substantial reductions in the workforce and accompanying pay-roll savings. Women were particularly hard hit and their employment tended to decline more than men's, especially as job losses were greatest amongst part-time workers.[37]

Public services unions were least effective in resisting contracting out in the most highly unionized workplaces.[38] The outcome was substantial employment reductions and worsening terms and conditions of employment, especially prior to the application of TUPE regulations.[39] Employee voice was also frequently curtailed because when a public service employer granted union representatives facilities time, it did not extend to members employed by a private services or voluntary services contractor, because this would effectively result in the public service employer subsidising the private services. However, as private contractors often do not recognize unions or provide facility time a representation gap emerges and union membership has declined.

Second, organizational reforms fragmented the public services with the establishment of more autonomous, commercially orientated enterprises, breaking up so-called monolithic public services into their constituent business units, as part of the creation of arm's length executive agencies, managed by contract-based forms of regulation. Many organizational units were reconstituted as employers, requiring unions to develop their workplace presence to ensure effective employee voice. These measures also included a blurring of the boundaries between the public, private, and voluntary services. The influence of senior managers was strengthened and human resource practices devolved, including enhanced responsibility for establishing pay and conditions on a more decentralized basis. Public services managers were encouraged to use managerial techniques typical of the private services with greater emphasis on leadership skills and the promotion of performance management, underpinned by targets to ensure compliance with government priorities.

Finally, several consequences for employee voice stem from these changes as the case of Britain illustrates. A key trend has been the development of employer-led direct systems of individual employee voice, such as the use of briefing groups and staff opinion surveys. For example, regular meetings between senior management and the workforce increased from 44 per cent to 54 per cent between 1998 and 2004. In the same period the number of public services workplaces with an on-site Joint Consultative Committee (JCC) declined from 39 per cent to 33 per cent.[40] In addition, as in many countries,

[36] N. Millward, M. Stevens, D. Smart, and W. Hawes, *Workplace Industrial Relations in Transition* (Routledge, 1992).

[37] K. Escott and D. Whitfield, 'The Gender Impact of CCT in Local Government' Equal Opportunities Commission Research Series No 12 (EOC, 1995).

[38] Millward et al. 342 (n 36).

[39] Deborah Foster and Peter Scott 'Competitive Tendering of Public Services and Industrial Relations Policy: The Conservative agenda under Thatcher and Major 1979–97' (1998) 6 Historical Studies in Industrial Relations 101.

[40] Stephen Bach, Rebecca Kolins Givan, and John Forth, 'The Public Sector in Transition' in William Brown, Alex Bryson, John Forth, and Keith Whitfield (eds), *The Evolution of the Modern Workplace* (CUP, 2009) 325.

there has been a process of decentralization of pay determination and the incentivization of pay through bonuses and other forms of performance related pay.[41] These trends combined with the marketization and fragmentation of the public services weaken the regulatory effects of sectoral agreements and made it more difficult for trade unions to maintain effective employee voice in the public services, a situation that became more acute after 2008.

Austerity

The economic and financial crisis that erupted during 2008 led to a rapid deterioration in the fiscal position of the public services in the majority of OECD countries. The preoccupation with public expenditure directed attention at the public services pay bill and, to varying degrees, the crisis has been used by governments to undermine employee voice. After several decades in which NPM reforms aimed to enhance the similarity of employment practices in the public and private sectors, the crisis has underlined the distinctive capacity of the state as an employer to act unilaterally to determine the terms and conditions of public services employment.[42] Many governments have asserted that they have little option but to implement austerity measures (vis-à-vis employment numbers and pay) as rapidly as possible to reassure financial markets and this has often resulted in established systems of tripartite discussion and collective bargaining being suspended or modified (for example, in Greece[43]). The ILO Committee of Experts has examined the conditions in which collective agreements can be limited in periods of economic crisis and suggested that they are admissible if there has been prior consultation with workers' and employers' organizations and certain conditions apply including: being applied as an exceptional measure that is time limited and safeguards exist to protect workers' standard of living.[44] The experience of austerity measures suggests that these conditions are not being fulfilled and the ILO recently expressed concern in its Oslo Declaration that 'social dialogue and collective bargaining serve as effective tools to mitigate the impact of the crisis, but in many countries they have been weakened'.[45]

Four main developments have occurred: a return to unilateralism and the erosion of employee voice; the repeal of collective bargaining arrangements; reduced scope of collective bargaining; and direct or indirect attacks on public services unionism. A large number of governments have imposed wage freezes or wage cuts without any prior consultation with employer or union organizations. In countries that have received external financial assistance such as Greece, Portugal, Romania, and Spain amongst others there has been negligible consultation or negotiation. In many cases, such as the wage freezes, pay caps, or increases in employee pension contributions, these measures have been announced in Parliament bypassing established channels of employee voice. Public

[41] Stephen Bach and Lorenzo Bordogna, 'Reframing Public Service Employment Relations: The impact of economic crisis and the new EU economic governance' (2013) 19(4) European Journal of Industrial Relations 279; and Organisation of Economic Cooperation and Development, *Public Sector Compensation in Times of Austerity* (OECD, 2012).

[42] Bach and Bordogna (n 41). [43] ILO 125 (n 4). [44] ILO 124 (n 4).

[45] International Labour Office, *The Oslo Declaration: Restoring confidence in jobs and growth* (ILO, 2013) 1.

services employers in Britain have been the main user of section 188 redundancies—a method by which to impose changes in terms and conditions of employment upon pain of a 'sign or be sacked' offer of new contracts.[46] In other cases such as Italy, the government simply cancelled the bargaining round and imposed pay cuts. These changes, therefore, reflect a new centralized unilateralism which resembles the traditional unilateral regulation of the public services industrial relations by central political authorities, but with a renewed emphasis on cost control. The assumption, however, reflected in the requirement on governments to return to Parliament to extend wage freezes is that these represent exceptional and *temporary* measures. By contrast, in some jurisdictions there has been a concerted attempt to *remove* collective bargaining rights.

Severe deficits at national or local level and an ideological climate hostile to the public services workforce and their representatives have been used to remove collective bargaining rights. In Britain, the Conservative-Liberal Democrat Coalition government abolished the School Support Staff Negotiating Body that was established by the Labour government to negotiate pay and conditions and provide a national framework for careers and salaries for school support staff. Republican governors in US states have been in the vanguard of highly contested legislative moves to repeal bargaining rights. In Wisconsin, Governor Walker enacted the 'Budget Repair Bill' that denied state and local employees the right to negotiate on issues like pensions, healthcare benefits, and working conditions and severely circumscribed the parameters of wage bargaining increases.[46a] Ohio and Michigan have moved in a similar direction. Two other states, Oklahoma and Tennessee, also curtailed collective bargaining rights, whilst states including Nevada removed bargaining rights for specific groups such as doctors.[47]

A third shift in policy has been the narrowing of the scope of collective bargaining and legislatures have removed and in many cases prohibited bargaining over a range of issues with health care benefits the most frequent item removed from the bargaining agenda in the US.[48] In several EU countries, such as Spain during 2012, an increased 37.5-hour working week was imposed on all public services employees. Another mechanism that has been used to amend collective bargaining has been the increased use of dispute resolution procedures including mandatory arbitration. In some jurisdictions, such as Canada, so-called 'back to work' legislation requires the resumption of work and changes to impasse procedures that increase significantly employer control over the final terms and conditions of employment; also a feature of recent US developments.[49] Finally, there have been concerted attempts to undermine the role of public services unions and to limit their scope to fund and organize their activities. In the UK the Conservative Coalition government has outlined plans to limit facilities time, that is, the provision of work time to carry out union duties. A prevalent characteristic of recent bills on collective bargaining has been measures that have an adverse effect on unions' ability to collect fees from non-members that are free riders.[50]

[46] Gregor Gall, 'The Fight Against Sneaky Pay Cuts', The Guardian's *Comment is free*, 7 July 2011, <http://www.guardian.co.uk/commentisfree/2011/jul/07/council-pay-cuts-unions>.

[46a] Freeman and Han (n 24).

[47] Martin Malin, 'The Legislative Upheaval in Public-sector Labor Law: A search for common elements' (2012) 27 ABA Journal of Labor and Employment Law 149.

[48] Malin, 149 (n 47). [49] Malin, 149 (n 47). [50] Freeman and Han (n 24).

Summary so far

To summarize, outright, formal or *de jure* derecognition (or decertification) of unions for representational and collective bargaining purposes has been rare for this involves an open and high risk strategy of assault upon unions. Instead, and apart from a few cases, different means of undermining the integrity of the institutions and processes by which unions bargain collectively have been used to affect varying forms of de facto partial derecognition, through studied neglect, hollowing out of institutions, reductions in the facilities granted to unions to allow them to engage in bargaining and representation, and management unilateralism. (Whether these prove to be permanent or merely contingent—or ideological or instrumental—features of the age of austerity remains to be seen.) The procedural and substantive outcomes have seen a clear reduction in not only the terms and conditions of employment of public services workers but also a diminution of their ability to positively influence these terms and conditions. Employers are not replacing the union-based system of collective bargaining with other means of (non-union) joint co-determination so that a 'representation gap'[51] is emerging in the public services (albeit it is far smaller than in the private services). In many countries of southern Europe as well as Britain and the United States, mass strikes as a tool of political exchange have been used by public services unions to try to resuscitate bargaining and political exchange called tripartism but without much success.[52] Similarly, the creation of new, leftist political parties (like Die Linke in Germany and Bloco de Esquerda in Portugal) has made relatively little impact in helping to combat the domination of neoliberalism amongst governments of a centre-right or centre-left hue. Indeed, the main form of social dialogue which exists is de facto bipartism, whereby government consults employers and business organizations or is open to lobbying from employers and business organizations. This is particularly evident in that performance indicators that are used by governments for the public services are increasingly based on those of the private services and treating citizens as consumers.

Resolving the Democratic Deficit

Pertinent and rigorous criticism can be made of the ineffectual responses of public services unions in industrial, political, and ideological terms to the reconfiguration of collective bargaining in the public services. Put another way, the success of neoliberalism is not merely attributable to just the strength of one side of the equation, namely, the forces of the neoliberals, but also the weakness of the opposing side too. Given that the modus operandi of public services unionism is primarily a political one—even where strikes are used because they represent a political rather than economic form of attempted leverage—it is useful to note that these unions have very much suffered

[51] Brian Towers, *The Representation Gap: Change and Reform in the British and American Workplace* (OUP, 1997).

[52] See, for example, G. Gall, 'Quiescence Continued? Recent strike activity in nine Western European economies' (2013) 34(4) Economic and Industrial Democracy 667.

from the implosion of traditional state-based social democracy at the same time as being unable (or unwilling) to articulate and prosecute a renewed form of popular and participative social democracy. Because the modus operandi of public services unionism has been (centralized) political exchange, there has been a relative under-development of its workplace unionism presence and prowess. This has not put public services unionism in a strong position to resist neoliberalism at either the national or local levels. Even though public services unionism has been weakened as a political and industrial force, we believe it still has a central role to play in resolving the democratic deficit and ordaining effective voice at work through re-establishing social democracy.

The hallmark of social democracy is the pursuit of social justice by regulating the processes and outcomes of market mechanisms so as to moderate and ameliorate them. As a state-based project (sometimes referred to as 'state socialism'), rather than one predicated upon organizations of popular participation in civil society, the colonization and takeover of the state by the forces of neoliberalism has rendered the idea and practice of existing social democracy ineffective. Concomitant, the trajectory towards building a non-state based form of social democracy through the organs of civil society (including unions and community organizations) has not been made any easier while unions themselves have overwhelmingly sought to retake the state by installing left-of-centre labour-type parties back in office. This is not least because, on the one hand, these attempts have been largely unsuccessful, and on the other hand, the left-of-centre parties are no longer social democratic parties but social liberal versions of neoliberalism so they did not fulfil the expectations of their union supporters. Cumulatively, public services unions have become increasingly disempowered and disenfranchised as a result.

Notwithstanding this, the weakness of public services unions—as well as unions in general—compels a two-pronged approach of a radical political economy perspective in order to re-establish the socialization of the economy, polity, and society, and of which the re-establishment of full collective bargaining and co-determination in the public services is a major component. The power of the state apparatus (and the social forces which have captured it) cannot be wished away nor can they be evaded by establishing autonomous spheres of existence. This is particularly true in the case of the public services which are part of the state. Thus, a strategy to recapture the state apparatus through the political process is required but where activities outside of the electoral and representative democracy arenas complement and reinforce this. Thus, parliamentary and extra-parliamentary means are required in a way which creates a counter force which is greater than the sum of its parts. The focus of extra-parliamentary activity would be to create progressive alliances between unions and other forces in civil society. Their purpose would be to help deliver and ensure control of the parliamentary means as well as to act as a support to it should resistance be met from the personnel of the state apparatus. But in order for this approach of a radical political economy perspective to become a possibility, the public services unions—in concert with all unions—are required to transform themselves from bodies which still work largely to the framework of the division of unions dealing with the economic/industrial issues affecting their members and Labour-type parties dealing with the political issues affecting their members. In other words, the unions must become more thoroughly political agencies. Through this radical political economy perspective the democratic deficit of the workplace and society in regard of worker/employee voice could be resolved. This highlights starkly that the problem of the democratic deficit in the workplace, epitomized by the concept of 'voice at work', cannot be resolved in the workplace alone. Nor can it be addressed exclusively within an industrial relations framework.

From here to there

There are two critical components to resolving the deficiencies in voice at work and the wider democratic deficit. The first is to create and articulate a compelling and credible vision of an alternative counter vision or narrative. The second is to construct the social forces that are capable of successfully prosecuting such a vision or narrative. The first is necessary but without being sufficient for success for the two components are not only organically and intimately linked but self-reinforcing. Thus, the credibility of the vision is central to creating the requisite social forces to pursue the vision. Concomitant, the credibility of the vision is vastly enhanced to a wider array of potentially supportive citizens when it becomes clear that the vision has begun to attract a critical mass of supporters.

Looking at the first component, the articulation of a desired or preferable 'model' or 'exemplar' which combines aspirations with existing practice elsewhere is one obvious option. Thus, counter-posing an alternative worldview of putting 'people before profit' and pointing to the best practice of an amalgam of the Nordic countries' version of socialized democracy would be one option (notwithstanding that the golden age of social democracy in the Nordic countries has passed). Taking the example of Britain, a political imagination is needed to connect existing material grievances and political discontent to a vision which does not rely upon returning to the past. Thus, envisaging the public services as nationalized industries and not as a system of public (or social) ownership would be to ignore that much of the appeal of Thatcherism was based on attacking what were seen as the failed projects of nationalization and state ownership. In other words, the participation of citizens and not the control of civil service mandarins would be essential to offering an attractive and revitalized vision of public ownership. The controlling influence of citizens by virtue of their participation would facilitate not just transparency, democracy, and accountability but these facets on the basis of the political values of social democracy such as 'people before profit'.

Turning to the second component, it becomes obvious that its achievement is far more challenging than attaining the first component. This is because it requires not just a huge shift in the consciousness of the mass of citizens but also their move from being passive bystanders to active participants in their own fates. The decline in mass political participation in the last 30 years, coupled with the inability of critical voices to undo neoliberalism despite its crisis since 2007, is testament to the scale of the challenge here. Yet such a decline in mass political participation is neither necessarily a permanent nor a secular phenomenon for mass political participation is subject to both upswings and downswings. The '$64m question' is to discover under what circumstances an upswing can or will occur[53] and what place civil society organization outside of the union movement can play.[54]

The means of creating social democracy at work

In order for the political vision and attendant social forces to co-join in re-establishing voice at work in the public services a more detailed menu of proposals needs to be laid out. The basis of this is that public services are those that are publicly owned, controlled, provided, and financed. One key part of a menu would be the obligation of public services employers to engage in meaningful sectoral collective bargaining with the union representative of workers and which can be imposed by a combination of legal and non-legal means (public policy)—as can the insistence for the condition of the awarding of any public services contracts, through public procurement, to the private services to include union recognition and provision for collective bargaining and living wage ordinances. However, rather than just see collective bargaining as the beginning and end of the means for work voice, legal and public policy means could be directed towards creating a framework of co-determination in terms of works councils and supervisory boards. This is important because collective bargaining can have a tendency towards economism, that is, an overdue focus upon wages and conditions that does not adequately address matters of the organization of work at the micro-level as well as issues of investment and policy matters.

In Britain, the Institute of Employment Rights considered that bipartite sectoral employment commissions—creating sectoral agreements—would be the best means by which to re-establish sectoral co-determination.[55] Their remit would extend beyond the normal 'pounds and pence' of traditional collective bargaining and include equal opportunities, training, pensions, establishing minimum employment standards, and implementing European Union directives. To this can be added broader quality of working life concerns which would require some degree of coordination between the sectoral employment commissions. Although this model was promulgated with the private sector in mind (and especially where collective bargaining had been denuded within it), the fragmentation, decentralization, and denudation of bargaining (and attendant structures) in the public services in many countries by the early 2010s as a result of contracting out as well as government reform suggests it could be usefully applied to the public services. Practical issues about the means of imposing obligations (to agree and to implement primarily) and extent of coverage of agreements (for example, by size of employing organization or workplace) would require careful thought but there is enough of a tradition in a handful of continental European countries and in Australia to give some indication about how these challenges may be best dealt with.

[53] See Dan Clawson, *The Next Upsurge: labor and the new social movements* (ILR Press, 2003) and John Kelly, *Rethinking Industrial Relations: Collectivism, mobilisation and long waves* (Routledge, 1998).

[54] See Amanda Tattersall, *Power in Coalition: Strategies for strong unions and social change* (ILR Press, 2010).

[55] See Keith D. Ewing (ed.), *Working Life: A new perspective on labour law* (Lawrence and Wishart, 1996).

16

Voice and the Employment Contract

Douglas Brodie

Introduction

A contract entered into by an employer and a worker is one where the interests and concerns of the latter may well be ignored in the conduct of the relationship. More fundamentally, the worker's interests may be cast aside at the very inception of the relationship and he/she may be unable to insist upon 'employment status', which would confer significant contractual entitlements and statutory rights. There may be no realistic alternative other than to become an independent contractor or be employed through an intermediary. The worker will have very considerable difficulty in influencing the nature and terms of the contract and, once the relationship is entered into, will not find that the position improves. Workers lack voice given the absence of 'the meaningful ability... to present their views and opinions regarding the governance of the workplace'.[1] Marked disparities in bargaining power play a huge part in all of this.

At one time collective bargaining would have been viewed as the primary means of redressing the balance and thereby allowing voice:

> By the organization of labor, and by no other means, it is possible to introduce an element of democracy into the government of industry. By this means only the workers can effectively take part in determining the conditions under which they work. This becomes true in the fullest and best sense only when employers frankly meet the representatives of the workmen, and deal with them as parties equally interested in the conduct of affairs.[2]

Collective bargaining no longer flourishes in any of the jurisdictions under review in this project.

At the same time, and there appears to be a causal connection,[3] judicial perceptions of the employment relationship have changed. In his 1972 Hamlyn lectures Kahn-Freund said that 'the relation between an employer and an isolated employee or worker is typically a relation between a bearer of power and one who is not a bearer of power'.[4] At that time the prospects of judicial endorsement of this passage would have seemed remote, but in more recent years the courts have done just that and accepted the validity of the

[1] Guy Davidov, 'The Goals of Regulating Work: Between Universalism and Selectivity', University of Toronto Law Review, forthcoming, available in draft at <http://www.upf.edu/gredtiss/_pdf/2013-LLRN-Conf_Davidov.pdf> at 14.

[2] XIX Final Report of The Industrial Commission, H.R. Doc. No. 380, 57th Cong., 1st Sess. (1902). The report is referred to in Clyde W. Summers, 'Industrial Democracy: America's Unfulfilled Promise' (1979) 28 Cleveland State Law Review 29, 30.

[3] *South Australia v McDonald* [2009] SASC 219, para. 233.

[4] Otto Kahn-Freund, *Labour and the Law* (Stevens and Sons, 1972) 8.

Kahn-Freund analysis.[5] This chapter compares the respective contributions of judicial intervention and collective bargaining in addressing the imbalance of power in employment relations and allowing the articulation of the employees' interests. The fundamental question posed is whether, and to what extent, the former can compensate for the demise of the latter. At the outset it may be said that collective bargaining would have been expected to perform the following functions: rule-making (both procedural and substantive), provision of the rule of law, and industrial self-government. [6]

Approaching the Imbalance

The judicial acknowledgement that power imbalance is relevant to the adjudication of disputes concerning the employment contract raises a number of difficult questions, such as when does an imbalance become material and how can it be measured. The judiciary have, to some extent, sidestepped these conceptual difficulties by making a number of broad brush assumptions in the interests of the efficient administration of justice. Thus the courts appear to operate on the basis that the distribution of power remains static for the duration of the relationship. This is despite the fact that in all relationships power 'may shift as an exchange relationship is first created and then continues'.[7] For instance, the employee may make himself indispensable to the employer's business (e.g. by achieving exceptional sales figures) and, as a result, the employer may be forced into renegotiating the remuneration package and conceding much better terms. Should the employer fail to recognize that the balance of power has altered, he may forfeit the services of the employee to a rival. It may be said that, a shift in power notwithstanding, the employer will normally remain the dominant party. It is also the case that the courts tend not to differentiate between the positions of employees (despite the infinite variety of circumstances that arise in working life) but view them as a homogeneous class.[8] This makes a good deal of sense from the perspective of the adjudicator who will wish for clear demarcation lines between cases where intervention is appropriate and those where it is not. The outcome in any given case may though be open to question. Finally, the courts appear to disregard the economic position at large at any one time even though this is very relevant to an employee's bargaining position. Where unemployment is low an employee will be less concerned about losing his job and may also be more assertive in setting out the terms upon which he is prepared to

[5] *Slaight Communications v Davidson* [1989] 1 SCR 1038; *Autoclenz v Belcher* [2011] ICR 1157.

[6] Allan Flanders, 'Collective Bargaining: A Theoretical Analysis' (1968) 6 British Journal of Industrial Relations (BJIR) 1, 7.

[7] Stewart Macaulay, 'Non-Contractual Relations in Business; A Preliminary Study' (1963) 28 American Sociological Review 55, 66–7.

[8] This is not always true: *Crimmins v Stevedoring Committee* (1999) 200 CLR 1, para. 44. It is worthy of mention that some highly significant decisions in recent years have resulted from claims made by highly paid employees whose circumstances might otherwise be regarded as atypical. *Société Générale v Geys* [2013] 1 AC 523 is but one example. Such a pattern of litigation may lead to employment protection rights being restricted. For instance, the benefits of the Australian legislation on unfair contracts have been tempered where highly paid employees are concerned. Section 108A of the Industrial Relations Act 1996 (NSW) precludes a claim by an employee whose remuneration package (which is payable to or received by the employee) exceeds the remuneration cap in the 12-month period immediately preceding the application or termination of the contract of employment, whichever is applicable.

be employed: 'a group of workers may have their bargaining position improved when the state of the labour market changes in their favour and employers are strongly competing for scarce labour.'[9]

Correcting the Imbalance

A number of tools are made available to the courts by the general principles of the law of contract should they wish to adjust contractual rights and duties. Much can be achieved through the implication of terms and construction of the contract. Concepts such as economic duress and unconscionability may also come into play where the employment contract is concerned. Resort to the law on implied terms has been a common occurrence. For instance, Australia, Canada, the UK, and a number of states in the USA have all, to varying degrees, gone down the road of regulating employer behaviour through an implied obligation of fair dealing.[10] The courts recognize that, where one party to a contractual relationship is markedly more powerful than the other, there is a real risk of abuse of power. Concern may often focus on contexts where the exercise of the employer's discretion may adversely affect the interests and expectations of the employee. Decisions over whether to allocate work under a zero-hours contract, or to sanction or withhold payment of a bonus or commission are hugely important to the employee. The courts acknowledge that, while the parties to an employment contract are likely to have conflicting interests, where 'the provisions of the contract effectively place the resolution of that conflict in the hands of the party exercising the discretion, it is presumed to be the reasonable expectation and therefore the common intention of the parties that there should be a genuine and rational, as opposed to an empty or irrational, exercise of discretion'.[11] Implied obligations of the fair dealing type may be deployed to challenge decisions (such as those in respect of termination) which go to the very core of the employer's prerogative and have the capacity to impose significant restrictions on an employer's room for manoeuvre. However, their application always involves balancing the conflicting interests of employer and employee and, on occasion, the public interest. Thus it has been said that mutual trust is 'apt to cover the great diversity of situations in which a balance has to be struck between an employer's interest in managing his business as he sees fit and the employee's interest in not being unfairly and improperly exploited'. The strength of the protection afforded very much depends upon how that balance is struck. This is likely to vary across jurisdictions and will fluctuate in any given jurisdiction over time.

The US case of *Fortune v National Cash Register* demonstrates the way in which an implied obligation of fair dealing may restrict the operation of the employment at will doctrine.[12] *Fortune* is worth highlighting given that the latter doctrine is an extremely cogent expression of managerial prerogative and embodies the view that the 'employer

[9] See Flanders (n 6). [10] The terminology may vary.

[11] *Horkulak v Cantor Fitzgerald International* [2004] IRLR 942, 948.

[12] *Fortune v National Cash Register* 373 Mass 96. See James J. Brudney, 'Reluctance and Remorse: The Covenant of Good Faith and Fair Dealing in American Employment Law' (2010) 32 Comparative Labour Law and Policy Journal 773 and Katherine V.W. Stone, 'Revisiting the At-Will Employment Doctrine' (2007) 36 Industrial Law Journal (ILJ) 84.

has sovereignty except to the extent it has expressly granted its employees rights. The doctrine thus expresses and implements the subordination of workers to those who control the enterprise.'[13] It is also the case that the doctrine is deeply engrained in the ideology of the US common law. In *Fortune* a former salesman brought an action to recover bonuses due for sales made while he was still employed. The Supreme Court of Massachusetts held that even though the salesman's contract was terminable at will, there was an implied covenant of good faith in the contract. In addition, the evidence demonstrated that termination had taken place in order to avoid payment of bonuses to the salesman. Dismissal in those circumstances was held to constitute a breach of the contract. The application of the implied obligation gave rise to a result which differed from that flowing from a literal reading of the contract. It should be said that any one decision, no matter how favourable to the employee, may reveal a limited amount about judicial attitudes and the likelihood of intervention in subsequent cases involving different circumstances. In *Fortune* the facts cried out for a remedy; the employer could be seen as confiscating money that the employee had, in substance, earned. Forfeiture of the benefits that the employee could expect to accrue from the work-wage bargain was seen as a wholly unacceptable abuse of power. The importation of the fair dealing standard was also facilitated by its general application in the law of commercial contracts.[14] The wider context is important; it is easier to invoke a norm of general application than to devise one peculiar to employment as judicial intervention then appears neutral. Indeed when other contexts are considered there was nothing unexceptional about the application of a norm of good faith to the circumstances in *Fortune*. In the earlier US agency case of *RLM Associates v Carter Mfg* it had been held that a sales representative, whose contract was terminated by the manufacturer, was entitled to recover as the termination had been in bad faith because the employer was motivated by a desire to avoid paying commission.[15]

Fortune indicates that the unrestricted operation of employer's discretion over termination of the employment contract is not acceptable. Given the very specific concerns which arose it gave little indication of the extent to which employers would be constrained in future cases. The court undoubtedly regarded its decision as compatible with very considerable scope being given to managerial prerogative: 'We do not question the general principles that an employer is entitled to be motivated by and to serve its own legitimate business interests; that an employer must have wide latitude in deciding whom it will employ in the face of the uncertainties of the business world; and that an employer needs flexibility in the face of changing circumstances.' In the US in the years since *Fortune* it has become abundantly clear that the employer retains that 'wide latitude'.

In the US the implied obligation of fair dealing has operated as a means of control over the termination process.[16] In other jurisdictions terms of this type have regulated

[13] Clyde W. Summers, 'Employment at Will in the United States: The Divine Right of Employers' (2000) 3 University of Pennsylvania Journal of Labour and Employment Law 65, 69.

[14] *Uproar v National Broadcasting* 81 F.2d 373, 377.

[15] 356 Mass 718.

[16] David Cabrelli, 'Comparing the Implied Covenant of Good Faith and Fair Dealing with the Implied Term of Mutual Trust and Confidence in the US and UK Employment Contexts' (2005) 21 International Journal of Comparative Labour Law and Industrial Relations 445.

the employer's conduct of the relationship. *Transco v O'Brien* concerned the offer of a new contract which, inter alia, provided for enhanced redundancy terms.[17] The employer was held to have breached the obligation of trust and confidence by failing, without reasonable cause, to offer the applicant such a contract. Collective bargaining could, of course, have protected an employee in the position of *Fortune* or *O'Brien* as it furnishes rules which 'are a means of preventing favouritism, nepotism, victimisation and arbitrary discrimination of any sort. Thus one great accomplishment of collective bargaining has been its promotion of the "rule of law" in employment relationships.'[18] Judicial control of discretion can be seen as functioning in a very similar way and thereby enhancing the dignity of the worker. Collective bargaining also operates to create procedural rules and a collective agreement may contain provisions governing grievance, discipline, and termination processes. Fair dealing type terms, too, may serve to provide an element of due process.[19]

The Canadian courts have been extremely active in extending the protection afforded by the common law. Whilst they have not adopted an obligation of mutual trust and confidence as such, they take the view that there is a fundamental implied term of the employment relationship which requires that the employer treat the employee with civility, decency, respect, and dignity,[20] an approach endorsed by the Court of Appeal for Ontario in *Shah v Xerox Canada*.[21] The court in *Shah* cited with approval the judgment in *Whiting v Winnipeg* which demonstrates that failure to adhere to due process may lead to a breach of the implied term of decency; the trial judge concluded that an employee had been constructively dismissed because of a series of incidents cumulating in the imposition of probation where the employer had unjustifiably criticized the employee, levelled vague and unfounded accusations against her, and created a hostile and embarrassing work environment.[22]

Similarly, in the UK case of *Gogay v Hertfordshire County Council* the issue arose whether the defendant local authority had acted reasonably in suspending the claimant from her post in a residential home while they investigated the circumstances surrounding a child living in that home.[23] The Court of Appeal held that the employers were in breach of the implied term of mutual trust and confidence because they had no reasonable grounds for suspending the plaintiff and had failed to carry out a proper investigation of the circumstances before suspending her. The term 'aims to ensure fair dealing between employer and employee, and that is as important in respect of disciplinary proceedings, suspension of an employee and dismissal as at any other stage of the employment relationship'.[24] Implied obligations can provide for employee voice in key processes such as discipline and grievance. A fair dealing term allows for expression of the employee's interests and thereby gives rise to the prospect of a different outcome. *W A Goold v McConnell*, for instance, accepted that there was an implied right to have a grievance heard.[25]

[17] [2002] ICR 721. [18] Flanders 12 (n 6).
[19] *Russell v Trustees of the Roman Catholic Church* [2008] NSWCA 217.
[20] *Lloyd v Imperial Parking Ltd* [1997] 3 WWR 697. [21] 2000 CanLll 2317 (ON CA).
[22] (1998) 159 DLR (4th) 18. [23] [2000] IRLR 703. [24] *Johnson v Unisys* [2003] 1 AC 518, 537.
[25] [1995] IRLR 516.

Limitations and Vulnerability

Developments of the sort outlined here have led to a clear improvement in the position of employees, but it would be wrong to claim that the common law has evolved in a manner whereby it has become a meaningful substitute for collective bargaining. Flanders took the view that the rule-making dimension of collective bargaining had no proper counterpart at the level of individual bargaining.[26] I would suggest that this criticism is overstated where process is concerned and that the common law is capable, at least to some extent, of providing procedural protection. The cases discussed in the preceding section evidence this. Flanders' views carry far more weight where substantive terms are in issue. There we immediately run up against common law reluctance to declare whether or not a bargain is reasonable; a position which tends to be replicated across jurisdictions. In *Commercial Bank of Australia v Amadio*, for example, the High Court of Australia made clear that a contract will not be set aside on the basis of unconscionability merely because one side has exploited their superior bargaining power to conclude a very one-sided bargain.[27] This means that common law protection falls far short of what would be expected from the outcomes of an effective collective bargaining process. In the absence of a collective voice, employees will, in general, only be able to secure changes at the margins through individual negotiation.

It would also be wrong to forget that progressive common law developments are always vulnerable to attack by employers. Victories may prove to be short-lived; the autonomy that the private law concept of contract affords to the parties has the inevitable corollary that contracting-out will always be an issue in common law jurisdictions that lack a concept equivalent to the civilian apparatus of the *ius cogens/ius dispositivum* distinction. If we return to the doctrine of employment-at-will it is worth paying some attention to the fortunes of the judicially forged exception of implied contract based on statements in publications such as an employee handbook. In a number of decisions the courts have afforded greater employment protection by giving legal effect to assurances about job security contained in material issued by the employer which fell outwith the four walls of the employment contract. The doctrine of employment-at-will notwithstanding, dismissal in breach of those assurances would be actionable. In *Woolley v Hoffmann-La Roche* it was said that a 'policy manual that provides for job security grants an important, fundamental protection for workers... If such a commitment is indeed made, obviously an employer should be required to honor it... [T]he judiciary, instead of "grudgingly" conceding the enforceability of those provisions, should construe them in accordance with the reasonable expectations of the employees.'[28] However, a common employer response to these developments, in the role of drafter of the contract, has been to exclude wording in a staff handbook that would indicate any such intention. Empirical evidence indicates that a significant number of employers have altered their staff handbooks to remove any language a court may interpret as giving rise to an implied contract.[29] Employers may be

[26] Flanders 4 (n 6). [27] (1983) 151 CLR 447.

[28] *Woolley v Hoffmann-La Roche* 491 A.2d 1257, 1264.

[29] Max Schanzenbach, 'Exceptions to At-Will Employment' (2003) 5 American Law & Economics Journal 470.

very quick to reject rules which favour employees and the benefits of common law evolution may be lost in the absence of legislative entrenchment. The point is reinforced when we look at entry into employment. Where employment rights are contingent upon a particular type of contract being in place, the employer may well be able to hire on a different contractual basis. It is a matter of speculation whether this might be mitigated by the common law adopting a requirement of good faith in contract negotiation. As matters stand, the move towards atypical labour—seen in so many jurisdictions—is a response to conferring extensive statutory rights on employees.

The Role of Legislation

I have indicated that the extent of judicial protection varies considerably between jurisdictions and, in explaining why this should be, the nature and extent of legislative intervention in employment relations is one of the most significant factors. Legislation can act both as a catalyst and constraint where development of the common law is concerned. Constraint may be prompted by respect for the democratic will of the legislature. Thus we find that in the UK and Australia the existence of a general scheme of statutory protection against unfair dismissal has served to ensure that the manner of dismissal remains beyond common law scrutiny.[30] The fear that a carefully crafted legislative structure might be undermined has played a large part in judicial thinking. In both jurisdictions the legislature had chosen to confer protection against dismissal on a particular class of workers and to restrict the levels of compensation that could be awarded. The common law should not then be used to subvert such an arrangement by 'allowing employees to make an end-run around the procedural requirements and specific remedies the ... statutes establish'.[31] It would of course be wrong to develop the common law in this way.

Matters though become highly problematic where the common law is hobbled in a context where it is not apparent that the democratic will would be thwarted. The UK decisions in *Johnson v Unisys* and *Edwards v Chesterfield* illustrate this very clearly.[32] In *Johnson* the essence of the claim was that a dismissal without a fair hearing constituted a breach of the implied term of mutual trust and confidence. The House of Lords were concerned that deciding in favour of the claimant would undermine the statutory scheme: 'A newly developed common law right of this nature, covering the same ground as the statutory right, would fly in the face of the limits Parliament has already prescribed on matters such as the classes of employees who have the benefit of the statutory right, the amount of compensation payable and the short time limits for making claims.'[33] It is notable that those concerns are premised on the basis that the mooted common law right would cover 'the same ground as the statutory right'. However, the claim was much more modest in scope and, once this is recognized, it may be doubted whether the concerns expressed carried much weight.

[30] Matters may well be different where the statutory scheme is not all-embracing: *Lennon v South Australia* [2010] SASC 272.

[31] *City of Midland v O'Bryant* 18 SW 3D 209.

[32] *Johnson* (n 24); *Edwards* [2012] 2 AC 22.

[33] *Johnson* 526 (n 24).

Endorsing a right to a hearing at common law would have increased the protection afforded to employees who do not qualify for unfair dismissal because of the rules on continuity of employment. This was rejected as being at odds with the will of the legislature but whilst Parliament may not have intended that the reasonableness of an employer's decision to dismiss be subject to scrutiny it may have believed that, in certain circumstances, a right to a hearing would be appropriate. After all, unfair dismissal law was enacted in the knowledge that some employees in the UK already had such a right and it is wrong to say that the legislature assumes that the common law is '... set in stone and incapable of principled development'.[34] Parliament may have anticipated that the courts would seek to address the inconsistencies referred to by Lord Wilberforce in *Malloch v Aberdeen Corporation*.[35] In addition, in most cases, the damages awarded would be the same as they would merely reflect the wages that would have been earned during the time it would have taken to go through due process. Recovery of a sum in excess of the statutory limit would only be likely to occur if the contractual claim concerned damage to reputation or psychiatric harm. Judicial angst was particularly driven by a perceived attack on the compensation limits but this was unlikely to be an issue in the vast majority of cases.

Deference towards the legislature may mean that courts will refuse to extend the protection of the common law even where it is not claimed that to do so would undermine the will of Parliament. The sheer extent of legislative intervention may be invoked to bar the common law from regulating a dimension of employment relations. The Australian case of *McDonald v South Australia* provides a good example.[36] There the Supreme Court of South Australia held that the respondent's contract of employment did not contain an implied term of mutual trust and confidence. Statutory regulation of employment in the field of education meant that implication was not necessary: 'statute... provides a variety of means by which employees may be protected from abuses of power by the employer, and provides means of redress to employees who are aggrieved by some conduct of the employer.' The court in *McDonald* took the view that the protection of the common law would have been superfluous. It is, however, not possible to foresee the full range of circumstances that might give rise to an abuse of power in any particular employment. The open-textured nature of the implied term of mutual trust and confidence can accommodate the infinite diversity of workplace issues without difficulty. An area may appear to be extensively regulated but the flexibility of the judicial formulation allows for situations that were not anticipated to be embraced. Some would defend decisions like *McDonald* on constitutional grounds: '... the objection is made that the analogical use of statute violates the doctrine of Parliamentary sovereignty to the extent that it involves the operation in some way of a statutory regime or a regime modelled on a statutory regime notwithstanding Parliament's legislative decision that the text of the statute was to be limited, for example to a particular context or to a particular period of time'.[37] This argument is misstated as, apart from anything

[34] *Johnson* 535 (n 24). [35] 1 WLR 1518 [171].

[36] [2009] SASC 219. See R. White, 'A Setback for Mutual Trust and Confidence' (2010) 23 Australian Journal of Labour Law (AJLL) 220.

[37] Jack Beatson 'The Role of Statute in the Development of Common Law Doctrine' (2001) 117 Law Quarterly Review (LQR) 247, 249.

else, Parliament legislates on the basis that the common law will continue to evolve in the area concerned.[38] It is also inconsistent with the 'courts fulfilling their time-honoured role of updating the common law and making it more suitable for modern circumstances'.[39]

It is important to recognize that a failure to develop the common law does not constitute a position of neutrality. In the face of marked disparities in bargaining power, judicial failure to intervene serves to maintain the status quo and hence the position of the employer. It is clearly correct that the courts do not undermine the democratic will of Parliament but, at least in the UK and Australia, judicial reticence would seem to be much more deeply engrained and the courts often appear to assume that, because some forms of common law development would be incompatible with the statute in question, it would be wrong to intervene at all. This degree of reticence is not always in evidence in other areas of the common law; nor was it to the fore in *Rookes v Barnard*.[40] It is worth recalling that an employee's action for breach of statutory duty thrives despite the fact that the statute will already have provided a remedy: 'the specific duties imposed on employers in relation to factory premises are enforceable by an action for damages, notwithstanding the imposition by the statutes of criminal penalties for any breach'.[41]

It will be unsatisfactory if the law of the employment contract constitutes 'merely an aggregate of non-contradictory but apparently arbitrary propositions of a relatively detailed sort'.[42] The desire for a coherent body of law mandates us to inquire whether any mooted development furthers the values of the employment contract. Oliver has drawn attention to the common law's desire to guard against threats to an individual's 'dignity, autonomy, respect, status or security'.[43] There are analogies to be made with the law of negligence where, to ensure that the law on duty of care develops in a consistent and coherent fashion, the courts look to identify and articulate the policy in prior cases.[44] A decision in favour of the claimant in *Johnson*, by allowing for a right to be heard, would have required employers to treat staff with dignity and respect. Again, a decision to the contrary in *Edwards* would have promoted procedural fairness. I would suggest that, in arriving at a decision, greater focus needs to be placed on core values; otherwise, in an age of extensive legislative intervention, it might always be said that regulation of employment relations has moved beyond the common law. In *Edwards* the court assumed, quite erroneously, that the sole reason for providing contractual procedures was to comply with the requirements of employment protection legislation.[45]

A more expansive approach to common law evolution can be seen in a number of decisions in the US which have been arrived at by gauging the merits of a claim for innovation against the demands of public policy. Thus common law remedies have been devised to supplement those contained in discrimination legislation. Further exceptions to the employment-at-will doctrine are justified as discrimination is 'obnoxious to the interests of the state and contrary to public policy and sound morality'.[46] In *City of*

[38] *Rookes v Barnard* [1964] AC 1129.
[39] *New Testament Church v Stewart* [2008] ICR 282, 301.
[40] *Rookes* (n 38).
[41] *X v Bedfordshire* [1995] 2 AC 633, 731.
[42] Neil MacCormick, *Rhetoric and the Rule of Law* (OUP, 2005) 202.
[43] Dawn Oliver, *Common Values and the Public-Private Divide* (Butterworths, 1999) 60.
[44] *Crimmins* para. 74 (n 8).
[45] And see Kevin Costello (2013) 76 Modern Law Review (MLR) 134.
[46] *City of Moorpark v Superior Court* 959 P.2d 752.

Moorpark v Superior Court an action was recognized in respect of wrongful discharge even though the Fair Employment and Housing Act provided remedies in respect of disability discrimination.[47] Public policy may be discerned not simply through construction of the Act in issue. In *Molesworth v Brandon* it was noted that section 14 of the Maryland Fair Employment Practices Act is one of 'at least thirty-four statutes, one executive order, and one constitutional amendment in Maryland that prohibits discrimination based on sex in certain circumstances. Together these provisions provide strong evidence of a legislative intent to end discrimination based on sex in Maryland.'[48] Such an approach offers the promise of coherent development through the identification of key policies and fundamental values. It can also lead to bolder outcomes. In *Molesworth* the employer argued that they should not be liable for wrongful discharge as they were a small employer for the purposes of the Fair Employment Practices Act. This was rejected as whilst the employer (as a small employer) was exempted from the administrative process of the Fair Employment Practices Act they were not excluded from the underpinning policy prohibiting discrimination in employment. An approach which failed to look beyond the statute in dispute would have been less likely to arrive at this result. The employer's defence would have seemed much more compelling if coherence was assessed within the four walls of a specific enactment. The argument for the employee gains strength through looking to a wider range of sources and thereby distilling the cogency of public policy in respect of anti-discrimination.

Striking the Balance: Judicial Values

Common law interventions require that a balance be struck between the interests of employee and employer. The balance may be struck at very different points on the spectrum and a fair dealing term may have a limited impact on managerial prerogative. Indeed, more fundamentally, in the US earlier progress has been halted and only a small minority of states have implied an obligation of fair dealing into employment contracts.[49] This restrictive stance is justified on occasion by reference to the public interest in a strong economy and not simply by the benefits to individual employers.[50] Injudicious evolution of the common law might mean that 'the very foundation of the free enterprise system could be jeopardized'.[51] The continued vitality of the employment-at-will doctrine in many US states indicates strong judicial support for wide scope being given to managerial prerogative. The pervasive influence of the ideology of the market economy means that the way in which the balance is struck between employer and employee interests in the US looks odd when the treatment of other contracts is considered. Section 205 of the Restatement (Second) of Contracts provided that '[e]very contract imposes upon each party a duty of good faith and fair dealing in its performance and its enforcement'. However, that provision has been held to be overly broad and not applicable to the employment-at-will contract.[52] Again, in a somewhat surprising contrast, we find that the courts have been more protective of

[47] *City of Moorpark v Superior Court* (n 46). [48] 341 Md. 621.
[49] *Suburban Hos. v Dwiggins* 324 Md. 294. [50] *Whittaker v Care-More* 621 S.W. 2d 395.
[51] *Whittaker v Care-More* (n 50). [52] *Morris v Coleman* 241 Kan. 501.

the consumer under an insurance contract. Thus *Egan v Mutual of Omaha* holds that an insurer may breach the implied obligation of fair dealing when it fails to properly investigate its insured's claim.[53] Indeed the insurer must give at least as much consideration to the welfare of its insured as it gives to its own interests. The departure from the conventional approach in contract law arises because the relationship of insurer and insured is inherently unbalanced. In *Arnold v National County* it was said that '[i]n the insurance context a special relationship arises out of the parties' unequal bargaining power and the nature of insurance contracts which would allow unscrupulous insurers to take advantage of their insureds' misfortunes in bargaining for settlement or resolution of claims'.[54] The position of the employee would seem closely analogous but a number of US courts find themselves able to differentiate. The failure to allow the fair dealing norm greater scope has been the subject of judicial criticism: 'Employment contracts... determine the standard of living and the quality of education for children, and affect the general welfare of all the people in this country. It is ludicrous that the covenant of good faith and fair dealing has been adopted pertaining to commercial transactions... but has not been adopted for transactions involving human working conditions'.[55] The US courts maintain a particularly strong commitment to the values of the market economy; the other jurisdictions under review show a greater willingness to recognize the interests of employees. On the whole the judicial response in the United States has been restricted to correcting some of the worst abuses of power. In *Monge v Beebe Rubber* it was said that 'the employer's interest in running his business as he sees fit must be balanced against the interest of the employee in maintaining his employment, and the public's interest in maintaining a proper balance between the two'.[56] The judicial understanding of the public interest is crucial; in the US the values of the market economy are seen as being central. As a result, where the employment contract is concerned, should the interests of employer and employee conflict there is a reluctance to restrain managerial prerogative. It is of course the case that the judicial conception of the public interest in the US is informed by further considerations. The pursuit of social justice requires, for example, that employees should be protected against detrimental action should they exercise their right under workmen's compensation legislation. Such schemes relieve 'society of the care and support of the unfortunate victims of industrial accidents'.[57]

The factors which inform the public interest and the weighting attributed to them vary between jurisdictions. On the face of it recourse to the public interest allows decisions to be reached which are not dictated by the interests of either employer or employee; there is a semblance of neutrality but the reality may be very different. Such decisions also raise difficult questions about the institutional legitimacy of the judiciary determining 'public interest' in a constitutional democracy.

[53] 24 Cal.3d 809. [54] *Arnold v National County* 725 SW 2d 165, 167.
[55] *Morris* (n 52) per Herd J (dissenting). [56] 316 A.2d 549.
[57] *Reteuna v Indus. Comm'n* 55 Utah 258.

Unconscionable Bargains

From the perspective of the employee a fundamental consideration is whether an unfair bargain can be challenged and improved upon. It is unlikely that the natural pattern of common law development (where progress is incremental and measured) will lead to a position where a court is prepared to intervene on the basis that the substantive terms are unfair. An exception to this might be the rule on sham contracts which permits the courts to look behind the written terms to establish the true nature of the agreement.[58] This can lead to a finding that a contract of employment does in fact exist and, as a corollary, the worker should benefit from the relevant common law and statutory rights. The radicalism of the approach is tempered by the fact that it does not require a court to determine whether specific terms are inequitable but rather whether their presence is a charade. Courts remain 'reluctant to call upon wider standards of equality to make decisions reasoned by substantive fairness'.[59]

If the contract of employment is to become an effective vehicle for the expression of the employee's voice then legislative intervention may be required. The New South Wales Industrial Relations Act of 1996 is of considerable interest in this respect as it gives extensive powers to the Industrial Relations Commission (the Commission) to address the problems flowing from unfair contracts.[60] Contracts where unfairness arises are defined as including those which are unfair, harsh, or unconscionable. By virtue of section 106 the Commission can determine that an unfair contract is void, in whole or in part; they also have power to vary the terms of a contract. The design of the scheme is striking; in particular the extent of empowerment of the adjudicator. The Commission may re-write the bargain for the parties and operates within the most open-textured of formulae. Instantaneously statute provides a doctrine equivalent to a full-blooded common law concept of unconscionability; a development that would have an extraordinarily long gestation period at common law.

The NSW scheme offers a basis for informed speculation as to the difference a common law concept of unconscionability would make to judicial regulation of the employment contract. Looking to the extensive jurisprudence of the Commission it must be said that in a quite a number of cases the solution arrived at would have been one open to the courts at common law. For instance, quite a number of the claims involve highly paid employees with attractive packages including elements such as share options. The issue in such cases is often whether on dismissal such benefits can properly be expropriated. For example, in *Westfield v Sidney Helprin* the employee had been granted share options but was dismissed before they had vested.[61] Crucially the employee had been dismissed without cause. In those circumstances it was regarded as unfair that the options be forfeited in their entirety when the scheme was intended to provide

[58] *Autoclenz* (n 5).

[59] Julie McClelland, 'A Purposive Approach to Employment Protection or a Missed Opportunity?' 2012 (75) MLR 427, 434.

[60] See Sally Gibson, 'Section 106: Calls for Legislative Reform Should be Silenced' (2002) 24 Sydney Law Review 231. The legislation has been amended so that it now has an extremely limited scope and is said to have been reduced to a narrow jurisdiction for a special group of workers.

[61] [1997] NSWIR Comm 36.

him with additional remuneration both for past performance and during its period of operation. At the point of termination the employee had been employed for almost three-quarters of the qualifying period. The contract was varied so that, on termination, other than for cause, the employee should be entitled to exercise 73 per cent of the 40,000 options granted to him under the option scheme, proportionately reflecting his period of employment during the operation of the scheme. At common law a court might well have acted to provide the same degree of employee protection by way of an implied term.[62] Certainly, some such term is appropriate to prevent the remuneration package being unfairly undermined without conferring such a degree of protection that would distort the bargain between the parties.

It is also the case that where procedural matters are concerned there may be little need for statutory intervention. A number of section 106 cases involve applications which seek to improve the procedural protection afforded by the contract. In *Westfield v Helprin* it was held that the conduct of the employment contract became unfair where punitive action was taken despite a failure to investigate the allegations and a denial of an opportunity to respond to the allegations.[63] Such behaviour would also be likely to give rise to a breach of contract on the basis that there had not been fair dealing. If we view implied terms as a means of construction then *Westfield* is really about determining what has been agreed.[64]

Matters become more interesting when substantive terms fall for consideration; the common law being content to leave the fairness of the bargain to the parties. The NSW legislation allows a term to be struck out on the basis that it is unfair and to be replaced by a more equitable obligation. The Commission may, for instance, decide to re-write a term of a contract dealing with the remuneration package on the basis that it was not sufficiently generous.[65] The complaint in *Payne v Foxboro* was of this nature and it was claimed that the express terms on redundancy were inadequate.[66] The court noted that 'while the benefits are certainly on the low side for corporations of the standing and size of the respondents and their US parent corporation/s and, indeed, for many employers of lesser standing, they are not so low as to be unfair'. A finding of unfairness was inappropriate 'in the absence of evidence of a higher and objective standard applicable to the circumstances of this case, or of some other comparative unfairness'. The question of substantive unfairness is addressed by comparing the position of the claimant to someone holding a similar position in the same employment or perhaps industry. The Commission does not appear to indulge in a wider exercise of addressing more fundamental inequities in the labour market by challenging assumptions that occupations of a particular nature are treated unfairly in comparison to other occupations. A more radical approach to section 106 would increase the prospects of significant changes to the terms and conditions of workers in employments where inequality of bargaining power is most marked. In fact the operation of the legislation involves a process that is closely analogous to that involved in implying terms on the basis of custom and

[62] *Briscoe v Lubrizol* [2002] IRLR 607. [63] (1998) 82 IR 411.

[64] See Douglas Brodie, *The Contract of Employment* (W. Green, 2008). And see now *AG of Belize v Belize Telecom* [2009] UKPC 10, paras 18–19.

[65] *Moray Vincent v Merrill Lynch* [2000] NSWIR Comm 160 (redundancy payment).

[66] [1998] NSWIR Comm 360.

practice or identifying a breach of an implied term of fair dealing on the grounds of disparate treatment.

Both at common law and under statute one is looking for consistency across a limited class of people. I would suggest that it is not reasonable to expect more in the absence of a much more detailed statutory framework:

> An open-textured power of review would invite comparison with salary packages in an industry as a whole. Assessing the merits of those challenges would be a Herculean task... Obtaining adequate evidence upon which to make a decision would, of itself, be an arduous task. Arriving at a credible determination would, in addition, often require voluminous quantities of evidence to be sifted and assessed.[67]

New South Wales experience suggests that the impact of any common law doctrine of unconscionability may be less than one would expect. Nevertheless, the current conceptual shortfall means that the gap between what the common law offers and what collective bargaining could be expected to do is very considerable and very central to the concerns of the employee. There is undoubtedly a very large deficiency in the common law armoury.

It is also the case that the NSW scheme is far better placed than the common law to control contracting-out. The most direct way for the employer to achieve this is by electing for a different form of contractual relation. The courts, in applying the common law tests to determine the existence of the employment contract, are limited in their capacity to regulate this aspect of managerial prerogative. The NSW scheme tackles these difficulties in a very different way. It combines a wide-ranging and highly inclusive statutory definition with very considerable judicial discretion. The scheme applies to any 'arrangement whereby a person performs work in an industry, that is, a transaction which directly leads to the performance of work in an industry'. The width of definition means that the scheme has the potential to be over inclusive in that it is capable of embracing contracts that would be widely regarded as purely commercial in nature. Much in the way of difficult demarcation decisions is then left to the Commission. This particular statutory framework has led to a wide variety of contractual arrangements being scrutinized.

Conclusions

The judges are acutely aware of the decline in the efficacy of collective bargaining at a time when the need to regulate the labour market and prevent worker exploitation is acute. Judicial innovations are an attempt to fill part of the gap created by the current weakness of collective regulation. What might be made of their efforts? Employees will be concerned to ensure that the contract is run fairly (as well as being concerned to know whether the bargain struck is fair). Where the former issue is concerned the role performed by collective bargaining does not seem very different from that undertaken by the courts. Judicial intervention addresses the need for due process and consistency

[67] Douglas Brodie, 'The Employment Contract and Unfair Contracts Legislation' (2007) 27 Legal Studies 95, 107.

of treatment. However, things change where it is claimed that the substance of an agreement is inequitable. The common law is unlikely to come to the rescue; an unfair deal is not seen as a wrong in itself but may be evidence that a wrong has occurred. The extent to which statutory empowerment of the judiciary (along the lines of section 106) would bring about radical change is open to argument. Admittedly, such an enactment would put in place a key conceptual tool that the common law lacks and simultaneously confer the legitimacy of the legislative process. However, I would doubt if such a reform would lead to decisions that were dissimilar to those handed down in Australia. In the absence of detailed legislative guidance the courts would be highly unlikely to go further. An open-textured provision on fairness would offer an inadequate basis upon which to build a policy on exploitative contracts. It would place an adjudicator in an invidious position unless clear direction was offered as to the basis of determination.

The current position means that the common law fails to protect employees where the employer uses his superior bargaining power to impose unfair terms and conditions. More was and is expected from collective bargaining which is a means to convert 'formal into factual freedom of contract as between employer and workman, by raising the latter to a level of equality of bargaining power'.[68] Collective bargaining involves a 'power relationship between organisations'; such a relationship may involve an imbalance of power but not to the same degree as is inevitably the case at the level of the individual employment relationship. It is also the case that some key issues affecting the conduct of the workplace and which impact on the life of the worker are collective in nature. Collective bargaining can, for instance, regulate and restrain the use of casual employment. Individual bargaining may only improve the lot of the individual concerned; not those around him. On the other side of the equation is the fact that the coverage of implied terms in law is universal. We should also be realistic about the limitations of collective bargaining. It was always the case that the power of the collective varied considerably and the outcome of collective negotiations would not necessarily have been satisfactory from a worker point of view. Indeed some critics did not regard 'collective bargaining, with its restricted agenda (which avoids fundamental political issues and does not equalise the balance of power between employers and workers), as an effective method of achieving social change and social justice'.[69] Such fundamental deficiencies are unlikely to be addressed by the law of the employment contract. The content of the contract looks very different compared to 30 years ago but more radical improvements in the position of the employee can only come from the legislature.[70]

[68] Otto Kahn-Freund, 'Collective Agreements under War Legislation' (1943) 5–6 MLR 112, 117.

[69] William Rees, 'Frames of Reference and the Public Interest' in Kenneth W. Wedderburn and W. T. Murphy (eds), *Labour Law for the Community* (Institute of Advanced Legal Studies, 1982) 132.

[70] I am very much indebted to the Editors for their highly insightful comments on earlier drafts; the usual disclaimer applies.

17

Common Law and Voice

Mark Freedland and Nicola Kountouris

Introduction

In 1992, Bill Wedderburn noted, in his uniquely perceptive and characteristically caustic style, that '[f]ifty years of labour law have scarcely dented the pachydermatous cornucopia of self-esteem that is the life style of the English common law'.[1] As labour lawyers we have long complained, but also long accepted, that the interaction between employment statutes and common law reasoning has been one in which the 'judicial tendency' to disregard the autonomous 'values and assumptions' underpinning statute, has almost invariably resulted in the latter being shaped by the pervasive force of common law values and doctrines.[2] It is tempting to look at the relationship between what Wedderburn described as 'common law life style' and public regulation in the sphere of labour relations from a Gramscian perspective, whereby common law reasoning imbues British society and exercises a hegemonic influence on the law of the state, reproducing but also shaping some of the fundamental economic needs of the British economic and social system. And it is equally tempting to take the further step of equating employment protective statutes with 'workers' voice' and common law reasoning with its contrary (be it worker's lack of voice or, much more simply, with 'employers' voice') and to draw the conclusion that English labour law is irredeemably condemned to silencing workers' voice, due to the hegemonic role of the common law life style just described. Let us therefore sit back, and let the pessimism of both intellect and will dominate our discipline.

In this chapter, however, we seek to escape from the latter suggestion by proposing a different conceptualization of the relationship between 'common law' and 'voice', by reference to a new type of distinction, the one between 'Private Common Law' and 'Public Common Law'. The former, we will concede, is intimately linked to 'freedom of contract' and structurally committed to sustaining interests that have little to share with workers' voice. In other words, if our policy goal is that of giving voice to workers, we might as well give up on doing so through Private Common Law. But Public Common Law is, or ought to be, more permeable to being shaped by a different set of values and assumptions (sometimes emerging from other, supranational, legal systems), which, while '(unhappily) deeply offensive to classical common law "freedom of contract"',[3] enjoy a sufficient degree of cogency and autonomy from Private Common

[1] Lord Wedderburn, 'Inderogability, Collective Agreements, and Community Law' (1992) 21 Industrial Law Journal (ILJ) 245, 249–50.

[2] The short quotations reproduce Steve Anderman's words, in Steve Anderman, 'The Interpretation of Protective Employment Statutes and Contracts of Employment' (2000) 29 ILJ 223, 223–4.

[3] Lord Wedderburn, 'Inderogability, Collective Agreements, and Community Law' (1992) 21 ILJ 245, 249 referring to the, in his eyes, very un-British notion of 'inderogability' ('Indeed, English contains no word, certainly no term of art, apt to describe one of the very starting points in the legal vocabulary elsewhere').

Law and could result, no doubt through a long 'war of position', in giving a certain degree of voice to the world of work, if not also exerting a certaining degree of influence on Private Common Law.

The chapter proceeds by first identifying the version of the Private Common Law and Public Common Law distinction which we shall use for the purposes of argument, and then by providing a series of examples where Private Common Law has effectively managed to disenfranchise workers from any ability to participate in the establishment, performance, or termination of their personal work contracts or relations. In the following section, the chapter moves on to illustrate a number of instances in which the emergence of a separate Public Common Law analysis demonstrated its potential to confer certain kinds of 'voice' upon workers, against the odds of Private Common Law. A brief conclusion then evokes the sense in which there has been a continuing contestation between Private Common Law and Public Common Law in the field of labour/employment law, but remarks upon the disposition of Private Common Law to assert itself as the dominant framework, with a systemically chilling effect upon 'workers' voice'.

Private Common Law and Public Common Law—a Working Distinction

There are many different ways in which we could distinguish between Private Common Law and Public Common Law. For our present purpose, it is not necessary to attempt a general or systematic differentiation; it will suffice to delineate two bodies of common law, one of a private law kind and the other of a public law kind, which both bear upon labour/employment law and serve to determine the extent to which 'voice' is accorded to workers in the shaping of their working lives and the conduct of their work relations.

The relevant body of common law which is of a private law kind consists primarily of the common law of contract and of tort bearing upon employment relations both collective and individual. Other aspects of common law are also in play, such as the law of trusts and of restitution. We shall argue that although this body of common law does have an impact upon workers' voice, that impact is of a largely negative kind, so that private common law does not on the whole accord voice to workers and in certain respects actively denies it to them.

The relevant body of common law which is of a public law kind consists, for its part, primarily of the principles and rules which give rise to judicial review of administrative action—hence the body of law generally thought of as 'administrative law' in particular—and secondarily of 'public law' more generally. We shall argue that the principles and rules of administrative law, albeit overlaid with various substantive and procedural legislative provisions, most especially those of the Human Rights Act 1998, still constitute a body of authentically common law—in the broad sense of judge-made law—which has some real potential, within its sphere of application, to confer voice upon certain workers and perhaps to reassure us that the common law does have some voice-conferring capacity in a more general sense. We will also point out, however, that Public Common Law inevitably comes into friction with, and may occasionally risk being hollowed out by, Private Common Law in the sense previously outlined.

Private Common Law—the Fallacy of 'Freedom of Contract' and its Corollaries

The negative impact of common law reasoning on workers' voice is so abundant and so well documented that one could easily write a 'text and materials' manual on labour law by elaborating exclusively on the disenfranchising effects that Private Common Law has had on workers. We will not attempt this particular exercise here, but it is good to be reminded of the pervasive effects that common law doctrines have in excluding, typically, the most vulnerable workers from accessing and obtaining justice in the workplace and in the courts.

Three well established common law doctrines, the doctrine of illegality, the doctrine on intentionality in the creation of legal relations, and the doctrine of 'mutuality of obligations', have invariably acted as the most effective gags preventing workers from even accessing justice, let alone receiving it. In recent times, even months, we have witnessed the ability of these two doctrines to keep vulnerable workers such as 'illegal' migrant workers and disabled volunteers outside the reach of employment and discrimination law. The *Hounga v Allen*[4] saga, now about to be litigated before the Supreme Court, provides a powerful reminder of the exclusionary effect that a finding of illegality in obtaining employment can have on what the Court of Appeal itself described 'as a young person of whom unfair advantage was probably taken'.[5] Judgments like the one in *X v Mid Sussex Citizens Advice Bureau*[6] exemplify the extent to which even what, in EU parlance, we could describe as general principle of law such as the equality principle, can be excluded by parties whose employment relations are designated, by 'agreement', as non-contractual in character. And finally, *Stringfellow Restaurants Ltd v Quashie*[7] re-establishes the orthodoxy that was only stirred, but not shaken, by *Autoclenz Ltd v Belcher*,[8] that the contract is what the contract says, since 'it is legitimate for a court to have regard to the way in which the parties have chosen to categorise the relationship, and in a case where the position is uncertain, it can be decisive'.[9]

These three doctrines, for all their diversity, share an important underlying assumption deriving directly from the common law legal culture that has accompanied and shaped the development of labour law in Britain. This is the assumption that worker and employer are, fundamentally, parties to a contract and thus by definition the beneficiaries of a power to shape the terms and conditions of their contractual arrangements that, if not equal, is considered to be at least symmetrical. This is an important feature of our 'common law lifestyle' that sets our system quite apart from other labour law systems, for instance in continental Europe, that do contemplate a role for contract law and common law conceptual building blocks in their labour law edifice, but at the same time negate this false symmetry that underpins our notion of Private Common Law, in employment relations. So in France for instance 'the existence of an employment

[4] [2012] EWCA Civ 609.

[5] [2012] EWCA Civ 609 [62] per Rimer LJ. Compare generally Alan Bogg and Tonia Novitz, 'Race Discrimination and the Doctrine of Illegality' (2013) 129 Law Quarterly Review 12.

[6] [2012] UKSC 59. [7] [2012] EWCA Civ 1735. [8] [2011] UKSC 41.

[9] In the *Quashie* case in the Court of Appeal, [2012] EWCA Civ 1735, para. 52 per Elias LJ.

relationship depends neither on the will expressed by the parties nor on the denomination that they have given to their contract but on the factual conditions under which the activity of the workers is exercised'.[10]

But the strictures of contractualism and 'freedom of contract' reverberate across the entire lifespan of an employment relationship, affecting its performance, and eventual variation and termination. We can see this latter point emerging in the most dramatic fashion in the now classic case of *Bateman v Asda.*[11] The presence of a contractual variation clause in a company handbook allowed the employer to proceed to a (de facto unilateral) variation of the terms and conditions of employment by means of a (*de jure* unilateral) variation of the handbook itself. This was the case because the handbook itself '"*permitted* [the employer] *as a matter of contract* to do what it did", namely to introduce the new regime without obtaining the consent of the Claimants'.[12] One could hardly find a more revealing example of the 'freedom of contract fallacy' than in this particular quotation, which also exemplifies the extent to which common law contractualism (in the sense of a common law construction of the relationship between intra-contractual and extra-contractual sources as being equally contractual in nature) can supersede that figment of the legal imagination that is the contract of employment as an expression of a symmetrical 'freedom'.

The other juncture where it is possible to articulate the dominance of Private Common Law over the overall architecture of English labour law is of course *Malik v BCCI*,[13] and the long shadow that Lord Steyn's obiter dicta have cast on the seminal and controversial decisions of *Johnson v Unisys Ltd*[14] and *Edwards v Chesterfield Royal Hospital NHS Foundation Trust.*[15] In *Malik*, Lord Steyn had no hesitation in suggesting that the implied term of mutual trust and confidence, while 'an incident of all contracts of employment', operated as a 'default rule' with the parties being 'free to exclude or modify [it]'.[16] In *Johnson*, his Lordship reiterated that this 'overarching obligation implied by law as an incident of the contract of employment', this 'legal duty imposed by law' merely 'requires... express words or a necessary implication to displace it or to cut down its scope'.[17] But in *Edwards* we see the emergence of a yet more powerful version of Private Common Law's shaping of the relationship and hierarchy of sources of English labour and a further consolidation of the central role of 'freedom of contract' as the central star of the system. In Lord Dyson's judgment we are told that '*unless they otherwise expressly agree*, the parties to an employment contract do not intend that a failure to comply with contractually binding disciplinary procedures will give rise to a common law claim for damages',[18] and that therefore the 'Johnson exclusion zone' extends beyond implied terms and also covers contractual ones, though it can be displaced by *express agreement*. Lord Kerr rightly questioned the rationality of this approach, noting that 'if it is the case that the [Johnson exclusion zone] is

[10] Our translation of Jean Péllissier, Alain Supiot, and Antoine Jeammaud, *Droit du Travail* (Dalloz, 2006) 330 (emphasis added).

[11] *Bateman v Asda Stores Ltd* [2010] UKEAT 0221_09_1102.

[12] *Bateman v Asda Stores* para. 5 (n 11) (emphasis added).

[13] [1997] UKHL 23.

[14] [2001] UKHL 13.

[15] [2010] EWCA Civ 571.

[16] *Malik v BCCI* [1997] UKHL 23.

[17] *Johnson v Unisys Ltd* [2001] UKHL 13, para. 24.

[18] [2010] EWCA Civ 571, para. 39 (emphasis added).

underpinned by a public policy consideration, it seems highly curious that it can be displaced by the express agreement of the parties'.[19] But this 'curious result', to use Lord Kerr's words, is probably yet another manifestation of Private Common Law's prowess, though, we should note, only a hypothetical one since it is rather difficult to imagine an 'express agreement' of the kind envisaged in *Edwards* effectively materializing in an individual contract of employment. Once the figment of symmetry sustaining the abstract notion of freedom of contract is removed, it becomes obvious that an employee is unlikely to be able to voice into a contract of employment an express agreement displacing the Johnson exclusion zone, though of course its mere hypothetical possibility gives legitimacy to the—far more likely—express 'agreement' envisaged in *Malik* and *Johnson*, displacing obligations of good faith and mutual trust and confidence.

An analysis of Private Common Law role as a hegemonic feature of English labour law would not be complete without an assessment of its impact on industrial relations and collective labour rights. The *locus classicus* at which to begin this particular inquiry can only be the doctrine of breach of contract as applying at which to strike action and to industrial action short of strike. This British peculiarity, poignantly—but ultimately unsuccessfully—highlighted and challenged by Lord Denning MR in *Morgan v Fry*,[20] is a powerful manifestation of Private Common Law dominance in the labour law domain. At a fundamental level it reveals the extent to which Private Common Law legal reasoning is unwilling to depart from the strictures of orthodox contractual analysis. But more generally, as best exemplified by cases such as *Secretary of State for Employment v ASLEF (No. 2)*,[21] *BT v Tichehurst*,[22] and *General Engineering Services v Kingston and St Andrew Corp*,[23] it also reminds us of the ability of Private Common Law to expand the contractual net of duties and obligations that workers withdrawing their labour in furtherance of a trade dispute, put simply exercising their fundamental right to strike, are likely to be accountable for.

We can therefore see Private Common Law operating at two levels. There is a shallow and strictly contractual level on which Private Common Law effectively coincides with a fictional notion of 'freedom of contract'. There is also a deeper level at which a number of contractual and common law doctrines are incorporated into the overall analysis, with a resulting expansion of the contractual duties that actually constrain workers' voice. This is rather a bleak conclusion, and one which some might regard as unduly pessimistic. Does it amount to an unnecessary abandonment of a conception of the common law of personal employment which the first author of this chapter was defending no more than a decade ago in his work on *The Personal Employment Contract*,[24] as something other than 'narrowly mercantilist' and relatively autonomous from the common law as it applies to ordinary commercial contracts? Possibly so; but even that more optimistic analysis hardly went so far as to attribute a workers'-voice-conferring potential to the common law of personal employment contracts: and, so far as it might have done so, that depended upon the view that there was a significant input or influence from what this chapter identifies as Public Common Law. It is to the assessment of that input or influence that we turn our attention in the succeeding sections of this chapter.

[19] [2010] EWCA Civ 571, para. 154. [20] [1968] 2 QB 710. [21] (1972) ICR 19.
[22] (1992) IRLR 219. [23] [1989] 1 WLR 69. [24] OUP, 2011; see especially at 194.

The Voice-conferring Possibilities of Public Common Law

In the second section of this chapter we summarily identified our working definition of Public Common Law as primarily amounting to the common law of judicial review of administrative action; in this section we consider the extent to which that body of law can be regarded as having the potential to confer voice upon workers. The argument is, it should be admitted at the outset, a more difficult one to make out than was the previous argument about the voice-denying capacity of Private Common Law. It often feels as if we are 'grasping at straws' in the search for the common law's support for workers' voice. Nevertheless, it is a search worth pursuing. The first stage of this argument consists of a demonstration of the capacity of Public Common Law to control the decision-making power of the employer in relation to public employment to which it applies (to the scope of which we shall of course revert). The second stage consists of an assessment of the extent to which such controls, upon the decision-making powers of the employer in relation to public employment, have the effect of conferring or the potential to confer voice upon the workers in whose interest those controls can be invoked.

The first stage of this argument is a relatively straightforward one, to the extent that it is uncontroversial to say that the trajectory of development of judicial review in the last half-century has been towards more searching scrutiny of the soundness and fairness of administrative decision-making. In its substantive dimension, judicial review has long since moved beyond a concern with formal *ultra vires* towards a more searching questioning of the soundness of decision-making, especially by reference to ideas of 'legality' in a general sense, 'reasonableness', and the upholding of 'legitimate expectations'. Moreover, since the *Smith and Grady* judgment[25] and especially in the post-Human Rights Act legal environment, judicial review has shifted towards the inclusion of various forms of 'proportionality' calculus in its scrutiny of decision-making of public authorities.

In its procedural dimension, judicial review has similarly moved beyond a narrow concern with 'natural justice' in 'judicial or quasi-judicial' decision-making to a rather more general concern with procedural fairness and the giving of reasons for decisions. The *GCHQ* case,[26] for all its vacuity in terms of a positive outcome for the workers affected, remains an example of the 'breakthroughs in principle', to quote Keith Ewing,[27] that judicial-review-based Public Common Law has accustomed us to in the past three decades.

Moreover, its principles and rules as to *locus standi* to seek judicial review have somewhat opened out so as to favour a reasonably broad notion of what constitutes sufficient interest to query an administrative decision.[28] Judgments such as the one in *R (Unison) v NHS Shared Business Services*[29] are a powerful reminder that a number

[25] *Smith and Grady v UK* (1999) 29 EHRR 493.

[26] *Council of Civil Service Unions v Minister for the Civil Services* [1985] AC 374.

[27] Keith Ewing, 'Prerogative, Judicial Review, National Security' (1985) 44 Cambridge Law Journal 1, 2.

[28] Compare *R (Unison) v The Secretary of State For Health* [2010] EWHC 2655 (Admin), para. 5; also *R (Public and Commercial Services Union) v Minister for the Civil Service* [2010] EWHC 1027 (Admin).

[29] [2012] EWHC 624.

of often insurmountable strictures remain. But even there, one cannot but draw some hope from the obiter dictum of Eady J that even though there is 'no previous example of a trade union seeking a public law remedy in the context of [the Public Contract Regulations 2006] that is no reason to suppose that it is not legally possible'.[30] All this constitutes a kind of conferring of countervailing power upon individuals and organizations to challenge and control administrative decision-making.

If that first stage of our argument as to the voice-conferring potential of Public Common Law is fairly plain sailing, the second step is an essentially more difficult one—namely that of establishing that the countervailing or challenging power, which Public Common Law creates, also amounts to a kind of conferment of voice upon persons and organizations such as, in the context in which we are interested, workers and trade unions. In seeking to make out this further case, we can find significant support from an unexpected quarter, namely Dawn Oliver's treatise on *Common Values and the Public-Private Divide*,[31] a major contribution to the literature on the way in which English lawyers handle the distinction between public law and private law. Support from this quarter is unexpected to the extent that Dawn Oliver's initial premise is that the distinctions which are made between public law and private law are essentially artificial ones, so that she, or at least that particular book of hers, might be supposed to be hostile to our argument which does indeed depend upon a mode of distinguishing between Public Common Law and Private Common Law. However, that divergence of approach between her treatise and this chapter is perhaps more apparent than real, to the extent that her book is in truth devoted to the development of a thesis that the English law of judicial review embodies a set of public values which in her argument could and should be regarded as infusing the whole of English common law (and for that matter statute law): it is an argument which, while ultimately denying the validity of a sharp 'public-private divide', nevertheless finds its starting points in a certain broad notion of public law centred upon judicial review in much the way that this present chapter does.

For Dawn Oliver, those starting points consist in particular of four 'parallel strands of constitutional and citizenship theory' which, she believes, underlie 'the functions of the courts as red lights and green lights in public law'.[32] One of those 'strands in democratic theory which may be seen to be at work in public law' is crucially supportive of our present argument; it consists of a notion of 'participative communitarianism' according to which 'individuals—and groups—affected by public decisions ought to have the opportunity to participate in those decisions, for instance by being given a hearing before the decision is made, having opportunities to put their own case or arguments, or being given reasons for the eventual decision'.[33] She is of the view that this participative communitarianism 'involves a model of citizenship of a "civic republican" kind, which emphasises involvement in politics as being of central importance, not only for particular individuals but also in the general public interest'.[34] It will immediately be apparent how closely Dawn Oliver's argument coincides with Alan

[30] [2012] EWHC 624, para. 11.

[31] Dawn Oliver, *Common Values and the Public-Private Divide* (Butterworths, 1999).

[32] Oliver 2 (n 31). [33] Oliver 5–6 (n 31). [34] Oliver 8 (n 31).

Bogg's articulation and defence of a 'civic republican philosophy in terms of freedom as non-domination, the intrinsic value of democratic participation through deliberative democracy, and community',[35] a set of ideas which he and Tonia Novitz have infused into the present 'Voices at Work' project. This fact, that Dawn Oliver so clearly saw this notion of participative communitarianism as one of the values which the public law of judicial review could contribute to the evolution of the common law as a whole, puts at its highest the argument about the voice-conferring potential of Public Common Law which we have sought to develop in this section of our chapter.

However, even to the extent that the foregoing arguments as to the voice-conferring potential of judicial review and Public Common Law are attractive ones so far as Voices at Work are concerned, we have to keep it in mind that much depends upon the kinds of organizations and decision-making processes which can be controlled by judicial review, or in a broader sense regulated according to the values or approaches of public law. This is the dimension in which are determined the respective spheres of Public Common Law and Private Common Law in the employment sphere, which we consider in our concluding section.

Conclusion—Voice Conferred or Voice Denied? The Respective Spheres of Public Common Law and Private Common Law

The foregoing analysis might appear to suggest a simple allocation of the voice-conferring capacities of the common law between a public sector in which the positive attributes of Public Common Law prevailed and a private sector in which the negative effects of Private Common Law prevailed. However, even that idea of an equilibrium between Public Common Law and Private Common Law may in a certain sense be too optimistic. Two relevant tendencies deserve attention. On the one hand, judicial review with its voice-conferring potential seemed to advance quite strongly from its narrow base in the regulation of the institutions of national and local government strictly defined into a larger sphere of institutions commanding public power in a more general sense—such as professional regulatory or self-regulatory bodies as in the *Datafin* case.[36]

On the other hand, the courts have carved out a Private Common Law enclave for employment relations within the general sphere of Public Common Law, denying the applicability of judicial review in employment-related applications even where the employing institution is a public body—as especially in *R v East Berkshire Health Authority ex parte Walsh*[37] with which we may compare *Evans v University of Cambridge*.[38] This we suggest is a powerful voice-denying approach and one that, in our view, is not wholly unrelated to the hegemonic role of Private Common Law and its contractualist legacy. The artificial watershed created by *ex parte Walsh* is premised on the existence of a contract or, in the alternative, with the exercise of expressly

[35] This is the declared *leitmotif* of his treatise, *The Democratic Aspects of Trade Union Recognition* (Hart Publishing, 2009).

[36] *R v Panel for Takeovers and Mergers; ex p Datafin plc* [1987] QB 815.

[37] [1985] QB 152.

[38] [2002] EWHC 1382.

or impliedly incorporated contractual rights, and is a manifestation of the ability of Private Common Law and contractualism to act as the central pivot in the English law system of sources, even at risk of jeopardizing the very principles and values that Public Common Law is designed to address.

There is moreover another sense, or another location, in which Public Common Law (with its voice-conferring implications) and Private Common Law (with its voice-denying implications) compete with each other as to which one will be the predominant mind-set. The location is the interpretation of the law of unfair dismissal by tribunals and courts that, in a way, has always been a zone of conflict between the influences of Public Common Law and Private Common Law. The first author of this chapter and Paul Davies identified the influence of Public Law upon the law of unfair dismissal as a very important one,[39] and Dawn Oliver even saw in it some vindication of her idea of the spreading of the value of participative democracy outwards from its public law base into the legal system as a whole.[40] Over the years, UK labour lawyers have developed a Beckett-like sense of anticipation for the influence that human rights legislation and doctrines were meant to have in respect of our domestic interpretation of unfair dismissal legislation. And, admittedly, judgments such as *Pay v UK*[41] and, perhaps more markedly, *Redfearn v UK*[42] and *Eweida & Ors v UK*,[43] might have rightly raised a certain amount of expectations in this respect. But judgments such as *Leach v OFCOM*[44] and *Turner v East Midlands Trains Ltd*[45] leave little or no room for optimism in respect of the voice-conferring potential of this particular understanding of Public Common Law and are a further evidence of the resilience of a number of Private Common Law inspired doctrines dominating our legal thinking when it comes to scrutinizing the exercise of the managerial prerogative.

One good way to draw up a concluding balance sheet between the 'credits' for workers' voice from Public Common Law and the 'debits' from Private Common Law is to consider the implications of the recent decision of the Court of Appeal in *R (Shoesmith) v OFSTED*.[46] This decision, it will be recalled, concerned the summary dismissal of Ms Shoesmith as the Director of Children's Services for the local authority regarded as culpable for failure to protect 'Baby P' from the mistreatment and neglect on the part of his mother and others which led to his death. The Court of Appeal accorded judicial review and a declaration of unlawfulness on grounds of procedural unfairness in respect of a ministerial direction to dismiss Ms Shoesmith, and the local authority's consequential decision to do so, without according her a hearing. This was a revealing sign of the uneasiness that the primarily or exclusively contractual approach to public sector employment relations occasionally creates on the part of senior judiciary, and an explicit recognition that 'there . . . still remain cases which are amenable to judicial review and in relation to which the alternative remedy in the Employment Tribunal [i.e. unfair dismissal proceedings] will be inappropriate or less appropriate'.[47]

[39] Paul Davies and Mark Freedland, 'The Impact of Public Law on Labour Law 1972–1997' (1997) 26 ILJ 311, 324 'Some of the central ideas which inform the law of unfair dismissal are derived from or inspired by public law notions.'

[40] Oliver 134 (n 31).

[41] [2009] IRLR 139 (ECtHR).

[42] [2012] ECHR 1978.

[43] [2013] ECHR 37.

[44] [2012] EWCA Civ 959.

[45] [2012] EWCA Civ 1470, CA.

[46] *R (Shoesmith) v OFSTED* [2011] EWCA Civ 642.

[47] *R (Shoesmith) v OFSTED*, para. 87 (n 46).

How far might we regard this decision as a vindication of the capacity of Public Common Law to prevail over Private Common Law in creating voice for workers? We must, as ever, be cautious in the claims that we make in this respect. On the one hand, it is true that *Shoesmith* does represent something of a *Ridge v Baldwin*[48] moment of vindication of natural justice and fairness in the sphere of public employment; and to require a hearing for an employee does in a sense accord a voice to that employee—it is his or her 'voice' that is 'heard'. However, all this is a world away from according voice to employees in general, even public-sector employees in general, in the way that the organizations in which and for which they work are governed and managed—almost as remote as was the House of Lords in *Ridge v Baldwin* from what they perceived as 'the ordinary law of master and servant'.

Thus when celebrating the willingness of the Court of Appeal in *Shoesmith* to respond to arbitrary and oppressive action by public actors in the employment sphere, and in so doing to transcend the limits and restrictions of the law of the contract of employment and of unfair dismissal, we have nevertheless to remember that this willingness is evinced with regard to a hierarchically very senior employee—a top manager who could as such be regarded as an 'office-holder' as well as being a contractual employee. For all the injustice or excessively harsh justice which seems to have been meted out to her, we cannot doubt that she had from the outset possessed a 'voice', indeed quite a decisive one, in the way that the organization in question was managed and run. We have to be very careful about assuming that the undoubted benefit from decisions such as that in *Shoesmith* to our system of governance of public organizations will in any sense 'trickle down' to rank and file workers in those organizations in such a way as to confer 'voice' upon them.

In a sense the same point had been made by Paul Davies and the first author of this paper in 1997, even at the zenith, as it now appears, of the influence of Public Law on Labour Law. In the article in which, as mentioned earlier, they had for instance proclaimed the formative influence of Public Law on the law of unfair dismissal,[49] they had at the same time distinguished between three distinct threads of Public Law, and recognized that their influence on labour law varied considerably. The three threads or trends in question were:

(i) the pluralist one in which public law is concerned with ensuring that the exercise of public power is responsive to the concerns of the groups and associations in civil society which are intermediate between the state and the individual citizen;
(ii) the individualist one in which the central concern is that of protecting individual citizens against the unauthorized or arbitrary exercise of public power; and
(iii) the human rights one, an intersecting one in which the central concern is with upholding the personal and human rights of citizens.

Of these three, it is of course the pluralist thread which corresponds most closely to the idea of the voice-conferring potential of Public Common Law which is under discussion in this chapter. The Davies and Freedland article was clear enough in its conclusion

[48] [1964] AC 40, 65 per Lord Reid.

[49] See Davies and Freedland 324 (n 39).

that it was this thread which was the thinnest of the three, increasingly incapable of bearing any great weight at a time when the individualist trend was constantly becoming more marked both in Public Law and in Labour Law and at the intersection between them. We think that is a conclusion which has withstood the test of time; for, even if the implied term of mutual trust and confidence has in the intervening years retained some of its functionality[50] as a bridge between public and private common law, invoking public law notions such as rationality in the exercise of contractual powers, protecting legitimate expectations, or the right to a grievance hearing, it is nevertheless difficult, for the reasons which we gave in the previous section of this chapter, to regard those elements as having been deployed in any serious way towards the vindication of workers' collective voice.

So, in overall summary, we find ourselves in the end locked in the eternal and necessary conversation for labour lawyers as to how best a legal system, and in particular a legal subsystem of judge-made 'common law', might best reconcile the value of 'freedom of contract' with those of (primarily individual) justice and fairness and (primarily collective) voice for workers. We have observed how Private Common Law is very good at and generally disposed towards vindicating the first of those values in the employment sphere, while Public Common Law is, in extreme cases at least, just occasionally good at vindicating the second of those values. We conclude with the suggestion that, in striving towards a reconciliation between all three values, in the interest of 'workers' voice', we may usefully invoke that ever-useful idea of the redressing of the inequality of bargaining power inherent in the individual contract of employment, and also the large notion of respect for 'personality in work' which we have put forward in our recent writings.[51]

However, to that conclusion there is an important postscript. Sixty years ago, Otto Kahn-Freund wrote that:

> It is essential to realize that English law, contrary to most of the legal systems of the European Continent, knows nothing or little of the factory or mine, office or workshop, as a community organized by legal principles. The legal constitution of that community, if one may use that term, is still that of an absolute monarchy to the rule of which its members have submitted by contract. [...] The law thus refuses to look upon the workers in a factory as one entity. It dissolves the existing workshop community in a series of individual contracts, and does not make its sanctions available to those organs of representation and joint consultation which play such an important role in the life of industry.[52]

If we are honest with ourselves, we have to recognize that the most significant changes away from that state of affairs in the intervening years have consisted in the de facto decline in the 'organs of representation and joint consultation' which Kahn-Freund

[50] As to which, compare the very interesting analysis advanced by Alan Bogg, in '*Bournemouth University Higher Education Corporation v Buckland*: Re-establishing Orthodoxy at the Expense of Coherence?' (2010) 39 ILJ 408.

[51] Mark Freedland and Nicola Kountouris, *The Legal Construction of Personal Work Relations* (OUP, 2011) ch. 9, sec. 4.

[52] Otto Kahn-Freund 'Legal Framework' in Allan Flanders and Hugh Clegg, *The System of Industrial Relations in Great Britain* (Basil Blackwell, 1954) 49–50.

could regard as so important. Moreover, so far as British labour law has evolved to nourish and protect those increasingly fragile institutional mechanisms, it has done so entirely through the medium of legislation, much of which has been enjoined upon it by EU law. Despite an occasional flash of inspiration from Public Common Law, the overall contribution of the Common Law, with which this paper has been concerned, has been at best a negligible one, arguably a negative one. That is a reality which we should strive to reform, but which we have first to accept in order to do so.

18

National and International Labour Rights

Lance Compa

Introduction

Can invoking international labour rights amplify workers' voice in national labour law systems? Not easily. National systems are shaped by country-specific history of social conflict and culture of labour-management relations. They are highly resistant to international influences.

But resistant does not mean impervious. Although labour and employment laws are deeply rooted in national systems, the pressures of globalization are prompting social actors and judicial authorities in many countries to take international labour law into account. This means that not all will be impervious to the same degree. A variety of contextual factors such as constitutional traditions, the role of regional human rights regimes (under the European and inter-American human rights conventions, for example), and, in the United States, a largely closed normative system, will affect national labour law and its application

In Canada, the Supreme Court accepted trade unionists' arguments in the 2007 *B.C. Health* case and invoked international labour standards to expand collective bargaining rights under that country's Charter of Rights and Freedoms. The court pointed to Canada's ratification of the International Covenant on Economic, Social and Cultural Rights, the International Covenant on Civil and Political Rights, and the International Labour Organization's Convention No. 87 on freedom of association and protection of the right to organize and concluded 'these documents reflect not only international consensus, but also principles that Canada has committed itself to uphold'.[1]

French courts found that a two-year probation period in a 2005 law on newly-hired workers was inconsistent with ILO Convention 158 on termination of employment.[2] Mexico's Supreme Court applied ILO Convention 87 to rule against restrictions on trade union organizing by state authorities.[3]

In a detailed analysis of ways in which international labour standards have penetrated national labour law systems, Constance Thomas, Martin Oelz, and Xavier Beaudonnet said:

> The legal reasoning used by the courts to justify the reliance on international labour standards as a source of inspiration can vary from a country to another... The reference

[1] *Health Services and Support—Facilities Subsector Bargaining Assn v British Columbia* [2007] SCC 27.

[2] Eric Gravel and Quentin Delpech, 'International Labour Standards: Recent developments in complementarity between the international and national supervisory systems' (2008) 147 International Labour Review 403.

[3] Ana Torriente, 'Study of Mexican Supreme Court Decisions Concerning the Rights of State Employees to Organize in the States of Jalisco and Oaxaca' (1997), at <http://www.dol.gov/ilab/media/reports/nao/TorrienteStudy.htm#I> accessed 26 March 2013.

> to international labour law ... proves useful when domestic courts,... facing insufficient statutory provisions, have to create jurisprudential principles to settle labour disputes. Under such circumstances, international human rights and labour standards are considered by some courts as a valid source of inspiration in order to develop their case law ...[4]

Those authors pointed to several examples of national labour law authorities applying international norms in a domestic legal context, including these:

- Spain's Constitutional Tribunal in 1981 cited ILO Convention No. 87 on freedom of association to widen the scope of protection against anti-union reprisals to cover candidates for union office in addition to office holders.
- In a 1990 Italian case on an issue as basic as the formula for using overtime hours to calculate employees' vacation pay, a court applied ILO Convention No. 132 on annual holidays with pay to fill in gaps in national legislation.
- Costa Rica's Supreme Court cited ILO norms in 1999 to overturn a national law infringing on rights of indigenous peoples set out in Conventions 107 and 169.
- In 2000, a Paraguayan court relied on Convention No. 111 on discrimination to interpret national law as encompassing sexual harassment.
- The Supreme Court of Madagascar invoked ILO Convention No. 111 in 2003 to find that provisions in a collective bargaining agreement setting a lower retirement age for female airline employees than for male employees was unlawful discrimination.
- In another case arising in the airline industry, South Africa's Constitutional Court in 2000 relied on Convention No. 111 to condemn a company's refusal to hire someone because of HIV/AIDS status.
- In 1998, the Industrial Relations Commission of Australia pointed to ILO Convention No. 100 on equal pay to establish a rule of equal pay for work of equal value in national legislation, which had not specifically addressed this issue.

The authors concluded: 'It appears that in practice the degree to which courts refer to international instruments is considerably determined by the prevailing "legal culture" with regard to openness and awareness of international law rather than the system of incorporation [monist versus dualist]'.[5]

The American Case

Other contributors to this volume are more knowledgeable than I about the interplay of international labour standards and national labour law systems in each of their

[4] Constance Thomas, Martin Oelz, and Xavier Beaudonnet, 'The Use of International Labour Law in Domestic Courts: Theory, recent jurisprudence, and practical implications' in J.-C. Javillier, B. Gernigon, and G.P. Politakas (eds), *Les Normes Internationales du Travail: Mélanges en l'honneur de Nicolas Valticos* (ILO, 2004).

[5] Thomas et al. (n 4). Monist countries' constitutional law makes international treaties effective in the national legal system upon ratification, without need for further implementing legislation. In dualist countries, national legislatures must take a further step of adopting legislation to implement a treaty's provisions and make them enforceable under national law.

countries. This chapter concentrates on the United States, both because it is the case I know best and because it demonstrates how voicing of a 'workers' rights are human rights' theme can resonate in ways that advance workers' cause in a national setting that is otherwise inhospitable to invocations of international norms.

The United States is probably the country most opposed to international influence in its domestic legal system, in the labour field as much as any. Outside a small cadre of comparative and international specialists, most actors in the US labour law system have little familiarity with ILO conventions and labour provisions in other international instruments. Labour law in the United States is all about the National Labor Relations Act (NLRA). As Cynthia Estlund has noted:

> The official American view is that international human rights are endangered elsewhere, and that American labor law is a model for the rest of the world.... American legal institutions and decisionmakers have thus far been deaf to the claim that international labor law provides a potential model for American labor law, or even a critical vantage point from which to view American labor law.[6]

In an official message to the US Senate preceding ratification of the International Covenant on Civil and Political Rights in 1992, the first Bush administration acceded to demands by anti-labour senators that 'ratification of the Covenant has no bearing on and does not, and will not, require any alteration or amendment to existing Federal and State labor law' and that 'ratification of the Covenant would not obligate us in any way to ratify ILO Convention 87 or any other international agreement'.[7]

Although the domestic labour law system reflects an 'American exceptionalism' syndrome, the US government and civil society actors in the United States have readily accepted and promoted international labour and human rights standards in many other forums. Many US trade laws, starting with the Generalized System of Preferences (GSP), require developing countries that want access to the American market to comply with 'internationally recognized worker rights'. The law defines these as rights of association, organizing, and collective bargaining; prohibitions on forced labour and child labour, and 'acceptable conditions of work' on wages, hours of work, and occupational safety and health.[8]

Under a congressional mandate, the United States insists that any free trade agreement with another country or group of countries require the parties (including the United States) to 'adopt and maintain' national labour laws consistent with ILO core labour standards.[9] The US Department of Labour devotes enormous resources to

[6] Cynthia L. Estlund, 'The Ossification of American Labor Law' (2002) 102 Columbia Law Review 1527.

[7] Appendix B, Senate Foreign Relations Committee, Senate Comm. on Foreign Relations, 'Report on the International Covenant on Civil and Political Rights (ICCPR)', S. Exec. Rep. No. 23, 102d Cong., 2d Sess. 25 (1992), reprinted in 31 I.L.M. 645, 660 (1992).

[8] 19 U.S.C.A. § 2462(b)(2)(G) (West 1999). Note that although they are labelled 'internationally recognized worker rights', these standards are not the same as analogous ILO conventions. For discussion on this point, see Lance Compa and Jeffrey S. Vogt, 'Labor Rights in the Generalized System of Preferences: A 20-Year Review' (2001) 22 Comparative Labor Law and Policy Journal 199.

[9] See Office of the United States Trade Representative, 'Bipartisan Agreement on Trade Policy' [May 2007] *Trade Facts* memorandum, at <http://www.ustr.gov/sites/default/files/uploads/factsheets/2007/asset_upload_file127_11319.pdf> accessed 10 April 2013; for discussion, see International Labour Organisation, 'United

combating child labour and forced labour, using international standards as an overarching frame of reference.[10]

Almost 300 US companies have joined the UN Global Compact, which declares that '[b]usinesses should uphold the freedom of association and the effective recognition of the right to collective bargaining'. The UN body notes that 'the labour principles of the Global Compact are taken from the International Labour Organization's Declaration on Fundamental Principles and Rights at Work' and that 'the Principles and Rights identified in the ILO Declaration comprise the labour portion of the Global Compact'.[11]

Many US companies have adopted 'codes of conduct' for themselves and their suppliers requiring compliance with international labour standards. This social compliance movement began in the apparel and footwear sector involving brand-name firms such as Nike, Levi's, Adidas, and others, and has lately spread to the electronics sector with companies such as Apple and Hewlett-Packard.[12] So-called 'multi-stakeholder initiatives' such as the Fair Labour Association (FLA), the Ethical Trading Initiative (ETI), Social Accountability International (SAI), and others have emerged, bringing companies, consumer groups, NGOs, trade unions, and other actors to the table. In every instance, international standards in UN covenants and ILO conventions are key reference points.

In sum, corporate and government actors in the US labour law system have a split personality. They make loud calls for international standards on human rights and labour rights in trade agreements, international organizations, codes of conduct, and other contexts. But when it comes to workers' organizing and collective bargaining rights inside the United States, they fall silent on international labour standards. They do not want to acknowledge that many features of US labour law violate these standards.

Key aspects of American law that violate ILO standards include:

- Denying organizing and bargaining rights to millions of agricultural workers, low-level supervisors, and so called 'independent contractors' who are completely dependent on a single employer for their jobs—they can be sacked with impunity for trying to form a union;
- In the name of 'free speech', allowing employers the right to campaign aggressively against workers' organizing efforts through interference and intimidation, including captive audience speeches and managerial pressure tactics;
- At the same time, denying workers the right to meet union representatives at the workplace to discuss forming a union;
- Allowing employers to fire undocumented immigrant workers for trying to form a union and denying those workers a legal remedy for such discrimination;

States Free Trade Agreements (FTAs)' (19 October 2009) at <http://www.ilo.org/global/standards/information-resources-and-publications/free-trade-agreements-and-labour-rights/WCMS_115531/lang--en/index.htm> accessed 26 March 2013.

[10] See, for example, <http://www.dol.gov/ilab/child-forced-labor/index.htm> accessed 26 March 2013.

[11] See <http://www.unglobalcompact.org/AboutTheGC/index.html> accessed 26 March 2013.

[12] See, for example, Charles Duhigg and Steven Greenhouse, 'Electronic Giant Vowing Reforms In China Plants' *New York Times* (30 March 2012) A1; Keith Bradsher and David Barboza, 'Hewlett-Packard Joins Push to Limit Use of Student Labor in China' *New York Times* (8 February 2013) A1.

- Prohibiting trade union solidarity through harsh secondary boycott laws;
- Allowing employers to permanently replace workers who exercise the right to strike;
- Denying federal government employees the right to bargain over wages and benefits and prohibiting them from striking under any circumstances;
- Denying collective bargaining rights to public employees in many of the fifty states.

These features of US law run counter to Conventions Nos. 87 and 98 on freedom of association, the right to organize, and collective bargaining. Other elements of American labour law breach different ILO conventions. For example, US law:

- Allows products of prison labour to enter the stream of commerce in competition with products of free labour (in violation of Convention No. 29);
- Denies the principle of equal pay for work of equal value, leaving in place pay disparities that result from systemic job segregation and pay discrimination (in violation of Convention No. 100);
- Allows massive use of child labour in agriculture (in violation of Convention No. 138).

American employers concede as much. As the US Council for International Business (USCIB), the US employer representative at the ILO, explained:

> Five of the ILO core conventions (87, 98, 29, 138 and 100) have been found to directly conflict with US law and practice and would require significant and widespread changes to US state and federal law if they were ratified. US ratification of Conventions 87 and 98 would require particularly extensive revisions of longstanding principles of US labour law to conform to their standards.... US ratification of the convention would prohibit all acts of employer and union interference in organising, which would eliminate employers' rights under the NLRA to oppose unions.[13]

Introducing an International Human Rights Voice

It is difficult to come in a 'hard law' front door to assert international norms and international mechanisms on behalf of workers' interests in US labour affairs. Most American judges are unfamiliar with international law and, if the question arises, are content to say 'we have our own constitution and laws; we don't need advice from abroad'. Nonetheless, advocates have found 'soft law' side doors to introduce international human rights into American labour law discourse.

The new human rights theme in the labour field is part of a broader effort by US-based activist and advocacy groups to 'bring human rights home'.[14] They point to the role played by Eleanor Roosevelt and her American team, along with experts from

[13] USCIB, 'US Ratification of ILO Core Labour Standards' [April 2007] Issue Analysis.

[14] For comprehensive discussion, see Catherine Albisa, Martha F. Davis, and Cynthia Soohoo (eds), *Bringing Human Rights Home* (3-volume edition, Praeger, 2008; abridged 1-volume edition, University of Pennsylvania Press, 2009); Shareen Hertel and Kathryn Libal (eds), *Human Rights in the United States: Beyond Exceptionalism* (CUP, 2011).

Europe and from many developing countries, in drafting the Universal Declaration of Human Rights. US government officials often hold out the United States as a beacon of human rights. The US State Department issues an annual report on human rights in countries around the world—except the United States. Many American activists are calling for more consistent US human rights policies to be applied domestically, not just to be demanded of other countries.[15]

In the labour arena, many new organizations emerged in the past decade under a workers' rights-are-human rights banner. At the national level, they include American Rights at Work (ARAW), Jobs with Justice (JwJ), Interfaith Worker Justice (IWJ), National Day Laborers' Organizing Network (NDLON), National Domestic Workers Alliance (NDWA), National Guestworkers Alliance (NGA), Food Chain Workers Alliance (FCWA), and United Workers Congress (UWC, formerly Excluded Workers Congress). At the local and regional level, they include groups like Restaurant Opportunities Centres (ROCs) in many cities, Coalition of Immokalee Workers (CIW), New Orleans Workers' Centre for Racial Justice (NOWCRJ), Southwest Workers Union, California *Carwasheros*,[16] taxi drivers' unions in many cities, and what are known as 'workers' centres' serving low wage employees around the country.[17]

The human rights community is also taking up labour concerns. Starting in 2000, Human Rights Watch published a series of reports on workers' rights in the United States under international human rights standards covering child labour, household domestic employees, immigrant workers' rights, and freedom of association.[18] Trade unions and civil society used these reports as major resources in their campaigns to reform practices in targeted companies and sectors.

Advocates find that analysing US law through a human rights lens and charging employers with violations of international human rights, not just violations of the National Labor Relations Act or the Fair Labor Standards Act, gives more force to their claims for support in the arena of public opinion. For example, the United Food and Commercial Workers *Justice@Smithfield* campaign for workers at the Smithfield Foods hog-slaughtering plant in Tar Heel, North Carolina made extensive use of the HRW meatpacking report, and featured it in a campaign video and on its website.

Adding this human rights voice to the Smithfield campaign helped bring an historic settlement between the company and the union to allow Tar Heel workers to

[15] A new US Human Rights Network brings together many national and local organizations undertaking a human rights agenda inside the United States. See <http://www.ushrnetwork.org/> accessed 24 April 2013.

[16] The name given to the 20,000 mostly Latino car wash workers in California, where a freshly-washed automobile is part of the local culture.

[17] Janice Fine, *Worker Centers: Organizing Communities at the Edge of the Dream* (Cornell University Press, 2007); updated at Janice Fine, 'Worker Centers: Entering a New Stage of Growth and Development' (2011) 20 New Labor Forum 44.

[18] *Unfair Advantage: Workers' Freedom of Association in the United States under International Human Rights Standards* (2000); *Hidden in the Home: Abuse of Domestic Workers with Special Visas in the United States* (2001); *Blood, Sweat, and Fear: Workers' Rights in US Meat and Poultry Plants* (2005); *Discounting Rights: Wal-Mart's Violation of US Workers' Right to Freedom of Association* (2007); *On the Margins of Profit: Rights at Risk in the Global Economy* (2008); *A Strange Case: Violations of Workers' Freedom of Association in the United States by European Multinational Corporations* (2010); *Cultivating Fear: The Vulnerability of Immigrant Farmworkers in the US to Sexual Violence and Sexual Harassment* (2012); all available at the Human Rights Watch website, <http://www.hrw.org>.

exercise their organizing rights in a climate free of intimidation. Each side agreed to the strongest positive case for its position without attacking or disparaging the other. Moreover, Smithfield agreed to let UFCW (United Food and Commercial Workers) representatives meet with workers inside the factory, in non-work areas on non-work time such as break and lunch periods. Such non-obtrusive access is required under ILO standards. But since they are not enforceable, employers almost universally deny such access in the United States, where property rights reign supreme.

Under these conditions, a majority of the 5,000 workers voted in favour of UFCW representation in a secret-ballot election in November 2008. Good faith bargaining ensued, and the parties reached a collective bargaining agreement in 2009 with no further disputes.[19]

In another important organizing advance, 30,000 school bus drivers gained bargaining rights with the Teamsters union in the past four years at First Student, the nation's biggest private school bus contractor. Responding to an innovative campaign at shareholders' meetings and other forums, the UK-based multinational firm pledged adherence to ILO standards on non-interference and no reprisals in employees' organizing efforts, and compelled local managers to behave accordingly.

In dozens of secret-ballot elections around the country, workers chose union representation. In 2011 the company and the union negotiated a nationwide master collective agreement setting basic conditions of employment for all workers and guaranteeing freedom of association.[20]

In 2011, 300 workers at an IKEA supplier factory in Virginia won an NLRB election by a 3-1 margin after the Machinists union built an international support alliance invoking ILO standards.[21] This effort convinced IKEA's top officials in Sweden to halt their US management's American-style anti-union campaign. Then in 2012, protected by the same application of international standards, hundreds more workers at three IKEA distribution centres in Maryland, New Jersey, and Georgia joined them, voting by a solid majority in NLRB elections in favour of IAM representation.[22] In a similar fashion, advocates targeting Wal-Mart's allegedly harmful impact in various social and economic arenas seized on HRW's report to support their calls for reform of company practices.[23]

Human rights advocates' new focus on workers' rights has given powerful impetus to the promotion of a combined human rights-labour rights agenda. Advocates have come far to overcome historic differences, and in some cases tensions. Earlier, many human rights advocates saw labour interests as strictly economic, not really human

[19] Catherine Pritchard, 'Union, Smithfield put differences in the past' *Fayette Observer* (2 September 2012).

[20] Ryan Gray, 'Teamsters, First Student Sign "Historic Agreement" for School Bus Driver Labor' *School Transportation News* (6 June 2011).

[21] Stuart Pfeifer, 'Workers at IKEA factory OK union' *Los Angeles Times* (29 July 2011) B2.

[22] Bruce Vail, 'Machinists Rapidly Unionizing Ikea Warehouses: 3 Down, 2 to Go' *Working In These Times* (10 December 2012), at <http://inthesetimes.com/working/entry/14275/machinists_union_scores_new_victories_in_ikea_warehouse_organizing_campaign/> accessed 9 April 2013.

[23] See (and hear), for example, 'Report: Wal-Mart Violates Worker Rights, Fosters "Culture of Fear" to Prevent Employees From Forming Unions' *Democracy Now* radio programme (1 May 2007), at <http://www.democracynow.org/2007/5/1/report_wal_mart_violates_worker_rights> accessed 29 February 2008; Carol Pier, 'Wal-Mart is a Poster Child for What is Wrong with Labor Laws' *The Huffington Post* (16 May 2007), at <http://www.huffingtonpost.com/carol-pier/walmart-is-a-poster-chil_b_48645.html> accessed 29 February 2008.

rights-related, and labour advocates thought international human rights discourse was too remote, abstract, and 'highfalutin'[24] to resonate in locally-rooted struggles.[25]

Human rights and labour rights advocates have in large part overcome these differences. But in terms of concrete results, an international human rights voice in US labour law discourse sounds outside the periphery of the labour law system strictly defined. The human rights voice has helped workers win single struggles, but does so by affecting public opinion, raising concerns among investors, and other efforts to move management away from typical anti-union practices. The human rights voice is heard at the margins, but rarely at the core of the labour law system.

International Norms and US Law

Only in a few instances have international labour standards had direct effect in American courtrooms. The best-known case involved a 1990s lawsuit in California against Unocal Corporation for forced labour abuses in Burma. The case was brought under the Alien Tort Claims Act, a federal law giving US courts jurisdiction over lawsuits in which a non-citizen plaintiff alleges a tort in violation of international law against a defendant located in the United States, even when the tortious conduct occurred outside the United States. It was a statute adopted in 1789 aimed principally at pirates and other 'enemies of all mankind', as a US federal court later put it in applying the law against a Paraguayan police official who tortured and killed the son of a human rights advocate.[26]

Unocal was not a labour law case as such, but a tort case that implicated international human rights standards. The Burmese military junta committed beatings, rapes, torture, and murder to force villagers to work on the pipeline project. Norms on forced labour and ILO findings on forced labour in Burma were central elements of the lawsuit.

Unocal raised several procedural defences seeking to have the suit dismissed. In one, the company said that the case should be heard in Burmese courts rather than American courts. Considering that Burma was at the time under a harsh military dictatorship with no functioning legal system, the US court gave that argument the short shrift it deserved.

The federal court of appeals ruled against the company's procedural moves and ordered the case to go to a trial on the evidence.[27] Faced with the prospect of a jury hearing powerful personal testimony about the abuses perpetrated against villagers, Unocal settled the case with millions of dollars in recompense to victims of forced labour violations.[28]

Another federal court confronted a more difficult question of the role of human rights in US law in a case that implicated workers' freedom of association, rather than the more obvious case of forced labour violations. The families of assassinated leaders

[24] An American slang word suggesting snobbish, pretentious, fashionable, posh and the like.

[25] Virginia Leary, 'The Paradox of Workers' Rights as Human Rights' in Lance A. Compa and Stephen F. Diamond (eds), *Human Rights, Labor Rights, and International Trade* (University of Pennsylvania Press, 1996).

[26] *Filártiga v Peña-Irala* [1980] 630 F.2d 876.

[27] *Doe v Unocal* [2002] 395 F.3d 932.

[28] Marc Lifsher, 'Unocal Settles Human Rights Lawsuit Over Alleged Abuses at Myanmar Pipeline; A deal ends a landmark case brought by villagers who said soldiers committed atrocities' *The Los Angeles Times* (22 March 2005) C1.

of a union at a Colombian coal mine owned by US-based Drummond Corporation brought a wrongful death tort lawsuit against the company in federal court. The families argued that the unionists were killed because of their trade union activity. Freedom of association was the international norm at issue in the case, because without an international law nexus, the killings remained a criminal matter within the Colombian legal system.

Professor Virginia Leary, a long-time advisor to the ILO, gave expert testimony arguing that workers' freedom of association was a universal human rights standard under international law, and therefore covered by the Alien Tort Claims Act. Her testimony convinced a federal judge to move the case to trial. The judge denied the US-based coal company's motion to dismiss the case, saying that 'the rights to associate and organize are generally recognized as principles of international law sufficient to defeat defendants' motion to dismiss'.[29]

At trial, the jury found in favour of defendant Drummond Coal. Its decision turned on the facts, not on the invocation of international norms on freedom of association. The jury was convinced by the company's argument that it was not complicit in the murders.[30]

Plaintiffs appealed the verdict, arguing that the trial court improperly excluded key testimony.[31] Their position was strengthened in early 2013 when a court in Colombia found a former Drummond contractor guilty of murdering the union leaders.[32]

Several more Alien Tort Claims Act lawsuits involving international labour standards have been winding their way through federal courts in recent years. But in 2013, the US Supreme Court suddenly slammed shut the door opening courts to such cases. In a case raising issues of alleged genocide, not labour issues, the Supreme Court said that the law only applies to allegedly tortious conduct occurring inside the United States, not violations of international human rights law taking place outside the United States.[33]

This decision does not mean that no more lawsuits can ever be brought, but that they will have to be brought in state courts raising traditional tort claims such as wrongful death or assault and battery, not international human rights violations. Freedom of association, therefore, will likely not be part of such lawsuits.

US Labour Law under International Scrutiny

One dramatic case brought US labour law directly up against international standards on freedom of association, but it happened in a foreign court, not a US court. Trico Marine Services, a Texas-based multinational company that supplies offshore oil facilities in the Gulf of Mexico, responded to an employees' organizing effort with the typical

[29] *Rodriguez et al. v Drummond Co.* [2003] 256 F. Supp. 1250.

[30] Kyle Whitmire, 'Alabama Company Is Exonerated in Murders at Colombian Mine' *The New York Times* (27 July 2007) C1.

[31] Russell Hubbard, 'Colombia case appealed; Company sued over 3 slayings' *The Birmingham News* (15 December 2007) 1C.

[32] Libardo Cardona, 'Murder conviction in Drummond union leader slaying' *Associated Press Financial Wire* (7 February 2013).

[33] *Kiobel v Royal Dutch Petroleum* [2013] Docket No. 10-1491.

American management-style anti-union campaign, taking advantage of US labour law features that violate ILO standards, but not US law.

Management hired consultants to script captive audience meetings attacking the union. Moreover, according to the union, management discharged employees who supported the union but who qualified as supervisors. No recourse could be had under the NLRA since these employees were excluded from protection of the Act.

The company also denied requests by union representatives for access to the employer's premises to meet with workers. ILO standards insist that employers should provide access to union representatives so that workers can hear from them at the workplace. In a case involving the United States, the Committee on Freedom of Association said:

> The Committee requests the Government to guarantee access of trade union representatives to workplaces, with due respect for the rights of property and management, so that trade unions can communicate with workers, in order to apprise them of the potential advantages of unionization.[34]

But US labour law does not provide for such access, and the CFA decision has no force of law inside the United States. Thus, the union had no basis for an unfair labour practice charge under US law.

But the union had another angle of approach. Trico Marine derived a large portion of its revenues from operations in the North Sea, serving offshore oil rigs of the Norwegian state oil company, whose employees are represented by NOPEF, the Norwegian oil workers union. A NOPEF delegation visited their US counterparts in 2001 and saw first-hand the effects of management's anti-union campaign. In line with procedures required by Norwegian labour law, the Norwegian union sought court permission to launch a boycott of Trico's North Sea operations.

US labour law strictly forbids such boycott actions and holds unions financially liable for losses a company incurs pursuant to them. However, Norwegian law permits such solidarity action by trade unions. A union must seek preliminary review and approval by a Norwegian court to undertake it.

The key issue in the Norwegian case was whether US labour law conforms to ILO freedom of association norms. The union's boycott would be legal under Norwegian law if it could show that US law violates ILO standards. If the Norwegian court made such a finding, the NOPEF boycott could proceed with sharp, direct consequences for Trico's operations and profits.

Trico's chief executive officer articulated the stakes in the case in testimony to Congress:

> NOPEF seeks court pre-approval of an announced boycott against Trico Supply's vessels operating in the North Sea. The only issue at trial in Norway will be Trico's conduct in the US...

[34] ILO Committee on Freedom of Association, *Complaint against the United States*, Case No. 1523, Report No. 284 (1992).

> Secondary boycotts are illegal under the US National Labor Relations Act, but may be legal in Norway if deemed fair and without a disproportionate impact.... NOPEF is asking the district court in Volda to rule that Trico's compliance with US law—the National Labor Relations Act (NLRA)—does not offer a defense to the boycott since US labor law does not adequately protect US citizens....
>
> NOPEF is contending that the NLRA is defective by the standards of the International Labor Organization Conventions 87 and 98, unratified by the U.S., that deal with the right to organize and freedom of association. NOPEF also contends that US labor law does not meet 'European humanistic standards'....
>
> Since the vast majority of US corporations operating in the offshore oil and gas industry in both the Gulf of Mexico and in the North Sea are non-union in their US Gulf operations, a successful boycott against Trico will likely spawn more boycotts against US companies that operate in both locations.
>
> Such a decision rejecting US labor law could also impact US corporations throughout the world. In addition to potential boycotts, the decision could be used by foreign companies against US companies competing for business. It could be argued that a particular piece of foreign business should not be awarded to a US company because US law has been found not to protect US citizens adequately by a competent European court.[35]

Both the company and the union engaged national and international labour law experts to testify about US labour law's compliance or non-compliance with ILO standards. However, NOPEF and Trico Marine Services settled the case on the day the trial opened. Under the settlement agreement, Trico promised (without conceding that it had acted unlawfully) to obey the law and refrain from use of what the unions called coercive tactics, such as threats and dismissals of organizing leaders. Although a boycott did not materialize, the Trico case signalled the potential impact of ILO core standards within the United States. As the company's president noted, similar cases could arise in the future as trade unions increase their cross-border solidarity work.[36]

Human Rights versus Labour Rights... Again?

This generally positive account of ways in which advocates have injected an international human rights voice into American labour discourse is challenged by a countervailing view from committed labour supporters. Some have suggested that the new emphasis on workers' rights as human rights undermines trade unions and worker solidarity because it stresses individual rights instead of collective power. In so doing, it plays into the hands of anti-labour forces that attack unions as violators of human rights and portray themselves as defenders.

Historian Nelson Lichtenstein has suggested that 'rights consciousness' reflected in new anti-discrimination laws in the 1960s and 70s and other laws protecting individual

[35] See testimony of Thomas E. Fairley, President and Chief Executive Officer, Trico Marine Services, Inc., before the House Committee on Education and the Workforce, US Congress, 8 October 2002.

[36] The organizing drive later ended without an election or other resolution. The unions say that the legacy of Trico's earlier tactics had a continuing effect of undermining the organizing campaign. Trico says that employees were not interested in union representation.

workers has at least coincided with, if not contributed to, the decline of trade union membership and collective bargaining in the United States.[37] Labour lawyer Jay Youngdahl argues that:

> [t]he reliance on reframing labor struggles as first and foremost human rights struggles is misplaced. It is not hyperbole to say that the replacement of solidarity and unity as the anchor for labor justice with 'individual human rights' will mean the end of the union movement as we know it. This is true tactically, strategically, and philosophically. Rights discourse individualizes the struggle at work. The union movement, however, was built on and nourished by solidarity and community.[38]

Historian Joseph McCartin correctly notes that 'anti-union forces have become adept at using the language of human rights, and especially the right of freedom of association, to attack unions as enemies of individual freedom'. He points out that 'sophisticated anti-unionists have developed a rights talk of their own that places freedom from union coercion at the pinnacle of workers' rights'.[39]

A long-sought goal of the National Right-to-Work Committee, an employer-spons ored organization devoted to undermining trade unionism in the United States, is a change in labour law allowing individual workers to opt out of union representation and bargain for themselves, in the name of individual freedom. In such a regime, highly-skilled employees could forswear collective bargaining to seek higher pay than that negotiated by the union. Alternatively, unskilled workers could agree to *lower* pay in exchange for a no-layoff promise or some other perceived benefit.

Arguing for such a change, the Right-to-Work Committee calls union representation:

> ... monopoly bargaining ... a special coercive privilege given to unions by federal law ... every worker loses his or her right to negotiate directly with the employer on his or her own behalf ... trampling of individual rights ... coercion to herd workers into collectives against their will ... enthrones union-boss control over workers ...[40]

The Importance of Alliance

Human rights advocates must modulate their voice in ways that make it resonate in the peculiar acoustics of American labour discourse. It is a challenge to have the Universal Declaration of Human Rights and ILO Conventions taken seriously (or for that matter, even to be known) in the United States. But most of the rest of the world takes them seriously, inside and outside labour movements.

Building alliances is important for advancing workers' rights. Organized workers cannot achieve their goals alone, even with high degrees of union strength and solidarity, in

[37] See Nelson Lichtenstein, 'The Rights Revolution' (2003) 1 New Labor Forum 60.

[38] See Jay Youngdahl, 'Solidarity First: Labor Rights Are Not the Same as Human Rights' [Winter 2009] 18 New Labor Forum 31.

[39] Joseph A. McCartin, 'Probing the Limits of Rights Discourse in the Obama Era: A Crossroads for Labor and Liberalism' [2011] contribution to 'Scholarly Controversy: Labor Rights as Human Rights?' 80 International Labor and Working-Class History 1.

[40] See National Right to Work Committee, 'The Problem of Compulsory Unionism', at <http://www.nrtwc.org/about-2/the-problem/> accessed 11 October 2012.

a political and economic system that keeps them constantly on the defensive. A human rights voice reaches an important intellectual and social force that can join civil rights, religious, feminist, immigrant rights, and other allied movements in support of labour's struggles and labour's goals.

The human rights framework is especially helpful in building alliances with European trade unions and allied groups. They are strongly attuned to fundamental rights arguments and knowledgeable about ILO standards. They constantly raise them in European Union labour affairs. In Latin America, too, ILO standards are a normal part of labour law debates and jurisprudence.

A human rights argument defending individual rights does not preclude equally honouring a right to solidarity. Human rights advocacy for workers and unions goes beyond classic individual rights because freedom of association at work inherently takes on a collective character. The rights of individual workers can only be realized collectively. As the European Court of Human Rights stated in a case involving the European Convention's Article 11 on freedom of association, 'Article 11 presents trade union freedom as one form or a special aspect of freedom of association.... [T]he Convention safeguards freedom to protect the occupational interests of trade union members by trade union action... A trade union must thus be free to strive for the protection of its members' interests, and the individual members have a right, in order to protect their interests, that the trade union should be heard.'[41]

Employers, not human rights advocates allied with the labour movement, are promoting a narrow, individualistic rights argument. But because a human rights framework starts with individuals does not mean we should abandon the field to employers to push their interpretation of workers' rights. Human rights advocates have to push back. Collective rights of workers in the employment context are also an exercise of fundamental human rights. Individual rights are a starting point, but in matters of freedom of association, these rights can only be made real in a group.

Advocates should not pit one set of rights against another. Instead, we should offer a generous version of rights embracing both individual and collective interests against a restrictive, self-interested employers' version that deprives workers of their right to defend themselves through organization and collective bargaining—the only way workers can gain a voice that carries in the American labour relations system.

Conclusion

Trade unions are in crisis. Much of this volume is devoted to alternative forms of voice for workers. But in our eagerness to find them, we should not turn away from the voice that endures in a market-driven economic environment: strong, independent, democratic trade unions that defend employees in the workplace.

Cooperatives and employee-owned enterprises offer nice examples of alternative worker voice. They should be encouraged and nurtured. But they are never going to be more than sideshows in a global economy dominated by powerful corporations that

[41] *Wilson & the National Union of Journalists and Others v the United Kingdom*, App Nos 30668/96, 30671/96, and 30678/96, 2 July 2002.

see their first mission as upholding shareholder value and ever-greater return on investment. Without strong unions, workers' consultation in these firms carries a serious risk of co-opting them into identification with the firm and throwing them into competition with other workers.

The real need is to identify with other workers in a class-based labour movement for social justice, starting inside the firm but extending to society as a whole through social protection and public goods. Insisting on an international 'floor' of labour standards through international labour rights advocacy can help build a general social movement to achieve these broader goals.

BEING HEARD—OBSTRUCTING AND FACILITATING VOICE

19

Regulatory Facilitation of Voice

*John Howe**

Introduction

A key issue for the 'Voices at Work' project is the possible institutional and regulatory mechanisms by which worker voice is, and could be, facilitated. In this chapter, consideration is given to this question in light of regulation and new governance perspectives.[1] It applies a broader conception of regulation than one confined to the state's efforts to regulate through formal legal mechanisms such as legislation which mandate or prohibit certain behaviours. Instead, the chapter considers the broad range of regulatory measures through which voice at work—as an objective of regulation—might be achieved or promoted. This includes legislation but also encompasses deployment of public wealth and other resources available to the state. The example of public procurement is discussed as an illustration of such an approach.

Beyond this, the chapter considers how voice might be facilitated through the nature of regulation itself. Theories of optimal regulatory design, including 'responsive regulation' and 'reflexive regulation', suggest that regulation is enhanced when regulated actors are engaged as participants in the regulatory process, both inside and outside the firm.[2] Where workers and their organizations and/or representatives have a regulatory role, then this constitutes some form of voice. The question then becomes one of: how strong is the voice of workers in this regulation? If voice is limited to a form of participation which allows for information sharing at the workplace level but which does not empower actors to engage in norm creation and/or enforcement, we might consider it less effective than voice which provides workers with legal rights over working conditions and their observance. Thus, laws facilitating collective bargaining might be considered stronger, or more empowering, than laws requiring businesses to share information and consult with their employees over change.

* Centre for Employment and Labour Relations Law, Melbourne Law School.

[1] For examples of the exploration of regulatory and new governance scholarship in relation to labour studies, see e.g. Hugh Collins, 'Is There a Third Way in Labour Law?' in Joanne Conaghan, Richard Michael Fischl, and Karl Klare (eds), *Labour Law in an Era of Globalization: Transformative Practices and Possibilities* (OUP, 2002) 449; David Weil, 'Public Enforcement/Private Monitoring: Evaluating a New Approach to Regulating the Minimum Wage' (2005) 58 Industrial and Labour Relations Review 238; Ralf Rogowski and Ton Wilthagen (eds), *Reflexive Labour Law: Studies in Industrial Relations and Employment Regulation* (Kluwer, 1994); Orly Lobel, 'The Renew Deal: The Fall of Regulation and the Rise of Governance in Contemporary Legal Thought' (2004) 89 Minnesota Law Review (Minn L Rev) 342; Cynthia Estlund, *Regoverning the Workplace: From Self-Regulation to Co-Regulation* (Yale University Press, 2010). In relation to Australia: see generally Christopher Arup et al. (eds), *Labour Law and Labour Market Regulation: Essays on the Construction, Constitution and Regulation of Labour Markets and Work Relationships* (The Federation Press, 2006).

[2] See, for example, Rogowski and Wilthagen (n 1); Ian Ayres and John Braithwaite, *Responsive Regulation: Transcending the Deregulation Debate* (OUP, 1992).

In exploring the question of how voice can best be facilitated through the regulatory process, it is argued that traditional debates about voice have largely been focused on the standard setting/norm creation aspect of regulation, to the neglect of monitoring and enforcement mechanisms.[3] The role of employees, trade unions, and other worker representatives in both monitoring compliance with employment standards and enforcing those standards is important in realizing worker voice. The chapter therefore considers the ways in which legal systems facilitate or obstruct employees and other non-state actors playing a regulatory role through monitoring and enforcement of standards.

Regulating for Voice

In exploring the role of regulation in facilitating voice, a broad understanding of regulation is adopted, whereby regulation is

> any process or set of processes by which norms are established, the behaviour of those subject to the norms monitored or fed back into the regime, and for which there are mechanisms for holding the behaviour of regulated actors within the acceptable limits of the regime (whether by enforcement action or by some other mechanism).[4]

Further, a pluralistic approach to regulation is taken, in that it is recognized that key regulatory resources 'such as legal authority, wealth, information and organizational capacities are fragmented and dispersed between the state and non-state actors'.[5] This approach acknowledges that the key regulatory functions of standard setting, monitoring, and enforcement may be performed by both state and non-state actors through a variety of regulatory instruments and tools.[6]

While regulation and new governance perspectives encourage consideration of the role of non-state actors as regulators, this part of the chapter is concerned with the role of the state and how it is understood to regulate or govern in contemporary societies. As discussed in the introduction, regulation and new governance perspectives suggest new avenues of inquiry into '*how* the state attempts to influence behavior in pursuit of its policy goals'.[7]

Before considering how the state might facilitate voice at work, it is first necessary to give brief consideration to the nature of voice as a regulatory goal and its various possible meanings and purposes. In this chapter, it is accepted that voice at work might encompass a number of meanings. Voice is recognized as being a broader concept than its historical association with legal mechanisms to address inequality of bargaining power between employers and employees, such as legal support for trade unions and

[3] See also Hardy in this volume.

[4] Colin Scott, 'Analysing Regulatory Space: Fragmented Resources and Institutional Design' [2001] Public Law (PL) 329, 331.

[5] Carolyn Abbot, 'Bridging the Gap—Non-state Actors and the Challenges of Regulating New Technology' (2012) 39 Journal of Law and Society 329 at 339; Scott (n 4).

[6] Abbot (n 5). See also Christine Parker, 'The Pluralization of Regulation' (2008) 9 Theoretical Inquiries in Law 349; and Julia Black, 'Enrolling Actors in Regulatory Systems: Examples from UK Financial Services Regulation' [2003] PL 63.

[7] Bronwen Morgan and Karen Yeung, *An Introduction to Law and Regulation* (CUP Press, 2007) 9; see also Arie Freiberg, *The Tools of Regulation* (Federation Press, 2010).

collective bargaining.[8] Drawing on Dundon et al.'s definition of voice, [9] state initiatives to facilitate voice might relate to: the capacity for individuals to express dissent in the workplace; the potential for collective action, for example through union membership and collective bargaining; voice through the involvement of workers in management decision-making concerning work organization and efficiency; and voice as a form of mutuality, expressed by cooperation and partnership between employees and the firm. However, as noted earlier, these forms of voice are largely confined to standard setting and norm creation. Thus, in the second section of the chapter, this definition is extended to encompass voice in relation to the realization of working conditions and standards through monitoring of compliance with standards, and where necessary, the capacity to enforce those standards *outside* the workplace through courts or tribunals.[10]

Although there is a strong case for seeing the purpose of voice as being the protection and empowerment of workers, by giving them a say in governance at work and, more broadly, politics and society, voice is also seen as having economic benefits. The HRM literature suggests that voice can foster employee loyalty and staff retention, and can provide useful feedback and information to improve the efficiency and profitability of an employer's business.[11] We can therefore expect that governments may be interested in facilitating various forms of voice, and for different reasons. Given that some of these reasons may be economic, we might also expect that government is likely to see its role, and the regulatory tools it uses, as different to where it is engaging in social protection.

Whether we see voice as necessary for industrial citizenship and the enhancement of civic democracy, or as serving economic objectives, worker voice must be 'amplified'[12] to ensure that it is effective. This amplification may be achieved through mechanisms which support the independence of voice from capital, and to address power imbalance between employers and workers. As already noted, discussion of the role of the state in facilitating voice has largely emphasized the importance of collective bargaining systems for giving workers some power over their employment conditions. Thus the focus has been on the role of law in facilitating a role for unions in the standard-setting or norm creation aspect of regulation. In some contexts, this has meant consideration of the role of law in establishing legal mechanisms through which collective determination of working conditions can be achieved, such as the Australian conciliation and arbitration system, or the US 'Wagner Act' model. In other more voluntarist systems, such as the UK, the historical focus has been on the role of law in ensuring that workers are free to engage in collective bargaining where they wish do so, in circumstances where private law may otherwise be an obstacle to voice.[13]

[8] Alan Bogg and Tonia Novitz, 'Investigating "Voice" at Work' (2012) 33 Comparative Labor Law and Policy Journal (CLLPJ) 323.

[9] Tony Dundon, Adrian Wilkinson, Mick Marchington, and Peter Ackers, 'The Meanings and Purpose of Employee Voice' (2004) 15(6) International Journal of Human Resource Management 1149.

[10] Hardy in this volume.

[11] For an overview, see Bogg and Novitz 340–7 (n 8).

[12] Estlund 162 (n 1).

[13] See, for example, Alan Bogg and Tonia Novitz, 'Recognition in Respect of Bargaining in the United Kingdom: Collective Autonomy and Political Neutrality in Context' in Breen Creighton and Anthony Forsyth, *Rediscovering Collective Bargaining: Australia's Fair Work Act in International Perspective* (Routledge, 2012).

As Estlund has observed, given the decline in trade unions and collective bargaining as a form of voice, it is important to look for other voice mechanisms, and to consider the role of the state in facilitating those mechanisms. However, the relative strength of these mechanisms must also be considered. Do alternative forms of employee participation in regulation and decision-making facilitate the protection and empowerment of workers through involvement in the processes of norm creation, monitoring and enforcement?

In seeking to influence behaviour, the state has available to it a number of regulatory techniques or tools. This includes the conventional 'command and control' style of regulation, in which formal rules are created, monitored, and enforced by the state through orders and sanctions. Of these alternative techniques, 'soft' or 'light touch' approaches to regulation are distinguished from 'hard' legal or centred command and control regulation on the basis that the former are less reliant on the imposition by the state of generally applicable mandatory legal standards as a means of regulating behaviour. These light touch approaches may have advantages (or disadvantages) over command and control style regulatory approaches in that they have the potential to be more reflexive—that is, the capacity to be more responsive to complex regulatory environments and the interests of non-state actors, whether firms or civil society.[14]

In the realm of labour law specifically, the traditional focus on 'hard' law—legislation, awards and enterprise agreements, and case law—has indeed provided an incomplete picture of the role of the state (and of non-state actors) in regulating work.[15] Between the regulatory extremes of 'hard' command and control legal regulation and voluntary self-regulation or 'corporate social responsibility' (no direct role for the state) are a number of regulatory approaches which can be classified as 'hard' or 'soft' according to the extent of government involvement and the coerciveness of that involvement.[16] For example, some approaches rely on 'procedural regulation', or in other words, facilitation of 'co-regulation' or corporatist arrangements, such as collective bargaining, and/or 'self-regulation' by requiring or encouraging firms and stakeholders to develop standards of behaviour which are better than state sanctioned minima.[17] Governments might also encourage non-state actors to regulate by providing them with standing to seek legal or administrative remedies in cases of alleged breach of the law. These approaches will be discussed later in this chapter.

Other initiatives rely on government deployment of its wealth resource to secure behavioural change, such as attaching conditions to government contracts, or through the offering of financial incentives or rewards.[18] Further, governments frequently use

[14] Rogowski and Wilthagen (n 1).

[15] John Howe, '"Money and Favours": Government Deployment of Public Wealth as an Instrument of Labour Regulation' and Peter Gahan and Peter Brosnan, 'The Repertoires of Labour Market Regulation' in Arup (n 1); Keith Ewing, 'The State and Industrial Relations: "Collective Laissez-Faire" Revisited' (1998) 5 Historical Studies in Industrial Relations 1; John Godard, 'Institutional Environments, Employer Practices, and States in Liberal Market Economies' (2002) 41 Industrial Relations 249; Mark Stuart and Miguel Martinez Lucio, 'The New Benchmarking and Advisory State: The Role of the British Advisory, Conciliation and Arbitration Service in Facilitating Labour-Management Consultation in Public Sector Transformation' (2008) 50 Journal of Industrial Relations 736.

[16] Anthony Ogus, 'Rethinking Self-Regulation' (1995) 15 Oxford Journal of Legal Studies (OJLS) 97, 100; Lester M. Salamon, 'The New Governance and the Tools of Public Action: An Introduction' in Lester M. Salamon (ed.), *The Tools of Government: A Guide to the New Governance* (OUP, 2002).

[17] This is sometimes referred to as 'proceduralisation' of regulation or 'constitutive' regulation.

[18] A more detailed discussion of this particular tool can be found in Howe (n 15), Arup (n 1).

education and informational strategies, or *communication*, to shape or steer behaviour by those they seek to regulate, whether individuals, businesses or other organizations.[19] Information strategies include those which impose public disclosure requirements on firms, including reporting on performance against environmental and social responsibility criteria, as well as governmental use of information as a regulatory instrument, including dissemination of voluntary codes of practice, 'best practice guidelines', or 'case studies' designed to promote or encourage take-up of decent work practices by presenting them in a way which suggests consistency with ideals of good corporate governance.[20]

Whether the shift to these approaches indicates that the state is embracing neoliberal market ideology, or is instead a shift in the nature of regulation which reflects the political economy in which states are operating, can be debated.[21] However, it is at least arguable that certain regulatory approaches might be better suited to particular regulatory objectives than others. For example, an approach drawing on economic instruments such as deployment of public wealth might be useful where it is being argued that voice will be mutually beneficial for employees and the profitability of businesses.

The assumption underpinning the use of deployment of wealth as a regulatory instrument is that it is an attractive alternative to mandatory legal regulation. Instead of mandating a change of behaviour, with punishment for non-compliance, economic instruments offer the firm an incentive to undertake desired behaviour, whether by making access to a market or financial support conditional upon the business meeting certain goals. The idea is that the conditional transfer of funds from the state will subvert the firm's 'economic license to operate'. Gunningham, Kagan, and Thornton have argued that the concept of the licence to operate best explains the external pressures that shape the extent to which an enterprise is socially responsible.[22] Their concept is broader than the conventional understanding of a licence as expressing a company's legal obligations, encompassing three broad categories of licence: legal, social, and economic. The notion of the social licence to operate expresses the demands of social actors and stakeholders such as communities, activists, and the voting public. However, Gunningham argues that a business' licence to operate also includes:

> 'economic reality' requirements such as the need to meet debt obligations, show growth in earnings, and maximise shareholder return on investment (or at least to provide a reasonable rate of return). The terms of this *economic license*—what is an adequate rate of return on investment or level of profitability—are not written down in detail like a regulatory permit, of course; they may vary over time, 'tightening' and 'loosening' with market conditions and each firm' economic performance.[23]

[19] Morgan and Yeung 96 (n 7); for consideration in the context of the UK, see Karen Yeung, 'Government by Publicity Management: Sunlight or Spin?' (2005) PL 360–83; in relation to the US, see Janet A. Weiss, 'Public Information' in Salaman (n 16).

[20] Ogus 100 (n 16). [21] Stuart and Martinez Lucio (n 15).

[22] Neil Gunningham, Robert Kagan, and Dorothy Thornton, *Shades of Green: Business, Regulation and the Environment* (Stanford University Press, 2003).

[23] Neil Gunningham, 'Corporate Environmental Responsibility: Law and the Limits of Voluntarism' in Doreen McBarnet, Aurora Voiculescu, and Tom Campbell (eds), *The New Corporate Accountability: Corporate Social Responsibility and the Law* (CUP, 2007) 482.

The economic licence can act either as a brake on, or as a spur to, compliance or 'beyond compliance' behaviour. Where the state makes transfers of wealth conditional upon, for example, recognition of employee voice, the regulatory licence is intended to directly impact on the company's economic licence to operate. It is anticipated that the lure of government expenditure will make it easier for the firm's managers to ensure that the business respects voice in circumstances where in the absence of an economic incentive, such activity would be inconsistent with short-term market demands or the profit maximization goal.[24]

A good example is the use of public procurement. Governments have long used their market power as a substantial purchaser of goods and services from the private sector to pursue social policy objectives secondary to the immediate goal of cost-effective government procurement.[25] The growth in public procurement has only increased the pressure on government to ensure that government contractors are subject to social performance criteria such as the observance of minimum labour standards and progressive employment practices. Where governments purchase goods and services from the private sector using taxpayer funds, it is argued that government should use its purchasing power to ensure that its suppliers follow decent employment practices.[26]

Moreover, procurement is seen as an important form of government regulation of the economy, in that by attaching labour standards as conditions to purchasing contracts, governments provide businesses with an economic incentive to comply with those standards. In other words, it is assumed that the existence of an economic incentive will make business more likely to comply with social regulation than might otherwise have been the case. On the other hand, critics note that businesses not dependent on government largesse are unlikely to be affected by contract compliance mechanisms, and have argued that for this and other reasons, procurement is a less effective and more inefficient way to regulate labour standards than legal regulation.[27] This is an assumption that has not yet been empirically tested.[28]

Voice and the Australian Fair Work Principles

An illustration of how public procurement might be used to promote voice at work is the Australian government's Fair Work Principles. The federal Labor government of 2007–2013 took the linkage between procurement and labour standards to a new level with the Fair Work Principles, which were introduced in 2009.[29] The Fair Work

[24] See Robert Howse, 'Retrenchment, Reform or Revolution? The Shift to Incentives and the Future of the Regulatory State' (1993) 31 Alberta Law Review 455–92; Peter Grabosky, 'Regulation by Reward: On the Use of Incentives as Regulatory Instruments' (1996) 17(3) Law and Policy 256–81.

[25] For a comprehensive, international study of the use of public procurement as an instrument of social policy, see Chris McCrudden, *Buying Social Justice: Equality, Government Procurement and Legal Change* (OUP, 2007).

[26] Howe (n 15); Catherine Barnard, 'Using Procurement to Enforce Labour Standards' in Guy Davidov and Brian Langille (eds), *The Idea of Labour Law* (OUP, 2011).

[27] McCrudden 114–22 (n 25).

[28] Jeffrey Dunoff, 'Linking International Markets and Global Justice' (2009) 107 Michigan Law Review 1039 at 1057.

[29] For a more detailed consideration of the Fair Work Principles, see John Howe, 'Government as Industrial Relations Role Model: Promotion of Collective Bargaining and Workplace Cooperation by Non-Legislative Mechanisms' in Creighton and Forsyth (n 13).

Principles represent the most substantial attempt by the Australian government to incorporate employment and labour relations criteria in Commonwealth public procurement in the history of Commonwealth.[30] They were adopted after extensive lobbying by the trade union movement, which sought to build upon innovations achieved in the incorporation of labour standards in procurement by some states over the previous four years.[31]

The Fair Work Principles require certain government contractors to demonstrate that their employment practices (and those of their subcontractors) are compliant with the federal labour relations legislation, the Fair Work Act 2009 (Cth) (FW Act), and consistent with the legislation's objective of providing 'a balanced framework for cooperative and productive workplace relations that promotes national economic prosperity and social inclusion for all Australians'.[32] It should be noted that they are only one element of the Australian government's procurement policy, which also expresses other goals such as value for money and better outcomes for small businesses. These are values which may conflict with the goal of fairness at work, which can involve an increase in business costs.

A key aspect of the Principles is the expectation that to be eligible for federal government contracts, tenderers must demonstrate their compliance with relevant labour and employment laws over the previous two years. The Fair Work Principles require Commonwealth entities to include in the tender documents for procurement a requirement that contractors and their subcontractors comply with 'materially relevant laws', including industrial laws, occupational health and safety laws, and workers' compensation laws. If tenderers disclose breaches of any of these types of regulation within the previous two years, they must demonstrate compliance with any tribunal or court orders that may have been made or be excluded from eligibility to tender. Upon securing a government contract, the successful tenderer will be subject to contractual requirements concerning ongoing compliance with relevant laws, and 'as far as practicable', must ensure that its subcontractors comply.[33]

As noted earlier, procurement linkages can be used both to promote compliance with the law, but also to foster 'beyond compliance' behaviour. In the remainder of this section, consideration is given to the extent to which the Fair Work Principles require or promote voice at work.

Like many other collective bargaining systems, the FW Act facilitates collective bargaining by providing that employers must not refuse to bargain collectively with employees and their representatives where a sufficient number of employees wish that to happen. Moreover, both employers and employees must bargain in 'good faith'.

The FW Principles do not require tenderers to bargain collectively. However, given the requirement of compliance with the FW Act, tenderers would have to demonstrate

[30] For many years, Australian governments at both federal and state level have been active in using public purchasing power to promote social objectives such as local employment creation, achievement of affirmative action targets, and compliance with labour and employment laws, although in a somewhat ad hoc manner. See John Howe and Ingrid Landau, '"Light Touch" Labour Regulation by State Governments in Australia' (2007) 31 Melbourne University Law Review 367; Howe (n 15).

[31] Howe and Landau 373–82 (n 30). [32] FW Act, s. 3.

[33] Department of Education, Employment and Workplace Relations (DEEWR), *Fair Work Principles—User Guide*, January 2010.

compliance with the good faith bargaining requirements applicable to bargaining representatives under the legislation. Although the Principles do not mandate that tenders require suppliers to demonstrate collective workplace relations practices, such as bargaining with unions, the Principles do mandate that tendering contractors provide confirmation that they 'understand and respect their employees' rights in relation to freedom of association and the right to representation at work'.[34]

Another innovation in the Fair Work Principles which might advance voice at work is a requirement that tenderers with enterprise agreements made and approved under the FW Act must confirm that the agreement has a 'genuine dispute resolution' procedure as required by the FW Act. The definition of 'genuine dispute resolution procedure' includes a requirement that there be capacity for binding arbitration by an independent third party, a requirement that has been criticized by employer bodies as going beyond what is required by the FW Act.[35]

The fact that the Fair Work Principles do not *require* collective bargaining with unions is perhaps due to concerns regarding the freedom of association protections in Australia's labour laws. Presently, the relevant provisions of the FW Act are known as the 'General Protections'.[36] The provisions protect employees from 'adverse action' (such as dismissal from employment) or coercion in relation to the exercise of a 'workplace right'. These provisions are based on both positive and negative concepts of freedom of association.[37] That is, they are intended to ensure that employees who are union members are protected against victimization on the basis of their union membership. However, the Act also protects employees against discrimination on the basis that they are not union members, or do not wish to participate in industrial activities. The concept of a 'workplace right' is broader than the right to join, or not to join a union. It includes an employee's right to have an enterprise agreement apply to them. A person will contravene the FW Act if they coerce another person to exercise or not exercise a workplace right. This would appear to prevent the government from mandating that contractors bargain for an enterprise agreement with their employees, as this would violate their entitlements (and those of their employees) not to associate.

Perhaps because of this difficulty, some Australian procurement programmes have made the existence of 'cooperative' workplace relations practices between employers,[38] unions, and other stakeholders a relevant consideration in procurement decisions, without specifying that cooperation is necessarily achieved through collective bargaining. Under the Fair Work Principles, suppliers are expected to promote 'fair, cooperative and productive workplace relations', and must confirm that they 'have consultation provisions which encourage cooperation and engagement of employees and management'.[39] This goal reflects one of the stated objectives of the FW Act mentioned earlier, the provision of 'a balanced framework for cooperative and productive workplace relations'. However,

[34] DEEWR: Cl. 5.3.2 (n 33).

[35] Workplace Express, 'Fair Work Principles Users' Guide Released', 15 January 2010.

[36] Div 3, Pt 3.1, FW Act. [37] See Creighton in this volume.

[38] Howe and Landau 378 (n 30).

[39] DEEWR: Cl. 5.3.2 (n 33). Section 205(1) of the FW Act requires enterprise agreements registered under the Act to include a 'consultation term' requiring any employers subject to the agreement to consult with employees covered by the agreement concerning 'major workplace changes that are likely to have a significant effect on the employees'.

the incorporation of this objective in the Fair Work Principles suggests that the government expects tenderers to demonstrate that their approach to employee relations goes beyond mere compliance with minimum employment standards. The inclusion of the requirements concerning consultation and cooperation at least promote the objective of voice at work.

It is noteworthy that the encouragement of workplace cooperation and consultation is not required to be incorporated as a condition in the contract between government and successful tenderers. In other words, tenderers will be assessed on these criteria in relation to the award of contracts, but will not be required to continue demonstrating their commitment to these ideals over the life of the contract.

This raises an important issue with respect to government use of procurement to facilitate voice, or other regulatory techniques which could be said to entail a 'lighter touch' —the extent to which these initiatives have sufficient teeth to bring about anything more than cosmetic compliance by firms. In other words, it is important to take account of the state's contribution to what Godard refers to as the 'broader normative cultural context' of industrial relations: the extent to which the state acts to 'shape the broader ideological climate within which employers act, thus indirectly influencing their industrial relations and human resource management strategies through symbolic effects of broader policy objectives and rhetoric'.[40] However, the extent to which such initiatives truly subvert firms' economic licence to operate and foster deeper commitment to voice requires regulatory infrastructure, such as monitoring arrangements and enforcement mechanisms, as well as significant resourcing and effort.

The implementation and enforcement of the Fair Work Principles is shared across a number of Departments and agencies. All Australian Commonwealth entities conducting procurement to which the Principles apply are required to implement and comply with the Fair Work Principles, and monitor compliance with the Principles by their suppliers. DEEWR has overall responsibility for the Principles, while the Department of Finance and Deregulation has overall responsibility for procurement. In addition, the government established two new entities under the Principles, the Procurement Coordinator (PC), and the Procurement Consultation Committee (PCC), which includes representatives of business, unions, and the community. It must be said that the role of these entities is limited. The PC is responsible for promoting the Fair Work Principles, and for handling complaints, and reporting on its activities, while the PCC's role is predominantly advisory in nature.[41]

The key sanction available under this public procurement scheme is ineligibility for government purchasing in the case of supply chains which do not meet the eligibility criteria under the Principles, or cancellation of the government contract in the event of breach. The Principles also incorporate a form of 'naming and shaming' in the case of contractors who fail to comply with the Principles. The Commonwealth reserves the right to publish the names of businesses that breach compliance requirements as a condition of procurement contracts subject to the Principles.[42] However, the Fair Work Principles User Guide does not specify where the names of non-complying

[40] Godard 267 (n 15). [41] DEEWR: Cl. 7.5.4 (n 33). [42] DEEWR: Cl. 6.2 (n 33).

contractors would be published. It is also unclear as to who will be responsible for imposing sanctions.

A lack of transparency concerning the implementation of the Fair Work Principles means that it is unclear whether government departments and agencies have observed the spirit of the Principles and placed sufficient emphasis on the requirements of the User Guide, given the many other factors which must be taken into account in government procurement—value for money being the most obvious. It is not known what resources were devoted to monitoring and enforcement of the Principles in both the assessment and award of tenders, and the observance of relevant contractual conditions. Tenderers were expected to volunteer information as part of the tender process, verifying the information they have provided by signing a statutory declaration. However, it is unclear whether the tenderers were required to provide any evidence of their compliance with relevant laws, or evidence of their cooperative and productive workplace relations practices, beyond these undertakings. It is difficult to assess whether this initiative has had a significant impact on the facilitation of voice at contracting enterprises.

Voice through Regulation

Having presented a pluralist understanding of the range of regulatory tools that might be deployed to facilitate voice, it is also important to recognize that there are many different 'regulators' involved in the process of regulation and governance. Advocates of 'decentred' perspectives on regulation highlight the state-centred, unilateral, and legalistic character of many 'command and control' regimes.[43] The advocates of more decentred regulatory models such as responsive and reflexive regulation have argued that it is important for regulation to foster self-regulation and co-regulation by regulated actors. Although these theories differ in many respects, they share a focus on the compliance motivations of firms, and suggest that the role of the state is to prompt firms to take compliance more seriously, but where possible to leave how this is done to the firm or industry itself.[44]

However, a significant strand of regulation and new governance literature emphasizes that regulation which facilitates participation of non-state actors *in addition to* the regulated firm in regulatory regimes improves the chances of effective regulation and contributes to a more participatory democracy.[45] This reflects a concern that these new approaches to regulation do not leave too much to the firm, given the potential for neglect of social objectives: 'a central challenge that new governance takes on is how to

[43] Julia Black, 'Decentring Regulation: Understanding the Role of Regulation and Self-Regulation in a "Post-Regulatory" World' (2001) 54 Current Legal Problems 103.

[44] A useful comparison of the theories of reflexive and responsive regulation can be found in Parker (n 6).

[45] Ayres and Braithwaite (n 2); Julia Black, 'Proceduralizing Regulation: Part I' (2000) 20 OJLS 597 at 597–8. Decentred or responsive regulation is thought to improve the effectiveness of regulatory regimes by making them more inclusive of interested actors, and encouraging dialogue and debate between those actors—a form of deliberative democracy. See also Vibeke Lehmann Nielsen and Christine Parker, 'To What Extent Do Third Parties Influence Business Compliance' (2008) 35 Journal of Law and Society 309; Bridget Hutter, 'The Role of Non-State Actors in Regulation', Discussion Paper No. 37, Centre for Analysis of Risk and Regulation, London School of Economics, 2006; Black (n 6); and Peter Grabosky, 'Using Non-Governmental Resources to Foster Regulatory Compliance' (1995) 8 Governance 527.

promote legitimate, effective and active participation in the work of regulation by the private regulated parties themselves without devolving into deregulation'.[46]

So what are the various avenues by which workers and their representative organizations might exercise voice *through* regulation? In this discussion, the focus will be on the role of workers and their organizations in monitoring compliance with employment standards by employers, and enforcing the law in cases of non-compliance. This focus is taken because, as discussed earlier, there is a relatively extensive literature on the role of workers and unions in determining working conditions and standards. It has been argued, for example, that collective bargaining systems are inherently decentred, responsive, or reflexive in nature.[47] There has been less consideration of the importance of voice through monitoring and enforcement processes. The emphasis on enforcement is consistent with recent regulatory scholarship which has focused on business compliance with regulation, or in other words the effectiveness of regulation in achieving its stated policy goals.[48] A key issue in this work has been the importance of regulatory enforcement in achieving behavioural change among regulated firms.

Workers are uniquely placed to monitor firm compliance with regulation. Thus, one aspect of the regulatory role that workers might play is the exercise of voice concerning their own working conditions, but also the employer's behaviour more generally. However, it is one thing to be aware of non-compliance, and another to exercise voice with a view to bringing about a change in the employer's behaviour. The role of employees in monitoring compliance is more complex in relation to the exercise of voice concerning one's own working conditions, as distinct from exercise of voice concerning employers' behaviour/organizational corruption more generally.[49] Estlund has observed that fear of reprisal is likely to dampen employee complaints about any form of firm non-compliance or misbehaviour, because employees are both the direct beneficiaries of employment law and also the victims of any non-compliance.[50] Also, non-compliance is most likely to occur in relation to the most vulnerable workers, who are the least likely to complain for fear of losing their job or to possess the resources to successfully challenge managerial decisions.[51]

Lobel draws a distinction between legal protection of the capacity of employees to engage in dissent and problem solving within the firm—that is, to participate in self-regulation by the firm—and legal protection of workers who take their concerns outside the organization by reporting non-compliance, and by extension, take legal action to enforce compliance.[52]

[46] Orly Lobel, 'New Governance as Regulatory Governance' in D. Levi-Faur (ed.), *The Oxford Handbook of Governance* (OUP, 2012).

[47] Catherine Barnard, Simon Deakin, and Richard Hobbs, 'Reflexive Law, Corporate Social Responsibility and the Evolution of Labour Standards: The Case of Working Time', Working Paper No. 294, ESRC Centre for Business Research, University of Cambridge, 2004, p. 2; John Howe, '"Deregulation" of Labour Relations in Australia: Towards a More Centred Command and Control Model' in Arup (n 1).

[48] See, for example, Christine Parker and Vibeke Lehmann Nielsen, *Explaining Compliance: Business Responses to Regulation* (Edward Elgar, 2011).

[49] Estlund 143 (n 1). [50] Estlund 142–3 (n 1).

[51] David Weil and Amanda Pyles, 'Why Complain? Complaints, Compliance and the Problem of Enforcement in the US Workplace' (2005) 27(1) CLLPJ 59.

[52] Orly Lobel, 'Citizenship, Organizational Citizenship, and the Laws of Overlapping Obligations' (2009) 97 California Law Review 433.

Focusing on the first of these, historically, as will be explained in what follows, union membership has been an important means by which worker voice concerning employer compliance with employment conditions has been expressed within the firm. However, in an era of declining union membership, and at a time when employment rights and standards have become increasingly individualized, consideration needs to be given to the legal mechanisms by which workers can enforce their rights both within and externally to the firm, and the extent to which the regulatory framework empowers this by harnessing the engagement of non-state actors, whether unions or otherwise.

Mandated employee participation in governance of compliance through workplace committees is a feature of occupational health and safety regulation in Australia and elsewhere.[53] When it comes to 'brightline' employment standards such as wages and working hours regulation, legal protection of individual worker voice has largely been confined to protection against employer retaliation, and conferral of standing to bring legal proceedings to enforce standards.[54]

Studies have shown that such legal protections have only limited impact on the willingness of individual employees to raise complaints about employer non-compliance with employment standards within the firm.[55] Even with legal protection against retribution, workers are unlikely to have the regulatory capacity to be effective enforcement agents.[56] Moreover, Estlund has argued that as employees are inside the firm, they may not be sufficiently independent from the firm to be an effective monitor of non-compliance. For example, Estlund is critical of internal compliance regimes, where 'the biggest risk... is that they will fit *too* comfortably within the institution, its reigning management, and its institutional culture'.[57]

Thus it is important to consider the extent to which a regulatory system facilitates or *empowers* employees to be participants in the regulatory process by protecting or supporting their rights to enforce working conditions externally to the firm. This will be an important measure of the strength of worker voice in relation to the realization of their employment rights and conditions. That is, the law can play a role in supporting the effective exercise of voice concerning the realization of working conditions.

One way that regulation does this is through the establishment of a public enforcement model, whereby a state labour inspectorate is responsible for monitoring employer compliance with employment standards. The inspectorate will have various powers to enforce the system when non-compliance is detected. The ability to take complaints

[53] See, for example, Richard Johnstone, 'Institutional Arrangements on Health and Safety Representation in Australia' in D. Walters and T. Nichols (eds), *Workplace Health and Safety—International Perspectives on Worker Protection* (Palgrave Macmillan, 2009); D. Walters, 'Workplace Arrangements for Worker Participation in OHS' in Elizabeth Bluff, Neil Gunningham, and Richard Johnstone, *OHS Regulation for a Changing World of Work* (Federation Press, 2004).

[54] Although see Alexander Colvin, 'Organizational Primacy: Employment Conflict in a Post-Standard Contract World' in Katherine Stone and Harry Arthurs (eds), *Rethinking Workplace Regulation: Beyond the Standard Contract of Employment* (Russell Sage Foundation, 2013).

[55] See, for example, Estlund (n 1); Weil and Pyles (n 51).

[56] Regulatory capacity is 'the actual or potential possession of resources plus the existence of actual or potential conditions that make it likely that those resources will be deployed... to further the identified goals of those seeking to regulate': Black 72 (n 6).

[57] Estlund 136 (n 1).

about employer non-compliance to a state regulatory agency will be one avenue through which workers can exercise voice to ensure that employment standards are respected and upheld. This avenue is considered in further detail by Tess Hardy in her chapter in this volume.

In this chapter, the focus is on the extent to which the legal system fosters corporatist or private models of enforcement which empower workers to exercise voice in relation to the realization of their employment conditions. Regulatory and new governance scholarship has suggested various approaches by which the state can facilitate non-government enforcement of legal standards.[58] In the labour relations context, the most relevant of these are the conferring of entitlements to monitor and enforce standards on private parties, or private enforcement; and by empowering third parties to undertake enforcement actions on behalf of the state, often in the context of corporatist models of governance.[59]

Consideration is therefore given to regulatory facilitation of enforcement by individual employees, but also by unions and other representatives of worker interests. As already noted, in countries with collective bargaining systems unions have historically played such an important role in labour regulation and enforcement. In Australia, for example, trade unions were for a long time 'joint regulators' under the conciliation and arbitration system, with a significant involvement in the setting of standards, monitoring compliance with those standards, and enforcement in cases of non-compliance.[60] This can be distinguished from the enrolment of trade unions in state-initiated regulation.[61] The enforcement role of unions has largely been neglected in relation to voice at work. Trade unions have historically 'played critical roles in interpreting and amplifying the practical effect of law within workplaces, a role that fell to centrally to unions by virtue of their "bridging capacity", the ability to link institutional developments at national or industry level to the workplace',[62] a role that has perhaps been more visible in relation to OHS compliance.[63]

However, it is also important to acknowledge the decline of union membership and coverage in many developed economies, and the rise in statutory individual rights that do not depend on the existence of collective bargaining agreements and unions. While the extent to which trade unions and other worker representatives have legal rights to

[58] Abbot (n 5); Neil Gunningham, Martin Phillipson, and Peter Grabosky, 'Harnessing Third Parties as Surrogate Regulators: Achieving Environmental Outcomes by Alternative Means' (1999) 8 Business Strategy and the Environment 211.

[59] Gunningham, Phillipson and Grabosky (n 58); Grabosky (n 45).

[60] See further Tess Hardy and John Howe, 'Partners in Enforcement: The New Balance Between Government and Trade Union Enforcement of Employment Standards in Australia' (2009) 22 Australian Journal of Labour Law 306.

[61] Tess Hardy, 'Enrolling Non-State Actors to Improve Compliance with Minimum Employment Standards' (2011) 22 Economic and Labour Relations Review 117.

[62] T. Colling, 'Trade Union Roles in Making Employment Rights Effective' in Linda Dickens (ed.), *Making Employment Rights Effective: Issues of Enforcement and Compliance* (Hart Publishing, 2012); see also Hardy and Howe (n 60).

[63] D. Walters and K. Frick, 'Worker Participation and the Management of Occupational Health and Safety: Reinforcing or Conflicting Strategies?' in K. Frick, P. L. Jensen, and T. Wilthagen (eds), *Systematic Occupational Health and Safety Management: Perspectives on International Development* (Pergamon, 2000); D. Weil, 'Enforcing OSHA: The Role of Labor Unions' (1991) 30 Industrial Relations 20.

enforce employment entitlements is an important avenue for voice, attention must also be given to the extent to which the legal system supports private enforcement by individual employees.

Voice and the enforcement of employment rights

The extent to which workers are able to exercise voice concerning their employment standards requires consideration of the various legal mechanisms by which employment rights might be enforced.

At one end of the spectrum will be *informal enforcement* inside the workplace, such as negotiation between employer and employee over the existence of a breach of employment standards and how it might be remedied. Where trade unions are present, the union might negotiate with the employer, and where necessary and possible, industrial action used to pressure a firm into compliance. The legal protections important to this type of enforcement include the protection of workers against retaliation by their employers, right of union entry to workplaces for monitoring purposes, and legal protection of the right to take industrial action where that would otherwise be unlawful.[64]

The relative power of relevant actors will be important to the success of informal mechanisms. It has already been noted that individual workers are unlikely to engage in direct negotiation of compliance issues, even with legal protections concerning retaliation. Studies in Australia and the UK have observed that the bulk of the informal enforcement of collectively negotiated terms of employment at the firm level in the twentieth century was likely achieved by unions,[65] what Colling calls 'organic enforcement'.[66] Awareness of legal employment rights is generally higher in unionized workplaces, and union members are more likely to seek advice on employment problems than non-union members. Union members are more likely to report non-compliance with minimum working conditions, and to pursue grievances.[67]

Nevertheless, studies of regulatory enforcement suggest that these informal forms of enforcement are unlikely to be successful without the threat of more formal enforcement processes and sanctions. This is best expressed by the concept of the enforcement pyramid articulated by Ayres and Braithwaite in their model of 'responsive regulation'.[68] The enforcement pyramid works on the basis that '[t]he more the regulated firm refuses to comply, the greater the sanction that should be adopted'.[69] Enforcement activity should commence and occur most frequently at the foundation of the pyramid, which provides for less interventionist techniques, including education, advice, and persuasion. If compliance is not achieved, the regulator escalates up the pyramid where

[64] For discussion in the Australian context, see Hardy and Howe (n 60).

[65] Hardy and Howe (n 60); Colling 188 (n 62).

[66] Colling 195–6 (n 62).

[67] Colling (n 62); David Weil, 'Individual Rights and Collective Agents: The Role of Old and New Workplace Institutions in the Regulation of Labor Markets' in Richard B. Freeman, Joni Hersch, and Lawrence Mishel, *Emerging Labor Market Institutions in the Twenty-First Century* (NBER, 2005).

[68] Ayres and Braithwaite (n 2).

[69] Julia Black, 'Managing Discretion', Paper presented at Penalties: Policy, Principles and Practice in Government Regulation, Sydney, 8 June 2001.

more formal enforcement mechanisms are available. At the apex of the pyramid sit the most punitive sanctions, such as penalties and prosecution. It is the availability of these sanctions which ensures that less formal enforcement activity is successful in most cases.

In considering more formalized enforcement action, a distinction can be drawn between administrative processes and judicial processes of enforcement.[70]

In many countries, enforcement may be carried out through the use of *administrative processes*. This includes the powers of labour inspectorates to investigate or respond to complaints by unions or individuals. A state labour inspectorate might rely on its authority and the sanctions available to it to persuade a firm to comply with legislation. Alternatively, it may have a number of administrative remedies at its disposal which can be used without recourse to the courts.

Of greater relevance to this chapter is the capacity of workers or unions to bring disputes and seek remedies from administrative tribunals. For example, under the Australian conciliation and arbitration system which operated in the twentieth century, an effective administrative process used by unions was the notification of a dispute to the federal tribunal about the application of an award or agreement. Prior to the introduction of tighter legal controls over industrial action, this may have occurred during or after a strike or other work ban relating to the same issues, when the tribunal frequently dealt with more or less spontaneous disputes without regard for technical jurisdictional considerations.[71] This use of the tribunal's dispute resolution powers was a relatively inexpensive and speedy avenue to seek leverage against non-complying employers.[72]

Many jurisdictions now offer administrative remedies for individual employees able to sustain a grievance against their employer.[73] However, these mainly relate to grievances concerning dismissal from employment. They do not offer employees the opportunity to raise grievances concerning their existing terms and conditions of employment.

For this and other reasons, *judicial processes* for resolution of enforcement disputes are considered the most effective avenue for achieving justice in relation to employment rights and conditions. The availability of court action, and the capacity to utilize it, is recognized as the most effective way to achieve full realization and recovery of employment entitlements.[74]

In public enforcement models, a labour inspectorate would normally have standing to prosecute employers for non-compliance, and to seek civil and/or criminal penalties as a form of punishment and deterrence. However, as noted earlier, some regulatory

[70] Christopher Arup and Carolyn Sutherland, 'The Recovery of Wages: Legal Services and Access to Justice' (2009) 35 Monash University Law Review 96. See also Jonas Malmberg, 'Enforcement of Labour Law' in Bob Hepple and Bruno Veneziani (eds), *The Transformation of Labour Law in Europe: A Comparative Study of 15 Countries* (Hart, 2009).

[71] Breen Creighton and Andrew Stewart, *Labour Law*, 4th edn (Federation Press, 2005) 154–5; Margaret Lee, 'Regulating Enforcement of Workers' Entitlements in Australia: The New Dimension of Individualisation' (2006) 17 Labour & Industry 41.

[72] For a discussion of the reference of compliance matters to industrial tribunals as a possible enforcement mechanism, see Arup and Sutherland (n 70).

[73] For example, the UK: Linda Dickens, 'Individual Statutory Employment Rights Since 1997: Constrained Expansion' (2002) 24 Employee Relations 619; and Japan: Takashi Araki, 'New Forms of Dispute Resolution: Japan's Labor Tribunal System' in Stone and Arthurs (n 54).

[74] Arup and Sutherland (n 70).

systems will encourage private enforcement or third party enforcement, either as an alternative to state enforcement, or in place of a role for the state.

Under this model, the state confers rights of action on employees who become aware of a breach of their employment rights, and are unable to remedy that breach by negotiation with their employer. This is achieved either by conferring standing on employees to bring private actions seeking compensation from employers in breach of their obligations, or by empowering private actors to undertake enforcement actions on behalf of the state. This has been described as the casting of plaintiffs in the role of a 'private attorney general', the term used in the US to describe a regime which allows individuals to perform a function which is otherwise assumed to be the province of the state. Giving employees the option of seeking legal sanctions will be an important element of a private enforcement model with respect to minimum working conditions. However, given the relative lack of power of many employees compared to their employers, studies have suggested that legal rights of action alone will be insufficient to render a private enforcement model effective in this context.[75] The capacity of employees to utilize judicial processes of enforcement will depend upon factors such as the legal consciousness of employees, the availability of information concerning their employment entitlements, and their access to legal advice.[76]

The extent of effective access to justice therefore becomes an important consideration in assessing the private enforcement of employment standards. The accessibility of useful information about employment rights and how to secure observance with them is a key access to justice issue. As already noted, where employees are members of an active union, they are likely to have access to information and advice concerning their entitlements and how to enforce them.

However, governments might also seek to address the availability of information to employees concerning their employment rights, so that employees are aware when their rights have been breached. For example, in Australia the FW Act requires all employers to provide new employees with a 'Fair Work Information Statement' setting out information about minimum employment standards.[77] The federal labour inspectorate, the Fair Work Ombudsman, also plays a key role in communicating with employees about their employment rights and entitlements.

In the absence of assistance of a state labour inspectorate, the ability of a worker to enforce employment standards through the courts will normally depend on whether they have access to a trade union, or otherwise to legal advice and assistance from community legal centres or private lawyers. Access to the latter will often depend on whether there is a system of legal aid offered by the state to mitigate the cost of court proceedings.

Alternatively, the state might facilitate private enforcement through the provision of financial incentives, either by allowing for recovery of legal costs or through tax incentives.[78] The United States is perhaps the best example of this. Enforcement of standards under the Fair Labor Standards Act (FLSA) is ostensibly based on a public enforcement

[75] Arup and Sutherland (n 70). [76] Arup and Sutherland (n 70). [77] FW Act, s. 124(1).

[78] Barton H. Thompson, 'The Continuing Innovation of Citizen Enforcement' [2000] University of Illinois Law Review 185 at 193–4.

model, as it provides for the enforcement of the Act by a federal agency, the Wages and Hours Division of the Department of Labor. However, in practice, WHD does not have the resources to prosecute all cases of non-compliance which come to its attention.

Given this background, the FLSA effectively relies on the private suit as its primary enforcement vehicle, given the Act's provision for 'prevailing parties' to claim attorney's fees.[79] In other words, the FLSA encourages private enforcement by adopting the 'English rule' on fee recovery—loser pays winner's legal fees—instead of the more common 'American rule', where each party bears its own costs.[80] When coupled with the ability of US attorneys to charge contingency fees, there is an incentive for employees to bring actions against their employers as they will be unlikely to be liable for any legal fees in the event that the suit is unsuccessful.

Another way that the state can foster private enforcement of employment rights is by the availability of class actions. Class actions are a device intended to:

> overcome the cost and other barriers which impede people from seeking a legal remedy. People who may be ignorant of their rights or fearful of embarking on proceedings could be assisted to a remedy if one member of a group, all similarly affected, could commence proceedings on behalf of all class members.[81]

Class actions can overcome a potential disincentive to employee litigation. The fact that individual claims are often small means that the cost of litigation outweighs any benefits. The combination of fee incentives, the availability of class actions, and the existence of large employers with labour cost-cutting strategies has led to a number of class actions in the United States.[82] However, in smaller jurisdictions such as Australia, there are fewer financial incentives for plaintiff law firms to bring large employment standards enforcement actions. Interestingly, however, trade unions in Australia have made use of the class action to enforce employment standards, a development to which we will return shortly.[83]

Finally, the state may seek to compensate for lack of legal assistance and representation on the part of workers in conjunction with the courts. For example, under the Australian FW Act, employees may elect to pursue their claim under a 'small claims procedure', where the maximum amount that can be awarded is $20,000.[84] Where proceedings are brought under this procedure, the court may act in an 'informal manner' and 'without regard to legal forms and technicalities'.[85] The Australian labour inspectorate, the Fair Work Ombudsman, in dialogue with the Federal Magistrates

[79] Sam Estreicher and Michael Harper, *Cases and Materials on Employment Law* (West, 2004) 1120. See also Steven Willborn, Stewart Schwab, John Burton, and Gillian Lester, *Employment Law: Cases and Materials* (Lexis-Nexis, 2006) 1122.

[80] See A. Mitchell Polinsky and Daniel L. Rubinfield, 'Does the English Rule Discourage Low-probability and Prevailing Plaintiffs?' (1998) 27 Journal of Legal Studies 519.

[81] Australian Law Reform Commission, *Grouped Proceedings in the Federal Court*, Report No. 46 (Australian Government, 1988); quoted in Jane Caruana and Vince Morabito, 'Australian Unions—the Unknown Class Protagonists' (2011) 30 Civil Justice Quarterly 382 at 384.

[82] C. Becker and P. Strauss, 'Representing Low-Wage Workers in the Absence of a Class: The Peculiar Case of s 16 of the Fair Labor Standards Act and the Underenforcement of Minimum Labor Standards' (2008) 92 Minn L Rev 1317.

[83] Caruana and Morabito (n 81). [84] FW Act, s. 548. [85] FW Act, s. 548(3).

Court, has sought to facilitate access to justice for employees whose legal entitlements have been breached while saving its own resources for more strategic litigation by encouraging claimants to commence a small claims action—either with the direct or indirect assistance of the FWO.

In particular, in 2010–2011, the FWO began a small claims procedure pilot in Australia's second largest city, Melbourne, as well as a regional centre, Coffs Harbour. As part of the pilot, a FW Inspector or lawyer from the FWO may seek leave to appear in the capacity of *amicus curiae* or 'friend of the court'. In this role, the FWO representative does not act for either party, but rather works to assist the court better understand points of law or the relevant facts in dispute. In practical terms, the FWO representative does not make submissions or cross-examine witnesses, but rather responds to specific questions from the magistrate. The pilot has been viewed as so successful that it has now expanded in scope and application.[86] In its most recent Annual Report, the FWO confirmed that, during the 2011–2012 financial year, ninety-two small claims applications were heard before the FMCA which resulted in $266,946 being ordered in favour of applicants during that period.[87]

Even in jurisdictions where these regulatory incentives to private enforcement are present, the barriers to employee enforcement of employment rights may still be significant. In these circumstances, third party enforcement by trade unions or other public interest groups becomes particularly important. In some jurisdictions, the state facilitates third party enforcement by affording trade unions or other representative organizations standing to seek judicial remedies for breach of collective agreements or legislated standards. In Australia, for example, unions have standing to bring enforcement proceedings in relation to both statutory and collectively negotiated standards, whereas in other jurisdictions, such as the US, they do not.[88]

The nature of the regulatory system may offer further incentives to union enforcement. The Australian legislation authorizes the court to order payment of penalties for breach of employment standards to a person or an organization, as an alternative to payment to the federal government.[89] For example, where an action is successfully brought by a trade union, the courts will frequently direct that the penalty be paid to the union instead of into consolidated revenue.[90] Such a direction is a positive incentive for unions to bring matters to court, and operates in lieu of an order that the losing party pay the winner's legal costs.[91] As noted earlier, unions may also have the capacity to bring class actions, again a feature of Australian union enforcement.[92]

[86] Nicholas Wilson and Lynda McAlary-Smith, 'The Fair Work Ombudsman: Litigation Policy in Practice' (Speech to Industrial Relations Commission NSW Annual Members Conference, 18 October 2012).

[87] *FWO Annual Report 2011–2012*, 59. Presumably, this amount ordered in favour of applicants does not account for amounts that may have been agreed as part of settlement discussions between the parties—a common process adopted in the small claims proceedings.

[88] Under the FW Act, a union can apply for court orders in relation to a contravention or proposed contravention of civil remedy provisions, industry level 'awards, and enterprise agreements': FW Act, s. 540.

[89] FW Act, s. 546(3).

[90] See, for example, *Australian Federation of Air Pilots v Leach Aero Services* (1988) AILR 388; *Printing and Kindred Industries Union & Ors v Vista Paper Products Pty Ltd & Anor* (1994) 57 IR 414.

[91] The relevant provision in the current legislation is FW Act, s. 570.

[92] Becker and Strauss (n 82); Caruana and Morabito (n 81).

However, it does not necessarily follow that regulatory facilitation of union enforcement through judicial processes results in unions making use of the courts. For example, in Australia, trade union use of court proceedings against employers in Australia has traditionally been a less favoured aspect of trade union enforcement.[93] It also appears to be the case that some unions are more willing to use litigation than others.[94] This may be a function of the high financial costs of legal action at a time when the decline in union membership has led to a contraction in resources and there are competing demands for expenditure of those resources. Nevertheless, perhaps a greater focus on enforcement may be a source of reinvigoration for the role that unions play in giving effect to voice at work.[95]

Conclusions

This chapter has considered the question of *how* regulation might facilitate voice. By considering the role of governments in promoting voice through public procurement mechanisms, emphasis was placed on the importance of looking beyond traditional legal mechanisms for facilitation of voice. However, in doing so, it is nevertheless important to consider the effectiveness of these approaches in amplifying voice.

The chapter has also explained how workers might be empowered to exercise voice *through* regulation with consideration of the administrative and judicial avenues by which workers and their representatives can engage in enforcement of employment rights and working conditions. Protection of rights of access to the workplace, standing to bring enforcement proceedings in tribunals and the courts, and protection of workers against employer retaliation are all essential supports to the right of workers to exercise voice concerning the observance of their legal rights and entitlements. Nevertheless, the extent to which regulation facilitates a role for unions, representative groups, and even private lawyers continues to be important in achieving voice at work in this context.

To conclude on a sobering note, at the time of writing, there has been a change in government at the federal level in Australia, with a conservative Coalition government replacing the previous Labor government. The new government is less likely to see facilitation of voice as a key priority. This serves as a timely reminder of the importance of the political context to regulatory facilitation of voice. In the absence of political will to promote voice by or through regulation, and given the decline of unions, and the slow emergence of alternative representatives, it is likely that many employees will find it difficult to uphold their legal entitlements at work.

[93] See, for example, Lee (n 71).

[94] For example, the secondary literature on union enforcement cites various cases brought by the Finance Sector Union and its predecessors, indicating that it is frequently before the courts on enforcement matters: see Hardy and Howe (n 60); Lee (n 71).

[95] Hardy and Howe (n 60); Estlund (n 1) 169; Weil (n 67); and Richard B. Freeman and Joel Rogers, 'Open-Source Unionism: Beyond Exclusive Collective Bargaining' (2002) *Working USA*, Spring, p. 8.

20

Employee Voice in Corporate Control Transactions

Andrew Johnston and Wanjiru Njoya

Introduction

This chapter considers the role of employee voice in promoting economic efficiency, justifying the need for stronger voice rights during corporate restructuring on grounds that this would enhance the firm's productivity, profitability, and competitiveness. To develop this argument we focus on the regulation of takeovers, situations where control of a company is acquired by a purchaser of that company's shares. Takeovers, especially hostile takeovers, are a characteristic feature of common law jurisdictions whose economies are dominated by large publicly traded companies with fragmented and dispersed shareholders. Takeovers are deemed to be a flexible and cost-effective means of reallocating the ownership and control of such companies without affecting the existing legal rights and obligations of the company as a distinct legal entity. Yet, after the takeover, the new managers often appear to achieve the enhanced profitability necessary to justify the takeover only by sacrificing jobs and breaching implicit contractual obligations owed to employees and other stakeholders. We focus on takeovers for two main reasons. First, takeover regulation casts the tension between employee and shareholder interests into sharp relief, allowing an incisive analysis of employee participation in corporate governance, and the role played by employee voice in facilitating such participation. Second, although there is a well-established legal framework of information and consultation of employees in most common law jurisdictions, particularly in the context of large scale redundancies, no attempt is made to safeguard jobs during takeovers; for instance in the UK transfers of undertakings effected by share purchase are excluded altogether from the ambit of the Transfer of Undertakings (Protection of Employees) Regulations (TUPE).[1] Similarly in the US the judicial interpretation of unfair labour practice claims under the National Labor Relations Act recognizes that after a takeover a new employer may be bound by a pre-existing collective bargaining agreement, but this does not extend to stock sales which entail substantial restructuring of the corporation.[2] The prevailing view in common law jurisdictions that

[1] See Simon Deakin and Giles Slinger, 'Company Law as an Instrument for Inclusion: Regulating Stakeholder Relations in the Context of Takeovers' (1999) ESRC Centre for Business Research Working Paper No. 145 September 1999, describing the exclusion of share transfers from TUPE as 'anomalous'. In the UK, general information and consultation rights vested in employees continue to have effect when takeovers are contemplated: see Regulation 20 of the Information and Consultation Regulations 2004, SI 2004/3426 and Regulation 17 of the Transnational Information and Consultation Regulations 1999, SI 1999/3323 (as amended).

[2] i.e. restructuring which will 'alter the basic structure of the business': Phillip M. Schreiber, 'Pre-Existing Collective Bargaining Agreements and Pre-Existing Unions: A Comparison of Labor Law Successorship

large corporations should be run in the interests of their shareholders, subordinating the claims of employees, reaches its apotheosis in takeover regulation.

The aim of this chapter is to assess the efficiency implications of enhancing worker voice in the context of takeovers, and on that basis to identify the potential scope for employee voice in corporate governance. The chapter justifies this focus on efficiency on two interrelated bases, one narrow and one broad. The narrow basis for employee voice is that employees who acquire specialized skills to meet the requirements of their employer are vulnerable to opportunism in the event of a change in corporate control. Where this is the case, voice rights which bring employment considerations within the ambit of corporate governance potentially offer protection to employees against the risk of expropriation. The broad basis is that the growing precariousness and uncertainty confronting employees under a system of shareholder value corporate governance undermines trust between employees and management, bringing the conflictual aspects of capitalist production to the fore and reducing employees' incentives to work towards the common goal of the long-term success of the company. In this broader view, greater voice rights in corporate control transactions would symbolize employees' stake in the firm, incentivizing employees to be more productive and perhaps to specialize their skills to the company's production processes (hence creating the conditions which would make the narrow basis applicable). Perhaps more importantly, voice rights would also operate as a 'beneficial constraint' on corporate managers, forcing them to look to productivity and quality improvements rather than cost cutting as a means of generating shareholder value.[3] Hence voice rights would produce micro and macroeconomic benefits in a troubled global economy, where high value added production appears to be the best—and perhaps the only—way of increasing exports and improving the national fiscal position.

We proceed as follows. First we sketch out the operation of shareholder value corporate governance and explore its effects on employees. Then we examine the economic arguments for and against this type of corporate governance, and suggest that employee voice has a role to play in correcting corporate governance failures. We offer a critique of the limited scope for employee voice in takeover regulation in the jurisdictions with which this work is concerned, focusing mainly on the UK but drawing comparisons with the law and practice in the USA, Canada, and Australia. Finally, we suggest proposals for making employee voice more effective in corporate control transactions.

Are Takeovers Efficient? The Market for Corporate Control and Employee Voice

Labour lawyers and corporate governance scholars in common law jurisdictions do not communicate very often or very well. Where labour law treats the 'employer' as a black box with considerable discretionary power over employees, against which employees

Doctrines in the United States and Canada' (1992) 12 Northwestern Journal of International Law & Business 571, 589. See also Edward B. Rock and Michael L. Wachter, 'Labor Law Successorship: A Corporate Law Approach' (1993-94) 92 Michigan Law Review (Mich L Rev) 203.

[3] Wolfgang Streeck, 'Beneficial Constraints: On the Economic Limits of Rational Voluntarism' in J. Rogers Hollingsworth and Robert Boyer (eds), *Contemporary Capitalism: The Embeddedness of Institutions* (CUP, 1997).

require protection, and with which they must bargain and contract, mainstream corporate governance opens up that black box to find a complex set of relations between shareholders and managers, but for the most part excludes employees from its analysis, assuming them to be fully protected by their employment contracts.[4] Where labour law has traditionally concentrated on inequality of bargaining power and 'social concerns', the main normative concern of corporate governance is economic efficiency, which is assumed to follow from managers exclusively furthering the interests of shareholders. The name of the game is to prevent managers imposing 'agency costs' on their 'principals', the shareholders, these concepts being understood in economic rather than legal terms. In order to achieve this goal, conventional corporate governance theory advocates, among other things, the use of incentives to align the interests of management with those of shareholders, including linking their pay to the creation of shareholder value, as expressed in the share price or other, more qualitative metrics; and, more importantly for our purposes, the creation of a market for corporate control through the removal of legal and other barriers to hostile takeovers.

A market for corporate control exists where takeover bidders, normally legal entities, identify target companies which are underperforming in terms of creating value for their shareholders, and approach the target shareholders with an offer to purchase their shares. The approach may be indirect, via the company's management, or direct to the shareholders, in which case the bid is termed 'hostile'. It is hostile because the bidder does not seek the cooperation of the incumbent management, and will be very likely to remove the senior managers in the event that they are successful.[5] The aim is to gain control of the general meeting of shareholders, which requires the bidder to acquire a majority of the voting shares. However, in the normal case, the bidder will want to acquire all the shares so that they can control the company without regard to the interests of any minority shareholders, and to enjoy the whole of any improvements in management. The acquisition of control is a first step to removing managers who are underperforming in terms of generating shareholder value, and, it is assumed, a more efficient allocation of control over the company's assets.

Company law is broadly sympathetic to this type of activity. The common law, by means of the fiduciary duty of loyalty which directors owe to the company, restricts the directors' ability to take measures intended to prevent the general meeting deciding on the takeover.[6] This means that in most common law jurisdictions, with the possible exception of the US, the 'gatekeeping' function of directors, by which they might potentially exercise their discretion in favour of preserving jobs for employees by resisting

[4] Marleen O'Connor, 'Labor's Role in the American Corporate Governance Structure' (2000) 22 Comparative Labor Law and Policy Journal 97; Margaret Blair and Mark Roe (eds), *Employees and Corporate Governance* (Brookings Institution Press, 1999).

[5] Shleifer and Summers explain that 'takeovers that transfer wealth from stakeholders to shareholders must be hostile', with incumbent managers removed because they will not go along with this redistribution. See Andrei Shleifer and Lawrence H. Summers, 'Breach of Trust in Hostile Takeovers' in Alan Auerbach (ed.), *Corporate Takeovers: Causes and Consequences* (University of Chicago Press, 1988).

[6] See for example, *Hogg v Cramphorn Ltd* [1967] Ch 254; [1966] 3 All ER 420; *Howard Smith Ltd v Ampol Petroleum Ltd* [1974] AC 821; [1974] 1 All ER 1126. For an overview of the common law approach to takeovers, see Andrew Johnston, 'Takeover Regulation: Historical and Theoretical Perspectives on the City Code' (2007) 66 Cambridge Law Journal 422.

a hostile bid which puts jobs at risk, is extremely weak. In the UK the pro-takeover approach of the City Code on Takeovers can be seen in its central provision, which truncates managerial discretion absolutely in the event of a bid, prohibiting directors of listed and other public companies from doing anything 'which may result in any offer or bona fide possible offer being frustrated'.[7] In a similar facilitative vein, statutory company law allows a bidder who acquires 90 per cent of a company's shares to squeeze out the remaining shareholders. This right was introduced in the name of facilitating industrial consolidation, but now operates as a cornerstone of shareholder value corporate governance.[8] Similarly Canadian securities law restricts directors' defensive tactics, giving shareholders of the target company the right to have the decision put to them,[9] whilst in Australia the policy of the Takeovers Panel is to 'generally require that shareholders be able to determine the control and ownership of the company', with frustrating action likely to be declared an 'unacceptable circumstance'.[10]

Taken together, these provisions establish a legal framework which allows a market for corporate control to operate. This favours shareholder primacy because this market disciplines managers who do not create sufficient value for shareholders, as expressed in the current share price.[11] Where a target company's share price is lower than it would be if its managers concentrated on enhancing shareholder returns, so the argument goes, a bidder can offer the target company's existing shareholders a premium over the market price for their shares. Since most shareholders in listed companies have diversified portfolios, their interest in the companies in which they invest is purely financial, and they will be likely to accept any offer giving them a substantial short-term gain. Their wholesale acceptance will allow the bidder to acquire control of the 90 per cent necessary to squeeze out any stragglers who hold out against the bidder. Once the bidder has acquired control, it can remove the underperforming managers and replace them with nominees who are more committed to the cause of shareholder value. Given the assumption that previous managers were underperforming, the extra returns generated by the new managers will be more than sufficient to repay the premium paid to the existing shareholders, leaving the bidder with a good return on their investment. The generation of those extra returns becomes even more imperative where the takeover is leveraged, that is, funded by significant quantities of debt, which is then transferred onto the target company's balance sheet. Improved returns are required to avoid defaulting on those debt obligations and wiping out the bidder's equity stake in the target.

Takeovers are, of course, very expensive, with bidders needing to pay investment banks, law firms, and other intermediaries for advice and other services throughout the process. To conventional corporate governance theorists, the beauty of the market for

[7] See UK Takeover Code, Introduction Paragraph 3 and Rule 21.1.

[8] See Companies Act 2006, s. 979, originally introduced in 1926 on the recommendation of the Greene Committee on Company Law.

[9] Robert Yalden, 'Competing Theories of the Corporation and their Role in Canadian Business Law' in Anita Anand and William Flanagan (eds), *The Corporation in the 21st Century* (Queen's Annual Business Law Symposium, 2003). Though it is now proposed to loosen this regulation to allow directors more time to consider their response to hostile bids, this is unlikely to go as far as the US 'just say no' defence.

[10] See Takeovers Panel, Guidance Note 12: Frustrating Action and Corporations Act 2001, s. 657A.

[11] The beneficial properties of the market for corporate control were first eulogized by Manne: see Henry Manne, 'Mergers and the Market for Corporate Control' (1965) 73 Journal of Political Economy 110.

corporate control is that the mere *threat* of hostile takeover is sufficient to encourage most managers to concentrate on generating immediate shareholder value through financial engineering techniques such as selling assets, increasing leverage, buying back shares and so on. Shareholder value can also be generated by cutting costs, so these same market forces also encourage managers to bargain hard with employees, outsource work wherever possible, casualize the work force, sell off non-core businesses and so on. It is these very patterns of management which are of concern to labour lawyers, who seek to influence them through collective bargaining between unions and management; however, they are also of concern to conventional corporate governance theorists, who praise them as resulting in the allocation of scarce resources to higher valued uses. This tension between labour law and corporate governance, compounded by disputes as to whether takeovers are purely a mechanism for redistributing wealth from workers to shareholders, lies at the heart of the efficiency debates which we address in this chapter.

There is increasing recognition that the market for corporate control results in a less than perfect alignment of management and shareholder interests. The reason for the imperfect alignment is that the share price, which is absolutely central to the market for corporate control, does not adequately reflect the interests of all shareholders. This is not the place to question the efficient markets hypothesis, which is fundamental to normative arguments about the desirability of hostile takeovers.[12] However, the problem is also commonly framed as one of short-termism, which operates to the detriment of longer-term shareholders.[13] Essentially, the ever-present threat of takeover puts managers under powerful pressure to take any action that they consider will be likely to raise the share price in the short term. In undertaking the financial engineering and cost-cutting strategies discussed earlier, corporate managers are behaving in a manner very similar to private equity firms. These are also the very strategies that activist hedge funds call for in the name of shareholder value in their direct communications with corporate managers. This is not to deny that these strategies result in the materialization of shareholder value in the short term in the form of share price increases and distributions of surplus assets. Rather, it is to emphasize that, in the longer term, they also create considerable social costs. High quality employment disappears from these shores, as does the spending capacity that accompanies it, while companies with fewer assets and more debt are less able to weather economic downturns.

In line with the focus of conventional corporate governance on shareholders, this dynamic is recognized as a potential source of prejudice to longer-term shareholders in UK-listed companies, such as UK-based pension funds and insurance companies. The policy prescription for dealing with short-termism driven by market imperatives is more active involvement of such long-term shareholders in corporate governance, coordinated through soft law in the form of the Stewardship Code, with the aim of articulating a longer-term perspective on corporate decision-making.[14] Considerable reservations have been expressed about the viability of this mechanism, given that

[12] Nor is this the place to discuss the argument that hostile takeovers frequently result in significant losses for shareholders in bidder companies: see for example Richard Roll, 'The Hubris Hypothesis of Corporate Takeovers' (1986) 59 Journal of Business 197.

[13] See for example Lynn Stout, *The Shareholder Value Myth* (Berrett-Koehler, 2012) ch. 5.

[14] See *The UK Stewardship Code* (Financial Reporting Council, September 2012).

UK-based institutional investors make up a declining proportion of the share registers of listed companies,[15] but institutional investor activism remains the dominant prescription for correcting these apparent failures of the corporate governance system.[16]

Turning now to examine how these practices affect employees, it can be seen that they are potentially impacted twice: directly in the form of material reductions in the quality and quantity of their employment and increases in precariousness and uncertainty; and indirectly through damage to their pension funds in the event that a company in which they have invested fails because it has leveraged its balance sheet and divested its assets in the name of shareholder value, and so no longer has the equity buffer needed to resist a sustained economic downturn. Indeed, the spread of shareholder value may be undermining the long-term prospects of the corporate sector as a whole, something in which diversified pension funds have a clear interest. This indirect damage lies beyond the scope of this chapter, and it will suffice to note here that further research is needed on the extent to which this broader interest is taken into account and articulated by institutional investors such as pension funds in their dialogue with corporate management.[17] Here we focus on the direct damage to employees, and the extent to which mechanisms of voice might mitigate that harm.[18]

Where employees are organized, some of these restructuring options may be hindered by collective bargaining or by the threat of collective action. The role of collective

[15] See Brian Cheffins, 'The Stewardship Code's Achilles Heel' (2010) 73 MLR 985.

[16] See *The Kay Review of UK Equity Markets and Long-Term Decision Making*, Final Report, July 2012 and the Government's response to it, *Ensuring Equity Markets Support Long-Term Growth*, Department for Business Innovation and Skills, November 2012. Both the Kay Report and the earlier Myners Report on *Institutional Investment in the UK* (March 2001) called for greater clarity between asset holders and asset managers as regards mandates, performance assessment and policies towards activism, but the essential assumption is that short-termism can be corrected by market participants themselves through voluntary coordination of collective action, rather than by means of more prescriptive regulatory interventions.

[17] Hawley and Williams argue that long-term institutional investors should be 'concerned not only with the long-term performance of individual firms, but also with the performance of the economy as a whole': see James Hawley and Andrew Williams, *The Rise of Fiduciary Capitalism* (University of Pennsylvania Press, 2000) 1. While this may be theoretically persuasive, it is far from clear that institutional investors are bringing such a macroeconomic perspective to bear on their investment activities, perhaps because of collective action or epistemological problems. Notably, the evidence from the build up to the financial crisis reveals wholesale complacency during the 'good times'. For an argument that fiduciary duty should be interpreted as requiring institutional investors to consider wider measures of their beneficiaries' well-being, and a discussion of Modern Portfolio Theory, which emphasizes individual investor rationality at the expense of public goods, as the main obstacle to this, see Steve Lydenberg, 'Beyond Risk: Notes Towards a Responsible Investment Theory' in James Hawley, Shyam Kamath, and Andrew Williams (eds), *Corporate Governance Failures* (University of Pennsylvania Press, 2011).

[18] The extent of the harm to employees from the activities of takeover bidders has been clearly documented by Conyon et al. They conclude that 'control changes do appear to be followed by substantial falls in labour demand, but no more so for hostile mergers than for friendly ones', with the immediate negative impact on labour demand being about 7.5 per cent compared with the pre-merger level. However, they also find that hostile takeovers lead to an immediate fall in output of 17.9 per cent and in employment of 15 per cent, something they suggest should be attributed to the post-merger divestment of businesses that characterizes management after a hostile takeover. See Martin J. Conyon, Sourafel Girma, Steve Thompson, and Peter W. Wright, 'Do Hostile Mergers Destroy Jobs?' (2001) 45 Journal of Economic Behavior & Organization 427, 433, and 436. The evidence in relation to takeovers by private equity firms is more contested. Goergen et al. conclude that private equity acquisitions of corporate control result in a 'significant decrease in employment in acquired firms' without 'any parallel or subsequent increase in firm productivity or profitability': see Marc Goergen, Noel O'Sullivan, and Geoff Wood, 'Private Equity Takeovers and Employment in the UK: Some Empirical Evidence' (2011) 19 Corporate Governance: An International Review 259. On the other hand,

bargaining may, broadly speaking, be facilitated by rights of information and consultation as well as the duty to bargain in good faith.[19] However, failure to comply with what amount to no more than procedural safeguards will not invalidate the managers' decision. Perhaps more importantly, following a hostile takeover, employees are likely to be dealing with newly appointed managers, who will be more focused than their predecessors on generating shareholder value, and will be unlikely to feel bound by their predecessors' informal commitments in relation to industrial relations. Moreover, as we will show in the third section, although in the UK the right of employees to express their opinion on a takeover bid was strengthened in 2012, the value of this right depends primarily on shareholders taking account of employee interests. As we saw earlier, and despite the numerous failures identified by the Myners and Kay Reports, this might be conceivable if a large proportion of the company's shares were held by long-term, UK-based institutional investors. However, as the share registers of UK companies become increasingly globalized, this becomes less likely as investors with global reach and limited jurisdictional commitments concentrate on benefits that accrue in direct, financial terms. Accordingly, we argue, employees have few, if any, meaningful rights to voice in the event of a takeover. For example, in the UK, in the event of a transfer of undertaking, employees have rights to information about the implications of the transfer, and must be consulted 'with a view to seeking agreement' in the event that the new employer 'envisages...measures in relation to the employees'.[20] It is significant that a transfer of control over a company by means of share purchase or takeover was excluded from the ambit of these information and consultation rights at the behest of the UK, with concerns expressed that it would interfere with share pricing on stock markets and discourage mergers.[21] Such concerns do not arise in relation to the Information and Consultation of Employees Regulations 2004, which impose an obligation on the 'employer' to consult its employees in relation to, inter alia, 'development of the undertaking's activities' and any 'threat to employment', because that obligation will only take effect after the takeover has been completed.[22] In the US, although both labour law and corporate tests recognize that in principle acquiring control of a company by purchasing its shares does not in itself defeat a pre-existing collective bargaining agreement (CBA) or duty to bargain, the key consideration is whether 'substantial continuity exists between the old firm's and the surviving firm's workers'.[23] Applying the test of substantial continuity, a CBA and the duty to bargain remain prima facie binding

Amess and Wright conclude that companies acquired by private equity 'do not have significantly different employment levels compared with a control sample of firms'. See Kevin Amess and Mike Wright, 'Leveraged Buyouts, Private Equity and Jobs' (2012) 38 Small Business Economics 419.

[19] For an illustration of this potential, as well as the limitations, see Charlotte Villiers, 'The Rover Case (1) The Sale of Rover Cars by BMW—the Role of the Works Council' (2000) 29 ILJ 386; John Armour and Simon Deakin, 'The Rover Case (2)—Bargaining in the Shadow of TUPE' (2000) 29 ILJ 395.

[20] Council Directive 2001/23/EC of 12 March 2001 on the approximation of the laws of the Member States relating to the safeguarding of employees' rights in the event of transfers of undertakings, businesses or parts of undertakings or businesses, OJ 2001 L82/16, Art. 7.

[21] See Bob Hepple, 'Workers' Rights in Mergers and Takeovers: The EEC Proposals' (1976) 5 ILJ 209. Fall-back information and consultation rights continue to apply under the Information and Consultation Regulations 2004, SI 2004/3426.

[22] See Regulation 20(1) of the Information and Consultation of Employees Regulations 2004, SI 2004/3426.

[23] Rock and Wachter 219 (n 2).

on a transferee following a share purchase, but significantly 'the stock purchaser has no greater *or* lesser obligation to abide by the CBA than the old firm. In *either* situation, a change of circumstances, sometimes initiated by the employer, may render the CBA inapplicable.'[24] This gives flexibility to the purchaser to avoid a pre-existing duty to negotiate with workers by introducing fundamental restructuring of the corporation during the takeover.[25]

This hands-off approach to institutions of voice during takeovers in itself serves to make takeovers more desirable from a shareholder value perspective than other forms of restructuring in which employees have voice rights. We argue that granting employees stronger voice rights in the corporate governance process itself, regardless of the means by which the change in the company's power structure is effected, would be an effective means of articulating and protecting employees' interests. In the next part we develop in more detail the argument that such voice rights can be justified on economic efficiency grounds.

Economic Arguments about Employment Restructuring Driven by Corporate Governance

From a corporate law perspective there does not seem to be any reason, in principle, why a change in the ownership and control of a company should in itself trigger employment protection entitlements, given that employees are just as vulnerable to being dismissed for economic reasons by the pre-existing controllers as by the new management. Indeed it is clear under the TUPE regulations that a dismissal for economic reasons incurs no penalty as long as the dismissal can be shown not to be by reason of the transfer, or if related to the transfer as long as it can be justified by reference to 'economic, technical or organisational' reasons.[26] Dismissals prompted by economic imperatives are largely unregulated apart from a basic framework of redundancy compensation, as the emphasis on flexibility and profitability prioritizes the most cost-effective restructuring mechanisms without regard to the potential implications for the firm's employees.[27] The rationale is that such dismissals are prompted by impersonal market forces whose effects are inevitable and unavoidable, for instance where declining product markets or changing technology threatens the survival of the firm. From a labour perspective the concern is with those opportunistic dismissals prompted by corporate restructuring which are strategically engineered purely to boost short-term share value.[28] Corporate restructuring achieved at the expense of large scale job losses allows corporations to maximize

[24] Rock and Wachter 218 (n 2), discussing *John Wiley & Sons, Inc. v Livingston* 376 U.S. 543 (1964).

[25] Schreiber (n 2). The situation under TUPE offers similar flexibility to the employer in relation to the pre-existing CBAs: Case C-426/11 *Mark Alemo-Herron and Others v Parkwood Leisure Ltd* [2013] CJEU.

[26] Regulation 7(1): where either before or after a relevant transfer, any employee of the transferor or transferee is dismissed, that employee shall be treated for the purposes of Part X of the 1996 Act (unfair dismissal) as unfairly dismissed if the sole or principal reason for his dismissal is (a) the transfer itself; or (b) a reason connected with the transfer that is not an economic, technical, or organizational reason entailing changes in the workforce.

[27] See discussion in Hugh Collins, *Employment Law* (Clarendon Press, 2009) 190–205.

[28] In the UK 'It has become accepted wisdom in parts of the City that companies in difficulty can restore share prices by instituting large-scale redundancies': Deakin and Slinger (n 1). The same is true in the US: see Marleen A. O'Connor, '"Organized Labor" as Shareholder Activist: Building Coalitions to Promote

shareholder returns by externalizing the costs onto society. In this way the corporation is 'effectively transferring to the public sector the costs of maintaining these displaced workers'.[29] Deakin and Slinger have compared this effect of takeovers to other contexts in which regulatory intervention is appropriate to constrain the externalization of the costs of production by private corporations:

> [T]his is a kind of 'social pollution' whereby institutions beneficial to many, such as implicit contracts, are damaged by the privately-interested actions of the few. Hence one company's emphasis on maximising returns to shareholders at the expense of the under-protected, 'implicit' interests of other stakeholders, has effects beyond the individual takeover situation, and is corrosive to the productive potential of many other, similarly-situated companies.[30]

If efficiency is understood as the maximization of society's overall wealth then the economic outcomes of such takeovers may well not be efficient; that question can only be answered by means of a methodologically difficult inquiry into whether the costs of the takeover exceed its benefits. Hence in justifying employee voice on economic efficiency grounds we emphasize the potential role of worker voice in correcting governance failures and ultimately maximizing social welfare.[31] In developing this argument further we rely on two main ideas about regulating the firm's labour inputs: first, that contract law is unable fully to protect employee investments in firm-specific human capital and second, that voice rights potentially function as beneficial constraints upon managerial discretion.

Implicit contracts and firm-specific human capital

In the dominant paradigm of corporate governance, cutting costs by outsourcing and offshoring jobs is justified by assuming that any existing entitlements of employees can be fully protected by contracts. This assumption has been challenged by the 'productive coalition' theory of corporate governance, which focuses on employee investments in firm-specific human capital (FSHC) that cannot be fully protected by explicit contracts.[32] The essence of this theory is that employees specialize their skills to the production arrangements of the firm that employs them: these skills become firm-specific rather than sector-specific or generic, making these employees particularly vulnerable

Worker Capitalism' (1997) 31 University of Richmond Law Review 1345, 1375, citing a study in which 'fewer than half of [downsizing] firms subsequently increased profits; only a third reported higher productivity'.

[29] Joseph W. Singer, 'Jobs and Justice: Rethinking the Stakeholder Debate' (1993) 43 University of Toronto Law Journal 475, 496: 'Mass lay-offs create substantial negative externalities, imposing costs on the workers' families, public services, and other businesses in the community. Because the costs of economic transition are partly borne by taxpayers, allowing employers to fire workers en masse without minimum levels of benefits subsidizes those employers.'

[30] Deakin and Slinger 9 and 10 (n 1).

[31] For a discussion of efficiency as a theoretical foundation for regulating labour markets see Juan Botero, Simon Djankov, Rafael La Porta, Florencio Lopez-di-Silanes, and Andrei Shleifer, 'The Regulation of Labor' (2004) Quarterly Journal of Economics 1339.

[32] See Margaret Blair and Lynn Stout, 'A Team Production Theory of Corporate Law' (1999) 85 Virginia Law Review 247. For an overview, see Andrew Johnston, *EC Regulation of Corporate Governance* (CUP, 2009) ch. 3.

if they lose their jobs. Employees put themselves in this vulnerable position in reliance on implicit promises by management that employees will share in the productivity gains referable to their acquisition of firm-specific skills. Workers are induced to develop their skills and experience at their own cost, in the expectation of future rewards such as promotions or pay rises.[33] Managers make these implicit promises because they are aware that FSHC adds value to the firm which could not be obtained from external labour markets.[34]

Why do employees not bargain for explicit contractual terms preventing managers from reneging on their promises? In most internal labour markets, contracting failures result from factors such as limited foresight, information asymmetries, bounded rationality and the deliberately incomplete design of the long-term, open-ended, flexible contracts underpinning the firm. It is in practice difficult to protect FSHC investments at the time an employment contract is concluded when it is not yet clear to what extent a particular employee will specialize their skills to the firm's needs, nor the extent to which those skills will enhance productivity. The employers' implicit promises rely only on social norms such as trust and reputation for their enforceability. The relations of trust between managers and employees are fragile. Newly installed managers will not feel bound by the informal promises made by their predecessors, while existing managers, facing the threat of hostile takeover, might find reneging on these unenforceable contracts the route of least resistance in terms of increasing the cash flow available to shareholders. In short, the vulnerabilities of employee investments in FSHC offer an explanation for why 'labour is usually the first casualty of restructuring at company-level', with job losses being seen as an inherent part of implementing the takeover.[35] Far from enhancing efficiency and productivity, takeovers may provide a tempting opportunity for managers to return short-term profits to the shareholders by breaching implicit promises made to employees to induce FSHC investments.[36] Moreover, if wage cuts fund the acquisition of control and restructuring process, this essentially constitutes a transfer of wealth from employees to shareholders which may have a negative impact on productivity if it undermines trust or the firm loses core, specialized labour inputs on which its competitive advantage depends.[37] Whilst this will not be in the long-term 'interests of the company', it will show up as a short-term gain to the new controller, attributable to their 'improved management'.

Beneficial constraints

Building on this theory of FSHC, we go further and argue that employee voice during takeovers can operate as a 'beneficial constraint' on takeover bidders,[38] forcing bidders to find alternatives to cost-cutting to justify the premia they pay for control over target

[33] Shleifer and Summers (n 5).

[34] Margaret Blair, 'Firm Specific Human Capital and Theories of the Firm' in Blair and Roe (n 4).

[35] Julie Froud, Colin Haslam, Sukhdev Johal, and Karel Williams, 'Restructuring for Shareholder Value and its Implications for Labour' (2000) 24 Cambridge Journal of Economics 771.

[36] Blair 58 (n 34).

[37] This is not uncontroversial, and others argue that takeovers are by no means always harmful to employee interests: see Til Beckmann and William Forbes, 'An Examination of Takeovers, Job Loss and the Wage Decline within UK Industry' (2004) 10 European Financial Management 141.

[38] The notion of beneficial constraint originates with Wolfgang Streeck, who coined the term to refer to the imposition of limits on economic freedom and the managerial prerogative 'to support high economic

companies. This is to a large extent a problem of short-termism. A company that cuts its wage bill by using less skilled employees in another jurisdiction to produce lower quality products will clearly be more profitable in the short term. Those profits may well be distributed to the company's shareholders at the time, rather than retained, which may benefit short-term shareholders, as well as executives whose remuneration is tied to short-term movements in the share price. In the longer term, the company may become less successful for a number of reasons: its lower quality products lose market share; its reputation becomes tarnished; and its cost-cutting, along with that of other companies also exposed to shareholder value imperatives, results in a reduction of the purchasing power of the core consumers of its products. Hence it is doubtful whether takeovers result in increased productivity, nor is it clear that the associated mass layoffs of workers add any real value to the firm.[39]

Viewed from a more positive perspective, companies which are constrained by employee voice mechanisms to create shareholder value without cutting costs and employment contribute to national prosperity. They are obliged to nurture employee FSHC investments in order to gain competitive advantage, and further create positive externalities because this high quality employment increases the level of effective demand in the economy.[40] By steering corporate governance in this way, and closing off micro- and macro-economically undesirable routes to the creation of shareholder value, employee voice can contribute to greater prosperity. Voice in this context constrains managers from needlessly undermining the value of the corporation.

To what extent does the law impose such beneficial constraints? The importance of preventing opportunistic breach of existing obligations to employees is reflected in US law where the key test determining the new employer's obligations to the old workforce is whether the collective agreement remains binding after corporate restructuring, a question which depends very much on the precise form which the restructuring took and whether that restructuring resulted in a new corporate entity rather than simply new managers at the helm of the old entity.[41] Both US and UK law have legislative frameworks which to varying degrees facilitate or allow the interests of various stakeholders, primarily employees, to play a role during the restructuring process. This may be institutionalized through legal mechanisms such as information and consultation rights, negotiation or collective bargaining rights, or rights to participate in decision-making. Whether the existing legal framework of employee voice rights extends to the takeover context is the question to which we now turn.

Employee Voice in Takeover Regulation

In takeover regulation the ideology of shareholder primacy prevails. Little regard is paid to employee interests. Since 1974, UK law has required the offeror to include a

performance', with codetermination possibly 'the most suitable mechanism for generating economically beneficial trust': see Streeck 200–3 (n 3).

[39] Shleifer and Summers (n 5). For critical perspectives see Conyon et al. (n 18) and Goergen et al. (n 18).

[40] Thomas Palley, *From Financial Crisis to Stagnation* (CUP, 2012) discussing a structural Keynesian perspective on the macroeconomy.

[41] Rock and Wachter (n 2).

statement in the offer document about its policy for 'the continuance of the business of the offeree company', including 'for the continued employment of existing employees of the offeree company, setting out the extent of any steps to be taken towards ceasing such employment'.[42] The rationale for these provisions was that

> [t]he intentions of the offeror as to the future conduct of the offeree's business, and the likely effect of any such intentions on the future livelihood of the offeree company's employees, may be a significant factor for shareholders in deciding whether or not to accept an offer.[43]

The Takeover Code now requires the offeror to 'explain the long-term commercial justification for the offer'; 'its intentions with regard to the continued employment of the employees and management of the offeree company and of its subsidiaries, including any material change in the conditions of employment'; and 'its strategic plans for the offeree company, and their likely repercussions on employment and the locations of the offeree company's places of business'.[44] Since 2011, offerors who foresee no repercussions for employees have been required to include a statement to that effect.[45] Such offerors are to be 'regarded as being committed to that course of action for a period of 12 months from the date on which the offer period ends... unless there has been a material change of circumstances'.[46]

In 2005, in order to implement the European Takeover Directive,[47] the Takeover Code was amended to give employees rights to information on a par with shareholders,[48] and to require the board to circulate, alongside its own opinion,[49] 'a separate opinion from the representatives of its employees on the effects of the offer on employment, provided such opinion is received in good time'.[50] These provisions were included in the Directive at the insistence of the European Parliament, against the objections of the European Commission, which insisted that 'employee voice rights' had 'no place in these provisions' because 'only the holders of securities can decide whether or not to sell them and they are therefore the only parties concerned by it'.[51] In 2011, those employee voice rights were bolstered to a limited extent when the Takeover Code was amended to require the offeree company to pay for the employees' costs of both publishing their opinion and 'for the costs reasonably incurred by the employee representatives in obtaining advice required for the verification of the information contained in that

[42] These provisions were originally set out in the Stock Exchange Rules on 'Admission of Securities to Listing', but were transposed to the City Code on Takeovers in 1974. See Annual Report of the Takeover Panel 1973–4, 9.

[43] See Annual Report of the Takeover Panel 1972–3, 10.

[44] Rule 24.2(a) of the Takeover Code.

[45] Rule 24.2(b) of the Takeover Code.

[46] See Note 3 to Rule 19.1. For further information on this change, see The Takeover Panel, *Review Of Certain Aspects Of The Regulation Of Takeover Bids: Response Statement By The Code Committee Of The Panel Following The Consultation On PCP 2011/1*, RS 2011/1 21 July 2011, 7.4–7.9.

[47] Directive 2004/25/EC of 21 April 2004 on Takeover Bids (OJ L142/12, 30.4.2004).

[48] Rule 2.12, implementing Article 6(2) of the Directive.

[49] The board is expected to give its opinion of the effects of the offer and the offeror's strategic plans on employment and location of the company's business: see Rule 25.2(a).

[50] Rule 25.9, implementing Article 9(5) of the Directive. See further The Takeover Panel, The Implementation of the Takeovers Directive (RS 2005/5, 21 April 2006).

[51] COM (2001) 77 final, 12.02.2001, 3.14.

opinion'.[52] This was not, however, intended to give the employees financial assistance in producing their opinion; it was aimed at ensuring that all documents published are prepared with care and fairly presented.[53]

Despite the Panel's 1998 claim that it has 'always been a Code principle that the interests of employees should be considered in addition to those of shareholders',[54] the disclosure obligations imposed on offerors before the introduction of the Takeover Directive were intended to facilitate shareholder decision-making. Information about an offeror's longer-term strategic plans will be highly pertinent to shareholders who are accepting shares in the offeror company in part or full consideration for tendering their shares in the target, because they will have an on-going interest in the viability of the business post-takeover. However, in practice, these provisions were 'easily satisfied with a boiler-plate formula' which 'simply undertakes to observe the employees' pre-existing legal rights' and makes no reference to implicit contracts or informal understandings.[55] The changes wrought by the Takeover Directive were part of a larger institutional squabble between the European Parliament, which viewed takeovers as posing a threat to employee interests, and the European Commission, which, during the 2000s, was strongly influenced by the ideology of shareholder value. Even at the very last stages of discussion about the Directive, the Parliament was arguing that employees should be informed and consulted 'in good time before any takeover' and 'during all stages of the takeover'.[56] The resulting deadlock was eventually broken by a compromise allowing Member States to opt out of a prohibition on defensive measures, allowing them to give managers greater autonomy to fight off unwelcome bids.[57]

Takeover regulation in the US gives much more discretion to directors in responding to bids.[58] The question is whether there is much scope to exercise this discretion in favour of employees. In most states directors have discretion to 'just say no' to takeover bids by rejecting the bid without putting the matter to the shareholders.[59] In principle this enables target directors to block bids with potentially adverse effects for employees even when the bid might have been attractive to shareholders.[60] In addition, state 'anti-takeover' or 'stakeholder' statutes explicitly permit directors to resist unwelcome advances on the grounds that they are likely to have adverse implications

[52] See Note 1 to Rule 25.9. [53] Rule 19.1. [54] Annual Report of Takeover Panel 1997–8.

[55] Simon Deakin, Richard Hobbs, David Nash, and Giles Slinger, 'Implicit Contracts, Takeovers and Corporate Governance: in the shadow of the City Code' in David Campbell, Hugh Collins, and John Wightman (eds), *Implicit Dimensions of Contract* (Hart Publishing, 2003) 3178.

[56] See European Parliament Report A5-0469/2003 FINAL, Amendments 427 and 428.

[57] Having rejected the second draft of the directive in July 2001 by a tied vote of 273 votes to 273, the Parliament accepted the compromise version of the third draft in December 2003 by 321 votes to 219.

[58] Bernard Black and John Coffee, 'Hail Britannia? Institutional Investor Behavior Under Limited Regulation' (1994) 92 Mich L Rev 1997. This is partly because of the more active role played by institutional investors in UK corporate governance. At 2006: 'British institutional investors are considerably more interested in corporate governance than most American institutions. Moreover, the expectation of oversight is embedded in British culture. If the British system does not work flawlessly, we think it works better at effecting managerial changes and making boards of directors sensitive to shareholder desires than do current practices in the United States. Significant efficiency gains seem obtainable if American institutions were more willing to press for change at troubled firms, in the way that British institutions now do.'

[59] Discussed in Marcel Kahan and Edward Rock, 'How I Learned to Stop Worrying and Love the Pill: Adaptive Responses to Takeover Law' (2002) 69 University of Chicago Law Review 635.

[60] See Katherine Stone, 'Employees as Stakeholders under State Nonshareholder Constituency Statutes' (1991) Stetson Law Review 45.

for stakeholders.[61] These statutes were passed in response to widespread criticism of the social effects of takeovers in the 1980s, notably concerns about job losses.[62] Following the lead of Pennsylvania, about thirty states allow directors to have regard to stakeholder interests in responding to takeover bids.[63] However these statutes do not prioritize stakeholders above shareholders. Instead, they approximate the UK's 'enlightened shareholder value' (ESV) approach in which directors are allowed and possibly even encouraged to have regard to the interests of employees and other stakeholders, but must ultimately act for the benefit of the company. The UK Companies Act has allowed or required directors to have regard to employee interests since the 1980s.[64] The 2006 reforms retained employee interests among the relevant considerations for directors, but clarified that those interests did not have independent weight and that the company was to be run 'for the benefit of its members as a whole'.[65] The same approach is reflected in Canadian corporate law, where the Supreme Court has upheld the principle that 'the directors had a fiduciary duty to act in the best interests of the corporation and that the content of this duty was affected by the various interests at stake', recognizing also that 'directors, faced with conflicting interests, might have no choice but to approve transactions that, while in corporation's best interests, would benefit some groups at expense of others'.[66] This suggests that while promoting the interests of employees is not in itself a breach of duty, directors risk being in breach if they simply prioritize employee interests as distinct from the interests of the company as a whole which generally means shareholder interests.[67] More specifically, directors must be able to make a credible argument that taking account of employee interests is capable of improving the returns to shareholders, either in the short or the long term. Stakeholder interests are therefore instrumental to the interests of shareholders, and the extent to which they are considered is a matter of business judgement with which the courts are highly reluctant to interfere. This is replicated in Australia by notions of corporate social responsibility, which highlight the commonality of interests between stakeholders and shareholders, but are nevertheless set in a legal context in which English law notions of enlightened shareholder value prevail.[68] In all these jurisdictions employee interests rank *pari passu*

[61] Mark Roe, 'Takeover Politics' in Margaret Blair (ed.), *The Deal Decade: What Takeovers and Leveraged Buyouts Mean for Corporate Governance* (The Brookings Institution, 1993).

[62] O'Connor 103 (n 4).

[63] Martin Lipton, 'Twenty Five Years after Takeover Bids in the Target's Boardroom: Old Battles, New Attacks and the Continuing War' (2005) 60 The Business Lawyer 1369.

[64] Section 309 of the Companies Act 1985 required directors to 'have regard to' the interests of the company's employees in discharging their duty to act in good faith in the interests of the company. This provision was not tested in court, but it was widely assumed that employee interests were not an end in themselves, and were only relevant to the goal of furthering the interests of the company.

[65] See section 172 of the Companies Act 2006 which provides that '[a] director of a company must act in the way he considers, in good faith, would be most likely to promote the success of the company *for the benefit of its members as a whole*, and in doing so have regard (amongst other matters) to ... the interests of the company's employees' (emphasis added).

[66] *In Re BCE, inc* (2008), 301 DLR (4th) 80, [2008] 3 SCR 560. See discussion in Jeremy D. Fraiberg, 'Fiduciary Outs and Maximizing Shareholder Value Following BCE' (2009) 48 Canadian Business Law Journal 213.

[67] Bill Wedderburn, 'Employees, Partnership and Company Law' (2002) 31 ILJ 99; Yalden (n 9).

[68] Jennifer G. Hill, 'Evolving Directors' Duties in the Common Law World' in Adolfo Paolini (ed.), *Research Handbook on Directors' Duties*, (Edward Elgar Publishing, 2013). For further discussion, see Corporations and Markets Advisory Committee, *The Social Responsibility of Corporations: Report* (December 2006).

with other stakeholders, notably suppliers, customers, and the local community. The Pennsylvania statute, for example, specifies that the directors shall not be required to regard any corporate interest, or the interests of any particular group, as a dominant factor.

Stakeholder statutes and ESV therefore highlight the broad scope of the directors' discretion to consider employee interests, but they do so without vesting any rights in stakeholders. Significantly, no enforcement rights are vested in non-shareholder groups in the event that the directors should fail to have regard to their interests. Enforcement rights are vested in the company itself, or exceptionally in shareholders acting on behalf of the company. Moreover, it is often argued by commentators such as Branson, who are critical of stakeholder statutes, that directors are unlikely to take stakeholder interests into account unless doing so would serve their own purposes such as entrenching their control or justifying their decisions.[69] Branson's argument echoes the mainstream corporate governance view that, in the absence of appropriate constraints, directors will serve their own interests and impose 'agency costs' on shareholders. For example they might resist a takeover bid, claiming that it puts employee interests at risk, whereas in reality they are simply concerned about losing their own positions as directors of the company.[70] From a standpoint such as that adopted by Branson, a decision taken to invest in new markets which subsequently proves to have been disastrous might be belatedly justified as having been taken in a bid to boost relations with stakeholders. Hence Branson's critique that in the final analysis these statutes might only serve to 'protect stupid decisions' by allowing directors to justify their responses to the threat of hostile takeover by reference to vague stakeholder interests which they were purportedly attempting to promote. The essence of these anti-managerialist critiques is that by making directors accountable to the interests of anybody and everybody, in the final analysis they are accountable to nobody.[71] It is argued that in the absence of a single unified reference point by which to assess the validity of the directors' decisions, there is no basis on which to criticize any decision they make.[72] From this, it is argued that the company's share price offers the best available metric by which to assess

[69] Douglas M. Branson, 'Corporate Governance Reform and the New Corporate Social Responsibility' (2000–2001) 62 University of Pittsburgh Law Review 605.

[70] See for instance the dispute in *Re Saul D. Harrison & Sons plc* where an allegation that the directors were running the company solely for their own benefit, continuing to trade when the company had no hope of turning a profit and ignoring interests of minority shareholders was defended on grounds, inter alia, that their decision took account of the interests of employees. In obiter dicta the court said: 'Under s. 309 of the Companies Act 1985 the directors of a company are required to have regard to the interests of its employees as well as the interests of its members. This company has over 100 employees and because it has been able to find new premises in the same neighbourhood, the company has been able to ensure that their employment has not been jeopardised. The company's duty to its employees was clearly a matter which the directors were entitled to take into account if they were of the opinion that there was a reasonable prospect that the company's business could be salvaged': [1994] BCC 475 at 483.

[71] See for example, Joseph F. Johnston, 'No Man Can Serve Two Masters: Shareholders versus Stakeholders in the Governance of Companies', 1998 *Social Affairs Unit Research Report* 25.

[72] This was the essence of the influential 1932 Berle-Dodd exchange in the *Harvard Law Review (Harv L Rev)*: E. Merrick Dodd Jr, 'For Whom are Corporate Managers Trustees?' (1932) 45 Harv L Rev 1145; Adolf A. Berle Jr, 'For Whom Corporate Managers are Trustees: A Note' (1932) 45 Harv L Rev 1365. It is also the essence of the on-going contest between managerialism and shareholder value in debates about corporate governance.

managerial performance. The threat of hostile takeover and the grant of stock options put this metric into effect and greatly reduce the likelihood of management acting in a self-serving way which harms shareholders in the name of furthering stakeholder interests. The result is that company law and takeover regulation currently give only the most tenuous protection to employee interests, reflecting this deeply entrenched pre-occupation with shareholder value. The arguments about adverse effects on employees and productivity discussed in this chapter receive very little discussion in the economic literature, and are simply assumed away.

Implications for Voice

In recent decades, and justified by the ideology of shareholder value, the legal framework in common law jurisdictions has increasingly shifted power away from managers towards shareholders.[73] None of these jurisdictions gives labour a formal participatory role in decision-making during restructuring. The main avenue of voice is collective bargaining, which is usually limited to terms and conditions of work rather than decision-making about the firm's strategy. Tentative attempts to forge labour–management partnerships have tended to be beneficial to management but to offer little as mechanisms for employee participation.[74] Against this background we suggest that employee voice mechanisms can effectively safeguard human capital investments as well as improve managerial accountability, by reducing the scope for managers to indulge in self-serving decision-making, ranging from excessive pay and empire-building to breaches of fiduciary duty.

Employee participation could play out in different ways. Employees might form coalitions with managers to resist short-termist shareholders who favour any takeover bid which promises a premium over the current market price of shares. Employees and managers as corporate insiders with investments in FSHC[75] often have shared interests in the long-term future of the firm, whereas many shareholders have diversified portfolios, making them outsiders, eager to cash out to the highest bidder.[76] Coalitions in which unions and management agree on a joint strategy to resist bids have proved particularly effective in the US, although such coalitions tend to be short-lived,

[73] For the US see Sanford M. Jacoby, 'Corporate Governance and Employees in the United States' in Howard Gospel and Andrew Pendleton (eds), *Corporate Governance and Labour Management: An International Comparison* (OUP, 2005) 33. For Australia see Richard Mitchell, Anthony O'Donnell, Shelley Marshall, Ian Ramsay, and Meredith Jones, *Law, Corporate Governance and Partnerships at Work* (Ashgate Publishing, 2011) 40–2.

[74] Tonia Novitz and Charlotte Villiers, 'The 2006 Higher Education Pay Dispute: the reality of partnership rhetoric?' (2007) 27 Legal Studies 486 referring to 'the particular version of partnership that has been promoted by New Labour in industrial relations, which involves an emphasis on shared commercial objectives, largely at the level of the enterprise, with limited scope for trade union influence...a New Labour view of partnership that contemplates only a restricted (and non-confrontational) role for trade unions' at 486. See also David E. Guest and Riccardo Peccei, 'Partnership at Work: Mutuality and the Balance of Advantage' (2001) British Journal of Industrial Relations 207 who find that 'the balance of advantage is skewed towards management and reflects generally low management trust in employee representatives', at 207.

[75] See for example, John Coffee, 'Shareholders Versus Managers—the Strain in the Corporate Web' 85 Mich L Rev 1, emphasizing managerial investments in FSHC.

[76] John Coffee, 'Unstable Coalitions: Corporate Governance as a Multiplayer Game' (1990) 78 Georgetown Law Journal 1495.

unstable, and unpredictable.[77] They would certainly be unlikely to thrive in the current Anglo-American corporate governance context where managerial remuneration takes the form of shares and share options, a practice explicitly intended to align their interests with those of shareholders. Similarly, such political strategies would be much less likely to be effective in jurisdictions where directors have little legal scope to frustrate bids, such as the UK and Australia.

A more fruitful avenue might lie in the dual role which employees often play as workers *and* shareholders. Pension funds, of which employees are the ultimate beneficiaries, are potentially powerful players as institutional shareholders. As shareholder activists, pension funds have the bargaining power to negotiate deals favourable to workers. A similar role is played, albeit indirectly, by employee share ownership schemes. These forms of 'labour-shareholder activism' by employee pension funds and employee shareholders harness what O'Connor depicts as the bargaining power of 'labour's capital'.[78] O'Connor proposes that pension funds as institutional investors can put pressure on managers to bargain with unions, to settle disputes when strike action is imminent and use their voting power 'to ensure that anti-union managers do not become entrenched'. The difficulty with these mechanisms is that they place labour representatives in a paradoxical position: 'unions face a difficult balancing act in pushing stakeholder values through shareholder activism because such activism lends credence to the shareholder value credo, a credo that delegitimizes the stakeholder approach.'[79] Moreover, there are difficult collective action problems here, with pension funds that seek to encourage a longer-term approach to corporate governance likely to underperform their peers in the short-term, whilst funds which defect from such an approach will be able to take advantage of greater returns and attract more pension savings. In addition, there are likely to be conflicts of interest as some pension funds aggregate savings from different industries and sectors.

This paradoxical trap can be avoided by adopting direct mechanisms of voice based on an explicit role for labour in its own right, rather than labour in its capacity as shareholder. In various European jurisdictions, mechanisms such as works councils or employee board representatives function as 'beneficial constraints' allowing employees

[77] Coffee (n 76). This phenomenon does not appear to arise in a continental jurisdiction like Germany for two reasons. First, hostile takeovers are still very rare; Vodafone's hostile bid for Mannesmann caused shockwaves which resonate to this day. Second, employees are represented on the supervisory board of larger companies, and have greater employment protection, which 'reduce[s] the capacity of hostile raiders to engage in ex post redistribution of wealth following takeovers': see Martin Höpner and Gregory Jackson, 'Revisiting the Mannesmann Takeover: how Markets for Corporate Control Emerge' (2006) European Management Review 142, 145. Höpner and Jackson note that labour representatives were 'justifiably afraid of job losses', but that they were unable to defeat the takeover, despite particularly far-reaching codetermination rights. However, once the takeover had taken place, labour and shareholders found that they had a common interest in greater managerial accountability and restructuring to protect the company's competitive position, and reached consensus on these matters. They note that, whilst co-determination has the potential to act as a 'poison pill', it has demonstrated greater 'consensus orientation' since the 1990s. More broadly, Vitols argues that what is emerging in Germany is 'negotiated shareholder value', with pro-shareholder value institutional shareholders being brought into the existing stakeholder coalition, which necessitates a greater emphasis on shareholder returns, but is far from identical to Anglo-American notions of shareholder value: see Sigurt Vitols, 'Negotiated Shareholder Value: the German Variant of an Anglo-American Practice' (2004) 8 Competition & Change 357.

[78] O'Connor 110 (n 4). [79] O'Connor 126 (n 4).

to influence corporate governance. In common law jurisdictions, there is no legal framework facilitating or requiring employee representatives on the board of directors. The election of board members is under shareholder control and the identity of board members is significantly influenced by boards themselves, albeit that in UK public companies non-executive directors have the main say in this through their membership of the nomination committee.[80] A few corporations in the US have a union representative on the board of directors;[81] in the UK there may be a board member whose specific remit is human resources or employment relations, recognizing, at least in principle, the relevance of employee matters in the boardroom.[82] A similar function may be played by non-executive directors on the board who are intended to be independent and could reflect a broader range of interests than short-term shareholder value. On the whole, however, legally mandated board representation as an avenue for employee voice is not a mechanism at the forefront of reform proposals across the common law world.[83] Even if there were legal requirements for employee representatives on the board of directors, the effectiveness of such directors in expressing workers' voice would be questionable.[84] The principle that directors are subject to the core duty of loyalty to the company means that by promoting union interests the employee board representatives would risk breaching their fiduciary duty to exercise independent judgment in making decisions in good faith in the interests of the company.[85] The current codification of enlightened shareholder value does not materially affect this position. The 2006 reforms, with their emphasis on promoting 'the success of the company for the benefit of its members as a whole', have, at least rhetorically, made the position of employee board representatives even more difficult.[86]

It must also be noted that corporate law avenues of employee voice such as works councils or seats on the board of directors risk undermining, instead of supporting, collective bargaining. This is often the effect of partnership models which involve employees in corporate decision-making.[87] It is difficult to reconcile the conflicting

[80] See Principle B.2.1 of the *UK Corporate Governance Code* (London: Financial Reporting Council, 2012).

[81] 'Several American unions, aware of the tenuous nature of negotiated partnerships, have sought to bolster their strategic influence further by seeking seats on the boards of directors of companies where they represent members' a few of whom have succeeded in including this as part of a collective bargaining agreement: Eileen Appelbaum and Larry W. Hunter, 'Union Participation in Strategic Decisions of Corporations' (2003) NBER Working Paper no. 9590 26. Jacoby (n 73), at 47 notes that '[a] few US companies, particularly those with substantial employee stock ownership, have created mechanisms for bringing employee views to senior management and to the board, including formal representation systems and board seats for employee or union representatives...of the Fortune 1000 companies, only six have their own HR manager on the corporate board, an absurdly small proportion, whereas ninety-two include their Chief Financial Officer on the board.'

[82] For the evidence see David Guest and A. Bryson, 'From Industrial Relations to Human Resource Management: the Changing Role of the Personnel Function' in William Brown, Alex Bryson, John Forth, and Keith Whitfield (eds), *The Evolution of the Modern Workplace* (CUP, 2009) 120.

[83] For the influence of European law on prospects for codetermination in the UK see Wanjiru Njoya, 'Employee Ownership in the European Company: Reflexive Law, Reincorporation and Escaping Codetermination' (2011) 11 Journal of Corporate Law Studies 267.

[84] Indeed their effectiveness is questionable even in European jurisdictions with mandatory codetermination: Michael Gold, '"Taken on Board": An Evaluation of the Influence of Employee Board-level Representatives on Company Decision-making across Europe' (2011) 17 European Journal of Industrial Relations 41.

[85] Otto Kahn-Freund, 'Industrial Democracy' (1977) 6 ILJ 65.

[86] See Companies Act 2006, s. 172.

[87] Harry Arthurs and Claire Mummé, 'From Governance to Political Economy: Insights from a Study of Relations Between Corporations and Workers' in Cynthia Williams and Peer Zumbansen (eds), *The Embedded Firm: Corporate Governance, Labor, and Finance Capitalism* (CUP, 2011) 350.

identities of employee representatives who join in solidarity with fellow workers and at the same time have a duty of loyalty to the employing entity.[88] Yet, despite declining levels of unionization, unions continue to provide the main avenue of voice for workers so it is essential that employee involvement in corporate governance should not impede this role. For these reasons, the commitment of UK unions to partnership-based models of joint decision-making appears to be receding in favour of revitalizing traditional forms of collective bargaining as British unions look more to Australia and the US, and less to Europe, for inspiration.[89] The same is true in the US where the AFL-CIO has traditionally stopped short of seeking a codetermination-style role in joint decision-making. This suggests that voice mechanisms in corporate governance should complement, not replace, the industrial democracy ideals of employee voice.[90] As O'Connor has argued, the most effective approaches to enhancing employee voice rely on multiple complementary mechanisms including both collective bargaining and involvement in corporate governance.

At present the approach most likely to allow multiple avenues of voice is one which relies on stronger rights of information and consultation. In the UK context this would require extending the TUPE regulations to takeovers that transfer corporate control by acquisition of shares.[91]An alternative—albeit one which would be strongly opposed—would be to incorporate employee voice rights in the Takeover Code itself, for example, by requiring managers to consult with employees during takeover bids 'with a view to reaching an agreement'.[92] Another alternative is the US practice of explicitly protecting employees' implicit contracts which are breached during takeovers, over and above the normal redundancy entitlement.[93] Similarly, disclosure requirements could be enhanced, targeting the information that independent employee representatives require. Even without formal consultation mechanisms, such information on the anticipated consequences of corporate restructuring for employees would allow worker voice to be targeted effectively at their core concerns.[94] This would have to go beyond the current requirements of the UK's Takeover Code, which elicit little of substance which

[88] See for a general discussion Silvana Sciarra, 'Notions of Solidarity in Times of Economic Uncertainty' (2010) 39 ILJ 223. As noted by Brown and Oxenbridge, '[u]nless the union can demonstrate to its membership that they gain from the relationship, that it is, as one union official described it, a "two-way street," there are likely to be serious internal tensions and, worse still, membership apathy, cynicism and loss': William Brown and Sarah Oxenbridge, 'Trade Unions and Collective Bargaining' in Catherine Barnard, Simon Deakin, and Gillian Morris (eds), *The Future of Labour Law* (Hart Publishing, 2004) 73.

[89] Edmund Heery, 'The Representation Gap and the Future of Worker Representation' (2009) 40 Industrial Relations Journal 324.

[90] Tonia Novitz, 'A Revised Role for Trade Unions as Designed by New Labour: The Representation Pyramid and "Partnership"' (2002) 29 Journal of Law and Society 487.

[91] Deakin and Slinger (n 1).

[92] The European Parliament attempted to amend the second proposal for a takeover directive to require the board to consult the employees before finalizing its opinion to shareholders (see OJ C222/24, 21.7.97), and subsequently sought to give employee representatives a right to require disclosure of all information in the possession of the parties to the bid (see OJ C232/171, 17.8.2001). All these changes were rejected by the European Commission.

[93] See the discussion of 'tin parachute rights' in Deakin and Slinger (n 1). The limitation of this approach is that it requires the parties to the agreement to anticipate the likely consequences of breach far in advance. The difficulty of anticipating these matters is the reason implicit contracts are used in the first place.

[94] Again, the European Parliament attempted to include more far-reaching disclosure requirements in the Takeover Directive (see OJ C232/169, 17.8.2001).

is useful to employees. More useful information could include, for instance, details about, and an estimate of the value of, the firm's FSHC. As Deakin and Slinger have argued, an emphasis on voice rights, through information and consultation, has the advantage of being both cooperative and creative. It is cooperative in that it facilitates partnership in decision-making by managers and labour representatives; it is creative in that it allows both parties to formulate mutually acceptable solutions tailor-made to the particular context of their own enterprise.[95] Disclosure relating to FSHC might even give bidder companies pause for thought as they contemplate ways of cutting costs in order to recoup the takeover premium.

Conclusion

In final analysis, as long as employees lack enforcement rights to hold directors accountable for their decisions, their voice in corporate governance is necessarily muted.[96] Introducing enforcement rights is in turn impossible without a fundamental revision of the idea that the 'interests of the company' can be equated only with the interests of the shareholders. There is an efficiency case for giving this concept greater autonomy, with its content elaborated according to the context and the interests at stake.[97] Company law already recognizes that the duty of loyalty to 'the company' as a separate legal entity shifts from shareholders to creditors in the context of insolvency, a doctrinal shift justified by reference to the vulnerability of creditors to managerial opportunism; a similar justification could be advanced in the context of restructuring where jobs are at risk, based on an evolving theory of stakeholder property rights in the firm. Joseph Singer has persuasively described many situations in which common law courts could develop the law in this direction, were they so minded.[98] But without a reconceptualization of directors' fiduciary obligations company law is unlikely to make meaningful inroads into the problem. As Jacoby observes:

> it is unlikely that the fundamental tenets of corporate governance will change unless and until there is an expansion of employee representation, either through traditional union-based structures or works councils and committees. At the same time, however, attention must be paid to corporate governance. Governance reform opens up additional channels for employee voice in situations where representational structures are ineffective or unsuited to handling strategic, company-wide concerns.[99]

[95] Deakin and Slinger (n 1).

[96] O'Connor 105 (n 4): 'Such a fiduciary duty could protect displaced workers by requiring directors to mitigate the harms of downsizing through severance payments and job retraining.'

[97] Gunther Teubner, 'Company Interest: The Public Interest of the Enterprise "in itself"' in Ralf Rogowski and Ton Wilthagen (eds), *Reflexive Labour Law* (Kluwer Law International, 1994).

[98] Joseph Singer, 'The Reliance Interest in Property' (1988) 40 Stanford Law Review 611. Armour and Deakin argue that, where employees are given rights in corporate governance contingent on the occurrence of certain events, such as a transfer of undertaking, this does allow for the protection of investments in firm-specific human capital. See John Armour and Simon Deakin, 'Insolvency, Employment Protection and Corporate Restructuring: the Effects of TUPE' (2001) Working Paper No. 204, Centre for Business Research. It would be open to the courts to extend this limited statutory protection by recognizing the existence of a fiduciary duty on directors towards employees where their interests are at stake.

[99] See n 73.

In this chapter we examined the challenges facing voice rights in the context of takeover regulation. Since coming to prominence in the 1980s and 1990s takeover regulation has been a crucial site of debates on the question 'in whose interests should the corporation be run?'[100] We suggested that it is doubtful that takeovers result in increased productivity, and that it is far from clear that the associated mass layoffs of workers add any real value to the firm. Going further, we argued that, rather than enhance productivity, takeovers provide a tempting opportunity for managers to breach implicit contracts made with employees in order to induce FSHC investments.[101] If shareholder value is generated by making cuts to wages and employment, this essentially constitutes a transfer of wealth from employees to shareholders which may have no impact on productivity or may indeed have a negative impact if the firm loses core specialized labour inputs on which its competitive advantage depends. In light of these arguments, we suggested that greater worker voice in the corporate governance context would constrain managers from undermining the long-term value of the corporation in order to produce short-term returns for shareholders.

The arguments we have advanced in this chapter have implications beyond the context of takeovers, extending to the broader mechanisms of employee participation in corporate governance. The chapter demonstrates that efficiency is an important part of the underlying normative justification for worker voice, arguing that in the long term worker voice is an essential component of corporate success. From the analysis of takeover regulation in common law jurisdictions it can be seen that the protection given to employees during corporate restructuring is very weak. Conventional corporate governance assumes that shareholders should have as much freedom as possible to decide on reallocations of corporate control, and justifies this on the basis that the market for corporate control focuses the attention of the company's directors on maximizing the share price, and with it, the value of the firm, thereby reducing agency costs. Employees enjoy only flimsy voice rights, depending on 'enlightened' shareholders to take their concerns into account as part of a long-term approach to corporate governance. This chapter has suggested various ways in which employee voice might be strengthened so as to make it more effective, and better articulate the employee interests which are at stake during takeovers. This offers a starting point from which voice can play a role in the quest to find a counterbalance and corrective to the social costs created by shareholder value corporate governance. It serves to emphasize that employee exit from a particular company is not costless, and that shareholder gains often come at the expense of employees' residual claims in companies. Efficiency therefore requires that employees' claims be accorded legal protection commensurate with that accorded to shareholders during takeovers.

[100] Lipton (n 63). [101] Blair 58 (n 34).

21

Competition Law and Worker Voice

Competition Law Impediments to Collective Bargaining in Australia and the European Union

Shae McCrystal and Phil Syrpis

Introduction

In this chapter we explore the extent to which competition laws may operate as an impediment to the expression of collective voice by workers via collective bargaining. It is of course true that workers can express their collective voice via mechanisms other than collective bargaining, for example, via systems of workplace consultation and codetermination, but given the centrality of collective bargaining in Australia and in much of the EU (including of course in the UK), our focus, in this chapter, is on the implications of competition law on the operation of collective bargaining. Collective bargaining is a collective voice mechanism expressly based on a rationale which can be construed as 'anti-competitive' —that labour is not a commodity and individual workers should not be required to compete over the terms and conditions on which they sell their labour. As such, it is vulnerable to a critique based in competition principles that a free market for labour produces optimal outcomes, maximizing society's scarce resources. Combination by workers through trade unions could be construed as a labour cartel, fettering the operation of free market forces between union members over the terms on which they offer their labour in the market for their services. The pursuit of collective bargains may be construed as conduct designed to lessen competition in the markets in which the hirers of labour operate, limiting the capacity of firms to compete through adjustments to the price of labour, in particular where collective bargaining occurs on an industry-wide scale.

Different jurisdictions approach the potential clash between regulating to facilitate and encourage worker collective bargaining and regulating for competitive markets in different ways. Generally speaking, legislatures implement an industrial relations regime of some sort, and, within that context, expressly regulate collective relationships and collective bargaining between workers and employers. They also implement competition (or 'anti-trust') regimes, specifically designed to promote competitive markets for goods and services, prevent collusion between competitor businesses and protect against the abuse of market power by businesses and monopolies. If individual workers selling their labour are construed as individual 'businesses' or 'undertakings' then collective bargaining by workers could constitute anti-competitive conduct. In most jurisdictions this is avoided by providing that certain labour market transactions are exempt from anti-competitive conduct prohibitions. Such exemptions may be expressly enacted or created through judicial interpretation. They may be general labour market exemptions, specific exemptions for certain labour market transactions, or exemptions that apply only if sought by individual actors.

Labour market exemptions from competition regulation allow for the expression of worker voice in the form of collective bargaining to take place without fear of breaching competition laws. However, over the past 20 to 30 years, significant changes within the labour market have challenged the relative isolation of labour law from competition law and the scope of protection offered by labour market exemptions. In particular, changes to the structure of the labour market have seen the decline of the long-term relational employment contract as businesses outsource and restructure.[1] Increased use of temporary, short-term, labour hire and self-employed workers involve more complex contractual forms being utilized for hiring labour, forms of engagement which often fall outside of the standard labour law paradigm.[2] These changes in the world of work have led to many workers being excluded from the coverage of labour laws and consequently being subject to laws, including competition laws, which govern entrepreneurial businesses. They have also fuelled an on-going debate over the purposes of regulating labour markets and the rationale for a distinct form of labour market regulation.[3]

Such debates over the appropriate scope of labour laws and the underlying purposes of regulatory intervention raise difficult questions over the intersection between competition law and labour law. If increasing numbers of workers are engaged under contractual arrangements that take them outside of the scope of labour laws, should those laws be reformulated or extended, or should competition laws be applied more extensively to labour markets?

This chapter examines the scope of labour market exemptions from competition laws in Australia, and the UK as governed by the competition laws of the European Union (EU). The competition laws in both jurisdictions contain exemptions for certain labour market relationships and arrangements, and also procedures to allow for the authorization of conduct that might otherwise breach competition law. We aim to illustrate how the rising prevalence of atypical forms of labour market engagement takes ever larger numbers of workers outside the scope of the competition law exemptions, in particular those workers engaged as 'independent contractors', and thereby risks limiting access to meaningful collective bargaining. Of course, that risk will only be realized to the extent that expressions of worker voice, which are not exempt from competition law, are not capable of being authorized or exempted by courts or competition authorities. Thus, we also examine the attempts of courts and regulators to assess whether the restrictive

[1] See Hugh Collins, 'Independent Contractors and the Challenge of Vertical Disintegration to Employment Protection Laws' (1990) 10 Oxford Journal of Legal Studies 353; Judy Fudge, 'Blurring Legal Boundaries: Regulating Work' in Judy Fudge, Shae McCrystal and Kamala Sankaran (eds), *Challenging the Legal Boundaries of Work Regulation* (Hart Publishing, 2012); Judy Fudge, 'The Legal Boundaries of the Employer, Precarious Workers, and Labour Protection' in Guy Davidov and Brian Langille (eds), *Boundaries and Frontiers of Labour Law* (Hart Publishing, 2006).

[2] A useful overview of the variety of contractual forms utilized in the modern labour market is set out in chapter 3 of Richard Johnstone et al., *Beyond Employment: The Legal Regulation of Work Relationships* (Federation Press, 2012). See, in this volume, A. C. L. Davies.

[3] See e.g. Guy Davidov and Brian Langille (eds), *The Idea of Labour Law* (OUP, 2011); Judy Fudge, 'Fragmenting Work and Fragmenting Organisations: The Contract of Employment and the Scope of Labour Regulation' (2006) 44 Osgoode Hall Law Journal 1.

effects on competition of expressions of worker voice can in some way be reconciled by countervailing benefits. It will become apparent that expressions of worker voice are extremely vulnerable when they fall outside the scope of the exemptions, as a result of the fact that courts and competition authorities in both Australia and the EU privilege economic, over social, arguments.

The chapter will begin by briefly exploring the underlying purposes of competition law and collective bargaining regulation. The discussion will then examine the scope of the labour market exemptions within the two jurisdictions, before considering the implications of competition law regulation for worker voice and the vulnerability of collective bargaining models to challenges from competition law.

Competition Law and Collective Bargaining

The underlying purposes of competition law and collective bargaining regulation are very different. Labour laws 'promote and encourage what... antitrust laws forbid: cartels, agreements to fix prices and control production levels'.[4]

This is at least in part as a result of the differences in the nature of the regulated exchange. In general terms, in markets for goods and services, the object of the regulated exchange is a fungible good or a particular service where the identity of the person performing the service is generally not important to the exchange and may only involve a brief interaction between the parties involved. In labour markets, the object of the regulated exchange is a person's labour. Such exchanges generally take place in the context of long-term relational contracts where the labour provider works for the labour hirer for an extended period and subject to the ultimate right of command vested in the hirer in respect of the work performed. The sale of a fungible thing or a depersonalized service is understood to be different to the sale of a person's labour to one hirer for a period of time.[5]

This difference in the nature of the exchange helps to explain the contrasting regulatory purposes of competition and labour laws. Competition regulation is concerned with maximizing public welfare through the promotion of competitive marketplaces. Free competition is understood to produce optimal economic outcomes in terms of maximizing resources—goods and services are produced only where there is a demand, and are supplied at a price that a consumer is willing to pay and which ensures an optimal return to the producer. However, this approach is ill-suited to labour markets and the logic does not automatically translate. A person's labour is not a commodity. You cannot separate the labour from the person or the need of the person to work to secure their livelihood. For most workers, their labour is their major asset and the means through which they support themselves and their dependents. It cannot be stored for future use or substituted for labour by another person.[6] It may not easily be redirected

[4] Daniel I. Bookner, 'Symposium: The Application of Antitrust Laws to Labor Related Activities' (1983) 21 Duquesne Law Review 331, 332.

[5] See Ian Mcneil, 'Contracts: Adjustment of Long-Term Economic Relations under Classical, Neo-classical and Relational Contract Law' (1977–78) 72 Northwestern University Law Review 854.

[6] See Simon Deakin and Frank Wilkinson, 'Labour Law and Economic Theory: A Reappraisal' in Hugh Collins, Paul Davies, and Roger Rideout, *Legal Regulation of the Employment Relation* (Kluwer, 2000) 42.

to another purpose if the market fails to provide a reasonable return, particularly if this requires expensive or time-consuming retraining. Labour market regulation in the form of collective bargaining alleviates inequalities of bargaining power in labour markets, providing mechanisms to facilitate workplace democracy and worker voice. It ensures workers have meaningful opportunities to affect the terms and conditions under which they work.[7] But, although collective bargaining has these social objectives, it may also achieve economic goals; in particular, collective negotiation of terms of conditions of employment may create efficiencies through reduced transaction costs, and direct worker input into arrangements for work may lead to the development of more efficient and effective work processes.[8]

Labour market exemptions from competition laws generally take one of three forms (or a combination thereof).[9] First, the labour market may be exempted from the operation of competition laws, either through a general exemption, or through an exemption tailored to specific forms of conduct within the labour market. This may be implemented expressly by statute, or may arise through judicial interpretation of the scope and application of competition laws.[10] Second, the labour market (or a part thereof) may be subject to the competition regime but labour market actors may be able to apply for an exemption from the application of those laws by demonstrating that their proposed conduct satisfies certain criteria related to the pro-competitive effect or potential public good of the proposed conduct.[11] Third, the labour market may be subject to competition regulation in the normal way, raising questions as to the nature of the balance between the conflicting objectives of competition and labour law.

In those jurisdictions which contain specific labour market exemptions, particular regulatory choices have been made with respect to the scope of labour market interactions which will be exempt from competition regulation. In such cases a range of questions may arise. Which workers and work relationships are exempt—workers generally or only a more narrow category—perhaps 'employees'? What forms of collective bargaining are exempt—collective bargaining generally or only 'formal' agreement making? What issues is it permissible to bargain over? Further, where competition laws allow for ad hoc exemptions, requiring conduct to be justified on public interest or other grounds (rather than general exemptions), how are these exemptions applied to labour market actors and are labour market actors treated differently to other business actors?

The discussion will consider these issues through an examination of the interaction of competition law and labour laws in Australia, and the UK as governed by the competition laws of the European Union. It will examine the scope of the relevant exemptions

[7] See e.g. Beth Bilson, 'Future Tense: Some Thoughts about Labour Law Reform' (2005) 12 Canadian Labour and Employment Law Journal 233; Adelle Blackett and Colleen Sheppard, 'Collective Bargaining and Equality: Making Connections' (2003) 142 International Labour Review 419.

[8] For further discussion see Guy Davidov, 'Collective Bargaining Laws: Purpose and Scope' (2004) 20 International Journal of Comparative Labour Law and Industrial Relations 81.

[9] For a useful discussion of approaches taken in different jurisdictions see Case C-67/96 *Albany* [1999] ECR I-5751, opinion of AG Jacobs, paras 80–111.

[10] For example, in the US there are specific statutory labour exemptions contained in the Clayton Act of 1914 and the Norris-LaGuardia Act of 1932; and a so-called 'nonstatutory' exemption first developed in *Apex Hosiery v Leader* 310 U.S. 469, 60 S. Ct. 982, 84 L. Ed. 1311 (1940).

[11] See the discussion of the relevant exemption in Australia later in the chapter.

and explain the way in which competition law and labour law intersect in those areas in which exemptions do not apply.

Australia

Regulation of competition between commercial entities in goods and services in Australia is governed by the Competition and Consumer Act 2010 (Cth), and the associated Competition Code. Part IV of the Act prohibits a range of anti-competitive conduct including practices that commonly form part of collective bargaining between workers and labour hirers including collective agreements over remuneration, arrangements which lessen competition and the withdrawal of labour in pursuit of a collective agreement involving both collective breaches of existing contracts or a collective refusal to deal (collective boycott).[12]

By contrast, industrial relations in Australia are regulated by the Fair Work Act 2009 (Cth).[13] The Act establishes a system of enterprise level collective bargaining for all covered employers, employees, and their bargaining representatives, including provisions for the negotiation, registration, and enforcement of collective agreements, and a right to strike in support of negotiations for collective agreements.[14]

The relationship between the two Acts is governed by an exemption contained within the Competition and Consumer Act which exempts certain employment arrangements from some anti-competitive conduct prohibitions.[15] A further provision allows collectives of businesses to engage in collective bargaining which would otherwise breach the anti-competitive conduct provisions of the Act where the applicants can demonstrate the 'public benefit' that will flow from their proposed conduct (the public benefit test).[16] Each provision will be discussed in turn.

The employment exemption

An employment exemption has been a feature of competition legislation in Australia since 1965.[17] The employment exemption is currently enacted as s. 51(2)(a) of the Competition and Consumer Act. It exempts collective bargaining conduct by employees from provisions prohibiting price fixing (agreements over remuneration); contracts, arrangements or understandings which lessen competition; and collective boycotts (strikes).

The exemption is limited in scope and operation. It applies only to conduct by employees and not to collective bargaining by self-employed/independent contractor workers. It is restricted to conduct undertaken with respect to remuneration, conditions

[12] Competition and Consumer Act 2010 (Cth), ss. 44ZZRD, 44ZZRF, 44ZZRG, 45.

[13] A small number of Australian employees are not covered by the Fair Work Act 2009(Cth), but generally have access to collective bargaining under state legislation.

[14] See generally Breen Creighton and Anthony Forsyth, *Rediscovering Collective Bargaining: Australia's Fair Work Act in International Perspective* (Routledge, 2012); Shae McCrystal, *The Right to Strike in Australia* (Federation Press, 2012).

[15] Competition and Consumer Act 2010 (Cth), s. 51(2)(a).

[16] Competition and Consumer Act 2010 (Cth), ss. 88, 90.

[17] Trade Practices Act 1965 (Cth), s. 38(c).

of employment, hours of work, or working conditions, and the connection between the conduct and the purpose of the bargaining must be direct and immediate.[18] Further, the exemption only protects against liability for certain restrictive trade practices. Consequently, employee collective bargaining remains subject to the remainder of the Competition and Consumer Act including statutory prohibitions against unconscionable conduct and secondary boycotts. The latter is particularly relevant in the labour market context as it prohibits virtually all secondary or sympathy strike action by labour market actors, leaving such action open to injunctive relief and substantial fines or damages orders.[19] Australian competition laws effectively impede collective worker voice expressed in the form of secondary or sympathy concerted action.[20]

In terms of ensuring that the expression of worker voice through collective bargaining is protected against potential incursions by competition law, the employment exemption within the Competition and Consumer Act has been generally effective, provided that collective bargaining is carried out by employees over the range of topics listed and does not involve secondary action. There is no significant history of litigation concerning the application of the employment exemption or its scope (although there has been substantial litigation against employees for engaging in secondary boycotts), and employee collective bargaining in the context of industrial relations legislation has generally been pursued without hindrance from competition laws.

The 'public benefit' test

The public benefit test allows for collectives of businesses or undertakings to seek permission from the competition regulator, the Australian Competition and Consumer Commission (ACCC), to engage in collective bargaining conduct which might otherwise breach the anti-competitive conduct provisions of the Competition and Consumer Act.[21] The test applied by the ACCC in assessing proposed collective bargaining conduct is that the conduct may not proceed unless the ACCC is satisfied that it will produce net 'public benefit'.

The public benefit test involves an analysis of the anti-competitive effect of the proposed conduct and an assessment of whether this is outweighed by any claimed public benefit. The accepted legal meaning of 'public benefit' comes from *Re Queensland Co-Operative Milling Association Ltd*,[22] and includes 'anything of value to the community generally, any contribution to the aims pursued by the society including as one of its principal elements... the achievement of the economic goals of efficiency and progress'.[23] This embraces both tangible and intangible benefits which can flow from permitting collective bargaining to occur. The claimed benefits must be direct

[18] *Ausfield Pty Ltd v Leyland Motor Corporation of Australia Ltd (No 2)* [1977] FCA 6 (1977); 30 FLR 477; *Re Phillip Adamson and Ors v NSW Rugby League Limited and Ors* [1991] FCA 425; (1991) 31 FCR 242.

[19] Competition and Consumer Act 2010 (Cth), s. 45D and associated sections.

[20] See further McCrystal 102–8 (n 14).

[21] Competition and Consumer Act 2010 (Cth), ss. 44ZZRL, 45(8A), 88, 90, 93AC, 93AD. There are further exemptions within the Act, but as they are not pertinent to this discussion they will not be explored.

[22] (1976) 8 ALR 481.

[23] (1976) 8 ALR 481, 510.

by-products of the bargaining process and cannot be ones which could otherwise be achieved through other means.[24]

The public benefit test involves an assessment of the efficiencies that can be gained through collective bargaining and how those efficiencies produce a 'benefit' to the public through 'the best use of society's resources'.[25] The efficiencies may arise from such things as reduced transaction costs associated with collective over individual bargaining; decreased information asymmetries between the collective and the hirer; or increased input into contractual arrangements allowing for greater efficiencies in the execution of contracts.[26] However, claimed public benefits cannot include increased bargaining power which is not considered to be a public benefit in its own right, or improved industrial harmony unless it can be directly linked to an efficiency gain or other public benefit.[27] Efficiency gains can be ones that flow directly to members of the collective themselves in the form of improved wages or conditions, but more weight is generally given to benefits that flow to the consuming public in the form of better services, reduced prices, or greater choice.[28]

The benefits claimed must be such as to outweigh the detrimental impact on competition that collusion would entail. For example, collective bargaining by independent contractors who are otherwise competitors in the market for their services is considered to reduce competitive pressures and price signals which direct resources to their most efficient use.[29] The extent of this detrimental impact will be determined by reference to the degree of existing negotiations in the market (existing negotiations suggest less need for the proposed arrangements), the size of the group relative to the market (density), any existing market power held by the group, and the potential for coercion or compulsion.[30] Any existing market power held by the individuals in the group will produce a high degree of anti-competitive detriment. Any compulsion in the proposed arrangements, such as a requirement that a target or the collective comply with a collectively bargained outcome, will generate a high degree of detriment. Further, while the Competition and Consumer Act allows the ACCC to authorize conduct which includes the use of coercion through a collective boycott, decisions in this area suggest that the potential anti-competitive detriment from such conduct will always be too high to be overcome by any potential public benefits.[31]

[24] (1976) 8 ALR 481, 510.
[25] *Re 7-Eleven Stores Pty Ltd* (1994) ATPR ¶41-357, 42,677.
[26] *Re 7-Eleven Stores Pty Ltd* (1994) ATPR ¶41-357, 42,677.
[27] Australian Competition and Consumer Commission (ACCC), *Guide to Collective Bargaining Notifications* (Commonwealth of Australia, 2011) 35–6.
[28] Shae McCrystal, 'Is there a "Public Benefit" in Improving Working Conditions for Independent Contractors? Collective Bargaining and the *Trade Practices Act 1974* (Cth)' (2009) 37 Federal Law Review 264, 278–9.
[29] See e.g. *Draft Objection Notice in respect of a collective bargaining notification lodged by the AMA (Vic) Pty Ltd on behalf of a group of doctors at Werribee Mercy Hospital*, CB00005, Public Register Number C2007/1930, 8 November 2007, para. 3.58; *Assessment: Collective Bargaining Notification lodged by the Australian Newsagents' Federation*, CB00003, Public Register Number C2007/1612, 13 September 2007, para. 3.25.
[30] ACCC 28 (n 27).
[31] ACCC 37 (n 27); and see Warren Pengilley, 'The Competition Tribunal and Chicken Meat: Do exclusionary provisions have any future hope of authorisation?' (2006) 14 Competition and Consumer Law Journal 196.

Unlike the employment exemption, the application of the public benefit test requires a collective to justify its proposed bargaining arrangements and the likely effect those arrangements will have on competition in the market in which it operates. Distinctions are drawn by the ACCC between potential bargaining groups on the basis of existing market power and levels of negotiation in the relevant industry, and the potential for the proposed arrangements to have a substantive impact on the members of the collective and the target. Features of proposed bargaining which would indicate the prospect of successful collective negotiations in the employment context (high membership density, scarcity of labour, capacity to coerce an employer) are the same factors in the competition law context which will almost guarantee that an application to engage in collective bargaining will fail. Applications that do succeed generally propose a form of collective agreement making that is stripped of the pre-conditions that collectives of labour consider essential for success—the potential for coercive collective action and the capacity to conclude binding agreements.

An example comes from the proposal of a group of self-employed journalists to bargain with large media outlets.[32] The vast majority of the journalists involved in the application had almost no bargaining power and were subject to take it or leave it contract arrangements which included oppressive terms assigning copyright in their work and restricting their capacity to work for other media outlets. Collective bargaining was only permitted by the competition regulator because the proposed bargaining and obligations under any resultant collective agreement were to be entirely voluntary on the part of the media outlets and any journalists. In the authorization process, the media outlets concerned had indicated that they would refuse to be involved in any collective negotiations.[33] Permission to bargain was granted, but the journalists were not permitted to engage in a collective boycott. This created the farcical outcome that while collective bargaining could potentially produce public benefit and was allowed, it would never actually proceed because the media outlets would not agree to negotiations and the journalists could not try to force them to the bargaining table through a collective boycott.

The European Union

The EU's values and aims are set out in Articles 2 and 3 of the Treaty on European Union (TEU). The statements one finds in the current Treaties, most recently amended by the Treaty of Lisbon which came into force in December 2009, have a rather more pronounced social flavour than those in previous Treaties.[34] Article 3(3) provides for the establishment of 'an internal market'. That Article provides that the Union 'shall work for the sustainable development of Europe based on balanced economic growth

[32] *Determination, Application for Authorisation lodged by MEAA in respect of collective negotiations of the terms of engagement of freelance journalists by Fairfax Media Limited, ACP Magazines Ltd, News Limited and Pacific Magazines*, 26 May 2010, Authorisation No. A91204.

[33] *Determination, Application for Authorisation lodged by MEAA* (n 32).

[34] See further Phil Syrpis, 'The Treaty of Lisbon: Much Ado... But About What?' (2008) 37 Industrial Law Journal 219.

and price stability, a highly competitive social market economy, aiming at full employment and social progress, and a high level of protection and improvement of the quality of the environment'. Protocol 27 makes it clear that the internal market continues to include 'a system for ensuring that competition is not distorted'. There was some debate about the possible significance of the 'relegation' of the commitment to undistorted competition, from the text of what was Article 3(1)(g) EC of the Treaty, to a Protocol.[35] However, as Protocols are said to form an 'integral part' of the Treaties (see Article 51 TEU), it seems that the Court must be correct in continuing to regard the commitment to undistorted competition as a key part of the internal market endeavour.[36]

Within the EU structure, there are 'rules on competition' and also separate 'titles' of the Treaties dealing with 'employment' and 'social policy'. The European Union's 'rules on competition' are to be found in Articles 101 to 109 TFEU. The provision which is of most relevance to the expression of collective voice by workers is Article 101 TFEU, which has direct effect in UK law. Article 101(1) prohibits 'agreements between undertakings, decisions by associations of undertakings and concerted practices which may affect trade between Member States and which have as their object or effect the prevention, restriction or distortion of competition within the internal market'. Article 101(3) provides that the provisions of paragraph 1 may 'be declared inapplicable' in the case of any agreement, decision, or concerted practice which fulfils four cumulative conditions: it must (i) contribute to 'improving the production or distribution of goods or to promoting technical or economic progress', (ii) allow 'consumers a fair share of the resulting benefit' and not (iii) impose 'restrictions which are not indispensable to the attainment of these objectives', or (iv) afford undertakings 'the possibility of eliminating competition in respect of a substantial part of the products in question'. Thus, to the extent that agreements may be caught by Article 101(1), businesses, potentially including workers in the labour market, may nevertheless seek to have that provision declared inapplicable by demonstrating that their proposed conduct satisfies the criteria in Article 101(3).

This section will focus first on the extent to which labour market agreements come within the scope of Article 101(1), and second, to the extent that they do, on the application of Article 101(1) and (3) to expressions of collective worker voice. It will become clear that there are a number of connections between the Australian and EU systems. Both have created exemptions for at least certain categories of collective agreements from the competition law rules; though, as we will argue later, it may be that the EU's judge-made exemption is more vulnerable than Australia's statutory exemption. And second, to the extent that expressions of collective voice do not benefit from an exemption, both the Australian and the EU legal framework assess expressions of collective

[35] See e.g. Alison Jones and Brenda Sufrin, *EU Competition Law: Text, Cases and Materials*, 4th edn (OUP, 2011) 38–41.

[36] See e.g. Case C-52/09 *Konkurrensverket v Tele Sonera Sverige*, Judgment of 17 February 2011, para. 20. The function of the competition rules is said to be 'to prevent competition from being distorted to the detriment of the public interest, individual undertakings and consumers, thereby ensuring the well-being of the European Union' para. 22. For a flavour of the debate surrounding the objectives of EU competition law, see Renato Nazzini, *The Foundations of European Competition Law: The Objectives and Principles of Article 102* (OUP, 2011) chs 1 and 2.

voice according to an essentially competition law paradigm emphasizing efficiencies and economic benefits, in which arguments labour lawyers typically deploy to justify and account for collective bargaining are, at best, marginalized.

Are labour market collective agreements exempt from the application of Article 101(1) TFEU?

The key case discussing the applicability of Article 101(1) TFEU to labour market collective agreements is *Albany International*, decided by the European Court of Justice in 1999. In *Albany*, the question was whether a decision taken by the organizations representing employers and workers in a given sector, in the context of a collective agreement, to set up a single pension fund responsible for managing a supplementary pension scheme, was contrary to what is now Article 101(1) TFEU.[37] After explaining the reasons why the agreement might be thought to be capable of infringing what is now Article 101 TFEU, the Court stated that it was 'important to bear in mind' that the Treaties contain not only competition law, but also social policy objectives. Thus, the Court was able to conclude that:

> [i]t is beyond question that certain restrictions of competition are inherent in collective agreements between organisations representing employers and workers. However the social policy objectives pursued by such agreements would be seriously undermined if management and labour were subject to [Article 101 TFEU] when seeking jointly to adopt measures to improve conditions of work and employment.
>
> It therefore follows from an interpretation of the provisions of the Treaty as a whole which is both effective and consistent that agreements concluded in the context of collective negotiations between management and labour in pursuit of such objectives must, by virtue of their nature and purpose, be regarded as falling outside the scope of [Article 101 TFEU].[38]

In order to assess whether the 'nature and purpose' of the agreement justifies its exclusion from the competition law provisions, the Court emphasized two aspects. First, in relation to the *nature* of the agreement, the Court noted that the agreement 'was concluded in the form of a collective agreement and is the outcome of collective negotiations between organisations representing employers and workers'. And second, this time in relation to its *purpose*, the Court stated that the scheme 'seeks generally to guarantee a certain level of pension for all workers' and 'therefore contributes directly to improving one of their working conditions, namely their remuneration'.[39]

Later case law has clarified the implications of *Albany*. *Pavlov* held that agreements aimed at improving terms and conditions of employment, but crucially not concluded

[37] Case C-67/96 *Albany International* [1999] ECR I-5751 para. 52. The case also discusses a second question: whether the decision to request public authorities to make affiliation to the fund compulsory for all workers in the sector is contrary to what is now Article 101 TFEU. The Court's conclusion on that flowed directly from its decision on the first question—it held that 'since the agreement at issue in the main proceedings does not fall within the scope of' what is now Article 101(1), 'the Member States are free to make it compulsory for persons who are not bound as parties to the agreement'.

[38] Case C-67/96 *Albany International* paras 59–60 (n 37).

[39] Case C-67/96 *Albany International* paras 62–63 (n 37).

in the context of collective bargaining, do not benefit from the *Albany* exemption.[40] On the other hand, *AG2R Prévoyance* confirmed that the *Albany* exemption applies notwithstanding the fact that 'affiliation to such an agreement is compulsory for all undertakings within the occupational sector concerned' and that there is 'no provision for exemption from affiliation'.[41] This makes it clear that the scope of the exemption is determined by the Court's assessment of the 'nature and purpose' of any agreement rather than by any in-depth assessment of the competitive effects which any such agreement may have. The scope of the *Albany* exemption is a formal matter; once the conditions in *Albany* are met, competition law principles are excluded.[42] Where, on the other hand, the *Albany* conditions are not met, the full force of competition law applies.

How are non-exempt agreements assessed under Articles 101(1) and (3)?

To the extent that expressions of worker voice fall within the scope of Article 101, and do not benefit from the *Albany* exemption, they fall to be assessed under Articles 101(1) and (3). Given the *Albany* exemption, it is perhaps not surprising that there is very little case law applying Articles 101(1) and (3) to collective agreements; but other cases can be used to illustrate the nature of the enquiry facing courts and competition authorities, which have, since 2004, been able to apply not only Article 101(1), but also Article 101(3).[43]

The first step is to determine whether an agreement infringes Article 101(1); that is to decide whether its object or effect is such as to restrict competition. At this stage, the burden of proof is on the person or authority alleging the infringement. If Article 101(1) is infringed, courts and competition authorities must decide whether the agreement can be saved by Article 101(3). At that stage, the burden of proof shifts to the parties seeking to claim the benefit of the Article 101(3) exemption.

The most directly relevant case is *Pavlov*. In *Pavlov*, a decision taken by the members of a liberal profession to set up a pension fund responsible for managing a supplementary pension scheme was, as already mentioned, held not to benefit from the *Albany* exemption. The Court went on to assess whether the decision infringed EU competition law. The Court's analysis made it clear that the case was concerned with a decision by an association of undertakings,[44] which was within the ambit of Article 101(1). Based on

[40] Case C-180/98 *Pavlov* [2000] ECR I-6451. The decision at issue in *Pavlov* was taken by a liberal profession's representative body. The Court chose to emphasize that the Treaty contains no provisions encouraging the members of the liberal professions to conclude collective agreements (para. 69), and so held that the decision taken by the members of a liberal profession to set up a pension fund responsible for managing a supplementary pension scheme, does not, by reason of its nature or purpose, fall outside the scope of what is now Article 101 TFEU (para. 70).

[41] Case C-437/09*AG2R Prévoyance*, Judgment of 3 March 2011, para 33.

[42] For similar exemptions (in very different contexts) from the scope of Article 101 TFEU, see Case C-309/99 *Wouters* [2002] ECR I-1577, in relation to the regulatory rules of the Bar in the Netherlands; and Case C-519/04P *Meca-Medina* [2006] ECR I-6991, in relation to the anti-doping rules of the International Olympic Committee.

[43] See Council Regulation 1/2003 [2003] OJ L1/1. Prior to 2004 the European Commission had the exclusive competence to rule on the compatibility of agreements with what is now Article 101(3). On the scope of the powers of national courts and competition authorities, see further Case C-375/09 *Tele2 Polska* [2011] ECR I-3055.

[44] Case C-180/98 *Pavlov*, para. 89 (n 40).

the economic context and the structure of the market concerned, the Court held that the effects of the decision in question were such as to restrict competition.[45] However, as there was no 'appreciable' restriction on competition within the market,[46] there was held not to be a breach of Article 101(1).[47] Thus, the agreement was held to be lawful, without consideration of Article 101(3).

The analysis under Article 101(1) is an economic one, with the focus squarely on whether there is, or is not, an appreciable restriction on competition. There is much debate within EU competition law, and in particular between the European Commission and the European Court, about the extent to which a US-style 'rule of reason' approach should be used within the Article 101(1) analysis, or whether the more appropriate forum for weighing the restrictive effects of the agreement against the economic benefits and efficiencies it creates is Article 101(3). Be that as it may, it certainly seems to be the case that the analysis under the combination of Articles 101(1) and (3), aims to assess whether the 'objective economic benefits' of agreements 'outweigh the negative effects of the restriction on competition'.[48] Crucially, the place for broader 'public policy considerations' within Article 101(3) is limited.[49] Although there are indications, in particular in some of the earlier decisions of the Court and the Commission, that social factors, such as 'the provision of employment',[50] 'the promotion of the harmonious development of the EU',[51] and even 'the social advantages resulting to employees',[52] may play a role in the assessment of whether the first Article 101(3) criterion is satisfied; they may only play a supplementary or what has been termed a 'supererogatory' role, and cannot lead to the Article 101(3) being satisfied in the absence of economic arguments.[53]

Comparative Analysis and Lessons

As seen from the foregoing analysis, both Australian and EU competition laws operate an exemption system—in which it is tolerably clear that many expressions of worker voice fall outside the scope of competition law. Beyond the exemptions, however, courts and competition authorities assess expressions of worker voice within what is essentially a competition law framework, focusing on the restrictions inherent in collective bargaining, and an economic analysis of its costs and benefits.

Labour lawyers, and those interested in the promotion of worker voice at work, may find significant comfort in the existence of an exemption approach in both Australian

[45] Case C-180/98 *Pavlov*, para. 93 (n 40).

[46] The requirement that an agreement affects the free play of competition to 'an appreciable extent' is a longstanding feature of EU Competition law; see e.g. Case 5/69 *Volk v Vervaecke* [1969] ECR 295.

[47] Case C-180/98 *Pavlov*, paras 94–99. The Court observed at para. 95 that 'the cost of the supplementary pension scheme has only a marginal and indirect influence on the final cost of the services offered by self-employed medical specialists'.

[48] See Commission Guidelines on the Application of Article 101(3) [2004] OJ C 101/97 [33].

[49] See Giorgio Monti, 'Article 81 EC [now Article 101 TFEU] and Public Policy' (2002) 39 Common Market Law Review 1057.

[50] Case 26/76 *Metro (No 1)* [1977] ECR 1857 para. 43.

[51] *Ford/Volkswagen* [1993] OJ L 20/14 para. 23.

[52] *StichtingBaksteen* [1994] OJ L 131/15 paras 27–28.

[53] See Case T-17/93 *Matra Hachette v Commission* [1994] ECR II-595 at para. 139.

and EU law, which operates so as to shield some collective agreements from competition law scrutiny. However, it is important that the existence of general exemptions for labour market collective bargaining does not lead to complacency over the potential threat posed by competition law to worker voice expressed through collective bargaining. This is for two main reasons.

First, an increasing number of workers may fall outside the scope of the exemptions. Both exemptions, in particular the one in Australia, are of limited scope. They only apply to certain categories of agreement, between employers and certain categories of worker, over certain terms and conditions of employment. As workers continue to move towards more atypical forms of work, and as collective bargaining continues to fragment in many sectors of the economy, the protection afforded by the exemptions becomes ever narrower.

Second, both the Australian statutory and the EU judge-made exemptions are vulnerable to challenge. Although the statutory exemption in Australia is of long standing, it has faced criticism. The exemption was the subject of a major review by the National Competition Council (the NCC) in 1999.[54] While the NCC ultimately recommended its retention, the discussion of the rationale for the exemption assumed that collective bargaining was anti-competitive (and that enterprise-level collective bargaining was less anti-competitive than industry-level collective bargaining); and focused only on whether there were compelling public interest reasons to retain it (in particular, coherence of industrial regulation and compliance with international standards).[55] There was no substantive consideration of whether bargaining is, on balance, anti-competitive.[56] This approach raises concerns should the exemption face a concerted challenge in the future, particularly in these straitened economic times. There have long been calls by sections of the Australian business lobby to revisit and tighten the exemption.[57] This could have the effect of making all collective bargaining subject to anti-competitive conduct prohibitions, requiring workers and trade unions to justify all proposed collective bargaining on the basis of its effect on competition and the existence of a public benefit. The discussion of attempts to collectively bargain by Australian freelance journalists illustrates the potential difficulties that this would raise.

In the EU context, the *Albany* exemption may also come under threat. The Court is of course right to say that the Treaties include both competition law and labour law objectives. However it is not clear that this demands an exemption for labour market collective agreements from the scope of Article 101(1) TFEU. Trade unions, in the now infamous *Viking* and *Laval* cases,[58] argued that the *Albany* exemption should also be

[54] National Competition Council, *Review of Sections 51(2) and 51(3) of the Trade Practices Act 1974* (Commonwealth of Australia, 1999).

[55] National Competition Council, *Review* 64, 71 (n 54).

[56] For discussion of the view that collective bargaining may be pro-competitive see e.g. Simon Deakin and Frank Wilkinson, 'Labour Law and Economic Theory: A Reappraisal' in Hugh Collins, Paul Davies, and Roger Rideout (eds), *The Legal Regulation of the Employment Relation* (Kluwer, 2000); Richard Freeman and James Medoff, *What Do Unions Do?* (Basic Books, 1984).

[57] See for example Peter Anderson, 'Trade Practices vs Industrial Relations: Changing Times—Does the Balance Need Revisiting?', Address to the Institute of Public Affairs Work Reform Unit Seminar, 28 July 2004; Australian Chamber of Commerce and Industry, 'Workplace Relations and Trade Practices: Reconciling Competition with Collectivism', ACCI Review No. 100, June 2003.

[58] See Case C-438/05 *Viking* [2007] ECR I-10779 and Case C-341/05 *Laval* [2007] ECR I-11767.

applied to the free movement provisions of the Treaties. This would have had the result that any decision to take collective action would not have been capable of being scrutinized under either those provisions or the competition law provisions of the Treaties. The Court rejected the argument and the parallel with *Albany* on the ground that it is not 'inherent in the very exercise of trade union rights and the right to take collective action that those fundamental freedoms will be prejudiced'.[59] This reasoning is unconvincing. If there is a difference between the way in which collective bargaining and collective action should be assessed under the competition law and free movement provisions of the Treaties, it is not that it is inherent that one (competition law) will be affected and the other (free movement law) will not. It is rather that the Court has made the decision to insulate certain collective agreements from competition law, but that it is not prepared to take the same step in relation to free movement law, in which it has instead decided, perhaps unwisely, to involve itself in what is bound to be a politically contentious balancing process.[60]

This discussion of the vulnerability of the exemptions in both systems raises questions over the different regulatory strategies employed in Australia and the EU. The Australian exemption is statutory and, as such, can only be changed through an Act of Parliament. It is, therefore, fairly well entrenched. The EU exemption, on the other hand, is a product of judicial interpretation. It is potentially more vulnerable, relying on a continuing shared judicial understanding of the nature of the relationship between competition law and labour law. However, the EU exemption is also more flexible than its Australian counterpart, and can better adapt to changes in the types of relationships formed between employers and workers. Unless amended (and any amendments in the current climate are unlikely to broaden the exemption) the Australian exemption draws the boundary between labour law and competition law on the basis of the existence of a contract of employment—a boundary line which increasingly excludes workers that we might legitimately consider should be covered by collective bargaining laws. The EU exemption can much more easily grow so as to encompass more atypical forms of employment relationship.

Given the vulnerability of the exemptions, it is perhaps appropriate that our final points should relate to the fate of expressions of worker voice through collective bargaining which do not benefit from the exemptions. One might imagine that it would be possible to find a test, and a forum, in which the arguments for competition law and collective bargaining, discussed at the start of this chapter, could be appropriately reconciled. However, the Australian and EU experience of applying 'public interest'

[59] Case C-438/05 *Viking* [2007] ECR I-10779 at para. 52. See also Case C-271/08 *Commission v Germany* [2010] ECR I-7091, Opinion of AG Trstenjak at para. 68.

[60] See further Phil Syrpis and Tonia Novitz, 'Economic and Social Rights in Conflict: Political and Judicial Approaches to their Reconciliation' (2008) 33 European Law Review 411, 419–20. On other institutions' attempts to reconcile the economic and the social in EU free movement law, see the Commission's proposed 'Monti II Regulation', COM(2012)130, in particular Article 2, which reads as follows: 'The exercise of the freedom of establishment and the freedom to provide services enshrined in the Treaty shall respect the fundamental right to take collective action, including the right or freedom to strike, and conversely, the exercise of the fundamental right to take collective action, including the right or freedom to strike, shall respect these economic freedoms.' The proposal was greeted with fierce opposition, and was withdrawn in September 2012.

based tests to bargaining that occurs outside of the labour market exemptions provides concrete examples of the difficulties that collectives of workers would be likely to face if required to justify each and every incidence of proposed collective bargaining in terms of the 'public interest'; in particular if the justification has to be one which would satisfy competition regulators. Both tests elevate the importance of economic efficiency, and relegate the types of benefit which in a labour law context would be seen as of primary significance: worker empowerment and voice. Once light has been shed on the anti-competitive effects of collective bargaining it becomes vulnerable and it is typically difficult to persuade courts and competition authorities of the overall benefits it may have.

22

Information and Communication Technology and Voice

Constraint or Capability?

*Tonia Novitz**

Introduction

By 1991, a Canadian academic was reporting that 'spectacular advances in microelectronic technologies are transforming the workplace'.[1] At that stage, in Canada, studies showed that over 37 per cent of women used computers in their work, compared with about 30 per cent of men.[2] Today those percentages seem miniscule, especially in any job going beyond bare provision of manual labour. Indeed, in 1993, a US senator was claiming that modern offices were turning into 'electronic sweatshops'.[3] For example, a 2009 survey of Australian nurses indicated that (of those who responded) while only 20 per cent of nursing assistants used computers on a daily basis, 75 per cent of enrolled nurses and 95 per cent of registered nurses reported that they did so.[4]

There are arguably at least two ways to see the development and growth of the new information and communication technology (ICT) workplace in the context of 'voice'. One is a familiar story of 'constraint', namely that computerization can enable employers more than ever before to track workers' movements and correspondence in ways which restrict communication between workers. There is, however, an alternative story to be told of 'capability', which offers a more positive view of the ways in which ICT can

* Many thanks go to the organizers of a stream (chaired by Seda Guerses, Katholieke Universiteit Leuven) who invited me to speak on the theme of 'Freedom of Association in the Networked Workplace' as part of the annual CPDP (Computers, Privacy & Data Protection conference) held in Brussels 2012, and who included me in a daylong workshop hosted by Constant VZW. I am also grateful to colleagues at the University of Bristol in the Commercial Relations and Private Law research group for their comments on presentation of a draft of this chapter; as well as to participants in the seminar on 'Labour Law and New Technologies' at the inaugural LLRN conference at Barcelona in 2013 and to Guy Mundlak and Alan Bogg for further advice. All errors and omissions are my own.

[1] Graham S. Lowe, 'Computers in the Workplace' (1991) 3(2) Perspectives on Labour and Income Summer Article No. 4 available at <http://www.statcan.gc.ca/studies-etudes/75-001/archive/e-pdf/66-eng.pdf>.

[2] Lowe Table 1 (n 1).

[3] 139 US Congress Record 10,354–10,355 (1993) (statement of Senator Paul Simon); cited in Alexandra Fiore and Matthew Weinick, 'Undignified in Defeat: An analysis of the stagnation and demise of proposed legislation limiting video surveillance in the workplace and suggestions for change' (2007–8) 25 Hofstra Labor and Employment Law Journal 525 at 530. In the US, there is empirical evidence that while, in 1997, 14.9 per cent of employers monitored employees' email messages, by 2004, 77.7 per cent of large employers did so. See Yohei Suda, 'Monitoring E-mail of Employees in the Private Sector: A Comparison between Western Europe and the United States' (2005) 4 Washington University Global Studies Law Review 209.

[4] R. Eley, J. Soar, E. Buikstra, T. Fallon, and D. Hegney, 'Attitudes of Australian Nurses to Information Technology in the Workplace: A National Survey' (2009) 27(2) CIN: Computers, Informatics, Nursing 114.

aid voice in both unionized and non-unionized workplaces.[5] It may be helpful, at this point, to give some examples that can demonstrate how technological developments have dual effects. These may be found in computerized mechanisms for time management, as well as email and internet activity.

New computer systems now record when a worker logs in and logs off. Security systems register when a worker enters or leaves their place of work using card access. For many of us, this is the new clocking in and clocking out. Similarly, use of shared electronic diaries (such as Google calendar) can document when we are in or out of the office and our stated reasons for doing so. This may have enabling or capability-building consequences, for we may know when a colleague is likely to be free and be able to plan ahead to meet with them. Gatherings addressing a particular workplace issue may be swiftly planned and coordinated. However, such diary systems, especially when tied in to other forms of scrutiny such as timesheets or electronic monitoring of movement through tracers, pagers, or satellite navigation, also enable a manager to identify when and where meetings have taken place (and between whom) in ways that are not conducive to free or confidential communication between workers.[6] The very fact of accounting for how time is spent, such as the computerized telephone systems which operate in call centres,[7] can inhibit discussion in the workplace. The emergence of a 'coercive supervisory style' focused heavily on monitoring does not necessarily lead to inhibition of communication between work colleagues, as staff can respond rebelliously, sometimes getting the better of and subverting systems for their own ends.[8] However, empirical studies indicate that excessive supervisory interference followed by retaliation can 'result in an escalating cycle of monitoring and resistance'.[9]

Email messages offer a swift and effective method of communication between workers, as can mobile phone 'texts' and pager 'messages'. This very accurate and lasting record of conversations may actually have some enabling effects, for example helping a worker who seeks to hold a manager to a commitment or even to demonstrate bullying or discrimination. Electronic communication systems, being frequently used by workers, may also be utilized by their organizations to recruit potential members and inform existing members.[10] Yet, such electronic communications systems may also allow scrutiny by an employer to identify 'troublemakers' or pursue some other business objective.[11]

[5] This is the approach to the 'spread of low-cost Internet-based information and communication tools' taken by Richard Freeman, 'What, If Anything, Can Labor Do to Rejuvenate Itself and Improve Worker Well-being in an Era of Inequality and Crisis-driven Austerity?' (2013) 14(1–2) Perspektiven der Wiirtschaftspolitik 41 at 46.

[6] Avner Levin, 'Big and Little Brother: The Potential Erosion of Workplace Privacy in Canada' (2007) 22 Canadian Journal of Law and Society 197 at 216.

[7] Kirstie Ball, 'Situating Workplace Surveillance: Ethics and Computer Based Performance Monitoring' (2001) 3(3) Ethics and Information Technology 211; and Kirstie S. Ball and Stephen T. Margulis, 'Electronic Monitoring and Surveillance in Call Centres: A framework for investigation' (2011) 26(2) New Technology, Work and Employment 113.

[8] Ball and Margulis 116 (n 7).

[9] Ball and Margulis 119 (n 7).

[10] See usage of text messages and information posted on the website in the context of the BA strike ballot and dispute in *British Airways v Unite (No. 2)* [2010] IRLR 809—agreed to be permissible by the Court of Appeal (after initial issue of an injunction at first instance on the grounds that this was insufficient notice). See also the UK Trades Union Congress (TUC) website in this regard: <http://www.tuc.org.uk> and the 'Stronger Unions' blog: <http://www.strongerunions.org/>.

[11] Kirstie Ball, 'Workplace Surveillance: An overview' (2010) 51(1) Labor History 87 at 96; also Lindsay Noyce, 'Private Ordering of Employee Privacy: Protecting Employees' Expectations of Privacy with Implied-in-Fact Contract Rights' (2011) 1 American University Labor & Employment Law Forum 27 at 28.

Social network sites, which could offer scope for organizing protest and dissent, are frequently scanned by employers both in advance of hiring and during employment to check a potential employee's reputation and activities.[12]

There is continuing debate regarding the legal responses appropriate to the enabling and coercive effects of ICT in the workplace. This chapter considers regulatory forms adopted primarily in the UK legal context, but seeks to draw on examples from the other countries at the centre of the 'Voices at Work' study: Australia, Canada, New Zealand, and the US.

In this chapter, it is readily observable that current constructions of individual employment law (adopted by courts the world over) tend to support managerial use of ICT to inhibit the voice of workers. Common law obligations subsisting across the common law world continue to require obedience to lawful and reasonable instructions[13] that, when translated into forms of electronic surveillance, have more profound effects than ever on curtailing worker voice. However, I shall also argue, from the perspective of employee capability, that there is scope for challenging the status quo through modification of common law principles.

The refusal of courts to do so, to date, has led to legislative responses, such as blacklisting, data protection, and privacy legislation, each of which has its limits. A further strategy, therefore, could be to campaign for legislation oriented towards promoting more proactive workplace-related collective communication and action. Currently, legislative recognition of the positive potential for ICT to further worker voice is centred only on the trade union recognition procedure, which as we shall see, affects only a relatively small number of workers in a minimal way. More may need to be done, which is not conditional on trade union membership or support for the same.

A further alternative source of redress is a human rights discourse. Indeed, a privacy-based approach is already familiar to those working in the ICT field. This strategy certainly has its uses and there is scope for its further development. Nevertheless, it is argued here that a human rights case should not be solely based on privacy. While important, that focus seems insufficient to establish workers' positive capability for voice. It is argued here that this could however be achieved were greater attention paid to two other basic human rights in this context: freedom of speech and freedom of association.

Freedom from and Capability to…

One vision of liberty is that encapsulated by Isaiah Berlin's potent vision of 'negative freedom', which is 'simply the area within which a man can act unobstructed by others…'[14] A fundamental idea of freedom from constraint leads him, ultimately, to advocate 'that there are frontiers, not artificially drawn, within which men should be inviolable'.[15]

[12] For the latter, in a New Zealand context, see Rebecca Britton, 'An Employer's Right to Pry: A Study of Workplace Privacy in New Zealand' (2006) 12 Canterbury Law Review 65 at 67 and 88–9.

[13] Simon Deakin and Gillian Morris, *Labour Law*, 5th edn (Hart, 2012) 302–4.

[14] Isaiah Berlin, 'Two Concepts of Liberty' in *Four Essays on Liberty* (OUP, 1969) 122.

[15] Berlin 165 (n 14).

We find echoes of the same sentiment in the foundational article written by Samuel D. Warren and Louis D. Brandeis on 'The Right to Privacy', which although drafted in 1890 was very much a response to the technological advances of their day. The authors commented that '[r]ecent inventions and business methods call attention to the next step which must be taken for the protection of the person, and for securing to the individual... the right "to be let alone"'.[16] They considered that the common law could provide the primary vehicle for protection of this privacy right, enabling an action in tort or issue of an injunction.[17] Yet, defences were considered to arise 'in the discharge of some public or private duty, whether legal or moral, or in the conduct of one's own affairs, in matters where his own interest is concerned'. Protection of property would clearly constitute an appropriate defence.[18] Further, any privacy rights would seem to be extinguished by the 'consent' of the individual affected.[19] There is no mention in this seminal piece of the obligations which an employer might owe to an employee at common law in line with this right to privacy, but we can take from the authors' sentiments, that *if* any liability could arise on the part of the employer, it should be subject to the employer's entitlement to defend legitimate property interests and limited in any case by an employee's consent to invasion of privacy. The dominance of this negative liberties approach in the UK and other common law jurisdictions is evident in this chapter.

Nevertheless, such an approach does not have to be adopted uncritically. In making this suggestion I seek to build (like many other labour lawyers before me) on a vision oriented towards 'capabilities' proposed by Amartya Sen.[20] Sen's vision of 'freedom' is not merely oriented to negative protections from the encroachment; nor does he subscribe simply to the planned economies to which Berlin was so deeply opposed.[21] Rather, Sen argues for the establishment of 'both *processes* that allow freedom of actions and decisions, and the actual *opportunities* that people have...'.[22] This is not merely a 'freedom from', but a 'freedom to do', which focuses on the ability to achieve human 'functionings', namely 'the various things a person may value doing or being'.[23] Personal liberty (in the sense of private space) and liberty to transact (to engage in contractual and property dealings) are acknowledged as part of this process, but so is what Sen has

[16] Samuel D. Warren and Louis D. Brandeis, 'The Right to Privacy' (1890) 4 Harvard Law Review (Harv L Rev) 193 at 195, citing Judge Cooley.

[17] Warren and Brandeis 219 (n 16).

[18] Warren and Brandeis (n 16), for example, at 195 and 200. They seek to distinguish 'privacy' from forms of 'property', but ultimately at 218 consider that rules of consent which apply in the sphere of property should apply in the context of privacy.

[19] Warren and Brandeis 218 (n 16).

[20] Amartya Sen, *Commodities and Capabilities* (North-Holland, 1985); Amartya Sen, *Development as Freedom* (OUP, 1999). For examples of (different) treatment of this theoretical frame, Alain Supiot, *Beyond Employment: Changes in Work and the Future of Labour Law in Europe* (OUP, 2001); Simon Deakin, 'Social Rights in a Globalized Economy' in P. Alston (ed.), *Labour Rights as Human Rights* (OUP, 2005). Note that the open-textured nature of Sen's approach, lying between traditional stances of liberalism and socialism, has led to suggestions that it can be sufficient to offer rather 'thin' negative entitlements, as claimed by Brian Langille, 'Core Labour Standards—The True Story (Reply to Alston)' (2005) 16 European Journal of International Law 409; discussed also by Judy Fudge, 'The New Discourse of Labour Rights: From Social to Fundamental Rights?' (2007) 29 Comparative Labor Law and Policy Journal (CLLPJ) 29. Cf for a richer approach taken in the context of the 'Voices at Work' study, Simon Deakin and Aristea Koukiadaki, 'Capability Theory, Employee Voice, and Corporate Restructuring: Evidence from U.K. Case Studies' (2011) 33(3) CLLPJ 427.

[21] Berlin 121–66 (n 14). [22] Sen (1999) 17 (n 20). [23] Sen (1999) 75 (n 20).

described as 'liberty to achieve'.[24] He envisages learning and discursive processes which enable any given individual, group, and society to determine what is to be valued as a goal, but also values such processes as conversion factors to achieve that goal. [25] In his account, the significance of workers' capabilities is also explicitly acknowledged.[26]

Martha Nussbaum, seeking to develop the application of Sen's ideas, has stressed that 'capabilities have a very close relationship to human rights'.[27] Further, she considers that Sen's approach to capability provides a basis on which to critique, interpret, and apply human rights, providing answers to what have previously seemed rather tired debates regarding civil and political and socio-economic rights. In her view, consistent with that of Sen (although perhaps she makes this more explicit), a focus on capabilities requires us to go beyond neoliberal insistence on negative liberty.

Unlike Sen, Nussbaum lists 'Central Human Capabilities' based on her understanding of human dignity[28] and places amongst these 'affiliation', which is clearly relevant for the purposes of voice at work. This is to include being able 'to engage in various forms of social interaction; to be able to imagine the situation of another'. She further explains that protection of 'affiliation' 'means protecting institutions that constitute and nourish such forms of affiliation, and also protecting the freedom of assembly and political speech'.[29] This chapter seeks to build on the potential affirming role of these human rights in enabling people to utilize ICT so as to promote voice at work.

Certainly, information technology has been observed to act as a means for development,[30] but also in so-called 'developed' states as a resource for the extension of human capabilities: 'When people are able to make use of ICT to maintain meaningful associations with one another or to express themselves or to earn a living when they could not before, we can legitimately claim an instrumental role for technology in expanding capability and achieving valued forms of functioning.'[31] ICT may not be a panacea for those seeking voice in the workplace. Indeed, it would be a shame were face to face meetings to be entirely replaced by virtual occasions in which less could be communicated. Nevertheless, new technologies may offer important facilitative means by which to enable workers' affiliative action. It is on this basis that I suggest using the frame of 'capability' to evaluate the legal treatment of workers' technological voice.

[24] Sen (1999) 117–18 (n 20).

[25] Sen (1999) 119 (n 20). Simon Deakin and Frank Wilkinson, *The Law of the Labour Market: Industrialisation, Employment and Legal Evolution* (OUP, 2005) 286.

[26] Sen (1999) 27–30 and 112–16 (n 20).

[27] Martha Nussbaum, 'Capabilities as Fundamental Entitlements: Sen and Social Justice' (2003) 9 Feminist Economics 33 at 36. See also Martha Nussbaum, 'Capabilities and Human Rights' (1997) 66 Fordham Law Review 273.

[28] Martha Nussbaum, *Women and Human Development: The Capabilities Approach* (CUP, 2000) ch. 1.

[29] Nussbaum (2003) 41–2 (n 27).

[30] See, for example, Erwin A. Alampay, 'Beyond Access to ICTs: measuring capabilities in the information society' (2006) 2(3) International Journal of Education and Development using ICT 4 at 10–12; and Richard Heeks, 'Do Information And Communication Technologies (ICTs) Contribute To Development?' (2010) 22 Journal of International Development 625.

[31] Justine Johnstone, 'Technology as Empowerment: A capability approach to computer ethics' (2007) 9 Ethics and Information Technology 73 at 79.

A Common Law Approach?

By virtue of the common law governing employment, employees hired under a contract of service are obliged to follow the lawful and reasonable instructions of their employer.[32] The contract of employment is a relational one in which the employer's 'control' of the employee is treated as a defining feature, and the forms that control takes are expected to change over time and according to the needs of the employer.[33] This is a matter of 'managerial prerogative', which traditionally (at least) has gone unquestioned in common law courts. On this basis, an employer can require an employee 'to adapt himself to new methods and techniques introduced in the course of his employment'.[34]

An employer can also state that any use of ICT (email, text or pager messages, internet activity, electronic diaries or calendars etc.) will be subject to scrutiny. Often, this is done by reference to a policy set in place for that particular workplace; [35] or practices may simply be implemented to which the employee is taken to have consented either through the commencement or continuation of their employment. This idea of implicit consent is a feature of the common law, which has been identified by commentators writing on the UK,[36] but also in Canada,[37] NZ,[38] and the US.[39] Whether there is true consent (or agreement between the parties) might be called into question, given the fundamental imbalance of bargaining between the parties identified elsewhere in this collection,[40] which has also been acknowledged by the UK Supreme Court.[41]

It would seem arguable that the common law treatment of an employer's ability to scrutinize ICT usage violates the negative liberties of employees, insofar as they have a legitimate interest in a certain sphere of privacy which they may be unable to defend, particularly in individual contractual negotiations with their employer. Moreover, the licence this gives to nefarious employer practices inhibits the capability of a worker

[32] The origins of this principle are frequently traced back to *Turner v Mason* (1845) 14 M & W 112, although now there is an argument that the order should be reasonable as well as lawful. For a review of relevant case law see Deakin and Morris (n 13).

[33] *Montgomery v Johnson Underwood* [2001] IRLR 270; and under EU law, subordination is considered a defining feature, see Case C-256/01 *Allonby v Accrington and Rossendale College* [2004] ICR 1328 cited in *Jivraj v Hashwani* [2011] IRLR 373 (SC). See for treatment of implicit contracts' 'relational nature', Mark Freedland, *The Personal Employment Contract* (OUP, 2003) 268 ff and his comments regarding a linkage to an 'obligation of fair work and performance' at 276 ff (discussed also previously at 186 ff).

[34] *Cresswell v Board on Inland Revenue* [1984] ICR 508 per Walton J at 518.

[35] For a compelling exposé of policies adopted by Australian companies, both reasonable and unreasonable, see Louise Thornthwaite, 'Chilling Times: Labour Law and the Regulation of Social Media Policies' delivered at the LLRN Inaugural Conference, Barcelona, 2013 available at <http://www.upf.edu/gredtiss/en/LLRN/conference.html>. Note that these policies are often the subject of data protection legislation and privacy challenges discussed later in this chapter.

[36] Michael Ford, 'Two Conceptions of Worker Privacy' (2002) 31 Industrial Law Journal (ILJ) 135 at 148.

[37] Levin 205 (n 6). [38] Britton 69 (n 12).

[39] Daniel P. Gorman, 'Looking out for Your Employees: Employers' Surreptitious Physical Surveillance of Employees and the Tort of Invasion of Privacy' (2006) 85 Nebraska Law Review 212 at 253–4.

[40] See Brodie, this volume.

[41] *Autoclenz v Belcher* [2011] UKSC 41, [2011] IRLR 820 per Lord Clarke at para. 35: 'So the relative bargaining power of the parties must be taken into account in deciding whether the terms of any written agreement in truth represent what was agreed and the true agreement will often have to be gleaned from all the circumstances of the case, of which the written agreement is only a part. This may be described as a purposive approach to the problem.' See for discussion Alan Bogg, 'Sham Self-employment in the Supreme Court'

(or workers) to (in Nussbaum's terms) 'affiliate' or (in the terms of our project) to exercise individual or collective 'voice'.

It remains open to the courts themselves to reconsider whether they wish to maintain the status quo, in the light of these concerns. For 'the beautiful capacity for growth which characterizes the common law' can still enable judges 'to afford the requisite protection'.[42] Judges could do so by scrutinizing the purposes for which an employer imposes surveillance on workers. Some surveillance might then be found to be illegitimate on public policy grounds, for example where it is designed to prevent trade union organization or whistleblowing. In the alternative, it could be held that the surveillance in question serves legitimate business purposes but is disproportionate bearing in mind other essential values served by the common law (such as liberty). Further, it is open to the courts to find that implicit consent is not sufficient where workers' personal data (including their political views and affiliations with other members of staff within or organizations—including a union—outside the workplace) is placed under employer scrutiny; but that express and informed consent is needed. Judges might even, as the UK Supreme Court has done, bring into question the reality or scope of apparent express consent. Other possibilities include the creation of a tort of privacy upon which workers can rely,[43] although this is not currently contemplated in the UK.[44] Certainly, there are indications that Parliaments across the common law world seek departure from the dominant common law approach, to the extent that these alternatives are emerging in legislation relating to blacklisting, data protection, and privacy across a range of countries.

Legislative Intervention

Through legislative intervention, there remains potential for unreasonable employer scrutiny through ICT to lead to a successful claim under legislation protecting from dismissal; for example, creating an actionable 'personal grievance' under the NZ Employment Relations Act 2000 or an 'unfair dismissal' under the UK Employment Rights Act 1996. Nevertheless, we find few concrete examples where such actions have been successful, without further reliance on claims relating to 'privacy' and even then such claims have tended to be approached cautiously by the courts. In New Zealand, the Privacy Act 1993 creates a series of 'Information Privacy Principles', which although not legally binding may be indicative of a breach of procedural fairness (or reasonable conduct) in a personal grievance.[45] In the UK, we expect treatment of unfair dismissal

(2012) 41(3) ILJ 328. However, the extent to which this view has firmly taken hold is uncertain. See *Quashie v Stringfellow* [2012] EWCA Civ 1735, para. 53 discussed by Freedland and Kountouris in this volume.

[42] See Warren and Brandeis 195 (n 16).

[43] See in a US context, *ICU Investigations Inc v Jones* 780 So. 2d 685, 687 (Ala. 2000) where an employee brought a successful action for invasion of privacy of his conduct at home (urinating in his front yard), discussed by Gorman (n 39) at 224 discussing William L. Prosser, 'Privacy' (1960) 48 California Law Review 383 and Matthew W. Finkin, 'Employee Privacy, American Values and the Law' (1996) 72 Chicago-Kent Law Review 221 which discusses the Restatement (Second) of Torts. Also see *Hosking v Runting* [2005] 1 NZLR 1 discussed by Britton 87 (n 12). For emergence of these torts in a Canadian context, see Levin 206–7 (n 6).

[44] *Wainwright and another v Home Office* [2003] UKHL 53; [2003] 3 WLR 1137.

[45] E.g. *Imperial Enterprises v Attwood* (2003) 7 NZELC; the limitations of this approach are discussed in Department of Labour: Employment Institutions Information Centre, 'Big Brother Goes to Work: Video Surveillance in the Workplace' (2005) Employment Cases Summary 16, 25.

to be informed by application of the Human Rights Act 1998, but the extent to which this has in fact occurred in relation to privacy (and other rights) is minimal.[46] Beyond statutory dismissal protection, other legislation offers workers some protection of voice in relation to blacklisting, data protection, and privacy.

Blacklisting

In the UK, some of the issues relating to information kept by employers and circulated regarding workers' trade union activities are now addressed by the UK Employment Relations Act 1999 (Blacklists) Regulations 2010. This regulatory initiative was taken following extensive blacklisting activities undertaken by the 'Consulting Association' in respect of blacklisting in the construction sector,[47] and arguably indicates the limitations of the Data Protection Act 1998 in addressing such conduct. The Regulations state that no one may 'compile, use, sell or supply' a 'prohibited list', which 'contains details of persons who are or have been members of trade unions or persons who are taking part or have taken part in the activities of trade unions' and has been compiled for a 'discriminatory purpose'. However, the Regulations operate more to control what employers do with the information which follows from workplace surveillance than exercise control over the form and scope of the surveillance itself. Further, the Regulations are restricted to 'trade union activity', as are the more general provisions relating to trade union discrimination which apply under the Trade Union and Labour Relations (Consolidation) Act 1992 (TULRCA).[48] Other forms of worker activism are not covered.

In the US, there is scope for broader protection of workers' affiliative or 'concerted' action. Under section 7 of the US National Labor Relations Act (NLRA), the National Labor Relations Board (NLRB) has established that workers who are not trade union members can still be protected when they take take action for their mutual benefit regarding terms and conditions of employment. Moreover, under the NLRA, 'illegitimate motives for surveillance' such as frustration of union attempts to organize or other forms of 'concerted action' can be the subject of a claim,[49] even if the penalties imposed are negligible in their effects.[50] Similarly, in this volume of essays, Breen Creighton points to the protective potential of the Australian Fair Work Act 2009, which provides workers with protection against 'adverse action' both associated with 'industrial' or rather trade union activity (Division 4) and where a worker is (or workers are) exercising a

[46] See, for analysis, Virginia Mantouvalou, 'Human Rights and Unfair Dismissal: Private Acts in Public Spaces' (2008) 71 Modern Law Review 912.

[47] See Charles Barrow, 'The Employment Relations Act 1999 (Blacklists) Regulations 2010: SI 2010 No 493' (2010) 39(3) ILJ 300 at 301–3 and House of Commons, Scottish Affairs Committee, *Blacklisting in Employment: Interim Report*, Ninth Report of Session 2012–13 HC 1071. For recent disclosures that the police may have been involved in assisting the Consulting Association in compiling this information, see Rob Evans, 'Police Spied on Activists for Blacklisting Agency' *The Guardian* 18 August 2013.

[48] Especially TULRCA, sections 146–152.

[49] Gorman 267 (n 39).

[50] E.g. *Colgate-Palmolive Co* 323 NLRB 515, 516 (1997), *National Steel Corp v NLRB* 324 F.3d 928, 934–935 (7th Cir. 2003) and *Anheuser-Busch* 342 NLRB 560 (2004), discussed by Fiore and Weinick (n 3) at 540–1 who find that: '[a]lthough there appears to be more protection afforded union employees, the reality is that employers violating surveillance law are only given a slap on the wrist'.

'workplace right' (Division 3); in this way individual trade union voice (or collective voices not necessarily involving a trade union) can receive protection in pursuit of their statutory claims.[51]

Data protection and privacy

Another avenue for protection of voice in the workplace is legislation specifically concerned with the handling of data, particularly personal information. In the UK, the Data Protection Act 1998 (DPA) transposes the Data Protection Directive 95/43/EC into domestic law.[52] In so doing, this legislation draws a distinction between 'personal data' and 'sensitive personal data' (to which additional protections apply); and places certain restrictions on the 'processing' of such data by a 'data controller'. The general principles governing such treatment of data are set out in Schedule 1 to the DPA and informed by Schedules 2 and 3.[53] In our workplace scenario, the data controller will be the employer, while records of correspondence between workers or their access to social networks can be regarded as ordinary 'personal information'. Trade union membership certainly constitutes 'sensitive personal information', which also covers personal details regarding a worker such as racial or ethnic origin, political opinions, and religious belief.[54] The legislation is enforced by an 'Information Commissioner', an office which now has extensive powers including that to issue monetary penalty notices of up to £500,000 for serious breaches.[55] Further, the Information Commissioner's Office (ICO) first issued 'The Employment Practices Code' (EPC) in 2003, which is non-binding but seeks to spell out for employers the extent of their obligations as data controllers to their workers as data subjects. The Code has since been revised and supplemented[56] (and even abridged for smaller employers).[57]

Two crucial issues arguably arise for the worker whose personal data is being processed by the employer. One is the issue of consent: should we be applying common

[51] Creighton, this volume. See also Victoria Lambropoulos, 'The Evolution of Freedom of Association in Australia's Federal Industrial Relations Law: From trade union security to workplace rights' (2013) 54 Labor History, forthcoming published online at <http://www.tandfonline.com/doi/abs/10.1080/0023656X.2013.804277>.

[52] Note the further constraints imposed by the Regulation of Investigatory Powers Act 2000 (RIPA) and the Telecommunications (Law Business Practice) (Interception of Communications) Regulations 2000; but neither is concerned specifically with workplace surveillance. See discussion in Aileen McColgan, 'Do Privacy Rights Disappear in the Workplace?' (2003) European Human Rights Law Review 120 at 133; and Hazel Oliver, 'Email and Internet Monitoring in the Workplace: Information Privacy and Contracting-out' (2002) 31 ILJ 321 at 339.

[53] Cf Data Protection Directive 95/43/EC, Article 6.

[54] DPA, s. 2.

[55] See amendment of the DPA by Criminal Justice and Immigration Act 2008, s. 144.

[56] Published November 2011 (96pp. in length) and available at: <http://www.ico.org.uk/for_organisations/data_protection/topic_guides/~/media/documents/library/Data_Protection/Detailed_specialist_guides/the_employment_practices_code.pdf>. Note that this is further supplemented by 'Supplementary Guidance' published June 2005 (86pp.) and available at: <http://www.ico.org.uk/for_organisations/data_protection/topic_guides/~/media/documents/library/Data_Protection/Detailed_specialist_guides/employment_practice_code_supplementary_guidance.ashx>.

[57] Also published November 2011 (but only 26pp. in length) and available at: <http://www.ico.org.uk/for_organisations/data_protection/topic_guides/~/media/documents/library/Data_Protection/Practical_application/quick_guide_to_the_employment_practices_code.pdf>.

law principles indicating that implicit consent is sufficient? The other key issue is the purpose (or purposes) for which data can legitimately be kept by the employer.

While 'consent' is stated as a precondition for collection of personal data (under Schedule 2 of the DPA) and 'explicit consent' for 'sensitive personal data' (under Schedule 3), this is deceptive. For, if any of the other exceptions apply (more generous for bare 'personal' information than that which is 'sensitive'), then consent is not needed, whether implicit or explicit. Where ordinary personal data is at issue and these exceptions do not apply, the EPC seems to indicate that the kind of implicit consent familiar at common law is sufficient. The employer does not need to seek permission to hold employment records but the EPC does encourage employers to ensure that employees are aware of the purposes for which data concerning 'employment records' are being kept and the nature of any intended disclosure.[58] Data management of sensitive personal information is clearly subject to different threshold requirements. Schedule 3 makes clear that 'explicit consent' is needed, but this is still not essential if any of the following other criteria are satisfied: necessity for compliance with employment law, necessity for protecting vital interests of the data subject, processing for associative activities (such as a trade union) or data already 'manifestly made public by the data subject' or necessary for 'establishment, exercise or defence of legal claims'. Hazel Oliver has expressed concern at this formulation. First, it offers potential for justification of usage of sensitive personal information without a worker's consent, which arguably reduces the worker's capacity for agency. Second, perhaps even more significantly, it enables a worker to 'contract out' of privacy rights, even if the further criteria are *not* met, without further justification.[59]

Under Article 6 of the EC Directive, data may only be used for 'specified, explicit and legitimate purposes and not further processed in a way incompatible with those purposes'. It is recommended as 'good practice' that employers 'consult workers, and/or trade unions or other representatives, about the development and implementation of employment practices and procedures that involve the processing of personal information about workers', even where this is not obligatory under legislation.[60] The EPC acknowledges that:

> [m]onitoring may, to varying degrees, have an adverse impact on workers. It may intrude into their private lives, undermine respect for their correspondence or interfere with the relationship of mutual trust and confidence that should exist between them and their employer. The extent to which it does this may not always be immediately obvious. It is not always easy to draw a distinction between work-place and private information. For example monitoring e-mail messages from a worker to an occupational health advisor, or messages between workers and their trade union representatives, can give rise to concern.[61]

This could be said to provide an indication that only light touch intervention by an employer is appropriate when it comes to data scrutiny; but at the same time the EPC does not envisage use of ICT to facilitate trade union engagement in the workplace. There is, for example, no comment on 'blacklisting', which is now (one presumes) to be

[58] EPC at 32. Note also similar advice re records kept for pensions or insurance purposes.
[59] Oliver 331 (n 52). [60] EPC at 13. [61] EPC at 56.

addressed by the Blacklisting Regulations of 2010 rather than the DPA. This is perhaps curious given that adoption of those Regulations was prompted by the prominent prosecution by the ICO of the Consulting Association concerning the holding and dissemination of information regarding 3,213 workers in the construction industry.[62]

In terms of what can or should be disclosed to a trade union in order to assist in recruitment or representation drives, the following observations are made in the EPC:

> Personal information about workers should only be supplied to a trade union for its recruitment purposes if;
>
> - the trade union is recognised by the employer,
> - the information is limited to that necessary to enable a recruitment approach, and
> - each worker has been previously told that this will happen and has been given a clear opportunity to object.[63]

This suggests that electronic access to the workplace is likely to be no more available than physical access is at present.[64]

The UK legislative approach does not compare that unfavourably to those adopted in other common law countries. In the US, for example, an Electronic Communications Privacy Act 1986 (ECPA) allows an employer to 'monitor an employee's telephone and wire communications' under a 'business extension exclusion'[65] which enables surveillance of the statistical aspects of for example, destination of calls, call duration, and number of calls. Also, where an employer has a reasonable business purpose, there can be monitoring of the *content* of employee communications,[66] as long as the methods and/or scope are not unreasonable and one of the parties (although not necessarily both the employees involved) consented to interception, whether expressly or implicitly. However, the existence of a policy informing the employee is seen as vital: 'An employer may be acting unlawfully, notwithstanding the ECPA's business extension exclusion, if it intercepts employees' private communications absent a published monitoring policy.'[67]

In Canada, the Personal Information Protection and Electronic Documents Act 2000 (PIPEDA) regulates storage and use of information regarding an 'identifiable individual', imposing what is essentially a 'reasonableness' test. If covered by PIPEDA then workers are entitled to ensure that their employer: explains the purposes for which personal information is gathered; does not retain more than is necessary for such purposes; keeps any information accurate; gains their 'consent'; and allows them access to the information kept and a chance to correct inaccuracies. The problem is that coverage

[62] See text accompanying n 47. [63] EPC at 51.

[64] Limited for non-recognized trade unions only to a balloting period under the statutory recognition procedure. See TULRCA, Sch. A1, para. 26 discussed in Alan Bogg and Tonia Novitz, 'Recognition in Respect of Bargaining in the UK: Collective Autonomy and Political Neutrality in Context' in Breen Creighton and Anthony Forsyth (eds), *Rediscovering Collective Bargaining: Australia's Fair Work Act in International Perspective* (Routledge, 2012) 233–4.

[65] Electronic Communications Privacy Act of 1986 (ECPA), § 2510(5)(a).

[66] ECPA, §2510(8).

[67] Satch U. Ejike, 'Workplace Privacy in Domestic and International Business: Employers' Rights and Liabilities' (2002) International Trade Law and Regulation 12 at 17.

is patchy. PIPEDA applies across the private sector, but by reason of the Constitutional division of powers, only to federally regulated workers. 'The majority of workers in each province are not protected by PIPEDA, although their employer might be bound by PIPEDA with respect to their customers' personal information.'[68]

In four provinces, a tort of 'invasion of privacy' has been established by legislation: British Columbia, Manitoba, Newfoundland, and Saskatchewan. However, once again, difficult issues of 'consent' arise here. As Avner Levin has observed, even when such privacy legislation is in place, workers still 'face a difficult decision', as 'either they continue to work and lose their ability to sue for invasion of privacy due to their "consent" to the new measures, or they must risk their employment and claim, without any guarantee of success, that the new measures have brought the employment relationship to an end'.[69]

The lack of an enabling approach in UK legislation

As is evident from the survey provided earlier, UK legislation is adept at providing various restrictions on the ways in which employer surveillance occurs in the workplace. This is very much a constraint-based approach as it is appreciative of the ways in which an employer's treatment of ICT can constrain workers' communications with each other and their affiliative action. However, the legislation does little to enable workers' use of ICT to achieve collective objectives.

The seeds of a legislative enabling approach may be detected in connection to trade union recognition. The UK operates a statutory procedure whereby a trade union may apply for statutory recognition where certain threshold requirements are met and a certain level of worker support can be demonstrated.[70] Unfair practices are prohibited in the context of preparation for a ballot (to determine worker support) and guidance is provided by the Code of Practice: Access and unfair practices during recognition and derecognition ballots 2005 (AUP).[71] What is interesting about the AUP is the extent to which it recognizes the significance of ICT in determining capacity for trade union recruitment and organization. However, that said, the AUP is remarkably moderate in the demands it makes of employers. The employer need only allow workers access to the union's website, if the employer usually allows such internet use. If it is not allowed, the employer should 'consider giving permission to one of his workers nominated by the union to down-load the material' and circulate it. Similarly, access to sending an email message should be allowed, but only if the employer generally allows email use for non-work related purposes or the employer is using email in a campaign in this way.[72] The Code states that campaigning by the employer or the union can 'be undertaken by circulating information by emails, videos or other mediums' as long as it is not intimidatory or threatening.[73] Still, the union is not necessarily to be given access to the

[68] Levin 199 (n 6). [69] Levin 205 (n 6).

[70] Trade Union and Labour Relations Act 1992 (TULRCA), Sch. A1. A straightforward summary is available in Pascale Lorber and Tonia Novitz, *Industrial Relations Law in the UK* (Intersentia, 2012) ch. 3; for thorough and comprehensive analysis of the procedure, see Alan Bogg, *The Democratic Aspects of Trade Union Recognition* (OUP, 2009).

[71] Available at <http://www.bis.gov.uk/files/file14418.pdf>. [72] AUP at 27. [73] AUP at 45.

workers' email addresses unless the workers concerned have authorized dislosure by the employer.[74]

It should be noted that the scope of these entitlements regarding ICT access for unions is extremely limited. The statutory recognition procedure is not utilized extensively. In 2012–13, only fifty-four applications were made under the procedure and ten ballots were held.[75] Moreover, these are only entitlements which apply for a short window of time and for a limited purpose (a 'period of access' leading up to a statutory recognition ballot)[76] and the Code only seems to envisage access by trade unions and not individual workers.

A Human Rights Approach: Beyond Privacy?

One outstanding question is whether a human rights-based approach can offer anything more than is currently contemplated under legislation. At present, the assumption seems to be that privacy protections are the only game in town, but it is argued here that recourse to freedom of speech and freedom of association may be more fruitful in securing a capability-oriented outcome.

Privacy, consent, and proportionality

This is not to say that the scope for protection of privacy should be overlooked; not least because, as has been observed already, it casts doubt on whether mere consent to workplace surveillance is sufficient if such surveillance is disproportionate in terms of the legitimate aims pursued by the employer. This is an issue which has obviously arisen where a privacy right is imported into UK law by virtue of the Human Rights Act 1998 (HRA), which gives legislative effect to Article 8 of the Convention for the Protection of Human Rights and Fundamental Freedoms 1950 (also known as the European Convention on Human Rights 1950 or 'ECHR'). Notably, prior to the enactment of the HRA, arguments made relating to privacy in respect of trade union membership 'met with short shrift',[77] but this may no longer be the case.

Article 8 of the ECHR provides that:

1. Everyone has the right to respect for his private and family life, his home and his correspondence.
2. There shall be no interference by a public authority with the exercise of this right except such as is in accordance with the law and is necessary in a democratic society in the interests of national security, public safety or the economic well-being of the country, for the prevention of disorder or crime, for the protection of health or morals, or for the protection of the rights and freedoms of others.

[74] AUP at 17. This is consistent with the text accompanying nn 63 and 64 relating to scope of the EPC.

[75] CAC Annual Report 2012–13 at 10–11 (available at <http://www.cac.gov.uk/media/pdf/5/s/The_CAC_Annual_Report_2012-2013.pdf>).

[76] CAC Annual Report 2012–13 at 19 (n 75).

[77] *Blackpool and the Fylde College v NATFHE* [1994] IRLR 227; discussed by McColgan 121 (n 52).

What is crucial for our purposes is the explicit recognition of right to respect for 'correspondence', which is what workers are seeking in an ICT context in terms of emails and other messages which are posted on websites. Paragraph 2 does offer the potential for limitations in accordance with 'the rights and freedoms of others', which must presumably be taken to include the right of an employer to defend their right to property under Article 1 of Protocol No. 1 to the ECHR. However, any such constraint must be proportionate.[78]

There have been successful claims made under Article 8, particularly against public employers in the UK. Some of the most notable have been concerned with sexual behaviour or identity.[79] Others have indicated that covert surveillance, without detection of a criminal act at stake, is inappropriate.[80] One case which highlighted the issues arising regarding a worker's behaviour in the digital era was *Pay v UK*.[81]

The case of *Pay* concerned 'affiliative' behaviour in the context of new technologies, although not that so much concerned with worker voice inside the workplace as sexual conduct outside. Pay was an employee of the Lancashire Probation Service. He had been dismissed for being a director of an organization 'Roissy' that operated a website (registered to Pay's address), which advertised making and selling items used in bondage, domination, and sadomasochism ('BDSM') and the organizer of BDSM events and performances. The website had placed photographs of Pay and others performing BDSM acts which had taken place at a local private members' club. This was not illegal conduct, but conduct which could cause embarrassment to Pay's employer. Pay denied that he had placed these pictures on the website and it was accepted that he had already notified his employer of his connection to Roissy. The European Court of Human Rights reversed the finding of the UK court that privacy under Article 8 was not engaged here. The internet was not to be treated as a 'public' space. Sexual life was one of a number of 'important elements of the personal sphere protected by Article 8'; further, the fact that private behaviour was recorded by others and displayed over the web did not make it any the less private. The Court also made the following observation, which is arguably significant for the future protection of 'voices at work', namely that Article 8 also protects:

> the right to establish relationships with other human beings and the outside world. It may include activities of a professional or business nature. There is, therefore, a zone of interaction of a person with others, even in a public context, which may fall within the scope of 'private life'.

Much turned on what could be regarded, on the facts, as a 'reasonable expectation of privacy'. However, in this particular case, 'given in particular the nature of the applicant's work with sex offenders and the fact that the dismissal resulted from his failure

[78] Mantouvalou 938 (n 46).

[79] App Nos 33985/96 and 33986/96 *Smith and Grady v UK* (1999) 29 EHRR 493. See for discussion, McColgan 135–40 (n 52).

[80] *Halford v UK* (1997) 24 EHRR 523; [1997] IRLR 471, at para. 45; cf *Kopke v Germany* (1992) EHRR 97 at 111, para. 29.

[81] App No 32792/05 *Pay v UK* [2009] IRLR 139.

to curb even those aspects of his private life most likely to enter into the public domain', the Court did not consider that the measures taken against Pay were disproportionate.

The Court's approach in *Pay* seems to support the assertions of academic commentators on the nature of the right to privacy, which they see less as a matter of maintaining personal secrecy, but pursuing communication and relationships. For example, Oliver understands privacy as not just 'freedom from' interference but 'freedom to' engage democratically: 'Privacy allows individuals to develop their ideas before "going public", and can be described as essential to democratic government due to the way in which it fosters and encourages moral autonomy.'[82] Further, Michael Ford has advocated an approach taken previously by the Court to privacy in *Niemitz v Germany*,[83] such that privacy is not solely concerned with an 'inner circle' within which an individual leads some kind of protected existence, but also must 'comprise to a certain degree the right to establish and develop relationships with other human beings.'[84] In this sense, the Court seems to offer scope for privacy rights to be connected to a right to associate or affiliative action, which suggests opportunities for more stringent control of employers' surveillance of communications in the ICT workplace.

The problem with the judgment in *Pay* is the mention of what may be regarded as a 'reasonable expectation of privacy'. As Oliver and Ford explain, this notion creates a kind of perverse incentive that the more that an employer makes explicit their surveillance of workers' behaviour, the less there may be a 'reasonable expectation' of privacy.[85] This is a concern which stems from the frequent use of this phrase in the context of US Constitutional jurisprudence. There is no explicit right to privacy under the US Constitution but, since *Griswold v Connecticut*,[86] such an entitlement has been acknowledged and protected by the US Supreme Court. The most recent Supreme Court judgment concerning protection of privacy in the context of new technologies is that of *City of Ontario v Quon*.[87]

Quon concerned an action for breach of privacy by a former police officer in relation to personal use of text messages at work on a 'pager' issued by City of Ontario Police Department (OPD). There was a broader computer and internet policy adopted by the OPD that 'the city reserves the right to monitor and log all network activity including e-mail and Internet use, with or without notice', which the OPD had made clear to employees would include text messaging. On appeal to the US Supreme Court, Justice Kennedy (giving the leading judgment) was reluctant to lay down general principles relating to use of new technology:

> The Court must proceed with care when considering the whole concept of privacy expectations in communications made on electronic equipment owned by a government employer. The judiciary risks error by elaborating too fully on the Fourth Amendment implications of emerging technology before its role in society has become clear... Prudence counsels caution before the facts in the instant case are used

[82] Oliver 323 (n 52). [83] (1992) EHRR 97 at 111, para. 29. [84] See Ford 139 (n 36).

[85] Oliver 336 (n 52) and Michael Ford, *Surveillance and Privacy at Work* (London: Institute of Employment Rights) 50.

[86] *Griswold v Connecticut*, 381 U.S. 479, 486 (1965), applied in *O'Connor v Ortega*, 480 U.S. 709, 714–19 (1987), discussed in Fiore and Weinick 533 ff (n 3).

[87] *City of Ontario v Quon*, 130 S.Ct. 2619, 560 U.S.

> to establish far-reaching premises that define the existence, and extent, of privacy expectations enjoyed by employees when using employer-provided communication devices.[88]

He preferred instead to address the case in a more narrow fashion. On this basis he concluded that Quon had only a limited expectation of privacy, given his knowledge of the employer's policy, and that the search of messages (covering only the last two-month period and redacting texts sent out of work) was reasonable. This cautious approach attracted some criticism from Justice Scalia who argued that 'the proper threshold inquiry should be not whether the Fourth Amendment applies to messages on *public* employees' employer-issued pagers, but whether it applies *in general* to such messages on employer-issued pagers' and considered that the court should provide greater guidance on 'privacy expectations for emerging technologies': '"The times-they-are-a-changin" is a feeble excuse for disregard of duty.'[89] Notably, comment in the Harvard Law Review also expressed disappointment at the narrow scope of the judgment.[90] What *Quon* does however suggest is that an employer is best protected from a privacy-related action when there is a workplace policy regarding ICT to which the worker can be said to have 'consented' (although what we regard as sufficient consent arguably remains an ongoing challenge) and that the surveillance will have to be proportionate to a legitimate interest of the employer.

There has also been one recent judgment of the European Court of Human Rights concerning workplace surveillance, which seems to confirm that this is also likely to be the approach of that court. *Kopke v Germany*[91] concerned the covert video surveillance of an employee working in a supermarket's drinks department, following irregular till receipts. Kopke was shown by the video to have taken money from the tills which she hid in her clothes. The Court was satisfied that a video recording made at her workplace 'without prior notice on the instruction of her employer' affected her 'private life' under Article 8. Moreover, Article 8 did not merely 'compel the state to abstain from such interference: in addition to this primarily negative undertaking, there may be positive obligations inherent in an effective respect for private life.'[92] It was stated that 'in certain circumstances, the state's positive obligation under art. 8 is only adequately complied with if the state safeguards respect for private life in the relations of individuals between themselves by legislative provisions providing a framework for reconciling the various interests which compete for protection in the relevant context.'[93] Yet, in this case, the employer's interference with Kopke's privacy was justified under Article 8(2), with reference to the employer's entitlement to its property rights under Article 1 of Protocol No. 1 to the ECHR.[94] The requirement of proportionality was satisfied because 'there

[88] *City of Ontario v Quon*, per Kennedy J at 2628–30 (n 87). Discussed by Noyce 51 (n 11).

[89] *City of Ontario v Quon*, per Scalia J at 2635 (n 87).

[90] 'Leading Cases: Constitutional law—Fourth Amendment—Reasonable Expectation of Privacy' (2010) 124 Harv L Rev 179 at 188: 'Subsequent cases involving Fourth Amendment privacy rights in the digital realm are inevitable, and the Court should prepare itself to address those issues more definitively.'

[91] App No 420/07, Judgment of 5 October 2010—admissibility decision.

[92] App No 420/07, Judgment of 5 October 2010, para. 41 (n 91).

[93] App No 420/07, Judgment of 5 October 2010, para. 42 (n 91).

[94] App No 420/07, Judgment of 5 October 2010, para. 49 (n 91).

had not been any equally effective means to protect the employer's property rights' which would have 'interfered to a lesser extent with the applicant's right to respect for her private life'.[95] The 'public interest in the proper administration of justice' was also taken into account.[96] The judgment did however contain the following obiter statement akin to that of Kennedy J in *Quon*: 'The competing interests concerned might well be given a different weight in the future, having regard to the extent to which intrusions into private life are made possible by new, more and more sophisticated technologies.'[97]

This judgment perhaps places a more stringent obligation on employers to justify their conduct than that acknowledged to date in the UK. Examples include the findings of the Scottish Employment Appeal Tribunal in *McGowan v Scottish Water*[98] where it was held that film surveillance of an employee's home to see how many times an employee left his house to assess the validity of his worksheets was defensible, as the employer was entitled to protect its assets; and *Fairstar Heavy Transport NV v Adkins and Anor*[99] when it was found by the Court of Appeal that an employee had an obligation to surrender emails and other documents stored on a home computer in England in relation to the employer's business.

Alternative approaches: freedom of speech and freedom of association

What then of other forms of human rights protections potentially available under the ECHR? These might include Article 10 on freedom of speech and Article 11 on freedom of association. Freedom of speech has often arisen as an issue alongside the right to privacy, and the European Court of Human Rights has preferred each time to deal with the latter, finding allegation was 'tantamount to restatement of the complaints under Article 8' and did not 'therefore find it necessary to examine them separately'.[100] This would seem to be due to the cross-over with 'communication' in Article 8(1), but it is possible to conceive of a scenario where a worker seeks to be able to make a very public statement on an employer's website so as to engage other workers in debate and surely, the question then is whether the employer's proprietary interests are sufficient to limit the worker's reliance on freedom of speech under Article 10(2). One possibility is that where workers have grounds for reliance on more than one ECHR Article, this should be seen as adding to the normative weight of their case, so that it gains additional persuasive force.[101]

Further, there is scope for protecting workers' communications through workplace ICT under Article 11 of the ECHR. The significance of Article 11(1) of the ECHR is

[95] App No 420/07, Judgment of 5 October 2010, para. 50 (n 91).
[96] App No 420/07, Judgment of 5 October 2010, para. 51 (n 91).
[97] App No 420/07, Judgment of 5 October 2010, para. 52 (n 91).
[98] [1995] IRLR 167.
[99] [2013] EWCA Civ 886, 19 July 2013. This was not a pure proprietary right, but was based on an agency argument for reasons of business efficacy.
[100] App No 20605/92 *Halford v UK*, Judgment of 25 June 1997 (1997) 24 EHRR 523 Court judgment at para. 72.
[101] I am grateful to Alan Bogg for this suggestion, which comes out of his research with Keith Ewing in Alan Bogg and Keith Ewing, *The Political Attack on Workplace Representation—A Legal Response* (Institute of Employment Rights, 2013), especially at 21–3.

that it states that '[e]veryone has the right to...freedom of association with others, including the right to form and join trade unions'. This wording indicates that current legislation predicated on the view that only trade union activity should be subject to protection from employer intervention is inappropriate. Rather, we should be looking towards broader protection of all workers' affiliative behaviour and concerted action which has yet to be supported by a trade union. Given the decline in trade union membership, the increase in a representation gap, and the growth in spontaneous action by groups of workers not able to access trade union representation,[102] this seems vital to worker voice. In this way, workers' capabilities for voice could be supported and built up, rather than abandoned where they do not fit a particular state-authorized mould.[103]

The difficulty with human rights litigation is that it is often defensive, rather than proactive.[104] For these reasons, we might want to see greater recognition of a potential role for collective worker voice in the regulation of workplace arrangements for employer policies regarding ICT. Indeed, this would seem to be consistent with what the ICO has identified as 'good practice' under the current Employment Practices Code under the DPA.[105] It would also tally with Ford's attempt to promote a procedural dimension to privacy rights 'imposing duties to provide information to workers and, above all, collective consultation in relation to forms of surveillance regardless of whether or not private life is engaged...'.[106] It may well be that collective engagement by workers with these issues, whether by a trade union or more spontaneous forms of workplace organization, may offer a different perspective on the appropriate treatment of ICT in the workplace to that of human rights organizations, which have less interest in the on-going success of the business of the employer.[107] Contrary to common assumptions, there may be a win-win scenario possible for the 'good' employer which enables capability.

Conclusion

This chapter has examined various legal dimensions of the ways in which ICT can inhibit and encourage worker voice. My suggestion is that there has been a legal preoccupation with setting limits on the ways in which employers can use ICT to constrain worker voice, while assuming that some constraint will be legitimate insofar as it protects employers' commercial and reputational interests. Legitimacy has often been determined according to rather questionable treatment of 'consent' and 'expectation', imported from

[102] Anna Pollert, 'Spheres of Collectivism: Group Action and Perspectives on Trade Unions among the Low-Paid Unorganized with Problems at Work' (2010) 34(1) Capital and Class 115.

[103] See Bogg and Estlund, this volume.

[104] For caution expressed in this regard, see Kevin Kolben, 'Labour Rights as Human Rights?' (2009–10) 50 Virginia Journal of International Law 449.

[105] See n 63.

[106] Ford 154–5 (n 36).

[107] Tel Aviv Labour Court 10121/06 *Issakov-Inbar v Ministry of Commerce, Industry and Employment, Commissioner for Women's Work* [2007] Israel; appealed to National Labour Court 90/08 312/08 06 *Issakov-Inbar et al v Ministry of Commerce, Industry and Employment, Commissioner for Women's Work* [2007] Israel; discussed in Guy Mundlak, 'Human Rights and Labour Rights: Why the Two Tracks Don't Meet?' (2012–13) 34 CLLPJ 217.

common law into the application of legislative standards. Nevertheless, it remains possible to improve upon the scope of current worker privacy by reference to human rights norms and the imposition of a requirement of 'proportionality'.

A further suggestion offered here is that we should look to move beyond negative protection of workers' liberty towards positive promotion of workers' capability for voice. This could, for example, lead to enactment of more proactive legislative measures aimed at securing worker access to communication and other electronic systems. Moreover, a human rights approach could entail recognition, not only of workers' rights to privacy, but also their freedom of speech and freedom of association. This could enable workers to communicate between themselves, to affiliate, and to act in combination.

23

Can Worker Voice Strike Back? Law and the Decline and Uncertain Future of Strikes

Eric Tucker[1]

Introduction

The relation between worker voice and strikes is a long and intimate one. For most of the past 200 years, the withdrawal of labour has been the principal, perhaps, quintessential expression of collective worker voice.[2] This was true whether workers were organized on a craft or an industrial basis, although the pattern of organization certainly affected the form that strikes took.[3] The frequency and length of strikes varied considerably over time and place, but the strike remained the weapon of choice if a weapon was needed to achieve common workplace objectives.[4] However, the venerable age of this practice does not guarantee its continuation. Like a roof with a slow leak, one day a storm may come and suddenly the roof collapses, its supporting structure irreparably weakened, the victim of rot gone undetected for too long. Have we reached this point with strikes? In most advanced capitalist countries, we have witnessed the collapse of the strike over the last few decades. Have the structural and legal conditions that supported strikes eroded so thoroughly that exhortations to revive the strike are as futile as planning to raise a roof without first making sure there is a structure in place that can support it?

The purpose of this chapter is not to provide a definitive answer to the question of the future of strikes as the quintessential expression of collective worker voice, but

[1] I would like to thank the editors of this volume, Tonia Novitz and Alan Bogg for their helpful comments on an earlier draft, as well as Shae McCrystal for her comments on the Australian law. I also want to thank Osgoode Hall Law School students Jeffrey Rochwerg and Njeri Damali Campbell for research and editorial assistance. Of course, I am responsible for any errors, infelicities, etc.

[2] Peter Rachleff, 'Is the Strike Dead? An Historical Look at the Future' (2003) 12(2) New Labor Forum 87. For a discussion of earlier forms of collective labour protest, including rioting and machine breaking, see Paul K. Edwards, *Conflict at Work* (Basil Blackwell, 1986) ch. 4. Edwards makes the important analytic point that forms of protest are linked to changing relations of production, so that strikes should not be seen simply as a 'drift to modernity' (112). This insight has important implications for discussions of the future of collective action, to which we will return in the last section of the chapter.

[3] Joe Burns, *Reviving the Strike* (Ig Publishing, 2012) 14–17.

[4] The incidence of strikes is not a good measure of the strength of worker voice. More important is the plausibility of the threat of the strike. Thus in a world in which workers' organization is strong, employers may find it is in their self-interest to cooperate with labour and make concessions, rather than to fight. See Erik Olin Wright, 'Working-Class Power, Capitalist-Class Interests, and Class Compromise' (2000) 105 American Journal of Sociology 957. It is very unlikely, however, that the current decline in strikes reflects growing working-class strength. For example, union densities are declining as is labour's share of national income. For Canadian data, see Gary Sran et al., *Unions Matter* (Canadian Foundation for Labour Rights, 2013). For US data, see Fred Magdoff and John Bellamy Foster, 'Class War and Labor's Declining Share' (2013) 64 Monthly Review 1.

rather to contribute toward a discussion of it by providing an overview of the literature in three strike-related areas: recent data on the incidence of strikes; an examination of the role that law plays in influencing strike incidence; and speculation on the future of collective worker resistance.

However, before launching into these topics, it will be helpful by way of introduction to spend a little time identifying the ways in which industrial relations scholars have connected worker voice to strike activity.[5] The most frequent and popular view of strikes is as an economic weapon that enables workers to enjoy some countervailing power and make collective bargaining meaningful. The absence of a right to strike, or more generally, the absence of an effective threat to collectively withdraw labour and put economic pressure on employers, is said to transform collective bargaining into 'collective begging'.[6] In Canada, the Woods Task Force, which in 1967 articulated the underlying principles of the post-World War II industrial relations system, stated that strikes are 'an indispensable part of the Canadian industrial relations system'[7] and that '[t]he acceptance of collective bargaining carries with it a concomitant recognition of the right to invoke the economic sanction of the strike and the lockout'.[8]

The connection between voice and strikes, however, is not just limited to the achievement of better terms and conditions of employment. Strikes are often viewed as a means for workers to exercise democratic voice. Thus, the Woods Task Force asserted that strikes had become 'a part of the whole democratic system'.[9] What they meant was that trade unionism contributed to the development of industrial democracy, the ability of workers to participate in workplace governance, and not just the determination of terms and conditions of employment. Of course, the forms that industrial democracy could take varied considerably, but in the North American context, where almost any form of codetermination or social dialogue was beyond the pale, collective bargaining and its associated institutions were the principal vehicle for worker participation in workplace governance.[10]

[5] For an excellent overview, see Tonia Novitz, *International and European Protection of the Right to Strike* (OUP, 2003) 39–73.

[6] The origin of the term is unknown. Its earliest use, identified through a search of Google Books Ngram Reader, was in 1921. It was popularized by an article in Time magazine, 'U.S. At War: No Collective Begging' *Time* (25 September 1944) quoting a disgruntled union member opposed to the wartime no strike pledge who declared, 'Hell, we haven't even got collective begging, let alone collective bargaining.' Barrett, Grant, 'Collective Begging' (Online Dictionary) <http://www.waywordradio.org/collective_begging_1/> accessed 16 September 2013. Its use declined in the 1950s, but attained even greater popularity in the 1960s and '70s as public-sector unions fought to obtain formal collective bargaining rights and the right to strike. See Google Ngram Viewer, 'Collective Begging' <http://books.google.com/ngrams/graph?content=collective+begging&year_start=1800&year_end=2000&corpus=15&smoothing=3&share> accessed 16 September 2013. (I am indebted to Bob Sink for providing me with this link.) The term is now generally used to describe collective bargaining schemes in which workers lack an effective right to strike. For example, see Daniel Pollitt, 'McKay Radio: Turn it Off, Tune it Out' (1991) 25 University of San Francisco Law Review 295, 297 ('In sum, without the right to strike, collective bargaining denigrates into collective begging.'). *NLRB v Mackay Radio & Telegraph Co.* 304 US 333 (1938) allowed employers to hire permanent replacement workers during a strike.

[7] Report of the Task Force on Labour Relations, 'Canadian Industrial Relations' PCO (1968) [39], [408].

[8] 'Canadian Industrial Relations' [605] (n 7).

[9] 'Canadian Industrial Relations' [608] (n 7).

[10] Nelson Lichtenstein and Howell J. Harris (eds), *Industrial Democracy in America* (CUP, 1993).

State policy, however, never fully embraced this goal, and in particular was deeply opposed to permitting strikes as a vehicle for the expression of worker voice over day to day workplace governance issues.[11] In the Wagner Act model, grievance arbitration was to be the mechanism for resolving these disputes and strikes during the life of the collective agreement were prohibited, either by legislation (Canada) or by the express or implied terms of the collective agreement (US). More recently Australia and New Zealand have also prohibited mid-term strikes. However, prohibitions on strikes do not always stop workers from engaging in unauthorized strikes to protest against managerial decision-making and, perhaps, official union inaction. Indeed, there have been times when so-called wildcat strikes were quite frequent and viewed with alarm by those who thought of institutionalized collective bargaining primarily as a means for maintaining industrial order.[12] In the UK, where strikes during the life of a collective agreement were not illegal, workers faced fewer impediments to engaging in direct action to express their dissatisfaction with management actions. Notably, most strikes before 1980 were not officially supported by trade unions. The situation under current UK law is quite different. Mid-term strikes are still not prohibited, but like other strikes they must be 'official' if participating workers are to be immune from the threat of dismissal for the protected period. Where strike action is 'unofficial' the employment tribunal has no jurisdiction to deal with an unfair dismissal claim by the dismissed striker. The result is that workers participating in unofficial strikes can be selectively dismissed. It is also important to note that there are significant hurdles to making strikes official.[13]

A related but far more controversial question is the link between strikes and political democracy and, in particular, the role of strikes aimed at influencing government policies. Leaving aside the question of strikes aimed at overthrowing governments, the major objection to political strikes that seek to influence government policies is that economic pressure may disrupt the 'normal' legislative and political process. The difficulty with that argument is that it fails to take into account the ways that capital routinely influences government policy by the threat to withdraw investment if business friendly policies are not pursued.[14] The fact that many individual capitals can be gathered within a corporation, which is a distinct legal person, may mask its collective character, but it does not change it.[15] Moreover, the boundaries between a political strike and a collective bargaining strike become blurred in the context of the public sector where

[11] Josiah B. Lambert, *If the Workers took a Notion: The Right to Strike and American Political Development* (Cornell University Press, 2005).

[12] For Canada, see Linda Briskin, 'Public Sector Militancy, Feminization, and Employer Aggression' in Sjaak van der Velden et al. (eds), *Strikes Around the World* (Aksant, 2007) 86, 95–6. (Overall, between 1960 and 2004, 18 per cent of strikes were wildcats. At their peak in 1974, 40 per cent of all strikes were wildcats.) Official statistics on wildcat strikes are not kept in the US. For a discussion, see Rick Fantasia, *Cultures of Solidarity* (University of California Press, 1988) 59–65. For the UK, see Dave Lyddon, 'From Strike Wave to Strike Drought' in *Strikes* (see earlier in this note) 338. In the UK, there is some evidence that younger workers engage in collective action to resolve workplace complaints, but this does not seem to include strikes. See Anna Pollert, 'Spheres of Collectivism: Group Action and Perspectives on Trade Unions Among The Low-Paid Unorganized With Problems at Work' (2010) 34 Capital & Class 115.

[13] Pascale Lorber and Tonia Novitz, *Industrial Relations Law in the UK* (Intersentia, 2012) 113.

[14] For an insightful discussion, see Novitz 54–64 (n 5).

[15] Claus Offe and Helmut Wiesenthal, 'Two Logics of Collective Action: Theoretical Notes on Social Class and Organizational Form' (1980) 1 Political Power and Social Theory 67.

'ordinary' government legislation and executive action, let alone 'special' legislation targeting particular negotiations, so pervasively influences bargaining outcomes.[16] The Woods Task Force anticipated this situation and seemed resigned to the inevitability of political strikes.[17] These arguments, however, have had little legal traction. In Canada, political strikes are almost always unlawful and, indeed, at one time were liable to be criminally prosecuted as seditious conspiracies.[18] In New Zealand and Australia political strikes are unlawful and participants are subject to various penalties.[19] In the United Kingdom political strikers lose their statutory immunity from unfair dismissal and unions may become liable for economic torts, although there is a very small chance this may change as a result of the UK's international obligations under the ILO and the European Convention on Human Rights. The situation is more ambiguous in the United States.[20]

Finally, strikes have been viewed not merely as a manifestation of collective worker voice, but as an activity that produces higher levels of class consciousness, organization and, ultimately, power. This Marxist notion views consciousness as the product of human activity, so that although workers' interests may be structurally in conflict with those of capital, it is through the process of confrontation that workers are transformed and become a class for themselves.[21] The dialectical relationship between social activity and consciousness, of course, is not uniquely linked to participation in strikes, but in a world in which the repertoire of confrontation practices was built around the strike, their disappearance is deeply concerning and raises pressing questions of whether the strike can be revived and if not whether new repertoires are in the making. We will return to these questions later in this chapter, but next we turn to evidence on the extent of strike activity.

The Withering Away of the Strike?

Anyone familiar with the literature on strike activity should be reluctant to use the subtitle 'The Withering Away of the Strike' lest they suffer the same fate as functionalist industrial relations scholars in the 1950s who viewed the decline in strikes they witnessed as evidence for their theory that industrial conflict would decline in advanced industrialized societies

[16] Leo Panitch and Donald Swartz, *From Consent to Coercion: The Assault on Trade Union Freedoms* (Garamond Press, 2003).

[17] 'The political strike cannot be done away with by legislation; and it is a phenomenon that might become more common as governments become increasingly involved in economic and social planning as well as in industrial relations.' '*Canadian Industrial Relations*' [610] (n 7).

[18] *Domglas Ltd* [1976] OLRB Rep, October 569 (Ontario Labour Relations Board Reporter); Reinhold Kramer and Tom Mitchell, *When the State Trembled* (University of Toronto Press, 2010).

[19] Brian Brooks, 'Australia' in R. Blanpain (ed.), *International Encyclopedia for Labour Law and Industrial Relations* (University of Leuven, 2009) 233; Gordon Anderson, 'New Zealand' in *Blanpain* (see earlier in this note) 206–7.

[20] Keith Ewing and John Hendy, *Days of Action: The Legality of Protest Strikes Against Government Cuts* (Institute for Employment Rights, 2011); Seth Kupferberg, 'Political Strikes, Labor Law, and Democratic Rights' (1985) 71 Virginia Law Review 685.

[21] Fantasia 3 (n 12). This is not to imply that structural processes are disconnected from cultural ones and that struggle emerges either spontaneously or under material conditions that impede social action. Rather, the emphasis is on their dialectical interaction and the possibility of vicious or virtuous circles.

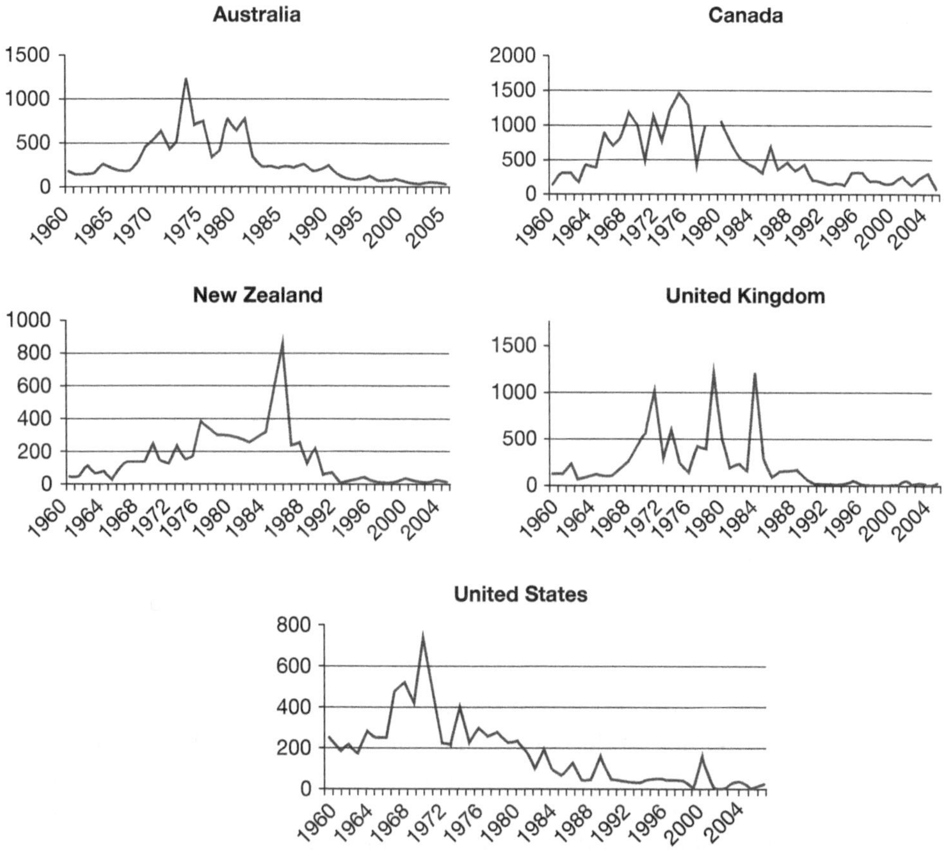

Figure 23.1 Days lost to disputes per thousand workers

Sources: van der Velden nn 12, 111, 152, 194, 365; Domenic Hale, 'International Comparisons of Labour Disputes in 2006' (2008) 2 ELMR 32.

which had become more adept at containing, redirecting, and controlling the sources and manifestations of unrest.[22] That prediction, of course, turned out to be spectacularly wrong soon after it was made, as a massive strike wave hit industrialized countries in the late 1960s and early 1970s. The discussion of recent strike trends here, therefore, disavows any broader claim about its significance for the future. Rather, Figure 23.1 simply presents, for the convenience of readers, previously published data on the decline in strike activity in the five common law countries covered by this project from 1960 to 2006.[23]

The strike data are, well, striking, but to make the evidence of decline even clearer Figure 23.2 presents the trend lines for the five countries. Regardless of the starting point, there is a convergence toward quiescence, bordering on disappearance, a trend noted by Shalev in the early 1990s.[24]

[22] Clark Kerr et al., *Industrialism and Industrial Man: The Problems of Labor and Management in Industrial Growth* (OUP, 1964) 184.

[23] van der Velden (n 12); John Goddard, 'What Happened to Strikes?' (2011) 49 British Journal of Industrial Relations (Brit J Ind Relat) 282.

[24] Michael Shalev, 'The Resurgence of Labour Quiescence' in Mario Regini (ed.), *The Future of Labour Movements* (Sage, 1992).

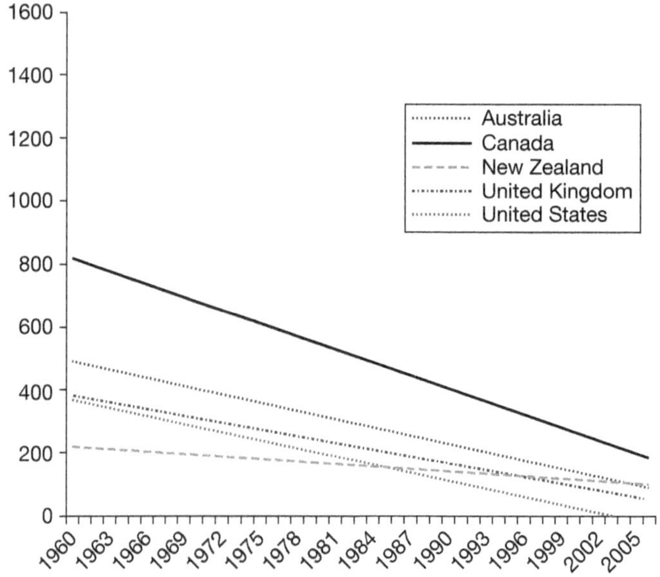

Figure 23.2 Trend lines

We will turn to discuss the reasons for this development, but first I want to explore whether national statistics hide within them distortions or variations that might be notable. A brief overview of this kind cannot undertake a review of each of the five cases, so I will only examine the Canadian data. In particular, I want to consider whether the declining strike rate is an artifact of the decline in union membership and whether there are different trends for public and private-sector strike rates.

Figure 23.3 presents a comparison of the strike rate calculated per 1,000 employees and the strike rate per 1,000 union members. If the decline was simply a function of the decline in union density, then one would expect the union member strike rate to remain flat while the employee strike late declined. However, the figure shows that the union member strike rate is declining more rapidly than the employee strike rate, indicating that the decline in union density explains very little of the total decline in strike activity.

Figure 23.4 compares changes in strike rates for public and private-sector workers. Given the great difference in the trajectory of union densities in these two sectors, with public-sector density remaining high, while private-sector union density is declining, it might have been thought that the public-sector strike rate would not decline as rapidly as the private-sector strike rate, especially given the findings of previous studies that strike activity varied with union membership.[25] But this is not the case for Canada over the period covered by this chart (1979–2007). While for the most part the strike rate of public-sector workers has been higher than that of private-sector workers, and more uneven because of the size of particular strikes, the strike rate is declining at about the same rate as it is for private-sector workers.[26]

[25] For example, see Shalev 118 (n 24).

[26] But see Morley Gunderson and Frank Reid, 'Public Sector Strikes in Canada' in Gene Swimmer and Mark Thompson (eds), *Public Sector Collective Bargaining in Canada* (IRC Press/Industrial Relations

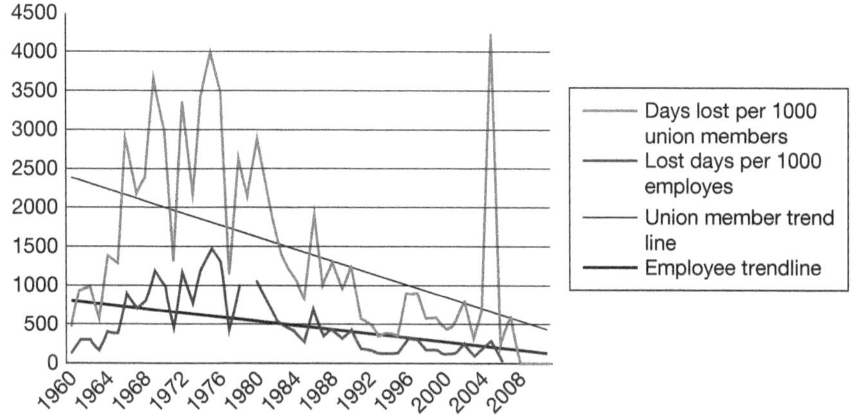

Figure 23.3 Comparison of strike rate per 1,000 union members and per 1,000 employees

Sources: Number of Unionized Workers from Historical Statistics of Canada, 2nd edn, F.H. Leacy, ed. (Ottawa: Statistics Canada, 1983), Table E175-177 (1960–1975); Statistics Canada, CANSM Table 279-006, (1976–1995): Table 282-0078 (1997–present). Days Lost Due to Strikes from: Briskin (n 12).

Of course, if we did a more refined set of sectoral trend lines, we might discover some differences, but the overall picture is unlikely to change. In Canada, and probably in the other jurisdictions, union members are striking less frequently now than they have in the past and the rate of public-sector strikes, despite higher union densities, is declining about as rapidly as the rate of private-sector strike. In short, the data suggest that the decline is real and pervasive.

The Causes of Labour Quiescence: What's Labour Law Got to do with It?

The challenge of explaining patterns of strike activity have intrigued numerous scholars. At certain moments, particular theories seemed to have a high order of explanatory power, but subsequent events defeated their predictions, sending scholars scurrying to find new theories that better fit the emerging data. For example, a consensus had emerged that there was an association between strike incidence and the business cycle.[27] Later, institutional factors came to be more heavily weighed, focusing initially on patterns of working-class mobilization and the extent to which labour was incorporated into political institutions. Yet this explanation too was found wanting a little over a decade after it was published.[28] Hence caution must be exercised by anyone offering to explain the pattern we have observed here.

The approach in this chapter builds on work by Michael Shalev, James Piazza, and Robert Brym. It starts from the proposition that there are structural factors that

Centre, Queen's University, ON 1995) 135. Their calculation is based on strike days as a percentage of days worked and their data run to 1991.

[27] For example, Albert Rees, 'Industrial Conflict and Business Fluctuations' (1952) 60 Journal of Political Economy 371.

[28] Walter Korpi and Michael Shalev, 'Strikes, Power and Politics in the Western Nations' (1980) 1 Political Power and Social Theory 301; Shalev 110 (n 24).

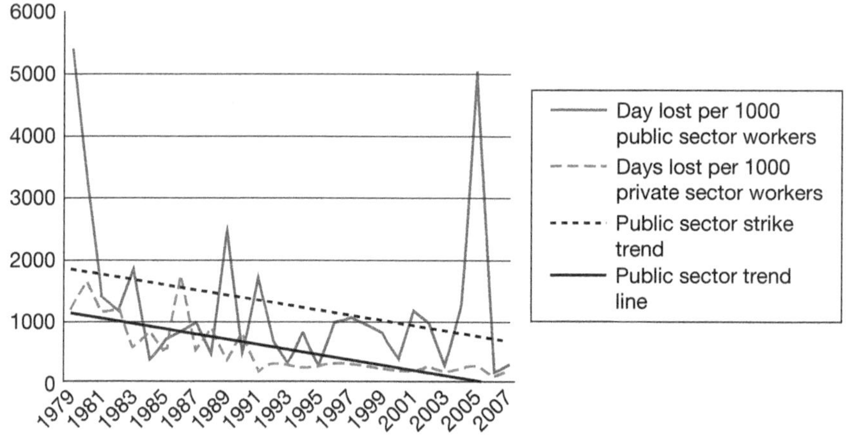

Figure 23.4 Public and private-sector strike rates per 1,000 workers

Sources: Days lost due to strikes by sector provided by Robert Hebdon; Public and Private Sector Employment from Historical Labour Force Review, 2010.

significantly shape the environment for strikes but that institutional factors mediate their effects to a degree.[29] At a structural level, the focus is on the ensemble of economic, political, cultural, and ideological arrangements that constitute a social structure of accumulation.[30] The dominant shift that has occurred since World War II is the shift from the social democratic or Keynesian welfare state to neoliberalism, which David Harvey has characterized as 'a *political* project to re-establish the conditions for capital accumulation and to restore the power of economic elites'.[31] A key strategy of this project was to strip away the buffers that protected workers from being fully exposed to capitalist market ordering. Internationally, this was achieved through globalization, a process that opened up national economies to greater international competition, while domestically the social wage, welfare provision, and other entitlements were scaled back to increase the labour market dependency of the vast majority of the population. At the same time, employers engaged in large scale workplace restructuring, relocating production in the global south, downsizing local operations, outsourcing into global production networks, substituting contractors for employees, making greater use of temporary employees, etc.[32] Although there are significant differences in the paths of the jurisdictions under consideration here, they are all operating within this global, neoliberal structural shift.

In the face of these challenges, the capacities organized labour had developed in the post-World War II era began to erode and with it their ability to buffer workers against

[29] Shalev (n 24); James A. Piazza, 'Globalizing Quiescence: Globalization, Union Density and Strikes in 15 Industrialized Countries' (2005) 26 Economic and Industrial Democracy 289; Robert Brym, 'Affluence, Power, and Strikes in Canada, 1973–2005' in Edward Grabb and Neil Guppy (eds), *Social Inequality in Canada: Patterns, Problems, Policies*, 5th edn (Pearson Prentice Hall, 2009).

[30] See generally Terrence McDonagh, Michael Reich, and David M. Kotz (eds), *Contemporary Capitalism and its Crises* (CUP, 2010).

[31] David Harvey, *A Brief History of Neoliberalism* (OUP, 2005) 19 (emphasis in the original).

[32] Guy Standing, *The Precariat* (Bloomsbury, 2011); Leah Vosko (ed.), *Precarious Employment* (McGill-Queen's University Press, 2006).

these changes. To a great extent, unions adopted a defensive posture, desperately trying to hold on to past gains often by accepting concessions, such as two-tier wages that protected existing members but put new hires on a lower wage scale with limited prospects for ever catching up. Resort to traditional repertoires of resistance, whether in the form of strikes, as we have seen, or other tactics such as work-to-rule campaigns and plant occupations became less frequent. Perhaps even more fundamentally, neoliberalism involved a cultural revolution that undermined the 'infrastructures of dissent' that had sustained the limited forms of union and working-class solidarity in an earlier era. The ability to imagine it was possible to challenge the neoliberal order was being lost.[33]

Labour law can be productively viewed as a mediating institution that can either buffer workers against these structural changes or enable them so that they bear more heavily on workers. For example, the law regulating strikes could be changed to prohibit replacement workers in the hope that it will help offset the unfavourable circumstances facing organized labour or strikes could be prohibited or picketing rights restricted to undermine the capacity of unionized workers to resist their greater exposure to market forces. As well, labour law may remain fairly stable, but because the environment in which it operates has changed dramatically, the ability of workers to strike successfully diminishes over time.

There are three dimensions of labour law that are most directly involved in this analysis. First, there is the freedom to strike, which refers to whether and in what circumstances strikes are legally permissible. Second, there is the right to strike, which refers to provisions in the law that protect the exercise of the freedom to strike, such as protection against dismissal or a right to reinstatement.[34] Finally, there is the law of industrial action that determines what actions striking workers can take to make their strike effective. In the section that follows, I offer a brief and preliminary assessment of the ways in which the law regulating strikes has operated as a mediating variable in the countries covered by this project.

Canada

It is important to note that most collective bargaining is governed by provincial law and so there are many collective bargaining statutes, although at least with the private sector all legislation is based on the Wagner Act model, which imposes significant restrictions on the freedom to strike. Most notably, recognition and mid-term strikes are prohibited and replaced by an administrative recognition procedure and binding grievance

[33] Sam Gindin, 'Rethinking Unions, Registering Socialism' in Leo Panitch, Gregory Albo, and Vivek Chibber (eds), *Socialist Register 2013: The Question of Strategy* (Merlin Press, 2013) 26; David McNally, *Global Slump: The Economics and Politics of Crisis and Resistance* (Fernwood Publishing, 2011); Alan Sears, 'The End of 20th-Century Socialism?' (Summer 2007) 61 New Socialist Magazine 5.

[34] Here I am drawing on Hohfeld's distinction between freedoms and rights, which I believe is helpful because it enables us to more precisely describe the way strikes are regulated by law. So when I say there is a freedom to strike I mean that the government and employers have no right to prohibit workers from striking or stop them from doing so. When I refer to a right to strike I mean that governments and employers have a duty not to retaliate or take other adverse action against striking workers or their unions for engaging in strikes. See Wesley Newcomb Hohfeld, 'Some Fundamental Legal Conceptions Applied in Judicial Reasoning' (1913) 23 Yale Law Journal (Yale LJ) 28.

arbitration respectively. Generally, strikes are only legal after recognition when no collective agreement is in force. But even then, there are procedural requirements that must be met, including completion of a conciliation process and the taking of a strike vote. Unlawful strikes can result in serious penalties for both the union and participating members.[35] Apart from restrictions on the freedom to strike, the law also protects striking workers in two ways. First, it provides that strikers retain their status as employees for the purposes of labour statutes and, second, workers have a right to return to their jobs within a certain time (e.g. six months). Only Quebec and British Columbia ban temporary replacement workers.[36] Finally, the law of picketing has become somewhat less restrictive over the last 30 years or so as some provinces have limited the availability of labour injunctions and the Supreme Court of Canada altered the common law so that secondary action is not per se tortious.[37]

The major change to private-sector collective bargaining legislation has been the abolition of card-count certifications in most provinces, resulting in a near exclusive reliance on certification elections. While this change does not directly affect the freedom to strike, studies have demonstrated that it has contributed to a decline in union density, which would undermine bargaining strength and make unions more reluctant to strike. Dachis and Hebdon found that the introduction of mandatory secret ballots results in a decrease in strike frequency, but that the effect is weakly statistically significant and so at best would explain only a small part of the decline.[38] More generally, it is fair to conclude that changes to private collective bargaining law have not been a significant cause of the decline in private-sector strike activity, but that in the context of less favourable structural conditions private-sector workers are less able to successfully use the limited freedom and right to strike and picket that the law provides.

The story is different for the public sector, where government intervention in strikes has increased over time, even though the baseline was more restrictive than in the private sector. When public-sector collective bargaining legislation was first enacted in the 1960s, not only did the law impose the same limits on the freedom to strike that were imposed in the private sector, but there were additional ones as well, including absolute prohibitions and essential service designations where the public interest could be adversely affected. Where strikes were prohibited or severely limited, binding interest arbitration by a neutral third party was the most commonly substituted dispute resolution mechanism. However, as Keynesianism began to be supplanted by neoliberalism, governments found that the already restrictive public-sector collective bargaining regime was not restrictive enough and they frequently imposed further limits on the

[35] For an overview, see Donald D. Carter et al., *Labour Law in Canada*, 5th edn (Butterworths, 2002); Judy Fudge and Eric Tucker, 'The Freedom to Strike in Canada: A Brief Legal History' (2010) 15 Canadian Labour & Employment Law Journal 333.

[36] Quebec since 1978 and British Columbia since 1993. Ontario had a partial ban on temporary replacements from 1993 to 1995.

[37] For an overview, see George W. Adams, *Canadian Labour Law*, 2nd edn (Canada Law Book, Aurora 2003) [11.720]; *R.W.D.S.U., Local 558 v Pepsi-Cola Canada Beverages (West) Ltd* 2002 SCC 8. Most recently, the Supreme Court held that privacy legislation restricting the freedom of trade unions to record people crossing the picket line was an unconstitutional limit on freedom of expression. They emphasized the importance of picketing as expression in the labour context: *Alberta (Information and Privacy Commissioner) v United Food and Commercial Workers, Local 401* 2013 SCC 62.

[38] Adams 13 (n 37).

freedom to strike in a number of ways. There has been increasing use of ad hoc measures, like back-to-work legislation ending strikes or wage restraint legislation that made strikes illegal either by outright prohibitions or by extending the term of existing collective agreements so that a strike would violate the ban on mid-term strikes. As well, governments have also expanded essential service designations, which deprive more workers of the freedom to strike and restricted or in some cases banned interest arbitration when strikes are prohibited. Leo Panitch and Donald Swartz have aptly characterized the sum total of these changes as 'permanent exceptionalism'.[39]

There is little empirical evidence on the combined impact of these interventions on strike incidence. Dachis and Hebdon find that an essential service designation does not significantly affect the likelihood of a strike and that following back-to-work legislation it is more likely that government will intervene in the next contract.[40] Presumably, it can be safety assumed that further restrictions on the freedom to strike will negatively affect strike frequency. Overall, it would be fair to surmise that changes in public-sector labour law make a marginal independent contribution to the decline in public-sector strike frequency. They are part of a larger government strategy of imposing public-sector wage restraint and creating an environment in which public and private-sector workers' expectations about the potential benefits of a strike will be diminished.

United States

The story in the United States is perhaps best understood as one in which the erosion of labour rights in the decades after the 1935 Wagner Act removed important institutional buffers that became increasingly significant in the late 1970s with the turn to neoliberalism, as the non-union employers more fiercely resisted the unionization of their employees and unionized employers fought to weaken the collective agreements that bound them. The result was a sharp decline in private-sector collective bargaining density and strike incidence.

It is notable that the Wagner Act imposed fewer restrictions on strikes than the Canadian law that was modelled on it. The power of federal courts to issue labour injunctions in non-violent strikes, including secondary action, was removed in 1932 by the Norris-LaGuardia Act.[41] The Wagner Act itself famously protected the right to engage in concerted activity in section 7 and section 13 specified that nothing in the Act should be 'construed so as either to interfere with or impede or diminish in any way the right to strike or to affect the limitations or qualifications on that right'.[42] Neither mandatory conciliation nor strike votes were stipulated as preconditions of strike legality.

[39] Panitch and Swartz (n 16). More generally, see Michael Thompson and Pierre Jalette, 'Public Sector Collective Bargaining' in Morley Gunderson and Daphne Taras (eds), *Canadian Labour and Employment Relations*, 6th edn (Pearson, Addison, Wesley, 2009); Joseph B. Rose, 'Public Sector Collective Bargaining: From Retrenchment to Consolidation' (2004) 59 Industrial Relations 271. In late 2013, the Alberta government substituted unilateral government imposition of contract terms for interest arbitration in the public sector and made more punitive the strike prohibition. See Bill 45, Public Sector Services Continuation Act (awaiting proclamation) and Bill 46, Public Service Salary Restraint Act, S.A. 2013, P-43.5.

[40] Adams 12, 17 (n 37).

[41] Michael H. LeRoy and John H. Johnson IV, 'Death by Lethal Injunction: National Emergency Strikes Under the Taft-Hartley Act and the Moribund Right to Strike' (2001) 43 Arizona Law Review 63, 92.

[42] 29 U.S.C. § § 151–69.

Despite the Act's broad statutory language, legislation and labour board and judicial decisions began to restrict the freedom to strike in the decades after its enactment.[43] The 1947 Taft-Hartley Act prohibited jurisdictional strikes, wildcat strikes, strikes by federal government employees and, most importantly, secondary action. It required unions and employers to give 80 days' notice before striking or locking out and authorized the President to intervene in strikes that imperilled the national health. This included the power to appoint of a board of inquiry and, more importantly, authorized the Attorney General to seek an injunction while the board sought to resolve the dispute. Finally, the law strengthened the powers of the National Labor Relations Board (NLRB) to enjoin strikes and gave employers the right to sue for damages resulting from secondary action or from strikes in breach of the collective agreement.[44]

The United States Supreme Court (USSC) also played a crucial role in restricting the right and freedom to strike. The Wagner Act neither prohibited mid-term strikes nor required binding interest arbitration to resolve disagreements over the interpretation and application of the collective agreements. While many collective agreements contained no-strike clauses, it was difficult to enforce them until 1957 when the USSC interpreted a provision of the Taft-Hartley Act as authorizing federal courts to enjoin strikes where the agreement contained a no-strike pledge. Three years later, in the so-called Steelworkers' Trilogy, the USSC ruled that even in the absence of a no-strike clause, there was a legal presumption that mid-term strikes were prohibited and disputes were to be resolved by arbitration. The court later held that unions that breached the collective agreement could be sued and that a strike in violation of the express or implied no-strike pledge could be enjoined, notwithstanding the Norris-LaGuardia Act.[45]

Another limitation on the right to strike developed out of the distinction between mandatory and permissive bargaining issues, a distinction not found in statute but created by the NLRB. Its power to make this distinction was upheld by the USSC in 1958. Mandatory issues are ones that the parties must bargain over if one of them wishes and can be bargained to impasse while permissive ones, which relate to matters that are at the core of entrepreneurial control, are not subject to the duty to bargain in good faith and cannot be bargained to impasse. As a result, unions cannot legally strike over crucial issues, such as technological change and changes in the production process, and the tendency over time has been for the scope of permissive bargaining issues to grow.[46]

The most significant judicial decision affecting strikes, however, has been the 1938 judgment in *Mackay Radio*, in which the USSC held that employers had the right to hire permanent replacement workers. Initially, the use of permanent replacements was infrequent, largely limited to the southern United States where opposition to

[43] Karl Klare, 'Judicial Deradicalization of the Wagner Act and the Origins of Modern Legal Consciousness, 1937–1941' (1978) 62 Minnesota Law Review 265; James Gray Pope, 'How American Workers Lost the Right to Strike, and Other Tales' (2004) 103 Michigan Law Review 544; Holly J. McCammon, 'Legal Limits on Labor Militancy: U.S. Labor Law and the Right to Strike since the New Deal' (1990) 37 Social Problems 206; Burns ch. 3 (n 3).

[44] LeRoy and Johnson (n 41).

[45] Katherine Stone, 'The Post-War Paradigm in American Labor Law' (1981) 90 Yale LJ 1509, 1523.

[46] Thomas T. Crouch, 'The Viability of Distinguishing between Mandatory and Permissive Subjects of Bargaining in a Cooperative Setting: In Search of Industrial Peace' (1988) 41 Vanderbilt Law Review 577.

unionization remained fierce. This began to change in the 1970s as employers more aggressively opposed unions, but it was after President Reagan ordered the hiring of permanent replacement workers in the 1981 strike by the Professional Air Traffic Controllers' Organization (PATCO) that the use of replacements became more widespread. At the same time, the Supreme Court issued a number of decisions that provided greater protection to permanent replacements.[47] The combination of low union density, weak bargaining power and a legal framework that provides striking workers with no buffers against hyper-competitive labour markets understandably has made unionized workers reluctant to collectively withdraw their labour.

With private-sector unionism weakened, politicians have increasingly focused attention on limiting public-sector unions and collective bargaining. The focus here, however, has not been on strikes, since the freedom of public-sector workers to strike was already quite limited. Rather, most changes in public-sector labour law have aimed to give government greater control over interest arbitration, the commonly provided dispute resolution mechanism when strikes are prohibited, so that they can impose wage restraint.[48]

In sum, the right to strike was incrementally eroded in the decades following the enactment of the Norris-LaGuardia and Wagner Acts. The cumulative potential of these changes to break strikes was not immediately apparent until the 1970s when employer resistance to collective bargaining increased dramatically. The union-avoidance industry, which grew to meet the demand, was able to exploit the law and raise the cost of strikes to unionized workers so steeply that the tactic often appears suicidal.

United Kingdom

Legal change has also played a significant role in reducing the incidence of strikes in the United Kingdom, but unlike in the United States it did not precede the neoliberal turn but rather was an expression of it. The starting point of UK strike law is also quite different. For most of the twentieth century, the law was based on a statutory immunity from the common law, which in the nineteenth century had constructed legal doctrines that exposed striking workers and unions to extensive legal liabilities for the harms caused by strikes. This approach is traced back to the 1906 Trade Disputes Act (TDA), which immunized trade unions taking industrial action in contemplation or furtherance of a trade dispute from tort liability. This produced a broad freedom to strike.

[47] *NLRB v Mackay Radio & Telegraph Co.*, 304 US 333 (1938); Michael H. LeRoy, 'Regulating Employer Use of Permanent Striker Replacements: Empirical Analysis of NLRA and RLA Strikes 1935–1991' (1995) 16 Berkeley Journal of Employment and Labour Law 169; John Logan, 'Permanent Replacements and the End of Labor's "Only True Weapon"' (2008) 74 International Labor and Working-Class History 171; Joseph A. McCartin, *Collision Course: Ronald Reagan, the Air Traffic Controllers and the Strike that Changed America* (OUP, 2011) and J. McCartin, 'Approaching Extinction: The Decline of Strikes in the United States, 1960–2005' in van der Velden 144 (n 12) ('most important single event in determining the subsequent fate of strikes in the US'); Matthew Finkin, 'Labor Policy and the Enervation of the Economic Strike' (1990) 3 University of Illinois Law Review 547.

[48] Joseph E. Slater, 'Attacks on Public-Sector Bargaining as Attacks on Employee Voice: A (Partial) Defense of the Wagner Act Model' (2013) Osgoode Hall Law Journal 875; Martin H. Malin, 'The Legislative Upheaval in Public-Sector Labor Law: A Search for Common Elements' (2012) 27 ABA Journal of Labor and Employment Law 149.

However, there was no legal right to strike in that striking workers could be dismissed for breaching their contracts of employment and their re-employment depended on the outcome of the strike. Moreover, collective agreements were not legally binding. The result was an industrial relations system in which strikes were quite frequent, many of them being unofficial actions undertaken locally to address workplace grievances.[49]

The 1968–74 strike wave triggered the first significant effort to use law to reduce the incidence of strikes. In 1971, the Conservative government enacted the Industrial Relations Act (IRA), which aimed to force unions into a legalized framework that drew on elements of American labour law: trade union immunities for strike activity were narrowed; state emergency powers to intervene in strikes were expanded and no-strike agreements were encouraged. Trade unions were having none of it and for the most part they boycotted the IRA's institutions. When the Labour Party formed the next government in 1974, it repealed the IRA, restored the TDA, and tried to close loopholes in the immunities opened up by a hostile judiciary. But no positive right to strike was enacted, in large measure because the trade union movement preferred the immunity-based approach. In retrospect this may have been a strategic mistake, but it provided the labour movement with the legal freedom it won in the early twentieth century to conduct strikes with limited exposure to legal liabilities.

This came to an end in 1979 when the Thatcher Conservatives came to power after a massive strike wave in 1978–79, triggered by union opposition to the Labour government's wage restraint policy in the so-called Winter of Discontent.[50] The Conservative government consciously set about to destroy the power of unions and undermine collective bargaining as part of a broader strategy of promoting neoliberal restructuring of the British economy. Beginning in 1980, the government passed a series of laws that made industrial action increasingly difficult. Trade union immunity for secondary action was stripped away, as was immunity for disputes that were not narrowly confined to immediate terms and conditions of work. Secondary picketing became unlawful and limits were placed on the number of pickets. Strike ballots were made mandatory and their requirements became stricter and more complex over time. Unions that failed to comply with the letter of the increasingly labrynthine law faced liability for damages resulting from an improperly called strike. Unions were required to prevent unlawful action by their members or face liability and a legal presumption was later enacted that industrial action was endorsed by the union unless it explicitly repudiated it, in which case the employer could selectively discipline the participants. Finally, all this statutory regulation provided courts with ample opportunities to become involved in strikes by issuing interlocutory injunctions. The combination of growing economic insecurity, more adverse labour laws, and major strike defeats, including the 1984 miners' strike, contributed to a major drop in strike frequency in the 1980s and 1990s.[51]

[49] See generally, Douglas Brodie, *A History of British Labour Law* (Hart Publishing, 2003); Keith Ewing (ed.), *The Right to Strike: From the Trade Disputes Act 1906 to a Trade Union Freedom Bill 2006* (Institute for Employment Rights, 2007).

[50] Chris Howell, *Trade Unions and the State* (Princeton University Press, 2005) ch. 4.

[51] Howell ch. 5 (n 50); Lyddon 339 (n 12); Bob Simpson, 'Strike Ballots and the Law: Round Six' (2005) 34 Industrial Law Journal (ILJ) 331; Gregor Gall and Sonia McKay, 'Research Note: Injunctions as a Legal Weapon in Industrial Disputes' (1996) 34 Brit J Ind Relat 567.

The election of a New Labour government in 1997 did not produce a distinctly different approach to strike regulation. Some greater employment protection was offered to employees engaged in union-endorsed strikes, undertaken for statutorily approved goals and complying with the balloting and notice requirements, but the government did little to alter the highly restrictive web of statutory rules that must be complied with for strikes to be protected, although the courts recently indicated they may interpret these statutory requirements less strictly than they have in the past.[52] Nothing has been done to loosen the tight limits on picketing. Bob Simpson aptly summarized the situation: 'Unions have the right to organize industrial action only when they have taken extensive steps to minimise its impact.'[53]

Australia and New Zealand

Australia and New Zealand broke with the prevailing common law approach to collective bargaining when it turned to the arbitration model in the late nineteenth century and consolidated it in the early twentieth. The arbitration model relied on a mixture of negotiation, conciliation, and arbitration. In the event a dispute was not resolved through negotiation or conciliation, either party could refer the matter to a tribunal which issued an award that set terms and conditions of employment that were not only binding on the parties, but that either applied across an occupation and industry and covered both unionized and non-union employees (as in New Zealand) or were made to apply by unions getting employers named in awards (as in Australia). One of the keys to the political success of the award system was its role in substantially reducing strikes. Registered unions were given the power to represent both members and non-members within their jurisdiction. Awards were enforced by an industrial relations inspectorate, assisted and, in some cases, largely supplanted by union officials who enjoyed wide powers of entry to speak to workers and monitor award compliance. Strikes were seen as unnecessary in such a system. Industrial relations statutes sometimes banned industrial action as did some awards, making unions liable for damages. As well, unions faced common law liabilities for unlawful industrial action and secondary action was prohibited by trade practices legislation. In practice, the award system did not prevent strikes, especially in Australia, and the legal sanctions for unlawful strikes were rarely invoked.[54]

The demise of the award system was part of a neoliberal project aimed at deconstructing institutional arrangements that insulated employment conditions from market forces. However, the move to a de-centralized collective bargaining system that

[52] Ruth Dukes, 'The Right to Strike under UK Law: Something More Than a Slogan? *NURMT v SERCO, ASLEF v London & Birmingham Railway Ltd.*' (2012) 40 ILJ 302.

[53] Simpson 337 (n 51). Generally, see Lorber and Novitz ch. 5 (n 13) and Shae McCrystal and Tonia Novitz, '"Democratic" Pre-conditions for Strike Action: A Comparative Study of Australian and UK Labour Legislation' (2012) 28 International Journal of Comparative Labour Law and Industrial Relations 115.

[54] Gordon Anderson and Michael Quinlan, 'The Changing Role of the State: Regulating Work in Australia and New Zealand 1788–2007' (2008) 95 Labour History 111; Chris Briggs, 'Strikes and Lockouts in the Antipodes: Neo-Liberal Convergence in Australia and New Zealand' in van der Velden (n 12); Anderson 206 (n 19); Breen Creighton, 'Enforcement in the Federal Industrial Relations System: a Paradox' (1991) 4 Australian Journal of Labour Law (AJLL) 197.

was more responsive to market conditions also required a market-based dispute resolution mechanism, which led to legal recognition of the right to strike. But in this context, the right to strike had to be tailored to insure that it did not empower unions to disrupt the economy in any significant way. Thus, there was a dual movement, legal recognition of strikes on the one hand but only within very narrow and effectively enforced limits on the other, the latter 'smothering' the former,[55] albeit more completely in Australia than New Zealand, particularly after the most recent wave of legislative reforms.

In New Zealand, the concept of a lawful strike was first introduced in 1987 but was substantially revised in the context of the Employment Contracts Act in 1991, which aimed to de-unionize workplaces and limit collective bargaining. Strikes were broadly defined to include almost any concerted action that interfered with the performance of work, the effect of which is to bring most forms of collective worker action within the restrictive strike regime. Strikes were unlawful if they occurred while a collective agreement was in force; they could not occur until a period of bargaining had elapsed; and secondary and sympathy strikes were prohibited, as were coordinated strikes for pattern bargaining and political strikes. Unlawful strikes could be enjoined by the courts and participants could be sued for damages and possibly dismissed. The strike regime was liberalized by the Labour government's Employment Relations Act in 2000. Strikes for multi-employer agreements were permitted and, most importantly, significant restrictions on the use of replacement workers were imposed. These legislative changes, however, have not prevented union density and strike frequency from declining.[56]

The strike regime implemented in Australia is more restrictive than the New Zealand one. A restrictive legal right to strike was first introduced in 1993 and then modified in 1996. It was the 2005 Work Choices Act, however, that dramatically altered the industrial relations regime and greatly increased the restrictions of lawful strike activity. As in New Zealand, industrial action is broadly defined. Before engaging in industrial action, a union must apply for permission to conduct a ballot. A condition of obtaining permission is that the union must demonstrate that it had been and continues to be genuinely trying to reach an agreement with the employer. If permission is granted, the union must arrange for an independent third party to conduct a secret ballot authorizing the proposed action. If the action is approved, the union must provide three days' notice to the employer and the strike must commence within 30 days of the ballot or the ballot must be conducted again. Strikes cannot be conducted for pattern bargaining, and mid-term strikes, sympathy strikes, secondary boycotts, and political strikes are prohibited. Picketing cannot impede the movement of goods and persons in and out of workplaces and injunctions and damages are available to remedy unlawful action. A cooling-off period can be ordered on the request of one of the parties and a strike can be stopped if it is determined that it is causing significant harm to a third party, the bargaining parties themselves, or to essential services (which includes the economy itself). Payment by the employer for periods of industrial action is prohibited, even as

[55] Shae McCrystal, 'Smothering the Right to Strike: Work Choices and Industrial Action' (2006) 19 AJLL 198.

[56] Anderson 210 (n 19); Barry Foster et al., 'Supportive Legislation, Unsupportive Employers and Collective Bargaining in New Zealand' (2011) 66 Relations Industrielles 192.

part of a settlement. In 2009 a Labour government enacted the Fair Work Act, which provides more support for collective bargaining but does not substantially change the strike regime.[57]

Conclusion

Our brief survey of legal regimes reveals that different jurisdictions have taken different approaches to the legal regulation of strikes. In Canada and the United States, the law regulating strikes has changed very little, perhaps because under the existing collective bargaining regimes unions were faring so poorly there was little apparent need to create even more restrictive ones. A partial exception to this pattern is in the public sector, where trade union densities have remained much stronger. In Canada exceptional interventions to prohibit or end strikes have occurred more frequently, while in the United States the focus has been on undermining strike alternatives, such as interest arbitration. By contrast, in the UK, New Zealand, and Australia, legislation was enacted to de-collectivize industrial relations and impose highly restrictive strike regimes. Thus it might be fair to say that law has played a more direct and significant role in these countries, but it is doubtful that changes in the law are the primary reason for the decline in strikes. Rather, it is more accurate to say that in jurisdictions where the law was not an effective buffer against market forces (Canada and the US), there was little need to change the law, while in jurisdictions where strong unions operated with legal immunities (UK) or where industrial relations regimes insulated workers against market forces (AU and NZ), legal changes were made to undercut trade union power and impose more restrictive strike regimes.

The Future of Strikes

Given the demise of the strike, what is to be done? One answer might be that nothing is to be done. Strikes have disappeared because the sources of conflict have diminished and the sources of peace have become more significant. The unitarist perspective has triumphed.[58] This seems unlikely in a world in which workers have seen their share of socially produced wealth decline and their standard of living is under attack. A more realistic starting point is that workers are frequently dissatisfied with their terms and conditions of work, but that strike activity is depressed because workers are also disorganized and disempowered. That dissatisfaction may remain latent or manifest itself in informal or non-union forms of collective action that do not develop into strikes or individualized forms of resistance or dysfunction. Where workers do act in these ways, individually or collectively, there is little evidence it leads to a successful resolution of the problem(s) they encountered, let alone fulfils the democratic or class-consciousness

[57] Shae McCrystal, 'The Fair Work Act 2009 (Cth) and the Right to Strike' (2010) 23 AJLL 3 and Shae McCrystal, *The Right to Strike in Australia* (Federation Press, 2010). Also, see McCrystal (n 55).

[58] The framework but not the conclusion is from Richard Hyman, *Strikes* (Fontana, 1972). For an insightful discussion of the issues touched on here, see Goddard 282 (n 23).

development functions of strikes.[59] If that is the case, there is indeed an urgent need to consider how collective worker voice might 'strike' again.

One focus might be on reforming laws that make strikes particularly difficult to win and risky to conduct. In the United States, for example, there is no doubt that the right of employers to hire permanent replacement workers, in conjunction with greater opportunities and motivation to do so, has undermined the ability of unionized workers to strike successfully.[60] In some countries, appeals to constitutional protection of freedom of association, whether in national or transnational law, may provide some leverage in limiting state restrictions on the freedom to strike, but the road ahead is uncertain.[61] In any event, as we have seen, unfavourable laws are not the primary cause of the demise of strikes, and so it can be anticipated that the impact of legislative reform or sympathetic constitutional interpretation would be modest.

Another possible area is the development of new strategies and tactics. Traditional strikes were successful in a world in which the collective withdrawal of labour inflicted or threatened to inflict significant economic costs on employers so that they preferred to settle on terms more favourable to the union. Moreover, through the act of striking, workers learned the practice of solidarity and were themselves transformed and made more class conscious. If traditional strikes no longer provide workers with leverage or collective voice, then new forms of collective action should be developed. Workplace occupations, bossnappings, and corporate campaigns have been identified as alternatives to traditional strikes, but as Gregor Gall concludes, '[s]o thus far, even sympathetic and engaged observers would have to conclude that the ability of organised labour to offer widespread, let alone effective resistance has been shown to be badly wanting.'[62]

Part of the problem is that unions have been shaped by the legal frameworks in which they operate. As a result, they often became narrowly focused on pursuing the interests of their members through collective bargaining and developed a repertoire of actions, permitted within the legal framework, to advance those interests. Reforming the legal framework and expanding the repertoire while keeping the same narrow focus is unlikely to lead to much change. Perhaps what is needed is a more fundamental shift that would see unions trying to rebuild as working-class movements more broadly focused on organizing and advancing the interests of working people outside of the framework of contract unionism.[63] Strikes may be an important vehicle for

[59] For a recent review, see Diane van den Broek and Tony Dundon, '(Still) Up to No Good: Reconfiguring Worker Resistance and Misbehaviour in an Increasingly Unorganized World' (2012) 67 Relations Industrielles 97. Also, see Anna Pollert and Andy Charlwood, 'The Vulnerable Worker in Britain and Problems at Work' (2009) 23 Work, Employment and Society 343.

[60] Logan (n 47).

[61] In Canada, for example, the Saskatchewan Court of Appeal recently overturned a lower court judgment that held the Canadian Charter of Rights and Freedoms protected the freedom to strike on the basis that this judgment was inconsistent with previous Supreme Court of Canada decisions. *Saskatchewan v Saskatchewan Federation of Labour* 2013 SKCA 43 (overruling 2012 SKQB 43). Undoubtedly, the Supreme Court of Canada will be asked to reverse these older judgments in the near future.

[62] Gregor Gall, 'Worker Resistance and Response to the Crisis of Neo-Liberal Capitalism' (2011) 33 Employee Relations 588. Also see Lucio Baccaro, 'Does the Global Financial Crisis Mark a Turning Point for Labour?' (2010) 8 Socio-Economic Review 341, 347 ('If strategy was at stake, one would expect to find that at least in some cases...unions were getting it right.').

[63] David Camfield, *Canadian Labour in Crisis* (Fernwood Press, 2011).

the achievement of these goals. Notable in this regard have been one-day strikes by Walmart and fast-food workers demanding higher wages, even though there is no prospect that they will be organized into dues paying bargaining units.[64]

Finally, there is the turn to international solidarity. Strikes were effective when the geographic scope of worker organization matched that of their employers. If locally organized unions could take on local, immobile employers and national industrial unions could take on national manufacturers, then international worker institutions are necessary to take on globally organized employers. No doubt this is correct and while global labour solidarity is being constructed, its slow pace and the difficulties facing this project leave little room for optimism that a globally organized working class is going to become the vehicle for collective worker voice and resistance in the near or medium-term future.[65]

Perhaps the answer to the question of what is to be done is that there is no good answer at this juncture. Reforming the law of strikes, launching constitutional challenges to restrictive strike laws, developing innovative strategies and tactics, and building international solidarity are all important projects that may help open up more space for collective worker voice now and in the future, but the inhospitable socio-economic climate severely limits what can be achieved.

[64] Karen McVeigh, 'Walmart workers protest over minimum wage in 15 US cities' *Guardian* (London 5 September 2013) <http://www.labourblawg.ca/strikeslockouts/fast-food-strikes-spread-to-new-us-cities-and-in-canada-baristas-seek-to-unionize/> accessed 10 September 2013; Atossa Araxia Abraham, 'Fast food workers begin strikes across U.S. over wages' *Globe and Mail* (Toronto 29 August 2013) <http://www.theglobeandmail.com/report-on-business/international-business/us-business/us-fast-food-workers-plan-nationwide-strikes-over-wages/article14018751/> accessed 10 September 2013.

[65] David Christopher Lier, 'Places of Work, Scales of Organising: A Review of Labour Geography' (2007) 1 Geography Compass 814. Law plays a role in this by, for example, forbidding secondary action that would enable workers in one country to disrupt the economic activity of a struck employer in another. See Bob Hepple, *Labour Laws and Global Trade* (Hart Publishing, 2005). For a prescient analysis, see Kenneth W. Wedderburn, 'Multi-national Enterprise and National Labour Law' (1972) 1 ILJ 12.

Index